INTRODUCTION TO PROGRAMMING USING VISUAL C++ .NET

T. Grandon Gill

University of South Florida

WILEY

John Wiley & Sons, Inc.

To Clare, with love. Thanks for being so understanding during those many days when my conversations were directed solely at my computer...

Acquisitions Editor	*Beth Lang Golub*
Editorial Assistant	*Ame Esterline*
Production Manager	*Pam Kennedy*
Production Editors	*Kelly Tavares*
	Sarah Wolfman-Robichaud
Managing Editor	*Kevin Dodds*
Illustration Editor	*Jennifer Wasson*
Cover Design	*Jennifer Wasson*
	Norm Christiansen

This book was set in Minion by Leyh Publishing, LLC and printed and bound by Malloy Lithograph. The cover was printed by Phoenix Color.

This book is printed on acid free paper. ∞

Gill, T. Grandon
  Introduction to programming in C++ / T. Grandon Gill
    p. cm.
  ISBN 0-471-48724-4 (pbk.)
  1. C++ (Computer program language) I. Title.

QA76.73.C153G58 2004
005.13'3--dc22
2003068694

ISBN 0-471-48724-4

Printed in the United States of America
10 9 8 7 6 5 4 3 2 1

CONTENTS

iii

PREFACE

Programming is more a matter of skill than knowledge. For this reason, the transformation from novice to effective programmer is far more similar to learning to play a musical instrument than it is to learning the basic principles of many other subjects, such as economics, biology, or physics. Books alone cannot make you a good programmer. Only time spent programming can do that.

This book is intended for individuals who expect they will want to (or need to) write computer programs before their career is over. Such individuals would, naturally, include information systems majors, in a college of business, and computer science majors, in a college of engineering. They could also be practically anyone in the natural or social sciences who recognizes that programming skills can benefit them in doing their jobs or in their research.

This book can be used in a variety of settings. On the one hand, its focus on teaching fundamentals makes it a good choice for a traditional foundation course at the undergraduate level. At the other extreme, its self-contained examples, video demonstrations, and walkthroughs—all tightly integrated with the text itself—make it a good choice for self-study. In between the two extremes, the book has been used effectively in distance learning settings, with the included student CD acting as substitutes for the "lab time" that is often incorporated into introductory courses.

THE CONCEPT OF THE BOOK

This book is intended to help the reader explore what it means to program computers. We first focus on structured programming technique—the building block for all styles of programming. Objects are introduced toward the end the book, focusing on introducing the three main features that differentiate object-oriented programming (OOP) from structured programming: encapsulation, inheritance, and polymorphism. Throughout the entire text, however, we do not forget that most programmers will ultimately be working in an OOP context. Thus, we adopt a programming style (e.g., use of very small functions, dividing projects into separate files, and creating functions to perform specific operations on structures) that will fit nicely with typical OOP approaches.

We conduct our exploration of structured programming using the C++ programming language. In doing so, we recognize that a trade-off is involved. The obvious downside of C++ is that it is definitely not the easiest language to learn. Few languages require the programmer to deal with the mechanics of computing (e.g., representing data and issues of scope, addressing, and the mechanics of function calls) as early and as often as C++. On the plus side, however, learning to program in C++ can help the programmer develop a mental model of how computers operate that is far richer than can be acquired when learning to program in other languages (e.g., BASIC). The result can be a far more capable programmer in the long term.

Throughout the book, a special effort is made to introduce the reader to programming techniques and problems that reflect today's commercial programming practices. The practical result of this philosophy includes the following:

1. *Focus on clarity rather than performance of code.* Clever programming algorithms can often shave precious milliseconds off high-performance code. We scrupulously avoid such algorithms and other tricks for two reasons. First, individuals who need to know these techniques (mainly computer scientists) are likely to have several subsequent courses specifically covering the creation of algorithms. Second, today's function and class libraries make it possible to purchase such sophisticated code at a fraction of the cost of developing it, rather than "reinventing the wheel." Nowadays, the trick is not to *build* a better mousetrap. For today's programmer the real trick is in identifying *when* you need a better mousetrap, knowing *where* to acquire it, and knowing *how* to splice that mousetrap into the program you are writing.

2. *Emphasis on activities that require the reader to incorporate existing code elements into his or her programs.* In today's development world, it is almost unheard of that a programmer should develop an application entirely from scratch. Much more typical is the case where a developer uses a wizard to generate a dozen (or so) program source files, after which the developer's task is to incorporate the necessary design elements into that generated code. For this reason, from the very start of the book, exercises and activities are designed that require the reader to comprehend some body of code that the book supplies, and then modify that code so as to make it perform some desired task.

3. *Use of graphic tools to generate code side-by-side with traditional code writing.* Large sections of code in today's applications are generated through graphical tools and other types of computer-aided software engineering (CASE) tools. This book is unique among introductory programming texts in that it incorporates such a tool, developed specifically for the book, into the exercises and text to allow students to thoroughly explore the relationship between their logical view of an application (e.g., a flowchart) and the actual program code for that same application.

4. *Integration of debugging tools in the text and exercises.* Debugging, like programming, is a skill that is acquired with time. Many books on programming, however, do not spend much time discussing debugging tools or techniques. Normally, this choice is justified by a stated desire not to make the book specific to a given vendor. In developing the current book, however, the opposite path was chosen. Sometimes you need to make choices—just as you cannot learn to play a generic musical instrument, you cannot program with a generic tool. The particular "violin" that we choose to play in this book is Microsoft's Visual Studio .NET environment, included in an optional edition

of this book (ISBN 0-471-68181-4). This choice was made because Visual Studio .NET is the most widely used and probably the most powerful development tool on the planet. By standardizing on the environment and walking the reader through it, we realize a number of benefits: the inexperienced reader can be provided with a concrete roadmap for getting started; the impressive capabilities of the debugger for showing us what's going on "behind the surface" can be harnessed to give the reader a clearer intuition of what happens as code is running; and the debugging skills learned early in the book will provide the reader with the ability to develop much more complex applications as the book progresses.

5. *Use of realistic exercises dealing with current issues:* Starting early in the book, exercises—reflecting many of the types of problems that today's programmers might be expected to work on—are incorporated, such as parsing user input, handling post strings from CGI applications (provided on the instructor's disk), and reading different file formats, both binary and text. We have also chosen to illustrate many techniques using examples drawn from business, such as loan amortization and Web-based interaction, which should be of particular benefit to business IS majors and those computer science majors seeking careers in industry, rather than in research institutions or highly specialized systems development shops.

What this book is definitely *not* intended to be is a primer on entire C++ programming languages. Although the code provided in this book is generally ANSI compliant, no effort is made to cover the C++ language and associated libraries systematically or exhaustively. Furthermore, many of the important capabilities of C++—such as templates—are almost entirely ignored. They will be the focus of a subsequent volume, specifically focused on object-oriented programming in C++.

AIDS TO LEARNING

After a (relatively brief) period of becoming acquainted with a language, the vast majority of subsequent learning comes from seeing examples of the language in use. Thus, when programming professionals need to figure out how to do something, they are more likely to consult sample code than any other source. It therefore makes sense that readers intending to acquire professional-level programming skills should be encouraged to get used to learning by example in this fashion. Thus, a book whose objective is to teach programming should be packed with code samples. As this book certainly is!

Unfortunately, if you are just getting started in the process of learning to program, unexplained listings of code generally do little but induce massive confusion and anxiety. Like programming itself, learning what to pay attention to in a code sample—and distinguishing that code from the code not really relevant to the problem at hand—is a skill that must be acquired. Toward this end, a wide array of learning tools—many of them unique to this book—have been developed to aid the reader.

FlowC

Perhaps the most unique aid to learning included with this book is FlowC. This applications is a Windows-based program (written in C++) that allow students to create flowcharts and then automatically transform them into C++ code, as well as pseudocode.

The development of FlowC took the author almost a year. This effort was motivated by a number of observations made during a decade of teaching structured C/C++ programming to MIS majors. The first of these observations was that, although logic flowcharts are practically never used these days to actually develop applications, they are extraordinarily useful in teaching students how to program. The second observation was that flowcharts are rather hard to draw and even harder to modify, even with tools such as Visio or PowerPoint. The third, and most critical, observation was that it is even easier to create bad flowcharts than it is to create bad code. As a consequence of these last two observations, the author found that a typical flowcharting exercise led to assignments being turned in that bore a closer resemblance to a plate of spaghetti than to a design that could lead to a working program.

The development of the FlowC tool dramatically changes an instructor's ability to use flowcharting as an effective learning tool. Its key features include the following:

- *It requires students to develop flowcharts using legal (and legally placed) constructs.* Because the tool limits insertions to those that are legal (e.g., a continue cannot be inserted unless it is within a loop), the hanging ends and multiple exits from statements that plague early student attempts to create flowcharts are eliminated.

- *It allows the user to transform flowcharts directly into C++ code.* An application developed in FlowC can be transformed into a C++ project that can be compiled and run with little or no modification. In addition, any function or construct selected in FlowC can be viewed as C++ code or pseudocode (as illustrated in Figures 1 and 2).

As a practical note, during the development of FlowC, a number of the author's colleagues expressed a concern that students would become too dependent on FlowC, and would therefore find that they could not read or write C++ code by the end of the course. The actual experience proved to be the opposite, however. In using FlowC, students quickly become of aware of the Achilles' heel of logic flowcharting: the size of the flowcharts produced (a typical FlowC diagram takes ten times more paper than the associated C++ source code). As a result, students quickly find that it is much more convenient to work with the C++ code when trying to diagnose problems than poring over the multipage charts.

FlowC also provides features related to OOP. It allows overloaded functions to be incorporated into a project. It also allows the user to represent objects using UML-consistent diagrams that can then be expanded into member functions and data declarations. Finally, it allows inheritance diagrams to be displayed.

Video Clips and Walkthroughs

Because this book is intended for individuals who are just starting to learn programming, the problem of how to get readers used to looking at code is addressed using a number of innovative teaching aids. Most significant among these aids are the almost twenty hours of

FIGURE I For Loop Selected in FlowC

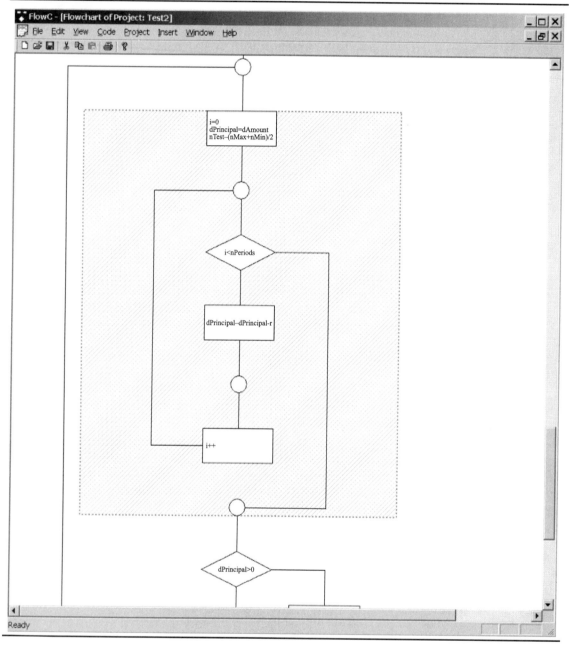

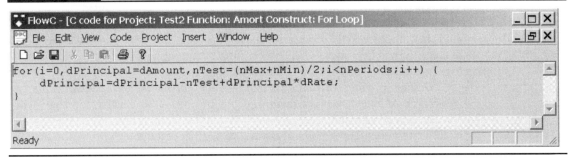

FIGURE 2   Associated C++ Source Code

video segments (ranging from a few minutes to an hour in length) found on the student CD that are tightly integrated into the text. These segments fall into a number of categories:

- *Tool demonstrations.* Using the same Visual Studio .NET tools that can be packaged with the book, narrated video clips walk the student through the use of the development environment, including project creation, editing, and debugging. Running these videos (with judicious use of the Pause and Rewind buttons on their media player), students can actually perform the activities being demonstrated as they run the clips. These segments are particularly valuable in situations where traditional labs are not available, or availability is limited.

- *Code walkthroughs.* Rather than simply listing code in the book, where important techniques are being illustrated using source code, narrated video clips— intended to be used in parallel with the textual material—are provided. Typically, the code being discussed is actually running (in the debugger) so that the actual activities of each statement can be explored and explained. Presenting the walkthroughs in this manner also encourages readers to employ debugging tools as a matter of routine in their own code.

- *Example walkthroughs.* A number of relatively complex programming projects are presented, from start to finish, in a video clip. By going through these clips, the reader is given insights into the techniques they must employ when solving the problems on their own.

- *Concept presentations.* Where a particular concept is known to be challenging to most students (e.g., twos complement, pointers, binary search), narrated video clips intended to supplement the text—and, perhaps, course lectures—have been provided.

In-Depth Learning

Throughout the text, sections providing in-depth learning opportunities are presented— at least one per chapter, often more. These sections provide the reader with the opportunity to develop a deeper understanding of some of the more technical aspects of the material than would normally be encountered in a first programming course. If the text is used in a survey course intended for individuals who have never programmed before and are taking the course without necessarily planning to further their programming education beyond the class, all sections beginning with "In Depth" can be omitted.

More often though, readers using the book may either have some programming background (in C or, more likely, other languages) or may be planning to pursue a career in an a computer-related field such as MIS, where further training in topics such as data representation, memory layout, and file organization may be limited. For these readers, the in-depth sections provide discussions that are of considerable practical value to programmers. Although some of these in-depth treatments are relatively independent, others may depend on material developed in previous in-depth sections. Coverage of some or all in-depth material is also appropriate in classes that prefer to delay the introduction of object-oriented programming to subsequent classes.

In addition to video clips, a variety of additional tools are introduced to teach readers about in-depth topics:

- *Memory grids for pointer problems.* Pointers, arrays, and structures often prove to be among the most difficult concepts for C/C++ novices to master. For this reason, a teaching aid referred to as memory grids has been developed to allow students to acquire a faster mastery of the subject.

- *Specification exercises.* As the book progresses, many chapters provide detailed instructions (i.e., specifications) for creating a nontrivial application or component of a larger application, with a working executable showing the finished product also being included on the instructor's CD. These types of exercises far more closely resemble the types of problems typical entry-level programmers will face than do the open-ended short problems that appear at the end of each chapter in many textbooks.

- *Specialized software.* In order to create a number of interesting exercises, the author has developed a number of programs (e.g., such as a Web server simulator, that allows CGI programs to be tested using a built-in browser) that students can use. Instructions for the setup and configuration of these programs are included on the student CD, making it relatively painless for students to use these programs to create more realistic projects.

ORGANIZATION

This book is organized into three main parts, to be covered consecutively (except the last). These parts are as follows:

1. **Introduction:** An overview of concepts that relate to all programming languages. Among the topics included are the nature of computers and how they are organized (Chapter 1), an overview of the Visual Studio .NET development environment (Chapter 2), how data is represented (Chapter 3), and the nature of functions and operators (Chapter 4).

2. **Structured programming in C++:** A summary of the material necessary to develop structured program code in C++. Among the topics included are program flow and flowcharting (Chapter 5), the organization of a C program and key programming constructs (Chapter 6), core library functions that programmers can't do without (Chapter 7), an overview of file I/O (Chapter 8), an

introduction to iterative techniques (Chapter 9), pointers and complex arrays (Chapter 10), structures (Chapter 11), and memory management (Chapter 12).

3. **Object-oriented programming in C++:** The heart of OOP using C++ is presented. Among the topics included are turning a data structure into a class using encapsulation (Chapter 13), function and operator overloading (Chapter 14), the STL string and vector template classes (Chapter 15), inheritance and polymorphism (Chapter 16), and the C++ file I/O system (Chapter 17).

In addition, a FlowC reference manual is provided on the student CD. There is also a collection of in-depth exercises and tools provided to instructors on their own CD.

TO INSTRUCTORS

Another important design feature of the book is how material is organized within chapters. Nearly every chapter is designed so that the beginning of the chapter presents material in an introductory or conceptual manner, whereas the materials toward the end of each chapter become considerably more advanced. As a result, some instructors may prefer to postpone later sections in some chapters until the material is needed in later chapters. For example, a reader wanting to understand the STL file I/O libraries (Chapter 17) needs to understand the bitwise operators (Chapter 4), but the section introducing those operators can be delayed until the operators are needed. In this regard, the book's organization sits between that of a traditional textbook (designed to be used in a pure sequential fashion) and a reference manual (organized entirely according to content areas). Where the book differs from a reference manual is in the richness of explanation provided whenever new content is introduced. A typical manual will provide an example of how a given task can be accomplished; this book, however, places greater emphasis on understanding why the approach works, and ways in which it could be extended.

This book's organization works well in a course that emphasizes programming assignments and projects. For such classes, students make most active use of the book when trying to figure out how to achieve some programming goal. Indeed—in more than a decade of using other textbooks for project-oriented programming classes—the author did not find any evidence that students *ever* read a textbook sequentially, regardless of how it was designed to be read.

In its entirety, this book is suitable for a motivated student with no experience in programming (but possessing considerable desire to learn) or for a student possessing a casual acquaintance with programming (e.g., a BASIC programming course in high school). With a mix of such students, the author has found two combinations to be equally feasible: (1) covering the entire book during a semester, omitting much of the in-depth material, or (2) covering only the structured programming portion of the book, incorporating most of the in-depth material. Naturally, what is feasible in other situations will depend on the nature and background of the students involved, as well as the amount of any additional materials to be introduced by the instructor.

A valuable instructor's CD includes: solutions to all end-of-chapter exercises; four sample project chapters with accompanying source code, applications, and multimedia files; a series of test generators; an entire sample course with lectures, lecture notes, assignments, and a syllabus; a PC assembler simulator; and server simulation software.

ABOUT THE AUTHOR

T. Grandon Gill is an Associate Professor at University of South Florida. His educational background includes three degrees from Harvard University: an undergraduate degree in Applied Mathematics (cum laude) from Harvard College, a Masters of Business Administration (high distinction) from Harvard Business School, and a Doctor of Business Administration in the Management of Information Systems, also from Harvard Business School. His teaching areas have included programming, management of information systems, database design, the Internet, and case method research. He has received numerous teaching awards, including the Florida Atlantic University award for excellence in undergraduate teaching. His research interests include expert systems, organizational learning, and MIS education and include numerous publications in prestigious journals, such as *MIS Quarterly*. He has also done extensive programming, in a variety of languages. Commercial software and educational software that he has developed include: 1) *The College Expert:* software that helped students choose what college to go to (marketed by Orchard House, Inc.), 2) *McMap:* a geographic information system that aided McDonald's (Latin American Division) in locating new restaurants in Mexico, 3) *PC Assembler-Simulator (PCAS):* an MS Windows-based simulator that displayed the inner functioning of Intel's 8086 processor chip, and 4) *FlowC:* a flowcharting tool used to teach C++ programming. He currently lives in Tampa, Florida, with his wife Clare, and his two sons, Tommy and Jonathan.

PART I

INTRODUCTION

What Is Programming?

EXECUTIVE SUMMARY

Chapter 1 poses and answers two questions: (1) What is programming? and (2) Why should we be interested in studying it? Before we can answer these questions, however, we need a basic understanding of the nature of a computer. To promote this understanding, the chapter presents a quick introduction to computer architecture and the processes involved in creating a computer program.

The chapter begins by explaining the basic stored program architecture employed by digital computers and its key components. It then traces the evolution of approaches to programming computers from the early 1950s to the present, noting the contributions made by C and C++ along the way. The role played by the **operating system** in programming is then explained. The terms *structured programming* and *object-oriented programming* (OOP) are then defined, and the two approaches are contrasted. Finally, a quick overview of programming style—emphasizing the range of styles commonly found in practice—is presented.

LEARNING OBJECTIVES

Upon completing this chapter, you should be able to:

- Explain what is meant by the "stored program architecture" of today's computers
- Distinguish between machine language, assembly language, and higher level languages
- Explain the roles played by C and C++ in the evolution of programming languages
- Identify key services typically provided by an operating system, and why such services are important to programmers
- Explain what is meant by the terms *structured programming* and *object-oriented programming*
- Justify why learning the techniques of structured programming is important even in a world increasingly dominated by object-oriented programming

1.1: WHAT IS A COMPUTER?

Our concept of how something works is sometimes called a *mental model*. Although such models can be right or wrong, it is usually more useful to ask the question: Is the model appropriate to the task at hand? For example, the "appropriate" mental model of an automobile depends on what the model needs to accomplish. If your purpose is to drive the car, you need to understand the purpose and operation of the key components of the car's user interface (e.g., the steering wheel, the brake, the accelerator, the directional, the gas cap, etc.). It probably wouldn't hurt to understand a little bit about the "implementation" of the engine as well—for example, to know that oil keeps the engine lubricated so it probably wouldn't hurt to check it and change it every once in a while or, at least, marry someone who will (as the author did). This example is not the only appropriate mental model of a car, however. The anxious parent of a toddler is likely to be perfectly content if the child's mental model consists entirely of "a car is something big that can move. You must stay away from a car if you're not holding Daddy or Mommy's hand." On the other hand, we would probably prefer that our auto mechanic have a slightly more sophisticated model.

Everyone who uses a computer—which, by definition, includes everyone who is learning to program—comes to the table with an existing mental model. Naturally, these models differ greatly, ranging from "the thing I use to connect to the Internet" to the highly technical view possessed by the designer of **CMOS** setup logic. In this section, our goal is to develop a mental model of a computer that is appropriate for the purposes of learning to program in C++. If you already have a more sophisticated understanding, great! But what we cover here is "good enough."

1.1.1: A Simple Computer

Much like driving a car, you do not need to know very much about what is "under the hood" of a computer before you can start driving it. In fact, you can usually program pretty effectively if you view the computer as having four key components:

- **Central Processing Unit (CPU)**
- **Primary Storage,** normally called Random Access Memory (RAM) on today's computers
- **Secondary Storage,** the various information storage systems (e.g., hard drives, floppies, CD-RW) that allow for long-term storage of information
- **Peripherals:** Other devices connected to your computer, such as a keyboard, a mouse, a monitor, a modem, and so forth

We now discuss these four components.

The CPU The CPU is like an elaborate calculator. In the simplest of calculators, for example, you have operators (such as the +, −, *, /, and = keys) and you have at least two temporary storage areas—one to hold the number you just entered or calculated, and the other to hold the number you are typing in. When you press a key, such as the * key, you tell the calculator to multiply the two numbers in temporary storage, then place the result on the display and in the first temporary storage area. At that point, you're ready to type in another number and press another operator key.

The CPU—such as Intel®'s Pentium® series of processors found in most of today's PCs—works in similar fashion. Specifically:

- The operators, referred to as the chip's **instruction set,** tell the chip what to do—just like the operator keys on the calculator. Although a calculator has a small number of operator keys, a normal processor supports hundreds of different instruction types.
- The temporary storage areas, known as **registers,** are used to store various types of information. Early PC processors had 10–20 registers, while today's Pentiums have dozens.

Each time the processor is given an instruction, it normally changes the value in one or more registers, a process called *executing* the instruction. The nature of the change depends on the specific instruction. A MOV instruction might copy a value from one register to another. An IMUL instruction might perform an integer multiplication and place the result in another register. A fast processor can execute hundreds of millions, or even billions, of such instructions per second.

Primary Storage   Primary storage, referred to as RAM in today's computers, is little more than a huge electronic scratch pad whose purpose is to hold information that the processor is likely to need as it executes. Although most processor operations tend to be performed using the contents of its registers, even several dozen registers are not nearly enough to hold all the information a program is working on. For example, if you are running a word processing program, your processor could probably hold a few lines of text in its many registers. If you want to hold the entire document, however, you need to use RAM.

Conceptually, RAM is a little like a bank of post offices boxes—each box being able to hold only a limited amount of information, just as you can only fit a limited number of letters into a PO box. On most of today's computers, the maximum amount of information that a single memory location can hold is a single character, also referred to as a *byte*. There is nothing magical about a byte, however. It is possible—even likely—that over the next few decades that standard "box" size may grow, to two bytes, four bytes, or even more.

Analogous to a bank of PO boxes, we need to be able to identify every "box" in memory. In a post office, we normally use a sequential set of numbers for identification, with one number assigned to every PO box (i.e., PO box numbers). In primary storage, we do the same thing. Every memory location has a unique *address* assigned to it. Using that address, we can:

- Retrieve its contents, referred to as a *read* operation
- Change its contents, referred to as a *write* operation

The temporary nature of primary storage cannot be overemphasized. It is there to act as a short-term scratch pad, not for long-term storage. It needs to be fast, so reading and writing from it does not slow down the processor, but it is usually **volatile.** Volatile means that if the power goes off, its contents are lost.

Secondary Storage   The difference between primary and secondary storage is largely logical rather than physical. Indeed, some of the physical approaches used in today's secondary storage, such as the hard disk drive, originated in the magnetic drum technologies used for primary storage in the early computers of the 1950s.

The logical differences between primary and secondary storage can be characterized as follows:

- Most forms of secondary storage are treated as being permanent, rather than volatile, in nature.
- We normally assume secondary storage to be much slower than primary storage, so we avoid programs that depend on constantly reading and writing small quantities of information to secondary storage (as is done continuously with primary storage).
- Whereas most transfer of information to and from primary storage is managed directly by our CPU, we normally use an intermediary—the computer's operating system—to manage our transfers to and from secondary storage.

The last of these characteristics, the use of the operating system, proves to be particularly important from a programming perspective. We will examine its implications in greater detail when we talk about the evolution of operating systems in Section 1.2.2.

In other respects, secondary storage is not so different from primary storage. Among the similarities:

- Both are designed to hold data that can later be read, and many—but not all—forms of secondary storage also allow data to be written (exceptions include read-only devices, such as CD-ROMs).

- Both use some form of internal addressing to identify where data is stored. Every physical location on a disk, for example, is assigned an address—although the form of the address can be more complicated than a single number.

Peripherals   The term *peripheral* usually refers to any component hooked up to a computer that is not part of the CPU-primary storage combination (although some definitions would exclude secondary storage, as well). Most peripherals (that are not secondary storage) are devices associated with:

- *Input:* Getting information into the system. Common examples include the keyboard and the mouse.

- *Output:* Getting information out of the system. Common examples include a printer and the display.

- *Input-Output:* Devices that transfer information in both directions, such as a modem, a network card, a touch screen, and a personal digital assistant (PDA) that can be synchronized to the PC.

Most commonly, a programmer will interact with peripherals using the operating system as an intermediary—just as was the case for secondary storage. A nice consequence of this fact is that many of the techniques employed for interacting with files (e.g., writing a line of text to a text file) are nearly identical to those used when interacting with a peripheral (e.g., sending a line of text to the screen or to a printer). We will discover that a number of benefits can be gained from exploiting these similarities when we look at files, first in Chapter 8 and then, in greater detail, in Chapter 17.

1.1.2: The Stored Program Concept

Just as it useful to have some understanding of the physical nature of the components we will be programming, it is also useful to have a conceptual model of how they are organized. This organization, sometimes referred to as the *stored program concept,* has tremendous implications for programmers.

For those of us born during the second half of the twentieth century, the presence of a device on our desk that can serve as a word processor, provide us with games and other entertainment, perform financial accounting, and enable communications across the globe seems entirely unremarkable. We've grown up with computers and take them for granted. It is hard for us to realize just how remarkable these devices are.

What makes computers so remarkable is their flexibility. Before computers first appeared in the late 1940s, our idea of a flexible device was a hammer. It could be used to pound nails, pound the lids of jars to loosen them, pound bugs walking across our workbench—the list of uses just went on and on. (And for a claw hammer, there was a whole other side to work with!) The fact that all the uses of any given device seemed to have a common theme—such as pounding—didn't seem like a limitation to us. That's just the way things were.

Computers totally changed our view of flexibility. It was not just that computers could perform calculations. Mechanical and electrical devices that performed some types of computations—such as Hollerith card readers and mechanical calculators—had been around for a century or so. Such devices, however, typically had to be set up to perform a specific task by their human operators, who would have to click switches, press buttons, connect patch cables, and so on before the device would perform its assigned task. What made computers different is the stored program concept.

What is the stored program concept? It is the notion (initially advanced in the late 1940s by von Neumann and others) that the instructions that are provided to the CPU—the part of the job that used to require operator setup—can be placed in the same primary storage where data are kept. In other words, we could tell the computer what to do without physically setting hundreds or thousands of switches. Doing so had enormous implications:

- It increased—by factors of millions, billions, or even trillions—the rate at which computers could be called upon to perform different tasks. A couple of centuries ago, it could take several months to do the physical set up on a loom so that it would weave a particular pattern of lace, one of the factors that made lace very expensive. Using a computer-controlled loom, the same setup could be accomplished in a few millionths of a second.

- It reduced, dramatically, the skills and patience required to set up a computer to perform a particular task. Because a single incorrect switch setting was sufficient to cause precomputer calculating machines (such as Aiken's Mark I, built in the mid-1940s) to fail, setup could not be left to unskilled individuals. Today, it is not unusual for six-year-olds to install complex software packages on their computers, at least in the author's home.

The stored program concept is nearly always implemented by organizing the contents of primary storage into three distinct areas: *program code, data,* and the **stack.** We will refer to these areas as the **code space, data space,** and **stack space,** respectively.

Code Space   The program space is that area of memory used by a particular application to hold processor instructions—in other words, the program itself. The amount of memory required for these instructions will, of course, vary according to the size of the program.

The contents of the program space are in the form of **machine language.** As a result, they are going to be different from the actual program code developed by the programmer. Machine language consists of a series of bytes in memory that represent:

- *Opcodes*: bytes that specify what processor instruction is to be performed
- **Arguments:** coded bytes that specify what the instruction is to be applied to, such as the **memory address** to be used in moving data from memory into a register

Fortunately, when we program in C and C++, the intricacies of machine language are hidden from us. It does not change the fact, however, that the only language the processor understands is machine language. We will return to this subject in Chapter 2 (Section 2.1), when we consider the compose-compile-link-load process.

Data Space   The data space is the block of primary storage that holds most of the data that our program will be using as it executes. We should, once again, reemphasize the fact that this storage is intended to be temporary—data we wish to save permanently should be placed in secondary storage instead of, or in addition to, primary storage.

As we already know, every byte in memory has its own unique address. As we shall see in Chapter 3, certain types of data—most notably individual characters—can be represented very nicely using a single byte. Often, however, we will need to store data that requires more than one byte. For example, a typical real number (i.e., a number that includes decimal places) is normally stored using eight bytes that are next to each other in memory—sometimes called *contiguous* bytes. In our PO box analogy, it is like having a single box that is made by combining eight individual boxes.

Stack Space   Although a stack space is not strictly necessary to implement the stored program concept, it is mentioned here for two practical reasons:

- Virtually every modern computer implements some form of a stack.
- The use of a stack has enormous practical implications for programmers.

A stack is best thought of as a place where your program places the data and other key information it is currently working on. Unlike the data space, where large blocks of information may remain throughout the course of running a program and never get used or changed, information stored in the stack is almost constantly changing.

Conceptually, the stack is like a giant "in-box" with four important characteristics:

1. We always focus our attention on the document—in other words, the data—that is at the very top of the stack.
2. Any time we complete working on a document, we throw that document away. Once thrown way, we can never get it back again.
3. If a document gets placed on top of the document we are working on, we must immediately turn our attention to that new document. We don't return to working on our previous document until we have completed work on the new document and have thrown it away.
4. Any time our in-box is empty, we sit around idly until a new document arrives, or we go home (depending on our contract).

The most important use of the stack, as it relates to programming, is to implement **functions.** Anyone who has taken elementary algebra is familiar with expressions such as:

$$y = f(x)$$

where the value of y is said to be a function of x. Many specific functions are defined in algebra, such as $y = \sin(x)$, which means the value of y is equal to the value of the sine function applied to the argument x.

The concept of a function in programming is much the same. Take, for example, the problem of computing a monthly payment—one that we shall return to later in the text (in Chapter 9). Most of us are aware that we need to know three factors to compute a loan payment:

1. The amount of money we need to finance (amount)
2. The number of months we will be taking to pay off the loan (periods)
3. The interest rate we will be paying (rate)

In algebraic notation, we would write this as:

```
Payment = f(amount,periods,rate)
```

or, more conveniently:

```
Payment = Pmt(amount,periods,rate)
```

where Pmt is the name we have chosen for our function and amount, periods, and rate are referred to as arguments.

How would we implement such a function on a computer? To begin with, we would probably want to have just one copy of the code that does the computations—even if our program needed to compute payments in many different places. Having just one copy of the code gives us two distinct advantages over rewriting the function every place we use it:

1. It reduces the amount of memory that must be used in the code space, because multiple copies of the same function are eliminated.

2. It means that if we make an error in writing the code, we only have to repair it in one place.

The relationship between functions and the stack stems from the need to hold information temporarily while a function is running. For example, when we call our function Pmt(), we know that we will need to hold, temporarily, the values of amount, periods, and rate. We may also need to hold other values within the function itself (such as a counter to keep track of what year we're computing). To hold values, we use a stack as follows:

- When a function is called, we make space for all the values we need to store temporarily on the top of the stack, called *pushing* the values on the stack.

- When a function has completed its calculation, it returns the calculated value (e.g., the monthly payment). At that time, the temporary values are removed from the top of the stack, a process called *popping* the values from the stack.

The advantage of using this technique is that it makes it easy for one function to call another function. This process is illustrated in Example 1.1.

TEST YOUR UNDERSTANDING 1.1:

What would the next stack illustration in Figure 1.1 look like (i.e., after Qualify() returns)?

The nice thing about using a stack to call functions is that no matter how many functions are called, we can keep pushing them on the stack. The only potential problem we might run into occurs if we run out of the memory set aside for the stack. This situation is called *stack overflow*.

1.1.3: Data and Representation

The final piece of our computer mental model involves understanding what we actually mean by *data*. In Chapter 3, we will discuss techniques for representing different types of data in detail. In this section, we mainly focus on understanding the need for developing representation techniques.

If we were to examine the internal construction of a computer's CPU or RAM, we would discover it consists of a large collection of microscopic electronic switches, each of which can be either on or off. In the case of a *microprocessor,* a chip such as the Intel Pentium 4 that serves as the CPU for some PCs, the connections made between the switches is very complex—designed in such a way that when instructions are placed in one

EXAMPLE 1.1

Function calls and the stack

 Walkthrough available in CallStack.wmv

Suppose we wanted to write a function that qualifies an applicant for a loan, called Qualify(). We might design the function so that it returns 1 if the applicant is qualified and 0 if the applicant is not qualified. It might also take arguments such as CreditScore, AnnualIncome, LoanAmount, InterestRate, and Periods. (Note that the last three of these values are also needed for our Pmt() function.)

Within our Qualify() function, in turn, we might call our Pmt() function—because computing the monthly payment for a given loan is an important part of determining whether an applicant is qualified. Using a stack, the following would occur when the program is running:

- When Qualify() is called, temporary variables for all the data used in that function are pushed on the top of the stack, such as variables to hold the five arguments and any other temporary variables required within the function.

- When Pmt() is called within Qualify(), the Pmt() temporary variables are pushed on top of the stack (i.e., on top of the Qualify variables(), which are still there). It means, for example, we might have two copies of the loan amount value on our stack—one being used by Qualify() and the other being used by Pmt().

- When Pmt() is done, it returns and its variables are popped off the stack. The Qualify() variables are still present, however.

- When Qualify() is done, it returns its 0 or 1 value, and all of its variables are popped from the stack.

This process is illustrated in Figure 1.1, where the stack is shown as growing "down"—a common convention. The "in-box" analogy comes from the fact as the stack grows (i.e., as functions are called) we normally only work with the values on the top of the stack. Only when a function returns—and its data are popped—do we return to working with the values further down.

set of registers, the chip automatically performs the specified operation (such as addition) in other registers. The circuitry for RAM chips is more straightforward, because the main operations that these chips need to be able to perform are reading the data at a particular address and writing values to that address. Thus, a key challenge in RAM design is seeing just how many of these switches can be placed on a single small chip (with the upper limit currently being somewhere well into the billions for a chip the size of a thumbnail).

Conceptually, we can think of each of these switches as having a value of either 0 or 1. In a digital system, values somewhere in the middle are not allowed. In other words, as soon as your computer powers up, every single one of the billions of switches incorporated into a typical computer has a value.

TEST YOUR UNDERSTANDING 1.2:

In programming, we sometimes make statements such as "this variable in our code doesn't have a value yet." If the aforementioned "variable" refers to a location in RAM, is it possible for it not to have a value? What would be a better way of expressing the situation?

FIGURE 1.1 Call Stack in Operation

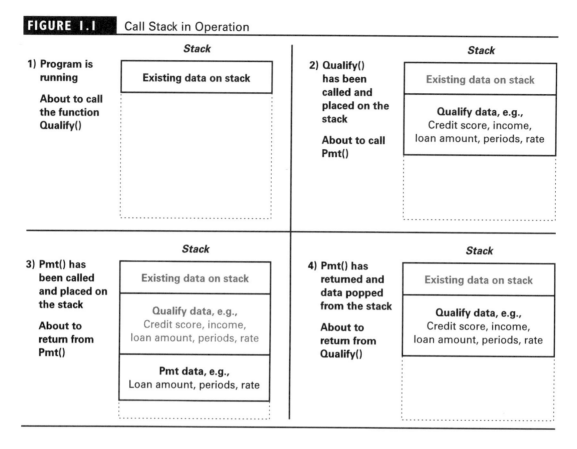

Given that primary storage is, conceptually, just a large collection of 0s and 1s, we are obviously going to need representation schemes to help us work with it. We have already seen one important representation:

> Within our code space, the 0s and 1s in RAM are often interpreted as instructions to the processor.

Within our data and stack spaces, on the other hand, these same 0s and 1s may be interpreted in other ways. The most common interpretations include:

- As text characters, or sequences of characters normally referred to as *strings*, such as "Hello, World"
- As integers
- As real numbers
- As addresses in RAM (i.e., a memory location can hold the address of another memory location)
- As TRUE/FALSE values, commonly referred to as *Boolean* values

A programming language provides you with ways of representing the information you need to work with. Specifically, nearly every programming language provides you with a way to do three things:

- Set aside space in memory to hold every piece of information that you need to keep in primary storage

- Provide a name to the storage location, known as a *variable name*, so you can refer to your information by name (e.g., X or Payment) instead of by its address in memory (e.g., 0x0126F36B)
- Declare what type of information is contained in the location (e.g., integer, real number, character)

Fortunately, as was the case with writing program code and implementing function calls, the tools provided by your programming language for setting aside, naming, and typing data storage make the process relatively painless. You will be a more effective C/C++ programmer, however, if you understand what is being accomplished as you apply the tools that the language supplies.

1.1: SECTION QUESTIONS

1. In what area of the computer are the code space, data space, and stack space located?
2. Why was it so significant that the three spaces could be put in the same general area?
3. If the data for a function are placed on the stack when a function is called, how long will that data stay around?
4. Can the same memory be used to represent both real numbers and text? If so, can it represent both at once?

1.2: A BRIEF HISTORY OF C/C++ PROGRAMMING

In this section, we will look at how programming has evolved from the early 1950s through the development of C++, in the early 1980s. In doing so, our focus is on understanding the following:

- The role of the operating system in programming
- The important roles played by C and C++ in the evolution of modern programming

Such understanding should help justify why it makes sense to learn C++. It also helps to explain some of the peculiar characteristics of language—such as its rather unique appearance—that have been both revered and despised by programmers and students alike.

1.2.1: Evolution of the 3GL

C and C++ are both examples of third generation programming languages (referred to as *3GLs*). The use of 3GLs to program commercial computers, however, was not widespread until almost a decade after the first commercial computers appeared. During most of the 1950s, first and second generation languages were more commonly used.

First Generation Language When commercial computers first appeared in the early 1950s, they were physically different from today's computers—although their logical organization and their application of the stored program concept was surprising similar.

Early processor circuitry, for example, was constructed using vacuum tubes. Such tubes were extremely unreliable—tending to overheat and then burn out. Any day when a computer was able to run for a few hours without a processor failure—requiring a shutdown followed by hours or days of maintenance—was a good day indeed. RAM on these machines tended to be implemented using slow magnetic drums, the precursor to today's hard drives. Secondary storage, if present, was typically in the form of card reader/writers that used punch cards. Such cards were a form of WORM (write-once, read many) technology, making them useful mainly for tabulating tasks, not data storage.

By today's standards, such machines were astonishingly expensive. Moore's law—developed by an Intel executive who charted the costs of computing over time—states that the cost of a given amount of computing power tends to fall by half over every 18-to-24-month period. This calculation roughly corresponds to a factor of 10 every five years. Thus over a fifty-year period, a decline in cost of roughly 10 billion (10^{10}) could be expected. In practical terms, that means the processing power embedded in today's typical digital wristwatch would have cost billions in the early 1950s.

The combination of unreliability over time (meaning you had a limited window of opportunity for your program to run in) and high cost of hardware had important implications for programming. Most importantly, it meant that a programmer's time was considered to be a negligible cost when compared with the cost of the computer's time. In other words, you'd never use the computer to do something a programmer could do. The result:

- When programmers wrote code, they wrote it in machine language—coding everything as 0s and 1s. Conveniences we take for granted, such as the ability to give values variable names, were nonexistent.

- When programmers tested code, they tested it on each other. You'd never run code on a computer unless you were "sure" it would work.

- A programmer had to learn the native "language" of any device connected to the computer. If you wanted to read data from a particular model of card reader, for example, you had to learn how to communicate with it. And every brand (and model) was likely to have its own language.

The inconveniences associated with such programming dramatically limited the number of applications that computers could be used for. As technologies advanced, however, the situation began to change.

Second Generation Language   By the late 1950s, some important new technologies began to change the cost and reliability of computing. The transistor, initially developed as a substitute for the tube at AT&T's Bell Labs, replaced the tubes in CPU components—increasing speed, reducing costs and, perhaps most importantly, dramatically improving reliability. Magnetic core memory, faster and more reliable than drums, was adopted for primary storage. Magnetic tapes, such as those used to record video in the emerging television industry, were adapted for the purposes of secondary storage—providing huge increases in capacity as well as read-write capability. With these new technologies, new uses for computers—such as in accounting applications—became feasible.

The rapidly dropping costs of computing, combined with the growing number of potential uses, lead to a fundamental change in the economics of computing. Specifically, the cost of programming computers could no longer be ignored in the equation. Indeed, it could actually exceed the cost of hardware over the life of a system. Furthermore, programmers who were sufficiently skilled (and sufficiently patient) to program in machine language were hard to find. Thus our approach to programming had to change.

The first shift in how we programmed was from machine language to **assembly language** (ASL), known as the second generation language (2GL). Although ASL is closely related to machine language, it offered a number of mnemonics designed to make it less cumbersome for programming, including the following:

- Instructions could be referred to by name (e.g., MOV or JMP) instead of requiring the programmer to remember numeric opcodes
- Registers could be referred to by name
- Memory for variables could be set aside, and variables could be given names that could be used within the program, as a substitute for remembering the address at which they were stored
- Locations in memory could be labeled—once again allowing the programmer to use names instead of addresses.

A side-by-side comparison of the 8086 machine language and assembly language equivalents is presented in Figure 1.2. On the left-hand pane, the machine language code is presented. On the right-hand pane, we see its assembly language equivalent. Examples of the benefits of ASL include:

FIGURE 1.2   Machine Language vs. Assembly Language

```
                          1 ;CHAR2INT.ASM is a file containinga rout
                          2 DATA SEGMENT
                          3     ; Data definition statements
                          4     DB TestString '1487'
                          5     DB 0                          ;Put in
                          6     DW IntVal 0                   ;Where t
                          7 DATA ENDS
                          8
                          9 STACK SEGMENT
                         10     DB 128 DUP(?)
                         11 STACK ENDS
                         12
                         13 CODE SEGMENT
                         14 MAIN PROC
0009:0000 B9 00 00       15              MOV CX,0
0009:0003 BB 00 00       16              MOV BX,0
0009:0006 8A 8F 00 00    17 LoadChar:    MOV CL,TestString[BX]
0009:000A 80 F9 00       18              CMP CL,0
0009:000D 75 03          19              JNZ NotZero
0009:0017 E9 38 00       23              JMP Done
0009:001A 80 F9 39       24 DigitTest:   CMP CL,0x39
0009:001D 76 03          25              JBE DigitOK
0009:001F E9 38 00       26              JMP Done
0009:0022 8B 06 05 00    27 DigitOK:     MOV AX,IntVal
0009:0026 BA 0A 00       28              MOV DX,10
0009:0029 F7 E2          29              MUL DX
0009:002B 80 E9 30       30              SUB CL,0x30
0009:002E 02 C1          31              ADD AX,CX
0009:0030 89 06 05 00    32              MOV IntVal,AX
0009:0034 43             33              INC BX
0009:0035 E9 06 00       34              JMP LoadChar
0009:0038 C3             35 Done:        RET
```

- *Setting aside and initializing a variable.* As an example, TestString is declared and initialized to the characters "1487" on the fourth line down in Figure 1.2. No machine language equivalent exists for that code, because it would be the programmer's responsibility to initialize those bytes before the program was loaded.

- *Refer to variables, by name, in operations.* To continue the previous example, the TestString variable is referred to in line 17 as an alternative to specifying its actual address in memory.

- *Ability to define labels within the code block.* For example, the JMP statement on line 34 causes the program to go to line 17 (which is the line labeled with LoadChar:). Once again, this label acts as an alternative to identifying the actual memory location of the line of code.

In order to write code in assembly language, you needed a special program called an **assembler.** The purpose of the assembler was to translate the programmer's assembly language into object code, a representation close to machine language, that could then be linked and loaded (Chapter 2, Section 2.1 provides further details on linking and loading). Running the assembler on the computer substituted the computer's time for the extra time it would take for the programmer to do the translation to machine language manually. As computers grew cheaper, this substitution made greater and greater economic sense.

Although ASL represented a major improvement in programming ease over machine language, it was still far from programmer-friendly. Assembly language programming also had two serious weaknesses:

- Even though mnemonics made it somewhat easier to program, ASL was still based entirely on the processor's instruction set. Thus, assembly language programming forced the developer to "think like a CPU."

- The CPU-specific nature of assembly language meant that each time a program was ported to a new type of machine (with a different instruction set), the program had to be rewritten.

The second of these weaknesses was particularly troublesome in the early 1960s. Before IBM introduced upward compatibility in its 360 series in the mid to late 1960s, every model of computer tended to have its own unique assembly language. Thus, acquiring new hardware often meant the need to throw away existing code and completely reprogram all existing applications.

Third Generation Languages   The challenges of porting code across different hardware systems and the increasing percentage of system costs that were the result of programming costs motivated the development of third generation languages (3GLs). The 3GLs—and there were many!—had two primary benefits over ASL programming:

- They were normally designed with a specific purpose, rather than a specific processor, in mind. For example, included among the languages developed in the late 1950s and early 1960s are:

    - FORTRAN (FORmula TRANslator), developed with mathematical computations and engineering applications in mind

    - BASIC, designed to aid in teaching elementary programming concepts

    - COBOL (COmmon Business-Oriented Language), developed to support business data processing applications

- LISP (LISt Processor), developed to support the complex data structures employed in artificial intelligence (AI)
- The languages were intended to be processor-independent. The features provided by these languages were task-oriented and did not assume the particular processor they would be running on.

The second of these benefits provided two advantages. First, it reduced the amount of reprogramming required to move applications from one machine to another. Second, it allowed programmers to move between systems (supporting the same 3GL) without having to relearn a whole new programming language.

As was the case with assembly language, a special program is required in order to translate 3GL code written by the programmer, commonly called *source code,* into executable code (machine language). In fact, two such programs are commonly used to translate 3GLs:

- **Compiler:** performs a source-to-object translation precisely comparable to that done by an assembler
- **Interpreter:** translates source code line-by-line while a program is running

Because compiled code is usually much faster than interpreted code, even 3GLs that were originally developed to run under an interpreter—e.g., BASIC and LISP—are increasingly being deployed using a compiler. For that reason, and because C/C++ is nearly always compiled, we will focus on compiled code throughout the rest of this book.

The fact that a compiler (or interpreter) must be developed for every platform on which a 3GL is to be used created some problems. Specifically, a natural tendency arose among compiler developers to "enhance" the language as they built the compiler. Such "improvements" could lead to language versions that became incompatible with each other. One way of avoiding those problems was to put the language in the hands of a standards board, as was done with COBOL. Another was for developers of the language to tightly control it, as IBM did for languages such as PL/1 and RPG. Unfortunately, even tight controls could not necessarily eliminate all problems associated with 3GLs. Part of the problem stemmed from the relationship between the 3GL and the host computer's operating system.

1.2.2: Operating Systems

Around the same time that 3GLs were becoming the dominant tool for programming, the use of operating systems became widespread. Operating systems (OS) are collections of programs, accessible by the programmer or user of a system, that provide various *services.* These services tend to fall into one or more of these categories:

- *Housekeeping services:* Performing tasks on the computer that keep it secure and in good working order. The range and scope of these services can vary greatly. For example, control of user access (security), timekeeping, and scheduled disk maintenance would all fall into this category.
- *Intermediary services:* Operating systems often act as an intermediary between the programmer and other attached devices. For example, when C programmers using early versions of DOS wanted to print graphics, they had to learn the printer's language and communicate various codes directly to the printer. When C/C++ programmers using MS Windows want to print, they tell MS Windows what to draw, and it translates the commands into the printer's language—

EXAMPLE 1.2

Operating system issues in the "real world"

No clear demarcation signals what belongs in the operating system and what does not. In the late 1990s, for example, Microsoft argued that access to a browser had become so important to programmers that the service belonged in the operating system—almost certainly true—so it began to bundle Internet Explorer into new versions of MS Windows. Netscape, in turn, argued that you could have MS Windows without Internet Explorer—also quite true—and that Microsoft's inclusion of Internet Explorer would dramatically reduce their ability to sell their own browser, Netscape Navigator. Thus, the case of what belongs and does not belong in an operating system went to court.

---

meaning the programmer only needs to know how to communicate with MS Windows, not with a thousand different printer models.

- *Organizational services:* Operating systems perform a wide range of tasks necessary to keep the system organized. Examples include organizing secondary storage (e.g., the folder system on a hard drive), keeping track of program locations and file associations, managing the flow of documents to the printer, ensuring memory and processor time is shared between programs, and managing the data flow through a user's Internet connection.

The fact that a 3GL programmer is likely to want to rely on the operating system creates major challenges when moving applications across platforms or operating systems. Microsoft Windows, for example, manages its display in a manner that is quite different from DOS, or even Apple's MacIntosh OS. Any program written in Windows using a 3GL—even written in C/C++, for which standards exist—that employs a graphic user interface (GUI) will therefore need to be rewritten to support the move across the platform/OS.

The problem of differences across operating systems has been difficult for 3GL designers to solve. One approach has been to give up on cross-platform compatibility. Microsoft's Visual Basic, for example, took a language notorious for lax and inconsistent standards (BASIC) and tailored it specifically to writing MS Windows programs on PC platforms. A radically different approach, adopted by Sun in designing Java, was to create a language that would only run on a Java virtual machine (a software-based emulator, similar in concept to the PCAS used to illustrate this chapter). Sun then went about developing virtual machines to run on different platforms and operating systems.

One of the most common ways of addressing the problem of cross-platform compatibility in 3GLs is to limit the functionality built into the language to the bare minimum that every operating system is likely to support. Constructed in this way, the 3GL is likely to provide built-in support for the following:

- User input and output from a line-oriented text device, such as a teletype
- Reading and writing data, in text or "raw" format, to secondary storage
- Ability to acquire blocks of memory (primary) storage from the operating system when needed and return such blocks of memory when done
- Access to a limited number of housekeeping services, such as date and time

Notably absent from this list are capabilities such as graphics, mouse I/O, Internet connectivity, and multimedia facilities—in other words, practically all the features that make today's programs engaging. Sadly, this omission was not accidental. Most 3GLs, including C/C++, treat these capabilities as if they do not exist.

The good news, however, is that even though certain capabilities are not present in a language that doesn't mean we can't use the language to create programs using those capabilities. It just means that we will probably need to extend the language by acquiring *libraries,* which are collections of functions and other code that add features to the "standard" language. If you want to write a snazzy Windows program using C++, for example, you might start by learning to use the **Microsoft Foundation Classes (MFC)** included with the Visual Studio.Net development tool (a process that will take you two or three months, once you're a decent C++ programmer—just in case you're wondering why we aren't doing it here). Because MFC is a class library that extends C++ by adding MS Windows functionality, once you bring it into your project, nearly all the features that MS Windows supports are at your fingertips. Of course, the drawback of proceeding down this path is that an MFC project will be incompatible with any platform except a Windows PC. But lack of PCs in the workplace is not usually a problem, so it's a trade-off.

1.2.3: Origins of C and C++

By the late 1960s, operating systems were used almost universally and were becoming increasingly sophisticated in the services they supplied—such as multitasking. At that time, the largest individual consumer and developer of computers in the world was AT&T (not IBM, as many people would assume). Despite its preeminence in the world of computing (both the transistor and the integrated circuit were developed at its Bell Labs), the company never sold a computer—all were used internally (mainly to manage its huge switching network that controlled the vast majority of U.S. telephone communications). AT&T's reason for not selling its computers was simple: it was prohibited by law from doing so. You see, AT&T was the world's largest monopoly, and was therefore heavily regulated.

Evolution of C   Because AT&T was continuously developing new computers, it constantly needed to develop new operating systems and to port old operating systems to new hardware. Toward this end, AT&T Bell Labs developed a prototype language, called B, that would be easy to move from system to system. Dennis Ritchie then created an enhanced version of this language specifically aimed for use in developing the Unix operating system. The language was called C.

The C programming language has a number of characteristics that are suggestive of its origins:

- It provides many capabilities, such as the ability to manipulate memory addresses directly, that are indispensable in assembly language programming but are not normally available in a 3GL because of their potential to wreak havoc when misused.

- It is an extremely small language, making it relatively easy to port from system to system. Even basic I/O capabilities are not part of the language, but are instead provided as part of a collection of standard libraries.

- Its syntax, with semicolons required at the end of each line and braces ({ and }) used to create blocks, was designed with ease of compiling—rather than ease of reading—in mind. Indeed, you have passed a major milestone in your progress in learning C/C++ when you can look at a typical C++ program and *not* grimace while saying to yourself: "Wow, this is the ugliest code I ever saw."

Three major factors kept C from becoming yet another page in the scrapbook of experimental languages that nobody remembers:

1. The Unix operating system was managed and extended by a number of groups, the most important of which was at UC–Berkeley. The intimate relationship between Unix and C guaranteed that the language would be kept alive.

2. The small size of C made it nearly ideal for porting to the new microcomputers (e.g., CP/M systems and IBM PC) that emerged in the late 1970s and early 1980s. At that time, the selection of languages on those machines was fairly limited (e.g., BASIC, FORTRAN, Pascal), and C proved to be a welcome addition.

3. Brian Kernighan teamed with Dennis Ritchie (C's original designer), to write a book called *The C Programming Language* in 1978. This book, whose target audience was experienced programmers, was probably the best book on any programming language ever written, and set a de facto standard for C until the ANSI standard was completed in 1988.

By the early 1990s, it is probably fair to say that C was the predominant language used by serious developers on every platform except IBM mainframes.

Evolution of C++ Bjarne Stroustrup, also of AT&T Bell Labs, developed the C++ language in the early 1980s. Its creation was motivated by two objectives (one major and one minor):

1. *Major: To add object-oriented programming (OOP) capabilities to the C programming language.* OOP capabilities, developed in the artificial intelligence (AI) community and implemented in languages such as SmallTalk, were intended to allow developers to create and manage more complex programs.

2. *Minor: To eliminate a few unnecessary limitations and to add a few capabilities to the structured programming side of C.* Because certain functionality was omitted from C to keep it small (e.g., passing variables by reference, flexibility in declaring variables, ability to overload functions and operators), the introduction of C++ was seen as an opportunity to expand the language.

The C++ language was developed as a superset of C, meaning a legal C program is generally a legal C++ program. The implications are that when you are learning C, you are also learning core elements of C++.

The C++ language was rapidly accepted in the computer science community. Its adoption in the business community was also relatively rapid, spurred by two developments:

■ The introduction of a low-cost C++ compiler by Borland in the late 1980s, Turbo C++.

■ The introduction of Microsoft's Visual C++ and the MFC in the early 1990s. Modeled after the company's popular Visual Basic tool for developing MS Windows applications, this tool made C++ the language of choice for developing complex MS Windows applications.

Present Day At the present time, three languages seem to be competing for the title of the dominant OOP language—C++ and two other languages that were both inspired by C++: Sun's Java and Microsoft's C# (C-sharp). The Internet capabilities built into both Java and C# give them an edge in that area of competition. On the other hand, Java and C# are both tightly controlled by their respective vendors, whereas the standard for C++ is controlled by ANSI. It is difficult to believe that the universe of programmers will stand by and allow a single vendor to dominate tomorrow's programming language of choice.

The case for the best structured programming language is much more straightforward. Both C and C++ can be used without reference to objects. Languages like Java and C#, on the other hand, are not designed to be used without objects. Thus, C/C++ would seem to be the best choice for performing structured programming, which happens to be the building block of all programming skills.

1.2: SECTION QUESTIONS

1. Given Moore's law, roughly how much do you think the power of a high-end PC increased between 1981 (the introduction of the PC) and 2001?
2. What was the main advantage of assembly language over machine language?
3. If one processor (e.g., a Pentium) is upward compatible from another (e.g., 486), what does that tell you about the assembly languages of the two processors?
4. What is the advantage of having a standard for a 3GL?
5. Why can operating systems make it more difficult to move applications and code between computers?
6. Would you expect to be able to compile a typical ANSI C program using a C++ compiler?

1.3: STRUCTURED VS. OBJECT-ORIENTED PROGRAMMING

Conceptually, you can think of programming approach as having passed through three major eras:

1. *"Anything Goes" era:* from the early 1950s to the mid-1960s. Programs tended to be small, loosely connected (if at all), and run in batch mode. During this stage, achieving hardware efficiency was often viewed as being more important than clarity and confusing jumps from place to place in code were the rule rather than the exception. This type of coding persists mainly in languages that are not well-designed for other styles, such as assembly language, FORTRAN, and early versions of BASIC.
2. *Structured Programming era:* from the mid-1960s to the early 1990s. Eliminated code jumps by organizing code into blocks, placing a premium on clarity over efficiency. Structured programming still persists in many places, particularly in legacy applications and low-level systems programming. Many languages support this style of programming, such as COBOL, PL/1, C, and C++.
3. *Object-Oriented Programming era:* from the early 1990s to the present. Changed the primary organizing mechanism for complex code from the function to the encapsulated object. Languages supporting this style of programming include C++, Java, and C#.

In this section, we focus on the relationship between structured and object-oriented programming. In the process, we discover that while they are often presented as competing approaches to programming, they are better thought of as being complementary. At the end of the section, we introduce "structured programming style." In doing so, we point

out the wide ranges of style that are likely to be encountered among professional programmers. We revisit that theme often in the book.

1.3.1: What Is Structured Programming?

The term *structured programming* usually refers to a particular type of logical organization that:

- Relies on three programming constructs (functions, branches, and loops) to
  control program execution, and strongly discourages the use of other constructs, particularly jumps (e.g., "go to" statements)
- Extends the concept of a simple variable by allowing many variables to be
  organized into logical groups called *structures*
- Uses functions (or subroutines) as its primary mechanism for organizing
  programs

Structured programming began to emerge in the mid-1960s. At that time, many of the
languages in common use, particularly assembly language and FORTRAN, made extensive
use of the jump instructions that are a central part of the machine language incorporated
into every processor (CPU). Although code written in this manner tended to run efficiently (critically important on the slower computers of the time), it also became
extremely hard to debug and maintain as programs grew larger. The term *spaghetti code*
was often used to describe such applications, because the path of control jumped back and
forth so many times that if you charted your program, it looked like a plate of pasta. As
companies and other organizations realized they were spending more time on debugging
and maintenance than on actual coding, they began to search for other approaches to
designing and writing programs.

By the late 1960s, structured programming became the dominant programming par-
adigm, particularly in business settings. The main difference between structured programming and previous programming approaches was the virtual elimination of jumps from
program code. (Indeed, structured programming is also called goto-less programming.)
Thus, even if a language supported a jump command (aka, a goto statement), individuals
using structured programming were prohibited, or at least strongly discouraged, from
using the capability. The resulting code proved to be much easier to understand and maintain. It also turned out that the "goto" statement was hardly missed at all. The capabilities
for branching and looping, to be introduced in Chapter 5, make such jumps entirely
unnecessary. Not using jumps mainly becomes a matter of habit. In this book, we encourage the habit by not introducing the goto statement supported by C/C++!

1.3.2: What Is OOP?

What OOP provides is another programming construct, the encapsulated *object*, as the
primary means of organizing programs. Objects allow the programmer to merge the functions and data structures used in structured programming. True OOP incorporates three
distinct capabilities that are not present in pure structured programming:

- **Encapsulation:** The ability to mix functions and data into a self-contained
  object that is, to the greatest extent possible, independent of other objects. The

philosophy behind encapsulation is a general principle of managing complexity in any situation. It is much easier to tackle a lot of independent small problems than to tackle a single large problem. In programming terms, this notion might be stated as preferring to write twenty small (500-line) programs to a single larger (5,000-line) program—even though you would end up writing more total lines in the first case. A language supporting OOP gives the programmer the tools necessary to implement encapsulation.

- **Inheritance:** A technique that allows you to define objects based on previously defined objects without making an independent copy. It doesn't take much programming experience to learn that it is much easier to copy and modify existing code than to create new code from scratch. After you've done it for a while, however, you start to notice a disturbing trend: every time you copy your old code you enhance it (or fix it) in the new copy but (somehow) you never get around to putting the revisions back into the original code. Using inheritance properly ensures all your code benefits from your enhancements and revisions and naturally leads you into taking a more abstract view of your data.

- **Polymorphism:** The ability to define objects so that they respond to the same signal in different ways. In MS Windows, for example, different things happen when you click different areas of the screen (e.g., a menu, a button, an edit box). In MS Windows, every control is actually a separate window object. The polymorphism comes from the fact that we can program each of these window objects to respond differently to the same signal from MS Windows (e.g., a WM_LBUT-TONDOWN message, which is sent every time the left mouse button goes down).

The advantages of using OOP techniques over pure structured programming approaches can become pronounced as code becomes more and more complex. Some estimates state that a single programmer can manage nearly twice as much OOP code (e.g., C++) as pure structured code (e.g., C). Committing to OOP does not, however, eliminate the need to develop good structured programming technique. Within the implementation of every object, structured programming techniques are invariably employed. Thus, the development of good OOP technique requires the mastery of *both* structured programming and the additional capabilities provided to implement objects.

1.3.3: Which Is It Better to Learn: Structured Programming or OOP?

Although structured programming is sometimes contrasted with *object-oriented programming (OOP)*, the two approaches are usually complementary, rather than competitive.

An easy way to view the relationship between the two techniques is to use a musical analogy. Think of structured programming as being like a piano. If so, object-oriented programming is like a feature-rich musical keyboard synthesizer (with rhythm accompaniments, automatic chords, multiple instruments, and MIDI hooks built in to allow it to connect to other instruments—all depending on the make of the keyboard, of course). Which of the two is better? It really depends on what your objectives are:

1. *You need to play at your sister's wedding next week and you've never played an instrument before.* In this case, the choice is obvious. You go with the full function keyboard and learn every feature you can so that you can play the wedding march with a single finger and still have it sound "okay." Naturally, using this

approach won't bring you much closer to being a musician, but it's the fastest way to get results. In the programming world, this approach is a bit like taking an environment such as Visual Basic and using it to tie a collection of prebuilt controls together. It's the quickest way to get something going and can lead to a pretty decent result (as long as you don't need to go outside the capabilities of the controls you've been given to work with).

2. *You know you want to become a classical pianist, and intend to spend years of practice getting there.* The choice is relatively obvious here as well. You go with the piano, because acquiring keyboard skill is your primary goal (and because not a lot of eighteenth-century music was composed for synthesizers). In the programming world, this choice might be analogous to certain (increasingly rare) careers in systems programming—where writing high-performance code is the primary objective, in which case it makes sense to focus on learning C and assembler, and not worry about OOP at all.

3. *You think you want to become a professional keyboard artist, but aren't sure what type or types of music you will eventually be playing.* Here the choice is much less clear. On the one hand, you may end up in a rock band—in which case you will be wanting to use the capabilities of the synthesizer. On the other hand, you could end up playing classical piano, in which case you won't be using those features as much—if at all. If you really plan to be a professional, however, one thing is common to all the paths you might take: you will benefit from a foundation of good keyboard skills.

Most students entering a computer science or MIS program are closest to the last of these situations. The field is changing too fast for any of us to know exactly what we will be doing in five years—this point is true even for those of us who have been in the field for decades. And, if you are just getting started in the field, you have many directions from which to choose. Fortunately, learning structured programming is like acquiring musical keyboard skills:

- If you end up writing nothing but object-oriented programs, you will still continue to use those structured programming skills every time you sit down at your computer.
- Even if you don't end up programming at all, but instead find yourself managing programmers or doing systems analysis, the skills and methods of thinking acquired in learning structured programming techniques will make you far more effective than individuals lacking that expertise.

Furthermore, even if you happen to be using a "synthesizer" to practice on, nothing will prevent you from turning off the bells and whistles (e.g., the OOP capabilities of C++) while you're acquiring these fundamental skills. Indeed, the experience of learning to program for the first time is a bit like taking the proverbial drink of water from a fire hose—the rapid influx of information that must be absorbed seems so enormous that you will probably not regret the absence of the few thousand extra concepts that object-oriented programming adds to those associated with structured programming.

And the good news is that plenty of time is available to go back and absorb the OOP "bells and whistles" when you're ready. And you *will* be ready by the time you have completed this volume!

1.3.4: Introduction to Programming Style

Structured programming was introduced to help ensure the development of more robust and maintainable code. On top of these general principles, however, many organizations (and pundits) proposed their own rules for what constitutes acceptable programming practices. These customizations are sometimes referred to as *programming style.*

What is meant by good programming style has generated a lot of controversy over the years. Styles have been characterized on a continuum of *scruffy* to *neat*.[1] Scruffy programmers tend to ignore any conventions that don't suit them, enthusiastically search all manuals for features that no one else knows about, and are willing to take any and all possible shortcuts to get an application working. In the extreme case, scruffy programmers can seem like miracle workers in their ability to get programs up and running in a short period of time—but their code is frequently undocumented, full of bugs, and nearly impossible for others to understand.

Neat programmers, in contrast, tend to follow programming rules religiously, use a limited set of language features to avoid confusing themselves and others, and will develop careful plans and documentation before even starting to write their programs. Their code tends to be bulletproof, easy to maintain, and easy to integrate with other applications. In the most extreme case, however, neat programmers can take so long designing applications that the tool set to be used in writing the program has become obsolete and the application itself has become unnecessary by the time they are ready to begin programming.

When you are just learning to program, it doesn't make a lot of sense to worry too much about style. Just getting the code to compile at all can seem challenging enough. As we look at various programming techniques, however, we will occasionally note where they fall on the scruffy–neat continuum. For example, some programmers believe that it is sensible to use "goto" statements to jump out of deeply nested loops (very scruffy!). Others believe that you should never use an "if" statement without adding an else block (obsessive-compulsive in its neatness!).

This text takes no position regarding what is too scruffy and what is too neat. To a great extent, the culture and rules of the organization employing a programmer will determine the appropriate balance. But you should be aware of how the techniques you are applying may be perceived. Otherwise, you may find yourself having to rewrite the first few programs you develop at your next job.

To illustrate attitudes on different programming styles, various "Style Sidebars" will appear throughout the book. Normally, these styles will consist of attitudes that the author has heard expressed by programmers or found in the programming literature. For the first of these sidebars, however, we will just take the liberty of imagining how the various camps might react to this discussion of style.

1.3: SECTION QUESTIONS

1. What is the driving force that moved us from "anything goes" to structured programming to OOP?
2. What is the primary organizing component of a structured program? An object-oriented program?

---

[1] A description of the scruffy–neat conflict in the field of artificial intelligence can be found in: Sowa, J.F. 1983. *Conceptual Structures.* Reading, MA: Addison-Wesley. p. 23.

3. Why is it useful to acquire some structured programming skills before learning object-oriented programming?

4. Why is it useful to know the general programming style preferred by a company (or an instructor) before you start writing your code?

5. What programming style is best?

1.4: IN DEPTH: A TOUR OF A SIMULATED PC

Walkthrough available in PCAS.wmv

In this section, we present a more detailed view of the internal functioning of a PC, using a tool that simulates a PC, called the PC Assembler Simulator.

1.4.1: The PC Processor

A simulated view of the original PC processor, the Intel 8086, is presented in Figure 1.3. In that processor, the general purpose registers have names such as AX, BX, CX, and DX. (For convenience, you could also access the values in half of these registers at a time. For example, AL was the lower half of the AX register, AH was the upper half). Other registers were typically used for more specialized purposes. The IP (instruction pointer) register, for example, was usually used to keep track of what instruction was currently being executed.

STYLE SIDEBAR 1.1	Attitudes toward discussions of programming style		
	Camp	**Position**	**Justification**
	Super Scruffy	What a waste of time! I clearly bought the wrong book.	Who is this author, an English major? I could be coding right now.
	Scruffy	Nice in theory, but...	Discussions of style are fine, as long as you remember that the job has to get done and are willing to do what it takes—even if it means bending a few of your precious rules.
	Middle Ground	Awareness that a range of styles exists is important if you are going to program in an organization.	Like it or not, everyone develops their own programming style. If you are not aware of the range of styles in use, you will seem naïve when you start programming professionally—and may inadvertently damage your reputation by violating organizational practices.
	Neat	Finally, someone has the courage to discuss styles.	I hope he really sticks it to those scruffies—they have it coming.
	Neat Freak	Totally inappropriate-it makes it sound as if there is a choice of reasonable styles	If you don't follow all the rules for pure structured programming, you are not only a bad programmer, you are a bad person.

| **FIGURE 1.3** | Key Registers in the Intel 8086 Processor |

1.4.2: PC RAM

Figure 1.4 shows the simulated contents of primary storage for a simple program running in the PC Assembler Simulator (PCAS). The two gray columns on the left contain the address of the memory, while the grid on the right contains the actual values. On the original PC, the actual address consisted of two numbers, a segment and an offset, that had to be combined to determine the actual address using the formula:

```
address=16*segment+offset
```

Fortunately, memory addresses on today's PCs are less complicated, consisting of a single number between 0 and about 4 billion. We briefly return to the implications of hardware addressing in our programming when we introduce the C/C++ pointer data type, in Chapter 3. We then return to the subject of addresses in Chapter 10.

1.4.3: PC Code Space

The size of a given opcode/argument combination varies according to the instruction to be performed. For example, on the 8086 processor, the command to add 1 to the value in the BX register (opcode 43, in hexadecimal) is a single byte. In contrast, an instruction to move 2 bytes from primary storage into the AX register (opcode 89 in hexadecimal) requires four bytes. As a result, machine language is difficult for a programmer to read directly. Furthermore, a single byte out of place can totally change the entire meaning of the program. That makes writing any nontrivial code directly in machine language a virtual impossibility. Where writing programs directly for a particular machine is necessary

| FIGURE 1.4 | Selected Bytes of Primary Storage Displayed in the PCAS |

Assem Windows Application - [Asm1:4]

File   Edit   View   Program   Window   Help

Segment	Offset	0	1	2	3	4	5	6	7	8	9	A	B	C	D	E	F
0000	0000	31	34	38	37	00	00	00	00	00	00	00	00	00	00	00	00
0000	0010	00	00	00	00	00	00	00	00	00	00	00	00	00	00	00	00
0000	0020	00	00	00	00	00	00	00	00	00	00	00	00	00	00	00	00
0000	0030	00	00	00	00	00	00	00	00	00	00	00	00	00	00	00	00
0000	0040	00	00	00	00	00	00	00	00	00	00	00	00	00	00	00	00
0000	0050	00	00	00	00	00	00	00	00	00	00	00	00	00	00	00	00
0000	0060	00	00	00	00	00	00	00	00	00	00	00	00	00	00	00	00
0000	0070	00	00	00	00	00	00	00	00	00	00	00	00	00	00	00	00
0000	0080	00	00	00	00	00	00	00	00	00	00	00	00	00	00	00	00
0000	0090	B9	00	00	BB	00	00	8A	8F	00	00	80	F9	00	75	03	E9

For Help, press F1

(e.g., to write certain critical components of an operating system) assembly language is more typically used. In Figure 1.5, the machine language (left pane) and corresponding assembly language (right pane) for a simulated program are displayed.

On most processors, certain processor registers are dedicated to keeping track of a program's position in the code space. In the original PC, for example, the CS (code segment) register was normally used to keep track of where the code began in RAM, while the IP (instruction pointer) kept track of the address of the instruction being executed. Execution would occur sequentially, that is, moving down line-by-line in Figure 1.5, unless some form of jump instruction (e.g., JMP, JNZ, JAE, JBE in the figure) was encountered. Such jumps would cause the program to begin executing at a different position in the code. When performed in conjunction with a test—a jump is specified to occur if some test condition is met, for example—the process is known as *branching*. Such branching is one of the primary ways we control the flow of our programs, a topic to which we shall return in Chapter 5.

1.5: REVIEW AND QUESTIONS

1.5.1: REVIEW

Upon completing Chapter 1, you should have developed a mental model of a computer that will help you understand the "big picture" of what you are doing when you start programming. The most important concepts presented in this chapter are as follows:

■   The primary components of a computer are the CPU, primary storage, secondary storage, and

peripherals. The CPU performs computations and sends directions to the remaining components. Primary storage, aka RAM, acts as readily accessible temporary scratch space used by the processor while performing its computations. Secondary storage is normally nonvolatile, meaning it can be used to hold information over long periods of time and does not reset when power is

FIGURE 1.5 Code Space (Machine Language) Bytes and Assembly Language

Brk?	Address	Codes	Line	Source Code
			14	MAIN PROC
	0009:0000	B9 00 00	15	MOV CX,0
	0009:0003	BB 00 00	16	MOV BX,0
	0009:0006	8A 8F 00 00	17	LoadChar: MOV CL,TestString[BX]
	0009:000A	80 F9 00	18	CMP CL,0
	0009:000D	75 03	19	JNZ NotZero
	0009:000F	E9 38 00	20	JMP Done
	0009:0012	80 F9 30	21	NotZero: CMP CL,0x30
	0009:0015	73 03	22	JAE DigitTest
	0009:0017	E9 38 00	23	JMP Done
	0009:001A	80 F9 39	24	DigitTest: CMP CL,0x39
	0009:001D	76 03	25	JBE DigitOK
	0009:001F	E9 38 00	26	JMP Done
	0009:0022	8B 06 05 00	27	DigitOK: MOV AX,IntVal
	0009:0026	BA 0A 00	28	MOV DX,10
	0009:0029	F7 E2	29	MUL DX
	0009:002B	80 E9 30	30	SUB CL,0x30
	0009:002E	02 C1	31	ADD AX,CX
	0009:0030	89 06 05 00	32	MOV IntVal,AX
	0009:0034	43	33	INC BX
	0009:0035	E9 06 00	34	JMP LoadChar
	0009:0038	C3	35	Done: RET

lost. It may be fixed (e.g., a hard drive) or removable (e.g., a CD or floppy disk). The term *peripheral* refers to any device attached to the system (e.g., a printer, modem, or keyboard) excepting the CPU and primary storage. These devices extend the capabilities of the basic computer system and are most commonly involved with getting information into the system (input) or getting it out of the system (output).

■ The stored program concept is at the heart of modern computer architectures. It most commonly involves organizing primary storage into three regions: code space, data space, and stack space. The code space holds the actual program (or programs) currently running on the computer. The data space holds information used by these programs in a way that is readily accessible to the processor. The stack space is a special region of memory that is used to hold the data and other information that we are actively focusing on, somewhat analogous to an in-box. It is most critical for implementing functions, which are conceptually similar to algebraic or financial functions, and are central to the organization and design of structured programs.

■ Today, the instructions that a processor executes, referred to as executable code, are very different from the instructions written by the programmer, called source code. This distinction was not always the case. In the early days of computers (the early 1950s), programmers actually placed executable instructions in memory, known as the first generation language, or 1GL. By the mid-1950s, a text-based mnemonic version of these instructions, known as assembly language or 2GL, had been developed for many processors. Code written in assembly language was translated into machine language using a tool known as an assembler. By the late 1950s, programming languages that were not processor specific, known as 3GL, were introduced. The tool used to translate these languages into machine language is called a compiler.

■ An example of a 3GL, developed by AT&T's Bell Laboratories in the late 1960s, is the C programming language. It was specifically designed to help move the Unix operating system across different hardware platforms. C became so popular as a general programming language during the 1970s that an object-oriented version of the language, known as C++, was introduced in the

1980s. C++ was specifically designed to be a superset of C, meaning that most C programs can be recompiled as C++ programs with little or no modification. As a consequence, learning C is often a first step to learning C++.

- Structured programming refers to a particular style of programming that is organized around functions and data structures. It differs from earlier, more ad hoc, programming styles in that it avoids explicit jumps within program code—such as the goto statement provided by many languages—in favor of more rigorous constructs.

- Object-oriented programming, in contrast, merges data structures and functions together into self-contained "objects," which then become the primary mechanism for organizing programs. It was developed to manage the complexity of applications that were ever-increasing in size. The three characteristics of OOP are (1) encapsulation, which means making objects as self-contained as possible, (2) inheritance, which is the ability to design objects using previously defined objects as a starting point, and (3) polymorphism, which is the ability to design classes of objects (e.g., types of windows) that respond differently to the same commands (e.g., windows messages). Although OOP is the preferred approach to most new program development, virtually all the skills associated with learning structured programming are applied while engaging in OOP. As a consequence, mastering structured programming is often the best first step in learning OOP.

- Programming style is the final topic addressed. A wide range of "appropriate" programming styles have been proposed, on a continuum ranging from scruffy to neat. What style works for a particular programmer will depend on the nature of program being written, the skills and preferences of the programmer, and, most importantly, on the organizational setting in which the program is being written. It is critical that programmers, particularly business programmers, understand the range of styles that are present, because many organizations have policies regarding acceptable programming practices that must be adhered to.

1.5.2: GLOSSARY

argument   A variable that is passed into a function

assembler   A program that takes assembly language (2GL) source code and translates it into object code suitable for the processor

assembly language   The second generation language that uses mnemonic instructions that translate to codes used by the CPU

central processing unit (CPU)   The "brain" of a computer; the main processing unit of a computer that allows for fast computations to be accomplished in a short period of time

CMOS   A chip on the computer that allows for settings to be stored

code space   Primary storage space used for the native executable code that a microprocessor understands

compiler   A computer program that translates 3GL computer programs into a form suitable for the central processing unit

data space   Space in the computer's primary storage used for holding data

encapsulation   The process of intermixing data and program code in order to produce a self-contained object that is completely independent of other objects to increase efficiency in program design

function   A defined portion of a program that performs a specific task; can also be referred to as a procedure or subroutine

inheritance   The process of using object code as a starting point for designing other objects

instruction set   A set of predefined commands that a processor can understand

interpreter   A computer program that translates a computer program into an intermediate form in order to execute the source code without any need to compile

machine language   The commands that are directly understood by the CPU

memory address   A logical unit or address where information is stored in the computer's RAM

Microsoft Foundation Classes (MFC)   Predefined classes developed by Microsoft to allow for the easier development of Windows-based applications

operating system   A computer program that regulates the functions of a computer and allows for memory management and for input and output mechanisms

peripheral   A device not directly connected to the computer's processing memory unit

polymorphism   Used by object-oriented programming languages, it allows for objects to exhibit specialized behaviors in response to signals from other objects

primary storage   Also referred to as RAM, it is the volatile scratch space that the computer's central processing unit uses in order to accomplish its computational tasks

registers   Storage facilities in the central processing unit allowing for fast manipulation of bytes for computation

secondary storage   Usually refers to the non-volatile storage devices connected to any computer, typically a hard drive or other type of media such as a floppy disk

stack   A technique for holding information that is used last-in, first-out, similar to an inbox

stack space   Primary storage space that is used as an inbox for holding information related to the active task

volatile memory   Memory that cannot hold a value when the power is removed

1.5.3: QUESTIONS

1.   If you were to create a function to calculate a person's age, what arguments would be needed and what type of value would it return? Would the manner in which the arguments were represented impact the number required?

2.   Create a chart identifying the evolution of hardware, programming languages, and programming approaches over time.

3.   If all memory can hold any type of data, do you suppose it is possible (in your program) to place data in an incorrect place as a result of a bug? What consequences could this cause when your program runs? (Hint: think about the types of information that primary storage holds.)

4.   Why does the operating system used by a computer have a profound impact on programming?

5.   What problems are likely to arise when developers and tool vendors "enhance" a language?

6.   Why does it make sense that compiled code runs faster than interpreted code? Given the speed difference, why are languages that are not compiled directly to machine language (such as Java and MS C# .Net) gaining in popularity?

7.   What are the pros and cons of programming using a language that is controlled by a particular vendor?

8.   The inventory term LIFO (last-in, first-out) is frequently used to describe a stack. Explain how this model fits a function call, as described in the chapter.

9.   In C++, a variable that holds an address is called a "pointer." If our "memory" is a bank of PO boxes, and we are told that Box 101 is a "pointer," what would we expect to find when we looked inside the box?

10.   Explain why there is probably no single "best" programming style.

CHAPTER 2

A Simple Project

EXECUTIVE SUMMARY

Visual Studio .NET is an extremely powerful development environment. With that power, however, comes significant complexity—unnecessary complexity for the purposes of what we need to accomplish in this textbook. In this chapter, we conduct a walkthrough of the bare essentials needed to create and debug simple C++ projects.

The chapter begins with an overview of the process of creating a program. We then turn to Visual Studio .NET, explaining terms such as *project*, *solution* and *configuration*. Next, we create the traditional first C/C++ program, a program that prints "Hello, World" on the screen. The concept of a multifile project is then introduced, beginning by bringing in a file of simple input/output functions supplied with the textbook. We then add our own file to the project and create a few simple functions. Finally, we look at some of the tools that are provided for the purposes of debugging projects: **breakpoints,** code stepping, inspection windows, and the **call stack.** These tools prove invaluable as we move on to more complex projects.

LEARNING OBJECTIVES

Upon completing this chapter, you should be able to:

- Describe what is being accomplished in each stage of the compose, compile, link, and load sequence of program development and operation
- Explain the purpose of Visual Studio .NET and the role of Visual C++ .NET within that environment
- Distinguish between the terms solution, project and configuration, as used in Visual Studio .NET
- Create a simple, single file console project in Visual Studio in C++
- Add additional files to the project
- Compile, link, and run your project, addressing a few simple errors along the way
- Use the debugger to step through your code as it runs
- Place breakpoints in your code to pause the debugger
- Use the inspection window to examine the values of variables
- Use the call stack window to see the sequence of functions being executed while your program is paused
- Use the help system to find out more information on the functions you are using

2.1: STEPS IN CREATING A PROGRAM

Before we create our first project, we need a basic understanding of the process through which **source code,** the program code that we type in, is transformed into **executable code,** the code that is actually run by our processor. In this section, we provide an overview of the process, which is illustrated in Figure 2.1. We refer to these steps as compose, compile, link, and load.

2.1.1: Compose

The first step in programming an application is, of course, writing the code for the application. As often as not, source code can be written in any text editor (such as MS Notepad). **Integrated development environments,** such as Visual Studio .NET, will normally provide their own editor. These included editors offer special features—such as keyword highlighting, auto completion, and automatic indentation—that make writing code somewhat easier.

It is important to realize that, for all but the simplest program, more than a single file of source code will normally be required. The use of multiple files both helps the programmer organize the project and speeds the compiling process (only recently edited files need to be recompiled when recreating a program to fix defects or change the code). In Figure 2.1, the collection of source files created by the programmer is illustrated by the row of .cpp files at the top.

One side effect of using multiple files is that some information may need to be shared across all the files. A common example of such information might be the names and types of individual variables that are used in all of the source files. Another example might be constants that we define, such as the maximum number of characters in a line of text. To ensure such consistency, most 3GLs provide a command that causes a file

FIGURE 2.1 Overview of Program Creation

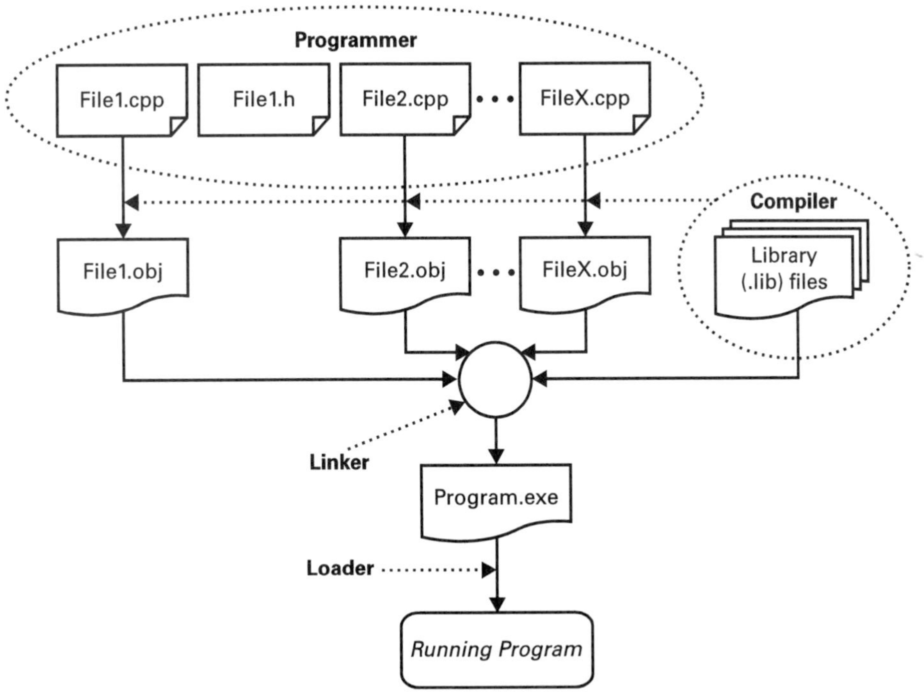

to be included—effectively pasting the included file into the source file when the compile process begins. In C/C++ such files are usually referred to as **header files,** illustrated by the .h file in Figure 2.1.

An analogy that can get us started toward a fuller understanding of the process is that of writing and editing a book. In this example, individual program files can be likened to chapters in that book. The common (included) files, on the other hand, might consist of lists—such as names of major characters, their sex, and their age—that can be used to ensure consistency across chapters. This analogy is illustrated in Figure 2.2.

2.1.2: Compile

After a programmer completes writing one or more source files, each file is compiled separately. The compiling process is intended to check the code for errors and—if no serious errors are found—generate a file containing object code, as illustrated by the .obj files in the second row of Figure 2.1. In addition to the .obj files created from the source code written by the programmer, a typical compiler comes with a collection of prewritten files, called library files, containing useful functions that the programmer can call from his or her programs. The .lib files in the second row of Figure 2.1 illustrate these precompiled function libraries.

FIGURE 2.2 Book Chapter Analogy

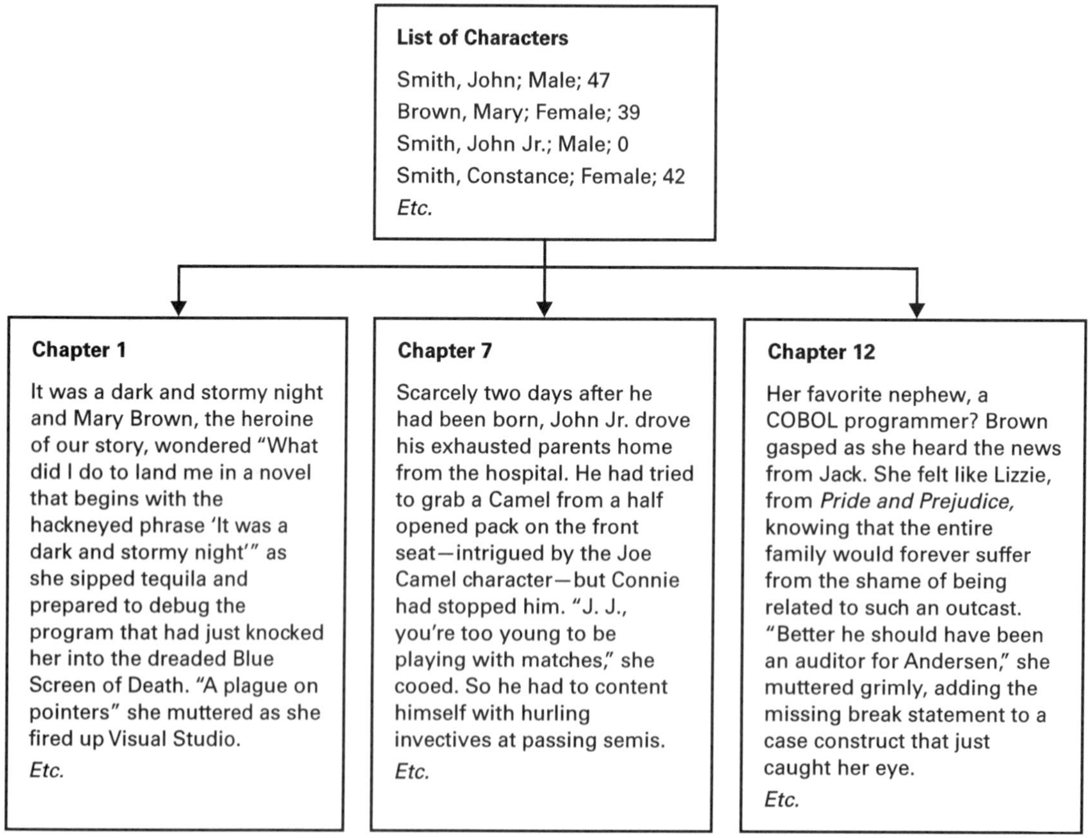

List of Characters

Smith, John; Male; 47
Brown, Mary; Female; 39
Smith, John Jr.; Male; 0
Smith, Constance; Female; 42
Etc.

Chapter 1

It was a dark and stormy night and Mary Brown, the heroine of our story, wondered "What did I do to land me in a novel that begins with the hackneyed phrase 'It was a dark and stormy night'" as she sipped tequila and prepared to debug the program that had just knocked her into the dreaded Blue Screen of Death. "A plague on pointers" she muttered as she fired up Visual Studio.

Etc.

Chapter 7

Scarcely two days after he had been born, John Jr. drove his exhausted parents home from the hospital. He had tried to grab a Camel from a half opened pack on the front seat—intrigued by the Joe Camel character—but Connie had stopped him. "J. J., you're too young to be playing with matches," she cooed. So he had to content himself with hurling invectives at passing semis.

Etc.

Chapter 12

Her favorite nephew, a COBOL programmer? Brown gasped as she heard the news from Jack. She felt like Lizzie, from *Pride and Prejudice,* knowing that the entire family would forever suffer from the shame of being related to such an outcast. "Better he should have been an auditor for Andersen," she muttered grimly, adding the missing break statement to a case construct that just caught her eye.

Etc.

Continuing with our novel analogy, let us assume a few things about the "legal" structure of our novel. Specifically, we are constrained in the following ways:

- Every character in our novel must be "introduced" somewhere in the novel, at which time a brief description of the character is given.
- No character may be introduced more than once in our novel—they may be used and developed throughout the novel, but more than one introduction would be considered patronizing to the reader, and would therefore be an error.
- Major characters may appear in more than one chapter. All of them should be listed in our "list of characters" document.
- Minor characters may be introduced locally within a chapter, then discarded (e.g., newspaper vendors, subway token takers), in which case they don't need to appear in our "list of characters" document. We will refer to them as local characters, for convenience.

Our "compiler" in this case would perform the task of getting each chapter ready for publication. In the course of doing so, it could run into four major categories of error:

1. *Grammatical errors:* problems with the grammar or spelling in the prose that render it inconsistent with proper English. The programming equivalent to this category of error is called a *syntax* error.
2. *Use of unknown characters:* Any individual whose name is mentioned but (a) is *not* on the "list of characters," and (b) has *not* been introduced locally, is not allowed.
3. *Improper use of characters:* In comparing the information from the "list of characters" and the chapters, some inconsistencies may surface. For example, having a newborn baby drive his two parents home from the hospital is impossible, and would therefore generate a *usage error.* The compiler may also identify situations in which the usage seems unlikely, but not impossible (e.g., a female character going into the men's room). These situations would be listed as *warnings.* Often, warnings can be removed by an appropriate explanation (e.g, "the line to the women's room extended across two county lines so she…").
4. *Introducing the same character more than once:* If the same character, local or major, should be introduced more than one time in the same chapter, a *multiple declaration* error would result.

Although the compiler can catch many errors, it cannot catch all errors. Among the "uncatchable" errors would be the following:

1. *Major characters that are never introduced:* If a chapter does not contain the introduction for a specific character in the novel, the compiler assumes the introduction will be performed in some other chapter. Thus, the compiler cannot determine whether we forgot to introduce the character anywhere.
2. *The same major character is introduced in more than one chapter:* Similar to (1), the compiler can only detect multiple declaration errors if both declarations are in the same chapter.
3. *Plot errors or inconsistencies:* Our compiler is not smart enough to know what we are trying to accomplish in our novel or chapter, so the compiler cannot detect anything but the most obvious *logic* errors.

Once we "compile" each chapter without any errors—and resolve all warnings to our satisfaction—the compiler is able to assemble the chapter into a unit that is closer to a state of readiness for publication. One piece of information that is necessarily missing, however, is page numbers—which correspond to memory locations in a programming example. Although we know the relative page numbers within each chapter once we compile it, we won't know the page number where the chapter begins until we compile all the chapters and place them in order.

2.1.3: Linking

The linking process involves taking all the object modules produced by the compiler, along with object modules stored in any library we choose to reference, and assembling them into a single executable program (normally a file with the .exe extension for the programs we will be creating). In doing so, it assigns the relative memory locations of all variables and functions that are used in the program. (Actual memory locations cannot be assigned until the final stage: loading.) This assignment is illustrated by the circle on the third row of Figure 2.1.

In our novel example, linking is the process of taking the individual chapters and assembling them into a complete book. In the linking process, we can catch two types of errors:

1. *A major character that is never introduced:* Having access to all chapters, the **linker** can ensure that every character is introduced once. If no introduction is found for a character used in the novel, an error is generated.

2. *The same major character is introduced in more than one chapter:* The linker can also go through all the chapters and ensure that an introduction to a given character does not appear in more than one place.

These errors, you may observe, are the same as the first two types of errors typically missed by the compiler.

Once all linker errors are resolved, our chapters can be assembled together into a single unit. At this point, certain blanks in the compiled chapters can be filled in—such as the relative position of each chapter in the book. We can also generate various tables, such as a table of contents and an index, if we are so inclined.

Even with the book assembled in this fashion, however, we may not know everything needed to assign page numbers. For example, our novel might be included in a trilogy, to be sold in the remainder racks of popular bookstores, in which case it might not begin on page 1. So, although our "linked" book is practically ready to publish, one final stage in the process still remains.

2.1.4: Loading

The loading process, normally performed by the operating system, takes the executable file produced by the linker, loads it into memory, then updates the addresses in the program so they reflect actual memory locations (as opposed to the memory locations relative to the start of the program, which were established by the linker). After a program is loaded, it can commence running. In MS Windows, for example, double clicking a program or document icon normally invokes the **loader** on the appropriate application, to start it running.

To complete our novel example, the loading process is analogous to placing the complete novel into our desktop publishing package, assigning a number to the first page, updating the page numbers in the table of contents and index to reflect the starting page, then pressing the print button.

Before leaving the subject of creating programs, we should emphasize, once again, that the travails associated with the compose-compile-link-load cycle represent only a fraction of programming time. At the front end, designing a program may take as long as composing it. At the back end, removing logic errors from code (i.e., debugging the running program) can easily take as much time as all the other stages put together—even more, when the programmer is just learning C/C++. These issues of design and debugging will be addressed frequently throughout the textbook.

2.1: SECTION QUESTIONS

1. What are some advantages of having a project consisting of many small source files, rather than a single large one?

2. If you were moving a project, such as that in Figure 2.1, from one computer to another, which files would you have to move, and which could you recreate?

3. What type of file in Figure 2.1 is a library file most like? What are some reasons for distributing code as library files, rather than as source code?

4. If a project only has one source file, do you still need to link the project before you run it? Explain why or why not.

5. When a program is loaded, will it always be loaded in the same location? Why or why not?

2.2: INTRODUCTION TO VISUAL STUDIO .NET

Visual Studio .NET is the newest software development environment in a long series of environments designed by Microsoft. It is built to accommodate programming in multiple languages (Visual Basic, Visual C++, and Visual C#—pronounced C-sharp—being the most tightly integrated) and is particularly targeted toward the creation of applications to be distributed across the Internet.

Visual Studio is an example of an integrated development environment (IDE). What distinguishes an IDE from other development tools is the tight coupling between all the components and utilities associated with developing a program.

To understand the benefits of an IDE, it is useful to consider the alternative. In the mid-1980s, for example, if you wanted to program in C you needed to acquire:

- A text editor, such as IBM's Personal Editor, to create your source code
- A compiler, such as the Lattice C compiler that later became Microsoft C (It was also often useful to have an assembler, such as Microsoft's Macro Assembler, to handle specialized code development, or mixed language programming.)
- A linker, normally provided with the operating system
- A **debugger,** such as the CodeView debugger, that could be used to examine your program while it was running
- If you wanted to program in Windows (late-1980s), you also needed to acquire the Windows SDK (software development kit)—a library of functions needed to write Windows applications

Many disadvantages came with using these tools. First, they were expensive, easily running upwards of $1,000 if Windows programming was your goal (of course, in the late 1980s, few people used the versions of MS Windows that were then available). Second, almost no online help was available, so you typically needed five or six reference manuals on your desk while you programmed. Third, each component had to be run separately. You would start by running your text editor, editing your code, saving your work, then exiting your editor. Then you would run your compiler. If there were errors, you would have to go back into your editor. If not, you could run the linker. If that worked, you could run the program, and so on. Although they seem archaic by today's standards, it is worth being aware that such separate tools existed—and continue to exist. Throughout the .NET C++ technical documentation, for example, references are frequently made to command line compiler switches. For some types of applications and development situations, using the standalone (command line) compiler continues to be recommended.

The experience of programming in an *integrated* development environment is entirely different from working with separate tools. To begin with, all the different components are incorporated into the same tool. In Visual Studio .NET, for example, you have:

- Source code editors that are aware of the language in use and that supply appropriate (yet customizable) indentation and highlighting (e.g., for keywords and comments)
- Online help—tied into Microsoft's MSDN library of technical documentation—that is equivalent to thousands of manuals
- Intelligent Make facilities that combine compiling and linking, using modification dates of the files to determine what files need to be updated each time a program is rebuilt (i.e., the executable is created)
- Debugging tools tightly coupled with the other development tools (Indeed, the .NET debugger is so sophisticated that it has the ability to make some code changes while a program is actually running.)
- Incorporated libraries and code generation Wizards that can be used to facilitate programming in environments that previously required expert-level skills (such as component development)

These tools dramatically increase a programmer's potential productivity. Of course, they also come with a downside—if you insisted on understanding every capability Visual Studio .NET offered, it would probably take you upwards of a year to start using it (and then, only if you were an expert programmer to begin with). So, the best way to proceed is usually to take on a few features at a time.

2.2.1: Projects and Solutions

The primary organizing elements of Visual Studio .NET are the *project* and the *solution*. These elements can be characterized roughly as follows:

- *Project:* A collection of files that, together, can be used to create and debug a single executable *target*. For our purposes, the *target* is always an executable program, although this does not always have to be the case. The files can include a variety of different types, including source code (e.g., .cpp and .h files), object files (.obj) created when source files are compiled, executable files (e.g., .exe, .dll files) produced by the project and a variety of project definition files whose purpose is to keep track of the other files in the project, and other information such as the location of breakpoints.
- *Solution:* A collection of one or more related projects. A solution also contains environmental information, such as the position of each open window. That

information is used to ensure that the programmer's *workspace* (the old name for solution) appears just as he or she left it each time it is retrieved.

The incorporation of multiple projects into a single solution is most useful when creating an application out of separate independent components. That programming approach is an advanced topic, far beyond the scope of this textbook. So, for our purposes, projects and solutions will always have a one-to-one correspondence (one project per solution), and we can think of the two as being effectively equivalent.

Real projects can include quite a few files (as illustrated in Figure 2.3, which shows the project folder used for a build of FlowC). Even simple projects contain more files than you might expect, when IDE-generated files are counted. For this reason, the standard behavior of Visual Studio .NET is to create a new folder for each project. Additional folders will then be created, if necessary, based on the project's *configuration*.

Project *configuration* allows the user to maintain different variations of a target program within the same project. The two most common configurations are Debug and Release. The Debug version of a target contains information that allows the debugger to synchronize the lines of source code with the machine code in the executable file. The Release version has no such information (and the .exe file it produces can be ten times smaller). Because Debug and Release mode targets must be compiled differently, a separate

FIGURE 2.3   FlowC Object Project Folder Created by Visual Studio .NET

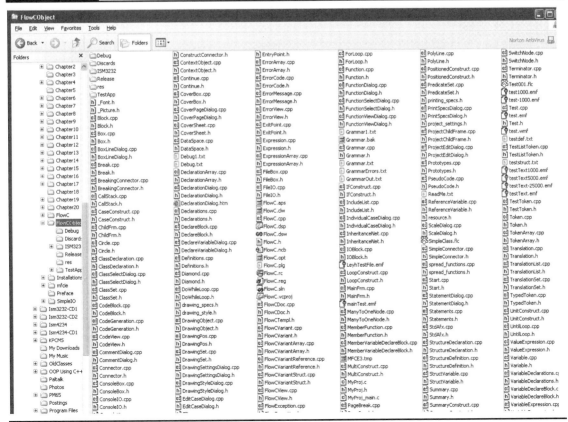

folder is used to hold the .obj and .exe files for each separate configuration (as can be seen in Figure 2.3, where both Debug and Release folders have been created).

For the purposes of this textbook, we will always be using the Debug configuration—because we have no reason to disable the tool most likely to help us get our programs working. Because Debug is the default, we will not normally need to adjust the configuration. It is wise to be aware that configuration settings exist, however, for several practical reasons:

- Should you accidentally set your configuration to Release, you won't be able to use the debugger until you return the setting to Debug and rebuild the project.

- If you need to copy your executable program—to hand in as part of an assignment or to show friends and family, for example—creating a release mode version may be the only way you can get it small enough to fit on a floppy.

- If you need to find the executable version of your program, you should be aware (a) that it will exist in the subfolder named after the configuration (e.g., the Debug folder), and (b) that where multiple configurations exist (e.g., Debug and Release), the version of the program in each subfolder will only be as recent as the last time you built the project while in that particular configuration.

Before leaving the subject of moving your programs around, it is also important to realize that projects can become quite large (even projects that do practically nothing can range from 3 to 10 megabytes in size). In the event that you need to move projects between machines, the *Build|Clean* option in Visual Studio deletes every file that can be recreated by the IDE (i.e., object files, executable files, etc.)—reducing the size of most small projects to a few hundred kilobytes. This excellent tool can be used for moving your work between home and work/lab computers, and sharing code during group projects.

2.2.2: Creating a Console Project

Throughout this text, we will be creating what are called console projects—applications that run in ugly black windows with I/O no more sophisticated than a teletype could manage. Such projects represent the "lowest common denominator" of C/C++ programming, and limiting ourselves in this way allows us to adhere pretty closely to ANSI standards—meaning the code we will write can be reused on almost any hardware/operating system combination that supports a decent (i.e., ANSI compliant) C/C++ compiler. Furthermore, it turns out that this plain vanilla approach to programming can still be used to create some pretty impressive I/O. For example, console C++ programs can generate CGI (common gateway interface) web forms.

Project Type Creating a new project begins by selecting a project type, which involves two steps. First, you must select the basic project category (Visual C++ Project) from the left-hand side of the New Project dialog. Then, from the list of templates that is presented on the right-hand side, you select the **Win32 Project** option, as illustrated in Figure 2.4. At that time, you should also give the project a name, which will be used to create a project folder, and also as the default name of the target (as an .exe file, used throughout this text).

Upon pressing OK, you will then be presented with a dialog (the *Win32 Application Wizard*). After choosing Application Settings from the left-hand panel in the dialog box, you will be given a choice of settings for your project. As illustrated in Figure 2.5, you should select the settings as follows:

- *Application Type* should be set to Console application.
- Empty Project box should be checked.

FIGURE 2.4   Creating a Win32 Console Project

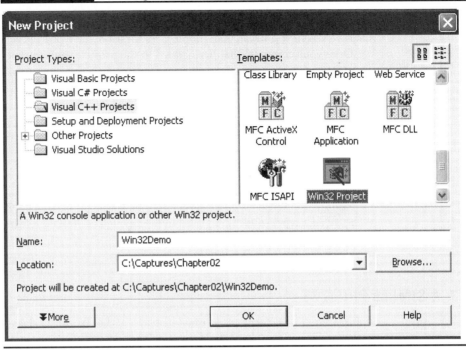

FIGURE 2.5   Application Settings Dialog Box

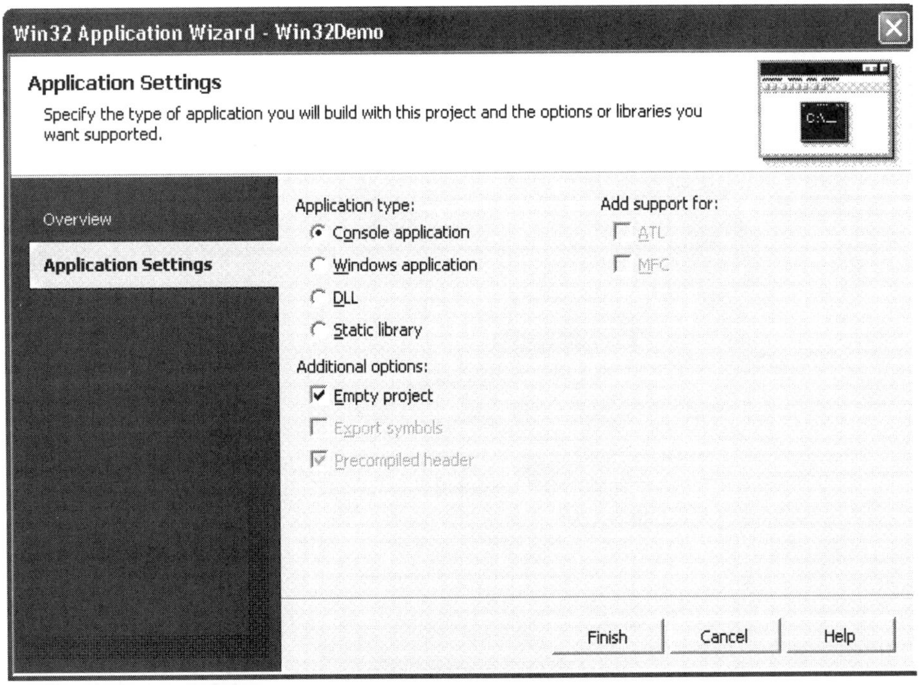

These settings will create a project into which you can place your C and C++ files.

Once your project has been created, you can right click the Source Files folder below the project icon (highlighted in Figure 2.6) in the Solution Explorer pane, and choose *Add|Add New Item*. You can then choose from the list of file types to create a new source file.

Once your empty file has been added to the project, you can type in your code and comments, as illustrated in Figure 2.6.

2.2: SECTION QUESTIONS

1. What's the difference between a C++ source file, a project, and a solution? Why won't the last of these differences be very important in this book?
2. What is a target? What type of target will we be focusing on?
3. What types of tools are incorporated into the Visual Studio .NET IDE?
4. What is the difference between Debug mode and Release mode?
5. What types of files are placed in the Debug and Release folders? Could you have the same file names in both folders?
6. Why will we need to adjust Application Settings every time we create a new project?

2.3: A SIMPLE PROJECT

In this section, we create a project that displays "Hello, World" to the screen in C++. This particular project has a long tradition of being the first C/C++ program taught in almost every course.

2.3.1: Hello, World in C++

Walkthrough available in HelloCpp.wmv

Creating a C++ console "Hello, World" project in Visual Studio is relatively simple. It involves:

FIGURE 2.6   Adding Simple Main Function

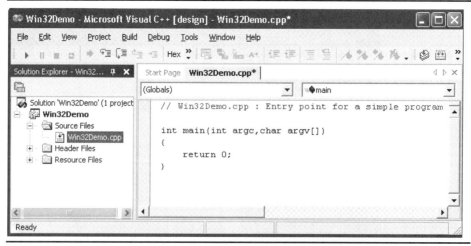

1. Generating a project with a skeletal main function
2. Editing the code so it prints "Hello, World"
3. Building the executable file
4. Running the program

We now look at each of these steps.

Generating a Project with a Skeletal Main Function   Follow the procedure in Section 2.2.2 to create an empty console project. Add an empty C++ source file, type in the contents as shown in Figure 2.6, and save it as "Hello.cpp".

Editing the Code to Print "Hello, World"   Modify the code so it matches that in Example 2.1. The lines being added are the following:

```
#include <iostream>
using namespace std;
```

above the line int main(int argc, char* argv[]), then

```
cout << "Hello, World " << endl;
```

within the { and }, above the line *return 0;*

Building the Executable File   Because Visual C++ has a sophisticated compiler/linker combination, we can perform our compile and link in a single step. This task can be done either using the toolbar, or by selecting Build|Build Solution from the menu. If you entered your changes properly, in an output box beneath the window you may see messages along the lines of those in Example 2.2 (with your paths being different, presumably).

Messages such as these are what might be termed a mixed signal. On the one hand, it completed compiling and linking your project. On the other hand it warned you about something—and you should *never* ignore a warning.

The particular message in question results from our main() function, the entry point for every C++ (and C) program, which has two arguments: *argc* and *argv*. The compiler noticed, however, that we were not using those arguments within our main function. It then wondered: Why would you define a function with arguments, then not use them? The warnings are just the compiler's way of trying to help us. In doing so, it also illustrates an important,

---

EXAMPLE 2.1

Modified C++ code

```cpp
// Hello.cpp : Defines the entry point for the console application.

#include <iostream>
using namespace std;

int main(int argc, char* argv[])
{
    cout << "Hello, World " << endl;
    return 0;
}
```

EXAMPLE 2.2

Build messages

Compiling...
Hello.cpp
Build log was saved at "file://c:
c:\YourFolder\Hello\Hello.cpp(6) : warning C4100: 'argv' : unreferenced formal parameter
c:\YourFolder\Hello\Hello.cpp(6) : warning C4100: 'argc' : unreferenced formal parameter
Linking...
\YourFolder\Hello\Debug\BuildLog.htm"
Hello - 0 error(s), 2 warning(s)

---------------------- Done ----------------------

    Build: 1 succeeded, 0 failed, 0 skipped

---

and nearly universal, law of compiler design: *never issue a message using language that a beginner can understand.* For further information, you can highlight the error code (C4100), then press F1 to bring up a help screen. Doing so will illustrate another important design principle: *When you're just getting started, don't expect the help screens to be of much use.*

> *Hint:* If you want more information on an error, try typing the error code into a search engine such as Google or Yahoo!. Frequently, more detailed explanations will be found.

Fortunately, the preceding message is relatively easy to get rid of. The main() function, it turns out, can also be defined with no arguments. So to make the warnings go away, just change the line that reads *int main(int argc, char* argv[])* to:

```
int main()
```
Build the project again and verify no errors and no warnings.

Running the Program   The last step in creating our first program is to run it. You can run the program in two ways, using the debugger and not using the debugger. Common sense would suggest that we need all the help we can get, so the first thing we will do is run it under the debugger, which can be done using *Debug|Start.* If you are quick, your eye might be able to catch the black screen appearing and disappearing, as the program ends. It turns out, if you want to run a console project under the debugger, you need to know something about breakpoints, which we will cover shortly.

The other alternative to running the program—an alternative you should almost never choose voluntarily when you're writing your actual programs—is to run without debugger support. This approach can be done using *Debug|Start without debugging.* As it happens, when a console project is run this way, the console window—which we might think of as "the black screen of despair" (so as to distinguish it from the ever-popular "blue screen of death" that appears when we've been *really* bad)—remains visible and the program doesn't end until we press a key, as illustrated in Figure 2.7.

| FIGURE 2.7 | Console Window When Program Is Run Without Debugging |

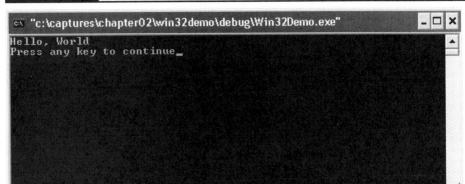

2.3.2: Anatomy of Hello, World

Although Hello, World is a very small program, it is nevertheless a complete program. For this reason, by examining it closely, we can learn a lot about how a C++ program is created.

We now go through the code originally presented in Example 2.1, line-by-line.

Explanation 1: Comments

The first line we encounter in the file is:

```
// Hello.cpp : Defines the entry point for the console
application.
```

This line is a comment, meaning it serves the purposes of informing the programmer, but has no effect on the actual program. There are two ways to define comments. The first, within /* and */ (traditional C comments), might look like the following:

```
/* anything between the comment delimiters,
   no matter how it is spaced, or how many lines it takes
   is a comment */
```

The other approach (which is technically a C++ standard) is the // (slash-slash comment)—as shown previously—which comments out the rest of the line.

Explanation 2: Preprocessor Instruction

What should first catch your attention about the next line is that it begins with the # (pound) character:

```
#include <iostream>
```

At the beginning of this chapter, we illustrated the concept of file inclusion using an analogy between a list of characters and chapters in a book. The file *iostream* contains similar information—most importantly, it tells the compiler what several dozen input and output functions in the standard libraries are supposed to look like. We need that information in order to run this program because C++ itself doesn't know what the **cout** we refer to in the program is. Without including the iostream file, the compiler would look at the line with the **cout** in it and say: "Hmm, I've never heard of it…"

<u>TEST YOUR UNDERSTANDING 2.1</u>

Try removing the #include statement (or commenting the line out) and building the project again. What does the error message tell you?

The # sign in front of the #include directive indicates that we are looking at a **preprocessor** directive. We will talk more about the preprocessor in a later chapter, but, for the time being, we can think of it as a sophisticated search and replace tool that works on your code before it is given to the compiler. The #include directive tells it to:

- Find the file *iostream* by looking in the standard include directories, which are specified deep within the IDE's project settings.
- Paste the entire file into the code you wrote, creating a temporary file that is then sent to the compiler.

Other preprocessor directives (most notably, #define) will be explained in later chapters, as they are needed.

Explanation 3: Namespace Directive Right under the preprocessor instruction is a **namespace** directive:

```
using namespace std;
```

To understand the purpose of this line of code, a little background is necessary. As C++ evolved, problems in keeping names unique began to emerge—especially since C++ allows several versions of a function to be defined using the same name. To help tell different functions and objects with the same name apart, the concept of a namespace was introduced. Using namespaces, it became possible to ensure high levels of uniqueness. For example, the iostream library defines **cout** to be in the standard namespace (**std**), that means its "real" name is **std::cout**, not just **cout**. This definition prevents any confusion with other **cout** objects that might happen to be hanging around.

Unfortunately, namespaces can be quite a pest. First, they make everything that you need to write longer, because you have to prefix the namespace name to objects. Second, old code—compiled before namespaces were incorporated into most compilers (which happened in the mid-1990s)—often won't work with the new libraries that use namespaces.

To reduce these problems, the **using namespace name;** statement can be employed. When present, the compiler takes every function and object that is not otherwise identified and tries prefixing the namespace *name* to it. Thus, when we have the statement **using namespace std;** in our file, whenever the unknown object (**cout**) is encountered, the compiler checks for **std::cout**, which it finds in the iostream library.

Although this problem seems like the type that falls under the heading of "C++ trivia," forgetting to put the **using namespace std;** statement into a program is a common error—one that can easily lead to hundreds of compiler errors, even in a short program. Thus, it is one of the pitfalls that even novice C++ programmers need to be aware of.

Explanation 4: Function Definition The next code comes in the form of a block:

```
int main(int argc, char* argv[])
{
    cout << "Hello, World " << endl;
    return 0;
}
```

The block of code at the end of the file is the definition of the function main(). The main() function is special in C++ because it defines the entry point for our program—

every stand-alone C++ program always starts running in main(). Other than that, however, it is a fairly typical C++ function.

Any function definition comes in two parts, the declaration line and the body. We now look at these separately.

Explanation 5: Function Declaration Line   The declaration line:

```
int main(int argc,char *argv[])
```

is extremely important. The declaration involves three parts, as illustrated in Figure 2.8.

- *Function name:* Declares the name to be used in calling the function. In C, only one function can have a given name in a project. In C++, it is possible for more than one function to have the same name—provided the functions have different arguments. In this case, the function's name is simply "main."

- *Return type:* After a function completes its activities, it can send a value back to the block of code that called it. For example, in the Pmt function, presented for discussion purposes in Chapter 1, Section 1.1.2, the function "returned" a value representing the monthly payment associated with a given loan amount, number of periods, and interest rate. The return type specifies what type of value is being returned by the function. In the case of main(), it returns an integer (the data type **int** in C++).

- *Arguments:* The values within the parentheses tell us about the arguments being passed into the function. In the case of our Pmt illustration, for example, we would need to declare three such arguments: amount (a real number), periods (an integer), and interest rate (a real number). In the case of main, we see it has two arguments. The first argument (argc) is an integer. The second argument (argv) is too complicated to figure out by simple inspection, but will become clear after we examine pointers and complex arrays in Chapter 10. (FYI, it is an array of character addresses used to hold the arguments typed by the user on the command line.)

TEST YOUR UNDERSTANDING 2.2

Real numbers are normally represented by the type **double** in C/C++, as will be explained in Chapter 3. Given this piece of information, what would the declaration line look like for the function Pmt, discussed in Chapter 1, Section 1.1.2?

A function declaration—which can actually extend over several lines, with the right parenthesis telling the compiler where it ends—can serve two purposes. First, it can be the beginning of the actual function definition, as is the case for main() above. Second, it can be a function **prototype,** signaled by a semicolon at the end, such as:

```
int main(int argc,char *argv[]);
```

The purpose of a prototype is to provide files that use the function with information such as (1) the number and type of arguments to be used in calling the function, and (2) the type of value being returned. Such function

FIGURE 2.8   Elements of Main Declaration Line

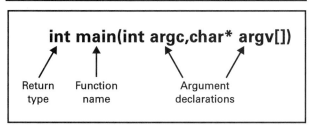

declarations are some of the most important contents of files such as stdio.h. Once the compiler sees a function declaration in a header (.h) file, it can check to make sure the function is being called appropriately, wherever it appears. We will examine such a file in Section 2.4. In our novel analogy at the beginning of the chapter, this process corresponds to making sure that the character's actions in a given chapter (the .cpp file) are consistent with the details of the character (e.g., age, sex) in the common list of characters (the .h file).

Explanation 6: Definition Body   The final piece of our simple C program is the body of main:

```
{
    cout << "Hello, World " << endl;
    return 0;
}
```

The code within the braces identifies what will happen when the function main is called. In this case, the action is simple:

- First, we send the string "Hello, World" to the output object **cout.** The << is sometimes referred to as the output or insertion operator and sending data to **cout** causes those data to be displayed to standard output—usually the console screen. The **endl** is what is called a *manipulator.* When it gets sent to **cout,** a new line character is sent to the screen, causing the cursor to move to the start of the next line. (You can do the same thing by sending a specific character, "\n" to **cout** as well.)

- Second, we return the value 0 (the **return value** of main is sometimes used by the operating system). What is important to note here is that the value being returned (0, which is an integer) matches the type of value we specified in the declaration. If it did not, we would get an error.

2.3: SECTION QUESTIONS

1. What is the one advantage of "executing" a console project with the exclamation point button, rather than running it in Debug mode?
2. Do the library "include" files that we reference in our programs contain function definitions?
3. What does the fact that the main() function is defined with arguments and a return value imply?
4. What is special about the function main()? Why must every stand-alone console project have one (and only one) main function?
5. What is *cout?*

2.4: MULTIFILE PROJECTS

Walkthrough available in Multifile.wmv

Just as it is hard to imagine a novel, of any length, without chapters, it is hard to imagine a program, of any substance, created using a single source file. Fortunately, the IDE makes multifile projects straightforward to create.

In this section, we will create a new project—called Multifile—that spans across three files:

1. The first file will contain main().
2. The second is a file that is supplied by the text.
3. The third file you will write.

Once complete, we will walk through some of the (very) simple functions we developed using the debugger in Section 2.5.

2.4.1: Adding Existing Files to a Project

After you have created a project using the procedure outlined in Section 2.3, out first goal is to add a couple of files to the project. These files, SimpleIO.h and SimpleIO.cpp serve three purposes:

1. They demonstrate the process of bringing existing code into a project.
2. They allow us to hide the complexities of I/O for a few chapters.
3. They let us keep C++ programs entirely structured—allowing us to ignore the fact that some of the things we are working with, such as **cout,** are actually objects—until we are ready to focus on how to work with objects.

Before actually adding the files, however, we will discuss their second purpose.

Contents of SimpleIO Files   The contents of the SimpleIO.h file are illustrated in Example 2.3.

EXAMPLE 2.3

Part of SimpleIO.h

```
// SimpleIO.h
#include <stdarg.h>

#include <fstream>
#include <iostream>
using namespace std;

#define MAXLINE 255

// Text Console I/O functions
void InputString(char str[]);
char InputCharacter();
int InputInteger();
double InputReal();
void DisplayString(const char str[]);
void DisplayCharacter(char cVal);
void DisplayInteger(int nVal);
void DisplayReal(double dVal);
void DisplayFormatted(const char *fmt,...);
void NewLine();
```

After our discussion of the Hello, World project, many of the components of the file should be familiar to us. The line at the top of the file:

```
// SimpleIO.h
```

is a comment line, telling us the name of the file. This line is followed by a series of #include statements, identifying libraries we will be using.

The lines at the bottom of the file are function prototypes. We can tell they are prototypes, as opposed to variable declarations or function definitions, by two characteristics:

1. The presence of parentheses in a declaration indicates a function is being declared.

2. The fact that a semicolon follows the declaration—as opposed to a function body within { and }—tells us we are just prototyping the function, not defining it.

The names of the functions should be fairly self-explanatory. The five functions we use in this chapter are:

- *InputInteger()*: waits for the user to type a line, then returns its integer value (or 0, if the user doesn't type an integer)

- *DisplayInteger(int nVal)*: is passed an integer (nVal) as an argument and prints its value to the console screen

- *DisplayString(const char str[])*: prints a string to the console screen (In this chapter, we create strings by placing text within double quotes. Later on, we will find other ways of doing so.)

- *NewLine()*: sends a line feed to the console (like the **endl** we already talked about in the Hello, World project)

One line in the SimpleIO.h file represents an instruction not seen in the Hello, World project:

```
#define MAXLINE 255
```

This example shows a preprocessor instruction (remember, the # symbol) called a macro. #define tells the preprocessor to do a search-and-replace within your source file. In this case, everywhere the symbol MAXLINE is encountered, it replaces it with 255. This instruction is a convenient way of specifying values that are not going to change during the program. (In SimpleIO.h, MAXLINE is used to represent the maximum number of characters we will accept in a line of text typed in from the user.)

TEST YOUR UNDERSTANDING 2.3

What are the advantages of defining a name, such as MAXLINE, and using it in your program, as opposed to just using the number 255?

The SimpleIO.cpp actually defines the functions that we prototype in SimpleIO.h. For example, the definition of DisplayInteger() in the .cpp file is as follows:

```
// Prints an integer
void DisplayInteger(int nVal)
{
    cout << nVal;
}
```

This definition uses the output operator to send the integer argument value (nVal) to cout.

Creating and Adding Existing Files to the Project The first step in our multifile project walkthrough is to create a C++ project, called Multifile, using the procedures outlined in Section 2.3.1.

Once created, we need to add our SimpleIO files to the project. The simplest way to do so, and the procedure we will follow throughout this text (to avoid wasting time on folder path problems), is to follow a two-step procedure:

- First, open Windows Explorer and copy the SimpleIO.h and SimpleIO.cpp files from the CD to the project folder.

- Second, right click the Multifile project name in the Solution Explorer, then select *Add|Add Existing Item* from the menu. You should see a dialog box like that in Figure 2.9. Select the two SimpleIO source files and press the Open button. These files are now included in the project.

Common Errors: If the files you just copied do not appear in the dialog box, the odds are high you forgot step 1, or did it improperly. It is important that these files from the CD be physically present in your project folder. If they are not, you might be tempted to browse the "Add Existing Item" dialog until you find them. Try to resist the temptation. If you succumb, you will almost certainly get "fatal" errors about missing .h files when you compile. The problem is that even though adding files outside the project folder tells the compiler where to find the .cpp files, it doesn't tell it where to look for the associated .h files. This problem is easy to solve (you can add folders as "default" include directories to your project), but the simplest approach—for now—is just to put every file we will be using in the project folder.

Also, just placing files in the project folder does not make them part of the project. You need to add them to the project, as well.

FIGURE 2.9   Add Existing File Dialog Box (in C++ Example

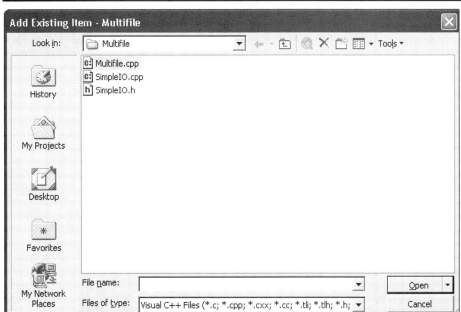

The final step of the process is to modify the main function. Change the main function so that it is the same as Example 2.4.

Run the program (without the debugger) and see what it does.

Discussion This initial stage of the multifile project demonstration illustrates a few new concepts. The first can be found in the line:

```
#include "SimpleIO.h"
```

This line was different from our earlier *#include <iostream>* because it uses quotation marks instead of < and > around the file name. The difference is significant:

- What an include file name in quotes tells the preprocessor is that the first place it should look for the included file is in the project folder that we created. If it does not find the file there, it then searches the default include folders (the locations of which are set in the compiler).

- Where an include file is between < and >, it tells the preprocessor it should *only* look for the include file in default include folders—it should not check the project folder.

In general, then, you should normally use < and > for standard include libraries, and quotation marks (often called double quotes, to distinguish them from apostrophes) for all other include files—such as the one you will create in the next section.

The code within the main function itself illustrates another new capability of C++—how to use newly defined functions. The functions InputInteger(), DisplayInteger(), and others that are used in main are not standard C or C++ functions. Instead, they are functions we incorporated into our project by adding SimpleIO.cpp. Our main function knows how they are supposed to be called because the SimpleIO.h prototypes tell it the number of arguments and types of return values. But the actual definitions of the functions are in the .cpp files.

2.4.2: Adding New Files to a Project

Having learned how to add previously written functions, the next stage of the walkthrough is to learn how to create our own new functions. We will do this in three steps:

EXAMPLE 2.4

New main function

```
#include "SimpleIO.h"

int main()
{
    int nVal;
    DisplayString("Enter an integer: ");
    nVal=InputInteger();
    DisplayString("You entered the integer ");
    DisplayInteger(nVal);
    NewLine();
    DisplayString("Congratulations. You did it!");
    NewLine();
    return 0;
}
```

1. Creating a header file
2. Creating a source file
3. Calling one of our functions from main

Creating a Header File   As soon as we start defining our own functions, we need to start worrying about creating our own header files. Fortunately, the process of header file creation is straightforward. Right click the Multifile item in Solution Explorer, then select *Add|Add New Item*. In the dialog box that appears (see Figure 2.10), select the Header File (.h) icon, type in the name FirstFunc, then press the Open button. This command will open the empty file FirstFunc.h.

Inside FirstFunc.h, type the code listed in Example 2.5.

FIGURE 2.10   Add New Item Dialog Box

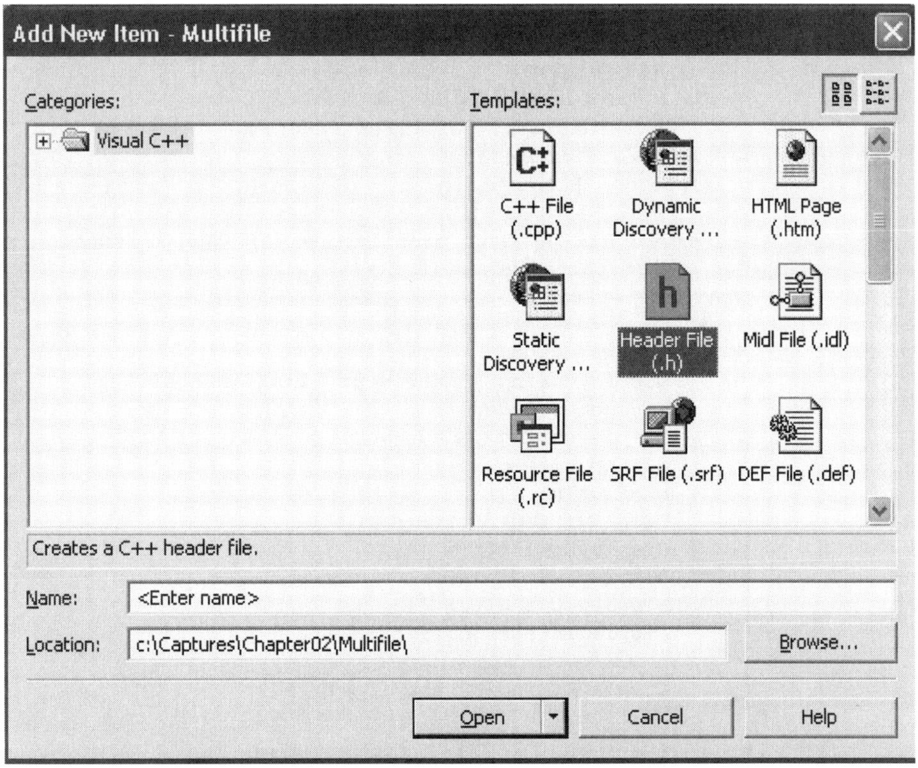

EXAMPLE 2.5

FirstFunc.h contents

```
// FirstFunc.h: prototypes for our first C/C++ functions

void TestFunc();
int Plus(int nArg1,int nArg2);
```

Looking at this file, you should be able to tell several things:

- We are going to write two functions, TestFunc() and Plus().
- TestFunc() takes no arguments. The **void** return type tells us it does not return a value.
- Plus() takes two arguments, both integers. It also returns an integer value.

Creating a Source File   Follow the process for creating a source file specified in Section 2.3.1. Once you have created your source file, type the code from Example 2.6 into it.

This source code is, once again, relatively simple. Nonetheless, it illustrates some important new concepts. Initially, we see two include directives:

```
#include "SimpleIO.h"
#include "FirstFunc.h"
```

EXAMPLE 2.6

FirstFunc.cpp

```cpp
// FirstFunc.cpp: Our first function
#include "SimpleIO.h"
#include "FirstFunc.h"

/* TestFunc(): Gets user inputs for Plus() function call,
   then displays results */
void TestFunc()
{
    int n1,n2,n3;
    DisplayString("Enter your first integer: ");
    n1=InputInteger();
    DisplayString("Enter your second integer: ");
    n2=InputInteger();
    n3=Plus(n1,n2);
    DisplayInteger(n1);
    DisplayString(" + ");
    DisplayInteger(n2);
    DisplayString(" = ");
    DisplayInteger(n3);
    NewLine();
    DisplayString("Pretty cool, eh?");
    NewLine();
    return;
}

/* Plus(): Takes its two integer arguments, adds them together
   and returns the value */
int Plus(int nArg1,int nArg2)
{
    int nTotal;
    nTotal=nArg1+nArg2;
    return nTotal;
}
```

We need both of these because we are calling functions prototyped in both SimpleIO.h (InputInteger(), for example) and FirstFunc.h (Plus(), for example). On the other hand, we are not using any standard library functions in this particular file, so we don't need *#include <iostream>*, as we did in our other files.

Two lines are of particular interest in our TestFunc() function. The first is:

```
int n1,n2,n3;
```

The purpose of this line is to define three integers. The definition does two things: (1) it sets aside enough memory to hold three integers; and (2) it *declares* that the names n1, n2, and n3 are to be used to identify each of the three locations, respectively. Because we are making this definition within a function, these variables will be local to the function—created when the function is called, eliminated when the function returns (see the discussion of the stack, in Chapter 1, Section 1.2, for an overview of this process).

> *Terminology:* The term *declaration* is used to refer to the process of specifying the data type associated with a given name. The term *definition* is used to refer to a statement that actually creates a variable, or other data element, of a given type in memory. As a result, a definition always incorporates a declaration, because creating a variable requires that we give it a name. A declaration, on the other hand, may be made without any variables actually being defined—for example, a function declaration (e.g., Example 2.5).

Our second line of interest is:

```
n3=Plus(n1,n2);
```

The purpose of this line is to call the function—also defined in the FirstFunc.cpp file—called Plus. Being passed into Plus() are the two values in n1 and n2 (which, if you look at the code preceding the call, have values that were input by the user). As you may recall from the function prototype, the Plus() function returns an integer value. It therefore makes sense that this return value will be placed in n3, because we wrote n3=Plus(n1,n2).

The final line of interest is at the end of the function:

```
return;
```

In our earlier main() functions, we saw *return 0;* at the end of the function. The reason no value comes after the return in this case stems from the declaration of the function:

```
void TestFunc()
```

As we said earlier, void here means the function does not return a value, therefore it follows that there should not be any value after the return.

The entire Plus() function is quite simple:

```
int Plus(int nArg1,int nArg2)
{
    int nTotal;
    nTotal=nArg1+nArg2;
    return nTotal;
}
```

We can interpret it as follows:

- nArg1 and nArg2 are **local variables** that take their values from whatever arguments the function is passed. In the case of the call in TestFunc(), they take their values from the values in n1 and n2 that were passed in.

- nTotal is defined as another local variable. It is then assigned a value equal to the sum of nArg1 and nArg2.
- The value of nTotal is then returned.

Effectively, then, the function Plus() takes its two arguments and adds them together. In other words, writing:

```
Z = Plus(X,Y);
```

is exactly the same as writing:

```
Z = X + Y;
```

From this, we can conclude that even after we write Plus(), we probably won't find a lot of demand for it in the real world. Still, it serves as a useful illustration, and we will refer to it frequently, particularly in Chapter 4.

TEST YOUR UNDERSTANDING 2.4

What would happen if the call Plus(12,17) were made inside a C/C++ program?

Modifying Main Function   The final step in this demonstration is to modify main so that it calls the TestFunc() function. Your new main() should look like that in Example 2.7. The modifications are simple:

- Add *#include "FirstFunc.h"* to the top, because main needs to know what TestFunc() looks like if it is going to call it.
- Add the line *TestFunc();* above the return statement to make the actual call to the function.
- You can now build and test the program.

EXAMPLE 2.7
Main function modified to call TestFunc()

```
#include "SimpleIO.h"
#include "FirstFunc.h"

int main()
{
      int nVal;
      DisplayString("Enter an integer: ");
      nVal=InputInteger();
      DisplayString("You entered the integer ");
      DisplayInteger(nVal);
      NewLine();
      DisplayString("Congratulations. You did it!");
      NewLine();
      TestFunc();
      return 0;
}
```

2.4: SECTION QUESTIONS

1. What is the purpose of the SimpleIO files?
2. Why should you copy files into your project folder before you add them, instead of adding them from whatever folder they happen to be located in?
3. When you start creating your own source (.cpp) files, what other type of file are you likely to want to create?
4. What are the two key objectives that are accomplished when you define a variable?
5. Explain the type of error you would have gotten if you had not included FirstFunc.h in Figure 2.6.
6. Why does it make sense to keep your main functions in source files by themselves?

2.5: IN DEPTH: INTRODUCTION TO DEBUGGING TOOLS WALKTHROUGH

Walkthrough available in DebugIntro.wmv

When you are just starting to learn programming, the debugging capabilities built into the IDE can serve two useful roles:

1. They can fulfill their stated purpose, which is to help you find bugs in your code.
2. They can provide a visual demonstration of the activities being performed as your code executes.

This second capability is often overlooked in programming courses, but it can be a powerful learning tool—one that we will utilize frequently throughout this text.

2.5.1: What Is a Debugger?

A debugger is not, as its name would seem to imply, a tool that removes bugs from your code. Sadly, the identification and removal of errors is still a task that is pretty much left to the programmer. A **debugger,** instead, is a collection of tools that can be used to help you locate bugs in your code.

Your typical debugger offers at least four capabilities that can be used to help identify bugs in your code:

1. *Breakpoints:* The ability to identify points in your code where the program will pause while it is running. Because modern computers run so quickly, without entering such a paused state it is impossible to use the remaining debugging features.
2. *Stepping:* The ability to execute your code line by line. It allows you to watch what happens in your computer one step at a time.
3. *Inspection:* The ability to examine the contents of memory (registers too, if you have a taste for trivia) using the variable names declared in your code.
4. *Call Stack:* The ability to examine the collection of functions in the process of being called (see Section 1.1.2 for a further explanation of stacks and their role in modern computers).

We now consider each of these features individually, using the Multifile project we developed in Section 2.4.

2.5.2: Breakpoints

Our early attempts to run the debugger have already underscored our need be able to pause the program: our console screen disappeared before we could read it. To solve that problem, all you need to do is click the mouse on the vertical bar to the left of the *return 0;* statement in main. When you then run the program, you will find it stops there, as illustrated in Figure 2.11 (note the arrow superimposed on the breakpoint dot).

When paused, you can then examine the contents of the console window by clicking on the appropriate button on the Windows task bar (the bar of buttons, normally at the bottom of the screen, used to control what program is active).

Breakpoints can be put on almost any line of code except variable declarations. Their presence will only pause the program if the line of code is encountered while the program

---

FIGURE 2.11 Program Paused at Break Point

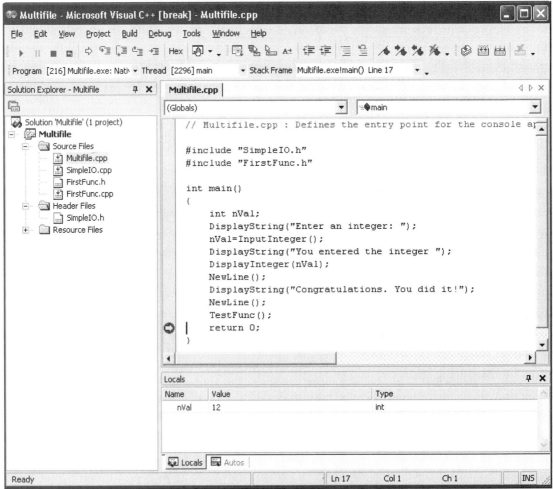

is running. What this capability is useful for will become more apparent in Chapter 5, when we introduce the concept of branching.

Some other useful facts about breakpoints:

- To remove a breakpoint, you can just click the breakpoint a second time.
- You can also deactivate a breakpoint (using a right click), which leaves the breakpoint in place but prevents it from stopping your program.
- It is possible to set *conditional breakpoints*—breakpoints that only stop the program if certain conditions are met. They can be useful, but are beyond what we need to know to get started.
- To resume running after pausing at a breakpoint, you can press the button (or select the same menu item) that you used to start the program running. The program will then proceed until either it ends (i.e., main() returns) or another breakpoint is encountered.

2.5.3: Stepping

Once you stop your code at a breakpoint, it is often convenient to watch what happens as your code executes, line by line. This process is referred to as stepping.

The most common forms of stepping include the following:

- *Step over:* The program performs the entire line of code, moving to the line below. It means that should a function be called in the line of code (e.g., in the line *n3=Plus(n1,n2);* within TestFunc), the function called will be completed as part of the step—unless there happens to be a breakpoint in the function that causes execution to pause.
- *Step into:* The program steps to whatever code is executed next, going into another function if necessary. For example, stepping into the line *n3=Plus(n1,n2);* would cause it to go to the first line of the Plus() function.
- *Step out of:* Causes the program to run to the point in our code just after the current function returns. This form is often used to get us out of functions we accidentally stepped into.

Stepping is straightforward, and can provide us with useful insights into how our code is running. Many common coding errors (e.g., missing break statements in a case construct, discussed in Chapter 6) are easily detected by stepping through the code. Stepping though an entire application is also a useful approach to testing software, because the stepping process tends to focus the developer's attention.

One common problem virtually everyone discovers within minutes of learning to step through code is accidentally stepping into a library function. What typically happens is that a dialog box (see Figure 2.12) prompts you that it does not know where the source code for the function is located—and because that code is probably not installed, you find your only viable alternative is to cancel. Once you cancel, the IDE will offer you the opportunity to look at the disassembly window.

Just say no! If you do not, you will find yourself deep in assembler code. (Should it happen, however, just Step Out, then go to *Debug|Windows* and close the Disassembly window.)

The reason for this bizarre behavior is that the debugger needs access to your source code in order to perform stepping. In installing the IDE, however, the library source code may not be copied—mainly to save space. As a result, the debugger does the only thing that

FIGURE 2.12 Accidentally Stepping into the strlen() Library Function

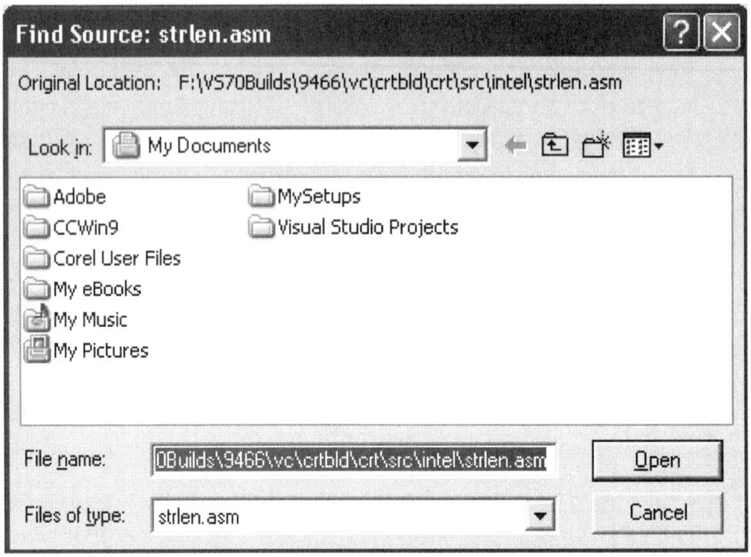

it can do: it takes the machine code it finds and translates it into assembly language—without the benefit of useful things like labels and variable names (a process called disassembly).

2.5.4: Inspection

An inspection window is just a name for a window that provides a list of variables and their values. Inspection is normally tied closely to stepping, because the type of information you are most likely to be interested in, while stepping through your code, is how variable values are changing.

Of the many different types of inspection windows, the most commonly used in this text are the Locals window and the Auto window. These windows appear by default when your program is paused in the debugger, tabbed so you can switch between them. Should you accidentally close them (a common occurrence, given Visual Studio .NET's huge selection of window types), you can find them under *Debug|Windows*. Because they show values in a running program, they only appear while the program is running under the debugger.

The main difference between the Locals and Auto inspection windows is that Locals displays values for all local variables, whereas Auto attempts to figure out the variable values you are most likely to be interested in. An example of the Locals window, paused at a breakpoint within a call to the function Plus() in our Multifile project, is presented in Figure 2.13.

As the yellow arrow on the breakpoint illustrates, we are about to execute the step of code:

```
nTotal=nArg1+nArg2;
```

To interpret the meaning of the local values, we have to consider where we are paused. At the highlighted point in the code, we have yet to place a value into nTotal (i.e., it has not been initialized). As a result, even though nArg1 and nArg2 had values assigned when the function was called, nTotal is—for our purposes—essentially a random number.

| **FIGURE 2.13** | Locals Window (Bottom of Screen) While Paused at Breakpoint |

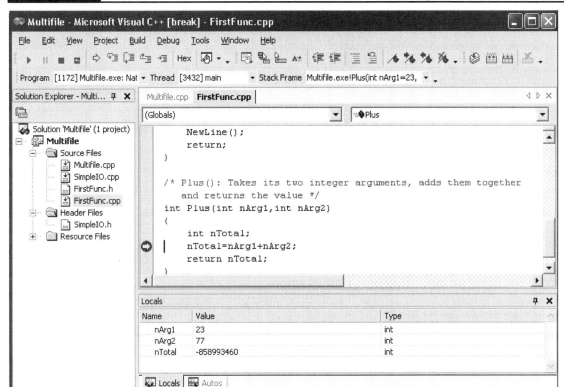

TEST YOUR UNDERSTANDING 2.5

What value for nTotal would appear in the Locals window if we were to step over the line of code where we were currently paused?

It is probably worth mentioning that just as you can view variable values in a properties window, it is also possible to change those values. This capability is rarely so useful to a novice programmer that it justifies the high risk of "shooting yourself in the foot" that accompanies using it.

2.5.5: The Call Stack

The final debugging feature to be presented at this time is the call stack, shown in Figure 2.14 (while the program was paused at the same breakpoint in Figure 2.13). The call stack window provides the programmer with a couple of useful facilities:

- It shows the functions currently being executed, along with the values of their arguments. For example, in Figure 2.14, it tells us:
  - we are in the Plus() function,
  - that was called from TestFunc(),

FIGURE 2.14 The Call Stack (Bottom Left Pane)

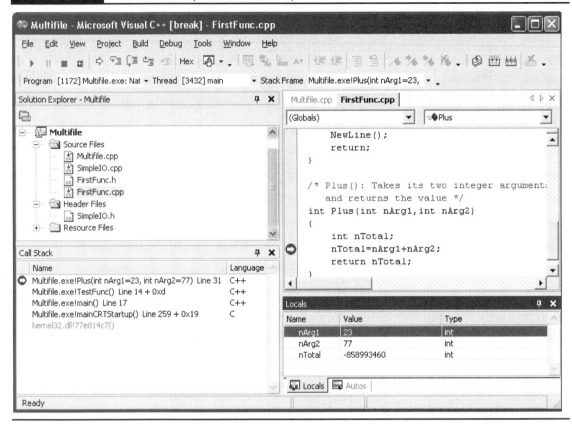

- that was called from main(),
- that was called from mainCRTStartup (a function MS Windows uses to get main() to run in the console window).

- Such information is often useful because, in a complex program, you will not always know how you got to a breakpoint when your program stops.
- It provides a convenient means of navigating between functions. For example, if you were to double click TestFunc() on the call stack, it would move the cursor to your current position in TestFunc() (which would be the line where it calls the Plus() function), and you could look at the values of variables local to TestFunc(), such as n1, n2, and n3.

As was the case with inspection windows, the call stack is only accessible when your program is actually running and paused in the debugger.

2.6: REVIEW AND QUESTIONS

2.6.1: REVIEW

Upon completing Chapter 2, you should be able to create a simple, multifile project in Visual Studio .NET and explain what you have done. The most critical concepts presented in the chapter are as follows:

The basic process through which a running program is created is called the compose-compile-link-load cycle. Composing is the process of writing your own source code, in a language such as C or C++, and saving it in files. Compiling is the process of taking a file containing source code and translating it into a file containing object code, which is similar to machine language except that certain key pieces of data, such as memory addresses, are left unspecified. In addition to object files created by compiling the programmer's source code, a typical program also uses library files (supplied with the compiler) that contain object code for standard functions. The process of merging object code files—both created by the compiler and libraries—is referred to as linking. This process is performed by a program known as a linker, and produces an executable (e.g., an .exe) file. A program called a loader, normally part of the operating system, can then be used to start the executable file running. In MS Windows, double-clicking an icon will normally invoke the loader on the associated program.

Visual Studio .NET is an integrated development environment, or IDE, which means the environment contains editors for composing source code, a built-in compiler and linker for creating executable code, and a debugger that can be used to load and test running programs. The primary organizing tool in .NET is a solution (sometimes referred to as a workspace), into which one or more projects can be inserted. A project, in turn, is an organized collection of source code and other files developed by a programmer that can be combined (e.g., compiled and linked) to create a single executable target. In the present text, we will primarily be interested in projects, so that all our solutions will consist of a single project.

To create a project in Visual Studio .NET, you must first decide on the appropriate target type. In this book, we will always be creating console applications, the simplest form of program. Once a new project has been created, you add new or existing source files to it (.c, .cpp, or .h files). You can then build the project (which causes the source files to be compiled and then, if the compile is successful, linked together). When getting started in programming, errors are commonly encountered during the compile and link stages. These errors need to be corrected before your program is ready to run. Once a build is successful, you can begin to debug the project.

The debugger that is built into .NET is one of its most powerful features. The term *debugger* is somewhat of a misnomer, however, because the tool does not remove bugs. Instead, it helps the programmer find bugs. The debugger provides four main capabilities that assist in finding bugs. Breakpoints allow the programmer to pause the program while it is running. Inspection and watch windows allow the programmer to examine the values of program variables while the program is paused. Stepping capabilities allow the programmer to execute code one step at a time, normally used in conjunction with inspection windows. Finally, the call stack allows the programmer to identify the sequence of function calls leading to a particular location in the program where it is paused, or where an error has been encountered. These debugging tools are invaluable in finding program errors. They also provide a window on program execution that can help novice programmers understand how their programs work.

2.6.2: GLOSSARY

breakpoint   A user-defined pause in the source code of a program written in Visual Studio .NET

call stack   A window in Visual Studio .NET that shows the functions called to reach a particular point in the code

debugger   A program designed to find errors in source code in order to make finding errors in an executable program easier

executable code   Code that can only be read by a computer; can also be referred to as a computer program

header file   A file used by C/C++ that allows for the declaration of functions, classes, and other predefined variables shared by other source code files

integrated development environment (IDE)   An environment or computer program that allows for easier transformation of source code to executable code by allowing for the editing, linking, loading, and debugging processes to be handled by one computer program

linker A program that combines objects to form the final executable program

loader Used by the operating system, it is a utility that transfers a computer program from secondary storage to primary storage in order to execute the program

local variable A variable defined in a function that can exist only when the function is being used

namespace A collection of code sharing a common name prefix to avoid ambiguity

preprocessor Program subroutine that cuts and pastes source code items in order to make the process of compiling a computer program easier

prototype A declaration of a function used to specify arguments and return types

return value A value returned by a function or procedure after the code has been completed and a result determined

source code A program written in a manner that is readable to humans and that can be compiled by a compiler in order to transform the code into an executable format

2.6.3: QUESTIONS

Questions 1-10: For each of the following errors that might be present in a program, identify where it is most likely to be detected:

A. By the compiler

B. By the linker

C. By the programmer

#	Error
1	A variable name is misspelled.
2	The programmer forgot to define one of the functions called in a project.
3	A variable is declared to be of type "integer" instead of "int."
4	A semicolon is missing at the end of a line.
5	A function is missing a closing brace (}).
6	A required library (.lib) file was accidentally deleted.
7	A function defined by the project (e.g., DisplayInteger) is called with the wrong number of arguments.
8	The "using namespace std;" is omitted after an include statement that requires it.
9	The programmer defined the same function twice, in separate files.
10	An incorrect formula is used to compute the return value of a function.

11. If you were to create a project with many .cpp source files, discuss the pros and cons of the following:

a. Creating a single .h file with every function declaration

b. Creating a separate .h file for every .cpp file you created

12. Explain why a definition implies a declaration, but a declaration does not necessarily imply a definition.

13. In a multifile project, does the compiler care what file contains a particular function definition. If so, why? If not, why should we care if it doesn't?

14. In a new single file project called *Doubler*, create a main function that:

■ Prompts the user to enter an integer

■ Reads an integer from the user

■ Multiplies the integer by 2

■ Displays "Your integer doubled is:" followed by the value

■ Ends

15. In a new single file project called *Circle*, create a main function that:

■ Prompts the user to enter an radius value

■ Multiplies the radius by 2*pi (3.1416)

■ Displays the circle's circumference

■ Ends

Although this issue is similar to *Doubler* (question 14), it can't be done with integers, which means you will need to use the real number data type (double) instead of the integer type (int). You will also need to choose the right functions from SimpleIO (from functions listed Example 2.3).

16. In a new multifile project, *MDoubler*, create a program that does what Doubler (question 14) does, except that a function you create called Double() is used. The Double() function should be declared as follows:

```
int Double(int arg);
```

It should take its argument, multiply it by 2, then return the result. (*Note*: This function will be quite similar to the Plus() function in the chapter, only even simpler.) Your project should have the same structure as the multifile project (Section 2.4), namely:

- A main() function defined in one .cpp file

- The Double() function defined in another .cpp file

- An include file, holding the declaration of Double()

17. In a new multifile project, *Circum*, create a program that does what Circle (question 15) does, except that a function you create called Circle()—which takes a radius value as an argument and returns a circumference—is used. Your project should have the same structure as the multifile project (Section 2.4), namely:

- A main() function defined in one .cpp file

- The Circle() function defined in another .cpp file (You should decide how it will be prototyped.)

- An include file, holding the declaration of Circle()

18. Explain what is meant when we say that "the debugger doesn't fix bugs"?

19. What are the four principal debugger capabilities that we covered?

20. In Figure 2.13, identify the source of each of the three values in the variable window.

Numbers and Data

EXECUTIVE SUMMARY

The objective of Chapter 3 is to develop an understanding of the basic types of data used in C++, sometimes referred to as the primitive types. As the book progresses, we will extend the types of data our programs work with to include complex objects. All data, however, ultimately turn out to be some form of integer, **real number,** bit, or address once we decompose them. They are the building blocks of programming. If you understand these primitive types well—particularly their peculiarities, such as the tendency to misbehave under certain circumstances—you will find that knowledge to be invaluable throughout your programming career.

We begin by reviewing the concept of variables and introducing the concept of **arrays.** The next section focuses on representing numbers, discussing how positive and negative integers can be declared, along with real numbers. The section on representing numbers is followed by a section on representing text, introducing the concept of a NUL terminated character string. The chapter concludes with two in-depth sections. The first examines the underlying mechanics of integer numbering systems, emphasizing two bases—**binary** (base 2) and **hexadecimal** (base 16)—that are particularly useful in understanding computers. We then consider the twos complement system for representing negative numbers, and its practical implications for programmers. The common integer forms (char, short, and long) are then presented and contrasted with the real number types (float and double). The second section presents a brief overview of pointers and other data types—with details on that important subject postponed until Chapter 10.

LEARNING OBJECTIVES

Upon completing this chapter, you should be able to:

- Distinguish between a scalar variable and an array
- Explain the nature of an array, and how to declare one
- Describe the basic data types in C/C++ and specify their ranges (in hexadecimal)
- Identify some of the pros and cons of using real numbers in a program
- Explain what is meant by a character string
- Explain the twos complement representation system and overflow
- Describe a pointer and how it is declared
- Explain why using a pointer is a convenient method for passing an array into a function

3.1: VARIABLES AND DATA TYPES

Data is the name we use to refer to the information that a computer program works with. Every program uses some data, so one of the first questions that must be addressed in the design of any programming language is: How do we get at the data?

As discussed in Chapter 1, in order to "use" data we need to be able to set aside memory for the data, and specify what type of data is being stored in that memory. In this section, we outline the basic approach for doing so in C/C++.

3.1.1: Scalar Variables

A *scalar variable* is the term used to refer to a single unit of data, within a program, that has its own name. In Chapter 2, we saw a number of cases where we created such variables, a process called defining a variable. For example:

```
int myvar;
```

serves to define a single variable, an integer, and declares its name to be *myvar*. C++ also gives us the ability to define more than one variable in a given line, for example:

```
int n1,n2,n3;
```

This line sets aside memory locations for three integers in a single statement, giving them the names n1, n2, and n3, respectively. Some programmers, particularly those from the "neat" community, believe that it is not a good idea to define more than one variable per statement, to prevent confusion and allow for easier commenting.

Initializing Variables   It is also possible to initialize variables when declaring them. For example, the declaration:

```
int n4=273;
```

This declaration sets aside enough room for one integer, gives it the name n4, and places the integer value 273 in the memory we set aside, all in one step.

If you do not initialize a variable when you create it, there is generally no guarantee as to what value will be present in the variable. In particular, do not suppose it will be some sensible value, such as 0.

If a variable is to be initialized when it is created, and then never changed, the **const** modifier can be used to tell the compiler to generate errors if modifications to the variable occur later in the code. For example, the statement:

```
const int nMyConstant = 32;
```

declares the name nMyConstant to be an integer with the value of 32. That value is then not allowed to change. As a result, a statement later in the program such as:

```
nMyConstant=31;
```

would produce a compiler error.

In some languages, such as Java, the declaration of const variables replaces #define preprocessor statements, such as we saw in Chapter 2. In C/C++, the most common use of const will be seen later, in function declarations.

Variable Names   In C/C++, the rules for naming variables are as follows:

- Variable names must begin with a letter or underscore (although the leading underscore is normally reserved for system-defined names, by convention).

- The initial character in a variable name can be followed by any combination of letters, numbers, and underscores.
- C++ is *case sensitive*, meaning a variable named X is entirely different from a variable named x.

In addition to the "rules," some common practices for naming variables also make a lot of sense:

- Variable names should be descriptive—a good practice for all but the smallest programs. A variable defined to hold the length of a string, for example, should be named something like length, or nLength, instead of x1.
- Some programmers precede variable names with a few characters indicating what type of variable they are. For example, strBuf (the str implies the variable contains a character string) or nLength (the n means the variable is an integer).
- Many C and C++ programmers name all their variables in lower case, using the underscore—where necessary—to separate words. For example, instead of naming a variable julyhightemp, it would be july_high_temp.
- Many C++ programmers use upper and lower case letters to break up variable names, instead of underscores (which don't always print properly). For example, JulyHighTemp.

Being consistent in your naming practices can be helpful in reducing complexity as your program grows. (Having given this advice, the present text uses a variety of practices—so you will not be surprised by what you encounter in "real-world" code.)

Naturally, the preceding discussions apply to all the data types we will discuss in this chapter, not just integers (which happen to be the only ones we've used so far).

3.1.2: Arrays

Although the notion of giving a name to each unit of data that we use sounds good at first, it doesn't take a programmer long to realize it is impractical. Suppose, for example, you wrote a program designed to analyze hourly temperature measurements over a ten-year period. Assuming roughly 8,000 hours a year, you would need to come up with 80,000 different names. This task would be inconvenient, to put it gently.

Declaring an Array   One approach to reducing the need to create unique names is to create an array. An array is a collection of data elements, all of the same type, accessible using a name and an index. We define an array just like a scalar variable, except we follow the name we are declaring by a number, in brackets, specifying the number of elements to be created. For example:

```
int arnTemp[80000];
```

would create an array of 80,000 integers, enough room to hold all the temperature measurements in our previous example. The name, arnTemp, might be used as a way of implying it is an integer array of temperatures, but we could call it anything we wanted.

Accessing Element Data and Array Storage   Once an array has been declared, the individual elements of it can be accessed using the same name/index notation we used in declaring it. For example, the expression:

```
arnTemp[0]
```

would refer to the first element in our previously declared array. It is very important to note that *every array in C++ is zero-based*, which means arnTemp[1] is actually the second element in the array, arnTemp[2] is the third, and so forth. In Chapter 10, we will discover the benefits of using zero-based indexing. For now, just take it on faith that it isn't done this way solely for the purpose of making it counterintuitive to novice programmers.

When C++ creates an array, it sets aside memory for the array in a single block. Doing so guarantees that the elements in the array are stored *contiguously*, meaning that element 1 is right next to element 2 is right next to element 3, and so on. Storing elements in this way makes it relatively easy for C++ to access individual elements. For example, if the memory address of arnTemp[0] is 1000000, and if we know that integers take up 4 bytes apiece, then we know we can find arnTemp[1] at 1000004 and arnTemp[2] at 1000008, and so forth. It also means that *the most critical piece of information about any array is the location in memory where it starts*. Once we know that, along with size of the data it stores, we could—in theory—locate the position of any element in the array based on its coefficient using the simple formula:

```
Position = Array Start Address + Element Size * Coefficient
```

In practice, we will normally let our programming language "do the math" for us.

Initializing an Array Just as we can initialize a scalar variable when we create it, we can also initialize an array. This initializing is done using braces to create a comma-separated list, such as:

```
int arInit1[5]={1,2,3,5,8};
```

This statement would create a five-element block of integers, with anInit1[0] being set to 1, anInit1[1] being set to 2, anInit1[2] being set to 3, anInit1[3] being set to 5, and anInit1[4] being set to 8.

Not all elements need to be initialized in the initialization list. For example, the following declaration is also legal:

```
int arInit2[10]={1,2,3,5,8};
```

In this case, the first five elements are initialized to 1,2,3,5,8 (as in the preceding example) and the remaining elements are zeroed out.

If an initialization list is included, C++ does not require you specify a number of values when you initialize the array—you can just specify []. The compiler will then compute the number for you. For example:

```
int arInit3[]={1,2,3,5,8};
```

This statement will cause the compiler to count the number of initialization elements (5), and then create a five-element array. In effect, it is exactly equivalent to the previous declaration of arInit1. It just allows us to be lazier.

Finally, just as was the case for scalar variables:

- If you create an array without initializing it, the likelihood is that the contents of that array will be whatever garbage happened to be in memory at the time the array was created. As long as you initialize at least one of the array's elements, however, the entire array will be initialized (to zeros, if values for higher coefficients are not specified).

- If you declare an array as **const,** then any attempts to change its values later in the program will result in a compiler error.

3.1.3: Where Are Variables Declared?

Variables are normally declared in four places:

- Within code blocks, such as the block used to define a function
- Within function declaration lines and prototypes
- External to all code blocks, within a source file
- Within definitions of complex data structures, such as **struct, union,** and **class** objects

We will delay discussing the fourth type of declaration to Chapter 11, where we introduce the C/C++ structure. Thus, we'll limit ourselves to the first three types of declarations here.

Local Declarations   We already looked at examples of the first two types of declarations in Chapter 2. For example, the function Plus() (presented in Chapter 2, Section 2.4.2):

```
int Plus(int nArg1,int nArg2)
{
    int nTotal;
    nTotal=nArg1+nArg2;
    return nTotal;
}
```

The variables nArg1 and nArg2 were declared in the declaration line. The variable nTotal, in contrast, was declared (and defined) at the beginning of the function body code block.

These declarations are both examples of local declarations. Within memory, these variables will normally be placed in the area known as the stack (see Chapter 1, Section 1.1.2 and Chapter 4, Section 4.1) when the function is called, and will be discarded as soon as the function returns. More generally:

> Anytime a variable or array is defined within a code block, it will continue to exist only as long as that code block remains active. As soon as the program leaves the code block, the data will be discarded.

Where local variables can be declared is one of the major differences between C and structured C++. In C, local variable declarations within a code block must always be the first statements within a code block—as was the case for nTotal, as already shown. Many C programmers go a step further and only define variables at the start of the function code block. C++, on the other hand, is much more flexible—you can declare a variable pretty much anywhere before you use it. For example, the following code would be legal in C++, but not in C:

```
int x,y;
x=3;
y=4;
int z=x+y; // illegal in C, but not C++
```

This format would not be legal in C, because the declaration follows code.

The ability to declare variables "on the fly" in C++ offers one key advantage and two potential disadvantages:

- *Advantage:* Declaring temporary variables immediately above the code that uses them leaves no question—to a programmer examining the code at some later time—that the variable is temporary in nature and is not being used to hold some important value.

- *Disadvantages:* Variables and initializations can surface all over the place in functions, making it more difficult to determine whether a function has been constructed according to its specification. The second disadvantage is that the **scope** of variables declared in some C++ constructs (most notably the "for loop," to be introduced in Chapters 5 and 6) has actually changed as the language evolved. It means code with local declarations that compiles under one version may not compile in another.

In either C or C++, however, as soon as the code block in which a variable is declared is finished (or we exit the code block, e.g., using a return), any variables or arrays defined in the code block are discarded.

Usually, the advantages of "on the fly" declarations outweigh the disadvantages. Having made this statement, the philosophy of this book is to maintain C/C++ compatibility wherever doing so does not introduce unrealistic programming practices. For this reason, we will not take advantage of the C++ extended variable declaration capability in the remainder of the text. We will, however, feel free to introduce new variables at the beginning of any new code block we create. (Chapter 6 covers the subject of such blocks in detail.) Because the code blocks we will create in the text tend to be quite small, we can limit ourselves in this way without giving up compatibility to C *and* without losing the spirit of C++.

Function Argument and Return Type Declarations We showed in Chapter 2 that the first line of a function definition declares the function's arguments and return type. The argument declarations are actually just another form of local variable. They differ from other local variables only in that they are initialized when the function is called. Thus, in Plus():

```
int Plus(int nArg1,int nArg2)
{
    int nTotal;
    nTotal=nArg1+nArg2;
    return nTotal;
}
```

nArg1, nArg2, and nTotal are all local variables. When we call the function as follows:

```
int Y;
Y=Plus(3,4);
```

the effect is the same as if we had the function defined as follows:

```
int PlusNoArgs()
{
    int nArg1=3;
    int nArg2=4;
    // The effect below this point is identical.
    int nTotal;
    nTotal=nArg1+nArg2;
    return nTotal;
}
```

Naturally, the advantage of supplying arguments (as opposed to defining a function such as PlusNoArgs() as we did) is that we can use Plus() with any combination of first and second values. In PlusNoArgs(), we are always stuck with adding 3 and 4.

The return type in a function declaration is used for two purposes. First, it allows the compiler to check to see whether what follows return statements inside our function is the right type of expression (or can be converted to the right type of expression). In our Plus() function then, the return statement:

```
return nTotal;
```

is legal because Plus() is supposed to return an integer, and nTotal is declared as an integer.

The other use for a return type is to make sure we are calling the function properly (argument types are used for the same purpose). For example, because Plus() returns an integer, the following call is legal:

```
int Y;
Y=Plus(3,4);
```

On the other hand, the call that follows would not be:

```
int Z[10];
Z=Plus(3,4);
```

If Z is an array, not a scalar integer, it makes no sense to assign an integer value to it. Thus, the compiler would generate an error. You could, however, write:

```
int Z[10];
Z[0]=Plus(3,4);
```

This format is legal because each element of Z[] is an integer (because Z[] is an integer array). Thus, the code would take the 7 returned by our call to Plus() and place it in the first element of the Z[] array.

Global Declarations It is also possible to declare variables and array outside of any functions. Such variables are often referred to as **global variables.** They are created and initialized when a program starts running, and are not discarded until the program exits.

The natural scope of global variables is called file scope, meaning they can be accessed by any function within the file that is defined after they are declared. Because files are compiled individually, however, creating a global variable or array in one file is not enough to let it be used by another. The problem is not with the variable itself—the problem is that the other file has no idea as to how the variable is named or defined.

To solve the problem of sharing global variables, we can use the include (header) file in much the same way that we did for function declarations. Instead of declaring the variable we want to share in the include file, however, we precede the declaration with the keyword **extern.** Thus, the statement:

```
extern int myarray[100];
```

in the .h file is a declaration that asserts that—somewhere in the project—an array of 100 integers named myarray has been defined. This declaration is enough to let other files use it by name.

Naturally, just putting extern declarations in an .h file is not enough to set aside memory for the variable or array being declared. In one—and only one—of the .cpp files, we must actually define the variable normally. If we fail to define it in any file, we get the ever popular "unresolved external" linker error. If we define it in more than one file, we get the "already defined" linker error. These errors are the same ones we talked about in the analogy presented in Chapter 2, Section 2.1.

Global variables are a form of *static* data. What this term means is that, once created and initialized, such variables remain in existence until the program stops running. In addition to local and static, a third type of data—dynamic—is provided by C++. This form of data will be addressed in a separate chapter (Chapter 12).

Choosing Between Local and Global Variables   In many cases, when you are declaring a variable in your program, you may perceive that a choice exists between making it local and making it global. Most people just beginning programming find that they gravitate toward global. Many factors make global variables *seem* easier to use:

- They never go out of scope.
- You don't have to pass them in as arguments to your functions.
- You don't have to worry about "running out of memory" while the program is running—once the program is started, the memory is already there.

As your programming experience grows, however, you discover that declaring lots of global variables is an extremely good way to shoot yourself in the foot. Two big problems arise with them:

- Because they can potentially be changed anywhere in your program, by any function, problems with them can be difficult to debug.
- Their presence can make dividing a project into independent components (e.g., for reuse) a real nightmare.

As a consequence of these issues, few serious structured programmers actually "like" global variables. What differs between programmers is how hard they will work to avoid them. The scruffy-to-neat continuum on this issue is illustrated in Style Sidebar 3.1.

STYLE SIDEBAR 3.1	Attitudes Toward Global Variables	
Camp	**Position**	**Justification**
Super Scruffy	Sure it makes sense to avoid global variables, but if you need them to get things up and running, then use them.	They're in the language for a reason, right? You can always take them out later, if you've got the time (or if you're being paid by the hour).
Scruffy	Avoid global variables except in situations where the application is small, and where reuse issues are not likely to be of concern.	Small applications, not intended for reuse, eliminate the two main arguments against using global variables.
Middle Ground	Avoid global variables where possible. If not, limit their use to data that are constant in nature.	If all global data elements are declared **const,** then there's no reason to worry about the debugging issues. It's still probably worth avoiding them for the reuse considerations, however.
Neat	Global variables should be avoided.	Their disadvantages far outweigh any benefits of convenience. Furthermore, many OOP techniques exist that make it easier to avoid them. Best not to get into the habit of using them at all.
Neat Freak	The capability to define global variables should not even be mentioned in a serious programming textbook.	Even if they help you get a project up and running, it's better to write no code than code that violates the strict rules of structured programming.

3.1: SECTION QUESTIONS

1. What is the principal benefit of defining an array, as opposed to defining ten individual scalar variables?

2. If we had an array (Test) that starts in memory address 1000, and each element was 4-bytes in size, where would element Test[2] begin in memory?

3. What are the two key pieces of data that we need to know about an array if we want to access data inside that array?

4. What would the values of each of the elements of the following array be after the following definition?

   ```
   int MyArray[5]={7,2,1};
   ```

5. What's the main difference between a local variable and a variable declared as a function argument?

6. Explain the two main uses of function declaration lines.

7. What is the purpose of the *extern* keyword?

3.2: REPRESENTING NUMBERS

C++ allows us to represent three basic classes of numbers:

- *Positive integers*: whole numbers that cannot take on a value less than 0
- *Integers*: whole numbers that can be either positive or negative
- *Real numbers*: floating point numbers stored internally in a sort of binary scientific notation

For all numeric data types, the type declared specifies the amount of memory each data element will hold. In this regard, numeric and textual data are quite different. Written as text, the integer 1,456,783,261 takes up substantially more space than the integer 3. On the computer, however, once you declare a piece of data to be of a given type, the amount of space it takes up is fixed. In other words, it takes the same amount of memory (e.g., 4 bytes) to hold an integer, whether its value is 1,456,783,261 or 3. (The latter memory, however, will probably have a lot more zeros in it than the former.) Furthermore, any given block of memory can only hold a finite number of different values, which means that every numeric data type comes with a built-in range of values it can represent. Getting a variable of that data type to hold values outside of its allowable range is impossible. Attempts to do so often lead to a condition called *overflow,* discussed in greater detail in Section 3.4.

In this section, we examine the different data types that C++ provides, and their ranges. In a later section (Section 3.4) we take a more in-depth look at the manner in which integers are actually stored on the computer, and its implications for programmers.

3.2.1: Integer Data Types in C/C++

Most of the data you will typically be representing in a C/C++ program will ultimately end up being one type of integer or another. In the design of C and C++, considerable flexibility was left for how such integers could be represented. As a result, the C/C++ standards do not specify what size the various types of integers must be—only their minimum size.

C/C++ provides four basic integer types, which identify the size of the integer:

```
char
short
int
long
```

Although **short** and **long** can be used in combination with **int** (i.e., **short int** or **long int**), doing so provides no extra information—so we usually don't bother. In addition to the types, the **signed** and **unsigned** keywords can be added in declaring an integer: **signed** means the integer can represent either positive or negative numbers, and is the default integer type; and **unsigned** means the integer can only represent positive numbers. If you know a value should never be negative (e.g., the value of a count), two advantages come from storing it in an unsigned data type: (1) you typically double the maximum value that can be represented in the variable; and (2) you never have to worry about the value being negative as the result of an error. If an integer is unsigned, it cannot hold a negative value.

Integer Limits   Whenever you declare an integer, the type of integer you declare determines the amount of memory available to hold values and, correspondingly, the range of values that integer can hold. C++ does not specify how many bytes each integer data type will use. The specific compiler we use, therefore, determines the sizes that are used by the different types. In Visual Studio .NET, the default sizes and ranges are listed in Table 3.1.

Aside from being familiar with the order of magnitude of the ranges (e.g., it is time to get very nervous when your **signed int** values start approaching 2 billion), one of the most important things you should take away from Table 3.1 is in the comments column. What it points out is that integer sizes are in a state of flux. Indeed, the "standard" size for almost every integer type has either changed within the past decade, or is likely to change in the next decade. As a programmer, this state of change means that you need to think carefully about any assumptions you make regarding the size of your data types. When you change compilers, you could easily discover you assumptions are no longer correct—and that your program does not run properly as a result. For example, you might save an array of 1-byte character data in one version of your program, then recompile your program using a compiler that assumes 2-byte characters. When you try to load in the previously saved array into your newly compiled

TABLE 3.1   C/C++ Integer Data Types and Their Current Sizes and Ranges

Type	.NET Size (in Bytes)	Minimum Value	Maximum Value	Comments
char	1	−128	+127	Two-byte characters are on the way, to support Unicode
unsigned char	1	0	+255	
short	2	−32768	+32767	Was the default size for **int** in pre-1995 MS compilers (v. 1.5 and below)
unsigned short	2	0	+65535	
int	4	−2147483648	+2147483647	**int** is currently the same as **long**
unsigned int	4	0	+4294967296	
long	4	−2147483648	+2147483647	8-byte **long** already used in C#; MS provides **_int64** 8-byte integer type
unsigned long	4	0	+4294967296	

program, the difference in assumed sizes causes a confusing mess. We will return to this topic when we discuss saving and loading information in files, in Chapters 8 and 17.

Declaring Integer Data We already saw examples of declaring integers in C++ presented in Chapter 2, and discussed what these declarations accomplish at the beginning of this chapter. The following would all be examples of legal declarations in C++:

```
int a1;
unsigned short s1,s2,s3=2;
char buf[80];
long mylong;
long bigarray[5]={1,3,5,7,9};
```

To repeat, for emphasis, what we already said several times: you must declare a variable or array in C++ before you use it.

TEST YOUR UNDERSTANDING 3.1:

In each of the preceding declarations, how much memory are we setting aside in Visual Studio .NET? Does our answer change based on the compiler we are using?

3.2.2: Real Data Types in C/C++

C/C++ offers three real number data types, only two of which are actually supported in Visual Studio .NET. The properties of these types are presented in Table 3.2.

Real numbers are internally represented in a form of exponential notation, with a single bit used to indicate whether the number is positive or negative, a collection of bits used to represent the number itself (the mantissa bits), and a certain number of bits used to represent the exponent. Because of this approach to representation, it is rare that a real number (float or double) would not be able to handle a value of a given size (short of programs computing the number of particles in the universe). On the other hand, if a limited number of bits are used to represent each number—the already-mentioned mantissa bits— then numbers cannot be completely accurate under many circumstances. For example, using a **float** you only get 6 or 7 significant digits. Thus, even a number like the price of a new house could not be represented to the penny with perfect accuracy.

Real Number Programming Issues The issues concerning real numbers are quite different from those involving the use of integers. Overflow conditions (or underflow—the

TABLE 3.2 C/C++ Real Number Data Types and Their Current Sizes and Ranges

Type	.NET Size (in Bytes)	Range	Significant Digits	Comments
float	4	$+/- 3.4 * 10^{38}$	~ 6–7	Not used that much anymore
double	8	$+/- 1.7 * 10^{308}$	~ 15	**double** and **long double** are same in .NET. 10 byte **long double** were used in some earlier versions
long double	8	$+/- 1.7 * 10^{308}$	~ 15	

presence of a nonzero number that is very small, such as 10^{-310}) rarely occur unless a serious logic error is present in the program—unlike the case for integer overflow. Twos complement issues, discussed later, are also irrelevant, as the real number implementation specified by the IEEE standards organizations uses a sign bit. Thus, at first glance, real numbers might seem preferable to integers from a programmer's perspective. They would appear to provide a lot fewer things to worry about.

Actually, real numbers tend to be used a lot less than integers in most programs. Two reasons explain why, with one becoming relatively minor, and one quite serious:

- *Performance:* Computations involving real numbers tend to be slower than integer calculations. This concern was once fairly serious, but performance issues associated with the use of real numbers declined significantly over the past decade. Although the use of real numbers on the original PC processor could reduce speed significantly—up to a factor of 100—today's architectures have circuitry built into the CPU that performs real number arithmetic. Furthermore, on today's machine it is rarely CPU speed that holds up a program—other components, such as memory and disk access, are much more likely to slow down the computer. Therefore floating point speeds and integer speeds are becoming reasonably comparable.

- *Accuracy:* The accuracy issue is the Achilles' heel of real number arithmetic. Even though 15 digits of precision is very good, for some numbers it may not be quite enough (e.g., the U.S. GNP in dollars and cents, the Italian GNP denominated in lire). Even worse, rounding errors can occur in arithmetic operations. For example, no guarantee holds that the expressions

    ```
    (X*Y)/Z and X*(Y/Z)
    ```

    will be exactly equal as a result of the rounding that occurs. They will be very, very close—but a big difference (in the way a program behaves) often separates close and equal.

As a result of these two issues, we find two things happening. First, because performance is almost never decisive and because memory and disk storage are so cheap, we almost always use the **double** in place of the **float**. Second, in applications where consistency counts, such as virtually all applications involving currency, we tend to use integers (e.g., amounts measured in pennies) rather than real numbers.

Declaring Real Number Data   No material difference arises between declaring real numbers and integers. For example, the following lines all define real numbers:

```
float a1;
double d1,d2,d3=2.0;
double buf[4] ={1.0,3.0,5.0};
float f2=125e-2;
```

When writing a real number constant in C++ (e.g., 3.00), it is usually a good idea to put in a decimal point, so the compiler knows that the value is not an integer. Exponential notation can also be used, using an E (or e) followed by an integer indicating the power of 10. For example:

```
1.25, 12.5E-1, 125e-2
```

are equivalent ways of writing the same number. (And 125e-2 is the same as writing the number $125*10^{-2}$.)

3.2 SECTION QUESTIONS

1. What is the difference between a signed and unsigned integer? Does the fact that an integer is signed impact the amount of space it takes to hold it?

2. Is it possible to do arithmetic operations on variables of type char?

3. Have the changes in integer sizes that occurred in Visual Studio .NET over the past decade made knowing the data ranges for each integer type more or less important?

4. Given that debits and credits must match exactly in an accounting application, would it make sense to use real numbers or integers to represent currency values in an accounting program?

5. Why are performance justifications for not using real numbers declining in importance over time?

6. Whenever you assign a real number to an integer, the compiler warns you. What two reasons (one major and one minor) justify the warning?

3.3: REPRESENTING TEXT

We have already defined the **char** data type as a 1-byte integer (for the current version of .NET, anyway). So, in a sense, we already know how to represent a single letter in C++. In this section, however, our principal focus will be on how we represent collections of letters that we refer to as text. C, and structured C++, normally accomplishes such representation using what is called a *NUL terminated character string*, or just *string* for short. After we explain how 1-byte integers become letters, we will focus on the nature of these strings.

3.3.1: Letters and the Char Data Type

Characters are just 1-byte integers. They can be added, subtracted, multiplied, and divided just like any other integers (although, in fairness, they do tend to overflow rather regularly if you use them in this way). What distinguishes characters from other integers, then, is mainly the way that we most commonly use them—as a convenient means to store text.

How do we move from integers to text? We need some sort of a coding scheme, allowing us to interpret numeric values as their text equivalents. Actually, three schemes for coding are, or were, in common use:

- **ASCII** *(American Standards Committee for Information Interchange) Character Set*: The most commonly used code, consisting of 128 integer-to-character conversions than include all the English alphabet, upper case and lower case, called ASCII for short. Another 128 characters—including non-English letters and drawing characters—are included in the extended ASCII character set, sometimes called the IBM character set (the original character set supported on the IBM PC).

- **EBCDIC** *(Extended Binary Coded Decimal Interchange Code)*: A system comparable to ASCII utilized by IBM mainframes.

- **Unicode**: A 2-byte character system including numerous non-English letter symbols and Asian word-character symbols. The first 128 characters of Unicode match those of ASCII.

Throughout this text, we will focus on ASCII—which is the character set traditionally used by C/C++. The specific mappings that ASCII provides are presented in Figure 3.1. The integer equivalents are presented both in **decimal** (base 10) and hexadecimal (base 16) format. (In C++, an integer can be identified as being written in base 16 by preceding it with 0x, for example 17 is equivalent to 0x11. A more thorough presentation of hexadecimal and its importance is presented in Section 3.4.)

Memorizing the values of the specific codes is an entirely unnecessary (and futile) exercise—it is what the chart is there for. Certain facts about ASCII are useful to know, however:

- All the characters less than or equal to space (aka ' ', 32) are nonprinting, sometimes called "white" characters.
- All the numeric digit characters are grouped together, stating with '0' (48).

FIGURE 3.1 Table of ASCII Character Codes (from Visual Studio .NET Documentation)

ASCII Character Codes Chart 1

Visual Studio
ASCII Character Codes Chart 1

Ctrl	Dec	Hex	Char	Code	Dec	Hex	Char	Dec	Hex	Char	Dec	Hex	Char
^@	0	00		NUL	32	20		64	40	@	96	60	`
^A	1	01		SOH	33	21	!	65	41	A	97	61	a
^B	2	02		STX	34	22	"	66	42	B	98	62	b
^C	3	03		ETX	35	23	#	67	43	C	99	63	c
^D	4	04		EOT	36	24	$	68	44	D	100	64	d
^E	5	05		ENQ	37	25	%	69	45	E	101	65	e
^F	6	06		ACK	38	26	&	70	46	F	102	66	f
^G	7	07		BEL	39	27	'	71	47	G	103	67	g
^H	8	08		BS	40	28	(	72	48	H	104	68	h
^I	9	09		HT	41	29	)	73	49	I	105	69	i
^J	10	0A		LF	42	2A	*	74	4A	J	106	6A	j
^K	11	0B		VT	43	2B	+	75	4B	K	107	6B	k
^L	12	0C		FF	44	2C	,	76	4C	L	108	6C	l
^M	13	0D		CR	45	2D	-	77	4D	M	109	6D	m
^N	14	0E		SO	46	2E	.	78	4E	N	110	6E	n
^O	15	0F		SI	47	2F	/	79	4F	O	111	6F	o
^P	16	10		DLE	48	30	0	80	50	P	112	70	p
^Q	17	11		DC1	49	31	1	81	51	Q	113	71	q
^R	18	12		DC2	50	32	2	82	52	R	114	72	r
^S	19	13		DC3	51	33	3	83	53	S	115	73	s
^T	20	14		DC4	52	34	4	84	54	T	116	74	t
^U	21	15		NAK	53	35	5	85	55	U	117	75	u
^V	22	16		SYN	54	36	6	86	56	V	118	76	v
^W	23	17		ETB	55	37	7	87	57	W	119	77	w
^X	24	18		CAN	56	38	8	88	58	X	120	78	x
^Y	25	19		EM	57	39	9	89	59	Y	121	79	y
^Z	26	1A		SUB	58	3A	:	90	5A	Z	122	7A	z
^[	27	1B		ESC	59	3B	;	91	5B	[	123	7B	{
^\	28	1C		FS	60	3C	<	92	5C	\	124	7C	|
^]	29	1D		GS	61	3D	=	93	5D	]	125	7D	}
^^	30	1E	▲	RS	62	3E	>	94	5E	^	126	7E	~
^-	31	1F	▼	US	63	3F	?	95	5F	_	127	7F	⌂*

*ASCII code 127 has the code DEL. Under MS-DOS, this code has the same effect as ASCII 8 (BS). The DEL code can be generated by the CTRL + BKSP key.

- All the uppercase letters are grouped together in sequence ('A'=65, 'B'=66, etc.).
- All the lowercase letters are grouped together in sequence ('a'=97, 'b'=98, etc.).

From time to time, we make use of these facts in our programming, as will become evident in later chapters.

One of the reasons it makes no sense to learn ASCII is that the C/C++ compiler gives us an easy way to access a letter's ASCII value without looking it up: just put it between apostrophes (single quotes). For example:

```
'A' is the same as writing 65 (or 0x41)
'a' is the same as writing 97 (or 0x61)
'3' is the same as writing 51 (or 0x33)
' ' (space) is the same as writing 32 (or 0x20)
```

Naturally, nonprinting characters are a bit harder to write in this way (except for the space as shown). To help us incorporate these characters in our programs, C/C++ gives us some common escape sequences, which are just sequences of characters beginning with a \ (backslash). Some common sequences are presented in Table 3.3.

Despite the fact that ASCII is used almost universally in ANSI-standard C/C++ programming, programmers need to be aware that Unicode is increasingly being used for data and operating systems, a fact that could cause serious problems if the one byte per character assumption is coded into programs that could be ported from system to system.

The use of apostrophes (single quotes) to represent characters, as opposed to quotation marks (double quotes) is significant here. To understand why, we need to turn to the subject of NUL terminated character strings.

3.3.2: NUL Terminated Character Strings

Characters don't really become *really* useful until you can group them together, to form names, words, sentences and, ultimately, complete documents. It is pretty obvious that the array, introduced at the beginning of this chapter, can be helpful to us here. Just put the sequence of characters that form your text into the array. Problem solved, right?

TABLE 3.3	Common Escape Sequences
'\t' is the tab character, the same as writing 9 (or 0x09)	
'\n' is the newline character, the same as writing 10 (or 0x0A)	
'\r' is the carriage return character, the same as writing 13 (or 0x0D)	
'\0' is the same as writing 0 (or 0x00), the NUL character	
'\c' (for any character c that is not predefined) refers to c that follows, e.g.,	
'\\' is the same as writing \	
'\"' is the same as writing "	
'\'' is the same as writing '	
'\%' is the same as writing %	
etc.	
'\xhh' (where h represents any hexadecimal digit) can be used for any character whose code we know (e.g., '\x33' is the same as '3' or 51)	

Actually, the pure array solution is not too bad. It is sometimes referred to as *fixed length strings* and is used by many early 3GL languages, such as FORTRAN, and is also common in database contexts (e.g., dBase III+, as we will see in various chapter examples). It has two disadvantages, however:

1. *Wasted space*: Often, when you store text, you don't know how much space you need in advance (e.g., How many characters will a person's last name be?). If you are going to store last names in a fixed length array, you need to set aside enough space for the "worst case" scenario—meaning you waste a lot of space when someone named "Lee" comes along.

2. *Need for padding*: Even if you don't care about space, short strings cause yet another problem. If you set aside 80 characters to hold a last name, and the name happens to be "Lee," what do you do with the remaining 77 characters? Something has to go there—memory can't be empty, it always holds some value. Normally, such a situation is handled by padding the end of the string with blanks (such as the space character, ASCII 32). Doing so, however, means that whenever you access the data in your array (e.g., to print a check), you need to do something to remove those trailing blanks (a process often referred to as trimming) if you want to avoid huge, ungainly spaces.

The way C and structured C++ handle the problem of variable string length is to define what is called a NUL terminated string. The concept is simple: whenever you create a string, you place a **NUL character** (ASCII value 0—see Figure 3.1) at the end. This NUL character, often written as '\0', should not be confused with the character '0' (ASCII value 48, 0x30). The NUL terminator normally is used for one purpose and one purpose only: to signal the end of string.

TEST YOUR UNDERSTANDING 3.2

Suppose we have a 10-character array in memory with the following contents:

65	66	67	68	0	0	0	0	0	0

How long is the string that starts at the beginning of the array? If we were to display the string on the console, what characters would appear? (*Hint*: In case you don't want to look back to Figure 3.1, 65 is the 'A' character.)

Initializing Strings We already talked about how to initialize an array using a brace enclosed list, for example,

```
int myarray[5]={1,2,3,5,8};
```

We can use the same technique for initializing strings, for example:

```
char mystring1[10]={97,98,99,100};
char mystring2[10]={'a','b','c','d'};
```

This approach is a bit cumbersome, however.

TEST YOUR UNDERSTANDING 3.3

Why are the initializations of mystring1 and mystring2 equivalent in the preceding example? (Consult Figure 3.1 for a hint.) Given what

was said about initializing arrays at the beginning of this chapter,
why will both of these initializations give us NUL terminated strings?

For this reason, C/C++ gives us an easier way of initializing arrays—using quotation marks (double quotes). For example:

```
char mystring3[10]="abcd";
```

does precisely the same initialization as was done for mystring1 and mystring2. Analogous to normal array initialization, we can also write:

```
char mystring4[]="abcd";
```

In this case, what happens is slightly different. The compiler counts the characters within the quotation marks. It discovers 4 and then adds 1 to that number (to provide room for the NUL terminator), meaning it needs to set aside room for 5 characters. Knowing this total, it then treats the declaration as equivalent to:

```
char mystring4[5]="abcd";
```

and proceeds as it would for the earlier case. What is important to note here is that when you are working with NUL terminated strings, you must always include a NUL at the end, even if you have the option of sizing the array to the precise size you need. No walls exist in memory to keep one array from flowing into another. So, if you leave off the NUL terminator, any of the C/C++ functions that assume NUL terminated strings (and there are many!) will not stop where your array ends. Instead, they will keep processing characters until a byte containing 0x00 is encountered.

Strings in C++ (Using OOP) NUL terminated strings are incredibly useful, but can also be a real pain in the neck. The problem with them, as we shall see in later chapters, is that many operators we use—such as assignment (=) and tests (<, >)—don't work with them. Instead, we need to define functions with names only a geek could love (e.g., strcpy, strcmp).

When we start programming using C++ objects, one of the first things we introduce is a **string** class (a class is a type of object) that remedies these defects. Even with such classes, however, it is not uncommon to use some C functions (such as the function that does case insensitive comparison) in an OOP application. Thus, understanding NUL terminated strings is important for both C and C++ programmers.

3.3.3: Summary of SimpleIO Functions

The SimpleIO.h and SimpleIO.cpp files, introduced in Chapter 2, provide a set of easy-to-use functions for getting information into and out of programs without worrying about the C++ IO libraries, which will be covered in later chapters (Chapters 7, 8, and 17). Some of the functions are summarized in Table 3.4.

Using the SimpleIO String Functions Two of the functions in the SimpleIO files, InputString() and DisplayString(), are intended to work with NUL terminated character string. A simple program that reads a line of code from the keyboard, then writes it back, is presented in Example 3.1.

Within the Example 3.1 code, a number of lines are worthy of comment.

```
(1) char strBuf[MAXLINE];
```

This line defines an array of characters to hold the string the user types in. The MAXLINE refers to a constant (255) that was defined in SimpleIO.h (see Chapter 2, Section 2.4.1 for an explanation) to specify the maximum number of characters we will allow the user to type in.

TABLE 3.4	Selected SimpleIO Functions

int InputInteger()

Reads an integer from the keyboard and returns its value.

char InputCharacter()

Reads a character from the keyboard and returns its value.

double InputReal()

Reads a real number from the keyboard, then returns its value as a double.

void InputString(char str[])

Reads a string from the keyboard, and places its value in the array whose name is passed as an argument.

void DisplayInteger(int nVal)

Writes an integer value to the console.

void DisplayCharacter(char cVal)

Writes an integer value to the console, displaying it as an ASCII character.

void DisplayRealNumber(double dVal)

Writes a real number to the console.

void DisplayString(const char str[])

Writes a string to the console. The string is passed in using the name of the array that contains it.

void NewLine()

Writes a newline to the console.

```
    (2) DisplayString("Input a line of text: ");
```

We are now in a position to provide a clearer explanation of the quoted string, already used in a number of earlier code examples in Chapter 2. When the compiler sees this code, it does the following:

1. It counts the number of characters between the quotes (22), then adds 1 (for the NUL terminator).

2. It creates a temporary array of at least 23 characters (normally on the program stack), and initializes it with {'I','n','p','u','t',' ','a', *etc.*}, ending it with a NUL terminator.

3. It passes the memory start address of that temporary array into the DisplayString() function.

Within the DisplayString() function, C/C++ library code then keeps printing characters to the screen (starting at the array address passed in) until a byte containing 0x00 is encountered (the NUL terminator), at which point it returns.

```
    (3) InputString(strBuf);
```

This line gets the starting address of the array strBuf and passes it into the function InputString(). Within InputString(), various C/C++ library code is called to read characters typed by the user (placing them in strBuf) until the user hits the *Enter* key. When the *Enter* key is pressed, the function then places a 0x00 (NUL terminator) byte at the end of

---

EXAMPLE 3.1

Simple program to read in a line of text and print it back

```
#include "SimpleIO.h"

int main()
{
    char strBuf[MAXLINE];
    DisplayString("Input a line of text: ");
    InputString(strBuf);
    NewLine();
    DisplayString("You just typed: ");
    DisplayString(strBuf);
    return 0;
}
```

---

the sequence of characters. In other words, it reads a line of text (typed in by the user), places it in the array strBuf, and puts a NUL terminator at the end to make it a string.

```
(4) DisplayString(strBuf);
```

This line passes DisplayString() the starting address of the array strBuf. It is similar to the earlier call (i.e., DisplayString("Input a line of text: "), already discussed) except that the compiler does not need to create and initialize a temporary array in this case. The location of strBuf has already been declared and defined in (1), and its contents have already been established in (3). It illustrates the fact that many string routines can either take arrays of characters created by the programmer (e.g., strBuf), or temporary arrays created by the compiler (quoted strings), as arguments.

TEST YOUR UNDERSTANDING 3.4

Given the preceding discussion, what is the difference in how 'A' and "A" are interpreted? What do you suppose would happen if you use the wrong one in calling a function?

3.3 SECTION QUESTIONS

1. Why do we need a coding system for **char** data, when we don't need one for other types of integers?
2. What is the difference between '1' and 1?
3. What are three different ways of writing the tab character?
4. What purpose does a NUL terminator usually serve in an array of characters?
5. What would the following lines display on the screen?
   ```
   char szBuf[20]={72,101,108,108,111,33,0};
   DisplayString(szBuf);
   ```

3.4: IN DEPTH: INTEGER NUMBERING SYSTEMS

The most common type of data that is represented on a computer is a number. Even data that we do not normally think of as being numeric—such as text—are treated as numeric data by the computer. All that we need is a coding system, such as ASCII or Unicode, for translating those numbers into symbols that can be printed or displayed on the screen.

In this section, we will examine different numbering systems and their properties. Developing an understanding of how we represent numbers on the computer can be especially useful in predicting when common programming problems, such as overflow, will occur. It can also help us understand some peculiar behaviors that can occur when we move between data types.

3.4.1: Numbering Systems and Bases

A numbering system is specific notation for representing numbers. Although we are used to one numbering system—base 10—many other systems are possible. Indeed, certain systems, such as binary, **octal,** and hexadecimal prove to be much more convenient for a number of computer-related purposes.

The key to any numbering system is its base. The base specifies the number of symbols that are used in the system. For example, base 10 uses 10 symbols:

         0, 1, 2, 3, 4, 5, 6, 7, 8, 9

Base 2 (also referred to as binary), on the other hand, uses 2 symbols:

         0, 1

For bases above 10, we need to make up symbols—typically using the letters of the alphabet. Thus, in base 16, the symbols we use are:

         0, 1, 2, 3, 4, 5, 6, 7, 8, 9, A, B, C, D, E, F

Base 16 is also referred to as hexadecimal, and is commonly seen when working in a debugger. For this reason, we pay particular attention to it as we examine the general topic of numbering systems.

How Numbering Systems Work   When using a number, it is important to realize that the numbering system we use influences how we display it—but not the actual value of the number. Thus, the number 63 (base 10) may be written as 3F in hexadecimal, or 1111111 in binary, or LXIII (Roman numerals). We mean the same thing by every one these different representations, all that is different is how each appears.

Although different numbering systems can appear quite different, all modern numbering systems (i.e., all discussed here except for Roman numerals) are constructed using the same basic principle. Specifically, the digit in each column represents the value times a corresponding power of the base. For example:

         $3478_{10} = 3*10^3 + 4*10^2 + 7*10^1 + 8*10^0$

In this example, the subscript indicates the number is written in base 10. We should also note that the farthest number to the right is always called the units column, as any number raised to the 0 power is 1.

The exact same approach can be generalized to all other numbering systems. For example:

         $1101_2 = 1*2^3 + 1*2^2 + 0*2^1 + 1*2^0$
         $3478_{16} = 3*16^3 + 4*16^2 + 7*16^1 + 8*16^0$

Note that the values 3478_{10} and 3478_{16} are significantly different. Thus to know the value of a number, you need to know the base in which it is written. Although looking at a number may give you information about what base it is *not* written in, it provides no information regarding what base it is written in (unless the base is provided).

TEST YOUR UNDERSTANDING 3.5

Explain why the number 12F5A gives us more about the base it was written in than the number 11011.

In C and C++, we most commonly use two bases to write numbers. To allow us to tell them apart, C/C++ provides the following rule:

- If an integer begins with the digits 0x, the digits that follow (normally 2, 4, or 8 digits) are interpreted to be in hexadecimal. Thus 0x4f31 and 0x1000 would both be viewed as hexadecimal numbers.
- If an integer does not begin with 0x, it is assumed to be written in decimal.

We will follow these rules throughout this text, unless we choose to specifically identify a base using a subscript.

Converting Numbers to Base 10 Once you know how to write out a number in its long form, converting it to base 10 is simple. All you have to do is figure out the powers. For example:

$$2^0 = 1$$
$$2^1 = 2$$
$$2^2 = 4$$
$$2^3 = 8$$

Therefore:

$$1101_2 = 1*2^3 + 1*2^2 + 0*2^1 + 1*2^0 = 1*8 + 1*4 + 0*2 + 1*1 = 13_{10}$$

Similarly:

$$16^0 = 1$$
$$16^1 = 16$$
$$16^2 = 256$$
$$16^3 = 4096$$

Therefore:

$$3478_{16} = 3*16^3 + 4*16^2 + 7*16^1 + 8*16^0$$
$$= 3*4096 + 4*256 + 7*16 + 8*1$$
$$= 13432$$

Converting Base 10 Numbers to Other Bases The two basic methods for converting numbers from base 10 to other bases are the power method and the remainder method.

The Power Method The power method of converting numbers from base 10 to other numbering systems is essentially the reverse of the process used to convert the numbers to base 10.

The process is simple:

- Take the base you are converting to and create a table of powers with enough entries so that the highest power is greater than the number you are converting.

- Divide the next highest power into the number you are converting. The result is your leftmost digit.
- Take the remainder and repeat the process on the lower powers. *Note*: Any time a power is higher than the number being converted, the digit becomes a 0.

Examples 3.2 and 3.3 illustrate this process.

The Remainder Method   The remainder method of converting numbers from base 10 to other numbering systems is easier to do, but harder to understand what you're doing. It builds digits from the right of the number as follows:

- Take the number and divide by the base. The remainder is the rightmost digit of the number.
- The process is repeated with result of the division, i.e., the quotient, and digits are built from right-to-left.
- The process ends when the quotient is 0.

The remainder method is illustrated, using the same two examples presented earlier, in Examples 3.4 and 3.5.

EXAMPLE 3.2

Converting 13610 to base 5

Suppose we want to convert 136 to base 5.
Create table of 5 powers:

Power	Value	Remainder/Value	New Remainder
4	625	136/625 = **0**	136
3	125	136/125 = **1**	11
2	25	11/25 = **0**	11
1	5	11/5 = **2**	1
0	1	1/1 = **1**	

Therefore, the new value is 1021_5.

EXAMPLE 3.3

Converting 5887_{10} to base 16 (hexadecimal)

Create table of 16 powers:

Power	Value	Remainder/Value	New Remainder
4	65536	5887/65536 = **0**	5887
3	4096	5887/4096 = **1**	1791
2	256	1791/256 = **6**	255
1	16	255/16 = 15 = **F**	15
0	1	15/1 = 15 = **F**	

Therefore, the new value is 0x16FF ($16FF_{16}$).

EXAMPLE 3.4

Convert 136_{10} to base 5 using the remainder method

136/5 = 27	Remainder: 1
27/5 = 5	Remainder: 2
5/5 = 1	Remainder: 0
1/5 = 0	Remainder: 1

Therefore, using the remainders and building from right to left, the new value is 1021_5.

EXAMPLE 3.5

Convert 5887_{10} to base 16 using the remainder method

5887/16	= 367	Remainder:	15 = F
367/16	= 22	Remainder:	15 = F
22/16	= 1	Remainder:	6
1/16	= 0	Remainder:	1

Therefore, using the remainders and building from right to left, the new value is 0x16FF.

Arithmetic in Different Bases   From time to time, we need to perform—or at least understand—arithmetic in different bases (most commonly hexadecimal). Complicated operations, such as multiplication and division, are normally easier to perform by (1) converting to base 10, (2) performing the operation, then (3) converting back to the original base. We can usually perform addition and subtraction, on the other hand, in the original base. The trick is remembering that when and what we carry (or borrow) depends on the base we are in.

- In base 10, we carry when the digits we add are greater or equal to 10. The 1 that we carry represents 10 units from the column to the right. Similarly, the 1 we borrow from the column to the left becomes 10 in the column we borrow to.

- In base 16, we carry when the digits we add are greater or equal to 16. The 1 that we carry represents 16 units from the column to the right. Similarly, the 1 we borrow from the column to the left becomes 16 in the column we borrow to.

- In base X, we carry when the digits we add are greater or equal to X. The 1 that we carry represents X units from the column to the right. Similarly, the 1 we borrow from the column to the left becomes X in the column we borrow to.

Some examples of this arithmetic are presented in Example 3.6.

3.4.2 Binary and Hexadecimal Bases

Sometimes, bases are related to each other by virtue of the fact that one base is a power of another. Where such a relationship occurs, a nice correspondence is evident between the digits of one and the digits of the other. The utility of hexadecimal in computers, for example, owes mainly to its close relationship to binary—the internal representation used by the computer. This relationship is illustrated in Example 3.7.

The reason this equivalence is so important on a computer is that, in representing an integer, the computer needs to allocate a certain amount of space. Traditionally, that space

---

EXAMPLE 3.6

Simple arithmetic done in different bases

1. 0x3421 + 0xBF21
   1 + 1 = 2
   2 + 2 = 4
   4 + F = 3, carry 1 (4 + 15 = 19, which is 16 + 3)
   3 + B + 1 = F
   = F342
2. 3425 + 1425
   2 + 2 = 4
   4 + 4 = 3, carry 1 (4 + 4 = 8, which is 5 + 3)
   3 + 1 + 1 = 0, carry 1 (3 + 1 + 1 = 5, which is 5 + 0)
   1 = 1
   = 1034

EXAMPLE 3.7

Relationship between base 2 and base 16

16 is 2^4, therefore any hexadecimal number can be translated, digit-by-digit, into a binary number.

Thus, if $1_{16} = 0001_2$, $D_{16} = 1101_2$, and $7_{16} = 0111_2$:

$1D7_{16}$ = $0001\ 1101\ 0111_2$
$D11_{16}$ = $1101\ 0001\ 0001_2$
$7D1_{16}$ = $0111\ 1101\ 0001_2$
etc.

The process also works in reverse. For example, suppose you wanted to find the hexadecimal value of the number:

`11001001111100101001`

The easiest way is to break it up into groups of 4 (starting from the right):

`1100 1001 1111 0010 1001`

then convert these directly into hexadecimal digits:

`C    9    F    2    9`

Joining these together, the equivalent hexadecimal number is C9F29.

---

has been allocated in *bytes*—groups of 8 bits. If each group of four bits (referred to as a *nibble*) represents a single hexadecimal digit, it stands to reason that when we allocate room for integers, whatever size we allocate will be an even number of hexadecimal digits. The practical effect of this logic is that it is much easier to express integer ranges in hexadecimal than it is in decimal, as illustrated in Table 3.5.

3.4.3: Twos Complement and Negative Numbers

The elegant system we just derived for representing numbers in hexadecimal has just one flaw. It assumes the numbers we want to represent are positive. As soon as we decide that we also need to represent negative numbers, we need to devise an entirely new scheme.

TABLE 3.5	Common Integer Sizes

Common Integer Sizes in Bytes	Range of Values (Expressed in Hexadecimal)
1	0x00-0xFF
2	0x0000-0xFFFF
4	0x00000000-0xFFFFFFFF
8	0x0000000000000000-0xFFFFFFFFFFFFFFFF

One scheme we might consider would be to take a single bit, and treat all numbers with the bit "on" as being negative, all numbers with the bit "off" as being positive. In essence, we do that exact thing when we write a negative sign. Unfortunately, a number of disadvantages are associated with such a solution:

- The approach would significantly complicate processor circuitry. It is important to realize that any system of numbering we devise needs to be handled by circuitry built into the processor. Using a single sign bit turns out to be a rather inefficient approach.

- We would lose our neat correspondence between bytes and hexadecimal digits. The leftmost digit of each number, in particular, would not be able to hold an entire hex digit—only the values between 0 and 7 (because the 8 bit would be reserved for use for the sign).

As it turns out, a much better approach can be used for handling positive and negative integers of a given size. It is referred to as *twos complement*.

For twos complement to work, you need to know how long your number is going to be. In today's computers, integers are almost always specified in one of three ways:

- 1 byte (8 bits)
- 2 bytes (16 bits)
- 4 bytes (32 bits)

Note: The use of 8-byte integers is also becoming increasingly common.

What twos complement does is to break the number line in half, with the numbers 0x00... to 0x7F being positive, and 0x80... to 0xFF being negative, which is illustrated for a 1-byte integer (also called a character) in Figure 3.2. The interpretation of the diagram is as follows:

- As we move from 0 in the positive direction, our normal number and its twos complement equivalent grow in parallel—for example 0x4A twos complement is just 0x4A (74_{10}). This pattern continues through 0x7f (127_{10}).

- At 0x80, however, the twos complement interpretation of the number shifts dramatically. Instead of being +128, it is interpreted as –128.

- From 0x80 on, the number line continues to rise (e.g., 0x81 is –127, 0x82 is –126, and so forth).

- This pattern then continues to 0xFF, which is –1. From there we go back to 0.

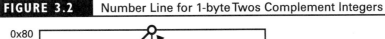

FIGURE 3.2   Number Line for 1-byte Twos Complement Integers

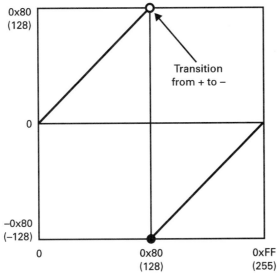

Precisely the same process is followed when we have more bytes to work with. For 2-byte integers:

- 0x0000 to 0x7FFF (0 to 32,767) are equivalent to the normal integer.
- 0x8000 to 0xFFFF (-32,768 to −1) are negative, rising to −1.

For 4-byte integers:

- 0x00000000 to 0x7FFFFFFF (0 to 2147483647) are equivalent to the normal integer.
- 0x80000000 to 0xFFFF (-2147483648 to −1) are negative, rising to −1.

Looking at it another way, the twos complement system reserves roughly half the number space for negative numbers. Therefore signed integers can represent:

```
1 byte:  -2⁷ to +2⁷-1
2 bytes: -2¹⁵ to +2¹⁵-1
4 bytes: -2³¹ to +2³¹-1
```

Computing Twos Complement Negative Numbers   The way twos complement works is by defining the representation for the negative numbers as follows:

```
1 byte:    -X  =    2⁸ - X
2 bytes:   -X  =    2¹⁶ - X
4 bytes:   -X  =    2³² - X
```

This format is allowable because the positive numbers are only allowed to go to $+2^7-1$, $+2^{15}-1$, and $2^{31}-1$, respectively. Thus, whether a number is positive or negative is never in question.

When computing twos complement, it is almost always easiest to work in hexadecimal. Using 0x notation to represent hexadecimal numbers, we find that:

```
1 byte:   -X  =    0x100 - X
2 bytes:  -X  =    0x10000 - X
4 bytes:  -X  =    0x10000000 - X
```

Some illustrations are provided in Example 3.8

The calculations in Example 3.8 suggest an important rule:

> To make a negative twos complement number fit into a larger memory location, you simply fill the new significant bits with Fs. To make a positive number fit into a larger memory location, you simply fill the new significant bits with 0s.

Understanding this rule can help you predict the types of changes that can occur in C/C++ as you move across data types.

Computing Positive Values from Twos Complement Negative Numbers

If you have a number in twos complement, how do you find its positive equivalent? The answer can be gleaned by the way twos complement numbers are constructed. For example, for a 1-byte number:

```
-X is represented as (2⁸ - X)
2⁸ - (2⁸ - X) = X
```

What this equation means, effectively, is that if we subtract a twos complement negative number from its base, we come up with the positive equivalent—exactly the same process we used to come up with the twos complement value. Some illustrations are provided in Example 3.9.

Benefits of Twos Complement   Using twos complement turns out to offer a major computational benefit over other techniques for representing negative numbers. If we represent negatives using twos complement, then the processor can just treat negative and positive numbers as if they were the same in performing its addition and subtraction. For example:

```
0x0010 + 0xFFFE = 0x000E
```

In twos complement, this is equivalent to saying 16 (0x0010) plus –2 (0xFFFE) equals 14 (0x000E). Similarly:

```
0x0003 + 0xFFF8 = 0xFFFB
```

EXAMPLE 3.8

Various twos complement calculations

What is the twos complement value of –1 (1 byte)?
    For 1-byte numbers: 0x100 – 1 = 0xFF
What is the twos complement value of –1 (4 byte)?
    For 4-byte numbers: 0x100000000 – 1 = 0xFFFFFFFF
What is the twos complement value of –127 (1 byte)?
    For 1-byte numbers: 0x100 – 0x7F = 0x81
What is the twos complement value of –127 (4 byte)?
    For 4-byte numbers: 0x100000000 – 0x7F = 0xFFFFFF81

EXAMPLE 3.9

Finding positive equivalents of twos complement negative numbers

What is the positive equivalent of 0xFF?
    For 1-byte numbers: 0x100 – 0xFF = 1
What is the positive equivalent of 0xFFC7?
    For 2-byte numbers: 0x10000 – 0xFFC7 = 0x0039 = 57

In twos complement, it is equivalent to saying 3 (0x0003) plus –8 (0xFFF8) = –5 (0xFFFB).

The only place where the arithmetic properties of twos complement break down is in situations where the result of the arithmetic is out of the bounds of the size of the integer we are using. This situation is called *overflow*.

3.4.4: Overflow

It is easy to dismiss the mechanics of twos complement as a form of geek trivia. After all, once you understand the allowable ranges for integers, does it really matter how they are actually represented in the machine? A good reason arises, however, for developing a clear understanding of how positive and negative numbers relate to each other. Such understanding tends to reduce the amount of time you spend dealing with one of the most common problems encountered by C/C++ programmers: integer overflow.

An *integer overflow* situation exists when we exceed the allowable limits of an integer that we are using in our program. Because of the nature of twos complement, this overflow is usually accompanied by an inappropriate sign change: either from positive to negative or from negative to positive. For example:

```
0x7F + 0x02 = 0x81
```

If these are twos complement 1-byte integers, it means that 127 + 2 = –127. On the other hand, the same arithmetic performed with 2-byte integers would be:

```
0x007F + 0x0002 = 0x0081
```

In this case, because the integers are longer, no overflow occurs. As a result, the arithmetic yields the proper result: 127 + 2 = 129.

Overflow can also occur where the numbers are negative. For example:

```
0xFF + 0x80 = 0x7F
```

(Although we probably would have wanted to carry in this situation, i.e., 0xFF+0x80=0x17F, on a computer you are limited by the size of the numbers you are working with. Thus bits that should have been carried beyond the available size are simply ignored.)

If these are twos complement 1-byte integers, it means that –1 + –128 = 127. Once again, however, if we did the same arithmetic using 2-byte integers, we would have gotten:

```
0xFFFF + 0xFF80 = 0xFF7F
```

In this case, the integers are long enough so that the results are the desired ones: –1 + –128 = –129.

TEST YOUR UNDERSTANDING 3.6

Why did we write 0x80 as 0xFF80 when converting it to a 2-byte integer? Show that 0xFF7F is, indeed, the same as –129.

Such overflows can create serious problems for programmers, and languages like C++ provide no automatic way of telling whether an integer overflow has taken place. Although some overflow exceptions (a form of error handling) are incorporated in libraries, it is fairly common that the actual occurrence of overflow will be undetected.

An argument can be made that programmers are responsible for understanding the limits of the data they are working with, and that all overflow can (and should) be avoided. Although admirable in intent, such a goal can be difficult to achieve. The problem is that sometimes calculations get performed where the result is within limits, yet some intermediate value may not be. For example:

```
char c1=5,c2=32,c3=10,c4;
c4=c1*c2/c3;
```

In this particular calculation, 5*32/10 (in decimal), the expected result (16) is clearly within the range of a 1-byte integer (the typical size of the **char** data type). Unfortunately, 5*32 gives us 0xA0 (160 in reality, but the value –96 in twos complement if we only have 1 byte to work with). Thus, if this particular arithmetic were performed single byte, our result is likely to be –9 (the result of –96/10, because integer division always truncates any remainder).

Recognizing that an overflow has occurred is usually harder than fixing it—the solution to overflow problems is nearly always the same: use larger integers.

3.4.5: The Convert Program

 Walkthrough available in Convert.wmv

The WinConvert program, supplied with the text, is designed to walk you through the calculations used in doing integer base conversions and moving to and from twos complement. The interface is a simple dialog box, shown in Figure 3.3, that allows you to specify a number to convert, a starting base, and an ending base. It then shows all intermediate calculations performed using the remainder method of converting between bases.

3.4 SECTION QUESTIONS

1. The IBM PC had 20 bits available to hold memory addresses. The IBM AT had 24 bits. Starting with the 386 series of computers, 32 bits were available. How much memory could each machine address?

2. If you take a number and reverse every 1 and 0 in its binary representation, you have the *ones complement* of the number. Explain why the ones complement of a 1-byte, 2-byte, and 4-byte number in hexadecimal can be computed by subtracting the original number from 0xFF, 0xFFFF, and 0xFFFFFFFF, respectively.

3. A mechanical shortcut is often used to compute twos complement: take its ones complement, then add 1 to the result. For example, suppose we wanted the twos complement of 5, for a 1-byte number:

```
Ones complement of 0x05 = 0xFF-0x05 = 0xFA
Adding 1: 0xFA + 0x01 = 0xFB
```

FIGURE 3.3	Convert Program

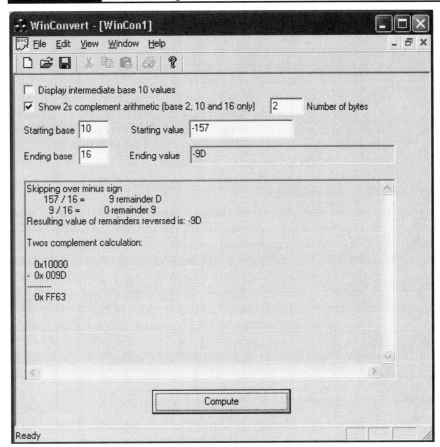

Explain why this gives the same result as the procedure given in Section 3.2.3 of this chapter.

4. What two places in the graph shown in Figure 3.2 are of particular concern to programmers working with integers?

5. Can you tell whether an integer is signed or unsigned by looking at its values in memory?

3.5: IN DEPTH: MORE COMPLEX TYPES

In addition to primitive data types, C/C++ provides the ability to define variables that hold memory addresses. C and, especially, C++ also provide means for defining more complex types of data. In this section we preview these capabilities just enough so that we can recognize their presence. Much more detailed discussions of these topics are presented in Chapters 10 and 11.

3.5.1: Introduction to Pointers

One of the most powerful, and potentially dangerous, capabilities provided by C/C++ is the ability to declare variables containing the addresses of other variables. What makes these variables so powerful is that they allow the programmer to manipulate the contents of memory directly, bypassing the safeguards a language typically provides to ensure the memory we are working with has been properly set aside and initialized. And that aspect, of course, is precisely what also makes the capability so dangerous.

A variable declared to hold an address of another variable, instead of a value, is called a **pointer.** It needs to be declared, like any other data type. What makes it different from other declarations, however, is that an asterisk (*) precedes the variable name. For example, consider the following two definitions:

```
char c1;
char *c2;
```

In the first, c1 sets aside 1 byte of memory that will hold a single character. In contrast, the second declaration specifies that c2 is a character pointer. That specification means it will set aside 4 bytes of memory on a typical system (like other data types, C++ does not specify the size of pointer variables, which depends on the size of addresses used by the CPU and operating system). Into that 4-byte variable, a memory address will be placed. Should we then go to the memory address in c2—the address that c2 "points" to—we would expect to find character data, assuming, of course, we put a valid address into c2.

We will go into the characteristics of pointers in considerable detail in Chapter 10. The only reason we need to introduce them here is that pointers are often used or generated when we work with arrays. For example, in Section 3.3.3, when we described what was accomplished in the function call:

```
DisplayString("Input a line of text: ");
```

we stated that the compiler created an array, initialized its contents to the string "Input a line of text: ", then passed its starting address into the function DisplayString(). What it means, in fact, is that the compiler created a temporary pointer variable to hold the address of the array it created, and that pointer was passed into DisplayString().

Indeed, the following rule is true throughout C++:

> Whenever an array name is used without following brackets, that name refers to the starting address of the array.

As we noted in the beginning of the chapter, the starting address of an array is the most critical piece of information we need to know about the array. Knowing that address, we can get to the remaining elements easily, because they are guaranteed to be next to each other in memory. For NUL terminated strings, the situation is even better. Not only does the array name give us the address where the array starts, the NUL terminator tells us where our string ends.

The practical effect of the relationship between arrays and pointers is that most C/C++ functions that are designed to work with arrays use pointers in their arguments. For example, the C/C++ library function strcpy() takes one string, its second argument, and copies its into another string, its first argument. It is declared as follows:

```
char *strcpy(char *a1,const char *a2);
```

Naturally, given our understanding of strings, what a1 and a2 point to are not likely to be individual characters. Rather, they are the start addresses of arrays of characters.

What is the purpose of the **const** in the declaration of a2? Given what the function does, why does it make sense to see **const** on the second argument, but not the first?

We might see strcpy() used in the following manner:

```
char buf1[80];
char buf2[80]="Hello, World";
strcpy(buf1,buf2);
```

The effect of this code would be to copy the string "Hello, World" into buf1. Because the array names buf1 and buf2 are not followed by brackets in the call *strcpy(buf1,buf2)*, the addresses where the arrays start are used to establish the values for a1 and a2 within the function.

The InputString() function, in SimpleIO, was declared as follows:

void InputString(char str[]);

Given what we just said (and using the example of the strcpy() function), what would be another way we could declare it, using pointer notation? What about for DisplayString()? What is different about the DisplayString() declaration, and why?

3.5.2: Enumerated Types

Frequently, in a C/C++ program, we use integers to code some useful piece of information—such as what department an employee is in. A convenient facility provided by the language for creating such a set of constants is the enumeration, or **enum**. An enumeration is declared as follows:

```
enum optional-name { Name1 [= val1], Name2 [=Val2], etc…} ;
```

The programmer has the option of whether or not to specify a name. In addition, values for each constant can be specified. If they are not specified, each constant has a value one higher than the previous constant. Example 13.10 shows an example enumeration being declared.

Once the enumeration in Example 3.10 is encountered by the compiler, any use of CHAR will be treated as if 0 was written, INT will be treated as 2, POINTER as 100, and so on.

Explain where the values of 0, 2, and 100 in Example 3.10 came from.

Once declared, enumerations can also be treated as if they were data types. For example, the variable x1 is declared to be of type *enum VTYPE* in the code that follows:

```
enum VTYPE x1;
int x2;
x1=CHAR;          // Will not produce an error
x1=0;             // Will produce an error
x2=CHAR;
x2=0;
```

EXAMPLE 3.10

Declaration of an enumeration

```
enum VTYPE {
    UNKNOWN=-1,
    CHAR,
    SHORT,
    INT,
    UCHAR,
    USHORT,
    UINT,
    FLOAT,
    DOUBLE,
    TEXT,
    POINTER = 100,
};
```

Even though x1=CHAR (where CHAR is equivalent to 0) and x1=0 do the same thing, the line x1=0 generates a compiler error because we haven't specifically said the 0 is an element of the enumeration. Because x2 is declared as an integer, on the other hand, both x2=CHAR and x2=0 are fine.

The advantage of declaring variables, such as x1, as enumerations instead of plain integers is that it allows the compiler to work for you—making sure you aren't accidentally confusing the purpose of your variable by assigning the wrong type of data to it. Much of the time, however, enumerations simply provide a convenient way of defining a lot of constants.

3.5.3: User-Defined Types

Although we covered the basic primitive data types (C++ has one more, **bool**, that will be introduced in Chapter 4), the C++ language provides a number of ways to create your own data types. In C, creating a data type is accomplished—to a limited extent—by the creation of structures (Chapter 11). In C++, the creation of entirely new **abstract data types** (**ADTs**) is at the heart of OOP.

As soon as you start to use the C/C++ standard libraries, you will start to encounter unfamiliar data types, with strange names like **size_t**, that we have not discussed. It turns out that some of these types aren't really new at all. Instead, they are synonyms for existing data types; **size_t**, for example, is really an unsigned integer (how many bytes depends on the compiler) that is used whenever a library function refers to a count of bytes.

The mechanism C/C++ uses to create such synonyms is the **typedef** declaration, which is a bit like the #define instruction we already mentioned (in Chapter 2), but is used only for creating type synonyms. It is of the form:

> **typedef** *type-specification new-name* ;

For example, an include file might include the declaration:

> `typedef unsigned int size_t;`

Thereafter, everywhere **size_t** was used, it would be the same as writing **unsigned int**.

We find little reason to resort to typedefs in this text. Nonetheless, if you are going to be programming in C/C++, you need to be aware of their existence. In C, they are easy to spot—just look for data type names we haven't mentioned in this chapter. In C++, a bit more detective work may be required, because unfamiliar data types could either be typedefs or ADTs.

3.5 SECTION QUESTIONS

1. Does the size of a pointer depend on the type of data it points to?
2. Is the size of a pointer likely to depend on the type of hardware it runs on?
3. Why does it make sense to identify the type of data a pointer points to?
4. If typedef statements and ADTs are used frequently by a programmer, what impact could that have on the resulting C++ code?

3.6: REVIEW AND QUESTIONS

3.6.1: REVIEW

Upon completing Chapter 3, you should have a good working knowledge of how data, particularly integer data, are stored and accessed by a program. The most critical concepts presented in the chapter are as follows:

A variable is a particular location in memory where data can be stored and accessed by name. Two types of variables are presented in the chapter. A scalar variable refers to a single location that is associated with a variable name. An array is a collection of locations, each of which can be accessed with a name and an integer offset—specified in the form:

```
variable-name[integer-offset]
```

In C/C++, the first element in an array is always an offset 0.

Variables must be declared before they are used. The declaration of a scalar variable takes the form:

```
variable-type variable-name = initial-
ization-value;
```

where the = initialization-value may be omitted. The declaration of an array takes the form:

```
variable-type variable-name[element-
count] =
{initialization-value1, initializa-
tion-value2,
initialization-value3,…} ;
```

where the = {list of initialization values} may be omitted.

The variable-type expression can include a fundamental data type (e.g., int, char, double float) that may also, in some cases, be preceded by a qualifier (e.g., short, long, signed, unsigned) or followed by an asterisk (*)—in which case the variable (or array) being declared holds an address (or an array of addresses).

Variables may be declared in a number of places within a program. Variables declared outside of any function are referred to as global or **static variables,** and may be used by any function defined within the file after the declaration. The extern keyword may be used to allow such variables to be shared between files. Variables defined within a function are said to be local to that function. Their values can only be accessed by name within the function where they are declared. As soon as a function returns, the memory locations used by all of its local variables are discarded and made available for reuse by other functions.

C has four fundamental data types: char, int, float and double. The char and int data types are integer data types. In Visual Studio .NET, they use 1 byte (char) and 4 bytes (int) of storage. Another integer type, short or short int, takes 2 bytes of storage. The number of bytes of storage available for an integer determines the range of values it can hold. If only positive numbers are represented (unsigned), the range is from:

$$0 \text{ to } 2^{\text{number of bits}} - 1$$

where there are 8 bits per byte. If positive and negative numbers are to be represented (signed), twos complement representation is used, meaning the values:

$$0 \text{ to } 2^{\text{number of bits-1}} - 1$$

are positive, and the remaining values are negative. Because a single byte can hold 2^8 (256) possible combinations, which is $2^4 * 2^4$ or $16 * 16$, each byte can conveniently be represented as a pair of hexadecimal (base 16) digits. For this reason, hexadecimal is frequently used to describe the contents of computer memory. Hexadecimal numbers are usually preceded with 0x (to signify hex) and may contain the letters a through f in addition to the digits 0–9 (e.g., 0x13f3). Hexadecimal is also useful when trying to remember integer limits. Such limits are important because twos complement integers can unexpectedly change sign if limits are exceeded, a condition referred to as overflow. Such overflows can cause serious problems when a program is running.

Although the char data type is really just a very small integer, it is mainly used for text purposes. When storing characters, letters are represented using the ASCII coding system. So that we do not have to remember the coding sequence, apostrophes around a character can be used to represent its ASCII value (e.g., writing 'a' is the same as writing 65 or 0x41). For text sequences, such as words or sentences, an array of char data elements is typically used. The C library makes extensive use of NUL terminated strings, which are arrays of characters with a NUL character (a byte with the value 0, or 0x00) used to mark the end of the text. Although

we will assume 1-byte characters throughout this text, it is likely that applications will transition to 2-byte characters over the next decade, and that ASCII will be replaced by the more flexible Unicode representation scheme.

The real number data types, float and double, store data using the IEEE scheme for encoding real numbers, which uses an approach similar to scientific notation. Unlike integers, real numbers do not change sign when they overflow. They are, however, subject to rounding errors that make them unsuitable for many currency-based applications, particularly accounting programs. Because the range of real numbers is quite large, precision is normally the issue when using real numbers in programs. The float data type uses 4 bytes, and provides 6–7 significant digits of precision. The double data type uses 8 bytes of storage, and provides about 15 digits of precision.

In addition to the fundamental data types, users may create their own types. More details on abstract data types will be presented in Chapter 11, which introduces C/C++ structures, and they will be the central focus of Chapters 13–16.

3.6.2: GLOSSARY

abstract data type (ADT) A user-defined data type derived from the primitive data types such as char, int, long, unsigned float, etc.

array A variable type that is of the same name and type but can hold multiple values

ASCII American Standard Code for Information Interchange; a code for representing the English language using a standardized set of numbers, in this case 0 to 127

binary A numbering system having only two unique digits 0 and 1

class A category of objects

decimal A numbering system having 10 unique digits, 0 to 9 inclusive

EBCDIC Extended Binary Coded Decimal Interchange Code; used by IBM as a way of representing characters on their large mainframe computers

extern A keyword used to allow variable declarations to be shared between files

global variable A variable whose scope extends across all files in a program

hexadecimal A numbering system having 16 unique digits, 0 to 9 and A to F

NUL character A character that represents the end of a string of characters in an array

octal A numbering system having eight unique digits, 0 to 7

pointer A variable type that holds a memory address

real number A number that will allow for fractions to be represented

scope The portion of code in a program in which a variable can be accessed by name

static variable A variable that exists throughout the execution of a computer program

Unicode A standard for representing characters that is 16 bits in length, allowing for up to 65,536 characters to be represented

3.6.3: QUESTIONS

1. Explain the pros and cons of local versus global variables?

2. When we say a variable goes "out of scope," what do we mean?

3. What do we mean when we say variables declared globally are, by default, static variables?

4. What does it mean to say a data type has a range? Why would we expect this range to depend upon the size of the data type?

5. Discuss the pros and cons of using integers versus real numbers to hold numeric data in a program.

6. What practical problems can result from the fact that integer sizes are not specified in C?

7. Explain what the ASCII coding system accomplishes.

8. Explain the difference between an array of characters and a character string.

In-Depth Questions

9. If a pointer is an address, and an address is represented as an integer, why not just treat addresses the same as integers?

10. Explain how using typedefs in your program could make the program easier to read and to modify.

In-Depth Exercises

11. Convert the following numbers, in column 1, into the bases specified in columns 2 and 3 [base is specified in brackets].

Number [Base]	Base 10 Value	Number [Base]
124 [8]	[10]	[12]
10011010 [2]	[10]	[16]
101 [6]	[10]	[2]
1G [20]	[10]	[4]
122 [5]	[10]	[11]

12. Convert the following numbers, in column 1, into the bases specified in columns 2 and 3 [base is specified in brackets].

Number [Base]	Base 10 Value	Number [Base]
216 [7]	[10]	[14]
11010010 [3]	[10]	[12]
101 [2]	[10]	[3]
1H [19]	[10]	[5]
12B [12]	[10]	[18]

13. Convert the following integers, written in hex, to their signed and unsigned decimal equivalents. You may assume that the number of digits specified is the number of bytes available.

Hex Value	Unsigned Decimal Value	Signed Decimal Value
0x010C		
0xB3		
0xFFFFFFB9		
0x0FF0		
0x90		

14. Convert the following integers, written in hex, to their signed and unsigned decimal equivalents. You may assume that the number of digits specified is the number of bytes available. (*Hint*: $2^{32} = 4294967296$)

Hex Value	Unsigned Decimal Value	Signed Decimal Value
0x7C		
0xA0B3		
0xB9		
0xFFFFFFF0		
0xC0		

15. Evaluate the following hexadecimal arithmetic expressions, specifying the result as indicated in the third column.

Expression	Value	Specify Your Results As:
0x44+0x7F		Hexadecimal integer
0x3E+0x83		Signed decimal integer
0xB4–0x4F		Unsigned decimal integer
0x94+0xAF		Hexadecimal integer
0x3F+0xC3		Signed decimal integer
0xA1–0x4F		Unsigned decimal integer

PART 2

STRUCTURED PROGRAMMING

Functions and Operators

EXECUTIVE SUMMARY

Chapter 4 explores functions and operators, the key elements of C++ expressions. For functions, we show how they can be defined and used—noting a few important extensions that were added to C++ beyond what is found in C. For operators, we focus on how they are used (noting, in passing, that C++ gives us the additional ability to define operators). We also examine some of the important issues associated with applying various types of C/C++ operators, such as assignment and testing.

The chapter begins with a systematic treatment of function definition and use—extending the ad hoc treatment presented in Chapters 2 and 3. In doing so, we specifically note the way C++ treats normal function arguments—making copies rather than passing them by reference. We also note the fact that C++ offers three major extensions: default arguments, passing arguments by reference, and function overloading. We then proceed to examine C++ operators, noting that operators are really just another syntax for calling a function. Assignment operators, arithmetic operators, relational operators, logical operators, and bitwise operators are then discussed, along with the concept of operator precedence. Finally, the notion of type conversions and type casts within operator invocation and function calls is introduced.

LEARNING OBJECTIVES

Upon completing this chapter, you should be able to:

- Identify the components of a function
- Explain the implications of passing copies of argument values
- Identify ways in which C++ extends the C function
- Describe the similarities and differences between operators and functions
- Explain operator precedence
- Use the assignment operator, understanding the difference between assignment and initialization
- Use the various arithmetic operators
- Apply prefix and postfix operators, distinguishing between their effects
- Understand what is meant by Boolean values, and how these values are generated by relational and logical operators
- Understand bitwise operators, and use them to set and read bits within an integer
- Explain how conversions are used in C/C++ to work with different value types, and how to force conversions

4.1: DEFINING A FUNCTION

The function, first introduced in Chapter 2, is our first example of a C/C++ construct. A construct, in any programming language, is a structural mechanism provided by the language for organizing code in order to perform a specific purpose. In the case of the function:

- The code we are organizing is individual code elements called statements.
- The purpose is to provide a self-contained unit of code that can be accessed from anywhere in our program.

In this section, we revisit the function—in order to examine it a bit more systematically than was done in Chapter 2.

4.1.1: Review: Components of a Function

In Chapter 2, Section 2.2.3, we identified the two key parts of a function **definition:**

- **Declaration:** The first portion of the function that specified the function name, number and type of return arguments, and the return value
- *Body:* A collection of statements, within braces (i.e., { and }) that defines what the function will do

An example of a function—originally defined in Chapter 2—is presented in Example 4.1. In this example, the declaration line:

```
int Plus(int nArg1,int nArg2)
```

tells us the function is called Plus, takes two arguments (both integers), and returns an integer value. Where a semicolon follows a declaration line (i.e., there is no definition) we have a function prototype. Such prototypes normally appear in header files—where they are used to tell the compiler what to check for when it sees function calls within your code.

The body, the **code block** that immediately follows the declaration line, defines what the function is supposed to do. Any time a statement beginning with the **return** keyword is encountered within a function body, it must be followed by an expression matching the **return type** of the function. Because the **int** that precedes Plus() in the declaration line tells us that Plus() is supposed to return an integer, it follows that whatever follows a **return statement** within the body of Plus() should also be an integer expression.

EXAMPLE 4.1

Typical function definition

```
/* Plus(): Takes its two integer arguments, adds them together
    and returns the value */
int Plus(int nArg1,int nArg2)
{
    int nTotal;
    nTotal=nArg1+nArg2;
    return nTotal;
}
```

An exception to the rule about expressions following the **return** keyword applies when a function's return type is specified to be **void**. Then the function does not return a value. In this case, the return statement is simply written as:

```
return;
```

If a return statement is omitted for a void function, the function simply returns when the end of the body is encountered. For any other function return type, a function without a return statement will produce an error.

4.1.2: Code Blocks and Indentation

We have now used the term *code block* several times to describe the function body. A code block is, itself, a construct used to group C/C++ statements together. A simplified way of looking at program code in C/C++ is as follows:

1. *Expression:* An expression is a legal combination of variable names, operators, keywords, and function calls. The *grammar* of a language determines whether an expression is legal. In this text, we mainly emphasize distinguishing legal expressions based on what seems to make sense. For example, of the two expressions:

    ```
    X = (Y+Z)/12
    ) X + / 12 Y Z ( =
    ```

    the first looks a lot more likely to be legal than the second—even though both contain the same set of symbols.

2. *Construct:* A collection of keywords and separators (e.g., (,), {, }) used to group expressions into more complex forms.

3. *Statement:* A statement is either:

    a. A declaration, followed by a semicolon

    b. An expression, followed by a semicolon

    c. A construct

Nature of Code Blocks A code block is just a construct that consists of a collection of statements, contained within braces. It has one very nice property:

> Anywhere the C/C++ language calls for a statement, a code block can be used instead.

As discussed in Chapter 3, Section 3.1.3, all declarations within a C-language code block must precede any other expressions. As also previously noted, C++ relaxes this requirement. Variables can be defined anywhere in the code block. Once defined, however, their existence is tied to the existence of the code block. As soon we exit the code block, they are discarded.

Because a code block can be substituted anywhere a statement is allowed—and because a code block consists of a collection of statements—it follows that code blocks can be placed within code blocks. This process of including code blocks within code blocks is a form of **nesting.** Thus, the following code structure would be perfectly legal with a C/C++ codeblock:

```
{
    some declarations...
    some statements...
    {
```

```
                some more declarations...
                {
                    some more statements...
                    {
                        even more declarations...
                        even more statements...
                    }
                }
            }
        }
```

Normally, you don't see a lot of pure code blocks nested within pure code blocks when the only benefit such a structure would provide would be in controlling the appearance and disappearance of local variables. The other major programming constructs—branches, loops, and so on as presented in Chapters 5 and 6—all typically use code blocks, however. Thus, such nesting is common. Indeed, it leads to the typical appearance of a C/C++ program—loved by its converts, hated and feared by all others.

Indentation   In the preceding example, it would be hard not to notice that the nested code blocks are written using indentation to keep them organized. The C++ compiler ignores all such forms of indentation. It cares about things such as braces and semicolons; how you choose to display your program is a matter of complete indifference. In fact, if it weren't for preprocessor statements, you could write your entire C/C++ application using a single line of text.

Hopefully, it is self-evident that *could* and *should* are entirely different notions here. Choosing a consistent style of indentation can help you navigate the complexities of C/C++ syntax. Being haphazard about it guarantees you will develop a close and intimate—but not necessarily friendly—relationship with your compiler, because a single brace out of place can generate hundreds of error messages.

The three common indenting styles shown in Example 4.2 for a hypothetical function definition are referred to here as Style 1, Style 2, and Style 3. Being consistent in indentation is probably the single most important guideline to follow. Being practical doesn't hurt either, however. For example, the author indented code using Style 3 for many years—until the desire not to engage in a constant battle with the Visual Studio built-in editor led to a change to Style 1.

Not surprisingly, the issue of indenting style has not been ignored in the scruffy and neat camps. A representative sampling of attitudes on the subject is presented in Style Sidebar 4.1.

4.1: SECTION QUESTIONS

1. What purpose does a semicolon serve in C++?
2. What is a code block?
3. Will the compiler be affected by the style of indenting you use when you write your program?
4. If you were to write a C++ program entirely on one line, what impact would likely result when you first compiled it?

EXAMPLE 4.2

Three common indenting styles

Style 1:

> *function-declaration*
> {
>> statement-or-codeblock
>> statement-or-codeblock
>> etc.
>
> }

Style 2:

> *function-declaration* {
>> statement-or-codeblock
>> statement-or-codeblock
>> etc.
>
> }

Style 3:

> *function-declaration*
>> {
>> statement-or-codeblock
>> statement-or-codeblock
>> etc.
>> }

---

5. What is the principal practical justification for adopting indenting style 1 or 2 from Example 4.2?

4.2: CALLING A FUNCTION

In Chapter 1 we introduced the concept of a program stack, and illustrated how a stack could be used to acquire temporary storage required during function calls. In this section, we examine function calls in more detail, focusing in particular on how arguments are passed into a function.

4.2.1: How Arguments Are Passed

Programming languages offer two ways to pass arguments into a function: **by value** and **by reference.** When arguments are passed by value, a copy of each arguments is made—and therefore all changes to the argument within the function are made to the copy, not the original value. The default behavior in C++ is to pass arguments in this manner.

When arguments are passed by reference, on the other hand, any changes made to an argument inside the function are reflected in the value of the variable being passed.

Unlike C++, most languages pass arguments in this way. (C++ also allows parameters to be passed by reference, to be discussed in Section 4.3.1.) Two main reasons support passing by reference:

STYLE SIDEBAR 4.1	Attitudes Toward Indentation

Camp	Position	Justification
Super Scruffy	Indent so it doesn't confuse you. Don't worry about other people reading your code—they're so far beneath you in talent they won't appreciate it no matter how you write it.	A whole table on indenting style? Can't we start a fund to get this guy some ExLax or anything else that will loosen him up?
Scruffy	Follow a consistent indenting style where it's convenient, and depart from it only where it makes sense.	Given that your editor even matches braces for you, a few variations for the sake of aesthetics aren't likely to cause any problems. Even if you are consistent in your approach, you'll still find yourself needing to use code from other sources.
Middle Ground	Choose a consistent style and stick with it. Change only if your tools or organization give you a good reason to.	Consistent practice never hurts, but which practice is chosen can, to some extent, be determined by convenience.
Neat	Choose a style and stick with it. You should also comment every ending brace.	Don't let your editor dictate your programming style. Editors can be customized (with a bit of effort) if you are unhappy about how it works. Commenting ending braces further reinforces where blocks start and end.
Neat Freak	Always use Style 3, because it's the way they taught us to indent in COBOL class.	Even if my company's too dumb to realize that COBOL was the pinnacle of all computer languages, that won't keep me from making my C/C++ look as much like COBOL as is humanly possible.

- A return statement can only specify a single value, therefore reference arguments can be used to allow functions to "return" more complex information—by changing argument values.
- Passing by reference does not require a copy of the argument to be made, therefore it is often more efficient to pass large amounts of data into functions using references.

As it turns out, the use of pointers (Chapter 10) in C++ allows us to gain many of the advantages of passing by reference. Furthermore, passing arguments by value also offers some valuable benefits:

- It avoids *side effects*—changes made by a function to variables that aren't directly related to its return value. Functions that only affect their return value tend to be the easiest for a programmer to work with, because you can call them without worrying about any changes they might make to the data in your own code. (This argument is the same one used against declaring global variables.)
- It allows values to be passed that aren't associated with any variables, such as function calls that return a value of the proper type.

These two benefits are now considered.

Avoiding Side Effects The most important implication of passing by value is simple:

> Any C++ function passing an argument by value cannot change the value of that argument. Any changes made within the function are made to a copy of the argument that is local to the function.

Although this rule has no exceptions, it does have a loophole so large that a good C++ programmer can—and frequently does—drive a truck through it. Even though a function cannot change the value of an argument, if you pass it an address, nothing will prevent you from changing value of the elements at that address—just as long as you don't change the address itself. In Chapter 3 we pointed out that when we pass an array into a function, what really gets passed is the address where the array starts—the one piece of information you really need. What this statement implies is simple:

> When you pass an array into a C/C++ function, you can change the values of the array elements. What you can't change is the address in memory where the array actually starts.

We will say more on this subject in Chapter 10, when we delve into pointers. For now, it is enough for us to realize scalar variables and arrays are handled quite differently by C++ functions.

Passing Expressions as Arguments Where arguments are passed by value, it is possible to substitute function calls (or other expressions) for variables in the function arguments. For example, you could call the previously defined function Plus() as follows:

```
int a0;
a0=Plus(Plus(3,4),Plus(5,6));
```

Because Plus(3,4) and Plus(5,6) both return integers, those values can be determined, then used in the top-level call. This type of call, with functions being used as arguments, is not always possible in languages that pass by reference—they might require the code to be written as follows:

```
int a0;
int a1;
int a2;
a1=Plus(3,4);
a2=Plus(5,6);
a0=Plus(a1,a2);
```

Naturally, the second example, which will lead to precisely the same value in a0 as the first example, could also be written in C/C++—and the neat community might justifiably argue that the second approach is clearer and easier to debug than the first. But it is certainly less concise than the first version.

Sadly—or happily, depending on your perspective—it is pretty common to see lines of code such as:

```
a0=Plus(Plus(3,4),Plus(5,6))
```

in actual C/C++ programs. What you need (to know to figure out what happens) is this:

> Before you can enter the body of a function, all of its argument values must be known.

In our current example, then, our "outer" call to Plus() can't begin work until the two inner calls—Plus(3,4) and Plus(5,6)—have been completed.

TEST YOUR UNDERSTANDING 4.1:

What would the return value for the call Plus(Plus(3,4),Plus(5,6)) be? Explain the call.

4.2.2: In Depth: Mechanics of a Function Call

Walkthrough available in FuncDemo.wmv

As we noted in Chapter 1, one of the main reasons we define functions is so that we can keep just one copy of code that is needed in many places within our program. Having just one copy of the code, however, means that we need to be able to:

- Pass parameters into functions—which we have called arguments—to allow the function to be applied to different values (e.g., different combinations of interest rate, periods and loan amount for a function that computes a mortgage payment).

- Tell the function where to return to (i.e., where it was called from) so that when the function's work is complete, the program can proceed.

Both of these problems can be solved through the use of a program stack. For example, suppose we had the simple function presented in Example 4.3. A typical procedure for implementing a function call (our mortgage payment function) using a stack might be as follows:

- Push the address of the code where you are currently located on to the program stack. This information will be used by the function to return to where it was called from when the function's work is completed.

EXAMPLE 4.3

Simple function example

```
#include "SimpleIO.h"  // Needed for output functions

// Prototype of Pmt function, presumably defined elsewhere
double Pmt(double dLoanAmount,int  nPeriods,double dInterestRate);

void VerySimpleFunction()
{
    double Rate,Amount,Payment;
    int Periods;
    Rate=0.065;
    Amount=100000;
    Periods=360;
    Payment=Pmt(Amount,Periods,Rate);
    DisplayString( "Payment is: " );
    DisplayReal(Payment);
}
```

- Place the values that you want used in the computation on the stack. For example, if you wanted to compute the payment for a $100,000 loan over a 30-year (360-month) period at 6.5%/year, you might place the values 100000, 360, and 0.065 on the stack—using the appropriate data type discussed in Chapter 2.
- You then jump to the function.
- The function knows where to find the key values it needs (e.g., amount, periods, and rate), because they are always at the top of the stack when it is called.
- The function then does whatever it takes to compute the payment.
- Once the computation is complete, the function can pop the local variables from the stack, and then place the computed value on top of the stack, so it is available to the calling function.
- The program then jumps to the return address (which was the first thing placed on the stack, and is retrieved during the return procedure).
- The calling code can then pop the returned data (i.e., the mortgage payment) from the stack and put it into another variable (Payment, in our example), if needed. If a function return value is not assigned or otherwise used, it is simply discarded when popped off the stack.

This process, which is a simplification of what actually happens in a C function call,[1] is illustrated in Figures 4.1 though 4.4.

In Figure 4.1, we are assumed to be stepping through some generic code, prior to calling our Pmt function. Existing data may be present on the stack, but we are not attending to that data.

In Figure 4.2, we are preparing to make the call to our function Pmt. At this time, we place the values we want to have used during the computation on our program stack, along with the address of the code we will be returning to (i.e., the address of the code that immediately follows the function call). By convention, stacks are usually shown to grow downwards, so the "top" of the stack is the bottom of the illustration.

In Figure 4.3, we enter the Pmt function as a result of the function call. Within the Pmt function, the values that were placed on the stack by the calling code are retrieved, and the payment value can be calculated.

FIGURE 4.1 Example Function Call, Before Call Is Made

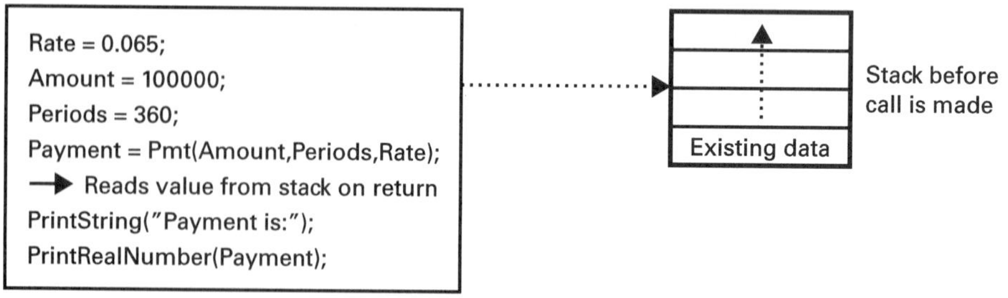

```
Rate = 0.065;
Amount = 100000;
Periods = 360;
Payment = Pmt(Amount,Periods,Rate);
→ Reads value from stack on return
PrintString("Payment is:");
PrintRealNumber(Payment);
```

Existing data

Stack before call is made

---

[1] For example, C pushes arguments in reverse order and also pushes register data to keep track of the position on the stack. It may also return some value types in registers, instead of placing them on the stack, depending upon the compiler. Fortunately, knowledge of such implementation details is nearly always unnecessary except when doing advanced mixed-language programming, which is far beyond the scope of this text.

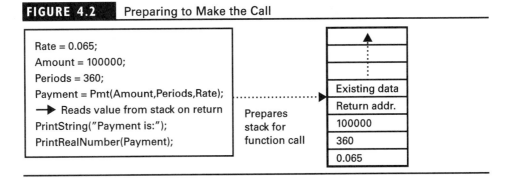

FIGURE 4.2   Preparing to Make the Call

FIGURE 4.3   Entering the Pmt Function and Retrieving Argument Values

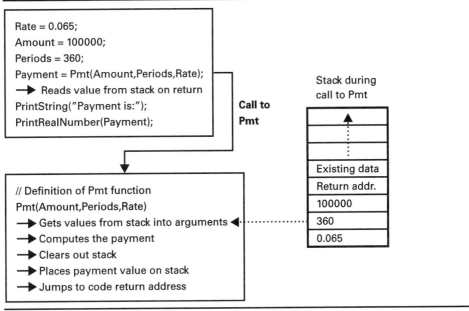

Once we have the computed payment, we can clear out the data that was placed on the stack, because we no longer need it. We can also place the payment value on the stack (another way of returning values is to put them in processor registers) and jump back to the location that the function was called from (the address of which was on the stack before we cleared it out). At this point, our function call is complete.

TEST YOUR UNDERSTANDING 4.2:

Suppose the Pmt function, during the course of performing its calculation, needed to call another function (e.g., to raise a number to a specific power). What would happen to the stack (a) before the call, (b) during the call, and (c) after the call, to that function within Pmt.

As a structured programmer using C++, understanding the mechanics of function call setup and unwinding is usually unnecessary. The C++ language itself handles these

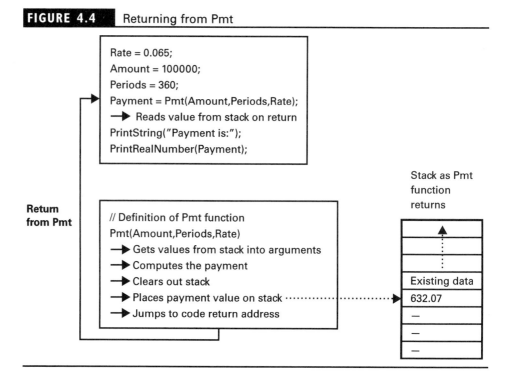

FIGURE 4.4 Returning from Pmt

details, so you don't need to worry about them. You must, on the other hand, recognize the practical implications of calling functions in this way. The values passed into the function are a type of *local* variable—so named because they can only be used locally, within the function that created them. Such variables come into existence while a function is being called, then cease to exist after the function returns. We use these types of variables a great deal in C++, so having a good mental model of how they operate can be extremely useful.

4.2: SECTION QUESTIONS

1. Explain why Plus(3,4) is called before the main (outer) Plus() function is called in the expression: Plus(7,Plus(3,4)).

2. What do we mean when we say that a C++ function cannot change the value of a normal (i.e., nonreferenced) argument?

3. What is different about the ways in which scalars and arrays are passed into a function?

4. If a function that has a local variable named *counter* calls another function that also defines a local variable named *counter*, will the two variables interfere with each other?

5. When variables are placed on the stack prior to a function call, how much space do they take up?

4.3: C++ FUNCTION EXTENSIONS

C++ provides three important extensions to the standard C function: the ability to pass arguments by reference, the ability to overload function definitions (declare multiple functions with the same name), and the ability to declare default values for arguments. In this section, we summarize these three capabilities.

Although the extensions we present here can all be useful in structured programming, none are critical. For this reason, we will use them only on a limited basis in the rest of the text until we get to the final part, covering OOP.

4.3.1: Passing Arguments by Reference

The ability to pass function arguments by reference is implemented in most programming languages, but is absent in C. C++ added this capability to the language. Because the array name (and pointer) loophole, mentioned at the end of Section 4.1.3, can be used to accomplish the same purpose as reference arguments, references are not critical for C++ structured programming. That situation changes when the language's OOP capabilities are used—certain types of functions (e.g., copy constructors) require references be used to define arguments. Even if you don't plan to use them, however, it is useful to understand them.

When an argument is passed into a function by reference, the parameter name given in the function declaration becomes an alias for the variable or other expression being passed in. Creating an alias is distinctly different from creating a copy:

- When changes are made to a parameter inside a function that was passed by value, the original variable expression being passed in remains unchanged—the changes affect only the copy that we made.
- When changes are made to a parameter inside a function that was passed by reference, the value of the variable or expression (e.g., array element) in the code that called the function changes as well.

To understand this distinction, lets contrast the function Plus() that we defined earlier to another function we might define, PlusEquals(). The idea of Plus(), as you may recall, was to return a value equal to its two arguments. For example, Plus(3,4) would return the integer value 7. Our function PlusEquals() on the other hand, is going to do something a bit more sophisticated—it will add the two arguments together, like Plus(), then place the result in the first argument. For example:

```
int X=3,Y=4,Z;
Z=Plus(X,Y); // returns 7, no change to X or Y
PlusEquals(X,Y); // returns 7, X becomes 7
// Equivalent to writing: X=X+Y;
```

The ampersand (&) operator is used in a declaration to identify the fact that a reference parameter is being created, rather than a normal parameter. We can therefore implement our function PlusEquals() as follows:

```
int PlusEquals(int &a1,int a2)
{
    a1=a1+a2;
    return a1;
}
```

The & in front of the declaration of a1 means it is being passed by reference. As a result, the line of code:

```
PlusEquals(a1,a2);
// equivalent to a1=a1+a2;
```

not only changes a1 inside the function, it also changes the value of what a1 was aliased to. In the block of code preceding it, for example, that was the variable X.

TEST YOUR UNDERSTANDING 4.3:

In the function PlusEquals(), why was a1 defined as a reference argument, while a2 was not? Could we have defined a2 as a reference?

If a reference is passed, but we do not want its value to be changed inside the function, we can use the **const** qualifier in front of the argument declaration. By using constant references in this way, we can eliminate one of the major criticisms of passing parameters by reference. Indeed, the program safety and memory management benefits that result from using references in places where we would otherwise have used pointers have led some newer languages based on C++ (such as Java and, to a large extent, C#) to eliminate the use of pointers altogether.

4.3.2: Overloaded Functions

C requires that every function have a unique name. Although this policy appears to be a sensible way of eliminating unnecessary confusion, it can actually create quite a drain on the programmer's mental resources as projects get large and complex.

To understand how this mental drain could occur, let us return to our workhorse Plus() function. As we defined it, the Plus() function takes two integers as arguments, and returns an integer. But, suppose:

- We also wanted a function to add two double values. Our problem here is that the name Plus() is already taken, so we need to choose a new name, and decide to call the function PlusReals(double a1,double a2).

- But now, we want another version to add two floats together. Fine, we define PlusFloats(float a1,float a2)—and rename our PlusReals(double a1,double a2) to PlusDoubles(double a1,double a2), annoyed at ourselves for not having realized the problem in the first place.

- Now it becomes really fun. We decide we want to be able to add a double to an int. So we define PlusDouble2Int(double a1,int a2). Then we realize we want to add an int to a double. So we also define PlusInt2Double(int a1,double a2).

- Then we realize we need to mix int and floats, floats and doubles, and so on, so we keep defining away.

The worst of it is, coming up with the names is the easy part. Next, you start using your functions and, every other minute, you find yourself asking the question: what did I call that stupid function? Was it PlusRealToInteger, PlusDoubleToInt, PlusDouble2Int, PlusDouble2Integer? After a full day of this kind of frustration, your head feels as if it will explode. When you get home, you find yourself searching the Internet for full-time sheep ranching job opportunities in Montana. Another sad casualty of too many darned names.

As it turns out, we find no "computational" reason that function names need to be unique. The purpose of function names is to give the programmer something to work with that is less cumbersome than memory addresses—as we pointed out in Chapter 1. It therefore stands to reason that as long as the compiler can tell our function calls apart, there is no reason they can't share the same name.

C++ provides the capability of different functions sharing the same name. As long as the functions have different arguments—different enough so that the compiler can figure out which version of the function you want when you make a call in your code—you can have as many functions with the same name as you want.

In the case of our Plus() function, then, we could define different versions of the function for all of our special needs. For example, we might have the following prototypes:

```
int Plus(int a1,int a2); // Our original version
double Plus(double a1,double a2);
float Plus(float a1,float a2);
double Plus(double a1,int a2);
double Plus(int a1,double a2);
float Plus(float a1,int a2);
float Plus(int a1,float a2);
double Plus(double a1,float a2);
double Plus(float a1,double a2);
```

Even though we would still have to define each function, it becomes much easier to work with them. Whenever you want to call your function, you just call Plus(). For example:

```
int ival1=1,ival2=4;
double dval1=3.5, dval2=9.0;
float fval1=6.0,fval2=4.1;
Plus(ival1,ival2);              // calls Plus(int a1,int a2)
Plus(dval1,dval2);              // calls Plus(double a1,double a2)
Plus(ival1,fval2);             // calls Plus(int a1,float a2)
```

This capability can dramatically reduce the cognitive load you experience while programming.

TEST YOUR UNDERSTANDING 4.4:

What would each of the three calls to Plus() in the preceding example probably return? How do you think the definition of the original version Plus(int a1,int a2) would differ from Plus(int a1,double a2)?

It turns out that being able to assign the same name to multiple versions of a function is also critical in implementing the OOP capability called *polymorphism*.

4.3.3: Default Argument Values

In a lot of applications—particularly when you start programming in MS Windows—you find yourself writing functions with lots of arguments (e.g., to specify the frame style, window type, window text). Frequently, however, you find that many of the arguments seem to have the same value, time after time. It can get tiring filling in these same values over and over again.

C++ provides a simple way of getting around the problem: the ability to define default values for arguments. Default values are assigned by initializing argument values in the function prototype. (Such initialization needs to be done in the prototype, because any file that calls the function needs to know what default values are assigned.)

To illustrate default values using a practical example, suppose we wanted to create a more sophisticated version of DisplayRealNumber(), discussed in Chapter 3, Section 3.3.3, called PrintDouble(). The difference between the two functions would be as follows:

- A second argument to PrintDouble(), called nMinLen, would be an integer, specifying the minimum number of characters to be printed. This argument could be useful, for example, in lining up columns of text. We could also specify that if –1 was specified for nMinLength, the program would just print as many characters as were needed.

- A third argument, called nPrecision, would specify how many decimal digits of precision (digits to the right of the decimal point) should be printed. We could also specify that if –1 was specified for nPrecision, the program would just print as many digits as were needed.

If we were to define the function, for example,

```
void PrintDouble(double dVal,int nMinLen,int nPrecision);
```

we would always have to call it with three arguments. Thus, if we just wanted it to print (as in DisplayRealNumber()), we would need to call it as follows:

```
PrintDouble(dVal,-1,-1);
```

using the –1 values to identify that we didn't care about its minimum length or how many characters to the right of the decimal were printed.

In C++, however, the ability to define default arguments would allow us to prototype the function as follows:

```
void PrintDouble(double dVal,int nMinLen=-1,int nPrecision=-1);
```

The presence of these arguments would mean the function could be called in three ways:

```
PrintDouble(dVal,10,3); // Both specified (e.g., 10 chars, 3
decimal places)
PrintDouble(dVal); // equivalent to PrintDouble(dVal, -1,-1)
PrintDouble(dVal,10); // equivalent to PrintDouble(dVal,10,-1);
```

Certain rules need to be followed in defining default values:

- As soon as a default value for an argument is specified in the declaration, all arguments to the right of it in the declaration must also have default values.

- When a function with default values is called, values are defaulted from right to left—you are not allowed to skip a value. For example, a call such as PrintDouble(dVal,,3)—presumably an attempt to get three digits of precision without specifying length—is not allowed.

- No variation on any function with default arguments can conflict with an over-loaded version of the function having the same name. The compiler does not respond well to such choices.

In the event that any of these three rules are violated, compiler errors will be encountered.

TEST YOUR UNDERSTANDING 4.5:

If we had named our more sophisticated function DisplayRealNumber(), and included it in a project that also had our SimpleIO files, which of the three rules would be violated, and why?

4.3 SECTION QUESTIONS

1. Explain the principal difference between passing function arguments by value and by reference.

2. What drawback of passing by reference can the **const** specifier address?

3. Is function overloading likely to be most useful in simple or complex programs?

4. If you were designing a function with a lot of default arguments, how would it be best to order the arguments in the function declaration?

5. What do you need to be careful about when defining overloaded functions that also have default arguments?

4.4: INTRODUCTION TO OPERATORS

Operators are special characters in C/C++ that can be applied to one, two, or (in one case) three expressions. Their purpose is to invoke code that would otherwise require a function call. The use of operators in programs offers a number of benefits:

- Use of operators can make expressions look less convoluted than function calls. For example, W+X+Y+Z is easier to understand than its functional equivalent might be, for example:

  ```
  Plus(W,Plus(X,Plus(Y,Z)))
  ```

- Use of operators provides some capabilities that are also available in complex C++ function declarations. For example:
  - Ability to access variables by reference
  - Limited overloading

The apparent naturalness of C++ operators disguises numerous activities going on beneath the surface. Up to this point in the text, where we used operators we relied on this naturalness to write expressions such as:

```
nTotal=nArg1+nArg2;
```

(which involves two operators: + and =) and then implied "you should be able to figure out what this operator does." In this chapter, however, it makes sense to be a little bit more systematic and rigorous in our approach. Toward this end, we first consider the fundamental equivalence between operators and functions, then address the specific issue of **operator precedence.**

4.4.1: Operators as Functions

Operators in C/C++ provide a convenient mechanism for invoking code that would otherwise require a function call. Indeed, throughout this text, we think of operators as being equivalent to functions—having both arguments and return values. For example, when we use the addition operator (+) operator:

```
int val1=1,val2=3,val3;
val3=val1 + val2;
```

we are effectively calling a function—a function we will refer to as operator+ (for reasons that will become clear when we discuss C++ **operator overloading**)—that could be prototyped as follows:

```
int operator+(int a1,int a2);
```

So prototyped, our code could be rewritten:

```
int val1=1,val2=3,val3;
val3= operator+(val1,val2);
```

By now, you should be able to recognize that our "operator+" function does exactly the same thing as the Plus() function we already talked about so many times. As it turns out, we find justification for using Plus() instead of operator+() as the name of that function: naming the function operator+ would not be legal, because you are not allowed to change the behavior of operators as applied to primitive data types. Otherwise, as we shall see in Chapter 14, you can call our "operator functions" as an alternative to using actual operators—although no obvious reason for doing so can be imagined.

Thus, our use of function names such as operator+(), operator<() and operator=() in this chapter will be for conceptual purposes only—to illustrate argument and return types. Why those particular names were chosen becomes apparent only when we reach the In-Depth section on C++ operator overloads at the end of the chapter.

In C++, the correspondence between operators and functions is nearly perfect. What confuses most people in seeing the relationship between operators and functions is the placement of operators. Function names are always placed in front of their arguments, which are kept separate from other pieces of code using parentheses. Operators, however, can appear in front of, behind, and between the arguments. In fact, the five legal placements of operators in C/C++ are listed in Table 4.1.

4.4.2: Operator Precedence

A final characteristic of operators that distinguishes them from functions is the concept of **operator precedence.** When calling a function, the use of parentheses unambiguously tells us the order in which the various expressions will be resolved. For example, if we call our function Plus() as follows:

```
Plus(3,4*5);
```

we know that 4 will be multiplied by 5 before the 3 is added to it. Written in operator form, however, it is less clear:

```
3+4*5
```

TABLE 4.1   Operators and Functional Equivalence

Type	Operator Appearance	Functional Equivalence	Examples	Comments
Unary (prefix)	**op** arg1	**op**(arg1)	+12, ++i and –3	
Unary (postfix)	arg1 **op**	**op**(arg1)	i++	In C++, a second argument is added to operator overload, to distinguish from prefix versions
Containment	**op1** arg1 **op2**	**op**(arg1)	val[3], (x+2)	Used to identify start and end of value, and to control execution order
Binary	arg1 **op** arg2	**op**(arg1,arg2)	X+3, i<100	
Ternary	arg1 **op1** arg2 **op2** arg3	**op**(arg1,arg2,arg3)	i<100 ? X :Y	Conditional operator is only ternary operator

Should the answer be 23 (3 + 20), or 37 (7 * 5)? In algebra, we learned we should do multiplication before addition. Thus, we'd probably guess (correctly) that the answer is 23. But what about an equally simple expression such as:

```
20/5*2
```

Should the answer be 8 (4 * 2), or 2 (20/10)?

Programming languages solve the problem of operator ambiguity by using a concept called *operator precedence* (or *operator priority*). Conceptually, we can think of each operator having a numeric rank. In any expression, operators having the highest rank get performed first. For example, * has higher precedence than +. That precedence means in 3+4*5, the functional equivalent becomes:

```
operator+(3,operator*(4,5))
```

If the plus operator had the higher precedence, the functional equivalent would have been:

```
operator*(operator+(3,4),5)
```

Where operators have the same precedence, operations are performed from left to right, In our example, then, the equivalent would have been:

```
operator*(operator+(3,4),5)
```

if + and * had the same precedence, since the plus sign appeared first.

TEST YOUR UNDERSTANDING 4.6:

Write the functional equivalents of 20/5*2 assuming (a) * has higher precedence than /; (b) / has higher precedence than *; and (c) * and / have the same precedence. Which of these orderings would you think is most likely?

Whatever an operator's precedence, parentheses—themselves a form of operator—can be used to change the order of execution. For example, (20/5)*2 is 8, while 20/(5*2) is 2.

Every C/C++ operator has an assigned precedence. Even though it is quite possible to create detailed tables of precedence, you will not be given one here. Memorizing such tables, and then relying on your memory of what gets done before what, is an invitation to hours of debugging pleasure. Even if your memory is so prodigious that you actually got the order right, nobody reading your code will be sure. Just put the parentheses in!

4.4: SECTION QUESTIONS

1. If it is possible to replace any operator with a function, why do we bother with operators at all?

2. Explain what we mean when we say the + operator is implicitly overloaded.

3. Why is it useful to think about operators in function form?

4. If a functional representation of an operator includes a reference as an argument, what does that imply about the operator?

5. If operators are just like functions, why don't we worry about function precedence?

4.5: ASSIGNMENT OPERATORS

C/C++ provides an **assignment operator** (=), plus a collection of assignment operators combined with other operators (e.g.,+=, *=, −=, /=, etc.) to be used in setting variable values.

4.5.1: The Pure Assignment Operator

The pure assignment operator takes an expression on the right-hand side (RHS) of the operator and evaluates it, then places the value in the variable or variable expression (e.g., array coefficient) on the left-hand side (LHS). Examples of its use include:

```
int x1,x2,x3;
int arVals[5]={1,2,3,5,8};
// Initialization is different from assignment
x1=1;
x3=x1+(x2=4);
// x1 is 1, x2 is 4, x3 is 5
arVals[2]=x3+8;
// And the third element of arVals (arVals[2]) is now 13
```

Structurally, it is applied as follows:

```
lvalue = expression
```

In functional form, the operator can be prototyped roughly as follows:

```
lvalue-type operator=(lvalue-type &lvalue,lvalue-type expression);
```

The functional form gives us a number of insights into the way the operator works. First, it shows us that the LHS argument is actually a reference—meaning its value can be changed during the assignment process (which, of course, is the purpose of the process). In fact, the LHS of an assignment operator is encountered so often in descriptions of C/C++ functions, it is sometimes referred to as a **lvalue** (or **l-value**) expression. Up to this point, we have seen two types of **lvalue expressions:**

- Variable names (e.g., x1=1)
- Array elements (e.g., arVals[2]=x3+8)

When we discuss pointers and structures (Chapters 10 and 11), we will find a number of other types of lvalue expression also exist.

Assignment Return Values   The second piece of information the functional form provides us with is the fact that an assignment operation returns a value (the same data type as the lvalue expression). The actual value returned is whatever value the RHS evaluates to. Thus, the operator X=4 returns the value 4. This aspect of the assignment operator is demonstrated in the line:

```
x3=x1+(x2=4);
```

This line not only assigns a value to x3, it also assigns a value of 4 to x2. Upon completion of that assignment, the value 4 is returned, which is then added to the 1 that was placed in x1, leading to the value 5 being assigned to x3.

The most common use of the return value of the assignment operator is in *chaining* assignments. For example, the expression:

```
x1=x2=x3=4;
```

would be accomplished first by evaluating x3=4, using the 4 returned by that to complete the assignment of x2, using the 4 from that assignment to complete the assignment to x1. Functionally, this would be constructed:

```
operator=(x1,operator=(x2,operator=(x3,4)))
```

which would force the operator= calls to be evaluated from right to left (because function arguments must be evaluated before outer functions can be called).

Distinction Between Assignment and Initialization The final point that needs to be made about the assignment operator is that its use in expressions is not the same as in declarations. For example, the appearance of an equal sign in the declaration:

```
int arVals[5]={1,2,3,5,8};
```

does not mean the assignment operator has been applied. Rather, the equal sign is used purely as a matter of C/C++ syntax to specify the initialization that is to take place.

This difference between assignment and initialization usually has limited practical impact in structured C++ programming—basically, it means you cannot use a brace delimited value list to assign values to an array (or structure) except when you are declaring it. In OOP C++, on the other hand, assignment and initialization are accomplished through calling entirely different functions (the assignment operator overload and the copy constructor, respectively). As a result, the difference can be quite significant.

4.5.2: Composite Assignment Operators

C++ allows many operators to be combined with simple assignments, for example:

```
int x=3,y=2;
x+=y;
// Same as writing x=x+y
```

Their structure and functional form are identical to the basic assignment operator. Their main purpose, then, is to save a few characters worth of typing.

All the **arithmetic operators** we will be discussing can be combined with assignment in this fashion, leading to:

- +=   Adds LHS to RHS and places value in LHS
- −=   Subtracts LHS from RHS and places value in LHS
- *=   Multiplies LHS by RHS and places value in LHS
- /=   Divides LHS by RHS and places value in LHS
- %=   Divides LHS by RHS and places the remainder in LHS

Assignment can also be combined with a variety of **bitwise operators.**

Most likely, at one point in the early days of C, the use of such composite operators could actually lead to more efficient machine code after a program was compiled. In the world of today's optimizing compilers, however, achieving any performance benefits by using these composite assignment operators is unlikely. As a result, their use will be minimized in this text.

4.5: SECTION QUESTIONS

1. What do we mean when we say the assignment operator returns its RHS value?

2. What is the significance of the fact that the first argument of the assignment operator functional form is a reference?

3. What is an *lvalue*?

4. What is the main practical difference between assignment and initialization for our current purposes?

5. Why do you need to be more careful in applying =– and =/ than you do applying =+ and =*?

4.6: ARITHMETIC OPERATORS

C++ provides the standard binary arithmetic operators, although more complicated operations (e.g., exponentiation) are accomplished using library functions, such as pow(), found in the math.h standard library. The language also provides a number of unary operators, for specifying positive and negative signs, and special unary operators for incrementing and decrementing integers.

4.6.1: Binary Arithmetic Operators

C/C++ provides operators for the four standard arithmetic operations (+, –, *, and /). It also provides a special operator, the modulus operator (%) that is used to return the remainder in a division operation. Some examples of the arithmetic operators in use include:

```
int x1=3,x2=7,x3=21,x4,x5;
double d1=3.00,d2=5.00,d3,d4,d5;
x4=x1+x2;
// x4 is now 10
d3=d1*d2;
// d3 is now 15
x5=x3 % x4;
// x5 is now 1
d4=x2*d1/x3;
// d4 is now 1
d5=x2/x3*d1;
// d5 is now 0
```

Structurally, the binary arithmetic operators are applied as follows:

```
numeric-value1 op numeric-value2
```

The exception here is the modulus operator, which is applied:

```
integer-type1 % integer-type2
```

Functionally, the operators call both LHS and RHS by value, and are functionally equivalent to each other (excepting %, which is limited to integers). Their function prototypes, shown only for +, are as follows:

```
promoted-type operator+(numeric-type1 arg1,numeric-type2
arg2);
```

The two major issues that programmers should be aware of when applying these operators deal with type promotion and various integer concerns.

Type Promotion   One of the most significant hassles of assembly language programming is the need to convert between similar data types. Taking a real value and placing it in an integer register, for example, could easily take 5–10 lines of library function calls. C++ eliminates most of these hassles through a process called *type promotion.*

Type promotion occurs whenever arithmetic arguments of two different types are encountered in an operation. Type promotion converts the return value of the operation to the most "capable type"—the type capable of holding the largest range and number of values. The rules of promotion are relatively simple:

- Smaller integers are promoted to larger integers (e.g., **char** and **short** become **int** and **long** when both types are encountered in an expression).
- **float** real numbers are promoted to **double.**
- Integers are promoted to real numbers.

Type promotion would occur, for example, in the line:

```
d4=x2*d1/x3;
```

because the RHS mixes integers (x2, x3) with a double (d1). The actual order of execution, using the values in the code fragment, would involve:

- Performing x2*d1 and promoting that result to a double (21.000)
- Initializing a temporary double to the value of x3 (21.000)
- Performing the division using the two doubles (21.000/21.000 ➜ 1.00)
- Returning the result and placing it in d4

Integer Issues Programmers need to be aware of certain issues in working with integers. One, which should be familiar from Chapter 3, is overflow. For example, look at the code fragment that follows:

```
char c1=20,c2=10,c3;
c3=c1*c2;
// c3 is now -56
```

When multiplying c1 and c2, we exceeded the limit of +127 for 1-byte integers. The result, –56, bears little resemblance to the expected value of 200.

TEST YOUR UNDERSTANDING 4.7:

Where did the value –56, which ended up in c3, come from?

Application of arithmetic operators, when using integers, can also be especially sensitive to ordering of operations. In particular, the programmer needs to be continuously vigilant about writing code where integers are divided by other integers within the calculation. *Whenever an integer is divided by a larger integer, the result is 0.* An illustration of this was present in the code:

```
d4=x2*d1/x3;
// d4 is now 1
d5=x2/x3*d1;
// d5 is now 0
```

According to the rules of algebra, d4 and d5 should have the same values: d4 is (x1*d1)/x3, which is the same as d5, which is (x1/x3)*d1. Both should result in a value of 1. But, if you actually run the code, d5 ends up with a value of 0.

The explanation speaks volumes about the need to be careful with integers. In computing the value of x2/x3*d1, the expression is broken into two parts.

- First, x2/x3 is evaluated. Because both x2 and x3 are integers, integer division is performed. Because 7/21 is 0—according to the rules of integer division—the result returns 0.
- Next, 0*d1 is evaluated. Because d1 is double and 0 is an integer, 0 is promoted to 0.000 before the multiplication is performed. But 0.000*7.000 is still zero.

What made the first code (x2*d1/x3) different from (x2/x3*d1) was that the double was in the middle, meaning everything got promoted earlier in the process and no problematic integer division was performed.

In Section 4.7, we examine the issue of conversions and a tool called type casting that can be used to avoid some of the problems associated with integers—provided we recognize that those problems exist.

4.6.2: Unary Arithmetic Operators

Two common categories of unary operators operate on numbers: those for assigning signs (negative or positive) and those that perform increment/decrement operations.

Sign Operators   The sign operators, + and −, are unary overloads of the addition and subtraction operators. They have a higher precedence than the various binary arithmetic operators, so the compiler can properly interpret expressions such as:

```
12 * -3 - +17
```

The sign operators cause relatively few problems. The − operator has the effect of multiplying the numeric value of the variable or value to the right by −1. The + unary operator serves no actual purpose, except perhaps to provide symmetry with the − operator.

TEST YOUR UNDERSTANDING 4.8:
What is the value of the expression 12*-3-+17?

Increment/Decrement Operators   The increment and decrement operators (from which C++ got its name), need a bit more explanation than the sign operators. The purpose of the two such operators, ++ and − −, is to increment or decrement the *lvalue* they are applied to (see Section 4.4.1 for explanation of *lvalue* expressions).

Each comes in two versions, a prefix version and a postfix version. Examples of the ++ operator in use are as follows:

```
int x1=3,x2=3,x3=10,x4,x5,x6,x7;
// Uses that are okay
x4=x1++;
// Results: x4==3, x1==4
x5=++x2;
// Results: x5==4, x2==4
// And some really "ugly" uses
++x6=10;
// Results: x6==10
x7=++x3=x1;
// Results: x7==5, x3==5, x1==4
```

Structurally, the prefix versions look like:

```
++ integer-lvalue
-- integer-lvalue
```

Structurally, the postfix versions look like:

```
integer-lvalue ++
integer-lvalue --
```

The functional forms of the prefix and postfix are similar, but subtly different. The functional version of the postfix forms can be thought of as:[2]

```
integer-type operator++(integer-type &lvalue);
integer-type operator--(integer-type &lvalue);
```

The prefix operator, in contrast, is more properly thought of as:

```
integer-type &operator++(integer-type &lvalue);
integer-type &operator--(integer-type &lvalue);
```

Differences Between Prefix and Postfix   The prefix and postfix versions of the increment/decrement operators differ in three significant ways:

- *Timing of application:* Postfix versions are applied to the lvalue expression after the expression is used in other contexts, while prefix versions are applied before the lvalue is used. In our sample code, for example:

  ```
  x4=x1++;
  ```

  causes x4 to get the value in x1 before the increment takes place. In contrast,

  ```
  x5=++x2;
  ```

  causes x5 to get the value in x2 *after* the increment has taken place.

- *Use of reference in return of prefix:* The functional form of the prefix versions of the operator returns a reference, rather than a value. The practical meaning of this is that the return value of the prefix operator can be thought of as an lvalue expression—meaning that it can be placed on the left-hand side of an assignment. Thus, the code:

  ```
  ++x6 = 10;
  ```

  is legal, while the code:

  ```
  x6++ = 10;
  ```

  is not, since x6++ returns an integer type, not an lvalue.

- The prefix and postfix versions have different precedence—of particular concern when we get to pointer dereferencing and structures (Chapters 10 and 11).

If the preceding differences seem rather technical, good! The lesson to be learned here is not to get caught up in the subtleties of prefix and postfix differences. Incrementing and decrementing integers are common enough procedures so ++ and – – get used a lot. *But use them on a line by themselves!* When you do, the differences won't matter.

TEST YOUR UNDERSTANDING 4.9:

What would be the value of x10 after the following fragment of code is executed?

```
int x10=10;
++x10=x10+5;
```

What good reason would there be to write code in this fashion?

---

[2] In C++ operator overloading, the postfix operator overload is specified as operator++(int &lvalue,int) to distinguish it from the prefix version. This distinction is relevant only in C++ operator overloading, described in Section 4.8, then revisited in greater detail in Chapter 15.

4.6: SECTION QUESTIONS

1. Why doesn't it make sense to define a modulus (%) operator for real numbers?
2. What is type promotion, and why is it important to understand when applying operators?
3. What two things do you need to be particularly careful about when writing complex arithmetic expressions using integers?
4. Why is the unary + operator unnecessary, even though it is supported by C++?
5. What is the difference between ++ postfix and ++ prefix operators? Is it a good idea to exploit this difference in your programs?
6. Why are ++ and – – reserved for integers and not real numbers?

4.7: RELATIONAL, LOGICAL, AND BITWISE OPERATORS

The ability to test values, and modify program execution accordingly, is fundamental to writing any nontrivial program. In this section, we examine the large collection of operators that C/C++ provides for performing testing. We begin by examining what constitutes a test—in the context of the **conditional** (ternary) **operator**—then we examine the operators available for relationship testing, logical testing, and bit testing.

4.7.1: The Conditional (Ternary) Operator and Boolean Values

Within a C/C++ program, most testing occurs with constructs—such as the branching (e.g., if) and looping (e.g., while) constructs introduced in Chapters 5 and 6. One C/C++ operator, however, employs tests directly: the conditional or ternary operator (?:). Although this operator is not normally of major importance in writing C/C++ programs, it provides a convenient starting point for our discussion of tests.

The ternary operator is the only three-part operator in C/C++. Its three parts are separated by two symbols, the ? (question mark) and the : (colon). Its purpose is identical to that of the =IF() function in spreadsheet tools such as MS Excel (see Figure 4.5). The first expression, to the left of the ?, is a test. The remaining two expressions, both to the right of the ?, are separated by a : symbol. If the test is true, the value to the left of the colon is returned. If the test is false, the value to the right of the colon is returned. Some samples of the conditional operator in action are provided here:

```
int x1=3,x2=3,x3,x4;
x3= (x1>4) ? 17 : 32;
// x3 is now 32
x4 = (x1<4) ? x2+4 : -1;
// x4 is now 7
```

Structurally, the conditional operator is applied as follows:

```
test ? expression1 : expression2
```

Functionally, the operator can be represented as follows:

```
promoted-type operator?:(test-type test,type1 expr1,type2
expr2);
```

The return type of the operator is determined according to the rules of type promotion, as described in Section 4.6.1. What we are really interested in, however, is the issue of what constitutes a *test-type*.

FIGURE 4.5	if() Function in Excel

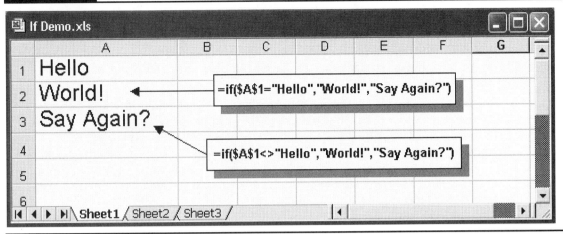

Boolean Data Data that can have two values—interpreted as True/False, Yes/No, On/Off, etc.—is frequently referred to as *Boolean* data. Conceptually, such data are different from all the other data types. For example, no logical reason would cause us to assume an expression such as:

```
x1 > 3
```

is equivalent to an integer, a real number, or a pointer. It's just a test whose result can either be true or false.

Many languages, such as Java and C#, offer a true Boolean data type—distinct from all other data types. C++, however, offers no true Boolean type—test expressions are evaluated as integers, with 0 being treated as false, all other values being treated as being true. For example:

```
int x1=3,x2,x3;
x2=(x1>3);
// x2 is now 0
x3=(x1<4);
// x3 is now 1
```

This code illustrates how relational tests (using the < operator) produce integer values in C++.

The equivalence of integer values and Boolean test results offered great convenience—for example, any function returning an integer (or a pointer, it turns out) could be used as a test. It also creates a number of potential problems. For one thing, it limits the compiler's ability to test for bizarre code. For example, the code:

```
int x1=3,x2;
x2=(x1>3)+(x1<4);
// x2 is now 1
```

is perfectly legal in C++ (it didn't even produce a warning when compiled in Visual Studio .NET), but would you really want such code in your applications?

Another problem with using integers as Boolean values is deciding what is true and false. 0 is normally chosen to mean false. But what about true? Most commonly, C++ uses

1 for true—but that is not guaranteed. Moreover, many languages (such as Visual Basic and Access) prefer to use –1 for true. So assuming 1 is the value for true is risky.

TEST YOUR UNDERSTANDING 4.10:

What property of –1 might make it a good choice for true—if we know that false is going to be represented by 0. (*Hint:* Think binary!)

bool Type in C++   The potential benefits of a pure Boolean type were recognized in the design of C++, but so was the need to maintain compatibility with C. As a consequence, a data type **bool** was added to C++, whose legal values were **true** and **false**. This data type, however, was not a true Boolean type because it could participate in integer promotion. In other words, if a **bool** data element is used in an integer expression, it would be promoted to integer—**false** being treated as 0, **true** being treated as 1 as illustrated by the following code:

```
int x1=3,x2,x3;
bool b1,b2,b3,b4;
b1=(x1>3);
// b1 is false
b2=(x1<4);
// b2 is true
x2=b1+b2;
// x1 becomes 1—integer conversion used
x3=true+true;
// x3 becomes 2
b3=b1+b2;
// b3 becomes true, but warning is issued
b4=4*3;
// b4 becomes true, but warning is issued
```

At first glance, the use of **bool** doesn't seem to offer us a lot of benefits. For example, we can still add two bools together and not get a warning, as in the lines:

```
x2=b1+b2;
// x1 becomes 1—integer conversion used
x3=true+true;
// x3 becomes 2
```

Some advantages come with using **bool** in place of **int**, however. To being with, we can be confident that any expression that returns **bool** will either return 0 (**false**) or 1 (**true**). Second, although the compiler will allow us to promote **bool** values to integers (as shown in the example), it will warn us if we try to place integer values into bool variables. For example, consider the following two lines:

```
b3=b1+b2;
// b3 becomes true, but warning is issued
b4=4*3;
// b4 becomes true, but warning is issued
```

Because the RHS in both assignments are integer types, warnings are issued for both lines. Furthermore, once the assignment is made, we can be assured that the values in b3 and b4 will either be 0 or 1 (i.e., **true** or **false**).

4.7.2: Relational Operators

Walkthrough available in RelationalOps.wmv

C/C++ provides the full complement of **relational operators** for testing equality (==), inequality (!=), and relative values (<, >, <=, >=). Some examples of their use (and misuse) are presented here:

```
int x1=3,x2,x3;
unsigned int u1=5;
double d1,d2;
bool b1,b2;
x2=(x1>3) ? 1 : 2;
// x2 now is 2
x3=(x1<u1) ? 10 : 20;
// x3 is 10, but warning is issued
d1=(5*4.5*7.33)/12.47;
//d1 is 13.225741780272655
d2=5*4.5*(7.33/12.47);
// d2 is 13.225741780272653
b1=(d1==d2) ? true : false;
// b1 is false
b2=(d1=d2) ? true : false;
// b2 is true
```

Structurally, the relational operators all fall into the form:

expression1 **op** *expression2*

Their functional form, shown for < operator, is as follows:

bool *operator<(type1 expression1,type2 expression2);*

If *type1* and *type2* are not the same, the less capable type is promoted to the more capable type before the comparison is performed. The return type is **bool** in C++ (0 for false and 1 for true in C).

Although the relational operators are usually fairly straightforward, three common issues are associated with their use:

- Comparing signed and unsigned integers
- Problems in equality testing of floating point numbers
- Accidentally confusing equality testing and the assignment operator

Signed/Unsigned Mismatch   A common, but often not serious, error can be encountered using the relational operators when signed and unsigned numbers are tested, as illustrated by the following code:

```
int x1=-1;
unsigned int u1=0xffffffff;
bool b1;
b1=(x1==u1);
// b1 is true
```

Although technically true (−1 does equal 0xffffffff in twos complement), the numbers aren't really the same. To alert the programmer to such potential problems, the compiler always issues a warning when signed and unsigned values are compared. Often, these warnings can be removed with a **type cast** (see Section 4.7), once the programmer is 100% confident that the signed/unsigned difference is not significant.

Rounding Errors and Equality Testing   Any real number that results from an arithmetic expression is potentially subject to rounding error. In our sample code, this phenomenon is illustrated by the lines:

```
d1=(5*4.5*7.33)/12.47;
//d1 is 13.225741780272655
d2=5*4.5*(7.33/12.47);
// d2 is 13.225741780272653
b1=(d1==d2) ? true : false;
// b1 is false
```

Algebraically, the expressions (5*4.5*7.33)/12.47 and 5*4.5*(7.33/12.47) are identical. In the computer, however, different orders of execution lead to different rounding errors. As a result, they are only equivalent to 16 digits—the seventeenth digit is different (see comments, which hold values observed in the debugger).

The practical impact of this rounding effect is that equality and inequality testing for real numbers should always involve a range (e.g., plus or minus some small percentage), rather than a test for precise equality. It is one of the main reasons that integers are so much preferred to real numbers whenever the choice is available.

Confusing Equality Testing and Assignment   Accidentally using an assignment operator in place of an equality test holds a place near the top of any "Top Ten Ways That C++ Says Gotcha!" list. Three factors conspire to make this error so inevitable:

- In natural language, we tend to use the term *equals* to mean both "set equal to" and "is equal to" in spite of the fact that they are distinctly different concepts.
- C/C++ uses similar symbols for assignment and equality testing (single equal sign versus double equal sign).
- Because the C/C++ assignment operator returns the value being assigned, and because any numeric value can be interpreted as a test result, assignments where tests were meant to be are often not detected by the compiler.

An example of the type of code that causes the problem was presented in our sample:

```
b1=(d1==d2) ? true : false;
// b1 is false
b2=(d1=d2) ? true : false;
// b2 is true
```

In this code, the result of the first test tells us that d1 doesn't equal d2. Yet the result of the second test suggests that it does. The problem, of course, is that the second "test" wasn't a test at all. It was an assignment. But, because the assignment returned a nonzero value, that fact was interpreted as a true value.

Unfortunately, decades of programming experience suggest that although the frequency of this error can be reduced, it can never be eliminated. Given that prevention is impossible, fast detection is the only cure.

4.7.3: Logical Operators

The **logical operators** are provided by C/C++ to work with Boolean values, such as those returned by the relational operators. A unary operator (! or **not**) reverses **true** and **false.** Two binary operators, **and** (&&) and **or** (||), combine logical conditions.

not Operator   The logical not (!) operator is a unary operator applied to a Boolean expression that reverses the expression value: **true** expressions become **false, false** expressions become **true.** In C or C++, the logical not operator is performed using the ! (exclamation point) symbol. In C++, the **not** keyword may also be used instead (provided the file *iso646.h* is included, in Visual Studio .NET). Some examples of the logical not operator in action follow:

```
int x1=3;
bool b1,b2;
b1= ! (x1>3);
b2= not (x1>3);
// b1 and b2 both true, because statements are equivalent
```

Structurally, the operator is applied before the test expression it is to negate:

```
! test-expression
```

Functionally, it can be presented as follows:

```
bool operator!(bool test);
```

As noted in Section 4.7.1, virtually any numeric (or pointer) expression can be converted to a **bool** value in C/C++. Therefore, the practical net effect of the operator is to turn any nonzero value to zero, and any zero value to 1.

In general, it is good programming practice to avoid the logical not operator. Even though its use is appropriate at times (e.g., when you are testing using a function that returns a Boolean value opposite of what you are interested in), most of the time logical nots can be avoided by changing the condition being tested. For example, !(x1>3) is the same as writing (x1<=3)—and the latter is much clearer.

Logical AND and OR

Walkthrough available in AndOrOps.wmv

Logical **and** (&&) and **or** (||) operators are used to combine the results of two Boolean expressions into a single Boolean expression. The logical **and** takes the two expressions and returns **true** only if both are true. If either is **false,** the return value is **false.** In contrast, logical **or** returns **false** only if the two expressions are both **false,** otherwise it returns **true.** As was the case with **not,** keyword versions **and** and **or** may substitute for their symbol equivalents, && and ||, in C++ (provided the file *iso646.h* is included, in Visual Studio .NET).

Some examples of logical operators in action are presented in Example 4.4. Structurally, the operators are invoked like standard binary operators:

```
test1 && test2
test1 and test2        // C++ only
```

EXAMPLE 4.4

and/or operator demonstration code

```cpp
// AndOrTest.cpp
#include "AndOrTest.h"
#include <ISO646.H>

int nSE1=0,nSE2=0,nSE3=0,nSE4=0;

void AndOrTest()
{
    bool b1,b2,b3,b4,b5,b6,b7;
    double d1,d2;
    double delta;
    d1=(5*4.5*7.33)/12.47;
    d2=5*4.5*(7.33/12.47);
    delta=d1*1E-15;
    // bring delta to 15 digits
    b1=(d1==d2);
    // b1 is false
    b2=(d1>d2-delta && d1<d2+delta);
    // equality test (to 15 places): true
    b3=(d1<d2-delta || d1>d2+delta);
    // Inequality test (to 15 places): false
    // ShortCircuit demonstration
    b4=(RetTrue1() and RetFalse3());
    // Returns false, both called
    b5=(RetFalse3() and RetTrue2());
    // Returns false—RetTrue2() never called
    b6=(RetFalse3() or RetTrue1());
    // Returns true, both called
    b7=(RetTrue1() or RetFalse4());
    // Returns true, RetFalse4() never called
    return;
}
bool RetTrue1() {
    nSE1++;
    return true;
}
bool RetTrue2() {
    nSE2++;
    return true;
}
bool RetFalse3() {
    nSE3++;
    return false;
}
bool RetFalse4() {
    nSE4++;
    return false;
}
```

```
test1 || test2
test1 or test2                // C++ only
```

The operators' function equivalents, shown only for &&, can be prototyped as follows:

```
bool operator&&(bool test1,bool test2);
```

As was the case for **not,** any numeric value can be converted to **bool,** so the operator can be applied to almost any pair of numeric or pointer values—although the propriety of doing so is questionable.

Short-Circuiting   The **and** and **or** operators exhibit a behavior sometimes referred to as short-circuiting. To understand this behavior, you must first realize that it is fairly common programming practice to include expressions (e.g., function calls) on one or both sides of a logical operator. As we discussed previously, the normal practice for a function is to evaluate all its arguments before entering the function body. The **and** and **or** operators in C/C++ are different, however. They only evaluate enough arguments to determine whether their answer is true or false. In some cases, that will mean that they only need to evaluate a single argument. For example:

- If the first (LHS) argument of an **and** operation is **false,** we know that the result will be **false**—no need to check the second (RHS) argument.
- If the first (LHS) argument of an **or** operation is **true,** we know that the result will be **true**—again, no need to check the second (RHS) argument.

C/C++ takes advantage of this knowledge, evaluating only those arguments that *need* to be evaluated. As a result, the && and || operators can be used to control program execution. This control aspect is demonstrated in the code, from Example 4.4, that follows:

```
// ShortCircuit demonstration
b4=(RetTrue1() and RetFalse3());
// Returns false, both called
b5=(RetFalse3() and RetTrue2());
// Returns false—RetTrue2() never called
b6=(RetFalse3() or RetTrue1());
// Returns true, both called
b7=(RetTrue1() or RetFalse4());
// Returns true, RetFalse4() never called
```

In the demonstration, the functions RetTrue1(), RetTrue2(), RetFalse3(), and RetFalse4() were defined to return either **true** or **false** (which is self-evident from the function name), and to increment a global variable: nSE1, nSE2, nSE3, or nSE4 (which, once again, is self-evident from the function name), used to keep track of the calls in the debugger.

Because of short-circuiting, in the assignments of b5 and b7, only the first of the two functions were called. In the case of b5, RetFalse3() returned a value of **false.** Because the operator was **and,** it meant the return value was going to be **false.** Similarly, in the case of b7, RetTrue1() returned **true**—meaning it was unnecessary to call RetFalse4() because the operator was **or.**

Not all languages short-circuit logical testing in this fashion, and some, such as Java, offer short-circuiting and non-short-circuiting operators. Thus, it is an important capability to be aware of, whether or not you decide to use it.

4.7.4: Precedence Ordering of Operator Categories

In introducing operator precedence, we stated that it was a poor idea to rely on precedence (and, especially, your memory of operator precedence) in writing expressions. Parentheses will make it easier for you, and for anyone who later reads your code, to understand what is going on.

Having made this disclaimer, it is usually reasonably safe to utilize precedence across major classes of operators. For the operators we have examined so far, precedence is as follows:

- Unary arithmetic sign operators (i.e., + and −) and increment/decrement operators (++, − −) get applied before arithmetic operators.
- Arithmetic operators (e.g., +,−,*,/) have a high precedence, with * and / being higher than + and -.
- Relational operators (e.g., <, >, ==) are the next level of precedence.
- Logical operators (e.g., && and ||) get done next. Because **and** and **or** have different precedence levels, use parentheses when forming complex logical expressions.
- Assignment operators (e.g., =, *=, +=) get done last.

You might also keep in mind that postfix and prefix versions of operators have precedences that are different (e.g., the ++ operator in ++X and X++ are effectively different operators), which means that you should probably use parentheses when applying them. Or, better yet, apply them on separate lines.

4.7.5: In Depth: Bitwise Operators

 Walkthrough available in Bitwise.wmv

Nothing underscores C++'s ancestry from a mid-level language designed for building operating systems more than the full complement of operators it provides for manipulating the individual bits of integers. Such capabilities were invaluable in the early days of programming, where they could be used for tasks such as performing multiplication and division in software, performing data translations and drastically reducing the space requirements of some types of data.

The capabilities of modern hardware and software have reduced the need for bit manipulations. Unfortunately, the need has not been entirely eliminated. In particular, any programmer planning to work in MS Windows needs to understand the use of these operators to pack and unpack data into integers that are then used as function arguments.

A second reason for being familiar with some of the bitwise operators—most notably bitwise-or (|) and bitwise-and (&)—is their unfortunate similarity to their logical operator cousins (|| and &&). Similar to the problem with the equality testing (==) and assignment(=), failing to "double up" on these operators when a logical test is desired can lead to unexpected results.

The bitwise operators are always applied to integer arguments. To actually predict what will happen when the bitwise operators are applied to their integer arguments, the best procedure is to:

- Convert the argument or arguments to hexadecimal bytes (using twos complement, if necessary).
- Convert the hex bytes to binary digits.
- Apply the operator to the binary digits individually.
- Convert the result back to hex.
- Convert the result back to decimal.

Normally, performing this procedure once or twice will satisfy a lifetime's worth of curiosity.

Bitwise Negation   The bitwise negation operator ~ (tilde) is a unary operator that takes every bit in its integer argument and reverses it, returning the resulting integer. In the questions in Chapter 3, we described such a reversal of bits as the "ones complement" of a number, further noting that the twos complement of a number could then be achieved by adding one to the ones-complement value. This procedure is demonstrated in the code that follows:

```
int val1=173,val2;
val2=~val1;
val2++;
// val2 is now -173
```

Structurally, the operator is applied as follows:

```
~ integer-expression
```

The functional prototype of the operator is roughly as follows:

```
integer-type operator~(integer-type expr)
```

As an example, suppose we wished to find the value of ~43. Our procedure would be as follows:

- Convert 43 to hex: 0x2B
- Convert 0x2B to bits: 0010 1011
- Reverse the bits: 1101 0100
- Convert back to hex: 0xD4
- Convert back to decimal:
  - 212 (unsigned)
  - −44 (signed)

Binary Bit Operators   C/C++ offers three binary operators used to manipulate bits: bitwise-or (|), bitwise-and (&) and bitwise-exclusive-or (^). Each operator takes two integer arguments and, bit-by-bit, returns a value computed from the original bits. The value is determined as follows:

- *Bitwise-or:* If either integer bit is on, the resulting bit is 1. Otherwise, the resulting bit is 0.
- *Bitwise-and*: If both integer bits are on, the resulting bit is 1. Otherwise, the resulting bit is 0.
- *Bitwise-exclusive-or*: If one, but not both, of the integer bits is on, the resulting bit is 1. If both or neither integer bit is on, the result is 0.

An example, illustrating the 43 & 31 computation for a 1-byte integer, is presented in Figure 4.6.

TEST YOUR UNDERSTANDING 4.12:

Compute the results for the 43 | 31 and 43 ^ 31 operations.

The structure of the bitwise operators is:

integer-expr2 **op** *integer-expr2*

Functionally, the bitwise operators can be prototypes as follows (shown for | case only):

promoted-integer-type operator|(*integer-type1* expr1,*integer-type2* expr2);

The operators all apply the same basic rules for promotion that we already discussed.

The most common use for bitwise operations is to pack a series of true-false values into a single integer. Although this approach may seem unnecessary, given today's RAM capacities, this capability is actually used quite a bit in functions, particularly in MS Windows and to set flags in various C++ standard I/O objects. The problem this practice solves is one of too many arguments. A typical window or font might have literally dozens of settings. It is, however, cumbersome to define functions with so many arguments. You can begin to sense the magnitude of the problem if you look at the function SetBits(), in Example 4.5, which has eight arguments (designed to represent each of the bits in an unsigned character). Imagine, now, a function with 30 arguments!

Using individual bits, 32 yes/no questions can be packed into a single int value. Thus, a function could have a single integer argument that contains the data that otherwise require 32 bool arguments. The trick then becomes how to set the bits, and how to retrieve them.

In SetBits(), we show how individual bits can be set using the | operator. We start with an integer value of 0, then we check each argument. Using the conditional operator, we bitwise-or the integer with the appropriate power of 2 (even powers of 2 always represent a single bit in binary). For example,

```
nRet=nRet | ((b5) ? 16 : 0);
```

The | leaves all bits already set in nRet untouched. Should the appropriate argument (e.g., b5) be true, the conditional operator causes the appropriate value (e.g., 16) to be turned on, in addition. If the argument is false, however, the conditional operator causes us to bitwise-or nRet with 0, which leaves it unchanged.

Just as | can be used to set bits, the bitwise-and (&) is used to see whether they are set. In the function DisplayBits(), we & the argument (containing the bits that have been set) with an even power of 2. Because the even power of 2 only has one bit set, it becomes a test for that particular bit. If it is off in the argument, the result is 0 (aka false). If the bit in the argument is set. We then use the condition operator to determine what gets printed. For example:

```
DisplayString((nVal & 16) ? "5. On\n" :
"5. Off\n");
```

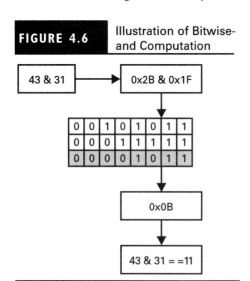

FIGURE 4.6 Illustration of Bitwise-and Computation

| 43 & 31 | → | 0x2B & 0x1F |

0	0	1	0	1	0	1	1
0	0	0	1	1	1	1	1
0	0	0	0	1	0	1	1

0x0B

43 & 31 ==11

EXAMPLE 4.5

Using bitwise | and & to set and display bits

```
// BitOps.cpp: Using | and & operators to set and extract bits
#include "SimpleIO.h"

/* SetBits(): uses bitwise-or to set bit values in an unsigned
char.
   returns the resulting unsigned char */
unsigned char SetBits(bool b1,bool b2,bool b3,bool b4,bool b5,
bool b6,bool b7,bool b8)
{
    unsigned char nRet=0;
    nRet=nRet | ((b1) ? 1 : 0);
    nRet=nRet | ((b2) ? 2 : 0);
    nRet=nRet | ((b3) ? 4 : 0);
    nRet=nRet | ((b4) ? 8 : 0);
    nRet=nRet | ((b5) ? 16 : 0);
    nRet=nRet | ((b6) ? 32 : 0);
    nRet=nRet | ((b7) ? 64 : 0);
    nRet=nRet | ((b8) ? 128 : 0);
    return nRet;
}

/* DisplayBits(): displays the individual bit values in an
unsigned char */
void DisplayBits(unsigned char nVal)
{
    DisplayString("Bits in ");
    PrintInteger(nVal);
    NewLine();
    DisplayString((nVal & 1) ? "1. On\n" : "1. Off\n");
    DisplayString((nVal & 2) ? "2. On\n" : "2. Off\n");
    DisplayString((nVal & 4) ? "3. On\n" : "3. Off\n");
    DisplayString((nVal & 8) ? "4. On\n" : "4. Off\n");
    DisplayString((nVal & 16) ? "5. On\n" : "5. Off\n");
    DisplayString((nVal & 32) ? "6. On\n" : "6. Off\n");
    DisplayString((nVal & 64) ? "7. On\n" : "7. Off\n");
    DisplayString((nVal & 128) ? "8. On\n" : "8. Off\n");
    NewLine();
}
```

In this case, if the bit 00010000 (binary 16) is on in nVal, the conditional operator causes "5. On\n" to be sent to DisplayString(). If the bit is not set in nVal, the string "5. Off\n" goes to DisplayString().

Confusing Logical and Bitwise Operators One of the biggest reasons to understand bitwise operators is to understand what happens when you accidentally confuse them with the logical operators && and ||. If you happen to be dealing with pure Boolean values, represented as 0 and 1, their behavior will be similar (because you are "and"ing and "or"ing only the first bit). The one difference will be that bitwise & and | do not short-circuit. They can't because doing a bitwise operation requires you to know the values of the integers on both sides of the operator.

A worse situation occurs when & is confused with &&, and we are not limited to 0 and 1 for our true/false values. Using the rules of C/C++, the value:

        1 && 2

is true, because both sides are nonzero. One the other hand, the expression:

        1 & 2

is 0 (or **false**), because the bits that are set on both sides miss each other when they are "and"ed together. Thus, as was the case with the assignment and equality test operators, not keeping the two operators straight can lead to hours of debugging pleasure.

WinBitwise Application   The Bitwise application, provided with the text, is a simple application for walking though bitwise computations. It is illustrated in Figure 4.7.

FIGURE 4.7   Bitwise Application

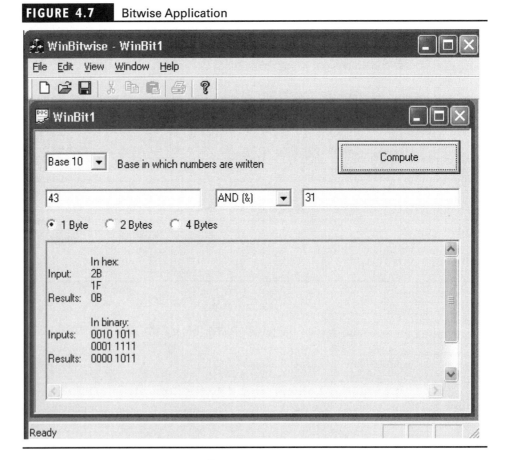

4.7: SECTION QUESTIONS

1. What's the difference between a true Boolean type and an integer Boolean type? Why does C++ have the latter?
2. Why is the compiler likely to warn you when signed and unsigned integers are used as part of relational tests?
3. Can the assignment X=3 also be treated as a test?
4. What is the difference between relational and logical operators?
5. What is logical operator short-circuiting? Why can it have a major impact on the way a program runs?
6. Why would it make sense for logical operators to have lower precedence than relational operators?
7. What is the difference between the | and || operators?
8. What are bitwise operators most commonly used for?

4.8: IN DEPTH: CONVERSIONS AND OVERLOADS

C and C++ provide a number of mechanisms that allow us to control how operators and functions are invoked. In this section, we examine type casting and the C++ capability of extending its operators to new objects—referred to as operator overloading.

4.8.1: Basics of Type Casting

In presenting the various arithmetic and relational operators, we already identified a number of situations where the default behavior of C/C++ was not precisely what we wanted. In some cases, the problem was that an arithmetic expression might not return the proper value. For example:

```
int n1=7,n2=21;
double r1=3.00,r2,r3;
r2=n1*r1/n2;
// r2 is 1.000
r3=n1/n2*r1;
// r3 is 0.000
```

The problem with this sample code is that r2 and r3 should be equal, according to the normal rules of algebra, but r3 ends up being 0 because the integer division (n1/n2) produces a 0 value. Another problem we noticed was compiler warnings that might, in some cases, tell us about problems that do not exist. For example:

```
int i1=5,i2;
unsigned int u1=7;
double d1=12.00;
bool b1;
i2=d1;
// produces warning: assigning double to int
b1=(u1<i1);
// produces signed/unsigned mismatch warning
```

As noted in the comments, the preceding code fragment creates two warnings—both justified. The first warning occurs for the statement i2=d1. Because the range of a **double** far exceeds the range of an **int**, the compiler alerts us to the potential problem. The second warning occurs because we test (u1<i1)—a signed integer compared with an unsigned integer. We already discussed the potential problems of mixing the two types of integers. Having applauded the compiler for doing its job, the fact remains that—in the preceding code—neither of these operations will lead to any actual problems. After all, we made sure our values are within acceptable ranges. So the question becomes: How do we get the compiler to shut up?

Type Casting C++ provides a mechanism, called type casting, that allows us to deal with many conversion issues and compiler warnings. The **type cast** operator—and yes, it is an operator—can be used to create a temporary value of a given type of data, or to force the compiler to change its interpretation of a given data type (used when pointers are type cast, discussed in Chapter 10). The most commonly used form of the operator is constructed by placing a type name in parentheses in front of the expression whose type is to be changed. Normally, this signal will force C++ to create a temporary variable of the desired type, initializing it using the value from the expression being cast. Some examples of type casts in action are presented next:

```
int n1=7,n2=21;
double r1=3.00,r2,r3,r4;
int i1=5,i2,i3;
unsigned int u1=7;
double d1=12.000;
bool b1,b2;
/***** Conversion problems *****/
r2=n1*r1/n2;
// r2 is 1.000
r3=n1/n2*r1;
// r3 is 0.000
r4=((double)n1/(double)n2)*r1;
//r4 is 1.000
/***** Compiler warnings *****/
i2=d1;
// produces warning
i3=(int)d1;
// no warning
b1=(u1<i1);
// produces warning
b2=((int)u1<i1);
// no warning;
```

Structurally, the type cast operator is applied as follows:

```
( data-type ) expression
```

The functional form of the operator can be prototypes roughly as follows:

```
target-type operator target-type(old-type expr1);
```

Naturally, for a type cast to be possible, the *target-type* and *old-type* must be compatible. This compatibility means you can move between numeric types, and you can move between pointer types, but you *really* don't want to move between pointers and numeric types. (Don't want to and can't are not the same, however. In the early days of C, type casting between integers and addresses, in both directions, was fairly common. It is, however, just about the most hardware-dependent code you could possibly write.)

Forcing Proper Operations   The sample code illustrates ways in which sensible type casting can eliminate some of the problems we ran into. For example, in the line:

```
r4=((double)n1/(double)n2)*r1;
```

we type cast both n1 and n2 to **double** temporary variables—naturally, n1 and n2 themselves are not changed. Doing so forces the division to use floating-point arithmetic (7.00/21.000==0.33333), leading to the result of 1.000. That particular expression also illustrates the use of parentheses to ensure operator application in the proper order. Actually, the same expression could have been written:

```
r4=(double)n1/n2*r1;
```

because the type cast operator has higher precedence than division (and because automatic type promotion will cause the division to be done in floating point if either argument is **double**). Writing the expression in the more lengthy fashion, however, avoids any chance that the expression would be interpreted as (double)(n1/n2)*r1, which would give us our original problem of returning 0 because (n1/n2) would be done before the conversion to double.

Removing Compiler Warnings   The sample code also illustrates how type casts can be used to remove compiler warnings (that we have determined to be okay). Consider the two examples from the code:

```
i3=(int)d1;
b2=((int)u1<i1);
```

In the first line, the (int) type cast tells the compiler we are aware of the conversion that will be taking place between **double** and **int.** As a result, it does not need to warn us. In the second line, the (int) type cast tells the compiler to interpret u1 as signed for the purposes of the comparison. Once again, this line eliminates the need for a warning.

Advanced Type Casting Issues   Type casting can have a number of effects in C++ that are not immediately obvious. They include the following:

- *Type casting can actually impact what functions are called.* In Section 4.3.1, we mentioned the C++ capability of function overloading. The particular version of a function to call is dependent on the arguments passed to the function, therefore, use of type casting can actually change the version of a function called by a particular line of code.

- *OOP inheritance can lead to defining objects that are multiple types.* Inheritance, introduced in Chapter 16, can lead to objects being defined based on the structure of other objects. For example, we might define an Employee based on how a Person is defined (i.e., using a Person object as a starting point). This structure would mean that any Employee object we created in our program would also, by definition, be a Person object. In such situations, type casting is sometimes needed to disambiguate what type of object we are talking about.

- *The type cast operators can be overloaded.* C++ allows operators to be overloaded, just like functions (to be discussed in Section 4.8.2). For this reason, the programmer can actually control what happens when objects are type cast.

As a result of the increased importance of type casting in C++, the language provides two special operators (**static_cast** and **dynamic_cast**) for safer type casting—while still supporting the type cast operators we just presented (originally introduced in C). The benefits resulting from the use of the advanced operators are limited mainly to advanced OOP programming situations. For this reason, they are not discussed further in this text.

4.8.2: Operator Overloads in C++

Operator overloading in C++ is a powerful capability that allows programmers to extend the capability of the C++ language, and write more natural code. In our first C++ program (Chapter 2, Section 2.3.1), we saw an example of such an overload in the line:

```
cout << "Hello, World "  << endl;
```

Although we referred to the << operator as the insertion or output operator, it is actually the little-used bitwise left shift operator in C (used to move the actual bits in an integer a specified number of positions to the left). In C++, however, the operator has been overloaded to allow it to serve the more common purpose of sending data to an output stream. Some of the common overloads in the iostream library might be prototyped as follows:

```
ostream &operator<<(ostream &out,int nVal);
ostream &operator<<(ostream &out,const char *str);
ostream &operator<<(ostream &out,double dVal);
etc.
```

The effect of an operator overload, like that of a function overload, is to cause C++ to call programmer-defined code where the operator is encountered (with matching arguments). The global variable **cout** happens to be an object of the *ostream* data type. As a result, any time the compiler sees:

```
cout << expression
```

it looks for an overloaded << operator where the first argument matches cout in type (ostream) and the *expression type* matches the second argument of one of the available overloads.

TEST YOUR UNDERSTANDING 4.13:

In the code *cout << "Hello, World"*, which of the overload versions (presented as prototypes) would be chosen?

Although operator overloading is a powerful capability, its use is mainly limited to OOP situations. To avoid creating massive incompatibilities, C++ does not allow already defined operators on the basic data types to be overloaded. Thus, we can't overload the == operator to test the equivalence of two character strings, no matter how much we would like to. For this reason, we do not return to operator overloading techniques until after we introduce objects (in Chapter 14), where we consider their implications in much greater depth.

4.8: SECTION QUESTIONS

1. Explain how type casting can be used to eliminate problems that occur when integers and real numbers are mixed in expressions.
2. When is it appropriate to use type casting to remove a compiler error?

3. What is the justification for the warning that is suppressed by the following type cast?

```
double d1=300;
int nVal;
nVal=(int)d1;
```

4. Why do we need to understand how to define objects before we are able to overload our own operators?

5. Given the prototypes for the << operator previously specified, how could we use a type cast to force a real number to display like an integer?

4.9: REVIEW AND QUESTIONS

4.9.1: REVIEW

Upon completing Chapter 4, you should have a clear understanding of the nature of C functions, and their close relationship to C operators, such as + and −. Every time you declare a function, you are identifying three key components for your program: the function's name, the function's arguments, and the function's return type. Knowing these three things, a compiler can determine whether a function call is legal even without knowing how the function is defined, or what it is supposed to do. Legal does not imply logically correct, however. In most cases, it is up to the programmer—often working with the aid of a debugger—to determine whether a function actually does what it is supposed to do.

The actual code associated with a function is specified when a function is defined. The syntax for defining a function is simply a declaration followed by a code block, which is a collection of one or more statements within enclosing braces {}. Such code blocks are critical in C/C++ syntax, because they can enclose multiple statements (semicolon-terminated expressions) anywhere a single statement can be used. Within functions, one or more **return** statements are normally present. Each return statement must be followed by an expression that matches the return type in the function declaration. The only exception to this rule is functions with a return type specified as **void**, which are functions that don't return any value. For such functions, a **return** statement does not need to be present. If one or more **return** statements are present, a semicolon—instead of an expression—must follow them immediately.

By passing arguments into a function, we allow the same program code to be used in many places. Arguments can be passed in by value and by reference. When function arguments are passed in by value, local copies of the arguments are made so that any changes to arguments made within the function affect only the copies—the original values passed into the function remain unchanged. It is the only way to pass arguments into C functions. The other way that arguments can be passed in is by reference. When passed in this way, the function creates an alias for its arguments instead of a copy. As a result, changes made to an argument within a function also affect the variable that was passed in. In C++, a reference argument can be declared by using an ampersand (&) in front of the argument name. C++ also provides two additional extensions to C: default values for function arguments can be specified when a function is declared, and allowing different functions to be defined with the same name—provided their arguments differ. This latter extension is called function overloading.

To sidestep the inability to change arguments passed by value, C and C++ both allow addresses of values to be passed into functions. Although the addresses themselves cannot be changed (i.e., only the internal copy of the address is changed within the function), the addresses can be used to access and change the values located at the specified address. When an array name is used as an argument—without accompanying brackets []—the address of the array is used in this fashion. Therefore, when you use an array name as an argument, you can actually change the values of the array elements within the function (but you cannot change the address where the array is located in memory). If you want to pass an address into a function, but also want to make sure the function does not change values pointed to by the address (avoiding what are called side effects), you can use the **const** keyword in front of the argument when you declare the function. If the keyword is present, any attempt to change the values at the address within the function will produce a compiler error.

The best way to think about operators is as a special type of function. For example, the + operator used to add two integers can be thought of as having the following declaration:

```
int operator+(int a1,int a2);
```

Six categories of operators are used most commonly in C and C++:

1. *Arithmetic operators:* This category includes: (a) five key binary operators +,-,*,/, and % (the first four are self-explanatory, and can be applied to both integers and real numbers; the last, the modulus (%) operator, returns the remainder resulting from an integer division); (b) + and – unary prefix operators, used to specify a number's sign; and (c) ++ and – operators, used to increment and decrement integers by 1, which can be applied either in prefix or postfix mode.

2. *Assignment operators:* This category includes the pure assignment operator (=) and a variety of composite operators (e.g., +=, –=, *=, and /=). The pure assignment operator takes the value on its right-hand side (RHS) and places it in its left-hand side (LHS) argument, which may be a variable, a reference to an array element, or certain other types of expressions (to be introduced in Chapters 10 and 11). The types of expressions that can appear on the LHS of an assignment are often referred to as l-values or lvalues.

3. *Relational operators:* Operators used to determine relative size of arithmetic arguments, such as >, <, >=, <=, ==, and !=. These binary operators return a Boolean (true or false) result based on the expressions on their LHS and RHS (e.g., 3 > 4 returns false, 3<4 returns true). A particularly common error using relational operators is to confuse the equality test (==) with the assignment operator (=).

4. *Logical Operators:* Operators used to combine test results, such as those returned by relational operators. The most common of these are two binary operators: logical AND (&&), which returns true only if both sides are true, false otherwise, and logical OR (||), which returns true if either or both sides are true, false only if both sides are false. A unary operator, NOT (!), is also provided that changes a true expression to false, and a false expression to true.

5. *Bitwise operators:* Operators that apply logical-style truth tables to the individual bits of integer arguments. This category includes the binary operators bitwise AND (&), bitwise OR (|), and bitwise exclusive-OR (^). It is important to be aware of these operators for two reasons: (i) they are often used to compress a lot of true-false information into a single integer argument (e.g., arguments to some MS Windows functions); and (ii) they can easily be confused with their logical counterparts, with results that can be difficult to detect. A bitwise unary operator, bitwise NOT, is also available that reverses all the 0s and 1s in an integer, returning the ones complement of that integer.

6. *Conditional operator:* The only ternary operator in C/C++, it is of the form:

```
test ? value1 : value2
```

and functions very much like the =IF() function in MS-Excel, returning the first value if the test is true, the second value if the test is false.

When operators are applied, the order in which they are applied is determined by operator precedence. For example, in the expression x1+x2*x3, the expression x2*x3 is evaluated before the + operator is applied because multiplication has a higher precedence than addition. Operator order can be forced using parenthesis—e.g., (x1+x2)*x3—which is recommended in this text to avoid programmer-created precedence errors that can waste hours of debugging time.

In addition to these six categories, C++ also supports a number of IO-driven operators (such as >> and <<). C++ allows programmers to overload operators in much the same way that its functions can be overloaded. These capabilities cannot be exploited effectively except when OOP is being used. As a consequence, they are not discussed in detail until the final part of this book.

4.9.2: GLOSSARY

arithmetic operators   Operators defined to perform mathematical computations on numeric data types

assignment operators   Operator that takes a value from the right-hand side (RHS) and places into the left-hand side (LHS) variable

bitwise operators   Operators that apply logical style rule tables to each bit in a byte to determine the final result

by reference   To pass a variable by reference means to create an alias for the variable, allowing the original to be changed within the function

by value   To pass a variable by value means to make a copy of the variable thereby preventing the original from being altered

code block   A collection of source code statements, delimited by braces {}, located within a function

conditional operator   A ternary operator that returns one of two possible values based on a Boolean condition

declaration   A formal way of expressing a function's name, arguments, and return type

definition   A function definition combined with a function body

logical operators   Operators used to combine Boolean expressions

lvalue expression   An expression that is evaluated on the left side of the assignment operator

nesting   The mechanism of placing constructs within other constructs

operator overloading   The ability to define different versions of the same operator that are called based on their arguments

operator precedence   The manner in which the order of operator calls is determined within an expression

relational operators   Operators used to determine the relative values of expressions, such as > or <

return   The keyword that C++ uses to pass a value back to the calling function

return type   The type of value a function returns when it is complete

type cast   Changing a value's type or interpretation within an expression

4.9.3: QUESTIONS

1.   Assume Array is defined as follows:

```
int Array[10];
```

Explain why passing Array[0] and Array into a function are different.

2.   Explain why a function that takes a reference as an argument would not normally be called with a function in that argument position. For example, if PlusEquals() were prototyped as follows:

```
int PlusEquals(int &arg1,int arg2);
```

we would normally not see the call:

```
PlusEquals(Plus(3,4),17);
```

3.   Why is it possible to change which version of an overloaded function is called by a using type cast?

4.   Explain why the following code sequence could cause a serious problem in a program:

```
short X=1000;
short Y=2000;
short Z;
Z = X*Y / 1500;
```

5.   Which of the two versions of the following functions is likely to work best, and why?

```
int Fahrenheit1(int Celsius) {
    int nTemp;
    nTemp=9*(Celsius/5)+32;
    return nTemp;
}

int Fahrenheit2(int Celsius) {
    int nTemp;
    nTemp=(9*Celsius)/5+32;
    return nTemp;
}
```

6.   What problem does the combination of (a) integer Boolean types and (b) the similarity of the assignment and equality test operators cause? Would the problem be as severe if C++ handled either differently?

7.   Other languages, such as Pascal, use an operator such as := for assignment, instead of =. What problems could such an approach help to solve?

8. Why is the conditional operator also called the ternary operator? What is it used for and what Excel function is it like?

In-Depth Questions:

9. Explain how type casting can change the version of an overloaded function that is called.

10. Why would it not make sense for bitwise operators to short-circuit?

Evaluate the following expressions:

11. 0x007A | 0x0013 = 0x_____

12. 0x9433 & 0x1C7E = 0x_____

13. ~0x332F = 0x_____

14. 0x72FB + ~0x332F = 0x_____

15. (0x0332 & 0x8B01) && (0xF111 & ~0xFFFD) = TRUE or FALSE

16. Evaluate the following hexadecimal arithmetic and logical expressions, specifying the result as indicated in the third column. Only use the number of bits available for your calculation.

Expression	Value	Specify Your Results As:
0x08 | 0x2E		Hexadecimal integer
0x73 & 0xF8		Hexadecimal integer
(0x08 | 0x2E) +(0x73 & 0xF8)		Hexadecimal integer
0xFF && (0x03 & 0xF8)		TRUE or FALSE
~0x0D + 0x01		Signed decimal integer
(0x0A & 0x05) || ~0xFF		TRUE or FALSE
0x15 & ~0x15		Hexadecimal integer
0x07 | 0x20		Hexadecimal integer
0x8C & 0xF8		Hexadecimal integer
(0x07 | 0x20) +(0x8C & 0xF8)		Hexadecimal integer
0xFF && (0x07 & 0xF8)		TRUE or FALSE
~0x0A + 0x01		Signed decimal integer
(0x0B & 0x05) || ~0xFF		TRUE or FALSE
0xF3 & ~0xF3		Hexadecimal integer

CHAPTER 5

Program Design and Flowcharts

EXECUTIVE SUMMARY

Chapter 5 examines how to organize a program, to be written in any structured programming language, with graphical flowcharts. Although flowcharting has fallen out of favor as a design tool (justifiably, since flowcharts can quickly become unmanageably large), it remains one of the best ways for individuals to learn the basics of programming in a visual manner. For this reason, flowcharts are used throughout this text to illustrate key programming concepts.

The chapter begins by introducing the "top-down" approach to program design. It then discusses how programs can be organized into functions and blocks of code. The main constructs used in structured programming—branching and iteration—are then presented using a graphical representation. Representations for several variations of each construct (e.g., if branches, multiway branches, while loops, until loops, and for loops) are provided. The FlowC program (included with the text), providing a convenient means of creating flowcharts, is then demonstrated. Finally, walkthroughs of several simple functions are conducted.

Chapter 5 is intentionally written to be applicable to nearly any programming language, and assumes the reader has little or no familiarity with programming. In Chapter 6, the same concepts are presented again, specifically for the C++ programming language.

LEARNING OBJECTIVES

Upon completing this chapter, you should be able to:

- Organize simple tasks into a series of subtasks, each of which is represented by a function or box in a flowchart
- Represent two-way (if) and multiway branches (case constructs) using a flowchart, explaining when it is appropriate to use each
- Represent three types of iterative constructs (while, for and until loops) using a flowchart, and describe appropriate uses for each
- Use the FlowC tool to create flowcharts
- Design simple applications (collections of functions) using FlowC, and walk through them step-by-step to explain how they are intended to operate

5.1: STRUCTURED PROGRAM DESIGN

Writing a program typically involves three steps:

1. Identifying what you need to accomplish
2. Creating a logical organization for achieving what you want to accomplish
3. Implementing your logical organization using the tools (e.g., language, libraries) that are available to you

The focus of this chapter is step 2, developing a logical organization for your program. In doing so, we adopt the principles of structured programming.

5.1.1: Working Definition of a "Program"

Before we can discuss how to design a program, it is useful to define what a "program" is. Unfortunately, the term means different things to different people. For some, the term *program* is used to describe any application that runs on a computer. For others, the term *program* is limited to a collection of code that can operate independently (e.g., a single executable file), with the term *system* being used to refer to collections of these programs working toward a common objective—such as the modules of an accounting system (A/R, A/P, G/L).

TEST YOUR UNDERSTANDING 5.1:

Would it be reasonable to call MS Windows a program? Does it depend on how you define a program?

For the purposes of this text, we will use the term *program* to refer to a collection of code that is designed to be compiled into a single unit to accomplish a specific task or set of tasks. This definition is certainly narrower than it needs to be for real-world situations, but reflects the type of applications we will be focusing on in this text.

5.1.2: The Top-Down Approach

When designing a structured program, a top-down approach is typically used. The principle of this approach is deceptively simple:

1. We take the task we are to accomplish and break it into a sequence of distinct subtasks, each of which accomplishes a clearly defined piece of the original task.
2. For each subtask, we identify the information that needs to be supplied to it.
3. For each subtask, we identify the information that will be produced by it.

Once we identify these tasks, we examine each subtask. If, for each subtask, we can identify a clear procedure for accomplishing part 1, and have clearly defined inputs (part 2) and outputs (part 3), we're done. If part 1 is not clear, we repeat the process on the subtask—breaking it down into further subsubtasks. This process of breaking down each task, called *decomposition,* continues until every element of our design is clearly defined—at which point we are ready to begin programming.

To illustrate this concept of decomposition, let us assume we wanted to program the apparently simple task of going shopping. We start with our initial program objective, illustrated in Figure 5.1.

Following part 1 of our principle, we next break this main task into a series of subtasks. For example, (1) Go to Store, (2) Shop, and (3) Return from Store. These subtasks are illustrated in Figure 5.2.

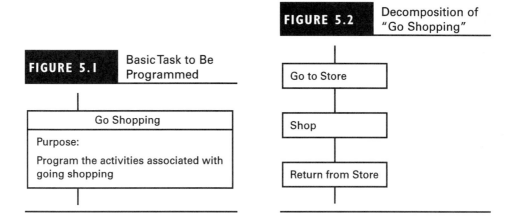

FIGURE 5.1 Basic Task to Be Programmed

Go Shopping
Purpose: Program the activities associated with going shopping

FIGURE 5.2 Decomposition of "Go Shopping"

Go to Store

Shop

Return from Store

Each of these tasks might, in turn, be further broken down. For example, "Go to Store" could become:

- Decide where to go shopping
- Decide how to get there
- Decide what to wear
- Travel to the shopping site

This additional decomposition is illustrated in Figure 5.3.

This process of decomposition is not arbitrary. Indeed a good decomposition should always possess these important characteristics:

- Each decomposition should lead to a set of subtasks, each of which seems slightly more manageable than the original.
- The sequencing of tasks produced by a decomposition should make sense. For example, deciding what to wear makes the most sense *after* we know where we are going (e.g., Are we going to be outside? Would excessively casual dress be inappropriate?) but *before* we travel to the store. In many cases, this sequencing will mean that the outputs of one subtask prove to be the inputs of a subtask that follows (e.g., choice of store is an output of the "where to shop" subtask, and an input of the "how to get there" subtask).

Unfortunately, a task such as "Go Shopping" is so loosely defined we could keep decomposing forever without reaching the level of precision required in order to write a program. This potentially unlimited decomposition is the principal reason that robots have not evolved to perform such "simple" tasks as cleaning, cooking, and shopping. Nonetheless, the same process of top-down decomposition that we just illustrated is the fundamental principle of structured design.

5.1: SECTION QUESTIONS

1. Explain the difference between top-down and bottom-up approaches to programming.
2. Does a top-down approach to programming guarantee that all programs so designed will look about the same?

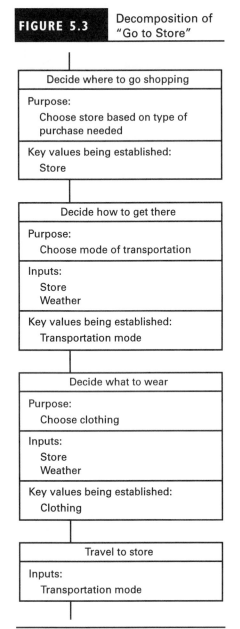

| FIGURE 5.3 | Decomposition of "Go to Store" |

Decide where to go shopping

Purpose:
    Choose store based on type of purchase needed

Key values being established:
    Store

Decide how to get there

Purpose:
    Choose mode of transportation

Inputs:
    Store
    Weather

Key values being established:
    Transportation mode

Decide what to wear

Purpose:
    Choose clothing

Inputs:
    Store
    Weather

Key values being established:
    Clothing

Travel to store

Inputs:
    Transportation mode

3. When might it make sense to consider a bottom-up, instead of a top-down, approach?

5.2: INTRODUCTION TO FLOWCHARTING

A **flowchart** (or, more precisely, a logic flowchart) is a graphical representation of the logical operation of a program, function, or block of code. Flowcharts have been around since the early days of programming, when they were routinely used in program design and were often required parts of program specifications. Since those days, however, use of flowcharts in actual program design has declined, replaced by **pseudocode** and other techniques.

In this section we compare flowcharts to another design technique, pseudocode. We then look at how to represent the programming **constructs** we covered previously, including declarations, statements, and functions using flowcharts. We then examine the use of **summary blocks** to reduce flowchart size. The particular style of flowcharting that we cover is fairly generic, and is not based on any particular standard (which is reasonable, because most standards in this area have long since been forgotten). Later in the chapter, we introduce FlowC, a tool that will allow us to create these flowcharts quickly and accurately—and do a lot of other interesting things as well!

5.2.1: Flowcharts vs. Pseudocode

Over the past few decades, flowcharts fell out of favor as design and documentation tools. Their principal weakness is their enormous size, with a typical flowchart being ten to twenty times larger than equivalent code. In other words, a modest program of 5 pages in length could easily lead to a 100-page flowchart—so large as to be unwieldy. Another weakness of flowcharts is the fact that they are generally not self-validating—meaning the author of a flowchart has no way of knowing if the chart represents a valid program, or even a legal flowchart. Problems of this sort are particularly acute when the analysts designing programs are not expert programmers, an all too common occurrence.

An alternative to flowcharting during program design is *pseudocode*, which involves writing out the activities that the code is to perform in a precise form of natural language. Even though pseudocode is not precisely a programming language, it should be specific enough so that a programmer familiar with the language to be used can translate it, almost line by line. For example, pseudocode for the decision as to what mode of transportation to take in the earlier example is provided in Example 5.1. **Structured pseudocode** is also used in some programming shops. This form of pseudocode has such a high level of formality that it is essentially another programming language.

Like flowcharting, pseudocode has its enthusiasts and detractors. On the plus side, use of pseudocode forces designers to think carefully and systematically about the code they

---

EXAMPLE 5.1

Pseudocode for choice of transportation mode problem

```
IF Is Raining?
THEN
      Mode = Car
ELSE
    IF Store = MiniMart
    THEN
        Mode = Walk
    ELSE
        IF Store = Downtown
        THEN
            Mode = Subway
        ELSE
            Mode = Car
        END IF // Store = Downtown
    END IF // Store = MiniMart
END IF // Is Raining?
```

---

are designing. It is much more compact than flowcharting, a major practical benefit. On the negative side, an inexperienced designer can easily write pseudocode that is of little or no value to the programmer expected to implement it. Moreover, as the rules for structured pseudocode become stricter and stricter, the advantages of using such code—versus just writing the program in the target language—become smaller and smaller.

5.2.2: Representing Statements and Declarations

In Chapters 3 and 4, we introduced the concepts of variable declarations and statements, as well as the general concept of a code block (e.g., a collection of statements between { and } in C/C++). In our flowcharting formalism, we represent these program elements as follows:

- A *code block* is represented by a vertical line. All program elements except functions and global declarations/definitions exist within code blocks.
- A *declaration* is represented by a polygon with angular edges, into which one or more variable declarations are placed. Initially, we will only allow declarations at the beginning of code blocks (to be consistent with C usage).
- A *statement* is placed in a rectangular box (which may hold more than one statement to keep the size of our flowcharts manageable). The three types of statement boxes are as follows:
  - **Statement boxes** contain general statements and function calls, such as the assignment statements already presented in previous chapters.
  - **Console I/O boxes** in the shape of parallelograms contain statements that take input from the keyboard or send output to the display, such as the DisplayString() function presented in previous chapters.
  - **File I/O boxes** in the shape of parallelograms contain statements that perform file I/O, to be covered in Chapters 8 and 17.

These elements are illustrated in Figure 5.4.

5.2.3: Representing Functions

In Chapter 4, we discussed how functions have a declaration, a body, and return statements. In our flowcharting formalism, we represent these basic elements as follows:

- An entry point, represented by an ellipse, signifies the name of the function.
- A declaration box contains any function arguments.
- A code block contains the body of the function.
- At least one exit point is necessary and is represented by an ellipse with a "return" in it.

An illustration of a function is presented in Figure 5.5. In C++, the declaration of this particular function would be:

```
int DemoFunc(int arg1,char arg2[]);
```

The code block that represents the body of the function is the line segment between the argument declaration and the return ellipse. Any code in the function would then be placed in this line segment, because the declaration of arguments is always the first element appearing after the function name.

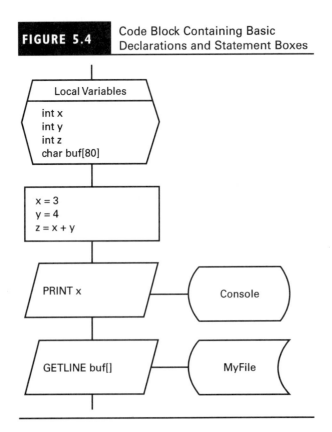

FIGURE 5.4 Code Block Containing Basic Declarations and Statement Boxes

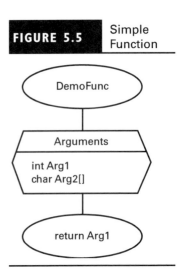

FIGURE 5.5 Simple Function

5.2.4: Summary Blocks

The final flowchart element to be presented in this section is the summary block. Designed to help us keep the size of our flowcharts manageable, a summary block is just a box that can be used to substitute for functions or code blocks, explaining their purpose but not going into details. For example, the function presented in Figure 5.5 could be summarized with the block shown in Figure 5.6.

Similarly, the code block in Figure 5.7 could be summarized as shown in Figure 5.8.

TEST YOUR UNDERSTANDING 5.2:

Why was the Local Variables declaration box in Figure 5.7 summarized in Figure 5.8, while the Arguments declaration box was not?

5.2: SECTION QUESTIONS

1. Give the main reason that flowcharts are unlikely to reemerge as an important tool in commercial application design.
2. How does a code block appear in a flowchart?
3. Why might pseudocode be preferred to flowcharts in commercial application design?
4. What is the advantage of representing functions so that local variables and arguments appear the same way in functions?
5. What is the main advantage of defining summary blocks?

5.3: BRANCHING

Although functions and the various forms of statement boxes provide a nice skeletal framework for designing a program, they limit what we can do. Some additional programming constructs can provide a number of interesting capabilities.

The first class of constructs we will discuss is *branching* constructs. A branch is simply a point in a program where a choice of alternative code blocks is available. In this section, we present techniques for flowcharting the two types of branches most commonly supported by programming languages:

FIGURE 5.6   Function Summary Block

Function: DemoFunc
Arguments ☐ int arg1 -- Integer first argument ☐ char arg2[] -- Character array second argument, showing how array is passed
Returns int ☐ Simple integer return value
Purpose: Demonstration function

FIGURE 5.7   Complete Main Function

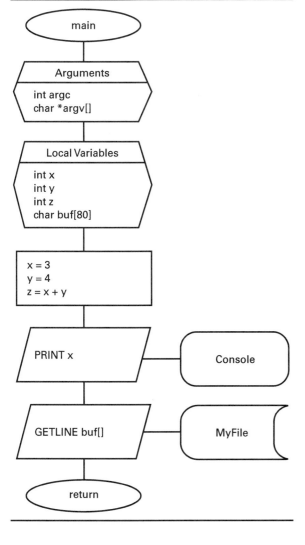

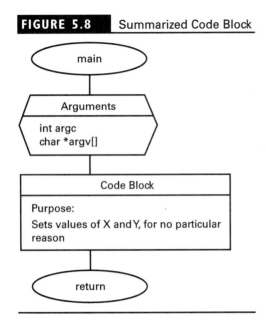

FIGURE 5.8 Summarized Code Block

- **Two-way branches:** Constructs that provide a choice between two code blocks, most commonly referred to as if…else constructs.
- **Multiway branches:** Constructs that provide a choice between an unlimited set of code blocks, sometimes referred to as case statements (C/C++), switch blocks, or computed gosubs (BASIC).

5.3.1: IF Construct

In programming parlance, the two-way branch is nearly always referred to as the *if construct*, or *if…else construct*. The construct consists of a test, the results of which determines which of two code blocks (the IF block or the **ELSE block**) is then executed. Either the IF block or the ELSE block of the construct could be empty but, under most circumstances, there will be code in the IF block. Having an empty IF block and an ELSE block containing code is legal, but it would be viewed as odd coding practice ("odd" being a coding style so peculiar it doesn't even fall on the scruffy–neat continuum).

In order to represent an if construct using a flowchart, we need a new type of element to represent a test. For this purpose, a diamond is used. In the flowcharting style we are using in this text:

- The entry point to the test is always the top of the block.
- The code block coming from the bottom of the diamond is *always* the IF block.
- The code block coming from the right-hand side of the diamond is *always* the ELSE block.

In addition to the test symbol, it is useful to have a node symbol (represented by a circle) showing where the IF and ELSE paths converge. This symbol allows us to distinguish situations where paths rejoin each other, versus those where they just happen to cross in the diagram.[1]

The skeletal framework for the if construct is presented in Figure 5.9, with the code blocks labeled. Because we will always follow these conventions, we will not need to label the IF and ELSE blocks in subsequent diagrams.

Sample Function with If Construct   To illustrate the use of the if construct, we can create a simple function to do temperature conversions. The function is specified as follows:

```
double ConvertTemp(double dtemp,int ntype);
```

where the two arguments are:

- dtemp: the temperature we want to convert
- ntype: the type of conversion we are performing, where 0 ➔ Fahrenheit to Celsius and 1 (or anything else) ➔ Celsius to Fahrenheit

---

[1] One of the advantages of the flowcharting standard we are using is that such crossings are actually quite rare. Indeed, they can only happen when *break* or *continue* statements are present, as will be discussed in the section on loops.

| FIGURE 5.9 | Basic if Construct |

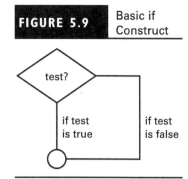

The return value is the converted temperature.

The flowchart for this function is presented in Figure 5.10.

Nested If Constructs In order to program complex logic, it is often necessary to nest one construct within another. The if construct, for example, provides two code blocks (the IF block and the ELSE block) into which other constructs can be inserted. These constructs could include other if constructs, potentially leading to a series of if…else if…else if branches, each being **nested** one level deeper. The pseudocode for the transportation mode decision, presented in Example 5.1, could be represented using the flowchart in Figure 5.11.

| FIGURE 5.10 | Temperature Conversion Function |

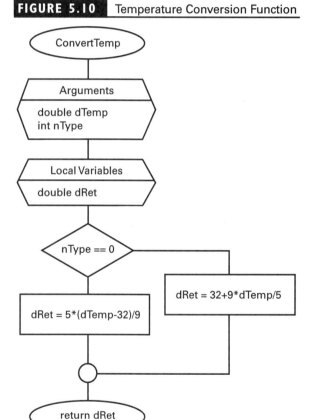

Return Statements in If Constructs In the flowcharts we have discussed so far, the IF and ELSE blocks always rejoin at the connecting node at the bottom. Such joining is a natural result of structured programming, and tends to encourage both clarity of code and clarity of thought.

When we discussed functions in Chapter 4, however, we encountered an element that could prevent such joining from occurring: the return statement. To illustrate how return statements could impact the structure of a flowchart, let us consider a revised version of the example presented in Figure 5.10 that incorporates some error checking. Specifically, our revised if construct will return –1000 whenever an illegal temperature is passed (i.e., any temperature less than absolute zero, which is –273 degrees Celsius). The new version of the if construct is presented in Figure 5.12.

TEST YOUR UNDERSTANDING 5.3:

Why does the IF block of the nType == 0 if construct test the value of dRet, while the ELSE block tests the value of dTemp?

The use of return statements within if blocks, as illustrated in Figure 5.12, would be extremely controversial among proponents of structured programming. They would make two arguments against such code:

- It is much easier to debug and understand functions if only a single return point is allowed per function.
- You can always rewrite a function to eliminate returns in the middle of the code (see Figure 5.13 for a rewritten version of the if construct that eliminates the return statement).

FIGURE 5.11 Nested if Blocks Equivalent to Pseudocode in Example 5.1

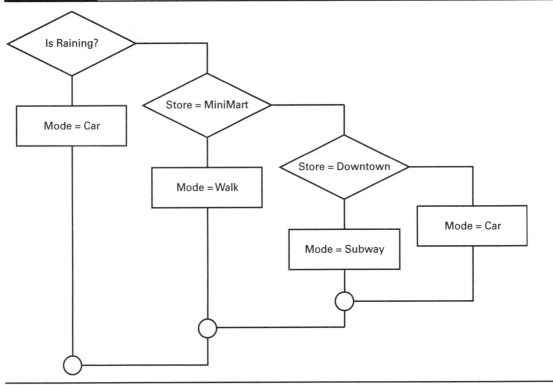

Members of the scruffy community, on the other hand, could make plausible arguments that one return per function is sometimes excessively limiting. In particular, they would argue that even though midfunction returns *can always* be avoided, that is not the same as saying they *should always* be avoided. Specifically, the types of deep nesting and special purpose temporary variables that may be required to avoid midfunction returns—particularly on error conditions or for special cases—can make the resultant "pure" code harder to read. The arguments of the various camps are summarized in Style Sidebar 5.1.

5.3.2: Multiway Branches

Although the **if branch** is sufficient to accomplish any branching requirement in a program, it can become very awkward when a large number of choices are present. Suppose, for example, you were to write a function that responded to the particular key pressed by the user (e.g., to implement a menu). Very quickly, your flowchart would degenerate into unimaginable levels of nesting, as conveyed by Figure 5.14.

Such a chart leaves the programmer with a number of concerns:

- *Readability:* What will the resulting code be like, with such complex nesting (twenty-six levels for the uppercase letters alone)?
- *Counterintuitive:* For a task like processing a letter, does it really make intuitive sense to do it using a long series of comparisons? When you are shown a letter on

FIGURE 5.12 Error Checking if Block with Return Statements

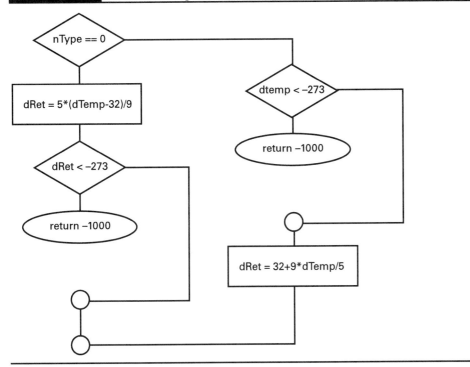

a flash card, for example, do you identify it by asking a series of questions such as "Is it an A? No. Then is it a B? No. Then is it a C? No. Then is it a D? No...."?

- *Inefficient:* Every time the processor does a test, it takes a certain number of cycles to perform the test. Would it make sense that processing a Z should take twenty-five more tests than processing an A?

These concerns all highlight the need for some form of construct that performs a multiway branch, offering the choice of more than the two possibilities provided by an if construct.

Most programming languages offer some form of multiway branching under a variety of names such as **case construct,** switch block, translation, and computed goto/gosub. Common to all these constructs is the use of an integer that contains a value that will be used to select the particular branch to be executed, each of which has a corresponding integer "case" value. We will use the term *case construct* to describe multiway branching constructs.

Because no generally accepted standard is available as a guide for how to flowchart such constructs, we will represent them as follows:

- A small diamond will indicate the start of the construct.
- Next to the diamond, we will place the expression used for switching.
- Each case will be represented by a small circle, next to which is the integer value or values (separated by commas). These integers can be actual integers or constants that evaluate to integers.
- A connector from each circle will lead to the code block to be performed in the event the case is selected. To avoid unnecessary line crossing, these blocks appear from right to left (i.e., the first case is connected to the rightmost code block).

FIGURE 5.13   Error Checking if Block with Return Statements Removed

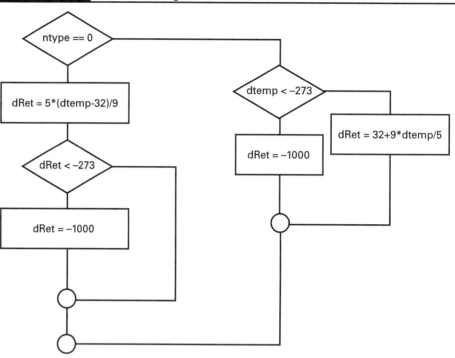

- A single unlabeled circle after the cases will represent the "default" case, containing the code block to be performed if none of the cases match the switching expression (the block may be empty).
- A larger node circle at the bottom of the construct represents the point at which all cases converge. The only thing that will prevent such conversion is a statement, such as a return statement, within a particular case.

For the sake of maintaining highly structured code, the representation presented does not allow for case fall through, a mechanism allowing the code in one case to continue into other cases. We will return to that topic in Chapter 6, when we discuss how cases are implemented in C/C++.

An illustration of a case construct skeleton, implemented to switch based on the value of the variable **key,** and to handle the letters A, B, and C (upper and lowercase) as well as the ? character, is presented in Figure 5.15.

Example Case Construct Function   In our earlier temperature conversion function, illustrated in Figure 5.10, a two-way branch was adequate because we were only interested in two scales, Fahrenheit and Celsius. Suppose, however, that we wanted to implement a general function for converting U.S. dollars to other currencies. Here, the number of possible conversions would be large, so using a case construct would be much preferred.

In order to set up such a function, we would first need to set up some data that our function can access, including the following:

STYLE SIDEBAR 5.1	Use of Return Statements		

Camp	Position	Justification
Super Scruffy	Return statements can be used wherever convenient.	It's my code and I'll return if I want to.
Scruffy	Return statements can be used at will, provided they simplify the functions where they are used.	As long as functions are kept small, it is not that difficult to identify more than one exit point.
Middle Ground	Return statements in the middle of a function should be used sparingly, and only for unusual cases (such as returning on an error condition).	Where avoiding a return makes the nesting structures in a function much more complex, the interests of clarity may be served by returning early. As long as functions are small, the presence of more than one exit point will probably not complicate debugging and maintenance excessively, if at all.
Neat	Multiple return statements are only appropriate at the very end of a function (e.g., to treat separate true and false cases).	Having a single point in the code where returns are allowed enforces good programming discipline, and will make debugging and maintenance easier in the long run.
Neat Freak	Every function should have one, and only one, return statement.	Returns are so messy we wouldn't let you use any at all if you didn't have to get out of the function somehow.

- Integer constants that could be used to identify each currency. (A fairly common C/C++ convention is to give such constants uppercase names, such as DOLLAR, UKPOUND, YEN, and EURO, to remind us that they are not variables.)
- Real values to hold the various currency conversion rates. For the time being, we can define these as global variables. (A much better approach, passing them into the function as a parameter, will become apparent once we have covered structures, in Chapter 11.)

Once we set up our data, the function can be declared as follows:

```
double Convert (double dVal,int nTarget);
```

where:

- dVal is the dollar value to be converted
- nTarget represents the integer constant assigned to identify the currency

The return value is the value of dVal converted to the specified currency (or −1, if an unsupported currency constant is passed into the function).

The function can be easily implemented using a case statement that includes a case for each currency type, as illustrated in Figure 5.16.

FIGURE 5.14 Deep Nesting in Response to Key Press

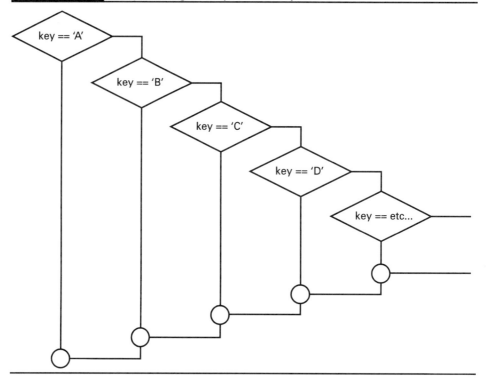

FIGURE 5.15 Skeletal Case Format

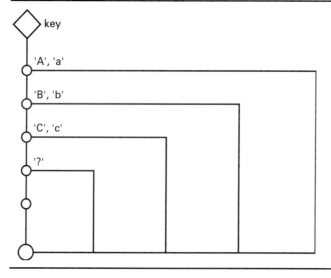

FIGURE 5.16   Currency Conversion Function

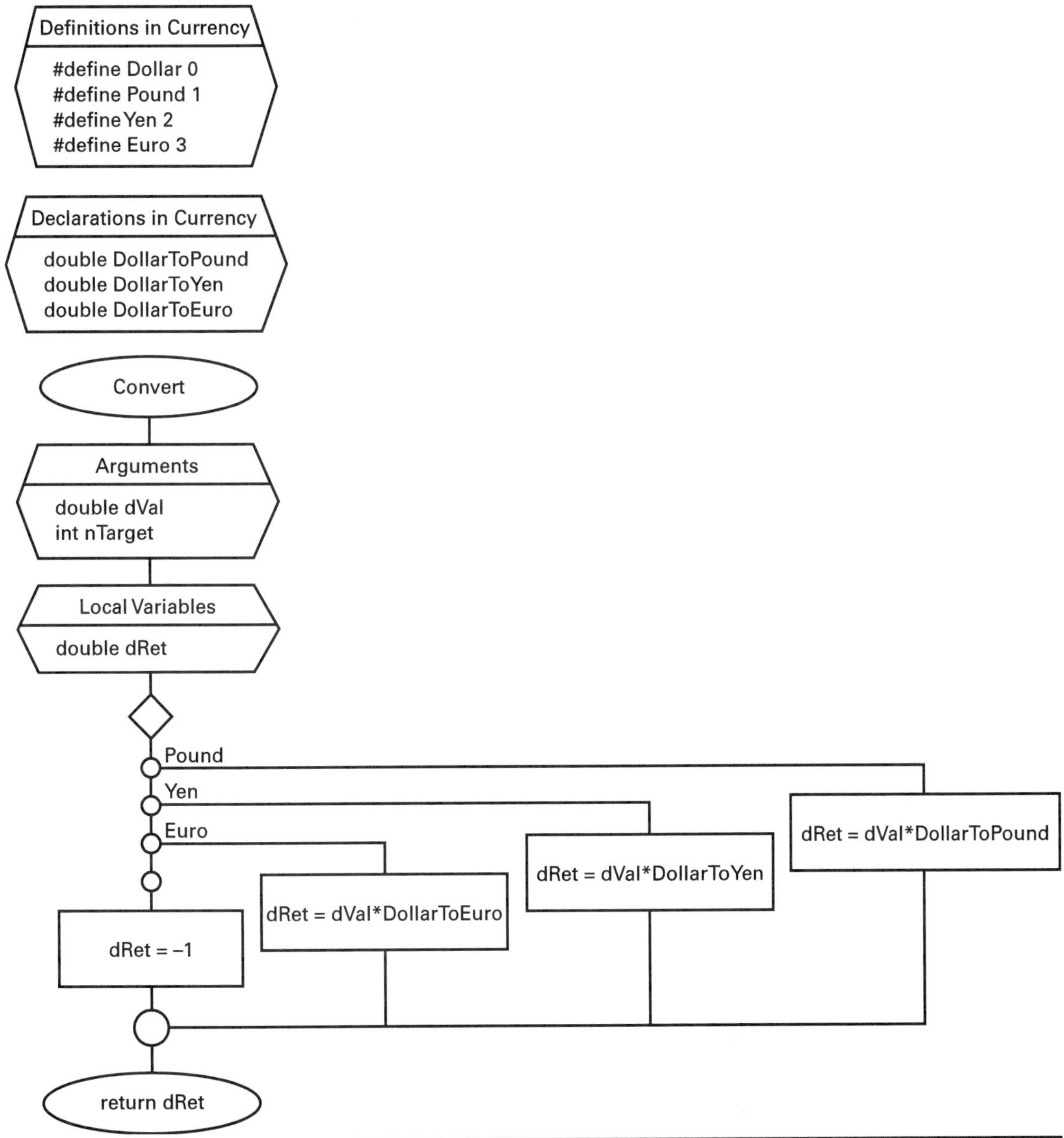

Definitions in Currency

#define Dollar 0
#define Pound 1
#define Yen 2
#define Euro 3

Declarations in Currency

double DollarToPound
double DollarToYen
double DollarToEuro

Convert

Arguments

double dVal
int nTarget

Local Variables

double dRet

Pound
Yen
Euro

dRet = -1

dRet = dVal*DollarToEuro

dRet = dVal*DollarToYen

dRet = dVal*DollarToPound

return dRet

TEST YOUR UNDERSTANDING 5.4:

Explain why the function in Figure 5.16 returns –1 if an unsupported currency is passed into the function. What, if anything, can we do to prevent possible ambiguity here?

5.3: SECTION QUESTIONS

1. What rules should you use in choosing between nested if constructs and multi-way branches?
2. What code blocks are associated with flowcharted IF constructs?
3. What code blocks are associated with the flowcharted CASE construct?
4. What are the pros and cons of using return statements within branching constructs?
5. If you wanted to add additional currencies to the function in Figure 5.16, what three things would you have to do?

5.4: ITERATIVE CONSTRUCTS

The final type of construct required for structured programming is the iterative construct, or *loop*. The basic idea behind a loop is that it allows us to apply the same block of code over and over again, until some condition causes the process to end. If no condition ever terminates the loop, we have an **infinite loop**—a programming condition so widely known that the term is frequently heard used among nonprogrammers.

Like branches, several looping constructs are available. In this section we look at four distinct versions of the loop—the **while loop, for loop, do...while loop,** and **until loop**—and learn how to represent them in flowcharts. Organizationally, we break these versions down into two general categories: loops that test first, and loops that test last. Despite the differences between the various flavors of loop, it will quickly become apparent that their similarities are far greater than their differences. As a result, thorough knowledge of how to apply any one of the four constructs is usually sufficient for nearly all programming situations.

5.4.1: Loops That Test First

Every looping construct has two key elements: a test (represented by a diamond) and a code block whose repeated performance depends on the results of the test. Two of the most common looping constructs, the *while loop* and the *for loop*, apply the test *before* the code block.

While Loop   The while loop is the simplest of the looping constructs. It consists of a test and a block of code that is performed as long as the test is true. In our flowcharting style, such a loop is represented in Figure 5.17.

The flowcharted version of the construct appears more complex than it actually is. As illustrated in the figure, the only code block in the loop is the vertical line that is connected to the bottom of the test (i.e., the corner of the test diamond that always represents true). The remaining lines simply serve as connectors, and no code can be inserted into them. The line on the left of the construct serves to bring us back to the test after our code block has been performed. The line on the right of the construct (coming out of a false corner of the test diamond) takes us down to the start of the next code block.

Looping constructs, such as the while loop, prove to be incredibly useful in many programming situations. As a simple example, suppose you were asked to print out the squares and cubes of all the numbers between 1 and 100. One way, of course, would be to write 100 statements, the "brute force" method. Much easier, however, would be to use a while loop, as illustrated in Figure 5.18.

FIGURE 5.17 Basic While Loop | **FIGURE 5.18** Code Block for Printing 100 Squares and Cubes

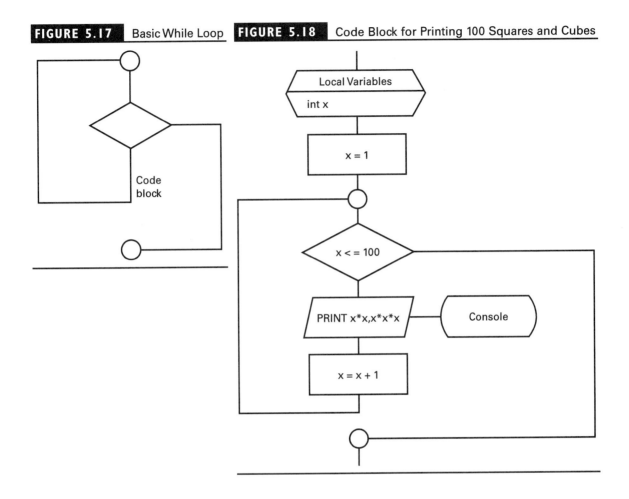

TEST YOUR UNDERSTANDING 5.5:

Precisely where does the while loop start and end in Figure 5.18?

For Loop The for loop is a close cousin of the while loop. Its main difference is that, for the sake of convenience, it contains two statement boxes that are built into the loop itself:

- The first box, the initialization box, contains statements (but no constructs) that are executed prior to the first test—and are only executed once.
- The second box, the iterator box, is applied after every loop (i.e., after the code block has been performed) immediately before the test is performed for the next pass.

In our flowcharting style, the basic for loop is illustrated in Figure 5.19.

It takes a sharp eye to distinguish a for loop from a while loop embedded in a code block on sight. For example, Figure 5.18 (the while loop for printing squares and cubes) could easily be written as a for loop, as illustrated in Figure 5.20. Indeed, given the need to initialize and increment X as part of the loop, the for loop is probably a more natural choice.

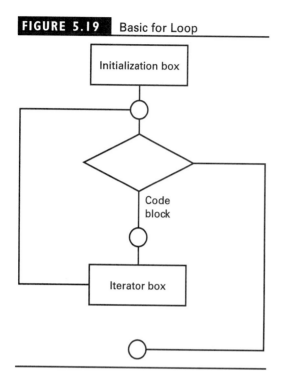

FIGURE 5.19 Basic for Loop

The principal practical difference between the two is the presence of a node between the print statement and the iterator in the for loop. Most of the time, this distinction is irrelevant. (The only time it becomes important is when a continue statement is present, as will be discussed in Section 5.4.3.) Thus, the choice between a for loop and a while loop is usually one of convenience. If values must be initialized before going into the loop, then the for loop is usually easiest. If not, the while loop is usually simpler.

5.4.2: Loops That Test Last

Although not as commonly needed as test-first loops, it is sometimes convenient to create loops in which the test to end the loop is performed *after* the code block has been executed at least once. Two examples of this type of loop are the *do…while* loop and the *until* loop.

Do…While Loop In appearance, the flowchart of the do…while loop construct is nearly identical to that

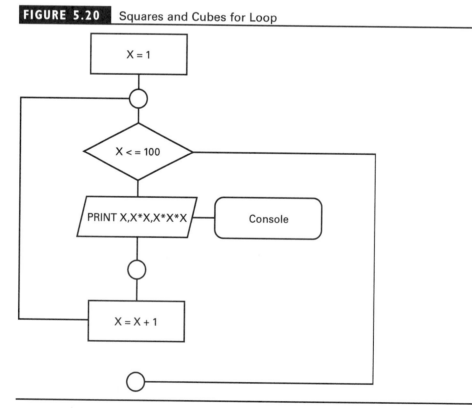

FIGURE 5.20 Squares and Cubes for Loop

of the while loop, as can be seen by comparing Figure 5.17 and Figure 5.21. The only difference between the two is that the code block comes before the test in the do…while loop, and after the test in the while loop.

An example of where such a loop might be convenient is in processing a text file. When reading lines from such a file, an end-of-file (EOF) marker is set after the last line has been read. As a result, in processing such a file, you might want a loop that keeps reading in lines of text until the EOF marker is set. Because the EOF marker is not set until you try to read past the last line, you need to read at least one line before making the test. Thus, it would make sense to position the test after reading the line, as illustrated in Figure 5.22.

Until Loop   Although the until loop pictured in Figure 5.23 looks rather different from the do…while loop of Figure 5.21, the two constructs are nearly identical. The only difference between a do…while loop and an until loop is that do…while keeps looping while the test is positive, whereas until keeps looping while the test is negative (i.e., *until* it is positive). For this reason, the two constructs can easily be substituted. All you need to do is reverse the test. For example, the until version of 5.22 would test for EOF==TRUE, breaking out of the loop when the condition was met.

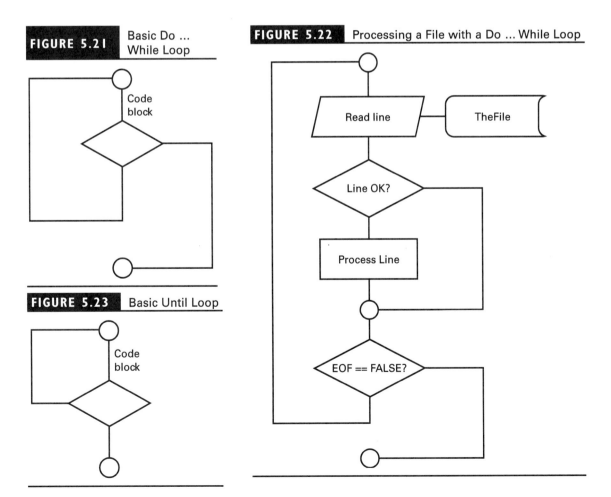

FIGURE 5.21   Basic Do … While Loop

FIGURE 5.22   Processing a File with a Do … While Loop

Code block

Read line

TheFile

Line OK?

Process Line

EOF == FALSE?

FIGURE 5.23   Basic Until Loop

Code block

Because of this similarity, most languages support only one of the two constructs. C/C++, for example, only offers a do...while construct. If you need an until loop, just remember to negate the test.

5.4.3: Breaks and Continues

Before leaving the subject of iteration, we must tackle, at least briefly, the thorny subject of *break* and *continue* statements. Few issues divide the scruffy and neat camps as sharply as the use of these constructs. Before we enter the debate, however, we need to understand what they do.

As already discussed in the case of branching, certain statements—most notably the return—can take the program out of a code block without following the well-ordered pattern of branching and rejoining that characterizes pure structured programming. When a code block is contained within a loop, however, two additional statements, the break and continue statements, can be used to jump out of a code block (and sometimes several nested layers of code blocks).[2] The statements work as follows:

- A break statement jumps to the node at the very end of the loop.
- The continue statement starts the loop on its next pass, skipping over any code beneath it.

The effects of the break and continue statements in a while loop and in a for loop are illustrated in Figures 5.24 and 5.25, respectively.

TEST YOUR UNDERSTANDING 5.6:

In the while loop (Figure 5.24), the connector from the continue statement (the dotted line) appears to go up, while in the for loop (Figure 5.25) it appears to go down. Explain why.

In many situations, the use of break and continue statements can be particularly convenient. For example, in a loop that reads lines from a text file and then processes them (e.g., extracts data), one of the first checks a program commonly makes is to see whether the line is blank. If so, the likely action will be to skip the processing part of the loop and read the next line. If so, using a "continue" on encountering a blank line eliminates the need to nest the entire processing block within an if statement (i.e., "if the line is not blank"). The alternative to using breaks in while loops is often to create flag variables, with names like bOK, that get incorporated into the loop test (and sometimes into tests nested inside the loop). A simple break at an appropriate exit point in the loop can eliminate the need for such hard-to-understand variables.

Having made a case for the convenience of break and continue statements, many advocates of structured programming view them to be nearly as evil as the hated goto statement. For one thing, as clearly illustrated in both Figures 5.24 and 5.25, they can cause lines to cross—an indication of their potential ability to jump across numerous code block boundaries. Although scruffies might view this as a plus, as soon as loops become nested within other loops, you face a very real possibility that you, the programmer, will entirely misinterpret what loop you are continuing, or breaking out of. These types of misunderstandings can lead to hours, or days, of extra debugging time—which is why the neat community feels so strongly that they should not be used.

---

[2] A more honest number is actually three—but even the author is not scruffy enough to include the goto statement in a treatment of structured programming.

FIGURE 5.24 Break and Continue within a While Loop

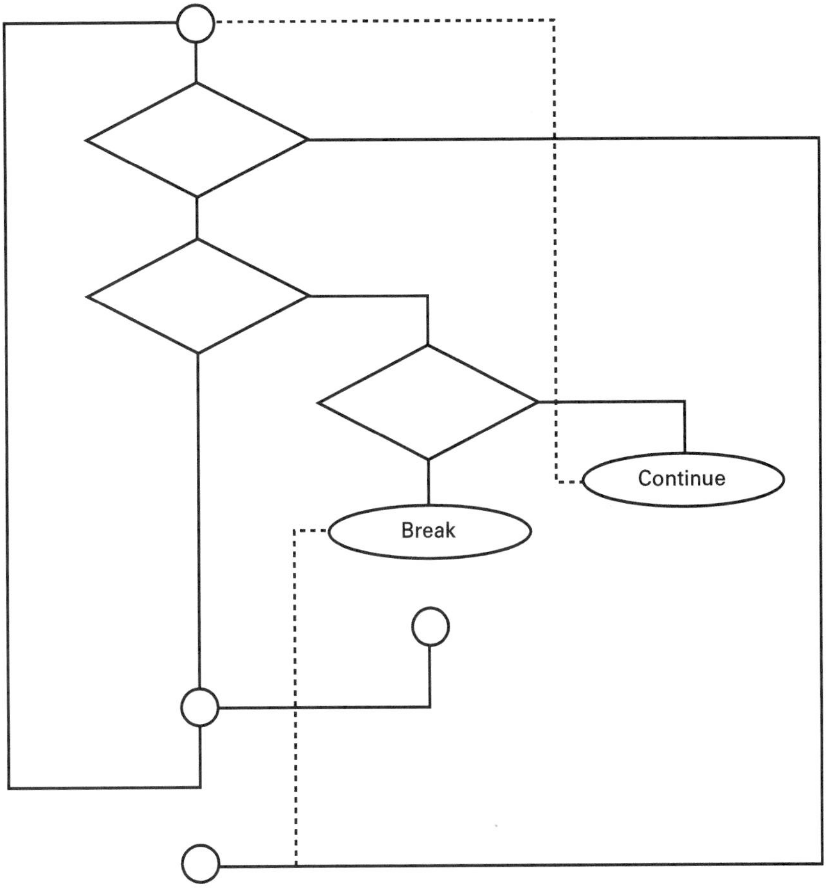

As an added bonus, we will discover in Chapter 6 that C/C++ uses the same break statement both to take you out of a loop *and* to prevent fall through in a case construct. This characteristic of the language—almost certainly designed to ensure that programmers (even experienced ones) will have countless opportunities to enjoy that euphoric sense of confusion and disbelief that accompanies multiday debugging sessions with no sleep—is another reason why the use of break statements, in particular, should be weighed carefully. Style Sidebar 5.2 summarizes some of the positions.

5.4: SECTION QUESTIONS

1. Where is the code block in a while loop?
2. Where is the code block in a for loop?
3. Where is the code block in an until loop?
4. Where is the code block in a do…while loop?

FIGURE 5.25 Break and Continue Within For Loop

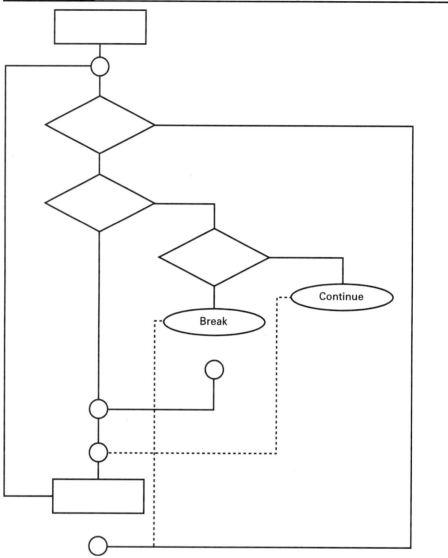

5. Why does a node symbol appear above the iterator box in a for loop?

6. What is the only statement for which while and for loops differ considerably?

5.5: USING FLOWC TO CREATE FLOWCHARTS

Walkthrough available in FlowC.wmv

As noted several times, even though flowcharts are useful tools for designing and explaining code, they are not widely used in real-world design, and even their use in teaching

STYLE SIDEBAR 5.2	Use of Break and Continue Statements

Camp	Position	Justification
Super Scruffy	Break and continue statements can be used wherever it's convenient.	If you're confused by my code, then you're not qualified to be reading it. Now get off my case.
Scruffy	Break and continue statements can be used anywhere where they simplify the code and are not too confusing.	In many loops, a continue or break is a more natural expression of what you are trying to do than defining peculiar flag variables.
Middle Ground	Break and continue statements in loops should be used as sparingly as possible, and only in situations where (a) the condition being tested is unusual enough to warrant disrupting normal flow (e.g., an error), and (b) no ambiguity exists about what loop the construct applies to.	If using the constructs makes the code clearer, then avoiding them as a matter of principle is too restrictive. On the other hand, using them too often can be indicative of sloppy programming.
Neat	Break and continue statements can always be avoided and should never be used.	Avoiding them forces you to write clearer code. Many times the apparent naturalness of a break/continue is really a symptom of sloppy coding and design.
Neat Freak	Even teaching what break and continue statements do should be prohibited.	If other neatniks see breaks and continues in your code, they'll think you're a bad person.

programming has declined significantly since the 1960s, when they were almost universally used. Three main drawbacks of flowcharts account for their decline:

1. They are a pain in the neck to create manually and—even with computer drawing tools—are a nightmare to modify.

2. They are easy to draw incorrectly. Particularly popular flagrant violations include multiple lines going into boxes or coming out of them, orphaned boxes and loops that never end (or don't even loop). Such errors are typically indicative of incorrect understanding of the problem being designed. Unfortunately, it is usually the attempt to write a program from the chart that uncovers these weaknesses of understanding, not the chart itself. Where a strict set of style guidelines is used to avoid such problems (such as those presented in this text), it is often easier to learn the programming language than to learn how to create the flowchart according to the guidelines.

3. They become so large for significant applications that their utility as a documentation tool is negligible.

The last of these drawbacks means that logic flowcharting will probably never resurge as a popular design tool. The first two, on the other hand, are mainly obstacles to using flowcharts in teaching programming.

5.5.1: What Is FlowC?

The FlowC program, included with this text, was developed to address the first two drawbacks of flowcharting. Designed specifically as a tool for teaching C/C++, FlowC:

- Makes it easy to create flowcharts and add constructs to them. Even complex constructs, such as case constructs and for loops, can be inserted in a fraction of a second.
- Ensures that any flowchart the user creates is legal, that is, it conforms to the rules of structured flowcharting set forth in this chapter. Naturally, being "legal" is different from being "right"—it is still completely possible to create flowcharts that are nonsensical. But at least it is a start.
- It allows its user to generate pseudocode and C/C++ code directly from a flowchart (or inspect the code that would be generated from any function or construct within the chart).

A short FlowC reference manual, explaining the menus and operation of the program, is provided on the CD that accompanies this book.

Creating a FlowC Project   When you create a new project in FlowC (e.g., File|New) you are presented with a dialog box asking for the project name and other information, as illustrated in Figure 5.26. For the purposes of getting started, the only elements of the dialog you need to worry about are the name (which must be supplied) and the Library Project check box. If you do not check it, a main function—with the standard argc and argv[] arguments discussed in Chapter 4—is automatically created, as shown in Figure 5.27.

Throughout FlowC, the contents of almost any box on the screen can be edited by double clicking it. As a first step, it probably makes sense to double click the legend box and enter information such as your name.

5.5.2: Inserting FlowC Constructs

The best way to learn to use FlowC is to play around with it. Before commencing to play, however, knowing a few principles of its operation is useful. First, FlowC maintains flowchart integrity by (1) limiting what you can add or delete to complete constructs, and (2) limiting where you can add them.

Basically only three types of objects can be added directly to FlowC projects: functions, classes (to be discussed when OOP is covered), and global project information (e.g., definitions, declarations). These objects can be added using the Insert menu (and in various other ways, such as right clicking an empty area of the screen).

Inserting Constructs   All of the other programming constructs we have discussed can only be added to existing code blocks. These code blocks are *always* represented as vertical lines in FlowC, such as the line between that connects the function name and return ellipses in an empty function. The slight problem created by this format is that while all code blocks are vertical lines, not all vertical lines are code blocks. For example, in the

FIGURE 5.26 New FlowC Project

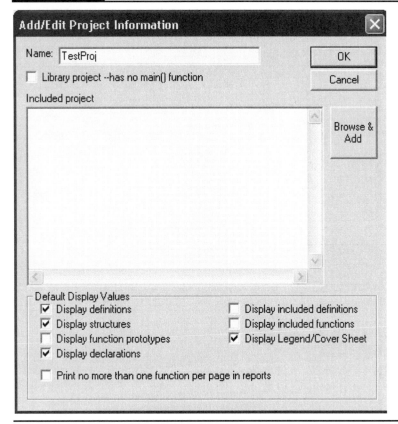

do…while loop shown in Figure 5.21, the vertical line above the test *is* a code block, while the vertical line below the test is a simple connector. To ensure that code is only added to code blocks, FlowC:

- Disables the insertion menu (accessed by right clicking the mouse) when the mouse is not over a code block.
- Changes the shape of the cursor when the mouse is not over a code block, as illustrated in Figure 5.28.

The insertion menu itself is also context sensitive. It will not, for example, present break and continue statement options unless the code block is nested within a loop.

To create a structured flowchart, then, you begin with a function (which can be main, or any other function you care to add). You then insert constructs into the function code block. Once inserted, you can then use the code blocks in the constructs themselves for further insertions, to create nesting. For example, Figure 5.29 shows how an if construct embedded within a while loop can be created in successive steps.

Editing Constructs   Once the desired construct is in place, the text in boxes, diamonds, ellipses, and so on can be filled in by double clicking them. For some boxes (e.g., declarations)

FIGURE 5.27 Project with Main Function

and constructs (e.g., functions, case statements), a specialized editor will be invoked designed to ensure the integrity of the charts is maintained. In case statements, for example, the specialized case editor:

- Moves code blocks when cases are repositioned.
- Allows new cases to be created.
- Ensures duplicate cases are not entered (although it is easily tricked with spaces and commas, should that be part of the user's nefarious plan).

Deleting Constructs Constructs are deleted by right clicking them, then choosing delete from the menu that is presented. Although a single level of Undo is usually available, it is wise not to count on it, because FlowC cannot always recreate every deletion. This fact is important because what construct is to be deleted is not always self-evident. For example, deleting the initialization box of a for loop will cause the entire for loop and all of its contained constructs—not just the box—to be deleted.

To avoid unpleasant and unexpected deletions, the *View|Box Selected Construct* option of the menu creates a crosshatched box that highlights the boundaries of the selected construct (see Figure 5.30).

FIGURE 5.28 FlowC Cursor Styles

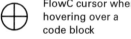 FlowC cursor when hovering over a code block

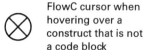 FlowC cursor when hovering over a construct that is not a code block

FIGURE 5.29   Creating a Flowchart Through Successive Insertions

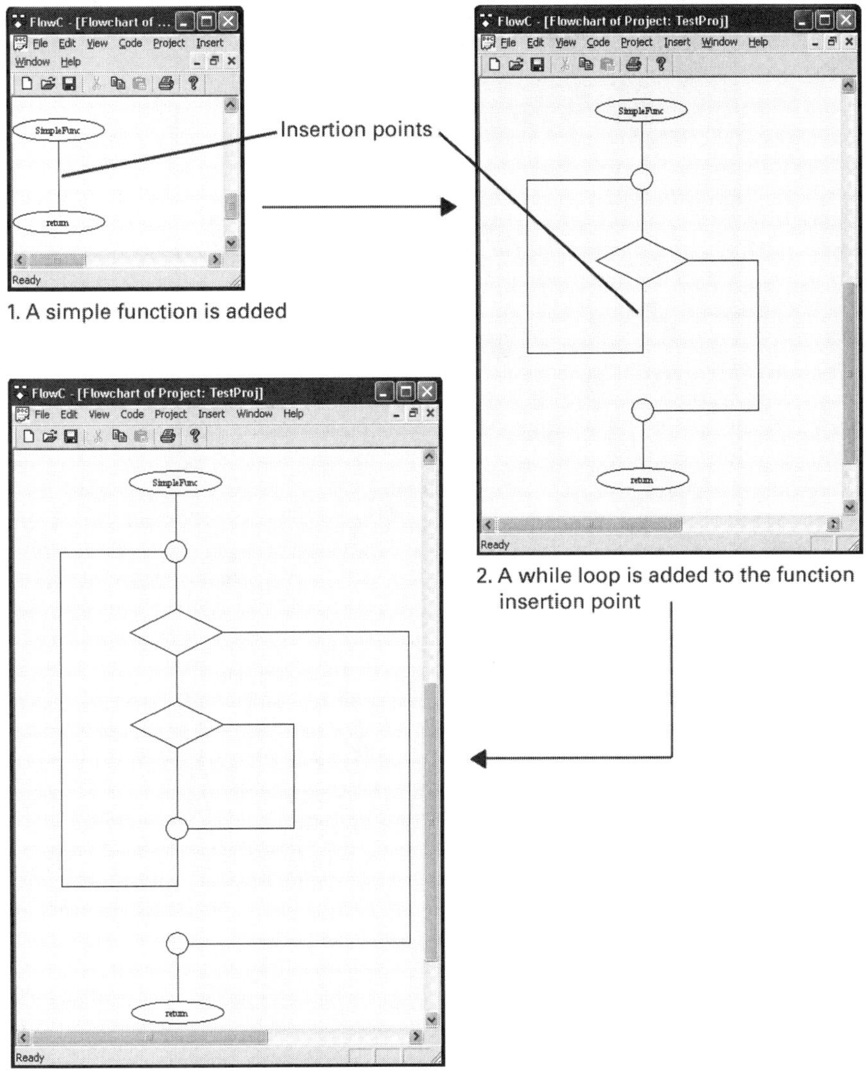

1. A simple function is added

2. A while loop is added to the function
   insertion point

3. An if construct is added to the insertion
   point of the while loop

This box identifies what would be deleted, if deletion is chosen. It is also useful for many other purposes, such as creating screen captures of specific constructs (Edit|Copy), displaying code and pseudocode, and creating separate editing windows, all of which are discussed in the documentation on the CD.

Certain types of constructs cannot be deleted directly, such as argument and local variable declarations. These boxes are an integral part of the construct they are embedded in (e.g., a function's argument box, a code block's local variables box). They will, however, be hidden if all the items in the box are deleted. Should they be hidden in this fashion, the right click menu is required to access them at a subsequent time.

FIGURE 5.30	For Loop Initialization Box Clicked with View|Box Selected Construct Set to ON

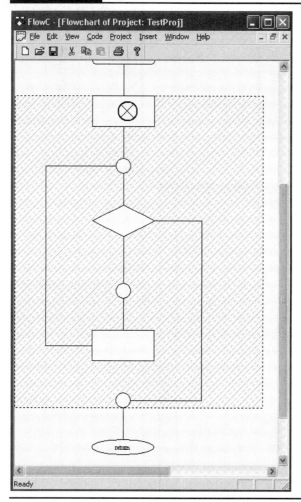

5.5.3: Styling and Printing FlowC Charts

FlowC offers a number of styling options that can be used for aesthetic purposes, to help fit text into the various boxes, and to allow for cleaner printing.

Aesthetic Styling The aesthetic styling options of FlowC are accessed through the View|Display Settings|Drawing Styles menu. The resulting dialog box, shown in Figure 5.31, provides control over colors, line widths, shadowing, and fonts for the selected view.

Sizing Options Because FlowC offers no discretion in positioning objects, the only way that any repositioning can be accomplished is through resizing the various objects. The dialog for doing so can be accessed through the View|Display Settings|Drawing Sizes dialog box, illustrated in Figure 5.32.

FIGURE 5.31 Drawing Style Dialog Box

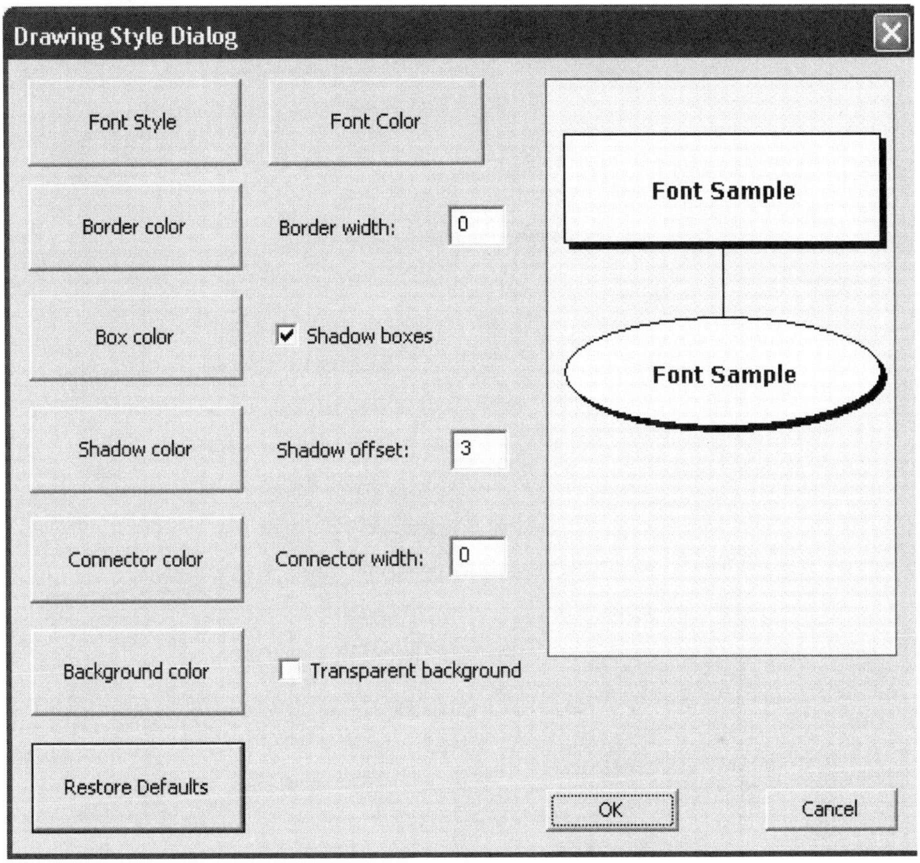

FlowC is conceptually organized into a grid of rows and columns, with each code block proceeding down a single column—although inserted constructs, such as loops and branches, may extend into columns to the left or right. The settings dialog is organized into four groups of settings:

- The physical size of the rows and columns, measured in pixels, is specified in the first group. (*Note*: Column width is equal to box width plus column space.)
- The height of the various flowchart symbols, designated in row units, is included in the second group. These height indications should always be even numbers (excepting node radius), or connectors may miss corners.
- The font height is measured as a percentage of row height (the height in the font dialog accessed through the styling window discussed previously is locked to 12). By changing values such as box width and font height, it is often possible to get truncated text to appear.
- The column group allows the width of a number of top-level constructs (i.e., constructs that aren't placed in code blocks) to be adjusted.

FIGURE 5.32 Drawing Settings Dialog Box

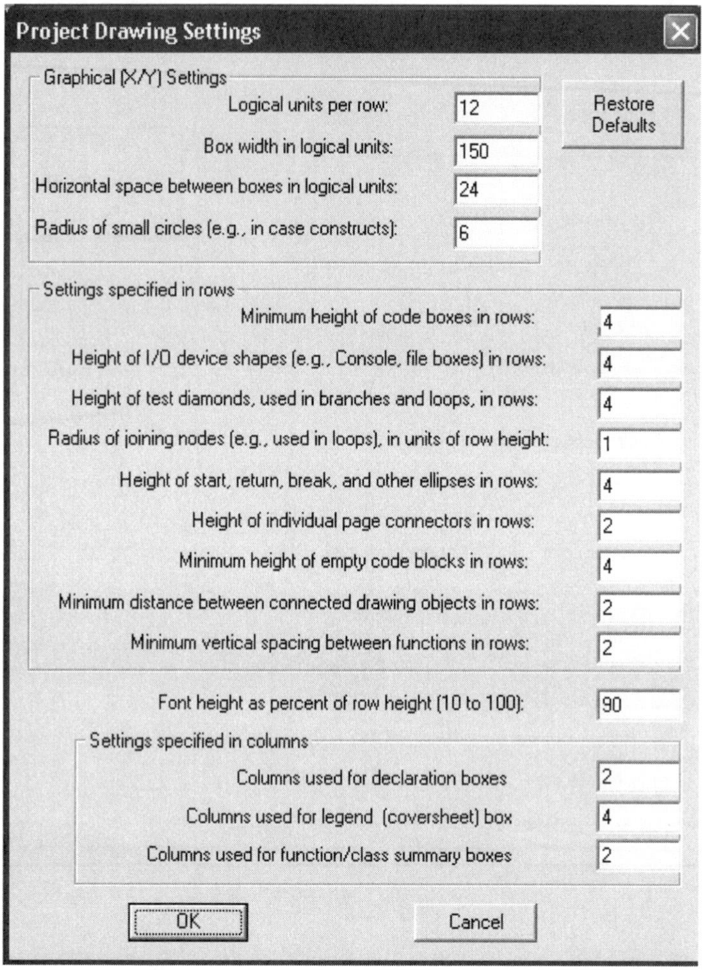

Project Drawing Settings	☒

Graphical (X/Y) Settings

Logical units per row:	12
Box width in logical units:	150
Horizontal space between boxes in logical units:	24
Radius of small circles (e.g., in case constructs):	6

Restore Defaults

Settings specified in rows

Minimum height of code boxes in rows:	4
Height of I/O device shapes (e.g., Console, file boxes) in rows:	4
Height of test diamonds, used in branches and loops, in rows:	4
Radius of joining nodes (e.g., used in loops), in units of row height:	1
Height of start, return, break, and other ellipses in rows:	4
Height of individual page connectors in rows:	2
Minimum height of empty code blocks in rows:	4
Minimum distance between connected drawing objects in rows:	2
Minimum vertical spacing between functions in rows:	2

Font height as percent of row height (10 to 100):	90

Settings specified in columns

Columns used for declaration boxes	2
Columns used for legend (coversheet) box	4
Columns used for function/class summary boxes	2

OK   Cancel

Printing Settings Because of the large amount of space that flowcharts take up, printing them has always been a challenge. In FlowC, three key settings are most important for printing:

- Setting rows per page
- Enabling pagination
- Enabling page connectors

The rows per page setting setting, along with enabling page connectors, is located in the View|Display Settings|Print Settings dialog box, illustrated in Figure 5.33.

No obvious way permits us to translate between screen presentation and printing, which means all print sizing is based on rows per page. Each row can be thought of as roughly equivalent to a line of text, and therefore some number in the range of fifty to sixty usually works best.

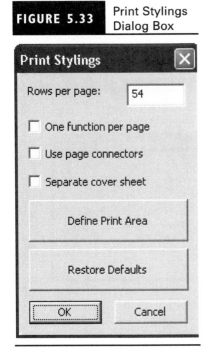

FIGURE 5.33 Print Stylings Dialog Box

The *View|Pagination* setting should normally be selected before printing. It does two things:

1. Places lines on the display that correspond to where page breaks would occur.

2. Adjusts the positions of boxes and other constructs that would be broken by pages so that they fall at the top of the succeeding page. Without pagination, some constructs may print more than once.

When the page connectors option is selected on the print stylings dialog, FlowC inserts page connectors wherever lines cross from one page to another. The page connector symbols contain the number of the page to which the line continues. These connectors only appear in the printed document (or in print preview).

5.5.4: Viewing Construct Pseudocode

At any time, structured pseudocode for the project, a single function, or a selected construct can be accessed using the Code menu. The basic process is to select a construct (which will appear boxed) then go to the Code menu and view the pseudocode for the construct itself, the function it is embedded in, or the entire project. Because the pseudocode is generated, it cannot be changed. It can, however, be selected and copied to another document, such as a text editor.

An illustration, showing how pseudocode was generated for the case construct originally presented in Figure 5.16 is presented in Figure 5.34.

5.5: SECTION QUESTIONS

1. What two specific problems with flowcharts is FlowC designed to address?
2. What is the difference between a regular FlowC project and a library project?
3. Can constructs be added to FlowC outside of a function?
4. When you click on a graphic element in FlowC, a diagonally striped box typically appears (unless the feature has been turned off). What is the significance of this box?
5. How do you find the code blocks associated with a construct?
6. How do you determine what constructs can be added to a code block?
7. How do you rearrange the elements in a FlowC diagram?
8. Will FlowC always generate valid pseudocode?

5.6: IN DEPTH: SAMPLE PROBLEMS

Three sample problems that examine flowcharting commonly used C/C++ library functions are now provided.

FIGURE 5.34	Example of Pseudocode Window

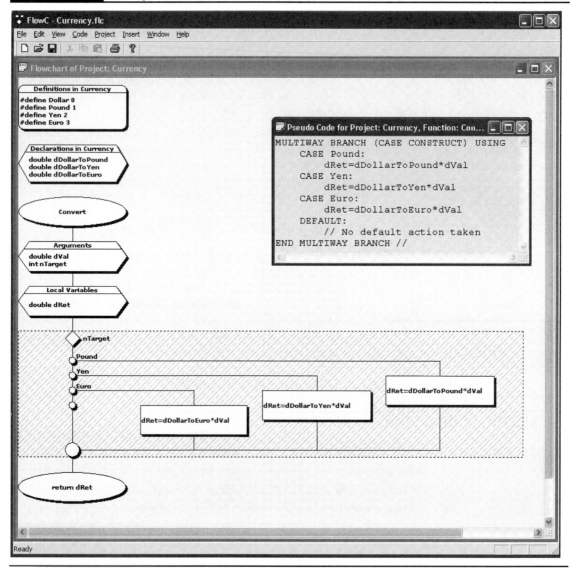

5.6.1: Strlen

 Walkthrough available in Strlen.wmv

The strlen function in C/C++ is used to determine how many characters are present in a NUL terminated string (see Chapter 3, Section 3.3.2 for a discussion of these strings). The function we will develop mimics this function and is prototyped as follows:

```
int Strlen(char str[]);
```

where the argument, str[] is an array containing a NUL terminated string, and the return value is the number of characters in the string.

The function is implemented in a straightforward fashion, as illustrated in Figure 5.35. We simply initialize a counter then test the array, character by character, until a NUL terminator (a byte with the value 0) is encountered. Then, we return the counter.

5.6.2: Strcmp

Walkthrough available in Strcmp.wmv

In C, we frequently find the need to check whether two character strings are equal to each other or to determine whether one is alphabetically greater than the other. The equality test, for example, might be needed if we wanted to find out if a particular name was in a list of names. Similarly, a test for greater than/less than would be critical if we wanted to search a sorted array of names. Unfortunately, C (and structured C++) does not allow us to use the standard operators (e.g., ==, !=, <, >) to compare strings—the best we can do with them is to compare their first characters. As a result, we use a library function called strcmp() to make the comparison. Our function Strcmp performs the same task as the library function, and is prototyped as follows:

```
int Strcmp(char sz1[],char sz2[]);
```

where sz1 and sz2 are the two strings to be compared. The return value of Strcmp has the following significance (which is the same as the library function):

- 0 means the two strings have the same characters (case sensitive) all the way to the NUL terminator.
- < 0 means the first string is alphabetically less than the second (e.g., Strcmp("abc","xyz"))
- > 0 means the first string is alphabetically greater than the second (e.g., Strcmp("xyz","abc"))

The Strcmp function is case sensitive, meaning that Strcmp("XYZ","abc") will return a value less than 0 (because capital X is less than lower case a in the ASCII coding scheme).

The Strcmp function, flowcharted in Figure 5.36, begins by declaring an integer local variable i to keep track of our position in the string. The variable i is then initialized to zero in the initialization block of a for loop, which keeps looping until either:

- A NUL terminator in the first string is encountered (meaning the end of the first string), or
- The difference between the characters at position i of each string is not 0 (i.e., the characters are not equal).

FIGURE 5.35   Strlen

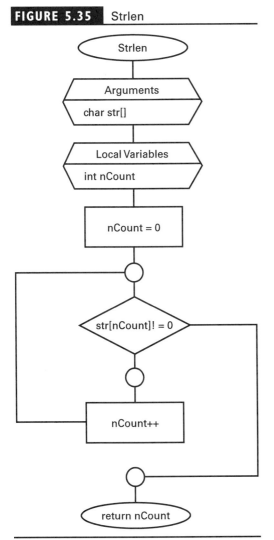

FIGURE 5.36 Strcmp

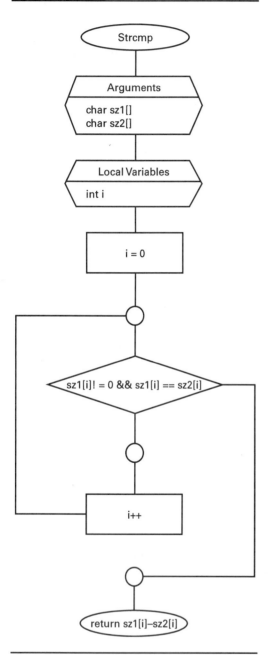

When we exit the loop, we return the difference between the two characters we were looking at.

TEST YOUR UNDERSTANDING 5.7:

Explain why returning the difference between the two characters after we break out of the loop meets the requirements for the return value set forth in our function definition.

5.6.3: Atoi Function

Walkthrough available in Atoi.wmv

The Atoi function mimics the C/C++ atoi() library function that takes a charter string and returns its integer equivalent. For example, the call Atoi("125") would return the integer 125. This functions turns out to be quite useful when we are faced with situations in which we are given character data (such as from the keyboard or a text file) that we need to transform into numeric data we can use within our programs.

Our version of Atoi, like the C/C++ library version, is prototyped as follows:

```
int Atoi(char str[]);
```

where str contains a string of characters that are numeric digits (i.e., 0 through 9) that may be preceded by either a plus (+) or minus (-) character. The return value is the integer equivalent of the string.

Just to have a little fun, we will also allow the user to put some spaces, tabs, or other nondisplaying characters before the number or between the sign and the number. In other words, the following strings would all be allowable:

```
"125"
"-125"
"   +125"
"-   125"
```

Skipping over such characters, often referred to as white characters (because they are white on the printed page—presuming you are using white paper!), requires us to know a little bit about how the ASCII system is organized. In particular, every character less than or equal to the space character (ASCII value of 32) is a white character. Thus, to skip over white characters, we just need to check to see whether a character's value is less than or equal to ' ' (or, equivalently, <= 32).

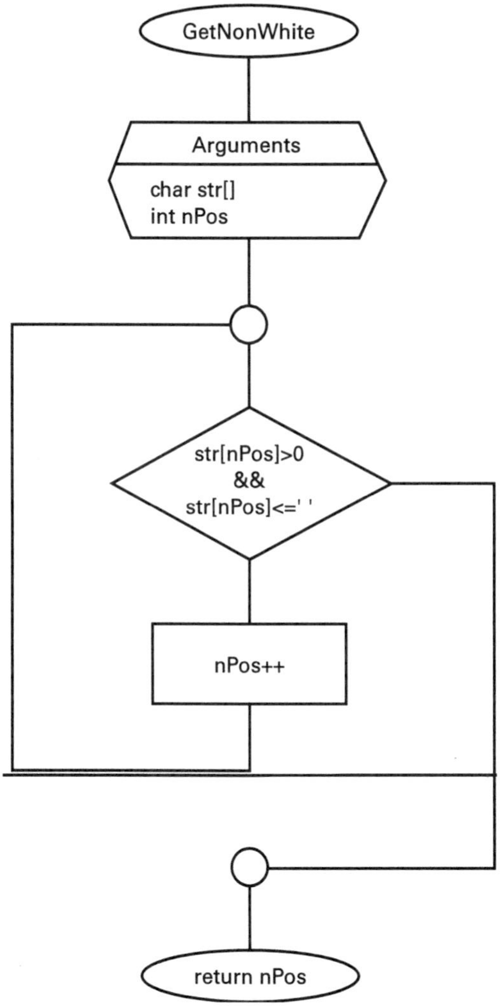

Because we need to do such skips twice in our Atoi function (once before and once after the sign, if a sign is present), it makes sense to define a separate function to do the skipping. So, before we write Atoi, we write GetNonWhite(), which is prototyped as follows:

```
int GetNonWhite(char str[],int nPos);
```

where:

- str is the string where we want to skip over white characters
- nPos is the position in the string where we start looking (0 if we are at the start of the string)

The GetNonWhite() function, illustrated in Figure 5.37, is a simple while loop that continues as long as the character at str[nPos] is white (i.e., <= ' ') and is *not* the NUL terminator. After each test, we increment nPos. When we break out of the loop, either because we reached the end of the string or encountered a nonwhite character, we return nPos.

TEST YOUR UNDERSTANDING 5.8:

What would GetNonWhite() return if the character at position nPos is not a white character?

Having defined GetNonWhite, we can now proceed to defining Atoi. The basic operation of Atoi is as follows:

- Three local integer variables are declared and initialized: nRet to hold our return value, nPos to keep track of where we are in the string—both initialized to 0—and nSign (initialized to +1), which keeps track of whether the number is positive or negative.

FIGURE 5.37 GetNonWhite Helper Function

- It calls GetNonWhite() to skip over leading blanks.
- It checks to see whether the first character is a sign (+ or −). If it's a minus sign, it sets nSign equal to −1, then moves to the next character. If it's a plus sign, it just moves to the next character.
- GetNonWhite() is called again, to move us to the first digit.
- We enter a while loop that continues as long as we are still reading digits, which are any ASCII characters between '0' and '9' (which is a result of how ASCII is laid out).
- During each pass of the loop, we take our old nRet value, multiply it by 10, and add the character minus the 0 character, which turns the character into its integer equivalent. For example, the ASCII character '2' is 50, and the ASCII character '0' is 48. Therefore '2' − '0' == 50 − 48 == 2. (This calculation works only because the character digits are coded in sequence; that is, '0' is 48, '1' is 49, '2' is 50, and so forth.)
- When any nondigit character is encountered, the function returns the accumulated value of nRet.

The least intuitive aspect of the Atoi function is how the digit-processing loop works. The easiest way to illustrate this looping is with a table of values as an example—say the string "125" (with a NUL terminator at the end):

nRet coming in	nPos	str[nPos]	str[nPos]–'0'	nRet coming out
0	0	'1'	1	1
1	1	'2'	2	12
12	2	'5'	5	125
125	3	'\0'	N/A	125

The Atoi function is flowcharted in Figure 5.38.

TEST YOUR UNDERSTANDING 5.9:

Given the way the Atoi function works, what would the string "12q47" return?

FIGURE 5.38   Atoi

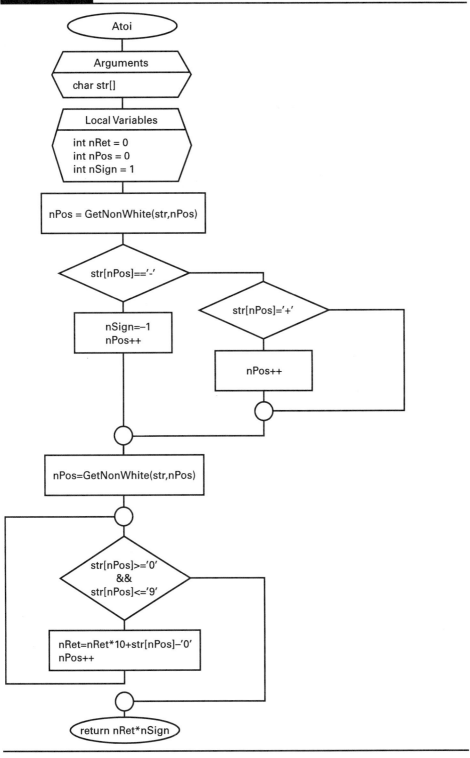

5.7: REVIEW AND QUESTIONS

5.7.1: REVIEW

A summary of the flowcharting elements introduced in this chapter is presented in the following table.

Symbol	Description
	Functions: An entry point (ellipse) with the function name and one or more exit points (ellipses) that return from the function. May also have argument and local variable declarations. The vertical line between the function and the return is a *code block*—the location where additional constructs can be inserted.
	Declarations: Box with angular edges used to declare variables. May be declared globally (at project level) or locally (within function).
	Statements: Three forms of statement boxes, containing one or more statements executed sequentially: • *Statement box:* holds all statements that do not perform I/O. • *Console box:* holds statements performing standard input (e.g., keyboard) and output (e.g., monitor). • *File I/O:* holds statements that take input from, or send output to, a file.
	If construct: A branch, using a test (diamond) that provides two alternative code blocks for execution. The IF block is always the block below the diamond, and is performed if the test is true. The ELSE block is the block to the right of the diamond, and is performed if the test is false.
	Case construct: A multiway branch controlled by a value of an integer. Provides access to as many code blocks as needed—each block associated with one or more integer values. They are always drawn to the right of the construct, coming out of a small circle (case node). Below the bottom case node is the "default" case, which may be empty.

Symbol	Description
	While loop: A code block that repeats as long as a particular test is true. The code block that is repeated is the vertical segment below the test (i.e., the diamond)—no constructs can be added to the code above the test. Normal behavior can be interrupted by two statements: ● **Break:** sends control to the bottom node, breaking out of the loop ● **Continue:** jumps to top, beginning next pass
	For loop: Similar to a *while* loop in that a code block repeats as long as a particular test is true. The code block that is repeated is the vertical segment below the test (i.e., the diamond)—no constructs can be added to the code above the test. It differs in two ways from the while loop: ● Prior to the first test, a collection of initializing statements is performed. ● After each pass, a collection of iterator statements is performed. Normal behavior can be interrupted by two statements: ● **Break:** sends control to the bottom node, breaking out of the loop ● **Continue:** jumps to node above iterator box, performing those statements then beginning next pass
	Do...while/until loop: Structurally similar to the *while* loop except the code block that is repeated is between the top entry node and the test, which means this code always gets performed at least once. No code that is part of the loop can be added below the test. A **do...while** loop repeats until the test is false. An **until** loop repeats until the test is true. Otherwise, they are identical.

The FlowC application, included as part of the text on the CD that accompanies this text, makes the preparation of flowcharts straightforward. It differs from traditional drawing tools in three important ways:

■ All drawing and editing is done using the flowcharting constructs (e.g., the elements in the table just presented) instead of drawing elements (i.e., circles, lines, diamonds, rectangles, etc.). As a result, it is much easier to add and remove flowchart elements.

■ It provides no discretion with respect to positioning flowchart elements, and therefore eliminates many problems associated with lines crossing and difficulty adding elements to existing charts.

■ The program will allow the user to generate pseudocode (a descriptive C++ language used to specify programs) and code for any construct, function, or application. The generation of C++ code is covered more fully in Chapter 6.

5.7.2: GLOSSARY

case construct A construct that evaluates a given term and executes the only single matching code block in a collection of code blocks; used to implement a multiway branch

console I/O box A graphical representation of how information is transmitted to and from a computer using the console (e.g., keyboard, display)

construct A formal way of identifying program elements code blocks by specific type

do...until loop A block of code that executes at least once and will repeat executions, stopping only when a statement or expression becomes true

do...while loop A loop of code that executes at least once and will repeat executions, stopping only when a statement or expression becomes false

ELSE branch A code block in an if construct that only executes if the expression or statement tested evaluates to false

file I/O box A graphical representation of the activities that perform input/output from or to a file

flowchart A graphical representation of how a program's logic is structured

for loop A loop that causes a code block to repeat for as many times as a test is true; also provides for an initializing sequence of statements that is performed only once, and a sequence of statements that is performed after each repetition and before the test

If branch A code block in an if construct that only executes if the expression or statement tested evaluates to true

infinite loop A loop with no way to stop, hence it will run on forever

multiway branch A point in a program that can lead to several different paths depending upon the input, normally implemented with a case construct

nested construct A construct that is placed within the code block of another construct

pseudocode Structured English used to specify the intended logic of an actual or desired program

statement box A graphical representation of a statement, or sequence of statements without intervening constructs, used in flowcharting an application

structured pseudocode Code that looks similar to structured source code yet illustrates the logic behind a block of program logic

summary box A box that summarizes the purpose and meaning behind program elements

two-way branch A point where a program can go either of two ways depending on the result of the expression or statement; normally implemented with an if construct

while loop A loop that examines an expression and, while the expression remains true, repeatedly executes that particular code block

5.7.3: QUESTIONS

1. *Printer failure:* One day you try to print a report on your desktop PC and nothing happens. Create a flowchart identifying the actions you would take.

2. *Phone problem:* You pick up the phone in your bedroom and discover there is no dial tone. Create a flowchart detailing the steps you might have to take.

3. *Job offer:* Write a flowchart that would identify the decisions you would need to make in the event you were given a job offer and needed to give a yes or no answer in 24 hours. Criteria you might want to consider include salary, location, industry, job description, and company size, among others.

4. *Min-max and average:* Create a flowchart for a function that reads in numbers from the user. As soon as the user types in "Done," it should display the minimum value the user gave, the maximum value, and the average value of the elements in the series.

5. *I'm thinking of a number:* Create a flowchart that implements a function that plays the game "I'm thinking of a number." The main construct of the chart should be a loop that asks the player for a number. The following rules apply:

- Any time the player guesses the right number (which should be stored in a local variable) the function says "You've got it" and returns.

- If the guess is the first guess, the system replies "Okay" (unless the guess was correct).

- If the guess is closer than the last guess, the chart should reply "Warmer."

- If the guess is farther away from (or equal in distance to) the answer, the system should reply "Colder."

- The function should return the number of guesses.

6. *White character counter:* Create a flowchart for a function that would count the number of white characters (ASCII codes <= " or 32) in its argument, a character array that holds a NUL terminated string.

7. *Line counter:* When characters are sent to a teletype (which pretty much describes C output), a newline (\n, ASCII 10) character moves the roll up a line and the return (\r, ASCII 13) character moves the print head to the left-hand side of the paper. As a result, it is fairly common to use the \n\r character sequence within text strings to signify the start of a new line. Create a flowchart for a function that goes through a string and returns the number of lines by counting occurrences of a \n character followed by \r character in the string. If no \n\r pairs are found, it should return 1.

8. *General Currency Converter:* Using the flowchart in Figure 5.16 as a starting point, write a flowchart for a function that converts between any two currencies. The function prototype should be as follows:

```
double GeneralConvert(double dVal,
    int nFrom,int nTo);
```

where dVal is the amount to be converted, nFrom is an integer constant for the currency we are starting with, and nTo is an integer constant for the currency we are converting to. *Hint:* This problem is much easier than it looks if you define two functions—one to convert from U.S. dollars (which you already have) and one to convert to U.S. dollars (which will be similar to the one you already have), then call the two of them from your GeneralConvert() function.

9. *LegalNumber:* Write a flowchart for a function that takes a string (i.e., char str[]) as an argument and returns TRUE if the string contains a real number and FALSE otherwise. We will define a legal number as follows (where anything in brackets is optional):

[WS] [+|-] [WS] digits [. [digits]] [WS] \0

In English:

- Optional white space or spaces

- An optional '–' or '+' character (but not both), followed by optional white space or spaces
- One or more digits (ranging from '0' to '9')
- An optional decimal point, followed by more (optional) digits
- Optional white space or spaces
- A NUL terminator

Unless a string follows this pattern precisely, the function should return FALSE. You are encouraged to assume a GetNonWhite() helper function (Figure 5.37) is available for you to use.

10. *Atof function:* Starting with the Atoi function that we designed in walkthrough 5.6.3, design and flowchart a function that takes a string and converts it to its double value (as opposed to the integer value returned by Atoi). The function prototype should be as follows:

```
double Atof(char buf[]);
```

where buf contains the string of numeric characters (perhaps including a +/– sign and a decimal point) and double is the real number value being returned. *Hint:* The only material way that this function differs from Atoi is the need to handle a decimal point. Two possible ways of doing this conversion are:

- In the loop that processes the digits, treat the real return value as if it were an integer—skipping over the decimal point but keeping a count of how many digits occur after the decimal point. Once all the digits have been accumulated, set up a second loop that divides the number by 10 the same number of times as there were digits to the right of the decimal point.
- In the loop that processes the digits, create a variable that is initialized to 1 but then gets multiplied by 10 each time we find another digit to the right of the decimal place. Divide the digit value by that number before adding it to the return value.

Programming Constructs

EXECUTIVE SUMMARY

Chapter 6 shows how the logical programming constructs presented in Chapter 5 are implemented in the C/C++ programming language. Along the way, it identifies more programming style issues that are encountered in using these constructs, and alerts the reader to some common sources of program bugs.

The chapter begins by demonstrating FlowC's ability to translate flowcharts into C++ code and C++ projects. It then follows the pattern of Chapter 5, presenting the C++ branching constructs (if...else, switch...case) and looping constructs (while, for, do...while). It then provides a series of examples. The first group of examples takes the flowcharts developed in Chapter 5 and shows how they translate into C++ code. The second group takes the code for C++ functions and translates them into flowcharts, accompanied by discussion and debugger walkthroughs.

Chapter 6 is C++ specific and assumes good working knowledge of the constructs presented in Chapter 5. The specific construct sections can also be read in parallel with the corresponding sections in Chapter 5. In fact, the examples were designed with doing so in mind.

LEARNING OBJECTIVES

Upon completing this chapter, you should be able to:

- Generate the C++ code corresponding to a FlowC flowchart
- Create an entire Visual Studio .NET project from a FlowC project
- Take any logical problem that involves branching and turn it into a C++ if construct or switch...case construct
- Take any logical problem that involves looping and turn it into a C++ while, for or do...while construct
- Translate flowchart specifications for functions into equivalent C++ code
- Translate C++ functions into equivalent flowchart representations
- Explain the purpose of a number of common C/C++ library functions, including strlen, strcmp, and atoi, and explain how they could be implemented

6.1: CREATING CODE FROM FLOWCHARTS (USING FLOWC)

 Walkthrough available in FlowCCode.wmv

Before proceeding to show how various programming constructs can be written in C/C++, we briefly return to FlowC (first introduced in Chapter 5). In this section, our specific interest will be the tool's ability to generate C++ code from your flowchart. We first consider how to generate the code for a selected block of the flowchart, then turn to creating complete projects that can be compiled using Visual Studio .NET.

6.1.1: Examining C++ Code for Constructs

Inspecting the C++ code that corresponds to a flowchart is almost the same as viewing pseudocode (see Section 5.5.4). The basic process is to select a construct (which will appear boxed), then go to the Code menu and view the C code for the construct itself, the function it is embedded in, or for the entire project. Because the C code is generated, it cannot be changed. It can, however, be selected and copied to another document, such as a text editor. It can also be used as the basis of a Visual Studio .NET project, to be discussed in Section 6.1.2.

In transforming a flowchart to C++ code, FlowC makes certain translations, such as adding semicolons to the end of statements and inserting appropriate braces (i.e., { and } characters) to denote block starts and ends. FlowC also has certain keywords (always written in uppercase, a complete list is found in Appendix B and is designed to correspond closely to the SimpleIO functions) that are translated in special ways. For example, if the line:

```
GETSTRING buf[],80
```

is encountered in a console I/O block, it will be translated into:

```
cin.getline(buf,80);
```

Other commands, also used in Console I/O blocks, include:

- PRINT, followed by a list of comma-separated arguments. Generates an unformatted text output for each variable. The NEWLINE keyword causes a **return** to be sent.

- PRINTF, followed by a printf-style formatting string (see Chapter 7, Section 7.3 for details) and a series of comma-separated arguments, which translates into a sprintf statement used to create a formatted string then sent to cout.

An example of a function that reads a string from the user, checks to see if it is "QUIT" (using strcmp), and prints out "Quitting" if it is, along with its associated C++ code window, is presented in Figure 6.1, with comments being automatically generated (based on variable names and descriptions entered when the function was created).

6.1.2: Generating a Visual Studio .NET Project

Complete projects can be generated using FlowC, accessed through the *Code|C++ Generation Settings* menu option. The dialog box is shown in Figure 6.2. The dialog provides the ability to enter a variety of settings, including #include statements to be placed at the top of each generated .cpp file, prototypes for functions used in the project but not included in it (relevant only if syntax checking is to be performed), and target file names. The default behavior of FlowC is to create a .cpp file using the name of the project, and an .h file containing prototypes for all project functions (except main), as well as definitions. If the project has a main function, the default behavior is to place it in a separate file, named using the project name concatenated with _main.cpp (as shown in Figure 6.2).

The procedure for creating a Visual Studio .NET project is straightforward:

- Create an empty Visual Studio .NET Win32 console project.

- Using the three browse buttons provided in the dialog box in Figure 6.2, redirect the output files to the project folder just created by Visual Studio .NET.

- In Visual Studio .NET, add the source files (.cpp and .h) to the project, using the Solution Explorer.

- Build the project, fix any compiler errors—either by going back to the flowchart or locally, in the code—then run the program.

FIGURE 6.1 Example of Function Code Translation

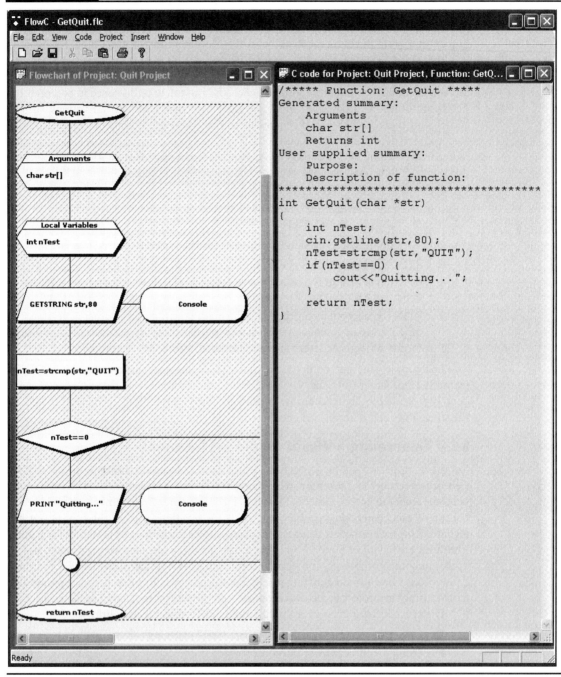

FIGURE 6.2   Project Generation Settings

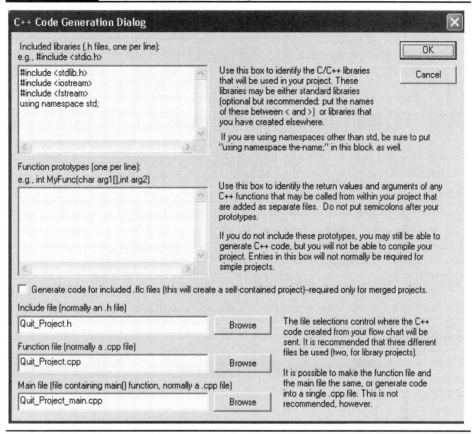

6.1: SECTION QUESTIONS

1. For what purpose are keywords, such as GETSTRING, used in FlowC?
2. What happens when you have a construct highlighted and display code?
3. What C++ files are generated for a normal FlowC project?
4. What C++ files are generated for a library FlowC project?
5. Where do FlowC comments come from?

6.2: THE IF…ELSE CONSTRUCT

The if…else construct is used to implement two-way branching in C/C++, and is probably the most commonly used construct in a typical program. The basic format of the simple if statement is:

```
if(test) statement-or-codeblock
else statement-or-codeblock
```

The *else* portion of the construct is optional. As was discussed in Chapter 4, Section 4.1.2, the statement-or-codeblock means that either a semicolon terminated statement or a brace-delimited sequence of statements (or nested code blocks) can be placed after the test and the else. As also mentioned in Section 4.1.2, three nesting styles are commonly observed where a code block is present, as reviewed in Example 6.1.

The main conclusion drawn about which of these three styles is preferred is that consistency is key. It is noted, however, that styles 1 and 2 are easily supported by the default behavior of the Visual Studio editor, whereas style 3 will require that you modify the editor or fight it every step of the way. The astute reader is left to draw his or her own conclusions.

These three styles can be applied to all the constructs discussed in this chapter.

6.2.1: The Basic if Construct

The basic if construct allows for a conditional test with or without an else block. To illustrate this test, flowcharts and associated code for two versions of a temperature conversion function—comparable to the one used in 5.3.1—are provided in Figure 6.3. The first version, ConvertToFahrenheit, looks at the nType variable (see the original definition of the function) and, if the incoming temperature is in Celsius, the temperature is converted. Otherwise no action is required, so the else block is omitted. In the second version of the function, a conversion always takes place, either from Celsius to Fahrenheit or from Fahrenheit to Celsius, so both the if block and else block are present.

In writing if constructs, some debate arises between the scruffy and neat camps regarding commenting and what to do with missing else blocks in if statements. Specifically, some practitioners and instructors recommend the following:

EXAMPLE 6.1

Review of common indentation styles

```
Style 1:
    if (test)
    {
        statement-or-codeblock
        statement-or-codeblock
        etc.
    }


Style 2:
    if (test)  {
        statement-or-codeblock
        statement-or-codeblock
        etc.
    }


Style 3:
    if (test)
        {
        statement-or-codeblock
        statement-or-codeblock
        etc.
        }
```

FIGURE 6.3	If Construct With and Without Else Block

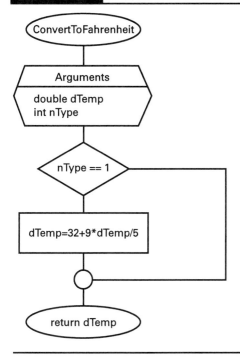

```
double ConvertToFahrenheit(double dTemp,int nType)
{
    if(nType==1) {
        dTemp=32+9*dTemp/5;
    }
    return dTemp;
}
```

```
double ConvertTemp(double dTemp,int nType)
{
    if(nType==1) {
        dTemp=32+9*dTemp/5;
    }
    else {
        dTemp=5*(dTemp-32)/9;
    }
    return dTemp;
}
```

- Commenting the beginning and end of each if construct to ensure that later readers of the code can identify the start and end of each construct—an issue that becomes important as if blocks are large and nested.
- Including an else block for every if construct, even if the else block is empty.

Applying these two rules, for example, the ConvertToFahrenheit C code on the left-hand side of Figure 6.1 would be rewritten, as it appears in Example 6.2.

The various positions on the appropriate way to write the if construct are summarized in Style Sidebar 6.1. One justification for these style recommendations is particularly relevant when indenting styles 2 or 3 are used (see Example 6.1), because the habit of putting semicolons at the end of each line can lead to the inadvertent writing of code such as:

STYLE SIDEBAR 6.1 | Writing the If Construct

Camp	Position	Justification
Super Scruffy	Just write the if statement.	Geez... the folks who invented these rules must have owned stock in a paper company.
Scruffy	Just write the if statement.	Comments in the code are nearly always unnecessary and blank blocks are confusing.
Middle Ground	Rewrite any code that is so confusing that such comments and empty if blocks are helpful to the reader.	Syntactical comments (i.e., comments about the mechanics of the code, and not about its intent) are patronizing to the reader and are often wrong, especially when seldom changed in maintenance. Unnecessary empty code blocks tend to produce confusion.
Neat	Start and end comments are useful in code walkthroughs and should be included.	Extra semicolons and other problems that lead to improper executions are most easily detected when the author's intent is clear.
Neat Freak	Commenting start and end and empty else blocks are mandatory.	Impure code suggests a deeper problem of impure thoughts and must be eradicated.

EXAMPLE 6.2

Writing if construct with empty else block using strict styling rules

```
double ConvertToFahrenheit(double dTemp,int nType)
{
    if(nType==1) { /* Start of temperature type if construct */
        dTemp=32+9*dTemp/5;
    }
else {
    } /*End of temperature type if construct */
    return dTemp;
}
```

```
if(nType==1);
{
    dTemp=32+9*dTemp/5;
}
```

In this code, the extra semicolon on the first line ends the if construct—so the block that follows is always executed.

An example of a simple function that can be implemented using an if block is the ToUpper function, which takes its argument (a character) and—if the character is a lowercase character—returns its uppercase equivalent (mimicking the C/C++ library toupper function). If the character is not an uppercase character, it is returned unchanged. The function is prototyped as follows:

```
char ToUpper(char val);
```

The argument val is the character to be transformed into uppercase, and the return value is the uppercase equivalent of the character (or the character itself). The function is flow-charted and its code equivalent presented in Figure 6.4.

The case change in the ToUpper function is accomplished as follows:

1. It relies on the fact that the ASCII code first codes all the uppercase characters together, in sequence, starting at 65, then codes all the lowercase characters together, in sequence, starting at 97.

2. The expression val-'a'+'A' uses this fact to accomplish a case change. For example, if the character were 'd', 'd'−'a' is 3 (100 − 97, using their ASCII codes). Similarly, because the letters are coded in sequence, 'A'+3 is equivalent to 'D' (65, the ASCII code for 'A', +3 is 68, which is the ASCII code for 'D').

We will use the library version of this function extensively when writing functions that are case insensitive.

TEST YOUR UNDERSTANDING 6.1:

The statement in the if construct of the ToUpper function could be written val=val−32. Explain why this alternative is true, and why writing val=val−'a'+'A' is probably preferable.

6.2.2: The if…else if…else Construct

Although we have treated the **case** construct as the best approach to implementing a multiway branch, the most general way is with a series of if statements, such as:

if (test0) statement-or-codeblock0
else if (test1) statement-or-codeblock1
else if (test2) statement-or-codeblock2
// …
else if (testN) statement-or-codeblockN
else statement-or-codeblockN+1

This construct performs a series of tests and performs the code block associated with the first test to be true, and then skips the remaining tests.

Although the **else if** appears as if might be a separate construct, actually it is not—the if…else construct itself is a form of statement. For example, the code:

if (test0) statement-or-codeblock0
else if (test1) statement-or-codeblock1
else if (test2) statement-or-codeblock2
else statement-or-codeblock3

is effectively the same as:

if (test0) {

FIGURE 6.4   ToUpper Function

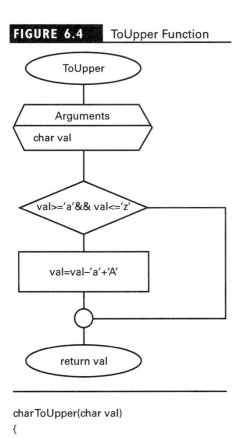

```
char ToUpper(char val)
{
    if(val>='a'&&val<='z') {
        val=val-'a'+'A';
    }
    return val;
}
```

```
            statement-or-codeblock0
    }
    else {
        if (test1) {
            statement-or-codeblock1
        }
        else {
            if (test2) {
                statement-or-codeblock2
            }
            else {
                statement-or-codeblock3
            }
        }
    }
}
```

which is just a standard nesting of code blocks.

An illustration of this construct, based on the temperature conversion with error checking introduced in Figure 5.13, is presented in Figure 6.5.

Stylistically, eliminating unnecessary blocks allows code to be rewritten in a more compact style, making it easy to skim. Doing so, however, runs the risk of confusion regarding what gets executed—especially when complex constructs, such as for loops, are not enclosed in braces. In the case of else if, the benefits of clarity probably outweigh the risks of confusion. An organization's coding standards (or lack thereof) are likely to be the deciding factor in determining how to code such constructs, however.

6.2: SECTION QUESTIONS

1. What are the advantages of placing empty else blocks in if constructs that only take action on the "true" case?
2. What happens if three of the conditions in a long if...else if...else if...etc. construct happen to be true?
3. How do you construct an if. . . else if. . . else if. . . construct so that code blocks associated with all true tests get performed?
4. What constitutes a legal "test expression" in an if construct?
5. What are the two most important factors to consider in deciding how to indent your code? What could dramatically change your choice?

6.3: THE SWITCH...CASE CONSTRUCT

The multiway branch in C/C++ is implemented with the switch...case construct. The construct is defined as follows:

```
switch (integer-value)
{
    case integer-constant1:
        statement-or-statements-or-empty1
    case integer-constant2:
        statement-or-statements-or-empty2
    case integer-constant3:
```

FIGURE 6.5   Same Flowchart Written with Nesting and Else If

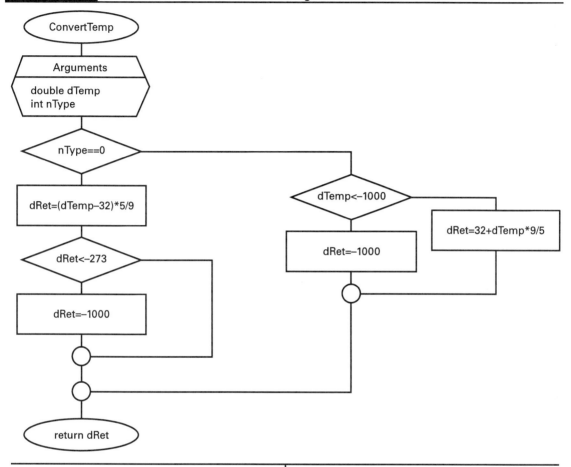

```
double ConvertTemp(double dTemp,int nType)
{
    if(nType==0) {
        dRet=(dTemp–32)*5/9;
        if(dRet<–273) {
            dRet=-1000;
        }
    }
    else {
        if(dTemp<–273) {
            dRet=-1000;
        }
        else {
            dRet=32+dTemp*9/5;
        }
    }
    return dRet;
} // Written with nesting (generated by FlowC)
```

```
double ConvertTemp(double dTemp,int nType)
{
    if(nType==0) {
        dRet=(dTemp–32)*5/9;
        if(dRet<–273) dRet=-1000;
    }
    else if(dTemp<–273)  dRet=-1000;
    else dRet=32+dTemp*9/5;
    return dRet;
}
// rewritten with unnecessary blocks removed
// using else if
```

```
                statement-or-statements-or-empty3
        // etc.
        case integer-constantN:
                statement-or-statements-or-emptyN
        default:
                statement-or-statements-or-emptyN+1
    }
```

Some comments:

- The *integer-value* can be any expression that evaluates to an integer, such as a variable, arithmetic expression or function call that returns an integer.
- The *integer-constant* associated with each case must be a value the compiler can determine, not an expression. Examples include:
  - Numbers, such as 17
  - Quoted constants, such as 'a' (same as writing 97) or '\t' (same as writing 9)
  - Hexadecimal numbers, such as 0x20 (same as writing 32)
  - Names created using a #define statement
  - Enumerated types (discussed in Chapter 3, Section 3.4.2)
- The statement-or-statements-or-empty can either be:
  - Individual or multiple semicolon terminated statements
  - A code block
  - Nothing at all—which has the effect of allowing multiple case labels to apply to the same collection of statements
- The *default* label is optional. If present, any **switch** value encountered that does not match any of the specific cases will go to the default block.

Unless a **break** statement (or return statement, or other statement that causes a code jump) is encountered, cases will fall through. In the case outline, for example, the case that matches integer-constant1 would do statement-or-statements-or-empty1, then statement-or-statements-or-empty2, then statement-or-statements-or-empty3, all the way through to statement-or-statements-or-emptyN+1.

6.3.1: The Structured Case Construct in C/C++

The C/C++ switch…case construct, used to its fullest level of flexibility, can produce pandemonium in code rivaling use of the vaunted goto statement. For this reason, a more structured approach to writing case statements is probably safer, and—in this book—we will always create case constructs according to the following framework:

```
        switch (integer-value)
        {
            case integer-constant1:
            {
                statement-or-statements-or-empty1
                break;
            }
            // for multiple cases doing the same thing
            case integer-constant2a:
            case integer-constant2b:
```

```
case integer-constant2c:
{
    statement-or-statements-or-empty2
    break;
}
// etc.
case integer-constantN:
{
    statement-or-statements-or-emptyN
    break;
}
default:
{
    statement-or-statements-or-emptyN+1
    break;
}
}
```

In this structure, the break statements prevent case fall through, and the explicit brace-delimited blocks after each case label help to reinforce the notion that each branch is distinct.

The construction of such a structured case construct is illustrated in Figure 6.6, which is derived from the currency conversion example developed in Chapter 5, Section 5.3.2.

6.3.2: Problems with Break

The flexibility provided by the C/C++ case construct implementation can lead to a number of common programming errors. The most common of these errors includes the following:

- Forgetting to put a break at the end of a structured case, causing unexpected case fall through.
- Using a break deeply nested within a case that is supposed to end a case and discovering it ends a loop nested within the case, or vice versa.

The second of these problems can be avoided by limiting the use of breaks to case constructs in all but the most extreme circumstances. The former is pretty much unavoidable, even among experienced programmers. The three most common reactions to discovering you have just lost three hours of your life—hours you will never see again—as a result of a forgotten break are: 1) laughing at yourself, because you've managed to nail yourself yet another time, 2) directing loud profanity at the case construct, the C/C++ programming language, along with anyone who had a hand in developing the language, and 3) perpetrating actual physical violence on your hardware. Of these responses, the third is not recommended.

As would be expected, some debate regarding what constitutes acceptable use of a case statement in a C/C++ exists between the scruffy and neat camps. Among the issues:

- Should case fall through be allowed?
- Must a default block be provided, even if it is not used?

The typical positions taken are summarized in Style Sidebar 6.2.

6.3: SECTION QUESTIONS

1. What is the only truly effective way to avoid leaving out break statements in C++ case constructs?

| FIGURE 6.6 | Currency Conversion Flowchart and Associated Structured Case Code |

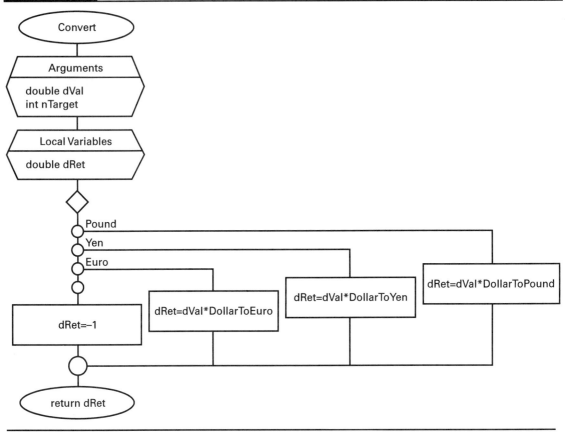

```
double Convert(double dVal,int nTarget)
{
      double dRet;
      switch()
      {
          case Pound:
          {
              dRet=dVal*DollarToPound;
              break;
          }
          case Yen:
          {
              dRet=dVal*DollarToYen;
              break;
          }
          case Euro:
          {
              dRet=dVal*DollarToEuro;
              break;
          }
          default:
          {
              dRet=-1;
          }
      }
      return dRet;
}
```

STYLE SIDEBAR 6.2	Writing the Case Construct

Camp	Position	Justification
Super Scruffy	Use any and all of the features C/C++ provides.	People should admire your cleverness when they read your code. The creative use of uncommented case fall through, in particular, will impress people who think you just forgot to put in the break.
Scruffy	Use all the features, but comment any use of case fall through.	Two weeks after you program a case statement with fall through, you'll have forgotten both *that* you did it and *why* you did it.
Middle Ground	Follow the guidelines for structured case statements, avoiding case fall through in all but the most extreme circumstances. The default label is required only where an actual default action needs to be performed.	Any benefits from case fall through tend to be minimal. Indeed, if lots of cases need to use the same code, a better approach is to write a function that performs the code. Even clever fall through that works when a case construct is initially constructed often fails when the code is modified. If fall through ever seems truly justified, it must be commented extensively.
Neat	Never use fall through and always include a default block.	You never go wrong by sticking as closely as possible to the structured programming model.
Neat Freak	Deep regret that the switch...case construct was ever implemented in C/C++.	The construct uses the break statement (which could encourage unstructured loops) and labels (which could seduce programmers into thinking about goto statements). Ignorance is the best defense against temptation.

2. Can any expression that evaluates to an integer be used after **case** labels in a case statement?

3. What is the relationship of an enumeration to a case construct?

4. Is there anywhere else in C++ that labels, like the **case** label, are used?

6.4: LOOPS

Two versions of the pure **while** loop are implemented in C++: the while loop, which tests before looping, and the do...while loop, which tests after at least one pass has been performed. In addition, a for loop is provided that extends the while loop with built-in initialization and iterator blocks.

6.4.1: The while Loop

The while loop construct is both simple and powerful. In C/C++ its structure is:

```
while(test) statement-or-codeblock
```

The while loop tests first, then performs the statement or associated code block that follows. The process continues until the test is false, at which time the loop ends. In addition:

- A break statement can also be used to cause the loop to end.
- A **continue** statement causes the loop to immediately go to the test and, if the test is true, start the next pass.

As was noted in Chapter 5, Section 5.4.3, use of statements such as break and continue to control loop behavior violates a number of premises of structured programming, and is likely to be controversial in many organizations.

Example While Loop   A flowchart for a simple while loop (introduced in Chapter 5) and corresponding C++ code are presented in Figure 6.7.

Common Looping Errors   A couple of errors are particularly common when using loops in C/C++:

- Prematurely terminating a loop with a semicolon
- Forgetting to increment a loop counter, leading to an infinite loop

The first of these errors is similar to what has already been observed for the if construct. For example, the code:

```
int x=1;
while(x<10);
{
    DisplayInteger(x);
    NewLine();
    x++;
}
```

would print a single integer, were it not for the fact that the statement:

```
while(x<10);
```

is an infinite loop and so the code path will never get to the DisplayInteger() statement. The reason is that the semicolon after the while completely disconnects the while loop from the block underneath it.

The typical C/C++ programmer gets so sensitized to such errant semicolons that he or she avoids them even where a semicolon would be legal. Thus, the following block of code:

```
char str[80]="Hello, World!";
int i=0;
while(str[i++]!=0);
```

which counts the number of characters in "Hello, World!" (including the NUL terminator), is legal, but would normally be rewritten:

```
char str[80]="Hello, World!";
int i=0;
while(str[i++]!=0){}
```

with the empty braces after the while serving the sole purpose of reminding the programmer that this particular while loop does not need a body.

TEST YOUR UNDERSTANDING 6.2:

Explain why the preceding block of code counts the characters in the string str (including the NUL terminator) and leaves their value in i.

FIGURE 6.7 Simple While Loop and Code

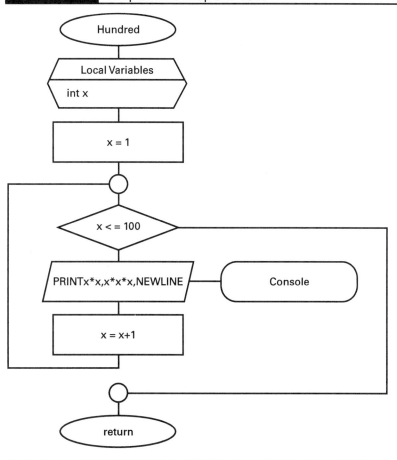

```
void Hundred()
{
    int x;
    x=1;
    while(x<=100) {
        cout<<x*x<<x*x*x<<endl;
        x=x+1;
    }
    return;
}
```

> Would this approach be a recommended way of writing such a loop if clarity is desired?

The other common problem in loops is to forget to do something in the loop that moves it toward its conclusion, such as incrementing a counter. For example, the code:

```
int x=1;
while(x<10)
{
    DisplayInteger(x);
    NewLine();
}
```

which is similar to an earlier example, will keep printing 1s forever because we haven't done anything to move X toward the >= 10 value that will cause the loop to end.

6.4.2: The do...while Loop

The C/C++ do...while construct takes the basic while construct and changes its position to the end of the loop. Its basic structure is:

```
do statement-or-codeblock
while (test);
```

Example do...while Loop   The while loop example of Figure 6.7 is rewritten as a do...while loop in Figure 6.8.

Usage of do...while Loops   Although the do...while loop is relatively simple, two specific reasons explain its infrequent use:

1. *Logical:* Most looping situations seem to benefit from having the test come first, rather than at the end of the first pass. Moreover, as you get used to writing loops that way, you tend to conceptualize your logic with the test first, even if the test coming afterwards is equally valid (as in the preceding example).

2. *Pragmatic:* Where code mixes while and do...while constructs, the fact that the while (test) components look the same, yet one almost never ends with a semicolon (while) and one must end with a semicolon (do...while) is a potential source of confusion. Indeed, many programmers choose to place the while clause after the closing bracket of the do block (as shown in Figure 6.8). This departure from normal indentation practices serves as a reminder that the while belongs to the end of a loop, and is not the start of a new loop.

Although C/C++ does not provide an UNTIL loop construct, the effect can be accomplished by negating the condition in the test of a do...while loop.

6.4.3: The for Loop

The C/C++ for loop is basically a while loop with initialization and iteration blocks. Its basic structure is as follows:

```
for (expression-list ; test ; expression-list) statement-or-
    codeblock
```

The two *expression-list* items are what make the for-loop unique. They make use of the comma operator, which allows a series of expressions to be placed on a single line—

FIGURE 6.8   Simple Do... While Loop and Code

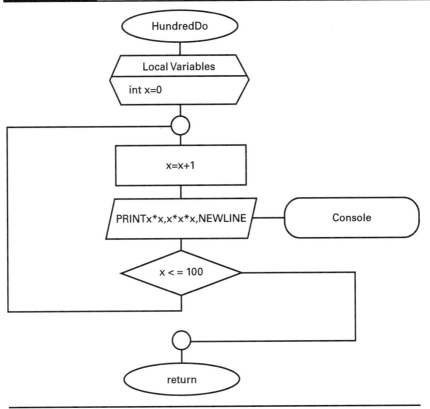

```
void HundredDo()
{
    int x=0;
    do {
        x=x+1;
        cout<<x*x<<x*x*x<<endl;
    } while (x<=100);
    return;
}
```

separated by commas—each of which is evaluated in sequence. Such expressions can, in turn, include assignments, function calls, and virtually anything that can be placed on the right-hand side of an assignment statement (as discussed in Chapter 4). In C++, these lists can also include variable declarations, a subject to be discussed shortly. In other words, almost anything except program constructs and preprocessor instructions can be placed in expression-lists. (The author has even heard of competitions to see how large a program could be constructed entirely within the two expression-lists of a single for loop. He suspects that the scruffy community was better represented in those competitions than the neat community.)

Neither expression-list need be present in a for loop. Thus, a for loop could be written in the form:

   for(;*test*;) *statement-or-codeblock*

making it precisely the same as a while loop. Usually, if one or more of the two expression-list blocks is empty, it is preferable—stylistically—to use a while loop.

FIGURE 6.9 Simple For Loop and Code

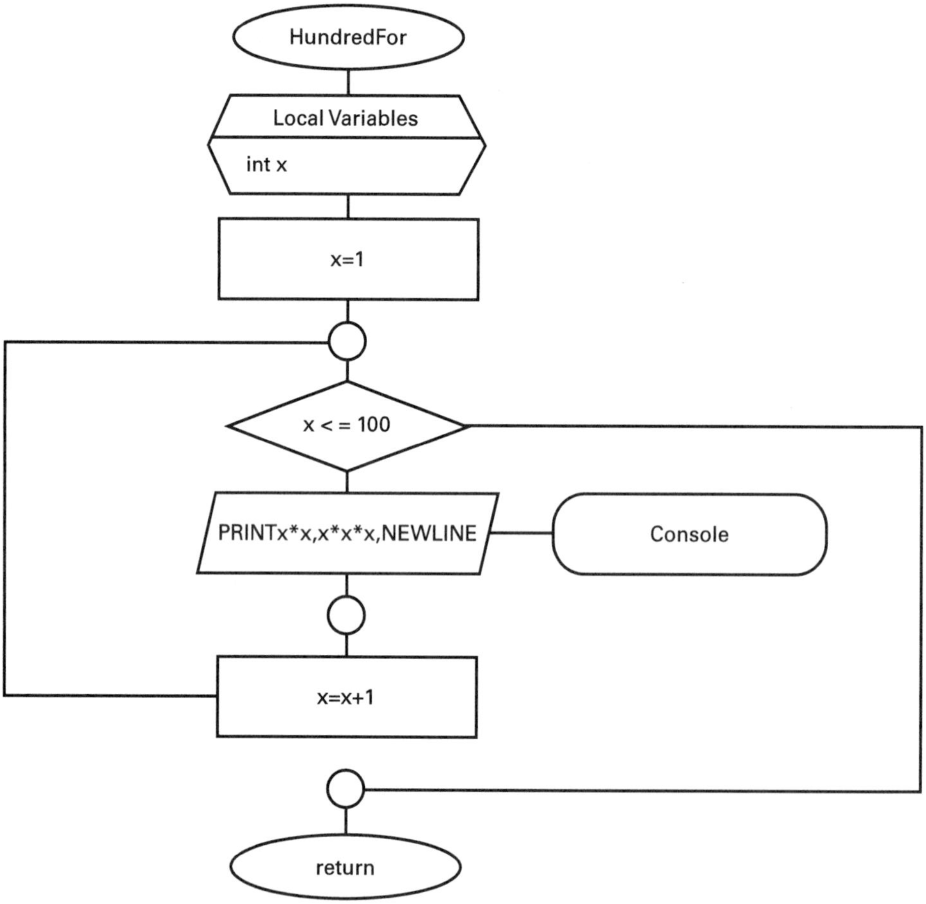

```
void HundredFor()
{
    int x;
    for(x=1;x<=100;x=x+1) {
        cout<<x*x<<x*x*x<<endl;
    }
    return;
}
```

Example for Loop   Figure 6.9 contains the Hundred example rewritten as a for loop.

Break and Continue Statements in for Loops   The break statement in the for loop works the same as it does in a while loop, causing the program to leave the loop. The presence of an iterator block, however, makes the behavior of the continue statement in for loops somewhat different:

- In the while loop, the continue statement leads directly to the test.
- In the for loop, the continue statement leads to the iterator block (i.e., the X=X+1 in the Figure 6.9 example) prior to the test.

Because structured programming style generally makes it preferable not to use either the break or continue statement regularly, this small difference between while and for loops is usually unimportant.

In-Depth: Declaration Scope in for Loop Initializer Blocks   Chapters 3 and 4, we noted that a major difference between C and C++, from the structured programming standpoint, is that C++ is much less restrictive than C regarding where variable declarations can be made. One consequence of this is that declarations can be made when initializing a for loop. For example, the code:

```
for(int i=1;i<=10;i++) cout << i << endl;
```

would be legal in C++ but not in C.

The ability to define variables in for loops is the type of capability that drives the neat community berserk, with considerable justification. One particularly serious problem with it is a widespread confusion with respect to variable scoping. Two schools of thought have always surrounded what the scope of a variable defined in a for loop initialization list should be:

- Conceptually, it would make sense to treat i as a variable whose existence was limited to the block within the for loop, which would mean its value could not be referenced after the loop was completed.
- Practically, it is often convenient to be able to look at the variable after the loop has ended, which would argue for a variable that continues to exist until the end of the code block containing the for loop. Under this scheme, code such as the following:

  ```
  for(int i=1;i<=10;i++) cout << i << endl;
  for(int i=11;i<=20;i++) cout << i << endl;
  ```

  would lead to a compiler error in the second for loop, because i was declared already. (Under the first school of thought, it would have been fine because the scope of the first i ends with the loop.)

So which approach was chosen? Both (unfortunately). In early versions of C++, the practical approach was preferred, and so variables remained in scope after the for loop. The C++ standard, however, deprecated that capability—and asserted that the conceptually cleaner limiting the local variable's scope to the for loop itself was the C++ standard (making it consistent with Java).

So which approach to for loops is supported by Visual Studio .NET? The answer is either, depending on what compiler switches you set. Such a situation is far from ideal for programmers and could require numerous revisions to old code.[1] For individuals just

---

[1] The author ruefully notes 274 local variable definitions within for loops were found in the FlowC code, found by searching files for "for(int".

starting out learning programming, it is obviously safer to stick with the C++ standard. And to hope that it doesn't change again.

6.4: SECTION QUESTIONS

1. Why might it be advantageous to write **while(test){}** instead of **while(test);** when writing an empty while loop?
2. What is the one behavior in a for loop that is hard to achieve in a while loop?
3. Give some examples of situations where it might be acceptable (to Middle Ground and scruffier, at least) to use continue statements in a loop?
4. What risks, if any, are present with break statements that are not present for continue statements?
5. What is the serious problem that can result from declaring variables in the initializer block of a for loop?

6.5: FLOWCHART TO CODE PROBLEMS

In this section we return to the flowchart samples of Chapter 5, Section 5.6, and present the code for each flowchart.

6.5.1: Strlen

The flowchart and code for the Strlen function, which counts the number of characters in a string prior to the NUL terminator, are presented in Figure 6.10.

6.5.2: Strcmp

The flowchart and code for the Strcmp function, which compares two strings character by character and returns an integer value indicating if they are equal (0 signifies they are equal, > 0 signifies the first is greater, < 0 signifies the second is greater), are presented in Figure 6.11.

6.5.3: Atoi

The Atoi function consisted of two parts, a helper function GetNonWhite() intended to skip over blanks, and the main Atoi function.

GetNonWhite   The flowchart and code for the GetNonWhite function, which returns the position of the first character greater than a space in a NUL-terminated string starting at a given position, are presented in Figure 6.12.

Atoi   The flowchart and code for the Atoi function, which returns the integer equivalent of a NUL-terminated string such as "125", are presented in Figure 6.13.

6.6: SAMPLE PROBLEMS

Having already done a number of examples involving transforming flowcharts to code, in this section we do some walkthroughs of taking C code, analyzing its logic, and transforming it into logical flowcharts.

| FIGURE 6.10 | Strlen Flowchart and Associated Code |

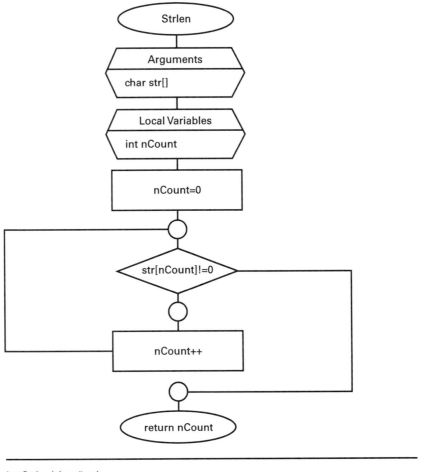

```
int Strlen(char *str)
{
    int nCount;
    for(nCount=0;str[nCount]!=0;nCount++) {}
    return nCount;
}
```

6.6.1: Strcat

Walkthrough available in Strcat.wmv

The Strcat function, modeled after the C/C++ library function *strcat*, takes a string—the second argument—and adds it to the end of another string, its first argument. It is proto-typed as follows:

```
void Strcat(char *s1,const char *s2);
```

FIGURE 6.11	Strcmp Flowchart and Associated Code

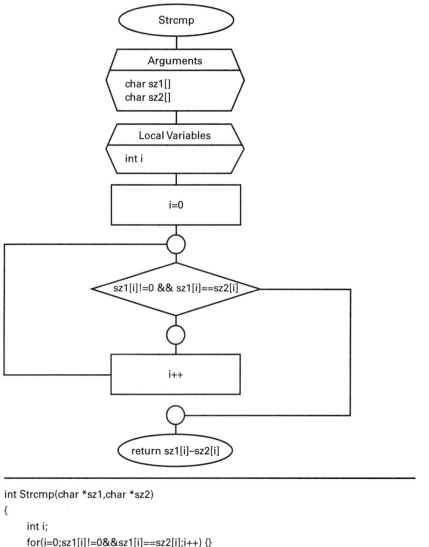

```
int Strcmp(char *sz1,char *sz2)
{
    int i;
    for(i=0;sz1[i]!=0&&sz1[i]==sz2[i];i++) {}
    return sz1[i]-sz2[i];
}
```

(the library version of strcat returns a pointer, however the return value is irrelevant to the function's normal use, so we won't bother).

Operation From a user's point of view, the operation of the construct is demonstrated by the following code:

```
char s1[20]="Hello,";
char s2[20]="World!";
```

FIGURE 6.12 GetNonWhite Function

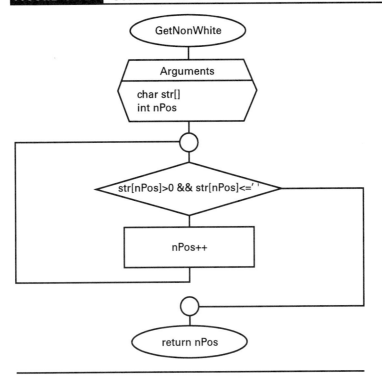

```
int GetNonWhite(char *str,int nPos)
{
    while(str[nPos]>0&&str[nPos]<=' ') {
        nPos++;
    }
    return nPos;
}
```

```
Strcat(s1,s2);
// If we look at s1, it will now contain "Hello,World!"
```

Implementation   This function can be implemented as follows:

```
void Strcat(char *s1,const char *s2)
{
    int i;
    int j;
    i=Strlen(s1);
    for(j=0;s2[j]!=0;j++) {
        s1[i+j]=s2[j];
    }
    s1[j+i]=0;
    return;
}
```

FIGURE 6.13 Atoi Flowchart and Code

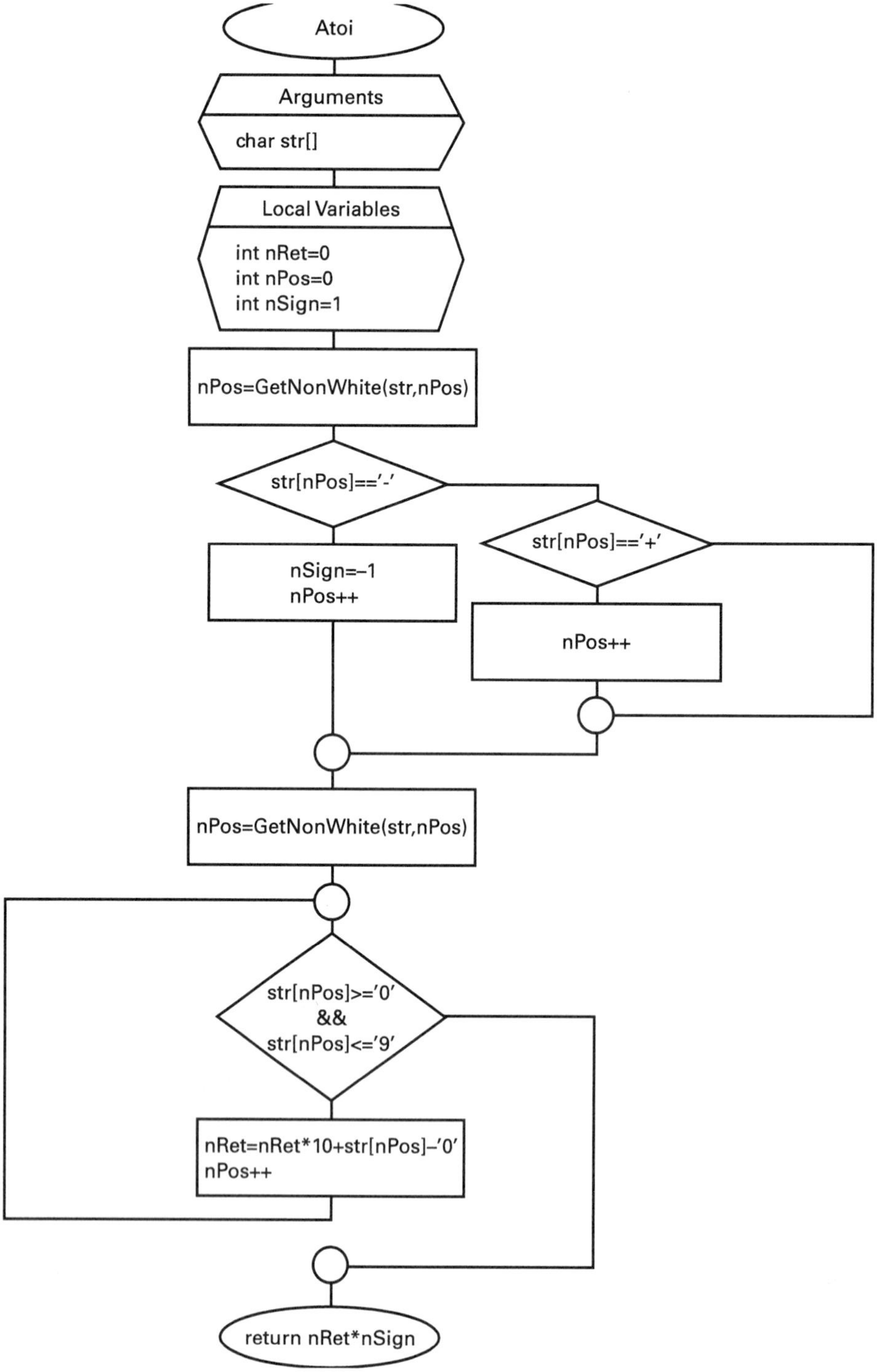

(Continues)

FIGURE 6.13   Atoi Flowchart and Code (Continued)

```
int Atoi(char *str)
{
    int nRet=0;
    int nPos=0;
    int nSign=1;
    nPos=GetNonWhite(str,nPos);
    if(str[nPos]=='-') {
        nSign=-1;
        nPos++;
    }
    else {
        if(str[nPos]=='+') {
            nPos++;
        }
    }
    nPos=GetNonWhite(str,nPos);
    while(str[nPos]>='0'&&str[nPos]<='9') {
        nRet=nRet*10+str[nPos]-'0';
        nPos++;
    }
    return nRet*nSign;
}
```

FIGURE 6.14   Position of s1[i], where i = Strlen(s1)

s1[]

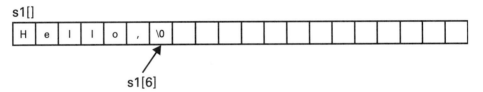

s1[6]

Discussion   Conceptually, we can break this function into three parts:

Part 1: Move to the end of s1

Although we could find the end of s1 with a loop, having already implemented our own Strlen function, it makes more sense just to call that function. Thus the line:

```
        i=Strlen(s1);
```

In our earlier example, the first string contained "Hello," so i becomes 6 when we call Strlen(). The position s1[i] is then illustrated in Figure 6.14, precisely on the NUL terminator that ends the string in s1.

Part 2: Move the characters from the second string to the end of the first

Here is the purpose of the loop. We use j to keep track of where we are in the second string, and i+j to identify our position in the first. Thus, the following loop will copy the characters over:

```
        for(j=0;s2[j]!=0;i++,j++) {
            s1[i]=s2[j];
        }
```

Continuing with our example, suppose we are on our third pass of the loop. At that point, j will equal 2 and i will continue to equal 6 because it is not changed by the loop. The resulting positions, and the character being moved are presented in Figure 6.15.

Part 3: Finish off the string

Unfortunately, as we copied the characters over from s2 to s1, we stopped upon hitting the NUL terminator in s2, as illustrated in Figure 6.16. As a result, we need to place a NUL terminator at the end of s1 to finish off the string. It is done with the statement:

```
s1[i]=0;
```

In the Figure 6.16 illustration, this statement would have the effect of placing a '\0' character in the gray cell in s1.

Flowchart of Strcat   The flowchart of the Strcat function is presented in Figure 6.17.

6.6.2: MainMenu function

Walkthrough available in Mainmenu.wmv

The MainMenu function allows us to illustrate how we can implement a simple menu using a case construct embedded within a while loop. We will be using this type of menu

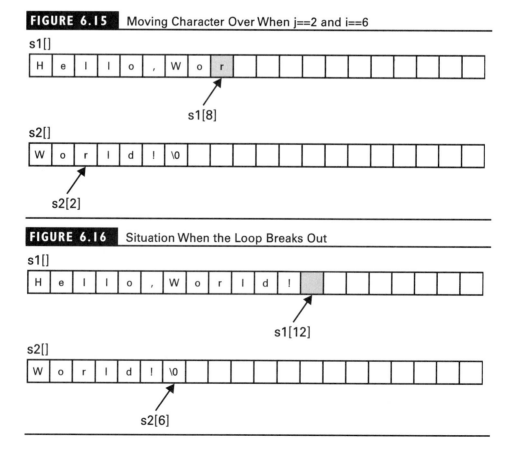

FIGURE 6.15   Moving Character Over When j==2 and i==6

s1[]

| H | e | l | l | o | , | W | o | r | | | | | | | | | | |

s1[8]

s2[]

| W | o | r | l | d | ! | \0 | | | | | | | | | | | | |

s2[2]

FIGURE 6.16   Situation When the Loop Breaks Out

s1[]

| H | e | l | l | o | , | W | o | r | l | d | ! | | | | | | | |

s1[12]

s2[]

| W | o | r | l | d | ! | \0 | | | | | | | | | | | | |

s2[6]

FIGURE 6.17   Strcat Flowchart

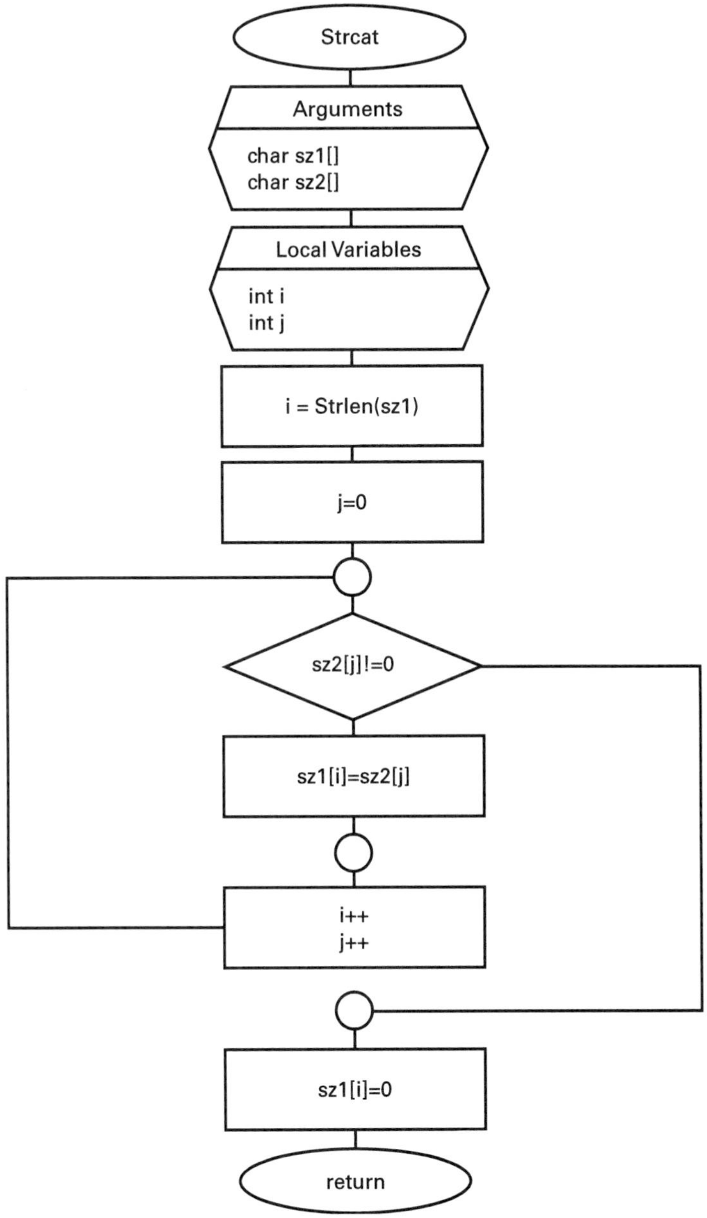

frequently in the rest of the text, because it allows us to insert test code for many functions that we might want to test.

Operation   The MainMenu function takes no arguments and returns no value. (Indeed, most of the time when we implement a menu, we won't write a separate function, but instead will place the code described here in main.)

The function does three basic things:

1. It prints out a menu of user options.
2. It reads a line of text from the user, then uses the first letter of that line as the option code.
3. It routes the code, using a case statement, using the option key.

Because the MainMenu provided here is intended to be a skeleton, rather than a real application, only the Quit (i.e., 'q') option is actually implemented. The framework for options 'A' and 'B' has been put in place, however, with comments showing where code would normally go. Additional options can easily be added by following this framework.

Implementation   The code for the MainMenu function is provided here:

```
void MainMenu()
{
    int nChar;
    int szIn[256];
    int nEnd=0;
    while(nEnd==0) {
        cout<<"A.ToDo"<<endl;
        cout<<"B.ToDo"<<endl;
        cout<<"Q.Quit"<<endl;
        cin.getline(szIn,80);
        nChar=szIn[0];
        switch()
        {
            case 'A':
            case 'a':
            {
                //Put code here;
                break;
            }
            case 'B':
            case 'b':
            {
                //Put code here;
                break;
            }
            case 'Q':
            case 'q':
            {
                nEnd=1;
                break;
            }
            default:
            {
                cout<<"Illegal!"<<endl;
            }
        }
    }
    return;
}
```

Operation   The operation of the function proceeds as follows:

1.   Before entering the main loop, a variable nEnd is initialized to zero.
2.   We enter a while loop that will keep looping as long as nEnd remains equal to zero.
3.   Within the while loop:
     a.   A menu of options is displayed, using a series of cout<< statements.
     b.   The user is prompted to enter an option, which is placed in the array szIn[].
     c.   The first character of szIn (i.e., the first character in the user's option string) is assigned to nChar.
     d.   A case construct, switching on nChar, is used to route the option. Upper and lowercase labels are used for each option.
4.   In the event the user chooses the option 'Q' (or 'q'), the case construct assigns nEnd to 1, which will cause the while loop to end.
5.   In the event the user chooses an option that does not exist, the default case is to print "Illegal" on the screen.

Flowchart   A flowchart for the MainMenu function is presented in Figure 6.18. As mentioned earlier, this particular model will be used for implementing many of the menus used for testing functions in future chapters. The reader is also encouraged to modify the function during the course of writing code in some of the sample questions at the end of this chapter.

6.6.3: In Depth: Int2String Function

Walkthrough available in Int2String.wmv

The Int2String() function takes an integer variable and creates its character string representation. For example, it would take the integer 125 and place the characters '1', '2', '5', '\0' into an array (the last character being the NUL terminator that ends the string). The function is prototyped as follows:

```
void Int2String(char szNum[],int nVal);
```

where str[] is the string array that we will place our characters into and nVal is the integer that we will be converting.

Operation   The Int2String function must be passed an array with sufficient room to hold the resulting string. It could be called as follows:

```
char num[20];
Int2String(num,125);
// contents of num[] would now be "125" (with a NUL termina-
tor at the end)
```

The function is essentially the reverse of the Atoi function already covered.

Implementation   The Int2String function implements the remainder method for converting an integer from one base to another, introduced in Chapter 3, Section 3.2.1. It could be implemented in C/C++ as follows:

```
void Int2String(char *szNum,int nVal)
{
```

FIGURE 6.18 Flowchart of Menu Skeleton

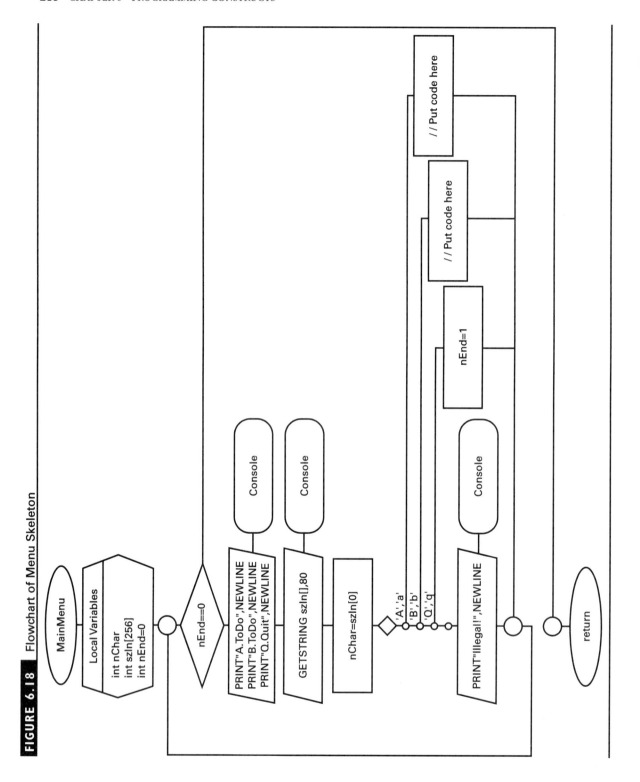

```
            char szN[80];
            int nDig=0;
            int nSign=1;
            if(nVal<0) {
                nSign=-1;
                nVal=-1*nVal;
            }
            do {
                szN[nDig]=nVal%10+'0';
                nVal=nVal/10;
                nDig++;
            } while (nVal>0);
            if(nSign<0) {
                szN[nDig]='-';
                nDig++;
            }
            szN[nDig]=0;
            Reverse(szNum,szN);
            return;
        }
```

As you may recall, the remainder method determines digits from right to left. As a consequence, it is convenient to define a helper function, Reverse(), that reverses the characters after we have assembled them. It is defined as follows:

```
        void Reverse(char *szTo,char *szFrom)
        {
            int nLen;
            int i;
            nLen=Strlen(szFrom);
            for(i=0;i<nLen;i++) {
                szTo[i]=szFrom[nLen-i-1];
            }
            szTo[nLen]=0;
            return;
        }
```

Discussion   *Reverse:* We begin by looking at Reverse(), which is used at the very end of Int2String to reverse the digits. For example:

```
        char szFrom[10]="521-";
        char szTo[10];
        Reverse(szTo,szFrom);
        // Will place "-125" in szTo[]
```

The function operates similarly to Strcat, in that we maintain different positions in different arrays. The function works as follows:

■   The variable nLen is set to the length of the szFrom string that we are reversing.

■   We enter a loop with a counter variable i. The loop proceeds as follows:

　■   A character at position nLen-i-1 in szFrom is placed at position i in szTo. Notice that when i is 0, this places us at the character directly in front of the NUL terminator in szFrom (i.e., at position nLen-1, the last actual character), while it puts us at the beginning of szTo.

- ▦ i is incremented. The effect of incrementing i is to move our position in szTo one character to the right (toward the end), while our position in szFrom is moved one character to the left (toward the beginning).

- ▦ When i=nLen, we have reversed the characters, and break out of the loop.

- ■ We place a 0 (NUL terminator) at the position i (which is equal to nLen when we break out of the loop) to terminate the string.

- ■ We return, because the function is complete.

TEST YOUR UNDERSTANDING 6.3:

What would happen if we changed the szFrom[nLen-i-1] in the function to szFrom[nLen-i], and changed the loop test to i<=nLen, so we could reverse all the characters, including the NUL terminator?

Int2String: As already noted, the function is essentially an implementation of the remainder method for switching between bases. However, one problem with the remainder method needs to be addressed: the method only works on positive numbers. For this reason, the function works as follows:

- ■ Local variables are declared as follows:

  - ▦ char szN[80], to hold our raw (i.e., reversed) number

  - ▦ int nDig, to keep track of the current digit we are processing

  - ▦ int nSign, which is initialized to 1 (indicating a positive integer)

- ■ We determine whether the argument nVal is negative using an if construct with no else block. If it is, we:

  - ▦ Set nSign to –1, flagging the fact we have a negative number.

  - ▦ Multiply nVal by –1, making it positive. Thus nVal of –125 becomes +125.

- ■ We implement the remainder method in the do…while loop—chosen because we want at least one digit stored, even if nVal is 0. Within the loop, we store each remainder—at position nDig in szN[]—as an ASCII digit by adding '0' (48) to it. (See the Atoi function, which works in the reverse direction, for the explanation.) We then increment nDig to position us on the next digit. Some of the key variables in the loop, for nVal starting at 125, are summarized in Table 6.1.

- ■ Once nVal==0, we break out of the loop because we have completed the remainder method.

- ■ We then check nSign, appending a '–' (minus sign) to our string in szN[] and incrementing nDig, which will cause our number to be preceded by a minus sign after the reversal.

TABLE 6.1			Key Values in Int2String Loop				
nVal Starting Pass	**nVal %10**	**nDig Starting Pass**	**szN[nDig] Before nDig++**	**szN[] at Test**	**nVal at Test**	**nDig at Test**
125	5	0	'5'	"5"	12	1
12	2	1	'2'	"52"	1	2
1	1	2	'1'	"521"	0 (ends)	3

- We place a 0 (NUL terminator) at position nDig of szN[], to end the string.
- We call Reverse() to reverse the string, placing the reversed string in szNum, our original argument.

FIGURE 6.19 Flowchart of Reverse Function

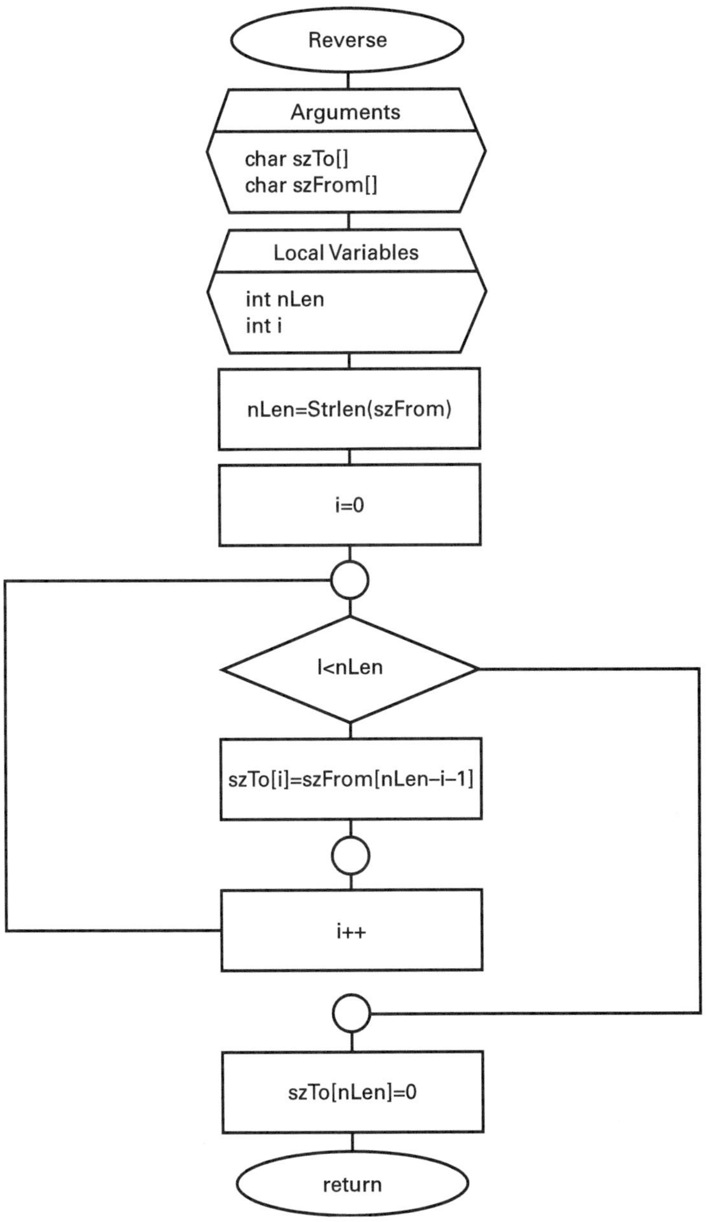

TEST YOUR UNDERSTANDING 6.4:

The size of the szN[] array was chosen to be 80 purely out of laziness. Will it always be long enough? What would be the minimum length required to guarantee that all values for nVal could be contained? Would that change if we modified the function to generate character strings in different bases (e.g., hexadecimal, octal, binary)?

Flowcharts The flowchart for Reverse() is presented in Figure 6.19. The flowchart for Int2String is presented in Figure 6.20.

FIGURE 6.20 Flowchart of Int2String

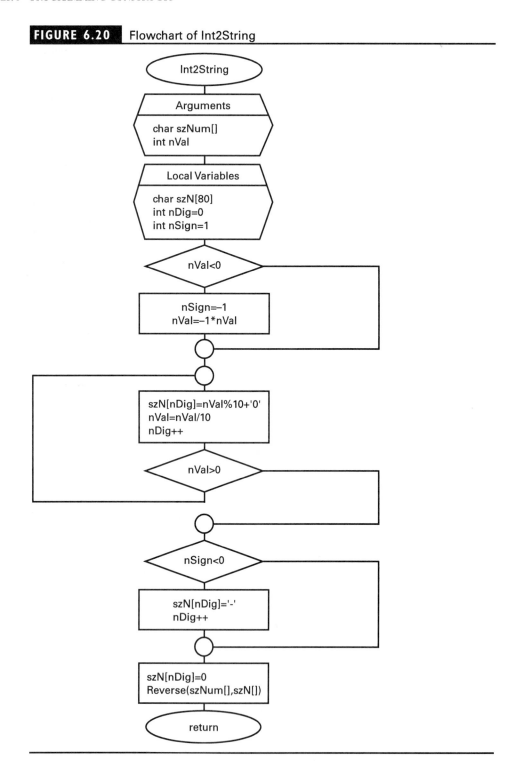

6.7: REVIEW AND QUESTIONS

6.7.1: REVIEW

Symbol	C/C++ Syntax

	Function:
	
	return-type **FunctionName**(*arg-list*)
	{
	    // code block
	    return *expr-matching-return-type;*
	}
	
	Notes:
	• **return** statements may appear anywhere in the function
	• ***arg-list*** is set of declarations separated by commas

	If construct: **if** (*test-expr*) *if-code-block* ; **else if** (*test-expr*) *else-if-code-block;* **else** *else-code-block;* Notes: • More than one **else if** test may be provided • Only **if** portion of construct is required

	Case construct:
	
	switch (*integer-expr*)
	{
	    case *int-const1:* {
	        // code block
	        break;
	    }
	    case *int-const2:*
	    case *int-const3:* {
	        // code block
	        break;
	    }
	    default: {
	        // code block
	    }
	}
	
	Notes:
	• If **break** (or **return**) not included, case fall through will occur
	• Multiple case labels may be associated with a single code block
	• **default** block is optional

(Continues)

Symbol	C/C++ Syntax

	while loop:
	
	while (*test-expr*) {
	    // code block
	}
	
	Notes:
	• **break:** sends control to the bottom node, breaking out of the loop
	• **continue:** jumps to top, beginning next pass
	• code block must change some value related to *test-expr* or infinite loop will occur (unless **break** is present)

	for loop:
	
	for(*initialize-code* ; *test-expr* ; *iterator-code*) {
	    // code block
	}
	
	Notes:
	• *initialize-code* is a comma-separated list of statements that are executed once, before the loop begins
	• *iterator-code* is a comma-separated list of statements that gets executed after the code block in each iteration
	• **break:** sends control out of the loop, bypassing *test-expr* and *iterator-code*
	• **continue:** sends control to *iterator-code* in preparation for next iteration of the loop

	do...while loop:
	
	do {
	    // code block
	} **while** (*test-expr*);
	
	Notes:
	• **break:** breaks out of the loop without performing any further test
	• **continue:** jumps to *test-expr* at the bottom, beginning next pass
	• code block is always executed at least once
	• code block must change some value related to *test-expr* or infinite loop will occur (unless **break** is present)

6.7.2: GLOSSARY

break A statement indicating the end of a loop or the end of a particular block in a multibranch construct

case A label, followed by an integer constant, used to identify where control should pass in switch block

continue A statement indicating that the next iteration of a loop should begin immediately, skipping the remainder of a code block

do A keyword signifying the beginning of a do...while loop, where the loop test is at the end of the loop

else A keyword signifying the start of a code block to be performed if no tests in an **if** construct are true

else if A pair of keywords specifying an incremental test in an **if** construct

for A keyword specifying the beginning of a test-first loop with an initializer block of statements performed

before entering the loop and an iterator block, performed after each pass

if A keyword, followed by a parenthesized test, signifying the start of an **if** construct

return A keyword specifying the completion of the function that contains it; if a function return type is specified, an expression compatible with that type must follow the keyword

switch A keyword signifying the outer boundaries of a case construct, followed by a parenthesized integer expression

while A keyword followed by a test expression that controls whether a loop continues repeating; **while** loops test before repeating a code block, whereas **do...while** loops test after the repeated code block has been done once

6.7.3: QUESTIONS

1. *MainMenu:* Create your own main menu function, modeled after the function described in Section 6.6.2 that can be used to test your functions. From this point on in the text, it is assumed that you will set up such a function, as needed, to conduct tests.

2. *FindChar:* Write and test a function called FindChar() that is modeled after the flowchart that follows on page 226. The function should look for a character (cChar) in a string (str[]) and return the position where it was found (of –1 if not found).

3. *CountColumns:* Write and test a function called CountColumns(), modeled after the flowchart on page 227, that estimates the width of a text string by adding 8 every time a tab character is encountered.

4. *CountColumnsExt:* Write and test a more sophisticated version of CountColumns() function, called CountColumnsExt(), which—instead of adding 8 for every tab—adds the number of characters to the next tab stop. For the purposes of this exercise, it may be assumed that tab stops occur at positions 8, 16, 24, 32, etc. (*Hint*: The % operator can be especially helpful here.)

5. *SumDigits:* Write and test a function called SumDigits, modeled after the flowchart on page 228, that sums every digit (i.e., character '0' through '9') encountered in a string—no matter what its position.

In-Depth Questions

6. *Int2OctalString:* Modify and test the Int2String function presented in Section 6.6.3 so it would produce strings

in octal (base 8). *Hint:* Look back at the remainder method and you will find it is a relatively trivial matter!

7. *Int2HexString:* Modify and test the Int2String function presented in Section 6.6.3 so it would produce strings in hexadecimal. *Hint:* This function is a bit harder than the Int2OctalString function, but is still relatively simple—the key difference is making sure you actually create hex digits.

8. *Int2BaseString:* Modify and test the Int2String function so it takes a third argument, the base of the number you want to display. The new prototype would be:

```
void Int2BaseString(char szNum[],
    int nVal,int nBase);
```

where nBase is a number between 2 and 36. *Hint:* Figuring out why nBase is limited to numbers less than or equal to 36 is a good starting point in solving this problem.

9. *Real2String:* Create and test a version of the Int2String function that displays real numbers as decimal numbers. The prototype of this function should be:

```
void Real2String(char szNum[],
    double dVal,int nPrecision);
```

where szNum is the location the resulting number should be placed, dVal is the double to be converted, and nPrecision is the number of decimal places. You may assume that it only needs to work for values of dVal between –2 billion and +2 billion. *Hint:* This function can be excruciatingly hard to write, or very easy, depending on how you approach it. The easy way

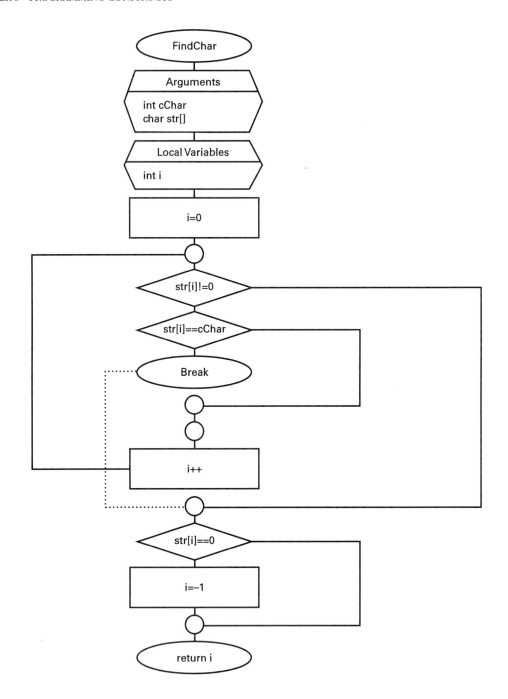

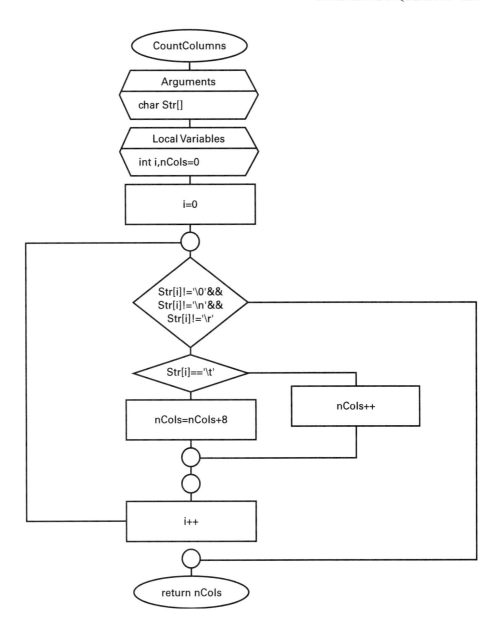

is to look at it as a problem of writing out two integers—one to the left of the decimal point, and one to the right of it:

a. The part on the left of the decimal point is easy (all you need to do is assign dVal to an integer). Get it working first!

b. The part to the right isn't that much harder, once you figure out how to use nPrecision.

c. Once you have both parts, tack a decimal point on the end of the left-hand part, then concatenate them (e.g., using Strcat).

Once you finish this function, you should have a pretty good idea how the formatting capabilities of sprintf work.

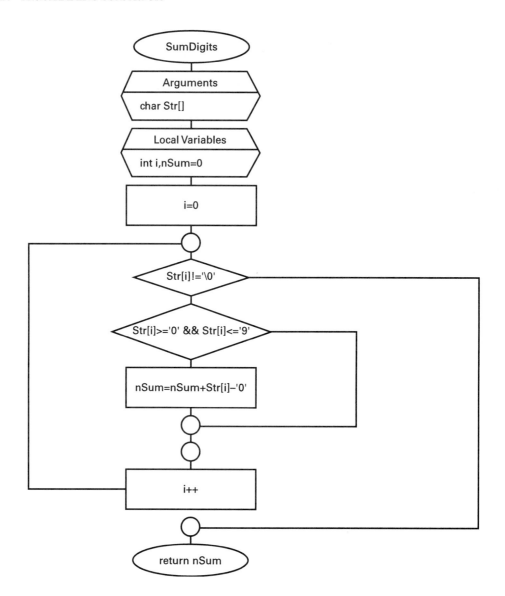

Elementary String Library Functions

EXECUTIVE SUMMARY

Chapter 7 introduces a number of useful functions in the standard C/C++ libraries, particularly relating to NUL terminated strings. In many languages, specific functions are considered part of the language. In C/C++, functions are normally added to the language in the form of libraries. The specific functions we cover in this chapter are functions that are used so commonly that it is difficult to write nontrivial programs without them.

The chapter begins with an explanation of the role played by libraries in C/C++ and a survey of the types of standard libraries available in C++. It then introduces a series of string-related functions—versions of many of which were already introduced in earlier chapters. We then turn to in-depth coverage of formatted console output using the **printf** family of functions. The use of the library function **sprintf** as a bridge between output techniques of C and C++ languages is discussed. Finally, some practice problem walkthroughs are presented.

LEARNING OBJECTIVES

Upon completing this chapter, you should be able to:

- Explain how a library-oriented language differs from other types of languages
- Describe the range of standard C/C++ libraries
- Understand the operation and implementation of a number of common string functions
- Explain the formatting argument in the printf function
- Explain how the sprintf function works, and how it can be used to perform line-oriented output in C++
- Discuss various data conversion functions, and explain why they are needed
- Explain the operation of a series of functions presented at the end of the chapter
- Apply the functions discussed in the chapter to programming situations

7.1: OVERVIEW OF C/C++ LIBRARIES

C and C++ were designed as library-oriented languages. Most early languages, such as FORTRAN and BASIC, incorporated a large collection of language-specific functions as part of their implementation. When

C was developed, however, the decision was made to leave such functions out of the language, making the language compact. Having made this design decision, a series of standard libraries were implemented to supplement the language.

In this section, we consider the practical implications of using C/C++ libraries and survey the range of these libraries. We also discuss, briefly, the difference between C function libraries (which also tend to be used in C++) and C++ **class libraries.**

7.1.1: What Are Libraries?

Before answering the question "What types of standard libraries does C++ provide?" we need to address the more basic question: "What are libraries?" Secondarily, it is useful to ask a more motivational question: "Why should we, as programmers, care?"

Nature of Libraries   In the programming context, *a library is a collection of functions and data definitions designed to be incorporated into other programs.* In today's programming environments, C/C++ libraries can be delivered in a variety of ways:

- *Full source code:* Where a library comes with full source code, all files needed to prototype and define functions (e.g., .h, .c, .cpp, .asm, etc.) are included with the library. An example of such a library is the SimpleIO files, used throughout the book to maintain C/C++ compatibility.
- *Object code:* Necessary header files are provided, but the actual function implementation is provided in object code form—without source code. A special file type, .lib files, allows many .obj files to be combined into a single file that can then be accessed by the linker.
- *Dynamic component libraries:* Mainly used in advanced programming, libraries can be supplied in the form of executable components (e.g., ActiveX controls) that can generate their own header files and are linked while the program is running, instead of using a linker. These types of libraries are beyond the scope of this text.

For several reasons, object code libraries might be supplied instead of full source libraries:

- *Proprietary concerns:* Once a programmer has been provided with a library's source code, it becomes much easier for the programmer to incorporate all or part of the library into applications without detection (and, therefore, without paying royalties). Source code also makes it much easier to understand how proprietary technologies work, when compared with trying to disassemble millions of lines of source code. Microsoft, for example, has steadfastly refused to open up the full source code for the Windows operating system, precisely for this reason.
- *Delivery concerns:* Many libraries are written in a mix of languages using a variety of tools. Delivery of source code may be impractical based on the fact that users may not have the required tools.
- *Revenue generation:* Many vendors will deliver library source code, but only for a higher price than would be charged for object libraries.

The main benefit of having library source code is that it facilitates debugging and understanding. For example, when library source code is available, the programmer can step into library functions using the debugger just as he or she does with his or her own functions. This capability often proves to be useful when code fails due to an exception or assertion failure within the library that occurs as a result of embedded error handling code. Library source can also help the skilled programmer understand what a library function actually does—when the documentation is limited or unclear. Finally, having library source can help an expert programmer identify problems that were caused by the library itself, rather than by his or her code. Unfortunately, such concerns about possible library defects are often justified when using third-party libraries.

In the case of the standard C libraries, proprietary concerns are not normally the issue. As a result, Microsoft supplies the source for these libraries with its professional versions. Source for the standard C libraries is often not installed, however, for student versions. As a consequence, problems sometimes occur when students try to step into library function—accidentally or on purpose.

7.1.2: C++ Function Libraries

The libraries of functions available in C++ are essentially the same as the libraries specified by the ANSI standard for C. They are summarized in Table 7.1.

In this text, we will concentrate on functions contained in stdlib.h and string.h. The remaining libraries are rarely used in C++, and their omission will have little impact on our discussions of structured programming.

C++ Class Libraries

Because C++ supports the C standard libraries, most of the functions presented in this text will prove useful in C++ as well as C. C++, however, has its own extensive set of standard libraries, such as the *standard template library,* that provides useful classes (a class in an object-type) in support of OOP. We begin introducing these classes in the final part of the text.

7.1: SECTION QUESTIONS

1. Why does a library-oriented language often seem more flexible than a language with specified built-in functions? What is a disadvantage of the library-oriented language?

2. What are the two key advantages of acquiring libraries with source code?

3. Does it make sense to customize library source code so it better fits your needs?

4. Why do you suppose that advanced capabilities—such as graphics and Internet capability—are not supported by C/C++ standard libraries?

5. If the focus of the book is C++, why do we cover the C standard libraries?

7.2: STRING MANIPULATION AND CONVERSION FUNCTIONS

String-related functions are mainly prototyped in *string.h* in the C standard library.

One of the things that makes C++ relatively unique is that many of its library functions, and nearly all of the functions prototyped in string.h, can be implemented using the language itself. For that reason, we will provide code that could be used to implement each function, and discuss the code for each of the functions we present.

TABLE 7.1 Standard C Libraries and Their Usage

Header	Usage	Description of Library Contents
asset.h	Used only in debugging	Contains assert macro, used to test for code problems and halt a program if the test fails (in debug mode)
ctype.h	Commonly used	Contains character-related functions, such as toupper
errno.h	Rarely used	Defines a series of constants used in systemwide error calls
float.h	Rarely used	Defines a series of implementation-based limit constants for floating point numbers, which can be used to determine information such as number of digits of precision
limits.h	Sometimes used	Defines a series of implementation-based limit constants for integer values, which can be used to determine information such as the number of bits in a character and the maximum value for a signed integer
locale.h	Rarely used	Defines structures and constants used for localization routines (e.g., currency and decimal conventions); such definitions are particularly useful in OS implementation uses of C
math.h	Commonly used	Contains all the mathematical functions provided by C
setjmp.h	Very rarely used	Support for nonlocal jumps—rarely required in C programs
signal.h	Very rarely used	Provides mechanisms for handling abnormal signals (e.g., execution failure signals) that occur during execution
stdarg.h	Sometimes used	Provides structures and macros for handling variable-argument functions
stddef.h	Rarely used	Contains definitions and typedefs for names such as size_t; many of these names are also defined in other header files, such as string.h
stdio.h	Generally not used in C++	Contains all C console and stream-based I/O functions and related structure definitions
stdlib.h	Commonly used	Contains a wide range of character-to-number conversion functions, memory management functions, and OS-related functions
string.h	Commonly used	Contains functions for string and memory manipulation
time.h	Commonly used	Contains date and time functions, along with structures for holding date/time information

7.2.1: strlen

size_t strlen(const char str[]);

Arguments	str—the string whose length is to be found
Return Value	Length of the string (see Chapter 3, Section 3.4.2, for discussion of size_t)
Purpose	Computes the number of characters in a string, not including the NUL terminator
Other Comments	Function usage and implementation discussed in Chapter 5, Section 5.6.1, and Chapter 6, Section 6.5.1.

7.2.2: strcpy

Walkthrough available in Strcpy.wmv

char *strcpy(char dest[],const char src[]);	
Arguments	dest – address of array that will hold the copied character src – address of the array holding the string to be copied
Return Value	Address of destination array (although the return value is almost never used)
Purpose	Copies a string from one array into another array, and acts as a substitute for the assignment operator (=) for strings
Other Comments	Perhaps the most commonly used of C functions—a version that only copies over a limited number of characters, strncpy, is provided as an exercise at the end of the chapter

The strcpy() function is used to copy a NUL terminated string from one array to another. The function is commonly used in C (and even in C++) because NUL terminated strings have no assignment operator.

In using the function, it is important to keep two things in mind:

- The src[] and dest[] arrays must not overlap. If they do, the function's behavior is "undefined" (never a good thing).
- The dest[] array must be large enough to hold the number of bytes in the src[] string. Because C++ won't check for array boundaries, if the string in src[] is too large, it will overflow the dest[] buffer and corrupt whatever memory follows.

A flowchart of the Strcpy() function and sample of how the strcpy function could be implemented is presented in Figure 7.1 and Example 7.1. (The name was altered to Strcpy() to prevent confusion with the actual library function.)

The function is about as simple as a C++ function can get. It has two basic parts:

1. A for loop copies individual characters from src to dest until the NUL terminator in src is encountered. The line src[i]!=0 could also be written src[i]!='\0' or src[i]!=0x00. On the other hand, src[i]!='0' would definitely *not* work!

2. A NUL terminator is placed at the end of the string in dest[], because we broke out of the for loop before that character was moved over.

TEST YOUR UNDERSTANDING 7.1:

In addition to the alternative tests for the NUL terminator listed in part (1) of the previous list, the for construct could have been written:

```
for(i=0;src[i];i++) {
    dest[i]=src[i];
}
```

Explain why this alternative would work. Why would it probably be preferable to write the test in the original form (or using one of the two alternatives provided)?

In-Depth: The Problem of Overlap The apparent simplicity of strcpy hides two potentially serious problems that were mentioned when we described the function. The

FIGURE 7.1 Sample Strcpy Flowchart

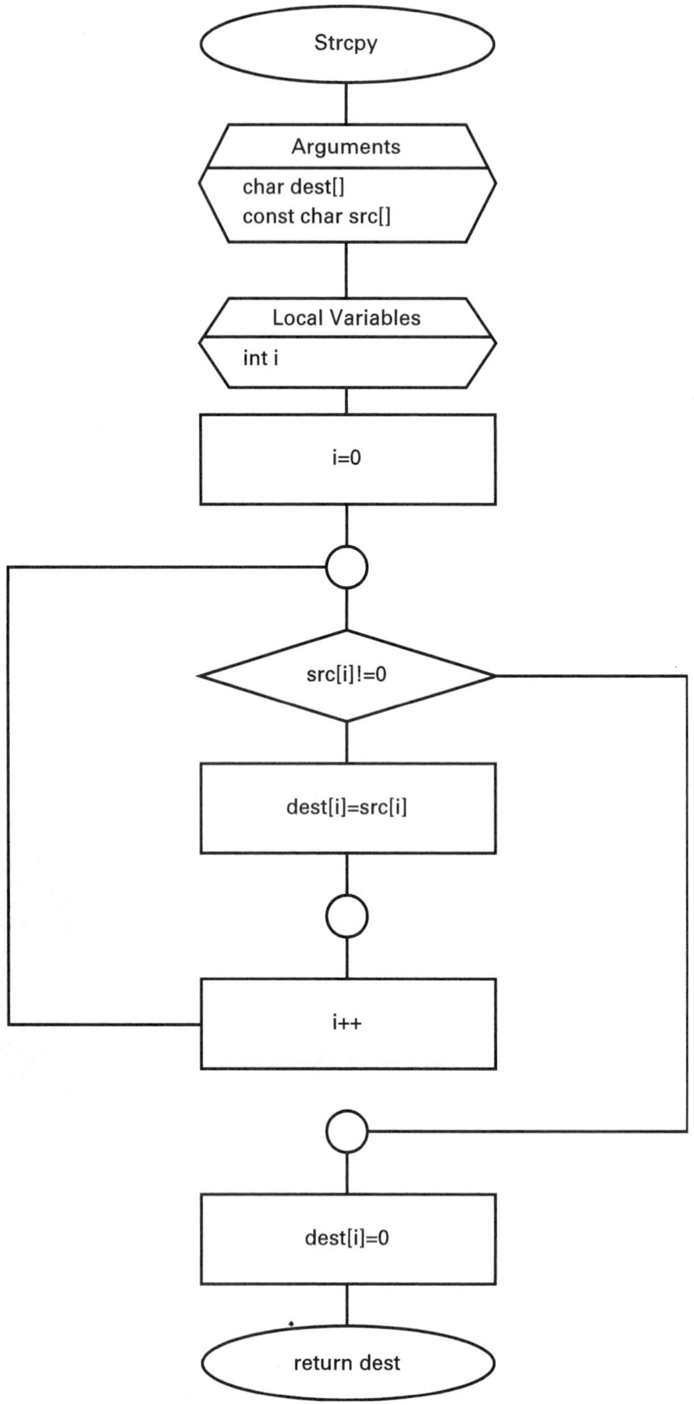

EXAMPLE 7.1

Sample implementation of strcpy() library function

```
char *Strcpy(char dest[],const char src[])
{
    int i;
    for(i=0;src[i]!=0;i++) {
        dest[i]=src[i];
    }
    dest[i]=0;
    return dest;
}
```

---

first, that the dest array must be large enough to hold the src string, should be self-explanatory by now. The second, the problem of the src[] and dest[] arrays overlapping, warrants additional discussion.

The first question, of course, is why would you ever overlap your source and destination in a string copy? Actually, it's pretty easy to come up with plausible examples. For example:

- When you type in insert mode in your word processor, each time you add a character, all the characters in the document to the right of your insertion point need to be moved one position higher in memory to make room for the new character.

- On the other hand, when you press the delete key, all the characters to the right of the deletion point need to be moved one position lower.

These two actions are illustrated in Figure 7.2. Thus, it would probably be nice if the strcpy() function were able to work with overlapping memory.

FIGURE 7.2   Overlapping src[] and dst[] in Insertion and Deletion

Add extra 'l' to string:

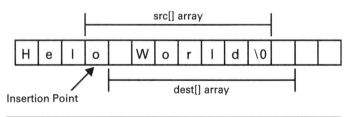

Remove extra 'l' from string:

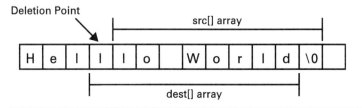

So what is the problem with src and dest overlapping when you use strcpy? First, let's consider what happens when we perform the deletion. In this case, the address of dest is one less than the address of src in our example. Thus, we move the characters over to the left, one by one. This process is illustrated for our example and several i values in Figure 7.3.

As we watch the deletion performing, it is natural to wonder "What's the problem?" In fact, the src[] and dest[] overlap isn't a problem at all here. Was the warning just excessive caution?

Before concluding that we can ignore warnings about library functions, it's probably a good idea to check insertion as well—just to be on the safe side. The same diagram, using our version of Strcpy() to make space for an insertion, is presented in Figure 7.4.

Pretty much as soon as we start copying characters, we can see that our insertion is running into problems. The source of the difficulty is that as i is incremented, it starts to run into characters it has already copied. Thus, it appears we're going to keep copying o's. Indeed, the situation gets worse, *much* worse. When i reaches 6, we will copy an 'o' on top of the NUL terminator. As a result, our function will not stop (at least in theory) until every byte of memory in RAM that is located after our insertion point contains the character 'o', which can't be good.

In practice, it is likely that your operating system might have something to say about your program's attempt to trash the entire contents of RAM. It might, for example, throw an exception. Protections against this type of error are virtually mandated in any multitasking OS—otherwise, a single student programmer (or expert programmer having a nostalgic moment) could bring down an entire server—and everybody on it! On the other hand, you'd be very optimistic if you believe you can do this sort of thing all the time and never experience adverse consequences outside of your own program. Which leads to

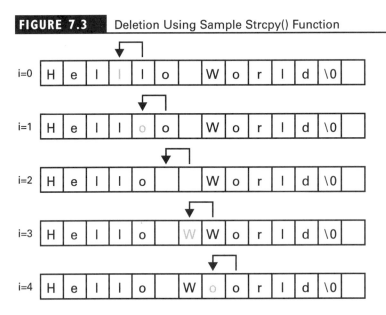

FIGURE 7.3 Deletion Using Sample Strcpy() Function

Etc.

| FIGURE 7.4 | Insertion Using Sample Strcpy() Function |

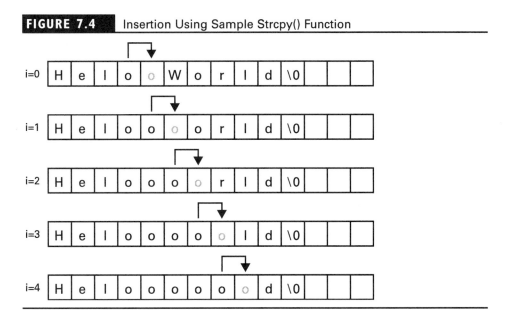

some practical advice: save that thirty-page end-of-term report that you happen to be writing in MS Word before you open up Visual Studio .NET and start writing C/C++ code. (Unless, of course, you enjoyed writing the report so much the first time that you'd relish the opportunity to write it again.) Enough said.

So, is this example what is meant by undefined behavior? Maybe yes, maybe no. It is the behavior that happens in our sample Strcpy during an insertion. However, strcpy could be written in many ways. Some might be implemented in a way that causes the problem during deletion, instead of insertion. Some might limit the damage to the length of the string, instead of going on a memory-eating rampage. The point is, what makes undefined behavior "undefined" is that it depends on how the specific compiler and libraries are constructed. We return to this subject in Section 7.4.1, where we implement a **Strmove function** that is able to handle overlapping memory.

7.2.3: strcmp

int strcmp(const char str1[],const char str2[]);

Arguments	str1, str2: Strings to be compared
Return Value	0 – characters in strings are equal >0 – first string is alphabetically (ASCII) greater than second <0 – first string is alphabetically (ASCII) less than second
Purpose	Performs a case-sensitive comparison of two strings for a limited number of characters (specified by the third argument)—effectively it is a case-insensitive substitute for the ==, !=, <, >, <=, and >= operators, which are only defined for integers, not NUL terminated strings.
Other Comments	Function usage and implementation discussed in Chapter 5, Section 5.6.2, and Chapter 6, Section 6.5.2.

7.2.4: strncmp

int strncmp(const char s1[],const char s2[],size_t len);

Arguments	s1, s2: Strings to be compared len: Number of characters to be compared
Return Value	0 – characters in strings are equal (through specified number of characters) >0 – first string is alphabetically (ASCII) greater than second <0 – first string is alphabetically (ASCII) less than second
Purpose	Performs a case-sensitive comparison of two strings for a limited number of characters (specified by the third argument)—effectively it is a case-insensitive substitute for the ==, !=, <, >, <=, and >= operators, which are only defined for integers, not NUL terminated strings.
Other Comments	Implementing a case-insensitive version of the function, **strnicmp()**, is provided as an exercise at the end of the chapter.

The **strncmp**() function provides case-sensitive comparisons over a limited number of characters, returning the same range of values as **strcmp**(). For example:

```
strncmp("Hello","Hello, World",4);
```

would return 0, because the first four characters are equal. On the other hand:

```
strncmp("Hello","Hello, World",8);
```

would return a value less than zero, because "Hello" is viewed as being less than "Hello, W".

A sample implementation of strncmp() is presented as a flowchart in Figure 7.5, and as C/C++ code in Example 7.2.

The implementation of Strncmp() is virtually identical to that of Strcmp() (Chapter 6, Section 6.5.2) with one exception: a test for i<len-1 is included as part of the for loop test. The reason that we need to subtract 1 from the number of characters to be tested is simple: we iterate starting at 0. Thus, if we are looking for a 5-character match, as soon as we know s1[4]==s2[4] without hitting any nonmatching characters, we are done.

EXAMPLE 7.2

Sample Strncmp() implementation

```
int Strncmp(const char *s1,const char *s2,int len)
{
    int i;
    for(i=0;s1[i]==s2[i]&&s1[i]!=0&&i<len-1;i++) {}
    return s1[i]-s2[i];
}
```

FIGURE 7.5 Sample Strncmp() Flowchart

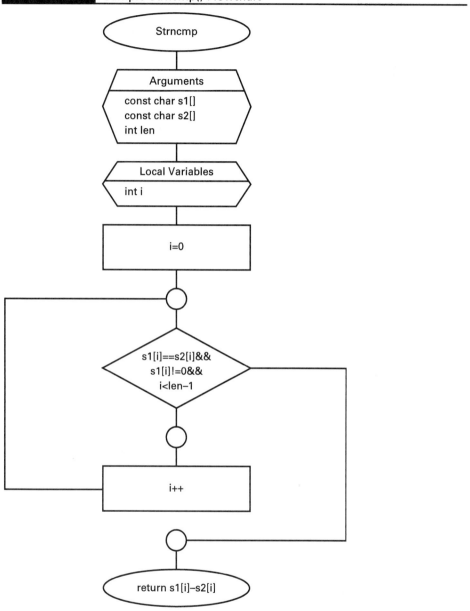

7.2.5: stricmp

int stricmp(const char str1[],const char str2[]);	
Arguments	str1, str2: Strings to be compared
Return Value	0 – characters in strings are equal, case insensitive
	>0 – first string is alphabetically (case insensitive) greater than second
	<0 – first string is alphabetically (case insensitive) less than second
Purpose	Performs a case-insensitive comparison of two strings—effectively it is a case-insensitive substitute for the ==, !=, <, >, <=, and >= operators, which are only defined for integers, not NUL terminated strings.
Other Comments	stricmp() is not part of the official ANSI string.h library, although it has a long history of being supported (also under the name strcmpi(), just to add to the confusion). In Visual Studio .NET, it is supported under the names stricmp(), strcmpi() and, the preferred usage, _stricmp(). Normally, a leading underscore on a function indicates some system-specific function.
	Implementing a limited length version of the function, strnicmp(), is provided as an exercise at the end of the chapter.

The **stricmp**() function performs case-insensitive comparisons of the same type performed by strcmp(), with the same interpretation of the return values. For example:

```
stricmp("Hello","hello");
```

would return 0, while strcmp("Hello","hello") would return a value less than 0, because 'H' is less than 'h' in ASCII. Similarly:

```
stricmp("Zoo","aardvark");
```

would return a value greater than 0 (because 'Z' > 'A', alphabetically), whereas strcmp("Zoo","aardvark") would return a value less than 0, because 'Z' is less than 'a' in ASCII.

stricmp() is not part of the ANSI standard for C/C++, perhaps because its interpretation is only meaningful for English. It is, however, widely supported by compilers. As a consequence, it is known under a number of names. For example, in Visual Studio .NET, the *string.h* header file prototypes:

```
_stricmp
stricmp
strcmpi
```

The first name is generally preferred, as leading underscores are normally used to identify system-specific functions and comments.

A sample implementation of stricmp() is easy to create. All that is required is to take the implementation of Strcmp() (e.g., found in Chapter 6, Section 6.5.2) and use the toupper() function—which takes a character and returns its uppercase equivalent—returning the value of its argument unless the argument is a lowercase character. (The function is described in Chapter 6, Section 6.2.1. The standard library version is prototyped in *ctype.h*.) This implementation is illustrated in Example 7.3.

EXAMPLE 7.3

Sample Stricmp() implementation

```
int Stricmp(char *sz1,char *sz2)
{
    int i;
    for(i=0;sz1[i]!=0&&toupper(sz1[i])==toupper(sz2[i]);i++) {}
    return toupper(sz1[i])-toupper(sz2[i]);
}
```

7.2.6: atoi and atof

int atoi(const char str[]);
double atof(const char str[]);

Arguments	str – the string whose value is to be converted, such as "125" or "125.03"
Return Value	atoi – integer value represented by the string atof – real number (double) value represented by the string
Purpose	Used to provide numeric equivalent for text input, such as a string entered by the user from the keyboard.
Other Comments	Function usage and implementation for atoi() discussed in Chapter 5, Section 5.6.3, and Chapter 6, Section 6.5.3. atof() presented as an exercise in the Chapter 5 and Chapter 6 end-of-chapter questions.

7.2.7: MatchType() Function Walkthrough

Walkthrough available in MatchType.wmv

The MatchType() function is a somewhat contrived function intended to demonstrate five of the string functions presented in this section. It takes two strings, compares them, then copies a message indicating the results of the comparison into a character array. Its prototype is as follows:

```
void MatchType(char szType[],const char sz1[],const char sz2[]);
```

The arguments are as follows:

- sz1[], sz2[]: The two strings to be compared.
- szType[]: The array that will hold the results of the comparison.

Examples of comparison messages include:

- Perfect match
- Case-insensitive match
- 5-character match
- 2-character case-insensitive match
- No match at all

An example of the function in operation, being called from a main() function that takes inputs from the user for the two strings, then prints the results, is shown in Figure 7.6. The code for the MatchType() function is presented in Example 7.4.

The MatchType() function uses all five of the functions presented in Section 7.2. Its basic operation is as follows:

- It does a simple string comparison of the two strings, sz1 and sz2. If this string comparison succeeds, it copies "Perfect match" into the szType array.

- If that fails, it does a case-insensitive comparison of the two strings, sz1 and sz2. If this comparison succeeds, it copies "Case insensitive match" into the szType array.

- If that fails, it compares the two first characters of the two strings, sz1[0] and sz2[0]. If these characters match, we proceed into the counting loop that checks how many characters match exactly. This loop is implemented as follows:

  - The length of sz1 is places in nLen, using strlen().

  - The local array buf[] is initialized to "? character match". (The '?' character will later be replaced with a numeric digit.)

  - Starting i at the length of the sz1-1 (i.e., the last character), we enter a loop that keeps calling strncmp(sz1,sz2,i) until it returns 0, making i smaller

FIGURE 7.6 MatchType Function Being Called

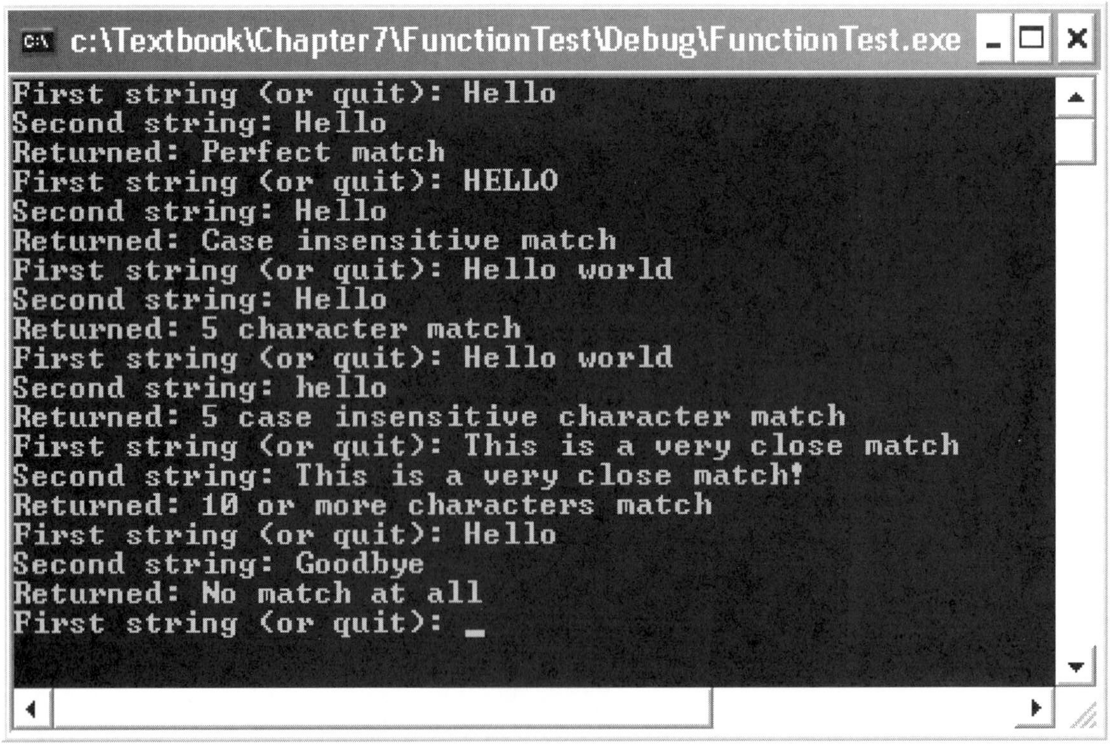

```
c:\Textbook\Chapter7\FunctionTest\Debug\FunctionTest.exe

First string (or quit): Hello
Second string: Hello
Returned: Perfect match
First string (or quit): HELLO
Second string: Hello
Returned: Case insensitive match
First string (or quit): Hello world
Second string: Hello
Returned: 5 character match
First string (or quit): Hello world
Second string: hello
Returned: 5 case insensitive character match
First string (or quit): This is a very close match
Second string: This is a very close match!
Returned: 10 or more characters match
First string (or quit): Hello
Second string: Goodbye
Returned: No match at all
First string (or quit): _
```

EXAMPLE 7.4

MatchType() Function Implementation

```
#include <string.h>
#include <ctype.h>

void MatchType(char szType[],const char sz1[],const char sz2[])
{
    if (strcmp(sz1,sz2)==0) strcpy(szType,"Perfect match");
    else if (stricmp(sz1,sz2)==0)
      strcpy(szType,"Case insensitive match");
    else if (sz1[0]==sz2[0]) {
        int i;
        int nLen=strlen(sz1);
        char buf[80]="? character match";
        for(i=nLen-1;i>1 && strncmp(sz1,sz2,i)!=0;i-){};
        if (i<10) {
            buf[0]=(char)i+'0';
            strcpy(szType,buf);
        }
        else strcpy(szType,"10 or more characters match");
    }
    else if (toupper(sz1[0])==toupper(sz2[0])) {
        int i;
        int nLen=strlen(sz1);
        char buf[80]="? case insensitive character match";
        for(i=1;i<nLen && toupper(sz1[i])==toupper(sz2[i]);i++){};
        if (i<10) {
            buf[0]=(char)i+'0';
            strcpy(szType,buf);
        }
        else strcpy(szType,
          "10 or more case insensitive characters match");
    }
    else strcpy(szType,"No match at all");
}
```

each time. (This process is actually much less efficient than the approach used in the case-insensitive loop, but it allows us to use strncmp()!)

- Upon breaking out of the loop, we check the value of i, which will be the number of matching characters.
  - If i is less than 10, we can turn it into a single ASCII digit (by adding '0') that then replaces the '?' in buf[]. We then copy buf[] into szType[].
  - If i is 10 or more, we "punt" and copy "10 or more characters match" into szType[]. (Fixing this shortcut using sprintf() is presented as an end-of-chapter exercise.)
- If that fails, it compares the uppercase versions of the two first characters of the two strings, sz1[0] and sz2[0], using the toupper() function (discussed in Chapter 6, Section 6.2.1). If these versions match, if proceeds into the counting

loop that checks how many characters match (case-insensitive). This loop, similar to the case-sensitive version, is implemented as follows:

- The length of sz1 is places in nLen, using strlen().
- The local array buf[] is initialized to "? case insensitive character match". (The '?' character will later be replaced with a numeric digit.)
- Starting i at 1 (because we know the first characters match), we enter a loop that keeps comparing the uppercase versions of sz1[i] and sz2[i], until they stop matching (making i larger each time).
- Upon breaking out of the loop, we check the value of i, which will be the number of matching characters.
  - If i is less than 10, we can turn it into a single ASCII digit (by adding '0') that then replaces the '?' in buf[]. We then copy buf[] into szType[].
  - If i is 10 or more, we "punt" and copy "10 or more characters match" into szType[]. (Fixing this shortcut using sprintf() is presented as an end-of-chapter exercise.)
- If all of the preceding operations fail, we copy "No match at all" into szType.
- The function then returns.

TEST YOUR UNDERSTANDING 7.2:

Explain why the use of strncmp() in exact match for loop is less efficient than the use of simple character comparisons, in the case-insensitive for loop.

7.2: SECTION QUESTIONS

Assume the following declarations followed by a code fragment:

```
char buf1[80],buf2[]="Hello, World";
char buf3[10];
int nFlag=0,i;
double dVal;
strlen(buf1);    // 1
strlen(buf2);    // 2
strlen(buf3);    // 3
strcpy(buf1,buf2); // 4
strcpy("Destination string",buf1); // 5
strcpy(buf3,buf2); // 6
nFlag=strcmp(buf1,buf2); // 7
for(i=0;buf1[i]!=0;i++) buf1[i]=toupper(buf1[i]); // 8
nFlag=strcmp(buf1,buf2); // 9
nFlag=strncmp(buf1,buf2,1); // 10
nFlag=stricmp(buf1,buf2); // 11
for(i=0;i<4;i++) buf3[i]=i*2+'0'; // 12
buf3[i]=0; //13
nFlag=atoi(buf3); // 14
buf3[4]='.'; // 15
strlen(buf3); // 16
for(i=5;i<9;i++) buf3[i]=(i%3)+'1'; // 17
```

```
buf3[i]=0; // 18
dVal=atof(buf3); // 19
```

1. Identify all the lines that would cause compiler problems and other issues that could be problems.

2. Assuming the bad code lines have been commented out, identify the effect of the remaining lines.

7.3: IN DEPTH: FORMATTED OUTPUT AND STRINGS

In C++, two distinct approaches can be used for formatting text output. The first approach, presented in Chapter 17, involves using the member functions and manipulations that are supplied with the C++ standard I/O classes. The second approach involves using functions from the C printf() function family.

In this section, we consider the second approach, which offers a number of advantages. First, using the printf family allows us to delay introducing objects and member functions until later in the text. Second, and more importantly, C++ programmers can benefit greatly from understanding how this important family of functions works. In Microsoft Foundation Class (MFC) programming, for example, a number of commonly used functions (e.g., the CString Format() member and the TRACE() macro) are modeled after printf. Finally, for many types of formatting, it is actually easier to use the printf family than to use the C++ library facilities.

7.3.1: DisplayFormatted() SimpleIO Function

The SimpleIO function DisplayFormatted(), which is what we use for formatting output, is modeled after the C function printf(). The actual prototype of the function is quite unusual, by C++ standards. It appears as follows:

```
void DisplayFormatted(const char fmt[],…);
```

What should immediately strike your eye about the prototype are the three dots (sometimes called an ellipsis). In a function prototype, the ellipsis signals that the function can have a variable number of arguments. Although the means of defining variable argument functions is beyond the scope of this text, it is critical to be aware of one fact: whenever a variable argument C/C++ function is defined, a built-in way is required for the function to figure out (a) how many arguments are coming, and (b) the type of data contained in each argument.

The DisplayFormatted() function determines what arguments are coming by using its first argument, the format string. The way the format string works is as follows:

- If the format string contains no % signs, then no more arguments are coming. In that case, DisplayFormatted() just prints the format string.
- If a % is encountered in the format string (followed by one or more special characters), DisplayFormatted() expects to see a corresponding argument passed in.
- If a double percent sign (%%) is encountered in the format string, DisplayFormatted() knows that what we really want it to do is display the percent sign, not specify an argument.

A more detailed discussion of what can follow the format string is presented in the next section (Section 7.3.2). One of the characters that must be present, however, is a character specifying what type of argument we are sending. A list of useful argument types is presented in Table 7.2.

All values passed into DisplayFormatted() come in either as int, double, or pointer (address) values. Thus, even if you pass printf a float variable, it is automatically promoted to **double** when the function is called (and **char** to **int, short** to **int,** etc.).

DisplayFormatted() is an extremely powerful function. The following code (the output from which appears in Figure 7.7) demonstrates its ability to create complex displays by mixing test and variables:

```
double dPi=3.1416;
int nPi=(int)dPi;
char szMyName[80]="Grandon Gill";
char szDumbComment[]=
  "he\'d ask you to write a function to compute it\n";
DisplayFormatted("Medieval officials once declared pi to "
  "be %i, instead of %f\n"
    "%s would never ask you to do that.\n"
    "More likely, %s", nPi,dPi,szMyName,szDumbComment);
```

TABLE 7.2   DisplayFormatted (printf) Type Character Codes

Symbol	Data Type of Argument	Comments
d, i	int	Outputs a decimal integer
x, X	int	Outputs integer value in hexadecimal; upper and lowercase versions indicate how a-f will appear (e.g., f or F)
u	int	Prints unsigned integer value
c	int	Prints the ASCII character equivalent of the integer
f	double	Prints the floating point number, using standard notation
e, E	double	Prints the floating point number, using exponential notation; upper and lowercase versions indicate whether it is printed as 1.774234e+03 or 1.774234E+03
g, G	double	Uses exponential numbers for very small numbers (E-4 or less), standard notation otherwise
s	char *	Prints the string starting at the address (e.g., array name or pointer)
p	void *	Prints the value of the address passed in (e.g., array name or pointer)

FIGURE 7.7   Output of DisplayFormatted() Sample

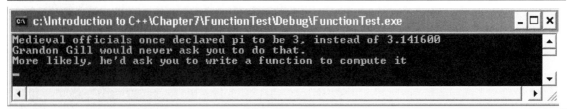

```
c:\Introduction to C++\Chapter7\FunctionTest\Debug\FunctionTest.exe
Medieval officials once declared pi to be 3, instead of 3.141600
Grandon Gill would never ask you to do that.
More likely, he'd ask you to write a function to compute it
```

The preceding DisplayFormatted() statement also illustrates a number of different practical issues, including the following:

- It shows how a single statement can hold more than one argument. In this case, it held four arguments: an int, a double, and two strings.
- It demonstrates how C/C++ can create long character strings—just place quotes strings next to each other, with no intervening characters.
- It demonstrates how the \ can be used to print special characters. For example, to get the apostrophe in he'd, the string was written as follows:

```
"he\'d ask you to write a function to compute it\n"
```

7.3.2: printf Family Formatting

The real power of the printf family of functions becomes apparent in their formatting capability (the 'f' in printf). In addition to the data type characters, the % sign can also accept a number of modifiers to provide fine-level control over formatting. These modifiers fall into three categories: flags, length.precision specifiers, and type modifiers, as summarized in Figure 7.8, which examines a typical full argument specification.

Example Specification   The interpretation of the example specification, *%-9.2li*, is as follows (moving from right to left):

- The i at the end specifies an integer type, as we have already seen.
- The letter l in front of the i specifies that it is a **long int.** Currently, the **long** data type is the same as **int,** so the type modifier would have no effect. It

FIGURE 7.8   Typical printf() Full Argument Specification

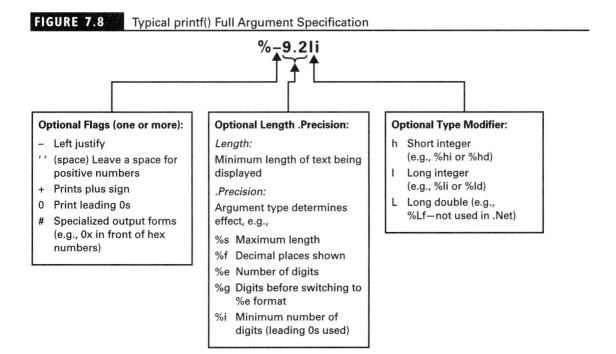

%-9.2li

Optional Flags (one or more):
- − Left justify
- ' ' (space) Leave a space for positive numbers
- + Prints plus sign
- 0 Print leading 0s
- # Specialized output forms (e.g., 0x in front of hex numbers)

Optional Length .Precision:

Length:
Minimum length of text being displayed

.Precision:
Argument type determines effect, e.g.,

- %s Maximum length
- %f Decimal places shown
- %e Number of digits
- %g Digits before switching to %e format
- %i Minimum number of digits (leading 0s used)

Optional Type Modifier:
- h Short integer (e.g., %hi or %hd)
- l Long integer (e.g., %li or %ld)
- L Long double (e.g., %Lf—not used in .Net)

could, however, when the program was ported to a new OS with 64-bit **long** data, or an old system (e.g., Windows 3.1) with 16-bit **int** data.

- The 9.2 is interpreted as follows:
    - 9 is the minimum number of characters to be printed.
    - 2 is the minimum number of digits. Should the integer be 7, for example, it would add a second digit to make 07. This particular setting, known as precision, varies according to data type. For f and e specifiers, it means number of decimal places. For the s (string) specifier, it is the maximum number of characters to be displayed (useful in aligning columns). For the c specifier, it has no effect.
- The – flag specifies that the 9-character integer is to be left justified, meaning that any trailing blanks will be placed at the end of the integer (as opposed to right justifying it, which is the standard behavior).

Demonstration of DisplayFormatted()

Walkthrough available in Printf.wmv

The easiest way to learn the basics of using the printf family is to try the DisplayFormatted() function. Example 7.5 contains a simple program that demonstrates a wide range of useful printf family formatting capabilities. Figure 7.9 shows how they appear on the console screen.

By matching the printf() statements in Example 7.5 to the output in Figure 7.9, you can see a practical demonstration of many of the most common printf formats. Within the valid statements, a few noteworthy results are worth mentioning specifically:

```
DisplayFormatted("Short (raw): %hi, (unsigned): %hu, (hex,"
"leading 0x): %#hx\n\n",s1,s1,s1);
```

In this line we first tell printf s1 is a **short,** then we tell it s1 is an **unsigned short.** The resulting output of –55 and 65481 indicates how DisplayFormatted() believes what you tell it.

```
DisplayFormatted("No flags:\n");
DisplayFormatted("\t%5i\n",i2);
DisplayFormatted("\t%5i\n",i3);
DisplayFormatted("Sign flags:\n");
DisplayFormatted("\t%+5i\n",i2);
DisplayFormatted("\t%+5i\n",i3);
DisplayFormatted("Space flags:\n");
DisplayFormatted("\t% 5i\n",i2);
DisplayFormatted("\t% 5i\n",i3);
DisplayFormatted("0 flags (seven digits):\n");
DisplayFormatted("\t%07i\n",i2);
DisplayFormatted("\t%07i\n\n",i3);
```

The series of statements illustrates various ways of aligning numbers in columns, which can be especially useful for creating reports. This alignment is normally done using *length.precision* specifiers and the *flags* column.

EXAMPLE 7.5

PrintFormatDemo() function

```
void PrintFormatDemo()
{
    int i1=76,i2=10000,i3=-10000;
    double d1=3.1415926535;
    short s1=-55;
    char szTest[]="This is a test of string printing";
    char szShort[]="Shorter test string";
    // simple number formatting
    DisplayFormatted(
      "Double (raw): %f, (exponential): %e, (formatted): %6.4f\n",d1,d1,d1);
    DisplayFormatted(
      "Integer (raw): %i, (formatted): %5.4i, (left justified): %-5i, (hex): %X\n",
        i1,i1,i1,i1);
    DisplayFormatted(
      "Short (raw): %hi, (unsigned): %hu, (hex, leading 0x): %#hx\n\n",
        s1,s1,s1);
    // test of flags in column (preceded by tab)
    DisplayFormatted("No flags:\n");
    DisplayFormatted("\t%5i\n",i2);
    DisplayFormatted("\t%5i\n",i3);
    DisplayFormatted("Sign flags:\n");
    DisplayFormatted("\t%+5i\n",i2);
    DisplayFormatted("\t%+5i\n",i3);
    DisplayFormatted("Space flags:\n");
    DisplayFormatted("\t% 5i\n",i2);
    DisplayFormatted("\t% 5i\n",i3);
    DisplayFormatted("0 flags (seven digits):\n");
    DisplayFormatted("\t%07i\n",i2);
    DisplayFormatted("\t%07i\n\n",i3);
    // Tests of string printing
    // No arguments
    DisplayFormatted(szTest);
    DisplayFormatted("\n");
    // %s format tests
    DisplayFormatted("%s\n",szTest);
    DisplayFormatted("%50s (no justification)\n",szTest);
    DisplayFormatted("%-50s (left justification)\n",szTest);
    DisplayFormatted("%.20s (maximum of 20 chars)\n",szTest);
    DisplayFormatted("%30.30s (guaranteed 30 characters, right justified)\n",szTest);
    DisplayFormatted("%-30.30s (guaranteed 30 characters, left justified)\n",szTest);
    DisplayFormatted("%30.30s (guaranteed 30 characters, right justified)\n",szShort);
    DisplayFormatted(
      "%-30.30s (guaranteed 30 characters, left justified)\n\n",szShort);
    // Typical error conditions
    DisplayFormatted("Common errors (not detected by compiler!):\n\n");
    DisplayFormatted("\tForgot to put in argument: %s\n");
    DisplayFormatted("\tFed it too few arguments: %i+%i=%i\n",5,3);
```

(Continues)

EXAMPLE 7.5 (CONTINUED)

```
    DisplayFormatted("\tFed it too many arguments: %i+%i=%i\n",5,3,8,23);
    DisplayFormatted("\tFed it double when integer was expected: %i\n",d1);
    DisplayFormatted("\tFed it integer when double was expected: %f\n",i1);
    DisplayFormatted("\tFed it integer when double was expected: %e\n",i1);
    // This one actually crashes the program with an access violation:
    DisplayFormatted("\tPassed character, instead of string: %s\n",'H');
}
```

FIGURE 7.9   Display of PrintFormatDemo() (Paused at Last Line)

```
c:\Introduction to C++\Chapter7\FunctionTest\Debug\FunctionTest.exe          _ □ ✕

Double (raw): 3.141593, (exponential): 3.141593e+000, (formatted): 3.1416
Integer (raw): 76, (formatted): 0076, (left justified): 76    , (hex): 4C
Short (raw): -55, (unsigned): 65481, (hex, leading 0x): 0xffc9

No flags:
        10000
       -10000
Sign flags:
       +10000
       -10000
Space flags:
        10000
       -10000
0 flags (seven digits):
       0010000
      -010000

This is a test of string printing
This is a test of string printing
                    This is a test of string printing (no justification)
This is a test of string printing             (left justification)
This is a test of st (maximum of 20 chars)
This is a test of string print (guaranteed 30 characters, right justified)
This is a test of string print (guaranteed 30 characters, left justified)
        Shorter test string (guaranteed 30 characters, right justified)
Shorter test string             (guaranteed 30 characters, left justified)

Common errors (not detected by compiler!):

        Forgot to put in argument: (null)
        Fed it too few arguments: 5+3=0
        Fed it too many arguments: 5+3=8
        Fed it double when integer was expected: 1413551940
        Fed it integer when double was expected: 0.000000
        Fed it integer when double was expected: 3.754899e-322
```

The most significant portion of the demo addresses various error conditions associated with DisplayFormatted(). It is essential to understand that *the compiler does not check for mismatches between the printf-family format string and its other arguments.* Therefore, any such mismatches could lead to serious program problems—even program crashes. Furthermore, DisplayFormatted() failures are another one of those "undefined" behaviors that we've come to know and love (e.g., see Section 7.2.2)—so there's no guarantee the behavior will be the same across compilers and operating systems.

The following statements demonstrate some of the more common errors:

```
DisplayFormatted("\tForgot to put in argument: %s\n");
```

In this example, we told DisplayFormatted() to expect a string, then didn't give it one. On this occasion, what was in memory where it expected to find the string address was 0x00000000. So, the MS Visual Studio .NET library version of the function printed (null) to indicate the fact—which was a lot nicer than some of the things it could have done.

```
DisplayFormatted(
    "\tFed it too few arguments: %i+%i=%i\n",5,3);
```

In this example, we told DisplayFormatted() to expect 3 integers, then gave it only 2. On this occasion, what was in memory where it expected to find the third was 0x00000000. So, it printed a 0.

```
DisplayFormatted(
    "\tFed it too many arguments: %i+%i=%i\n",5,3,8,23);
```

In this example, we told DisplayFormatted() to expect 3 integers, then gave it 4. Because it found what it needed, the result printed out okay—on this compiler.

```
DisplayFormatted(
    "\tFed it double when integer was expected: %i\n",d1);
```

In this example, we told DisplayFormatted() to expect an integer, then fed it d1 (a double). It therefore took the first four bytes of d1 and printed them as if they were an integer.

```
DisplayFormatted(
    "\tFed it integer when double was expected: %e\n",i1);
```

In this example, we told DisplayFormatted() to expect a double, then fed it i1 (an integer). It therefore took eight bytes (i1 and whatever else happened to be next to it in memory) and printed them as if they were a double. The actual value was not exactly zero (0.000000), as displayed in the first statement. Instead, it was a number with a large negative exponent—making it zero when displayed in standard form to the default 6 digits of precision, which could be verified by looking at the output from the second statement.

```
DisplayFormatted(
    "\tPassed character, instead of string: %s\n", 'H');
```

It was not possible to show output from the last statement—it generated an exception that crashed the program. The problem here is that it was passed a character ('H') where the address of the start of a string was expected (for example, "H" would have been fine). This command caused DisplayFormatted() to try to access a memory location whose value was nonsense, such as the address 0x00000048 (where 0x48 is 'H'). This location wasn't "owned" by the program. As mentioned in Section 7.2.2, advanced operating systems typically have built-in protections against such activities by rogue programs. Thus, the OS stepped in.

7.3.3: Printing to a String with sprintf()

Walkthrough available in Sprintf.wmv

Although the C++ STL provides many formatting capabilities, in some situations the printf family of functions is more convenient to use. Fortunately, the C++ programmer can still tap the power of printf using the library function sprintf.

Once you are familiar with DisplayFormatted(), sprintf() is easy. The sprintf() function works exactly the same way—except it sends its output to a character array (creating a string), instead of sending it to standard output. The prototype for sprintf() is as follows:

```
int sprintf(char dest[],const char format[],…);
```

The first argument (*dest*) is the address of the array to which output is to be sent. Its remaining arguments (or argument) are exactly the same as those of DisplayFormatted(). The function returns the number of characters "printed"—which will be the same as the length of the output string.

To use sprintf(), you need to create an array large enough to hold your output, then use that array as the first argument of the function. For example:

```
int dest[80];
int i1=125;
sprintf(dest,"%5i",i1);
```

Upon running this code fragment, the buffer dest[] will contain the string " 125" (with two leading spaces, because %5i was specified for formatting). This fragment illustrates the most important capability of sprinf()—to convert numeric data types to their text representation. In essence, then, sprintf() acts as the inverse to functions such as atoi()—which converts a text string to an integer (see Chapter 6, Section 6.5.3). Similarly, the Int2String() function, presented in Chapter 6, Section 6.6.3, shows how sprintf() might be implemented for integer data types.

The sprintf function can be employed in many creative ways. An example of such a use of sprint() is presented in Example 7.6.

The example function, FloatFormat(), is designed to allow the programmer to control how a **double** (dVal) is formatted using integer values for length (nLen), precision (nPrec), and a flag (cFlag). Up to this point, we have hard-coded such information into a printf() format string, e.g.:

```
DisplayFormatted("%+7.4f",dVal);
```

What the FloatFormat() does is to create its own format string, using sprintf(). The key line of the function is:

```
sprintf(szFormat,"%c%c%i.%if",'%',(cFlag==0)?'':
   cFlag,nLen,nPrec);
```

EXAMPLE 7.6

FloatFormat() function

```
void FloatFormat(double dVal,int nLen,int nPrec,char cFlag)
{
    char szFormat[80];
    sprintf(szFormat,"%c%c%i.%if",'%',(cFlag==0) ? ' ' :
     cFlag,nLen,nPrec);
    DisplayFormatted(szFormat,dVal);
}
```

Matching the formatting codes with the arguments, we discover:

- The first %c is replaced by '%'.
- The second %c is conditional: if argument cFlag is NUL (0), we put a space there. If not, we use whatever character was passed in (e.g., '+').
- The first %i is matched to the argument nLen (e.g., 7).
- The next %i is matched to nPrec (e.g., 4).
- The last character is an f.

Putting these all together, szFormat[] will contain the string "%+7.4f" after the command. We then call DisplayFormatted():

```
        DisplayFormatted(szFormat,dVal);
```

This call causes the contents of szFormat to be used for formatting purposes. The result: dVal is printed with our desired formatting.

As an example, Figure 7.10 shows FloatFormat() stopped in the debugger after it was called using:

```
        FloatFormat(3.14159,7,4,'+');
```

In the inspection window, we can see the szFormat[] that we constructed. After stepping over the printf(), **3.1416** was displayed on the console.

TEST YOUR UNDERSTANDING 7.3:

Why did we pass a '%' as our first argument in the sprintf() call, instead of just putting it in the formatting string? How could we have included the '%' szFormat[] without passing it as an argument?

7.3: SECTION QUESTIONS

Assume the following declarations and statements are run:

```
        char buf[80]="Hello", str[80],dest[80];
        int a1=30,a2=252;
        char c1=66,c2=0x35;
        double d1=3.14159;
        DisplayFormatted(buf); // 1
        DisplayFormatted("%s\n",buf); // 2
        DisplayFormatted("%i %04x %f",a1,a2,d1); // 3
```

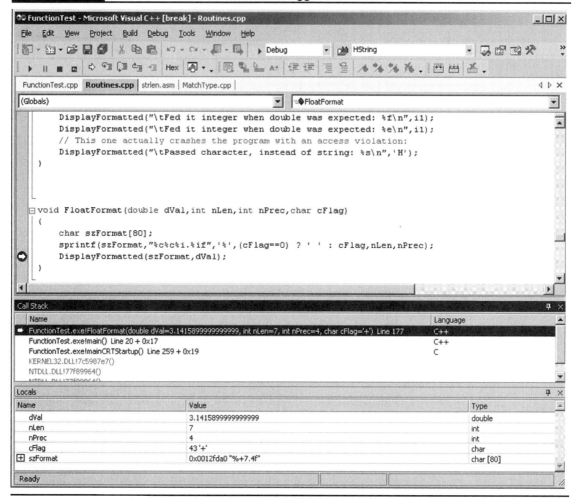

FIGURE 7.10 FloatFormat() Paused in the Debugger

```
DisplayFormatted("%i: %s\n",c1,str); // 4
DisplayFormatted("%s: %f\n",c1,d1+7.0); // 5
DisplayFormatted("%c: %s\n",c1,strcpy(str,buf)); // 6
DisplayFormatted("%i %04x %f",a1,a2,d1,str); // 7
DisplayFormatted("%10s\n%-10.10s\n",buf1,str); // 8
DisplayFormatted("%i %04x %c\n",c2,c2,c2); // 9
DisplayFormatted("%f %i %c\n",d1,d1,d1); // 10
// sprintf functions
sprintf(str,"%%%i.%if",10,7); // A
sprintf(dest,str,d1); // B
sprintf(str,"%c%c%i%c%i%c%c",'%','-',10,'.',10,'s','\n'); // C
sprintf(str,buf1); // D
DisplayFormatted(str,buf1); // E
```

1. Identify any illegal or inadvisable statements among the group labeled 1–10.

2. Assume inappropriate statements have been commented out. Explain what would happen for each of the remaining statements labeled 1–10.

3. Explain what would be accomplished by the statements labeled A–E.

7.4: SAMPLE PROBLEMS

In this section, we present two library-related sample problems. The first involves the definition of a function Strmove(), which performs the function of strcpy() even if overlap between source and destination exist. The second implements a function Doublecmp(), which compares two floats with a given degree of accuracy, and returns values analogous to those of strcmp() to indicate their relative values (with 0 being equal).

7.4.1: Strmove()

Walkthrough available in Strmove.wmv

The Strmove() function is intended to operate exactly the way *strcpy()* operates—except it will work properly if source and destination overlap. (It is named after a library function *memmove()* that works the same way). Its prototype is as follows:

```
void Strmove(char dest[],char src[]);
```

To begin writing the function, we would do well to recall our analysis of the sample we developed in Section 7.2.2. That function seemed to solve half our problem—it worked fine on deletion, but trashed the string upon insertion. The way that particular function worked was to begin copying characters at the beginning of the string and then proceed to the end of the string (i.e., front to back). An obvious question to ask would therefore be: What if we defined a function that copied from back to front (e.g., starting at the strlen and moving towards position 0)? Conceptually, such a function would work on our 1-character insertion example as shown in Figure 7.11.

Based on the example, it appears that the insertion actually works properly—by the time it is complete, we will have a space (currently occupied by the first o) where we can add the second l.

TEST YOUR UNDERSTANDING 7.4:
What happens when we do a back-to-front deletion of a character?

It would seem then that we could write two versions of Strcpy()—one that copies from front to back, one that copies from back to front. This approach is illustrated in Example 7.7, where the two functions are called Strcpy1() and Strcpy2().

The problem is, of course, which one to call. We could get our application to prompt the user each time it had to copy strings, but most consumers would probably not regard this reminder as a strong product feature. In fact, we could reasonably expect them to get quite annoyed if their word processor asks them in what direction they want to copy memory *each time they press a key.* A better solution would, therefore, be to have our function figure it out automatically.

This task, it turns out, is pretty easy. You need to remember four things:

1. If the arrays don't overlap, it doesn't matter which direction we go.

FIGURE 7.11 Insertion Example Moving From Back to Front ofArray

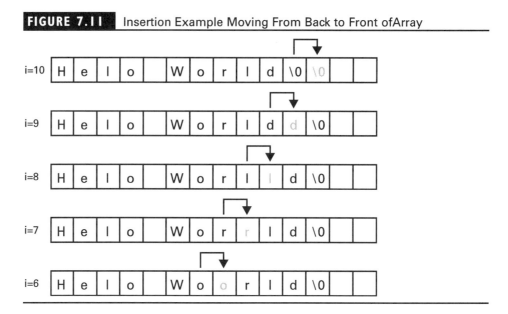

2. If it's an insertion, and we are moving memory to make room, then the destination is going to be in a higher memory address than the source.

3. If it's a deletion, we will be moving memory to the left and the destination is going to be at a lower address than the source.

4. Whenever an array is passed in, we pass the address where it starts.

Knowing these guidelines, we can figure out what version of the Strcpy() function to call if we can compare address values. And, as it turns out, the < operator works just fine for this task (as we will discuss at greater length in Chapter 10). Thus, we can write a simple Strmove() function, as shown in Example 7.8.

A test of the function, using our example test data, is shown in Figure 7.12. It should be noted that in the insertion case, the Strmove() function does not make the actual insertion. Instead, it makes room so that the character or characters to be inserted can be placed in the string at the right position (as was done with the 'l' in the example).

7.4.2: Doublecmp()

Walkthrough available in Doublecmp.wmv

As we observed in Chapters 3 and 4, one of the problems with floating point numbers is that miniscule rounding errors, which are unavoidable, can lead to problems with tests, particularly equality and inequality tests. One way to avoid such a problem would be to design a function along the lines of strcmp() that could compare two doubles and return:

- 0: if they are equal—within specified limits
- 1: if they are not equal, and the first is greater than the second
- −1: if they are not equal, and the second is greater than the first

---

EXAMPLE 7.7

Two versions of Strcpy() function

```
// Performs front-to-back copy
void Strcpy1(char dest[],const char src[])
{
    int i;
    int nLen=strlen(src);
    for(i=0;i<=nLen;i++) {
        dest[i]=src[i];
    }
    return;
}

// Performs back-to-front copy
void Strcpy2(char dest[],const char src[])
{
    int i;
    for(i=strlen(src);i>=0;i--) {
        dest[i]=src[i];
    }
    return;
}
```

EXAMPLE 7.8

Strmove() function

```
void Strmove(char dest[],char src[])
{
        if (dest==src) return;
        if (dest<src) Strcpy1(dest,src);
        else Strcpy2(dest,src);
}
```

FIGURE 7.12   Sample Test of Strmove()

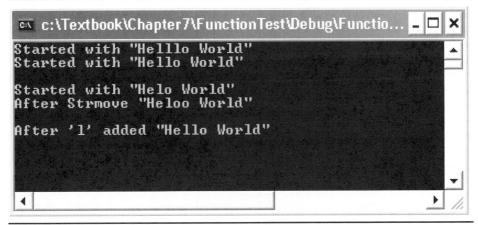

```
c:\Textbook\Chapter7\FunctionTest\Debug\Functio...
Started with "Helllo World"
Started with "Hello World"

Started with "Helo World"
After Strmove "Heloo World"

After 'l' added "Hello World"
```

Such a function could be prototyped as follows:

```
int Doublecmp(double d1,double d2,unsigned int nDigits);
```

d1 and d2 would represent the numbers to be compared, while nDigits would be the number of significant digits. For example, 2 would mean that at least two digits should match—implying an accuracy of around 1 percent (10^{-2}).

In Chapter 4, Section 4.6.3, Example 4.3, some code was presented that illustrates how the core of such a function could work. Specifically:

```
bool b1,b2,b3;
double d1,d2;
double delta;
d1=(5*4.5*7.33)/12.47;
d2=5*4.5*(7.33/12.47);
delta=d1*1E-15;
// bring delta to 15 digits
b1=(d1==d2);
// b1 is false
b2=(d1>d2-delta && d1<d2+delta);
// equality test (to 15 places): true
b3=(d1<d2-delta || d1>d2+delta);
// inequality test (to 15 places): false
```

The way this code worked, we defined a value delta—equal to the first value times a significance number, in this case 10^{-15}—that represents 15 decimal digits of accuracy. We could then test that the two values were within delta of each other and, if they were, we would call them equal.

The problem with the preceding code is that the 15 digits of precision are locked in. To make it more flexible, we want to be able to change:

```
1E-15 (in delta = d1*1E-15) to d1*1E-{our number of signif-
icant digits}
```

Now an experienced programmer would know that a pow() function in math.h would be perfect for this task. We, however, only know about sprintf(). So, how can we use sprintf() to help us here? It is similar to our formatting example in Section 7.3.4. First, assuming our precision is in nDigits, we create a text representation on the number in the following manner:

```
char num[20];
sprintf(num,"1E-%i",nDigits);
```

Then, we use the atof() function to convert the text representation to a number, for example:

```
delta=0.5*(d1+d2)*atof(num);
```

(By taking an average of d1 and d2—0.5*(d1+d2)—we ensure that our accuracy test will not vary depending upon the order of the numbers we use to call our function.)

At this point, it becomes easy to write our function, which is illustrated in Example 7.9.

Example 7.10 is a simple test function used to test Doublecmp() using the same calculations we used earlier. Figure 7.13 shows that test function halted in the debugger.

Examining the inspection window, we see that n1, our test result for the first test, was 0. Because the first test checked for 5 significant digits, this result is correct. Similarly, our test result n2 was 1—meaning the first value was larger than the second—to 20 significant digits. This result also turns out to be correct, because the two values d1 and d2 diverge after 15 places and the first is slightly greater than the second. Thus, the function appears to be working properly.

EXAMPLE 7.9

Doublecmp function

```c
int Doublecmp(double d1,double d2,unsigned int nDigits)
{
    double delta;
    char buf[20];
    // No significant digits means they're always equal
    if (nDigits==0) return 0;
    sprintf(buf,"1E-%i",nDigits);
    delta=0.5*(d1+d2)*atof(buf);
    if (d1+delta>=d2 && d1-delta<=d2) return 0;
    return (d1-d2>0) ? 1 : -1;
}
```

FIGURE 7.13   Doublecmp() Function Stopped in the Debugger

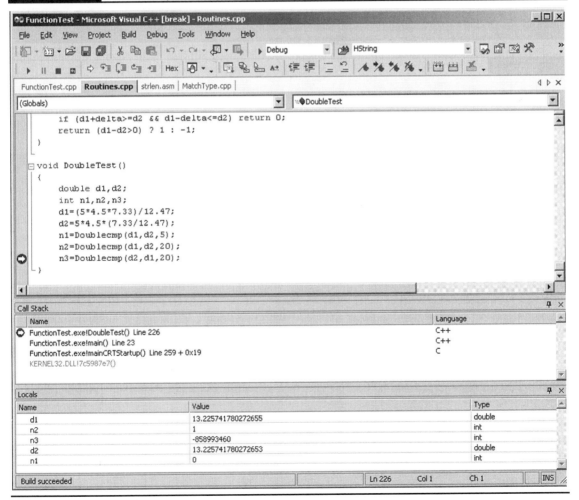

EXAMPLE 7.10

DoubleTest() test function

```
void DoubleTest()
{
    double d1,d2;
    int n1,n2,n3;
    d1=(5*4.5*7.33)/12.47;
    d2=5*4.5*(7.33/12.47);
    n1=Doublecmp(d1,d2,5);
    n2=Doublecmp(d1,d2,20);
    n3=Doublecmp(d2,d1,20);
}
```

7.5: REVIEW AND QUESTIONS

7.5.1: REVIEW

In Chapter 7, we focused on introducing a collection of library functions used so commonly that it would be difficult to proceed to future chapters without them. We began by introducing, and reintroducing, a number of functions that operate on NUL terminated strings:

Function	Purpose
size_t strlen(const char *str);	Returns the number of characters in the string pointed to by str, not including the NUL terminator
char *strcpy(char *dest,const char *src);	Copies a string, character by character (including the NUL terminator) from src to the array that dest points to
int strcmp(const char *s1,const char *s2);	Compares strings s1 and s2 character by character, signaling the result with the return value; the return has the following significance: 0 means the strings are equal, character by character >0 means s1 is lexically greater than s2 <0 means s1 is lexically less than s2 The term *lexically* refers to ASCII sort order—meaning the function is highly case-sensitive
int strncmp(const char *s1,const char *s2,size_t n);	Same as strcmp() except the comparison stops after n characters, returning the result at that point
int stricmp(const char *s1,const char *s2);	Same as strcmp() except case-insensitive comparison is used (e.g., uppercase values of all characters may be compared)
int atoi(const char *s1);	Returns the integer equivalent of a string such as "721"
double atof(const char *s1);	Returns the double (floating point) equivalent of a string, such as "3.14159"

In addition to the string functions, the printf family of functions was introduced. The key to DisplayFormatted() and sprintf() is the formatting string. Whenever a % sign is encountered in the formatting string, it is broken up into a series of data elements that tell the function what to print, and how to print it. These elements are illustrated in the figure at the top of the next page.

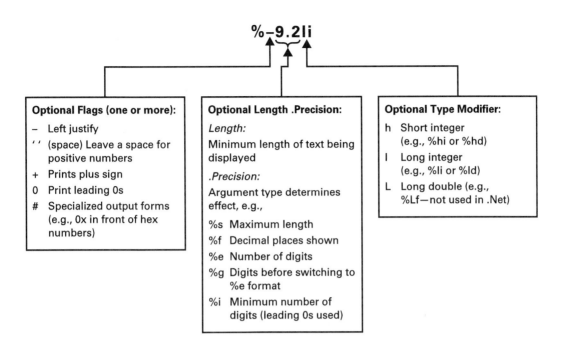

The final character in the formatting for each argument indicates the type of data being sent. Allowable choices include the following:

Symbol	Data Type of Argument	Comments
d, i	int	Outputs a decimal integer
x, X	int	Outputs integer value in hexadecimal; upper and lowercase versions indicate how a-f will appear (e.g., f or F)
u	int	Prints unsigned integer value
c	int	Prints the ASCII character equivalent of the integer
f	double	Prints the floating point number, using standard notation
e, E	double	Prints the floating point number, using exponential notation; upper and lowercase versions indicate whether it is printed as 1.774234e+03 or 1.774234E+03
g, G	double	Uses exponential numbers for very small numbers (E-4 or less), standard notation otherwise
s	char *	Prints the string starting at the address (e.g., array name or pointer)
p	void *	Prints the value of the address passed in (e.g., array name or pointer)

7.5.2: GLOSSARY

class library A predefined set of C++ classes (i.e., object definitions) used by the compiler in order to speed up development time

printf library function A C-defined function used to display information to the user on the screen but can be redirected to other output devices

sprintf library function Similar to the printf function, this function will write output to a given file or stream

strcmp library function A function that is used to compare two strings for any differences and subtracts the resulting differences to determine the level of equality

stricmp library function Similar to the strcmp function, however does a case-insensitive version of comparison in which the resulting differences determine the level of equality

string overlap Occurs when two strings share part of the same memory area (e.g., during an insertion or deletion); failure to take overlap into account when copying a string can corrupt the resulting and original strings

strncmp library function Compares n number of characters in the string to determine the equality of the two strings

strnicmp library function Compares n number of characters in a string insensitively to determine the equality of the two strings

7.5.3: QUESTIONS

1. *Strncpy:* The strncpy() library function works like strcpy(), except it stops copying after a specified number of characters (n, an unsigned int, or size_t). It is prototyped as follows:

```
char *strncpy(char dest[],const char
*src[],unsigned int n);
```

In the event strlen(src) < n, the function fills all the remaining characters in dest (up to n characters) with NUL terminators ('\0' characters, or just plain 0s). If strlen(src)>=n, it copies over n characters and does not add a NUL terminator to the end of dest.

2. *Strnicmp:* The strnicmp() function does a case-insensitive comparison of two strings, using the same arguments as strncmp(), e.g.,

```
int strnicmp(const char s1[],const
char s2[]);
```

Implement your own version of this function, called Strnicmp() and test it.

3. *UpperCount:* Suppose we needed a modified version of the strlen function so that instead of counting the number of characters in the string, it counted the number of uppercase characters in the string. For example:

```
UpperCount("Hello, World!")
```

would return 2 (reflecting the 'H' and the 'W'). Write and test the function.

4. *VowelCount:* Suppose we needed a modified version of the strlen function so that instead of counting the number of characters in the string, it counted the number of vowels (a,e,i,o,u) in the string. For example:

```
VowelCount("Hello, World!\n")
```

would return 3, reflecting the 'e' and two 'o's. Write and test the function.

5. *BadStrlen:* The following function, BadStrlen() is supposed to work like strlen() but has one or more bugs that cause it to lock up each time it is run. Identify the problem or problems (line numbers are provided).

Line	Code
1	int BadStrlen(const char s1[])
2	{
3	int i=0,nCount=0;
4	while(s1[i]!='\0')
5	{
6	nCount=nCount+1;
11	}
12	return nCount;
13	}

6. *BadStrcpy:* The following function, BadStrcpy(), is supposed to run like strcpy but has one or more bugs that will cause it to run improperly. Identify the problem or problems (line numbers are provided).

Line	Code
1	void BadStrcpy(char s2[],const char s1[])
2	{
3	int i;
4	for(i=0;s2[i]!='\0';i++)
5	{
6	s2[i]=s1[i];
11	}
12	s2[i]='0';
13	}

7. *ReplChar:* Write and test a function ReplChar that takes a string and replaces all the occurrences of one character with another. The function should be prototyped as follows:

```
int ReplChar(char str[],char cOld,char
cNew);
```

The arguments are as follows: str[] is the string in which the replacements are to be made, cOld is the character being replaced, and cNew is the character we are replacing it with. For example:

```
char buf[80]="3/4/2003 to 3/7/2003";
ReplChar(buf,'/','-');
// would return 4 and buf[] would
// now hold "3-4-2003 to 3-7-2003"
```

8. *MakeUpper:* Write and test a function MakeUpper that goes through a string and makes every lowercase character uppercase. The function is prototyped as follows:

```
int MakeUpper(char str[]);
```

The function should return the number of characters made uppercase. For example:

```
char buf[80]="Hello Bye";
MakeUpper(buf);
// function returns 6 and buf[]
// contains "HELLO BYE"
```

In-Depth Questions

9. *Enhanced MatchType() function:* Show how sprintf() could be used to eliminate the restriction of no more than 9 matching characters in the MatchType() function presented in Section 7.2.7. Modify the MatchType() function and test it.

10. *ReplString:* Create and test a function ReplString(), that goes through a string and replaces every occurrence of one string with another string. The function prototype is as follows:

```
int ReplString(char szMain[],const
char szOld[],const char szNew[]);
```

The arguments are szMain[], the string in which the replacement is to occur, szOld[], the string being replaced, and szNew[], the replacement string. The function should return the number of replacements made. (*Hint:* You will probably want to use the Strmove() function, shown in Example 7.8, to make room in the event szOld[] and szNew[] are not the same length.)

Introduction to File Stream I/O

EXECUTIVE SUMMARY

Chapter 8 examines how we can use files to load and save data in our applications. Without the ability to use files, computers are pretty much limited to computational activities—the information system activities that represent most of today's technology applications need to load and save data. The chapter introduces the idea of a generalized file stream, defined to accomplish I/O without knowing the precise characteristics of the device being used. It also explains how text and binary files differ, noting the compatibility and speed characteristics of the two approaches. The view of file I/O presented in this chapter is a general one, with SimpleIO functions being used to hide the object-oriented nature of file I/O in C++. The specific I/O classes available from the C++ standard template library are presented in Chapter 17.

The chapter begins by introducing the concept of a stream, noting that many I/O functions are defined in three forms: standard I/O form, file stream form, and buffer form. It then introduces the notion of a text file, showing its basic equivalence to console I/O. The topic of binary files is then presented, demonstrating how such files allow rapid storage and retrieval of data. The use of such files as substitutes for in-RAM arrays is also illustrated.

LEARNING OBJECTIVES

Upon completing this chapter, you should be able to:

- Describe what is meant by a file stream
- Explain why standard I/O and text file I/O are actually equivalent
- Open and close streams
- Write programs that write text data to a file
- Write programs that read text data from a file
- Identify key differences between text and binary files
- Explain the types of functions used to access data and navigate around binary files
- Write applications that incorporate binary files

8.1: I/O STREAMS

The underlying mechanics of reading and writing information using files and the console tend to be complex. Fortunately, in C++ these mechanics are completely invisible to the programmer. Instead, C++ employs the concept of **I/O streams,** which we examine in this section.

8.1.1: Generalized Stream I/O

The idea behind generalized stream I/O is relatively simple. If you look at a typical computer, information can be retrieved from or sent to three types of places:

- Attached devices, or peripherals, such as the keyboard, monitor and printer
- Disk files
- Memory buffers (i.e., blocks of memory containing data)

The principle used by C++ in designing its I/O libraries is that the functions used to input and output data should be as similar as possible, regardless of destination. As a consequence, most of the I/O capabilities in C++ are provided in three versions:

- A console or standard I/O version, designed to take input from the keyboard and/or send output to a text-based screen
- A file version, designed to go to a designated disk file opened as a stream, identified with a special file object
- A memory buffer version (for text I/O functions), where output is directed to an area of memory instead of a file or device

Stream-oriented operating systems, such as UNIX and DOS, were specifically designed to support C++'s view of I/O. Indeed, special file names (such as PRN and COM1) are assigned to specific devices (e.g., attached printers) and ports (e.g., the serial port) so that input from and output to these devices can be accomplished using the same commands used for moving data to and from files.

Unfortunately, GUI-based operating systems, such as MS Windows, are slightly more complex. Unlike console I/O—which closely resembles both a teletype and a **text file** that can be read line-by-line—graphic activities typically do not correspond closely to any normal file activities. In addition, many devices (e.g., printers, modems) and ports (e.g., COM ports) are managed by the operating system in a manner not consistent with the way files are opened and closed in stream I/O. As a consequence, stream-based I/O tends to be mainly limited to file activities on these operating systems. Console programs created under Windows, however, are specifically designed to mimic the behavior of earlier operating systems. Thus, the programs we write in this text follow the traditional UNIX/DOS model reasonably well.

8.1.2: SimpleIO Stream Objects

Before we can worry about moving data between file streams and our programs, we need to know how to associate a file with a stream. This process actually involves two issues:

- How do we identify a stream in our program?
- How do we associate a stream with a specific file?

Every operating system has a specific object it uses to keep track of all the information necessary to manage a specific file or device attached to the stream. The name of the structure is unimportant (an _iobuf structure in Visual Studio .NET), and its specific elements even less so. The reason we do not care about the structure itself is that the language provides us with encapsulated objects (C++) that we can work with, without worrying about the mechanics, which are handled by the operating system.

In C++, a variety of different object types are defined to allow us to work with file streams. To fully understand these object types, however, requires fairly substantial knowledge of how C++ objects are constructed, and how they inherit characteristics from other objects. For this reason, we delay their introduction to a later chapter (Chapter 17).

In order that we may discuss files in a general way (that applies to C++, C, and many other languages), a series of elementary file functions have been included in the SimpleIO files. Using these functions and type definitions, we can study the nature of file I/O without initially worrying about the complexities of the C++ class libraries.

Before we can work with a stream, we need to be able to associate it with a file, which is typically done as a two-step process. First, we need to declare a stream object variable as follows:

```
STREAM fobj;
```

We must keep such a variable for every stream that we have open. If you lose the variable, you can no longer use the stream.

TEST YOUR UNDERSTANDING 8.1:

If you want to see how SimpleIO data types and functions are defined, where should you go?

Opening a Stream   How do we associate a file with our stream variable? We call the SimpleIO Open() function, prototyped as follows:

```
bool Open(STREAM &file,const char *szName,
    bool bRead,bool bWrite,bool bTrunc,bool bText);
```

When we call Open(), we need to specify the following arguments:

- **file:** The STREAM variable we have previously declared
- **szName:** The file name (including a path, if desired) to be associated with the stream
- **bRead:** Is the file to be open for reading (input)? If **true,** we will be able to read data from the file. If **false,** we can only write data to the file.
- **bWrite:** Is the file to be opened for writing (output)? If **true,** we will be able to write data to the file. If **false,** we can only read data from the file. It is permissible for both the *bRead* and *bWrite* arguments to be true—in that case we can both read data from the file and write data to it. At least one (*bRead* or *bWrite*) must be true however.
- **bTrunc:** Is the file to be erased when it is opened? Many times, when you open a file (e.g., doing a "Save As…" for a document), it makes sense to erase anything that is already there. On the other hand, you would certainly not want *bTrunc* set to **true** if you were opening an existing document and you wanted to read the data from it.
- **bText:** Is the file to be opened for text I/O (i.e., is it to be a text file or **ASCII file**), or is it going to hold raw (i.e., binary) data?

The function returns **true** if the opening operation is successful, **false** if it is not. Reasons an open operation might fail could include incorrect file name, incorrect path name, incompatible device (e.g., opening a file for writing on a read-only CD), the file is already open somewhere else (especially if sharing is not set), as well as other types of problems. For this reason, you should always check to see whether an open operation has succeeded before going on to use the file.

Text Files The final argument to Open() warrants a bit more explanation. Its origins go back to the early days of C, when I/O was frequently performed using teletype-style devices. To start a new line on these devices, two characters were required: a newline (\n), which moved the role up a line, and a return (\r), which moved the print head to the left-hand side of the paper. For this historical reason, many operating systems require that each line of a text file end with a "\r\n" pair of characters.

The problem with having two characters at the end of each text line is that when you read data from a text file (which is often done line-by-line, as we shall see), these characters can be read as well—meaning that you end up with at least one extra white (non-printing) characters at the end of each line you read in. The purpose of opening a file in text mode (*bText* set to **true**) is to eliminate the extra character (the \r) when a line is read in. Specifically:

- When a file is designated as a text file, single '\n' characters are replaced by "\r\n" pairs in text files when outputting data. Conversely, "\r\n" pairs are replaced by '\n' characters when reading data from files.
- If a file is opened as a binary type, no translations are made.

Thus, even though you can read lines of a text file that is opened as a **binary file,** if you do so, you will often get an extra character at the end of each line you read. That difference, however, is the only major one between files open in text and binary modes.

Closing a Stream The SimpleIO Close() function is used to close an open file stream. Its prototype is simple:

```
void Close(STREAM &file);
```

The file argument must point to a stream opened by using Open().

Three reasons explain why you should always close files when you are done with them:

- Because open files consume resources, most operating systems have a limit on how many files are open at once. Keeping a file open unnecessarily may impact other programs if that limit is reached.
- If your program has a file open using one stream, chances are it will not be able to open it using another (an O/S protection that may be disabled under certain circumstances). The practical result is that if you open a file, then lose track of its stream variable without closing it, you may not be able to access the file again until you shut down your program, which automatically closes all open files.
- To avoid slowing down your program by waiting for leisurely file accesses (and to avoid making your disk sound like a hummingbird from all the activity), file buffers in memory often hold output waiting to be sent to a file. When a file is closed, those buffers are flushed to the file. Until they are flushed, it is possible that data your program has written to disk may not have actually reached the disk, which means it could be lost in the event of a system crash or power failure.

8.1: SECTION QUESTIONS

1. What is the purpose of the bTrunc argument to Open()?
2. Are text files produced under different operating systems necessarily byte-for-byte compatible with each other?

3. Why should you *always* check the return value of Open() after you call it?

4. What are the key problems of opening a file stream and not closing it when you are done?

8.2: TEXT FILE I/O

Up to this point in the text, all of our input and output has been in the form of collections of ASCII characters to and from the console. In this section, we extend this text-based I/O to files.

8.2.1: Text Output

In this section, we examine how to write text to an open file stream. First we examine unformatted text, then we briefly consider formatted text.

Unformatted Text Output The SimpleIO PrintLine() function writes a string to a text file, followed by a newline. It is prototyped as follows:

```
void PrintLine(OUTPUT &out,const char *szOut);
```

In addition, SimpleIO provides a series of functions that write individual data elements to a file, without a newline:

- *void PrintString(OUTPUT &out,const char *szOut):* Writes a text string to the text stream *out*.
- *void PrintInteger(OUTPUT &out,int nVal):* Translates an integer to a string, then writes the integer to the text stream *out*.
- *void PrintCharacter(OUTPUT &out,char cVal):* Writes an ASCII character to the text stream *out*.
- *void PrintReal(OUTPUT &out,double dVal):* Writes an unformatted real number to the text stream *out*.
- *void EndLine(OUTPUT &out):* Sends an end of line to the text stream *out*, which is basically equivalent to PrintCharacter(out,'\n').
- *void WhiteSpace(OUTPUT &out):* Sends a space to the text stream *out*, which is basically equivalent to PrintCharacter(out,' ').

In all of these cases, the *out* argument can be one of two things:

- A STREAM variable that has been opened for writing in text mode
- A predefined object, such as **cout** or **cerr**

The second of these alternatives is particularly important to note because it means that these functions can be used for console, as well as file, output. For example:

```
PrintString(cout,"Hello, World");
```

is equivalent to both:

```
DisplayString("Hello, World");
```

and

```
cout <<  "Hello, World";
```

The ability to treat the console as just another form of file is one of the principal benefits of defining streams.

In addition to treating the console as file stream, the operating system may provide other specialized file names. For example, in DOS any data directed to a file called PRN actually gets sent to the default printer. Thus, the code:

```
STREAM myPrn;
// open printer stream for text output
if (!Open(myPrn,"PRN",false,true,false,true)) return;
PrintLine(myPrn,"Hello World");
```

would cause "Hello World" to be sent to the printer. (It's probably not a good idea to try printing this way in Windows, because it can lead to problems with the print queues. For Windows printing, the best approach is to print to a file, then open the file in a program such as MS Word or MS Notepad and print from there.)

TEST YOUR UNDERSTANDING 8.2:

What advantage might there be to using a function such as EndLine() in place of printing "\n" directly when you want to start a new line?

In-Depth: Formatted Text Output As we shall see in Chapter 17, C++ provides a large range of options for formatting text output. For the time being, however, we can accomplish significant formatting using the same principles presented when the DisplayFormatted() function was introduced in Chapter 7, Section 7.3. **Formatted output** to a text file is accomplished using PrintFormatted() SimpleIO function. The function is prototyped as follows:

```
void PrintFormatted(OUTPUT &out,const char *szFmt,...);
```

Its usage is precisely the same as that of the printf() function, discussed at length in Chapter 7 (Sections 7.3). In fact, the following two forms are identical:

```
PrintFormatted(cout,fmt,args…)  ≡  DisplayFormatted(fmt,args…)
```

8.2.2: Text Input

Text input from a file can be accomplished by reading individual data elements, or by processing the file line by line. The SimpleIO functions for reading individual data elements are as follows:

- *void GetString(INPUT &in,char szIn[]):* Reads a string from the text stream *in* and places it in the array szIn, which must be large enough to accommodate it.
- *int GetInteger(INPUT &in):* Reads an integer from the text stream *in* and returns its value.
- *double GetReal(INPUT &in):* Reads a real number from the text stream *in* and returns its value.
- *char GetCharacter(INPUT &in):* Reads a character from the text stream *in* and returns its value.

These functions work by skipping over any white characters in the stream (i.e., spaces, tabs, returns) then reading data until the next white character is encountered.

Unfortunately, the way input is processed leads to difficulties when dealing with text strings (problems that impact C++ I/O as well). The problem can be easily illustrated. Suppose we have an open text output stream (*tout*) and write a string to it as follows:

```
PrintString(tout,"Hello World");
```

Later, we reopen the file for text input as *tin*, and try to read the string back:

```
char arIn[80];
GetString(tin,arIn);
```

When we look at the contents of arIn after the GetString() function has been called, we see the string "Hello". What happened to the "World"?

The nature of the problem is that GetString() assumes any white space terminates a string. That means that since original string, "Hello World", had a white space in it, when read back it appears as two separate strings, "Hello" and "World".

Getting around this problem can be done in a number of ways that are illustrated in Chapter 17. You can use delimiters—such as the tab character—to start and end data elements. You can use characters such as " and ' to mark the start and end of strings. You can even save text in such a way that different pieces of data align in columns (as illustrated in a walkthrough at the end of this chapter, Section 8.4.1). None of these solutions, however, are supported directly by C++. Instead, they tend to require the programmer to read in data line by line, then process the lines within the program. As a result, most of the time when you are working with text files, you will find it is easier to work with lines than with individual data elements.

Line input from a file into a character array can be performed using the GetLine() SimpleIO function. It is prototyped as follows:

```
bool GetLine(INPUT &in,char szIn[],int nMax);
```

The function reads a line from any file stream (e.g., STREAM variable) or from **cin,** which is the standard input object that corresponds to **cout.** Upon reading the line, no more than nMax-1 characters are then placed sIn, with a NUL terminator at the end. The function returns **true** unless the end of the file has been reached (or some error occurs, such as passing in a stream not opened for reading), in which case it returns **false.** This fact can be used in reading lines from a text file. For example, the following loop will read lines from "testfile.txt" until the file is empty:

```
STREAM infile;
char buf[255];
// open existing text file for reading
if (!Open(infile,"testfile.txt",true,false,false,true)) return;
while (GetLine(infile,buf,255)) {
// code to process lines goes in here
}
```

The function behaves similarly to the already discussed InputString(), which reads a line from the console. It differs in two ways:

- The nMax argument limits the number of characters that are read. This feature is important because it is easy for a file to accidentally overflow the destination buffer (e.g., if a binary file—lacking \r\n characters to make the end of a line—was accidentally read, instead of a text file).
- The in argument identifies a file stream.

The following call to GetLine() would be roughly equivalent to a call to InputString():

```
char buf[80];
GetLine(cin,buf,80);
```

The GetLine() call would actually be somewhat safer, however, because it would guarantee the input would not overflow the buffer.

8.2.3: Example of Text I/O

Walkthrough available in TextIO.wmv

In this section we look at a simple text I/O demonstration program, focusing on element-oriented I/O. (In 8.4.1, line-oriented file processing will be considered.)

The SaveText() function, presented in Example 8.1, takes a set of arrays (set up as global variables, for convenience) and writes them to a text file. Its sole argument is the name of the file to which the data is to be saved. It returns **true** if successful, **false** otherwise.

The SaveText() function operates as follows:

■   The file named szFile is opened for writing as a text file. The bTrunc argument of Open() is set to **true,** so that any existing data will be erased. If the file fails to open, the function returns false.

EXAMPLE 8.1

SaveText() function

```
#include "SimpleIO.h"

int arID[10]={101,102,103,104,105,106,107,108,109,110};
double arHeight[10]={6.1,5.8,5.05,6.3,5.9,5.4,6.0,4.95,6.6,5.3};
char arSex[10]={'M','M','F','M','F','M','F','M','M','F'};
int arWeight[10]={225,190,98,307,210,145,215,110,280,165};

bool SaveText(const char *szFile)
{
    STREAM out;
    int nCount,i;
    if (!Open(out,szFile,false,true,true,true)) return false;
    DisplayString("How many values do you want to save? (1 to 10): ");
    nCount=InputInteger();
    if (nCount<1 || nCount>10) {
        DisplayString("Illegal value: must be between 1 and 10");
        return false;
    }
    PrintInteger(out,nCount);
    EndLine(out);
    for(i=0;i<nCount;i++) {
        PrintInteger(out,arID[i]);
        WhiteSpace(out);
        PrintReal(out,arHeight[i]);
        WhiteSpace(out);
        PrintCharacter(out,arSex[i]);
        WhiteSpace(out);
        PrintInteger(out,arWeight[i]);
        EndLine(out);
    }
    Close(out);
    return true;
}
```

- The user is prompted to identify how many values are to be saved, which is verified to be between 1 and 10. This information is then written to the text file (where it will be useful when it comes time to read the data), followed by an EndLine().

- A loop is performed whereby the ID, height, sex, and weight data are all saved, followed by an EndLine(), which causes each set of data to be given its own line in the file.

- Upon completion of the loop, the stream is closed and the function returns true, indicating success.

A data file produced by SaveText() function is displayed, in MS Notepad, in Figure 8.1.

The function DisplayText() takes a file created by SaveText() and displays it to the console. This function is presented in Example 8.2

The DisplayText() function operates as follows:

- The file stream is opened for the szFile argument. The call to Open() specifies a readable text file, not truncated. If the open fails, the function returns **false.**

- The integers specifying the number of data items stored is read from the text file. This information is used to control the file reading operations.

- Column headers, separated by tabs, are displayed to the console.

- A loop is performed whereby the ID, height, sex, and weight elements are read from the file, then displayed (separated by tabs) to the console. It is interesting to note that although the ID was saved as an integer, it is loaded as a string. When dealing with text I/O, this type of switch presents no serious obstacles, because anything in a text file can be read as if it were text.

FIGURE 8.1   Contents of File Created by SaveText()

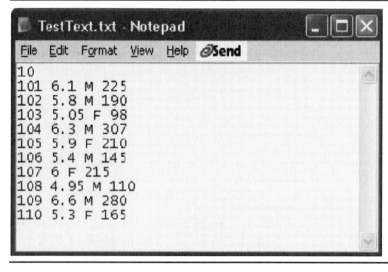

EXAMPLE 8.2

DisplayText() function

```
bool DisplayText(const char *szFile)
{
   STREAM in;
   int nCount,i;
   if (!Open(in,szFile,true,false,false,true)) return false;
   nCount=GetInteger(in);
   NewLine();
   DisplayString("ID\tHeight\tSex\tWeight\n--\t------\t---\t------\n");
   for(i=0;i<nCount;i++) {
      char szID[20];
      double dHeight;
      char cSex;
      int nWeight;
      // reading data
      GetString(in,szID); // Note: ID read as string for demo purposes
      dHeight=GetReal(in);
      cSex=GetCharacter(in);
      nWeight=GetInteger(in);
      // displaying data
      DisplayString(szID);
      DisplayCharacter('\t');
      DisplayReal(dHeight);
      DisplayCharacter('\t');
      DisplayCharacter(cSex);
      DisplayCharacter('\t');
      DisplayInteger(nWeight);
      NewLine();
   }
   Close(in);
   return true;
}
```

■ Upon completion of the loop, the input stream is closed and the function returns **true.**

The console output from running SaveText() then DisplayText() is shown in Figure 8.2.

It is worth noting, once again, that text files can be created using many techniques. Example 8.3 contains a revised version of the text saving function, called SaveFormattedText(), that uses a single call to PrintFormatted() (see Chapter 7, Section 7.3, for explanation of formatting arguments) instead of saving the data elements individually.

This function produces a text file that is nearly identical to the one produced by SaveText(), except that the real numbers saved for height measurements are all displayed to two decimal places (as a result of the %6.2f formatting used). The output file produced by the function, shown in MS Notepad, is presented in Figure 8.3.

FIGURE 8.2   Console Display of SaveText() Followed by DisplayText()

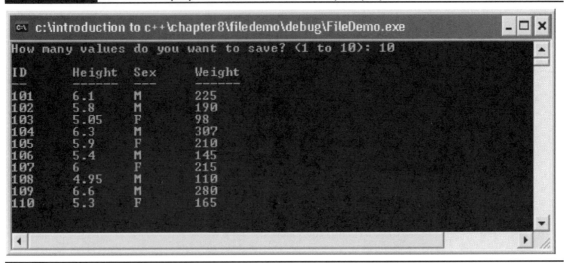

EXAMPLE 8.3

SaveFormattedText() function

```
bool SaveFormattedText(const char *szFile)
{
    STREAM out;
    int nCount,i;
    if (!Open(out,szFile,false,true,true,true)) return false;
    DisplayString("How many values do you want to save? (1 to 10): ");
    nCount=InputInteger();
    if (nCount<1 || nCount>10) {
        DisplayString("Illegal value: must be between 1 and 10");
        return false;
    }
    PrintInteger(out,nCount);
    EndLine(out);
    for(i=0;i<nCount;i++) {
        PrintFormatted(out,"%i\t%6.2f\t%c\t%i\n",
            arID[i],arHeight[i],arSex[i],arWeight[i]);
    }
    Close(out);
    return true;
}
```

8.2: SECTION QUESTIONS

1. Why is using GetLine(cin,...) safer than using InputString()?
2. How can the contents of a string interfere with our ability to read it?
3. Why is GetString() not a mirror image of PrintString()?

FIGURE 8.3 File Generated by PrintFormattedText()

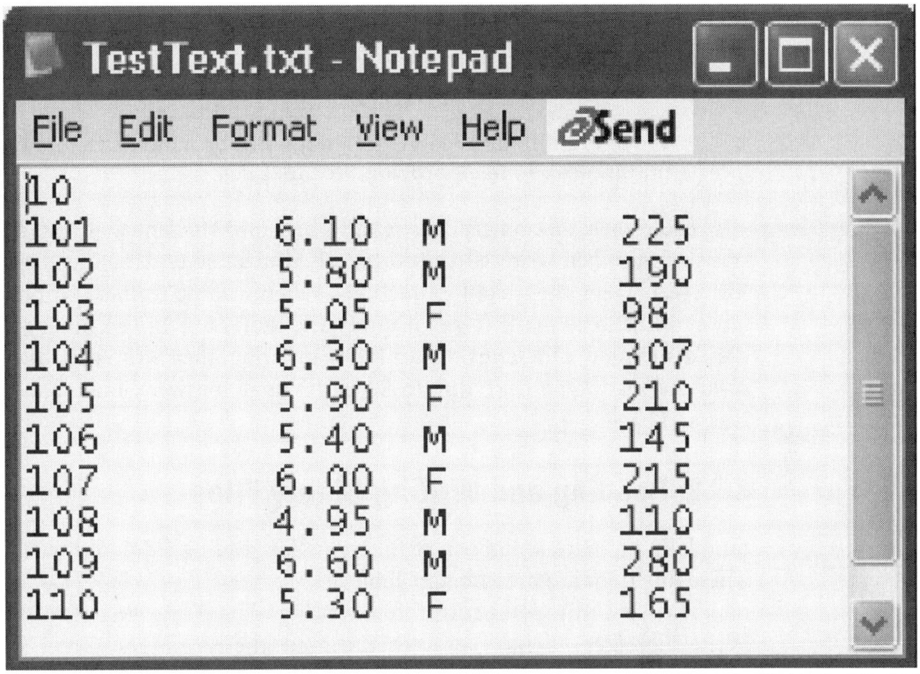


```
10
101        6.10  M       225
102        5.80  M       190
103        5.05  F       98
104        6.30  M       307
105        5.90  F       210
106        5.40  M       145
107        6.00  F       215
108        4.95  M       110
109        6.60  M       280
110        5.30  F       165
```

4. What is the basic procedure for reading all the lines in a text file?
5. If you are not sure about the format of a text file, how do you examine its format?

8.3: IN DEPTH: BINARY I/O

Although text files are used extensively for transferring data between systems and between applications, binary files are much more commonly used to store internal application data. Among the reasons:

- Binary file data can usually be processed much faster than text data.
- Many data types, such as graphics, have no natural text representation.

In this section we explore what we mean by a binary file. We then present some SimpleIO functions for working with such files.

8.3.1: Text vs. Binary Files

What is the difference between a text file and a binary file? It's actually pretty simple. A text file is a file created with two important characteristics:

- All nontext data contained in the file are represented using text equivalents (e.g., 125 would be represented by the three characters '1', '2', and '5').
- The separation between lines is indicated by specific characters, which may vary by operating system. Normally, the ends of line are indicated either by a

single '\n' character, or by a "\r\n" combination. (The PC normally uses the two-character combination.)

A binary file is any file that is not a text file.

TEST YOUR UNDERSTANDING 8.3:

Why would binary file I/O functions not provide the same type of formatting capabilities provided for text I/O.

The reason that binary files tend to be more efficient than text files has to do with translation. When writing to a text file, all noncharacter data must be translated into text form (e.g., using the sprintf() function). When reading from a text file, the reverse translation needs to be made (e.g., the atoi() and atof() functions). Binary files normally handle data entirely differently. Instead of translating, they write data directly from RAM to disk, and read them from disk to RAM. It's as if you were doing a memcpy() directly to disk and back.

8.3.2: Reading and Writing Binary Files

SimpleIO provides a number of functions for reading from and writing to a binary file. These functions are presented in Table 8.1.

The first three functions for writing data (i.e., WriteInteger, WriteReal, and WriteCharacter) behave exactly the way their SimpleIO text counterparts (i.e., PrintInteger, PrintReal, and PrintCharacter) do. The only difference is that raw data are written, instead of character strings. The same is also true of the first three functions for reading data (i.e., ReadInteger, ReadReal, and ReadCharacter), which correspond to the text input functions (i.e., GetInteger, GetReal, and GetCharacter). An additional group of functions (WriteFloat, ReadFloat, WriteShort, and ReadShort) is also provided. Such functions were unnecessary in text I/O, because of little need to distinguish between float (4-byte) and double (8-byte) reals, or short (2-byte) and regular (4-byte) integers when going back and forth to text. In a binary file, however, it is critical that any data be read exactly as they were saved. We will see an example of the use of these functions in the binary file example presented in Section 8.4.2.

Block Writing and Reading   What is really different about the binary file I/O functions are the two block functions, WriteBlock and ReadBlock. These functions are particularly important for two reasons: (1) they are particularly well-suited to saving array data, and (2) they most closely correspond to the binary I/O functions that are provided by the C++ library, which will be discussed in Chapter 17.

The WriteBlock and ReadBlock functions are, effectively, mirror images of each other. Both take three arguments:

1. *file:* The open binary file stream object.
2. *buf:* The address in memory where the block to be written from, or read to, begins. For our purposes, we will assume that it is an array name that—as you may recall—identifies the location in memory where the array starts. (Later, in Chapter 10, we'll discover that a pointer can also be used.)
3. *nBytes:* The number of bytes to be written or read.

| **TABLE 8.1** | SimpleIO Functions for Binary File I/O |

bool WriteInteger(STREAM &file,int nVal);

Writes a single integer to the open binary file stream. It returns **true** if the operation is successful, **false** otherwise.

---

bool WriteReal(STREAM &file,double dVal);

Writes a single double real number to the open file stream. It returns **true** if the operation is successful, **false** otherwise.

---

bool WriteFloat(STREAM &file,float dVal);

Writes a single float real number to the open file stream. It returns **true** if the operation is successful, **false** otherwise.

---

bool WriteCharacter(STREAM &file,char cVal);

Writes a single character to the open file stream. It returns **true** if the operation is successful, **false** otherwise.

---

bool WriteShort(STREAM &file,short nVal);

Writes a short (2-byte) integer to the open file stream. It returns **true** if the operation is successful, **false** otherwise.

---

*bool WriteBlock(STREAM &file,const void *buf,int nBytes);*

Writes an array of any type of data, starting at position *buf,* to the open binary file stream. The amount of data to be written is *nBytes.* It returns **true** if the operation is successful, **false** otherwise.

---

int ReadInteger(STREAM &file);

Reads an integer from the open binary file stream, returning its value.

---

double ReadReal(STREAM &file);

Reads a double from the open binary file stream, returning its value.

---

float ReadFloat(STREAM &file);

Reads a float from the open binary file stream, returning its value.

---

char ReadCharacter(STREAM &file);

Reads a character from the open binary file stream, returning its value.

---

short ReadShort(STREAM &file);

Reads a short (2-byte) integer from the open binary file stream, returning its value.

---

*bool ReadBlock(STREAM &file,void *buf,int nBytes);*

Reads an array from the open binary file stream, copying *nBytes* of data from the file to the memory location beginning at position *buf.* It returns **true** if the operation is successful, **false** otherwise.

The last of these arguments is, to a great extent, the most problematic because it requires us to figure out how much memory the data we are saving/loading require. Fortunately, C/C++ gives us a convenient means of doing so, the **sizeof** operator.

sizeof Operator   The C/C++ **sizeof** operator is a special type of operator that is evaluated by the compiler and returns the number of bytes required for its argument. The operator may be applied to variables, expressions, and data types. In each case, it returns the following result:

sizeof scalar-variable-name	➔ returns size of variable's data type
sizeof array-name	➔ returns number of bytes to hold entire array
sizeof (data-type)	➔ returns size of the data type
sizeof other-expression	➔ returns size of the return type

Parentheses are only required when the operator is applied to a data type, for example **sizeof**(int) or **sizeof**(STREAM).

Suppose, then, we wanted to save an array of 10 integers to an open file stream bintest. We could use one of two ways (that are completely equivalent):

```
int arTest[10]={1,3,5,7,9,2,4,6,8,0};
// Method 1: Writes entire array arTest to file stream bintest
WriteBlock(bintest,arTest,sizeof arTest);
// Method 2: Writes entire array arTest to file stream
// bintest (a second time)
WriteBlock(bintest,arTest,10 * sizeof(int));
```

Reading is accomplished in the same manner. In fact, the WriteBlock() and ReadBlock() functions are specifically designed so that writing and reading looks the same. For example:

```
int arTest[10];
// Method 1: Reads bytes from disk into arTest
ReadBlock(bintest,arTest,sizeof arTest);
// Method 2: Reads bytes from disk into arTest a second time
ReadBlock(bintest,arTest,10 * sizeof(int));
```

In using **sizeof,** it is important to recognize where it is and is not appropriate. Despite its appearance, **sizeof** is an operator, not a function. For this reason it can be applied without parentheses (except when a data type is specified). More importantly, the actual value returned by **sizeof** is computed by the compiler—it is not computed while the program is running, the way a function call is. Thus, when **sizeof** is applied to an array of characters, it returns the size of the entire array—not the length of any string that happens to be in it. Similarly, when applied to a character pointer that contains the address of a string, it returns 4—or whatever the size of a pointer is. It does not return the length of the string! Do not make the common mistake of confusing **sizeof** and strlen() in your code.

8.3.3: Moving Around in a Binary File

Text files tend to be processed sequentially—with each line being read in then discarded. Binary files, in contrast, are often read randomly—meaning that we move around in the file to find specific data. By doing so, we can use our binary files as a substitute for RAM—any data we need we can read from the file, it just takes longer. Virtually all real-world databases are constructed on this principle: keep data on disk until they are specifically needed.

Concept of File Position Before discussing the functions SimpleIO provides for navigating within a file, it is useful to consider the key similarities and differences between RAM and file storage. The two most important similarities are the following:

- Both files and RAM store data using digital representation, which eliminates any problems moving data back and forth between files and RAM (as we saw using the ReadBlock() and WriteBlock() functions).

■ Like RAM, every byte in a file has an address. The addressing scheme for files is simple: the first byte is 0, and the remaining bytes are numbered accordingly.

One important difference between files and RAM bears mentioning, however. Files always keep track of their current "position"—a concept that is not meaningful in RAM. Virtually every file operation takes place relative to its current position (sometimes called the file cursor, file window, or file pointer). Thus, we need to explore the concept more fully.

The reason files keep track of a position is fairly easy to understand. In the early days of computing, card readers and tape drives were the most common devices used for mass storage. These devices are as different from today's hard drives as a cassette recorder is from a CD. You cannot just jump from point A to point B in a cassette drive—it takes time because you have got to go through all the intervening tape. (Or, in the case of a card reader, go through the stack of cards.) For such devices, a huge advantage comes from keeping track of where you are. If, for example, you are at position 10,000 and need to go to 10,001, it would be highly inefficient to rewind the tape to 0, then count 10,001 bytes from the beginning.

When a file is opened, it normally starts at position 0 unless the file is opened for appending—in which case the starting position is the end of the file, whatever that happens to be. From that point on, every read or write operation updates the position (just the way that *listening* to a song or *recording* a song changes the position on a cassette tape). Thus, after the following code:

```
STREAM in;
char buf[256];
if (Open(in,"Example.bin",true,false,false,false)) {
    ReadBlock(in,buf,250);
}
```

our new position in the file would be 250 (assuming the file opened properly). Our next read would take place at that position.

Setting File Position   In C++, the position for the next read and position for the next write are set separately. SimpleIO, therefore, provides two functions for setting **file position:**

```
bool SetWritePosition(STREAM &file,int nPos);
bool SetReadPosition(STREAM &file,int nPos);
```

Both functions set file position using a 0-based system, where 0 is the first byte in the file. Although, as we will discover in Chapter 17, C++ provides more options for positioning (e.g., positioning relative to the current position, positioning relative to the end of the file), setting position relative to the start of the file is the simplest approach, and by far the most commonly used.

8.3.4: Binary File Demonstration

Walkthrough available in BinaryIO.wmv

For purposes of comparison, we can compare the functions used to create text and binary files. In Example 8.4, the SaveBinary() function is presented, designed to save exactly the same data saved in the SaveText() function presented earlier (Example 8.1).

The function is similar to its text counterpart, first opening the file (this time, in binary mode), then prompting the user for the number of values to be saved. Among the key differences that need to be noted are the following:

EXAMPLE 8.4

SaveBinary() function

```
bool SaveBinary(const char *szFile)
{
    STREAM out;
    int nCount,i;
    if (!Open(out,szFile,false,true,true,false)) return false;
    DisplayString("How many values do you want to save? (1 to 10): ");
    nCount=InputInteger();
    if (nCount<1 || nCount>10) {
        DisplayString("Illegal value: must be between 1 and 10");
        return false;
    }
    WriteInteger(out,nCount);
    for(i=0;i<nCount;i++) {
        WriteInteger(out,arID[i]);
        WriteReal(out,arHeight[i]);
        WriteCharacter(out,arSex[i]);
        WriteInteger(out,arWeight[i]);
    }
    Close(out);
    return true;
}
```

- The binary SimpleIO functions (i.e., Write...) are used to save data to the file, instead of the text functions (i.e., Print...).

- No lines or spacing characters are inserted into the file. Such characters are unnecessary, because the data size of each element being saved is fixed (i.e., integers are 4 bytes, doubles are 8 bytes, characters are 1 byte), which means that separators to tell us where each data element starts and ends are unnecessary.

The DisplayBinary() function, presented in Example 8.5, is also similar to its text counterpart, DisplayText() (Example 8.2). In fact, the function calls to display text to the console are identical. What is different, however, is how data are read.

The key differences in the data reading are as follows:

- Binary SimpleIO input functions (i.e., Read...) are used in place of text input functions (i.e., Get...).

- ID must be read as an integer. When we read the text file, we could choose to interpret the data as text or numeric, but that choice is not available in a binary file. Because the value was saved as a 4-byte integer, it must be read that way.

The difference in text and binary files can be understood by looking at the actual bytes in binary and text files. Visual Studio .NET makes this task easy, because it allows any file to be opened in a binary display format in the following manner:

- Select File|Open.
- Click "Open With..." (as shown in Figure 8.4).
- Select "Binary Editor" from the resulting list of options.

EXAMPLE 8.5

DisplayBinary() function

```
bool DisplayBinary(const char *szFile)
{
    STREAM in;
    int nCount,i;
    if (!Open(in,szFile,true,false,false,false)) return false;
    nCount=ReadInteger(in);
    NewLine();
    DisplayString("ID\tHeight\tSex\tWeight\n-\t——\t--\t——\n");
    for(i=0;i<nCount;i++) {
        int nID;
        double dHeight;
        char cSex;
        int nWeight;
        // reading data
        nID=ReadInteger(in);
        dHeight=ReadReal(in);
        cSex=ReadCharacter(in);
        nWeight=ReadInteger(in);
        // displaying data to console
        DisplayInteger(nID);
        DisplayCharacter('\t');
        DisplayReal(dHeight);
        DisplayCharacter('\t');
        DisplayCharacter(cSex);
        DisplayCharacter('\t');
        DisplayInteger(nWeight);
        NewLine();
    }
    Close(in);
    return true;
}
```

The text file TestText.txt (generated by running SaveFormattedText(), in Example 8.3) is presented in a binary file viewer in Figure 8.5. A binary file containing the same data (generated by calling SaveBinary(), in Example 8.4) is shown in Figure 8.6.

The differences between the two files are immediately apparent. In the text file, the first piece of information is the number of data items followed by a newline pair, presented as the bytes:

0x31 ('1'), 0x30 ('0'), 0x0D ('\r') , 0x0A ('\n')

(ASCII equivalents of printable characters are printed in the right 16 columns, with periods used to signify that a character is not printable). We then see the data elements separated by tab (0x09) characters. Because the file contains text, most of the ASCII equivalent area on the right-hand side of the viewer contains printable characters.

In the binary file, on the other hand, the first four bytes are:

0x0A 0x00 0x00 0x00

FIGURE 8.4 Opening File Using "Open With" Option

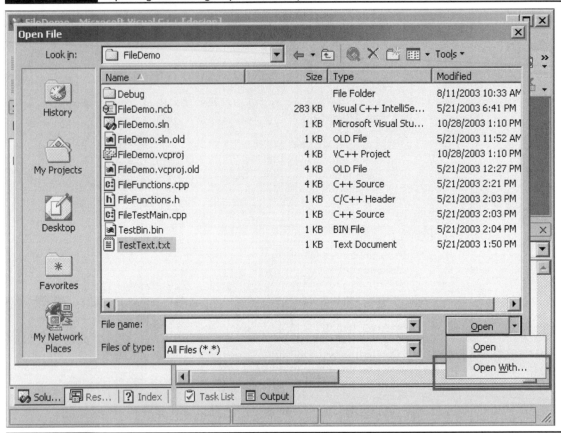

FIGURE 8.5 Binary View of Text File TestText.txt

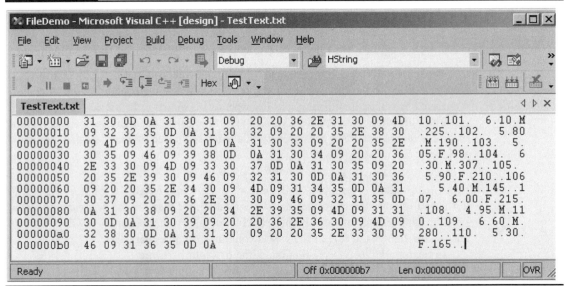

FIGURE 8.6 Binary View of TextBin.bin

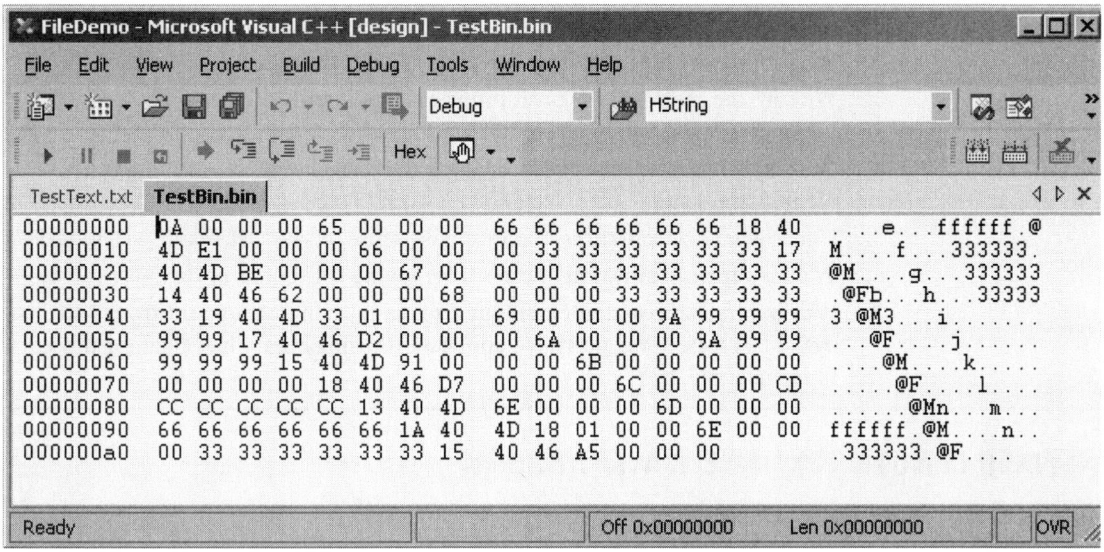

This 4-byte integer is saved in reverse order (which is how such integers are saved in a PC), meaning it is equivalent to writing the hex number:

0x0000000A

It is the same as 10 in decimal. It is, of course, the number of data elements saved—just as it was for the text file. Following that:

- The next 4 bytes are the integer 0x00000065, which is 101 in decimal—the ID of the first element.
- The next 8 bytes are a double, which is nearly impossible to interpret.
- The next byte (first byte of the second row) is the character data identifying sex, which happens to be 0x4D, or 'M'.
- This byte is followed by the 4-byte weight integer 0x000000E1, which is 14*16+1 = 225 in decimal.

That file item is followed by the information for the next data item. You can get a sense of the layout of the overall layout file by looking the text side. Each item that we saved required 17 bytes (4 for ID, 8 for height, 1 for sex, 4 for weight). Because each row in the display shows 16 bytes, the diagonal pattern in the left-hand side reflects the position of the sex character within each item, one byte further over in each row. Most other characters on the right-hand side are purely coincidental, values contained in integers or real numbers that happen to correspond to ASCII characters.

TEST YOUR UNDERSTANDING 8.4:

What is the significance of the 'e' that appears in the first row of the Figure 8.6 display?

8.3 SECTION QUESTIONS

1. Explain why reading and writing binary data is similar to the C function memcpy.

2. Why are binary files usually faster to work with than text files?

3. Why are the functions for positioning a file pointer nearly always reserved for use in files opened in binary mode?

4. What is the difference between saving a structure as a block and saving it element by element?

5. Under what circumstances might it make sense to save a structure as a block?

6. What is the near-universal approach for saving collections of data (e.g., arrays)?

7. Why might changes in integral type sizes (e.g., changing **long int** from 4 to 8 bytes) be of greater concern for applications using binary files than for those utilizing text files?

8.4: FIXED LENGTH TEXT FILE WALKTHROUGH

 Walkthrough available in FixedFilm.wmv

In this section we present a walkthrough that shows how information can be extracted from a text file where the data are laid out in columns of fixed width. In a business context, this type of data file is fairly common, as a fixed width layout can be produced directly by many applications (e.g., MS Access) and is also sometimes created by printing data from an application to a text printer whose output is directed to a file—something that can easily be set up in MS Windows.

8.4.1: Processing a Fixed Width Text File

The particular file we will be working with contains a collection of some of the films released in 1999. It is a pure text file, with data laid out in columns. A section of the file is presented in Example 8.6.

The definitions of the data elements in the file layout are presented in Table 8.2, which identifies the 0-based start column for each data element, its length, and a description. This type of table can be easily prepared using a text editor, such as MS Notepad or the editor in MS Visual Studio .NET, which displays the column position of the cursor.

Application Description   The application being presented takes the text file and displays the film title, along with its categories of classification. It pauses every 24 lines (i.e., when the screen fills up) and prompts the user for a key. Sample output is displayed in Figure 8.7.

The TextViewer application consists of three functions:

- *ListFilms:* Reads each line of the text file into a buffer, then calls DisplayFilm() to cause it to be displayed on the console.

- *DisplayFilm:* Takes a text string containing a single line from the file and displays the desired data elements to the console.

- *GetField:* Retrieves the data for a specific element (e.g., title) from a string containing all the data for the file.

EXAMPLE 8.6

Sample of Films1999.txt

```
1   1999 200 Cigarettes                               0 1 0 1 0 0 0 0 0 0 0 0 0
2   1999 2001 Yonggary                                0 0 0 0 1 0 0 1 0 0 0 0 0
3   1999 8MM                                          0 0 0 0 0 0 1 0 0 0 0 0 0
4   1999 Magical Legend of the Leprechauns, The       0 0 0 0 1 0 0 0 0 0 0 0 0
5   1999 Storm of the Century                         0 0 0 0 0 0 0 0 0 0 0 0 1
6   1999 10 Things I Hate About You                   0 1 0 0 0 0 0 0 0 0 0 1 0
7   1999 13th Warrior, The                            1 0 0 0 1 0 0 0 0 0 0 0 0
8   1999 Alice in Wonderland                          0 0 0 0 1 1 0 0 0 0 0 0 0
9   1999 All the King's Men                           0 0 0 0 0 0 0 0 1 0 0 0 0
10  1999 American Beauty                              0 0 0 1 0 0 0 0 0 0 0 0 0
11  1999 American Pie                                 0 1 0 0 0 0 0 0 0 0 0 0 0
12  1999 Analyze This                                 0 1 0 0 0 0 0 0 0 0 0 0 0
13  1999 Angela's Ashes                               0 0 0 1 0 0 0 0 0 0 0 0 0
14  1999 Animal Farm                                  0 0 0 0 1 0 0 0 0 0 0 0 0
15  1999 Anna and the King                            0 0 0 1 0 0 0 0 0 0 0 1 0
16  1999 Any Given Sunday                             0 0 0 1 0 0 0 0 0 0 0 0 0
17  1999 Anywhere But Here                            0 0 0 1 0 0 0 0 0 0 0 0 0
18  1999 Apartment Complex, The                       0 0 0 0 0 0 1 0 0 0 0 0 0
```

TABLE 8.2   Films1999.txt Layout

Start Column	Data Length	Description
0	5	ID code for the file
5	4	Year film was released (always 1999 in this file)
10	40	Film title
50	1	Action (1 if TRUE, 0 if FALSE)
52	1	Comedy (1 if TRUE, 0 if FALSE)
54	1	Cartoon (1 if TRUE, 0 if FALSE)
56	1	Drama (1 if TRUE, 0 if FALSE)
58	1	Fantasy (1 if TRUE, 0 if FALSE)
60	1	Family (1 if TRUE, 0 if FALSE)
62	1	Mystery (1 if TRUE, 0 if FALSE)
64	1	SciFi (1 if TRUE, 0 if FALSE)
66	1	War (1 if TRUE, 0 if FALSE)
68	1	Western (1 if TRUE, 0 if FALSE)
70	1	Musical (1 if TRUE, 0 if FALSE)
72	1	Romance (1 if TRUE, 0 if FALSE)
74	1	Horror (1 if TRUE, 0 if FALSE)

These functions are now presented.

TextViewer Functions   The driving function for the TextViewer application is the ListFilms() function, presented in Example 8.7. The function is prototyped as follows:

```
void ListFilms(const char szFile[]);
```

Its argument is the name of the file containing the film data.

| FIGURE 8.7 | Sample Output from TextViewer Application |

```
c:\Introduction to C++\Chapter8\TextViewer\Debug\TextViewer.exe          _ □ ×
1      200 Cigarettes                              Comedy Drama
2      2001 Yonggary                               Fantasy SciFi
3      8MM                                         Mystery
4      Magical Legend of the Leprechauns, The      Fantasy
5      Storm of the Century                        Horror
6      10 Things I Hate About You                  Comedy Romance
7      13th Warrior, The                           Action Fantasy
8      Alice in Wonderland                         Fantasy Family
9      All the King's Men                          War
10     American Beauty                             Drama
11     American Pie                                Comedy
12     Analyze This                                Comedy
13     Angela's Ashes                              Drama
14     Animal Farm                                 Family
15     Anna and the King                           Drama Romance
16     Any Given Sunday                            Drama
17     Anywhere But Here                           Drama
18     Apartment Complex, The                      Mystery
19     Arlington Road                              Action Drama
20     Astronaut's Wife, The                       SciFi
21     At First Sight                              Drama
22     Austin Powers: The Spy Who Shagged Me       Comedy
23     Baby Geniuses                               Comedy Family
24     Babylon 5: A Call to Arms                   SciFi
Hit enter to continue!_
```

EXAMPLE 8.7

ListFilms() function

```
void ListFilms(const char szFile[])
{
    STREAM in;
    char szIn[4000];
    int nCount;
    // open existing file for text reading
    if (!Open(in,szFile,true,false,false,true)) {
        DisplayString("File could not be opened!");
        NewLine();
        return;
    }
    for(nCount=1;GetLine(in,szIn,4000);nCount++) {
        DisplayFilm(szIn);
        if (nCount%24==0) {
            DisplayString("Hit enter to continue!");
            InputCharacter();
        }
    }
    Close(in);
}
```

The function illustrates a fairly common approach to reading a text file. It works as follows:

- It opens the file by calling the SimpleIO function Open(), specifying the file is to be read, is not to be truncated, and is a text file.
- It enters a loop that reads each line into a buffer by calling GetLine(). The maximum line length was arbitrarily set to 4000—although 80 would have been more than enough for the file in question.
  - The loop takes each line and sends to DisplayFilm()—which performs the actual display activity.
  - Every time the line number is an even multiple of 24 (computed using the remainder operator) it prompts the user to hit enter. This keeps the list from scrolling off the screen before it can be seen.
  - When GetLine() fails, which will occur when the end of the file is reached, the loop ends.
- The file is closed.

Before discussing the DisplayFilm() function, it is helpful to skip to the GetField() function, presented in Example 8.8, which extracts a single data element from the line that is read from the file. It is prototyped as follows:

```
void GetField(char szTarget[],const char szBuf[],int
nStart,int nCount);
```

The *szTarget[]* argument will be used to hold the extracted data (e.g., similar to the first argument of the strcpy() library function). The second argument, *szBuf[]*, contains the line loaded from the file (in the ListFiles() function, that was passed into the DisplayFilm() function). The third argument, *nStart*, contains the starting position of the data, the fourth argument, *nCount*, the number of bytes of data to be copied. Appropriate values for these two arguments can be found in Table 8.2. For example, if szIn[] contained a line of text read from the file and szField[] was our target string, then the call:

```
GetField(szField,szIn,10,40);
```

would cause the 40 bytes of "Film title" information to be copied from szIn into szField.

EXAMPLE 8.8

GetField() function

```
void GetField(char szTarget[],const char szBuf[],int nStart,int
nCount)
{
    int i;
    for(i=0;i<nCount;i++) {
        szTarget[i]=szBuf[i+nStart];
    }
    szTarget[i]='\0';
}
```

The function's operation is very simple, and reminiscent of many of the string functions introduced in Chapter 7. It works as follows:

- Starting at nStart in the szBuf[] array, it copies over nCount characters to szTarget[].
- It places a NUL terminator at the end of szTarget, to make it a NUL terminated string.

The final function to be discussed is DisplayFilm(), shown in Example 8.9. This function is prototyped as follows:

EXAMPLE 8.9

DisplayFilm() function

```
void DisplayFilm(const char szBuf[])
{
    char szTarget[256];
    // ID
    GetField(szTarget,szBuf,0,5);
    DisplayString(szTarget);
    // title
    GetField(szTarget,szBuf,10,40);
    DisplayString(szTarget);
    // film types
    GetField(szTarget,szBuf,50,1);
    if (szTarget[0]=='1') DisplayString(" Action");
    GetField(szTarget,szBuf,52,1);
    if (szTarget[0]=='1') DisplayString(" Comedy");
    GetField(szTarget,szBuf,54,1);
    if (szTarget[0]=='1') DisplayString(" Cartoon");
    GetField(szTarget,szBuf,56,1);
    if (szTarget[0]=='1') DisplayString(" Drama");
    GetField(szTarget,szBuf,58,1);
    if (szTarget[0]=='1') DisplayString(" Fantasy");
    GetField(szTarget,szBuf,60,1);
    if (szTarget[0]=='1') DisplayString(" Family");
    GetField(szTarget,szBuf,62,1);
    if (szTarget[0]=='1') DisplayString(" Mystery");
    GetField(szTarget,szBuf,64,1);
    if (szTarget[0]=='1') DisplayString(" SciFi");
    GetField(szTarget,szBuf,66,1);
    if (szTarget[0]=='1') DisplayString(" War");
    GetField(szTarget,szBuf,68,1);
    if (szTarget[0]=='1') DisplayString(" Western");
    GetField(szTarget,szBuf,70,1);
    if (szTarget[0]=='1') DisplayString(" Musical");
    GetField(szTarget,szBuf,72,1);
    if (szTarget[0]=='1') DisplayString(" Romance");
    GetField(szTarget,szBuf,74,1);
    if (szTarget[0]=='1') DisplayString(" Horror");
    NewLine();
}
```

```
void DisplayFilm(const char szBuf[])
```

Its argument is a single line read from the film file in ListFilms().

The function works by calling GetField() to extract the data for each field that needs to be displayed. ID and title are extracted first, as these are displayed for every film. After that, each of the film type specifiers is checked. If a '1' is present, a type string is added to the display line.

8.4.2: Lab Exercise: Displaying a List of Films by Category

Another useful way to display the information in the Films1999.txt file is to organize it by category. In this lab exercise, you will create three functions that can be used for this purpose.

Objective   The objective of this exercise is to create a function that reads the film input file (i.e., Films1999.txt) and writes the data to an output file, organized by category. An extract of some of the output file, taken from the middle, is presented in Example 8.10. It should be noted that films may appear in more than one category.

Functions   The functions needed to implement the exercise are presented in Table 8.3.

EXAMPLE 8.10

Extract from output file, organized by category

```
War
        9       All the King's Men
        44      Bravo Two Zero
        46      Bridge of Dragons
        77      End of the Affair, The
        101     Hornblower: The Frogs and the Lobsters
        104     Hunley, The
        133     Messenger: The Story of Joan of Arc, The
        157     One Man's Hero
        202     Tea with Mussolini
        206     Three Kings
        223     Wing Commander

Western
        112     Jack Bull, The
        171     Ravenous
        174     Ride with the Devil[vI]
        222     Wild Wild West

Musical
        82      Fantasia/2000
        187     South Park: Bigger Longer & Uncut
        212     Topsy-Turvy

Romance
        6       10 Things I Hate About You
        15      Anna and the King
etc...
```

TABLE 8.3   Functions to Implement "Films by Category" Lab Exercise

void CreateCategoryFile(const char szInFile[],const char szOutFile[])

The driver function for the application, it takes the name of the input file (i.e., Films1999.txt) and the name of the file to which output is to be directed. The function should:

- Open the output file as a truncated text file for writing.
- For each category:
    - ○ Print the name of the category to the output file (e.g., the "War," "Western," etc., in Example 8.10).
    - ○ Call CreateCategoryList(), passing it to the column where the category type is located (which can be found in either Table 8.2 or Example 8.9).
- Close the output file prior to returning.

void CreateCategoryList(STREAM &out,const char szInFile[],int nStart)

Prints all the films matching a particular category. Its arguments are the open output file stream (out), the name of the input data file, and the column position of the type indicator for the particular category. The function should:

- Open the input file as a nuntruncated, readable text file.
- Read each line of the input file (in a loop similar to that of the ListFilms() function in Example 8.7).
    - ○ Determine whether the data at the specified column is '0' or '1'.
    - ○ If it is '1', call PrintFilm() to add it to the list in the output file.
- Close the input file prior to returning.

void PrintFilm(STREAM &out,const char szBuf[])

Prints the film to the output file. The function takes the open output file and a text string containing the data for a given film as arguments. It should:

- Print a tab("\t") to the output file.
- Extract the ID from szBuf using a call to GetField() and send it to the output file.
- Extract the title from szBuf using a call to GetField() and send it to the output file.
- Send a line end to the output file.

Procedure   The easiest way to implement the lab exercise is as follows:

- Set up the TextViewer project.
- Add a new .cpp file to the project, with a name such as CategoryFile.cpp.
- Write the PrintFilm() function, using DisplayFilm() (Example 8.9) as a model. The main changes are that the category display statements can be eliminated and the Display… statements become Print… statements directed to the output stream passed in as an argument.
- Write the CreateCategoryList() function, which will be similar to the ListFilms() function (Example 8.7) except that it will only call PrintFilm() for files where the category column passed in as an argument is '1'. (*Hint*: The value of the category column can be determined by calling GetField() or it can be looked at directly.)
- Write a text version of CreateCategoryFile() that opens the output stream, and calls CreateCategoryList() for a single column (e.g., 50, the "Action" column). Test this function by calling it from your main() function.
- When the single column version of CreateCategoryList() works, expand it by making calls to the remaining categories.

8.5: IN DEPTH: BINARY .DBF FILE WALKTHROUGH

Walkthrough available in DBFFilm.wmv

In this section we present a walkthrough that shows how information can be extracted from a binary file organized in a known way. It will demonstrate the reading of binary data and navigating within a binary file.

8.5.1: The .DBF File Format

Before packages like MS Access, MS SQL Server, and Oracle were on the scene, the most common PC database file format was based on Ashton Tate's dBase. The key building block of dBase was the .DBF file, which was used to hold data for a single table.

In many ways, actual data is stored in a .DBF file in a manner similar to that found in the fixed length text format presented in Section 8.4. A key difference between DBF and text files, however, is that DBF files contain information about how the file is laid out in a section of the file known as the header section. Specifically, the header contains information such as:

- The date when the table was last modified
- The number of records (rows) in the table
- The length of each record
- The size and type of each data element

This header information is stored in binary format, organized into 32-byte chunks of information.

The overall organization of a DBF file, used in dBase III, is presented in Figure 8.8. The overall organization is as follows:

- The file begins with 32 bytes of information related to the organization of the entire file, including date modified, record length, and number of records.
- Definitions of individual fields (up to 128) then follow. Each definition is 32 bytes and contains information about the field name, data type, and size.
- A single carriage return, '\n' follows the field definitions.
- The actual data for the table then begin.

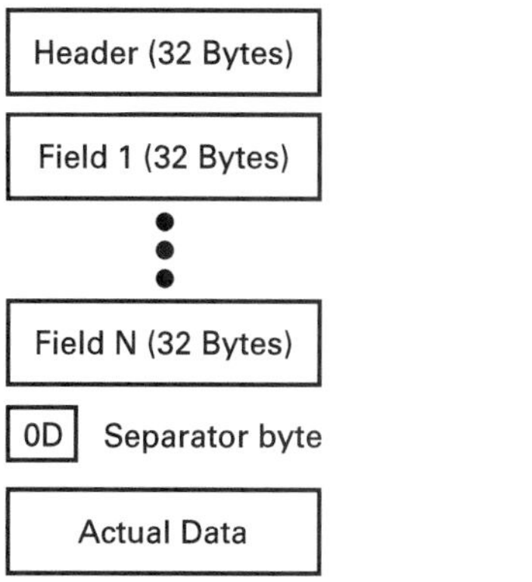

A binary display of the contents of an actual DBF file (Films1999.DBF) is presented in Figure 8.9. This file contains the same data as the Films1999.txt file discussed in Section 8.4.

Because the MS Visual Studio binary viewer displays 16 bytes per row, it is relatively easy to locate data in the file. The first two rows correspond to the header block of information. The key elements of the header are as follows:

- **Byte 0:** Should be 0x03 for dBase III files. (0x83 is also legal, but it implies a separate memo file, which will not be relevant here.)
- **Byte 1:** Year the file was last modified (1900 is 0). In Figure 8.9, the value 0x67 corresponds to 103 decimal, or 1900 + 103 = 2003.
- **Byte 2:** Month the file was last modified. In Figure 8.9, the value 0x05 signifies May.

FIGURE 8.8 DBF File Organization

Header (32 Bytes)

Field 1 (32 Bytes)

•
•
•

Field N (32 Bytes)

0D Separator byte

Actual Data

FIGURE 8.9 Binary Display of Films1999.DBF File

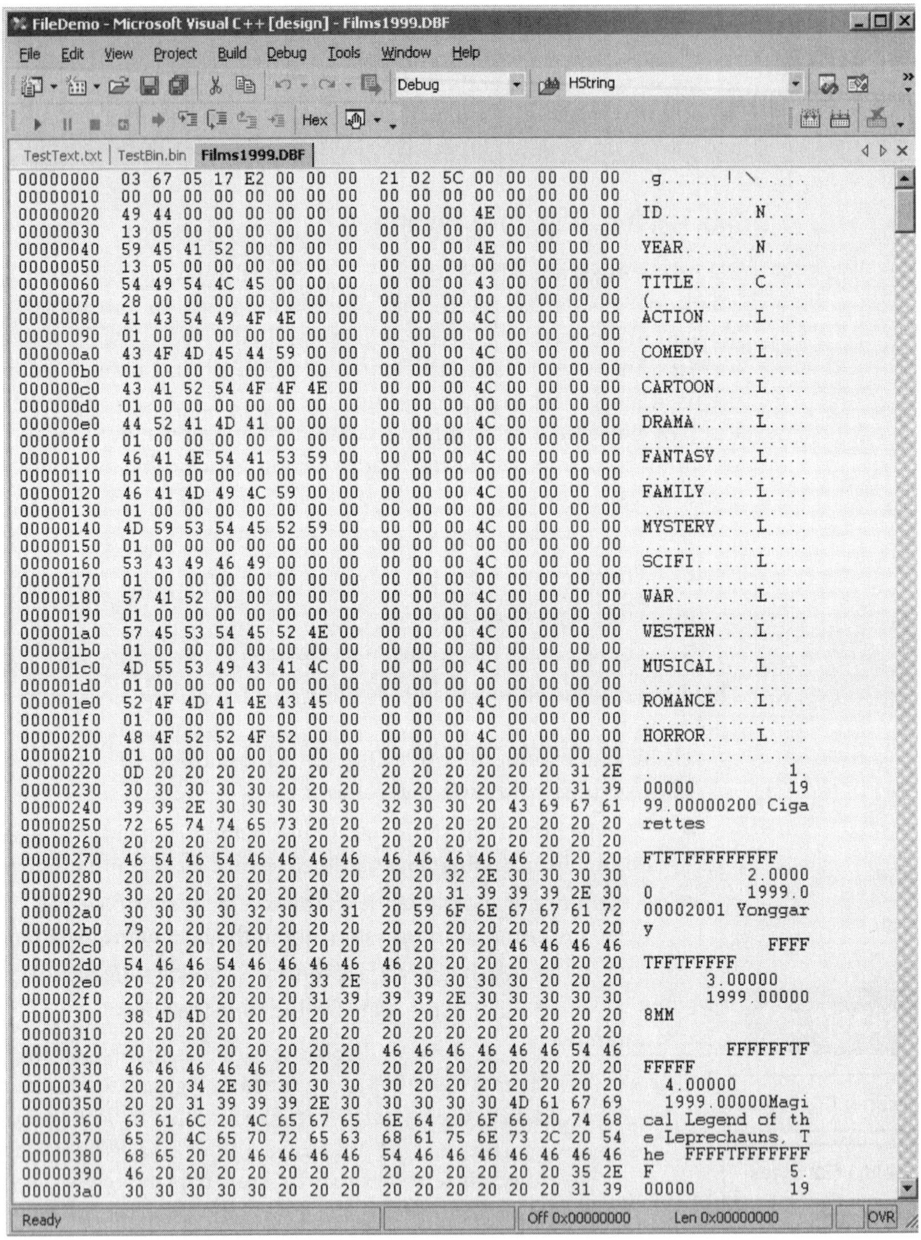

- **Byte 3:** Day the file was last modified. In Figure 8.9, the value 0x17 signifies 23. Thus, the file was last modified on May 23, 2003.
- **Bytes 4–7:** A 4-byte integer indicating the number of records in the file. Reversing the bytes (as discussed in Section 8.3.4), this number becomes 0x000000E2, which is 226.

- **Bytes 8–9:** A 2-byte integer specifying where the actual data in the file begins. In this case (reversing the bytes), the position is 0x0221. Looking at the addresses on the left, you can verify that it is, in fact, the actual location where the data appear to be located (immediately after the 0x0D separator byte shown in Figure 8.9).
- **Bytes 10–11:** A 2-byte integer specifying the record length. In dBase III, the maximum record length was 4000, so this number should always be less than or equal to that value. In Figure 8.9, the value 0x005C specifies that each record is 92 bytes long.

The remaining bytes in the 32-byte header are ignored. Following the header block comes the field definitions. The number of fields defined for the table can be computed from the information in the header block. Specifically, you take the location where the data begins (0x221) and subtract the bytes used for the header (0x20 bytes) and the separator byte (0x01 byte), which leaves 0x200 bytes for all the field definitions (512 bytes, in decimal). We then divide this total by the size of each field definition (0x20 bytes, or 32) and the result is 16 fields (512/32 = 16).

Each 32-byte field definition is laid out as follows:

- **Bytes 0–10:** A NUL terminated string containing the field name. In dBase III, field names were limited to 10 characters (with the additional byte allocated for the NUL terminator). For example, the field beginning at 0x00000020 is named "ID," the field beginning at 0x00000060 is named 'TITLE," etc.
- **Byte 11:** A single character indicating the field type. Allowable types included 'N' (numeric), 'C' (character, or text), 'D' (date) and 'L' (logical, or TRUE/FALSE). For example, the ID field has a value of 0x4E (ASCII for 'N'), meaning it is numeric. The TITLE field has a value of 0x43 (ASCII for 'C'), meaning it is a text field.
- **Byte 16:** A single character specifying the field length (individual dBase III fields were limited to 255 bytes). For example, the ID field is 0x13 (19) characters long. The TITLE field is 0x28 (40) characters long.
- **Byte 17:** Relevant only for numeric fields, it is the number of places to the right of the decimal place—roughly equivalent to the precision of a numeric field. For example, the ID field has a precision of 0x05 (5), meaning it is written with 5 decimal places. (This precision can be verified by looking at the actual data.)

The remaining bytes in each field definition are ignored.

8.5.2: The .DBF File Header Viewer

Creating an application that displays the definitions (header and fields) for a DBF file is relatively simple. The DBFHeader application, which can be used to display the structure of any dBase III file, uses two functions: DisplayHeader() and DisplayFieldDef(). Its output is presented in Figure 8.10.

Functions Only two functions were required to implement the application. The first, DisplayHeader(), displays information from the top 32-byte block, then calls the second, DisplayFieldDef() to display each field definition. It is prototyped as follows:

```
void DisplayHeader(const char szFile[]);
```

It takes a single argument: file name for which the header will be displayed.

The function is presented in Example 8.11.

FIGURE 8.10   Output from DBFHeader Application

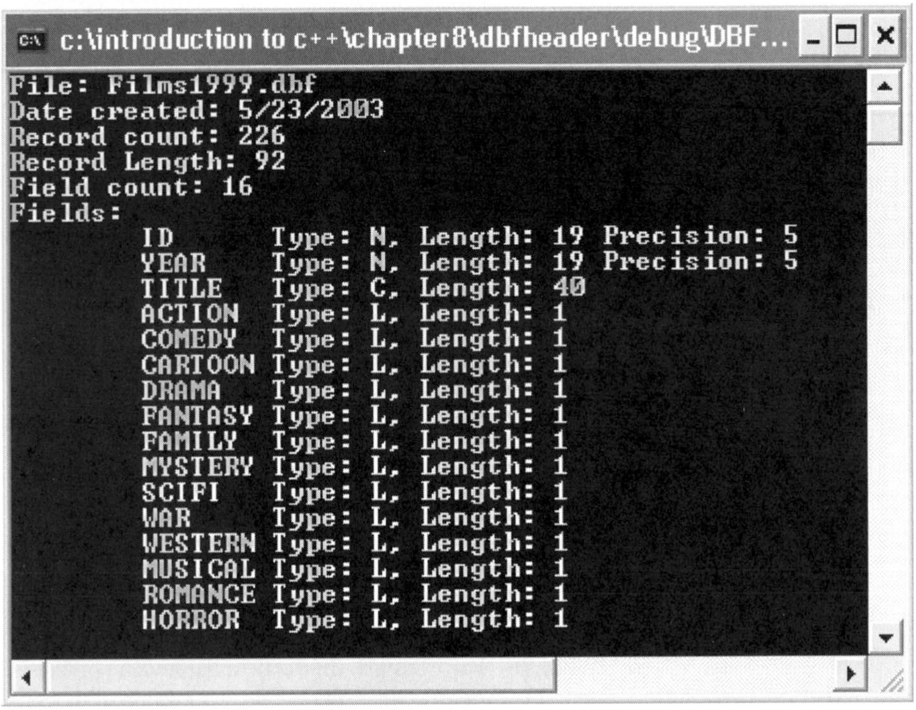

```
c:\introduction to c++\chapter8\dbfheader\debug\DBF...  _ □ ✕
File: Films1999.dbf
Date created: 5/23/2003
Record count: 226
Record Length: 92
Field count: 16
Fields:
        ID      Type: N, Length: 19 Precision: 5
        YEAR    Type: N, Length: 19 Precision: 5
        TITLE   Type: C, Length: 40
        ACTION  Type: L, Length: 1
        COMEDY  Type: L, Length: 1
        CARTOON Type: L, Length: 1
        DRAMA   Type: L, Length: 1
        FANTASY Type: L, Length: 1
        FAMILY  Type: L, Length: 1
        MYSTERY Type: L, Length: 1
        SCIFI   Type: L, Length: 1
        WAR     Type: L, Length: 1
        WESTERN Type: L, Length: 1
        MUSICAL Type: L, Length: 1
        ROMANCE Type: L, Length: 1
        HORROR  Type: L, Length: 1
```

The function works as follows:

- It opens the file as a binary file for reading (not truncated) using the SimpleIO Open() function.
- It reads the first byte to ensure it matches the expected value of 3.
- It reads the year, month, and day bytes. After adding 1900 to the year, it displays the file name and date.
- It reads the number of records as a 4-byte integer, then displays it.
- It reads the start position of the data as a 2-byte integer, then uses the formula presented earlier (nStartPos-33)/32 to compute the number of fields. It then verifies that a legal number of fields is specified.
- It reads the record length data as a 2-byte integer, then displays it.
- It loops though the fields one-by-one, calling DisplayFieldDef() specifying the starting position of each field definition.

The second function, DisplayFieldDef(), is designed to output the definition for a single field. It is prototyped as follows:

```
void DisplayFieldDef(STREAM &in,int nStart);
```

Its argument is the open DBF file stream and the position in the file where the field definition starts. It is presented in Example 8.12.

The function works as follows:

- The file read position is set to the offset specified by nStart. (This offset was computed in the loop contained in the DisplayHeader() function.)

EXAMPLE 8.11

DisplayHeader() function

```
void DisplayHeader(const char szFile[])
{
    STREAM in;
    int nRecords,nReclen,nFieldCount,nStartPos;
    int nYear,nMonth,nDay;
    int i;
    if (!Open(in,szFile,true,false,false,false)) {
        DisplayString("DBF File could not be opened!");
        NewLine();
        return;
    }
    // check that first byte is 0x03
    if (ReadCharacter(in)!=3) {
        DisplayString("Illegal DBF file format");
        NewLine();
        return;
    }
    // next data element is date created
    nYear=ReadCharacter(in)+1900;
    nMonth=ReadCharacter(in);
    nDay=ReadCharacter(in);
    DisplayFormatted("File: %s\n",szFile);
    DisplayFormatted("Date created: %i/%i/%i\n",nMonth,nDay,nYear);
    // next data element is number of records
    nRecords=ReadInteger(in);
    DisplayFormatted("Record count: %i\n",nRecords);
    // next data indicate position where data start
    nStartPos=ReadShort(in);
    // to compute number of fields, subtract 33 bytes for header and separator
    nFieldCount=(nStartPos-33)/32;
    if (nFieldCount<1 || nFieldCount>128) {
        DisplayString("Illegal DBF file format");
        NewLine();
        return;
    }
    // next data element is record length
    nReclen=ReadShort(in);
    DisplayFormatted("Record Length: %i\n",nReclen);
    DisplayFormatted("Field count: %i\nFields:\n",nFieldCount);
    for(i=0;i<nFieldCount;i++) {
        DisplayFieldDef(in,(i+1)*32);
    }
    Close(in);
}
```

EXAMPLE 8.12

DisplayFieldDef() function

```
void DisplayFieldDef(STREAM &in,int nStart)
{
    char szName[20];
    char cType;
    int nLen,nPrec;
    SetReadPosition(in,nStart);
    ReadBlock(in,szName,11);
    cType=ReadCharacter(in);
    SetReadPosition(in,nStart+16);
    nLen=ReadCharacter(in);
    nPrec=ReadCharacter(in);
    DisplayFormatted("\t%s\tType: %c, Length:
    %i",szName,cType,nLen);
    if (cType=='N') DisplayFormatted(" Precision: %i\n",nPrec);
    else NewLine();
}
```

- It reads the field name as an 11-byte block into a local array, szName.
- It reads the field type as a character, assigned to cType.
- It repositions the pointer to offset 16 (where the field length is stored).
- It reads the field length byte and places the value in nLen.
- It reads the precision byte and places it in nPrec.
- It displays the name, type, and length of the field.
- If the field is of type 'N' (numeric), it also displays the precision.

8.5.3: Lab Exercise: The .DBF Record Viewer

In this exercise, we create a simple file viewer that displays the data from dBase III records. The interface is a simple loop that prompts the user for a record number, then displays the field names and associated data for that record, as illustrated in Figure 8.11.

Functions The DBF Record Viewer can be implemented using two functions. Their prototypes and descriptions are presented in Table 8.4.

The one aspect of these two functions that warrants some additional explanation is the determination of where each field starts and ends in DisplayData(). Each dBase III record is stored entirely in text form, as is evident from Figure 8.9. Within the text for each record, which is loaded in DisplayLoop(), the first byte is reserved—having one of two values:

- ' ' (space): Indicates the record is active.
- '*' (asterisk): Indicates the record is marked for deletion.

It means that the actual field data begins a position 1 in the record, not the usual position 0. The first field, ID, therefore occupies positions 1–19 (because its length is 19 bytes); the second field, YEAR, occupies bytes 20–38 (again, a 19-byte field length); TITLE occupies bytes 39–78 (40-byte length); and so forth. As you iterate through the field definitions, then, you need to:

FIGURE 8.11   DBF Record Viewer in Operation

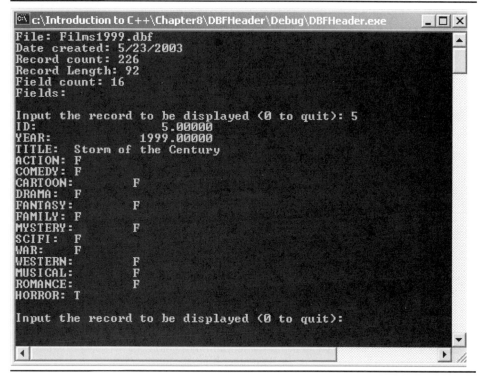

- Start at position 1.
- Add the length of the current field to the starting position to determine where the next field starts.
- If you use GetField() to extract the data, the arguments will be the starting position (*nStart)* and the field length (*nCount).*

Procedure   To build the DBF Record Viewer, the following procedure is recommended:

- Make a copy of the DisplayHeader() (Example 8.11) function and name it DisplayLoop() to provide an excellent starting point for the first function.
- Remove the loop from the original function that displays field definitions and replace it with a loop that:
  - Prompts the user for a record number and verifies the record number is valid (or 0, in which case you can break of if the loop).
  - Loads the record data into a buffer (which should be defined to be at least 4000 characters long, for safety's sake).
  - Calls DisplayData().
- Write the DisplayData() function. The DisplayFieldDef() (Example 8.12) provides a good starting point for extracting the two key pieces of information required (field name and field length). The loop that displays field definitions in DisplayHeader() (a loop removed in the previous step) also is useful in figuring out how to identify the starting point of each field definition in the file.

| **TABLE 8.4** | Functions to Implemented "DBF Record Viewer" Lab Exercise |

void DisplayLoop(const char szFile[])

The driver function for the application, it takes the name of the DBF file (i.e., Film1999.dbf) as its only argument. The function should:

- Open the DBF file for reading, as a binary file.
- Load much of the same header information as was loaded in DisplayHeader(). Of particular importance is the data starting position, number of records, number of fields, and record length.
- Enter a loop that prompts the user for a record number. Within that loop:
  - ○ If the user enters an invalid record number, it should display an error message.
  - ○ If the user enters 0, it should break out of the loop.
  - ○ If the user enters a valid record number, it should:
    1. Move to the appropriate position in the file (computed using the data start position and the record length).
    2. Load the record data into a buffer, which can be done with ReadBlock() and the record length. If you size the buffer at 4001 characters (the maximum dBase record size), you should never have to worry about too many bytes being read.
    3. Call the DisplayData() function to cause the actual record data to be displayed.
- Close the file stream, once the user ends the loop.

void DisplayData(STREAM &db,const char szRecord[],int nFieldCount)

Displays all the field data for a given record. Its arguments are the open file stream for the DBF file (*db*), a character string containing the currently active record (*szRecord*), and a count of the number of fields. The function will consist of a single loop, which iterates through the individual field values. Within the loop, the function will:

- Load the name and field length of each field definition (the DisplayFieldDef() function provides a good model for getting this information).
- Extract the actual data from the szRecord[] array. The GetField() function, presented in Section 8.4.1, Example 8.8, could be used to extract the data.
- Display the field name, followed by the associated data.

8.6: REVIEW AND QUESTIONS

8.6.1: REVIEW

Without the capability of file reading and writing, it would be almost impossible to construct today's information systems, and computers would be little more than fancy calculators. To facilitate using files, C++ offers an extensive class library, covered in detail in Chapter 17. In this chapter, we focused on understanding the essential nature of file IO, hiding the specific implementation through the use of the SimpleIO functions provided with the text.

The key to file I/O is the creation of a stream, which is a place to which information can be sent or from which information can be retrieved. To attach a file to a specific stream, we use the Open() function, prototyped as follows:

```
bool Open(STREAM &file,
const char *szName,
bool bRead,bool bWrite,
bool bTrunc,bool bText);
```

The arguments to Open() are as follows:

- *file*: A previously declared stream variable.
- *szName*: The name of the file (including path, if desired, of the file to be attached to the stream).
- *bRead*: Will we be able to read from the file?
- *bWrite*: Will we be able to write to the file?
- *bTrunc*: Should we erase (truncate) the file when we open it?

■ *bText:* Should the file be opened for text processing, as opposed to binary processing?

The function returns **true** if successful, **false** otherwise. Once a file is no longer needed by the program, its stream can be closed with the Close() SimpleIO function, prototyped as follows:

```
void Close(STREAM &file);
```

Text files contain stored data translated into ASCII character format. They are also line oriented, meaning that they tend to be organized into variable-length lines that are ended with a sequence of newline and carriage return characters (in MS Windows, "\r\n" pairs signal the end of each line, but this command can vary according to operating system).

SimpleIO Functions commonly used in text files include those in the table at the bottom of this page.

In the table:

OUTPUT is either a STREAM variable open for writing, or cout.

INPUT is either a STREAM variable open for reading, or cin.

In general, text IO is performed using line-oriented functions (e.g., the GetLine() and PrintLine() functions). The reason is that white characters, such as space and tab, are treated as end of string markers when reading strings. Therefore, data saved as a single string, e.g., "Hello, World" using PrintString(), would be read as two separate strings ("Hello," and "World") using GetString(). Using **line-oriented IO** permits more sophisticated processing of text files (e.g., see the fixed file processing example in Section 8.4).

Binary files differ from text files in that the data placed in them are usually a direct copy of data in memory (instead of being translated to text form). As a result, they tend to be much more efficient to work with than text files. Implicit in any binary file is a pointer, identifying the position from which the next read or write will start. Functions commonly used with binary files include those in the table on the following page.

SimpleIO Text Stream Functions

Output Functions	***void PrintString(OUTPUT &out,const char *szOut):*** Writes a text string to the text stream *out*.
	void PrintInteger(OUTPUT &out,int nVal): Translates an integer to a string, then writes the integer to the text stream *out*.
	void PrintCharacter(OUTPUT &out,char cVal): Writes an ASCII character to the text stream *out*.
	void PrintReal(OUTPUT &out,double dVal): Writes an unformatted real number to a file.
	void PrintLine(OUTPUT &out,const char *szOut): Sends a string (*szOut*), followed by a newline, to the text stream *out*.
	void PrintFormatted(OUTPUT &out,const char *szFmt,...): Writes formatted text data to the text stream *out,* using a printf style formatting string (see Chapter 7, Section 7.3 for in-depth discussion of formatting).
	void EndLine(OUTPUT &out): Sends an end of line to the text stream *out;* basically equivalent to PrintCharacter(out,'\n').
	void WhiteSpace(OUTPUT &out): Sends a space to the text stream *out.* This is basically equivalent to PrintCharacter(out,' ').
Input Functions	***void GetString(INPUT &in,char szIn[]):*** Reads a string from the text stream *in* and places it in the array szIn, which must be large enough to accommodate it.
	int GetInteger(INPUT &in): Reads an integer from the text stream *in* and returns its value.
	double GetReal(INPUT &in): Reads a real number from the text stream *in* and returns its value.
	char GetCharacter(INPUT &in): Reads a character from the text stream *in* and returns its value.
	bool GetLine(INPUT &in,char szIn[],int nMax): Reads a line from the text stream *in* and places it in szIn, followed by a NUL terminator. No more than *nMax* characters are read.

SimpleIO Functions for Binary File I/O

Output Functions	*bool WriteInteger(STREAM &file,int nVal);* Writes a single integer to the open binary file stream. It returns **true** if the operation is successful, **false** otherwise.
	bool WriteReal(STREAM &file,double dVal); Writes a single double real number to the open file stream. It returns **true** if the operation is successful, **false** otherwise.
	bool WriteFloat(STREAM &file,float fVal); Writes a single float real number to the open file stream. It returns **true** if the operation is successful, **false** otherwise.
	bool WriteCharacter(STREAM &file,char cVal); Writes a single character to the open file stream. It returns **true** if the operation is successful, **false** otherwise.
	bool WriteShort(STREAM &file,short nVal); Writes a short (2-byte) integer to the open file stream. It returns **true** if the operation is successful, **false** otherwise.
	*bool WriteBlock(STREAM &file,const void *buf,int nBytes);* Writes an array of any type of data, starting at position *buf,* to the open binary file stream. The amount of data to be written is *nBytes.* It returns **true** if the operation is successful, **false** otherwise.
	bool SetWritePosition(STREAM &file,int nPos): Sets the 0-based file position to be used for the next write operation.
Input Functions	*int ReadInteger(STREAM &file);* Reads an integer from the open binary file stream, returning its value.
	double ReadReal(STREAM &file); Reads a double from the open binary file stream, returning its value.
	float ReadFloat(STREAM &file); Reads a float from the open binary file stream, returning its value.
	char ReadCharacter(STREAM &file); Reads a character from the open binary file stream, returning its value.
	short ReadShort(STREAM &file); Reads a short (2-byte) integer from the open binary file stream, returning its value.
	*bool ReadBlock(STREAM &file,void *buf,int nBytes);* Reads an array from the open binary file stream, copying *nBytes* of data from the file to the memory location beginning at position *buf.* It returns **true** if the operation is successful, **false** otherwise.
	bool SetReadPosition(STREAM &file,int nPos): Sets the 0-based file position to be used for the next read operation.

Using binary files effectively typically involves some general principles, which include the following:

- Unlike text files, the organization of binary files cannot necessarily be determined by inspection. When working with files that you did not create, some roadmap is normally needed.

- Binary data need to be retrieved in exactly the same format that they were saved in. If data are saved as 2-byte integers, for example, they cannot be read back as 4-byte integers.

- Whereas text files are usually processed sequentially, a file pointer is often used in binary files to allow random access of data contained within the file.

8.6.2: GLOSSARY

ASCII file   A file containing data that have been translated into text characters, using the ASCII coding scheme

binary file   A file containing data in their original (byte) form, as opposed to being saved as ASCII characters

cin   The default input stream for functions such as InputString()

close a stream   Release the association between a file and a given STREAM, so the file is not locked to prevent access by other programs and to reduce operating system resources (Close() function)

cout   The default output stream for functions such as DisplayString()

file position   The logical location (an integer address), within an I/O stream, for the next read or write operation

formatted output   Text output that is presented in a manner that is specified by the programmer (e.g., a fixed number of decimal places for real numbers, a fixed length for strings), rather than relying on default presentation

I/O stream   A general method of characterizing an input-output area, such as a display, hard drive, or RAM

line-oriented I/O   Input/output done on a line-by-line basis, rather than on a data element by data element basis

open a stream   Associate a file with a given STREAM, so it can be used for subsequent I/O (done with Open() function)

open mode   How a stream is opened (e.g., for reading, writing, or read/write), the type of stream being opened (e.g., binary or text) and whether the file is to be erased upon opening (i.e., truncated)

STREAM   A SimpleIO typedef used to identify a file stream variable

text file   An alternate name for an ASCII file

8.6.3: QUESTIONS

1. *Line Counter.* Write and test a function that counts all the lines in a text file. The function should be prototyped as follows:

```
int LineCount(const char *szFileName);
```

where szFileName is the name of the file, and the function returns the number of lines.

2. *Word Counter.* Write and test a function that counts all the words in a text file. The function should be prototyped as follows:

```
int WordCount(const char *szFileName);
```

where szFileName is the name of the file, and the function returns the number of words in the file. For the purpose of this function, any cluster of nonwhite characters separated by one or more white characters from any other cluster is considered a word. For example:

```
"Hello World 123 it's me!"
```

would be considered to have 5 words. (*Hint:* Write a second function that counts the words in a line and the entire process becomes much easier.)

The next two questions deal with the file GradesFixed.txt, in the Chapter 8\Exercises folder. The file contains grades from a course, where each row represents the grades for a particular student, whose ID is the first item on the row. If a grade is missing, it is left blank. A segment of the file is displayed in Notepad at the top of the following page.

3. *Summing Rows of a Fixed Text File.* Write two functions, TotalGrade() and DisplayTotals(), prototyped as follows:

```
bool TotalGrade(STREAM strm);
bool DisplayTotals(const char
  szFileName[]);
```

The TotalGrade() function should read a line from the file, then print out the student ID (the first column from the

```
GradesFixed.txt - Notepad                                    _ □ X
File  Edit  Format  Help
ID      Ex1      Ex2      Ex3      MT      Ex4      Ex5      Ex6      Ex7
1001     50       45       43      68      100       40       69
1002     50       28       34      84       82       30       87       10
1003     50       34       24      77       82       46       73      120
1004     50       40       26      65       81       42       93       50
1005     50       39       30      65       85       26       95
1006      0       39        6      41      100       40       61       90
1007     50       38               88       83                56       20
1008     40       39       34      38       70       44       45      120
1009     50       34       23      52                         38       30
1010     50       41       41      47       65       42       67
1011     50       45       48      83       86       40       93       97
```

file) and the total of the remaining columns, treating any empty column as 0. It should return false if the line cannot be read, or if there is no ID. The DisplayTotals() function should open a file, skip the first line (containing the headers), then call TotalGrade() on each line until it returns false. Use the SimpleIO functions and the GetField() function (Example 8.8) to help you. You will need to open the file in a text editor to determine where each grade starts and ends. You will also need to write a small main() function to test your application.

4. *Averaging Columns of a Fixed Text File.* Write two functions, TotalCols() and DisplayAverages(), prototyped as follows:

```
bool TotalCols(STREAM strm,int
nStart,int nCount,double dTotals[],int
nVals[]);
bool DisplayAverages(const char
szFileName[]);
```

The TotalCols() function should read a line from the file, then take the values of nCount columns, starting at column nStart, and add them to the values in dTotals[], incrementing the corresponding value in nVals[] if the column is nonblank. For example:

```
double dTotals[8]={0.0};
int nVals[8]={0};
STREAM strm;
// missing code to open file, etc.
TotalCols(strm,1,8,dTotals,nVals);
```

The call to TotalCols() here would cause a line from the file to be read, the first column (column 0) to be ignored, and

the values of subsequent columns to be added to dTotals (column 1 value is added to dTotals[0], column 2 added to dTotals[1], etc.). For any column that is not all spaces, nVals[Column number-1] will be incremented, which prevents blank cells from being used to compute the average.

The DisplayAverages() function is like DisplayTotals() function of Question 3 except that after TotalCols() has been called on each line, it then computes the average by taking the total in dTotals[] and dividing it by the corresponding count in nVals[]. A simple main() driver function will also need to be written to test the application.

5. *Creating a Fixed Text File.* Write a function, ComputeTotals(), that computes the total grade for each student, then writes the student ID and associated grade to a fixed text format file, one line per student. The function should be prototyped as follows:

```
bool ComputeTotals(const char
szInputFile[],const char
szOutputFile[]);
```

The argument szInputFile[] contains the name of the input data file (i.e., "GradesFixed.txt") and the name you chose for the output file. A simple main() driver function will also need to be written to test the application. You should also feel free to use any functions written in Questions 3 and 4.

The next two questions deal with the file GradesTab.txt, in the Chapter 8\Exercises folder. The file contains the same data used in GradesFixed.txt except that date elements are

```
GradesTab.txt - Notepad                                          _ |□| ×
File  Edit  Format  Help
ID      Ex1     Ex2     Ex3     MT      Ex4     Ex5     Ex6     Ex7
1001    50      45      43      68      100     40      69
1002    50      28      34      84      82      30      87      10
1003    50      34      24      77      82      46      73      120
1004    50      40      26      65      81      42      93      50
1005    50      39      30      65      85      26      95
1006    0       39      6       41      100     40      61      90
1007    50      38              88      83              56      20
1008    40      39      34      38      70      44      45      120
1009    50      34      23      52                      38      30
1010    50      41      41      47      65      42      67
1011    50      45      48      83      86      40      93      97
```

separated by tab (0x09) characters. A segment of the file is displayed in Notepad at the top of this page

6. *Summing Rows of a Tab-Delimited File.* Write three functions, TotalGradeTab () and DisplayTotalsTab(), prototyped as follows:

```
bool TotalGradeTab(STREAM strm);
bool DisplayTotalsTab(const char
    szFileName[]);
void GetFieldTab(char szTarget[],const
    char szBuf[],int nField)
```

The TotalGradeTab() function and DisplayTotalsTab() function should perform the same functions as those defined in Question 3. GetFieldTab() is the only different function. It will replace GetField() and—instead of copying a range of characters from szBuf—it will count tabs until it reaches nField (e.g., nField of 0 starts at szBuf[0], nField of 1 starts immediately after the first tab, nField of 2 starts immediately after the second tab, etc.), then copy all the characters until the next tab (or end of the line) is reached. You will also need to write a small main() function to test your application.

7. *Averaging Columns of a Fixed Text File.* Write two functions, TotalCols() and DisplayAverages(), prototyped as follows:

```
bool TotalColsTab(STREAM strm,int
    nStart,int nCount,double
    dTotals[],int nVals[]);
bool DisplayAveragesTab(const char
    szFileName[]);
```

These functions should do precisely what their counterparts did in Question 4.

8. *Creating a Tab-Delimited File.* Write a function, ComputeTotalsTab(), that computes the total grade for each student, then writes the student ID and associated grade to a tab-delimited format file, one line per student. The function should be prototyped as follows:

```
bool ComputeTotalsTab(const char
    szInputFile[],const char
    szOutputFile[]);
```

This function should do precisely what the function defined in Question 5 did, except the output file fields should be separated by tabs.

In-Depth Questions:

9. *Creating a Binary File.* Write a function, TranslateToBinary(), that reads the GradesFixed.txt file and saves each element as a binary file. The function should be prototyped as follows:

```
bool TranslateToBinary(const char
    szTextIn[],const char szBinOut[],
    int nCols);
```

where szTextIn is the name of the input file (i.e., "GradesFixed.txt"), szBinOut is the name of the output file you create and nCols is the number of columns of grade data to be saved (allowing flexibility in using the file for data on more or fewer items). The function should return true unless it cannot open one of the files. The binary file should include the following data:

- Number of columns
- Number of student records
- Name of each column (stored as a string)
- Data for each student (with –1 used to indicate missing values) and student ID saved as a string (rather than as an integer)

You should also write a simple main() driver function for test purposes.

10. *Loading a Binary File.* Write a function, CreateReport(), that reads the binary file created in Question 9 and displays summary statistics. The function should be prototyped as follows:

```
void CreateReport(const char*szBin);
```

where szBin is the name of the file created in Question 9. The function should return true unless it cannot open the file. The report generated by the function should be displayed to the screen, and (at a minimum) should contain:

- A list of average grades for each assignment
- A list of total grades for each student
- An average across all students

In defining arrays, you may assume that no more that 256 assignments will ever be present. You should also write a simple main() driver function for test purposes.

CHAPTER 9

Iterative Techniques

EXECUTIVE SUMMARY

Chapter 9 introduces the topic of algorithms, focusing on a number of commonly used iterative techniques. The emphasis of the discussion is on learning a few basic techniques, then applying them to different types of situations. The specific topics to be discussed include iterating over time, searching using divide-and-conquer strategies, and iterative approaches using successive approximation.

The chapter begins by explaining what is meant by an algorithm—pointing out that most programming problems can be solved by employing a relatively small number of generic approaches. It then turns to the specific topic of working with time series, and how to formulate problems where an element of an array depends on the value of a previous element or elements. A practical demonstration, the creation of a principal and interest table for a loan, is presented. The next section introduces divide-and-conquer techniques for searching, analyzing the huge performance benefits of an ordered search space. A simple algorithm for binary search is presented as an example. Finally, the general technique called successive approximation is discussed. The information needed to set up a successive approximation problem is then identified, and two different examples of the technique—computing a square root and determining an appropriate pension fund contribution—are presented.

LEARNING OBJECTIVES

Upon completing this chapter, you should be able to:

- Define the term *algorithm*
- Explain the role algorithms play in programming
- Identify the issues associated with sequenced (time-ordered) arrays
- Construct functions that iterate through arrays using lagged variables
- Explain the benefits of ordering a search base
- Implement binary search of an array of different data types
- Describe a typical successive approximation problem
- Explain the prerequisites for setting up a successive approximation problem
- Apply successive approximation techniques to computing various mathematical functions
- Apply successive approximation techniques to various business problems
- Discuss the relationship between representation and complexity in the context of the Roman numeral translation problem

9.1: WHAT ARE ALGORITHMS?

An **algorithm** is a procedure for solving a general problem and can be applied to a variety of situations. In many of the previous chapters, we introduced examples of simple and not-so-simple algorithms—converting strings to numbers, numbers to strings, insertion and deletion of strings within strings, and so forth. In this chapter, we take a more general view of algorithms, focusing on some algorithms commonly employed in iteration (looping) problems.

9.1.1: Algorithms and Intuition

During your early encounters with computer programming, it is easy to find yourself believing that writing code, developing and applying algorithms, is somehow entirely different from anything you've ever done. Nothing could be further from the truth. We are applying existing algorithms and devising new ones all the time. Every time we look up a number in a phone book, for example, we are applying a variation of the binary search algorithm we discuss later on in this chapter. Every time we project out our expenses and income to see whether we have enough money to pay our bills, we are using sequence iteration algorithms. Every time we try to figure out how to get from "here" to "there" using a road map, we apply forms of successive approximation.

Our intuition can also be helpful in devising new algorithms. As an illustration, suppose I gave you the following task:

I have created a deck of 1,000 cards, each of which has a number between 1 and 1,000,000 written on it. The cards are currently in random order. Your task is to sort them, and return the sorted deck to me.

Take a minute or so to think about this problem. If you are like most people, your intuition will guide you to a general way of approaching the task that is much better than a brute force approach. The "typical" approach that most people devise is presented at the end of the section, in Example 9.1. But do try to figure out how you would do it before checking the answer.

It is important to understand that it is fairly unusual to come up with radically new algorithms. Indeed, inventing a single new algorithm with practical applications can permanently establish a programmer's reputation. What is much more common is the process of modifying existing approaches to make them more effective in a given situation, or applying existing algorithms to novel situations. Thus, it is extremely beneficial for programmers to have a grasp of a variety of these techniques. Naturally, in an introductory programming course, we will not be able to cover all the algorithms a programmer needs to know. But we can start the process. Even more important, we can help you begin to identify situations in which looking for an algorithm is warranted. Indeed, in most situations, recognizing that you need to find an algorithm to apply is even more critical than designing the algorithm.

9.1.2: Overview of Techniques in the Chapter

In this chapter, we look at algorithms related to iteration. We focus on three different categories of algorithms:

1. *Algorithms involving sequences of values:* Such sequences, such as values that change over time, often require us to use values of elements ahead or behind in

the sequence. In doing so, we specifically present code for computing a *Fibonacci* series, developing a principal/interest table for a loan, and—as a particularly challenging in-depth example—computing the integer value of a Roman numeral.

2. *Divide-and-conquer techniques:* Algorithms that successively try to break our initial "large" problem into smaller and smaller problems—until the problem we are solving becomes trivial. We demonstrate this task using a technique called binary search, used to find an element in an ordered array.

3. *Successive approximation techniques:* Algorithms that use a guided form of trial and error to find a value. Examples we present include computing a square root and determining an appropriate pension contribution to receive a desired payout.

9.1: SECTION QUESTIONS

1. What is the best way to figure out an algorithm to solve a particular problem?
2. Why is the intuition that an algorithm is needed just as important as knowing the algorithm?

9.2: ITERATING THROUGH A SEQUENCE

For the purposes of this text, we define a **sequence,** or *series,* of values as a collection of values that:

- Must be presented in a particular order
- Are computed in a manner such that individual values in the sequence can be computed based upon other values in the sequence

Because sequences are ordered, it makes sense to give each element in a sequence a sequence number. The most common type of sequence is probably values that vary over

---

EXAMPLE 9.1

Sorting the deck of 1,000 randomly numbered cards

After thinking about this problem for a short time, most people come up with a solution along the following lines:

- Take the deck and divide it into 10 piles, one containing 0–99,999, one containing 100,000–199,000, and so forth.
- Keep repeating the process on the individual piles (until the piles become so small we can order them quickly, in our hands).
- Reassemble the sorted piles in the appropriate order.

In devising such a strategy, you are intuitively recognizing an important fact: *it is much easier to sort a lot of small piles than it is to sort a single large pile.* In fact, this algorithm is an example of a divide-and-conquer technique, and is known under a number of names—such as the "bucket sort" algorithm.

time—with the sequence number representing the time elapsed (in whatever units are convenient) since the sequence began.

The second requirement—that sequence elements depend on each other—is more restrictive than most sequence/series definitions. It is, however, what is of particular interest to us in examining some of the techniques for computing sequences.

For the types of sequences that we are considering, we typically require two key pieces of information in order to define the sequence:

1. A formula specifying the relationship between sequence elements. For example, when you leave money in an interest bearing account, the amount in the account at time t is computed as follows:

$$\texttt{amount}_t \;=\; \texttt{amount}_{t-1}\texttt{(1 + interest rate)}$$

2. Initial values for one or more elements of the sequence, for example, $\texttt{amount}_0 = \$10,000$.

9.2.1: Scalar and Array Sequences

When computing sequences, we often can choose to use either scalars (e.g., individual variables) to hold the sequence elements or an array. To illustrate this choice, let's consider a simple sequence, the Fibonacci sequence. The definition of this sequence is presented in Example 9.2.

Defined in this way, we can easily write two versions of a function that computes the nth element in a Fibonacci sequence: one using scalars, one using an array. Both approaches are presented in Example 9.3.

In the scalar approach, we use local variables (n0 and n1) to hold the values of two elements of the sequence. They are both started at 1. Within the loop:

- We need to use a temporary value to hold n1 (whose value we will still need).
- We set n1=n1+n0, which is the next element in the sequence.
- We set n0 to the old value of n1.

We can then repeat the process until we reach the desired sequence number, at which time we return n1.

In the array version, we are populating an array with the sequence, in addition to returning the value. We start by placing a 1 in element 0, then—if the desired element number in nPos is 1 or greater, we also place a 1 in arFib[1].

EXAMPLE 9.2

Fibonacci sequence definition

A **Fibonacci sequence** $(F_0 \ldots F_N)$ is a series of N integers defined as follows:

- Each element of the sequence is the sum of the previous two elements.
- F_0 and F_1 are both equal to 1.

A Fibonacci sequence of 10 elements $(F_0 - F_9)$, for example, is:
$\{1, 1, 2, 3, 5, 8, 13, 21, 34, 55\}$

EXAMPLE 9.3

Two ways of computing Fibonacci series

```
// two ways of computing Fibonacci sequences

unsigned int Fib1(unsigned int nPos)
{
    unsigned int n0=1,n1=1;
    if (nPos<2) return 1;
    while(nPos-- > 1) {
        int nTemp=n1;
        n1=n1+n0;
        n0=nTemp;
    }
    return n1;
}

unsigned int Fib2(unsigned int nPos,unsigned int arFib[])
{
    unsigned int i;
    arFib[0]=1;
    if (nPos<1) return arFib[0];
    arFib[1]=1;
    for(i=2;i<=nPos;i++) {
        arFib[i]=arFib[i-1]+arFib[i-2];
    }
    return arFib[nPos];
}
```

TEST YOUR UNDERSTANDING 9.1:

Why do we know we will always need a value in position 0, and that we will never get a negative coefficient passed in?

We then use iteration to compute the remaining elements, starting at i=2 and ending when i>nPos. To find the value of element i, we use the formula:

```
arFib[i]=arFib[i-1]+arFib[i-2]
```

This formula bears a nice resemblance to our original definition.

Choosing Between Array and Scalar Versions   So which is better, the array or scalar version? Because this choice is available for nearly all sequence problems, it is a reasonable question to ask. The answer really depends on what we need the sequence for—forgetting, for the moment, the dubious likelihood that any of us would ever really *need* a Fibonacci series. The pros and cons of each approach are as follows:

- Computationally, the two approaches are pretty close—so that issue is not a concern.
- Memory-wise, the array-based approach is more expensive.
- Simplicity-wise, the array-based approach is probably a bit easier to understand and debug, because it doesn't involve the use of temporary variables.

The most decisive issue is probably how often we will need to use the values in the series. If we will need them often, it might make sense to compute the array once, then look up the value whenever we need it. If it is a one-time thing, the scalar approach might be preferable (although we could also use the array internally to the function, by making it a local array instead of passing it as an argument).

9.2.2: Computing a Principal and Interest Table

Walkthrough available in PandI.wmv

When a loan is made, one document that often accompanies the transaction is a principal and interest table (also referred to as a loan amortization table). This table is basically a simple pair of related sequences, wherein:

```
Interest_t = Principal_{t-1} * Interest rate
Principal_t = Principal_{t-1} + Interest_t - Payment
Principal_0 = Loan amount
```

To understand the sequence, look at it as follows:

- The principal (remaining amount of the loan to be paid) at time 0 is the entire loan amount.

- In each period, interest is computed by multiplying the loan amount at the end of the previous period by the interest rate. Once again, interest is pretty self-explanatory.

- To compute the principal at period t, we need to look at what comes in, and what goes out, applying the proper sign to each:

    - *Comes in (+):* amount we owed in the previous period

    - *Comes in (+):* amount of interest accrued in this period

    - *Goes out (–):* the actual payment that we made

Suppose, then, we wanted to design a function that would compute an amortization table for a particular loan amount, interest rate, and payment amount. We would need to create the actual table, therefore, we are obviously going to want to use arrays (a scalar version of the function is specified as an end-of-chapter exercise). Thus, we could prototype the function as follows:

```
unsigned int PandI(double dAmount,double dRate,double
    dPayment,double dPrincipal[],double dInterest[],unsigned
    int nMaxPeriods);
```

The arguments of the function are as follows:

- *dAmount:* Amount of the loan. Must be positive.

- *dRate:* Amount of the interest rate, expressed as a fraction. Must be consistent with the payment (e.g., if a monthly payment is specified, the interest rate must be the annual interest rate/12).

- *dPayment:* Amount we are paying each period.

- *dPrincipal[]:* An array to hold the end-of-period principal amounts.

- *dInterest[]:* An array to hold the interest accrued each period.

- *nMaxPeriods:* The maximum number of periods to be computed. This is needed to protect the dPrincipal[] and dInterest[] arrays from overflowing, and to avoid an infinite loop if a loan is negative amortizing (which occurs if the payment is less than the interest accrued each period—causing the loan to get bigger, not smaller).

The function returns an unsigned integer representing the period in which the loan is fully paid off (i.e., principal value becomes 0). If the loan is not paid off by the end of nMaxPeriods, it returns nMaxPeriods. The remaining principal, at that time, can be determined by looking at the value in dPrincipal[nMaxPeriods].

A simple implementation of the PandI() function is provided in Example 9.4.

The main challenge associated with this function is the fact that we need to simultaneously compute two related sequences, instead of just one. Actually, though, the dPrincipal[] sequence is the most important one—it is easy to compute the interest in any period if you have the dPrincipal[] sequence.

TEST YOUR UNDERSTANDING 9.2:

Why is it easier to compute interest from the dPrincipal[] than principal from interest?

The other interesting aspect of the function is how negative principal is handled. This situation is encountered only for the final payment of a loan—because principal going negative indicates the loan is paid off. Thus, the statement:

```
if (dPrincipal[i]<0.00) dPrincipal[i]=0.00;
```

appears at the bottom of the loop. It has the effect of terminating the loop (which tests for positive principal), as well as making sure we don't overpay.

EXAMPLE 9.4

PandI() function

```
unsigned int PandI(double dAmount,double dRate,double dPayment,
    double dPrincipal[],double dInterest[],unsigned int
    nMaxPeriods)
{
    unsigned int i;
    // ensure legal values
    if (dRate<0 || dAmount<=0 || dPayment<=0 || nMaxPeriods==0)
    return 0;
    // initialize period 0
    dPrincipal[0]=dAmount;
    dInterest[0]=0.00;
    for(i=1;dPrincipal[i-1]>0.00 && i<=nMaxPeriods;i++) {
        dInterest[i]=dPrincipal[i-1]*dRate;
        dPrincipal[i]=dPrincipal[i-1]+dInterest[i]-dPayment;
        // when principal goes negative, assume partial payment
        was made
        if (dPrincipal[i]<0.00) dPrincipal[i]=0.00;
    }
    return i-1;
}
```

9.2: SECTION QUESTIONS

1. Besides financial applications, what other problem types would follow the cumulative comes-in goes-out model we presented for designing our series?
2. When would it make sense to start saving the values for any series in an array?
3. Should we feel any concern about using doubles in our financial calculations?

9.3: DIVIDE-AND-CONQUER TECHNIQUES

Divide-and-conquer techniques are usually employed in situations where data are involved, such as searching and sorting problems. The basic philosophy behind the techniques is to take the collection of data you are working with, such as an array, and break it up into smaller and smaller pieces, each of which becomes easier to work with. The approach to sorting a deck of cards, presented in Example 9.1, was an example of this type of technique.

In this section, we focus on a particular divide-and-conquer approach to searching an already sorted array, called **binary search.**

9.3.1: Binary Search

Despite its technical-sounding name, binary search is an extremely intuitive technique that can be employed in searching almost any sorted array. We begin by illustrating the technique in action, then by considering its performance compared with other strategies.

Example of Binary Search Strategy The easiest way to visualize the binary search technique is to think about how you would play the following game:

"I'm thinking of a number between 1 and 1,024. What is your first guess?"

So, what's the best first guess you could make? Well, assuming "I" will tell you if you're too high or too low, the best place to guess is right in the middle.

512

"You're too high. What's your next guess?"

Well, you have essentially the same problem you started with, except now the number is between 1 and 511. So you guess in the middle again.

256

"You're too low. What's your next guess?"

Now you know the number is between 257 and 511. The middle of these numbers is (257+511)/2, which is 384.

384

"You're too low again. What's your next guess?"

Now you know the number is between 385 and 511.

General Binary Search Problem   The general binary search problem requires three things:

1.   We have a search space (a collection of items to be searched) that is ordered and in which each item can be identified by some index. In our example, the search space was the collection of integers, and the index was just the integer itself.

2.   We have an initial upper bound and lower bound for the index. In our example, these bounds were 1 and 1,024.

3.   We have a function that tells us whether a particular index corresponds to a value that is too high, too low, or equal to the value we are looking for. In our example, that function was performed by asking "I" to tell you if your guess was too high, too low, or just right.

It is important to recognize that nothing requires that the value we are searching for be a number. For example, consider the question:

"On what page is Henry James in the phone book?"

Applying the same technique, you could:

- Open the phone book to the middle. You observe the first name on the page is "Mandeville, Shirley." Recalling your alphabet, you think to yourself, too high!
- So you take the first half of the book, open it in the middle (i.e., a quarter of the way into the book) and hold it with your thumb—keeping a finger in the halfway point. You see the name, "Foster, Reginald."
- You take the right-hand group of pages, splitting the portion between your thumb and finger in half and open it up. You see the name "Kanter, G. S."
- And so forth…

Once again, the approach is the same—as long as you can identify the range of your search (i.e., page numbers) and whether a given item is too high or too low (alphabetical order). The binary search algorithm is simple:

- Test the element halfway between the top and bottom index numbers.
- If the element you tested is what you're looking for, you're done.
- If the element you tested is too high, make your current index the new top.
- If the element you tested is too low, make your current index the new bottom.

The algorithm stops under two conditions: (1) you find what you're looking for, or (2) the top and bottom are next to each other—in which case the element is not present.

Performance of Binary Search   Before actually implementing a simple binary search function, it is useful to ask the question, how much does a binary search actually save us—compared with linear search (i.e., starting at the bottom and searching until we reach the top). Our intuition tells us that there must be some savings—otherwise, we'd look for names in the phone book by starting at the beginning and reading through it, name by name. But just how big are those savings?

Our number guessing game can be used to give us a pretty good sense of the amount of savings we get. What is the maximum number of guesses it would take before we find our number? Since each guess divides the number of values in our search space by one-half, another way of asking the same question is:

How many times can we divide 1,024 by 2 before we end up with 1?

As it turns out, this question is pretty easy to answer: 1,024 just happens to be 2^{10} power (possibly not a coincidence). What that means is that we can divide 1024 by 2 precisely 10 times before we get to 1. Now, we could get lucky and find it earlier. But it will never take more than 10 probes.

Ten probes as a maximum versus 1,024 as the maximum for linear search, this is a pretty good savings. But it gets better.

Stating this conclusion in another way, for a search space the size of 2^k, it will take no more than k probes to reach our solution. There happens to be a function that relates 2^k and k: the *logarithm* (base 2). So, for any binary search problem, the maximum number of probes k can be found by the formula:

```
k=log₂(Number of elements)
```

It also happens that all logarithms are proportional to each other. So, when we want to compare relative search times, we can use $\log_{10}$ instead of worrying about powers of 2. Suppose then, we have a computer that takes 1 unit of time, using binary search, to search through 10 elements. To give linear search a head start, let's also assume it takes linear search the same amount of time to search through 10 elements. What happens to relative search times as the number of elements in our search space grows? The answer to this question is illustrated in Table 9.1.

By looking at the table you see a huge difference between search times as search spaces get larger. To interpret this table, think of it in the following way:

- If you could scan 10 names in a second, it would take you about 11 days—1 million seconds, scanning round the clock, with no breaks—to read through the greater NYC phone books (~10,000,000 entries) to find a particular name.
- Using a binary search technique, it would take you about 7 seconds to find the name you were looking for.

Naturally, binary search only works if your search space is sorted in some intelligent fashion. This qualification, perhaps, explains why they alphabetize phone books (in case you had any doubt). It also explains why binary search is such an important technique in computer programs.

TABLE 9.1	Growth in Search Times	
Number of Elements	**Linear Search Time**	**log(elements)— Binary Search Time**
10	1 (given)	1 (given)
100	10	2
1,000	100	3
10,000	1,000	4
100,000	10,000	5
1,000,000	100,000	6
10,000,000	1,000,000	7
100,000,000	10,000,000	8

9.3.2: Binary Search of an Integer Array

Walkthrough available in BinarySearch.wmv

The binary search algorithm for searching an integer array is just a straightforward implementation of the general algorithm. The function can be prototyped as follows:

```
int BinarySearch(int nTarget,int arInts[],int nCount)
```

The arguments are as follows:

- *nTarget:* The integer we are looking for
- *arInts[]:* A sorted array of integers we want to search
- *nCount:* The number of integers in our array

The return value is an integer, representing a coefficient between 0 and nCount. It can mean one of two things:

1. The position in the array where a match was found.

2. The position in the array where the item would need to be placed, if it were there.

This positioning provides slightly more information than just returning the coefficient's value if it is found, and something else (e.g., –1) if it isn't. If such a function (that flags missing values with –1) is desired, however, it would be easy to write once BinarySearch() is implemented. For example:

```
int ModifiedBinarySearch(int nTarget,int arInts[],int
nCount)
{
    int nFound=BinarySearch(nTarget,arInts,nCount);
    return (nFound==nCount || arInts[nFound]!=nTarget) ? -1
      : nFound;
}
```

The flowchart for the BinarySearch() function is presented in Figure 9.1. The code is provided in Example 9.5.

The only aspect of the BinarySearch() code that is not completely straightforward is the test at the end. This particular test is required only for situations in which the element we are looking for happens to be less than or equal to the value at position 0. In this case, nUpper can reach 1, and we will break out of the loop before we ever get to test the 0th element. The test ensures such a situation never happens.

TEST YOUR UNDERSTANDING 9.5:

Why isn't a test similar to the one made for nLower also made for nUpper at the end of the function?

9.3: SECTION QUESTIONS

1. Suppose you had an array of integer date values, stored as MMDDYYYY (e.g., 7/4/2003 would be represented as the integer 7042003, 31 December 2003 would be 12312003) that was sorted according to chronological order. How would we need to modify the binary search algorithm to handle this array? Can you think of a better way of representing the dates that wouldn't have this problem?

FIGURE 9.1 Binary Search of Integer Array

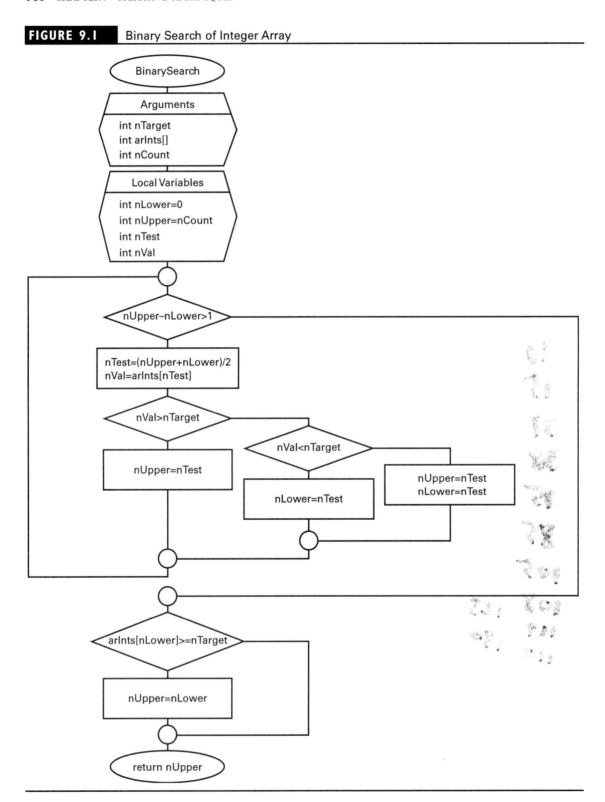

EXAMPLE 9.5

BinarySearch() function

```
/***** Function: BinarySearch *****
Generated summary:
    Arguments
        int nTarget-Integer we are looking for
        int arInts[]-Sorted array of integers
        int nCount-Number of elements in sorted array
    Returns int - position of found element or insertion pos
    ****************************************************/
int BinarySearch(int nTarget,int *arInts,int nCount)
{
    int nLower=0;
    int nUpper=nCount;
    int nTest;
    int nVal;
    while(nUpper-nLower>1) {
        nTest=(nUpper+nLower)/2;
        nVal=arInts[nTest];
        if(nVal>nTarget) {
            nUpper=nTest;
        }
        else {
            if(nVal<nTarget) {
                nLower=nTest;
            }
            else {
                nUpper=nTest;
                nLower=nTest;
            }
        }
    }
    if(arInts[nLower]>=nTarget) {
        nUpper=nLower;
    }
    return nUpper;
}
```

---

2. What would we need to do to change the BinarySearch function so it searches an array of doubles?

3. Can binary search be used on nonnumeric data?

9.4: IN DEPTH: SUCCESSIVE APPROXIMATION

Successive approximation is, at heart, a guided form of trial and error. It is typically used to find continuous values, such as values for a numeric function. In this section, we use iteration to solve some simple successive approximation problems, using the same types of techniques we used in binary search.

9.4.1: Introduction to Successive Approximation

Successive approximation is a technique employed to estimate the values that we cannot compute directly. Normally, these values are continuous quantities (i.e., real numbers). In order to make an estimate using successive approximation techniques, we normally need two things:

- A function we can use to tell us whether our estimate is getting closer. At a minimum, it is enough if our function can tell us whether our estimate is too large or too small.
- A range of values that brackets our estimate.

Prerequisites to Successive Approximation Problems   Technically, a lot of theory is related to whether successive approximation techniques can or cannot be used in a particular situation (e.g., the function we are estimating being continuous, monotonic, and having a provable inverse over the range pretty much nails it down). Because this text does not cover number theory, however, it is enough to say:

- You need to be able to establish clear upper and lower bounds for your estimate, which is the range of the estimate.
- You need to understand the quantity you are trying to estimate, and know that it doesn't have any weird behaviors over the range you are using to estimate it (e.g., it doesn't suddenly change signs, the way signed integers do upon reaching the overflow point).
- The values you are estimating should either be going up or going down over the entire range

These guidelines are rather abstract, so let's take a concrete example. Suppose you wanted to estimate the mortgage payment for a particular term, interest rate, and loan amount (an example is presented as an end-of-chapter exercise). For a given loan amount, term, and interest rate, we can clearly bracket the payment range. The simplest range would be to set 0 as the "minimum" payment and the loan amount as the "maximum" payment—and this approach would work, although a bit slowly. A slightly more informed range would be as follows:

- *Minimum payment:* The {interest rate} * {loan amount} is clearly a lower bound for the payment, because it would not amortize any of the principal.
- *Maximum payment:* The {Minimum Payment} + {loan amount}/{# of periods} is a reasonable upper bound. The minimum payment covers the maximum possible interest we could pay over the term, and the {loan amount}/{# periods} would amortize the whole loan—so we would obviously be paying less in interest than our estimate.

Over the range we computed, higher payments mean the loan gets paid off faster, so the function is well behaved.

Now, what about a function to tell us whether our estimate is too high or too low? It turns out, we already wrote such a function: the *PandI()* function developed in Section 9.2.2. When we call that function:

- If the number of periods returned is too low, then our estimate is too high.
- If the number of periods is too high, then our payment estimate is too low.

- If the number of periods is exactly right:
  - If our last period principal reduction + interest payment is significantly less than our payment, then our estimate is still a bit too high.
  - If our last period principal reduction + interest payment is approximately equal to our payment, then we got it!

Thus, we have all the elements in place to be able to estimate mortgage payments (without looking up the formula in a finance book, which would be like giving in to the dark side of the force).

A Simple Successive Approximation Algorithm Although sophisticated approximation algorithms are available—employing approaches such as Newton's method—a simple approach will do the job for us:

- Take the average of your upper and lower range estimates as a test approximation.
- Determine whether your test approximation is too low or too high:
  - If your approximation is too low, it becomes the new lower bound.
  - If your approximation is too high, it becomes the new upper bound.
- Continue the process until your upper and lower bounds are within the desired accuracy of your estimate.
- Return the average of the upper and lower bound.

If this technique seems familiar, it should. Basically, it is the same technique we used for binary search, adapted for continuous variables. Indeed, we can imagine a general functional framework, as illustrated in Figure 9.2 (shown with a function EvalEst() that returns **true** if our estimate is too low).

9.4.2: Computing a Square Root

Walkthrough available in Sqrt.wmv

Needless to say, functions are already available in the math.h library to compute square roots (*sqrt*() being the most obvious of these). Nonetheless, computing a square root is an easy way to demonstrate successive approximation. We implement two functions to perform the computation:

```
double ApproximateSqrt(double dAccuracy,double dVal);
bool EvalEstSqrt(double dRoot,double dVal);
```

The first of these functions implements the successive approximation algorithm, passing in an extra parameter to hold the value for which we will be computing the square root. It returns the value of the square root to a specified precision. In other words:

```
ApproximateSqrt(1E-10,25)
```

would return a number close to 5—to at least 10 digits of precision—such as 5.0000000000181899.

The second function, EvalEstSqrt(), takes our estimate of the square root (dRoot) and the value whose square root we are estimating, and returns **true** if our estimate is too low.

The only slightly nonobvious thing about the implementation is the estimate of the upper bound for the square root function, which is shown in Example 9.6. Normally, using

| **FIGURE 9.2** | Framework for Successive Approximation |

```
                    ╭─────────────────╮
                   (    Approximate    )
                    ╰─────────┬─────────╯
                    ╱─────────┴─────────╲
                   ╱      Arguments       ╲
                  ╱────────────────────────╲
                  ╲    double dAccuracy     ╱
                   ╲  ...Other Parameters...╱
                    ╲──────────┬───────────╱
                    ╱──────────┴──────────╲
                   ╱      Local Variables   ╲
                  ╱──────────────────────────╲
                 ╱       double dLower         ╲
                 ╲       double dUpper         ╱
                  ╲      double dTest         ╱
                   ╲     bool bTooLow        ╱
                    ╲─────────┬────────────╱
              ┌───────────────┴───────────────┐
              │       Compute dLower           │
              │       Compute dUpper           │
              └───────────────┬───────────────┘
                             (○)
              ┌───────────────┴───────────────┐
              │  dTest=(dUpper+dLower)/2        │
              │  bTooLow=EvalEst(dTest,...)     │
              └───────────────┬───────────────┘
                        ◇─────┴─────◇
                       <    bTooLow    >
                        ◇───────────┬─◇
              ┌───────────────┐  ┌──────────────────┐
              │  dLower=dTest  │  │   dUpper=dTest    │
              └───────┬────────┘  └──────────────────┘
                     (○)
                ◇─────┴─────────────◇
               <  dUpper−dLower>dAccuracy >
                ◇───────────────────◇
                     (○)
                    ╭─────────────────╮
                   (    return dTest   )
                    ╰─────────────────╯
```

the value we are estimating is a perfectly good upper bound for our square root (e.g., 25 is a good upper bound for the square root of 25). If our square is less than 1, however, this is no longer the case. 0.25 is not a good upper bound for the square root of 0.25 (which is 0.5). So, if dVal is less than 1.0, we set the upper bound to 1.0.

EXAMPLE 9.6

ApproximateSqrt() and EvalEstSqrt()

```
double ApproximateSqrt(double dAccuracy,double dVal)
{
    double dLower;
    double dUpper;
    double dTest;
    bool bTooLow;
    if (dVal<0) return -1;
    dLower=0;
    dUpper=(dVal>1) ? dVal : 1.00;
    do {
        dTest=(dUpper+dLower)/2;
        bTooLow=EvalEstSqrt(dTest,dVal);
        if(bTooLow) {
            dLower=dTest;
        }
        else {
            dUpper=dTest;
        }
    } while (dUpper-dLower>dAccuracy);
    return dTest;
}

bool EvalEstSqrt(double dRoot,double dVal)
{
    double dTest=dRoot*dRoot;
    return (dTest<dVal);
}
```

9.4.3: Computing a Pension Contribution

Walkthrough available in Pension.wmv

A slightly more interesting problem we can compute using successive approximation techniques is that of a pension contribution. Suppose we are just starting out, and need to decide how much to contribute to a 401(k) or other pension plan with defined contributions. We would probably start by making assumptions about the following facts:

- The number of years until we retire
- The interest rate, over and above the inflation rate, we expect to earn
- The amount of income, over and above inflation, we would like to have when we retire

To compute our retirement income, given an annual contribution, we can use the following approach:

```
RetirementIncome = PensionBalance * InterestRate
```

which assumes we don't want to dip into principal during our retirement. Our PensionBalance, in turn, can be computed using a sequence defined as follows:

$$PensionBalance_0 = 0$$
$$PensionBalance_t = PensionBalance_{t-1}(1+InterestRate)+Contribution$$

with t going from 0 to the number of years until we retire.

With these definitions in mind, we can set up our successive approximation problem. The two functions we will be defining are as follows:

```
double ApproximateContribution(double dAccuracy,double dRate,
    unsigned int nYears,double dIncome);
bool EvalEstContribution(double dPayment,double dRate,
    unsigned int nYears,double dIncome);
```

The ApproximateContribution() function takes the accuracy of the desired estimate (e.g., 0.01) and the parameters of the problem: interest rate (dRate), periods (nYears), and desired income (dIncome). It returns the target payment. For example:

```
ApproximateContribution(0.001,0.06,30,100000)
```

returns a value of 21081.52. That result means we need to contribute $21,081.52 a year into our pension plan every year if (1) we expect to earn 6% on that money, (2) we expect to retire in 30 years, and (3) we want to make $100,000/year for an indefinite retirement period.

The EvalEstContribution() function takes an estimated annual contribution and returns **true** if it is too low to meet our income objectives, given the number of years we have to retirement and our interest rate expectations.

The two functions are presented in Example 9.7. Once again, they are straightforward. The upper bound payment estimate in ApproximateContribution():

```
dUpper= dIncome/(dRate*nYears);
```

is simply a formula for our contributions assuming we make 0 percent interest on any money we put in between now and retirement (which should not happen). The lower bound of 0 is self-explanatory.

The EvalEstContribution() function just sums our series to get our principal at retirement, then compares that amount * the interest rate (our interest-only payout) with our test payment.

9.4: SECTION QUESTIONS

1. Explain the three requirements for a successive approximation problem.
2. Why is it easy to construct a successive approximation problem if you have the inverse function of the value you are estimating (e.g., the squared function for computing square roots)?
3. Does successive approximation work for discrete values, or just continuous values?

9.5: IN DEPTH: COMPUTING ROMAN NUMERALS

Walkthrough available in Roman2Int.wmv

In most of the sequences we have examined, the value of sequence elements has been a function of previous elements of the sequence. In converting Roman numerals, however, we get to write a function that needs to look at elements ahead of the element being computed

EXAMPLE 9.7

Pension contribution functions

```
double ApproximateContribution(double dAccuracy,double dRate,
  unsigned int nYears,double dIncome)
{
    double dLower;
    double dUpper;
    double dTest;
    bool bTooLow;
    if (dRate<0 || nYears<1 || dIncome<0) return -1;
    dLower=0;
    dUpper=dIncome/(dRate*nYears);
    do {
        dTest=(dUpper+dLower)/2;
        bTooLow=EvalEstContribution(dTest,dRate,nYears,dIncome);
        if(bTooLow) {
            dLower=dTest;
        }
        else {
            dUpper=dTest;
        }
    } while (dUpper-dLower>dAccuracy);
    return dTest;
}

bool EvalEstContribution(double dPayment,double dRate,
  unsigned int nYears,double dIncome)
{
    unsigned int i;
    double dTotal=0.00;
    for(i=0;i<nYears;i++) {
        dTotal=dTotal*(1+dRate)+dPayment;
    }
    return (dIncome > dTotal*dRate);
}
```

in the sequence. In this example, what we should really be focusing our attention on is the role played by representation in determining how we write our programs.

9.5.1: Roman Numerals 101

The basic Roman numbering system constructs a number using a set of symbols, each of which has a value. In our function, the symbols we will support are:

```
I = 1
V = 5
X = 10
L = 50
C = 100
D = 500
M = 1,000
```

Higher symbol values were achieved by overlining to multiply by a factor of 1,000. For simplicity's sake, however, we'll content ourselves with handling numbers of 4,999 or less.

The basic framework for creating a number is that symbols are written in descending order, and their values are added. For example, LXXVIII would be 78 (50 + 10 + 10 + 5 + 1 + 1 + 1). We must, however, make some complex observations about any numeral that is legal:

1. No halfway symbol (e.g., V, L, D) may appear more than once in a numeral, nor can it appear in front of a larger symbol.

2. If a single symbol—representing an even power of 10 (i.e., I, X, C) is placed to the left of a symbol of greater value, the lesser symbol's value is subtracted from the greater symbol's value. Thus, 9 is normally written IX (10 − 1) instead of VIIII (5 + 1 + 1 + 1 + 1), and 4 can be written IV instead of IIII, although both forms are legal.

3. Any symbol to the left of another symbol can be no less than 1/10th of the value of any symbol to its right. Thus, IX, IV, XC, and XL are okay, but IC, IM, IXC, and XM are not.

4. Once a symbol has been placed to the left of a greater symbol, it cannot be repeated in the number (e.g., XIXI is not legal) except when it follows a lesser symbol (e.g., repeating the C in MCMXCVII is permissible because the repeated C comes after an X), nor can the symbol five times its value be used (e.g., XIXV is not legal).

5. If a lesser symbol is placed in a series of higher-value symbols, it must be in front of the right-most of the higher value symbols (e.g., CCXC is legal, CXCC is not).

6. No single symbol may appear more than four times in a numeral.

These exceptions provide some interesting sequencing issues, because they mean an X in our number could either add 10 or −10 to the total, depending upon what comes next.

TEST YOUR UNDERSTANDING 9.6:

For each of the following Roman numerals, identify whether it is legal and its value (if it is legal):

- XLVIII
- MIM
- CLXIXX
- MCMXCIX
- CVLII
- LIIII

The translation of a Roman numeral is an example of a general class of translation problems. In tackling the problem of translating a sequence, it is usually a good idea to break it down into two separate problems:

1. Is the input legal?

2. What is the value of the input?

Doing so has two benefits. First, it simplifies the function for evaluating the value—because that function can assume its input is legal without doing any testing. Second, it forces us to address the problem of what to do about illegal input. By organizing our code in this way—a good practice whenever user input is involved—we can avoid problems like the assertion failures or exceptions that may be embedded in library code and could occur if an illegal digit has been supplied by the user.

9.5.2: Finding Numeral Value

In order to solve this problem, we need a series of functions. The first, obviously needed, is a function that returns the value of any symbol. We can prototype that function as follows:

```
unsigned int NumeralValue(char cNum);
```

The argument *cNum* contains a symbol—'I', 'V', 'X', 'L', 'C', 'D', 'M'—which can be either uppercase or lowercase. It returns its integer value—1, 5, 10, 50, 100, 500, 1000—or 0, if an illegal numeral (e.g., 'G') is supplied. If there was ever a natural fit with a case statement, it is this function, which is provided as Example 9.8.

9.5.3: Testing for Legal Numerals

Our next function, IsLegalRoman(), is intended to test whether a Roman numeral is legal. It is prototyped as follows:

```
bool IsLegalRoman(const char szNum[]);
```

The argument szNum[] contains a string representing a Roman numeral (e.g., "MMIII"). It returns a Boolean value of 1 (true) or 0 (false).

We will implement two versions of the same function:

- A **"brute-force" method** that attempts to employ our rules for Roman numerals exactly as they were written
- An "elegant" method in which we revisit how Roman numerals are presented and come up with a method of testing that takes half as much code (and is 10 times more likely to be bug-free)

IsLegalRoman1(): Brute Force Method   In doing a straightforward application of our rules for Roman numerals, it is useful to have a function that tells us whether a numeral is a halfway symbol (e.g., V, L, D). Thus, we define a short test function:

```
bool IsHalfWaySymbol(char cSym)
```

This function takes a character argument and returns **true** if it is 'V', 'v', 'L', 'l', 'D' or 'd', **false** otherwise.

IsHalfwaySymbol() is presented in Example 9.9.

Our brute-force approach to determining whether a numeral is valid, called IsLegalRoman1(), is presented in Example 9.10.

The basic logic of the function is as follows:

- We have a local variable, bRet, that becomes **false** as soon as evidence that our numeral is not valid is encountered.
- We go through our sequence of digits until we reach the NUL terminator or until bRet becomes **false,** which occurs when any of our tests for a legal numeral fails.
- We test first for an illegal numeral digit (e.g., 'K'), which can be determined by the fact that NumeralValue() returns 0.
- If the digit we are looking at is a halfway symbol, we make sure:

EXAMPLE 9.8

NumeralValue() function

```
// NumeralValue(char cVal) returns the integer equivalent of the
character cVal
unsigned int NumeralValue(char cNum)
{
    unsigned int nVal=0;
    switch(cNum)
    {
        case 'I':
        case 'i':
        {
            nVal=1;
            break;
        }
        case 'V':
        case 'v':
        {
            nVal=5;
            break;
        }
        case 'X':
        case 'x':
        {
            nVal=10;
            break;
        }
        case 'L':
        case 'l':
        {
            nVal=50;
            break;
        }
        case 'C':
        case 'c':
        {
            nVal=100;
            break;
        }
        case 'D':
        case 'd':
        {
            nVal=500;
            break;
        }
        case 'M':
        case 'm':
        {
            nVal=1000;
            break;
        }
    }
    return nVal;
}
```

EXAMPLE 9.9

IsHalfwaySymbol()

```
bool IsHalfWaySymbol(char cSym)
{
    char cUp=(char)toupper(cSym);
    return (cUp=='V' || cUp=='L' || cUp=='D');
}
```

- That it does not precede a larger symbol (Rule 1b), and
- That it is the only digit of that type present in the numeral (Rule 1a).

■ If the digit is not a halfway symbol, we look ahead at the sequence and ask: Is the digit that comes after it (nNext) a higher value than the current symbol (nVal)? If so:

- We check to make sure it is no less than 1/10th the value of the higher symbol by computing nNext and nVal (Rule 3).
- We loop through the remaining symbols to be sure:
  - nVal is not present, except where it is preceded by a lesser digit, such as the C in 1997—MCMXCVII (Rule 4a).
  - nVal*5 is not present (Rule 4b).
  - nNext is not present (Rule 5).

■ If our digit is not out of numeric order (relative to the digit to the right), we check the remaining digits to ensure the same symbol does not appear more than four times (Rule 6).

If our original string was empty or bRet got set to **false** in the loop, the function returns **false,** otherwise it returns **true.**

As you look over the code for the brute force version of IsLegalRoman1(), an uncomfortable feeling should start creeping up the back of your neck. Even though the function is small (without comments, the function is fewer than 40 lines), it is packed full of characteristics that might provoke anxiety:

■ *Serious inefficiencies:* The code has no less than three loops that look ahead through the digits in the numeral looking for violations. Although we are not particularly concerned with software performance in this text, such inefficiency is suggestive of sloppy thought processes.

■ *Numerous in-code comments:* Throughout this book, the philosophy has been to minimize in-code comments except in situations where the code is not easily understood. The in-code comments in this particular function were critical, however, because none of the code was easily understood (even to its author!).

■ *Deep nesting:* Some of the code in the routine was nested in branches and loops five levels deep (in fact, the FlowC chart took six pages). At such depths, the potential for logic errors to creep in is extremely high.

Having mentioned all these aspects, worse ways to implement Roman numeral translation are certainly available. Probably, with extensive testing, we could develop a high confidence level that the routine works. But imagine an application consisting of 1,000 functions written this

EXAMPLE 9.10

IsLegalRoman1()—brute force approach

```cpp
bool IsLegalRoman1(const char szNum[])
{
    int i;
    bool bRet=true;
    for(i=0;bRet && szNum[i]!=0;i++) {
        unsigned int nVal=NumeralValue(szNum[i]);
        unsigned int nNext=NumeralValue(szNum[i+1]);
        // Illegal digit
        if (nVal==0) bRet=false;
        else if (IsHalfWaySymbol(szNum[i]))
        {
            // halfway symbols can never precede larger symbols
            if (nVal<nNext) bRet=false;
            // check for repeated halfway symbol
            else {
                int j;
                for(j=i+1;bRet && szNum[j]!=0;j++) {
                    if (nVal==NumeralValue(szNum[j])) bRet=false;
                }
            }
        }
        // symbol prior to higher symbol
        else if (nVal<nNext)
        {
            // test for no less than 1/10th rule
            if (nNext/nVal>10) bRet=false;
            else {
                // need to catch problems like CXCC instead of CCXC
                // and CXCL, which can't really be interpreted
                int j;
                for(j=i+2;szNum[j]!=0;j++) {
                    unsigned int nDownStream=NumeralValue(szNum[j]);
                    if (nNext<=nDownStream || nVal*5==nDownStream) bRet=false;
                    // Check repeated digit exception
                    // e.g., MCMXCVII repeated C is okay
                    if (nVal==nDownStream && NumeralValue(szNum[j-1])>=nVal) bRet=false;
                }
            }
        }
        // Check for more than 4 non-halfway symbols
        else {
            int j,nCount=1;
            for(j=i+1;szNum[j]!=0;j++) {
                if (nVal==NumeralValue(szNum[j])) nCount++;
            }
            if (nCount>4) bRet=false;
        }
    }
    if (i==0) return false; // Romans have no 0, so empty string is not allowed!
    return bRet;
}
```

way—still a "small" application by most standards. Yikes! You would have to clone yourself for ten successive generations to test it enough to get the whole thing running.

The bottom line is: Whenever you write a function like this one, you should immediately start thinking to yourself, "How can I make it simpler?" You can think of your entire software project as having a budget limit for "nasty" functions like this one; go over a certain number—say five or ten—and you've got yourself a testing nightmare. Don't squander your precious "nasty function" budget on functions that can be cleaned up!

IsLegalRoman2(): The Elegant Approach   In the vast majority of situations, simplifications to a problem come about as a result of changing the way we look at the problem. In our brute force approach, we applied the rules we were given pretty much as stated. In what other ways could we look at the problem? In particular, can we find the "holy grail" of simplification: *taking a single complex problem and then breaking it up into a collection of simpler problems that can be solved independently?*

As it turns out, a nice simplification for Roman numerals immediately suggests itself with a slight change in the way we write the numerals. Take, for example, the year 1997. Normally, it is written:

> MCMXCVII

Suppose, however, we were to break it up into decimal groups. In this case, it becomes:

> M-CM-XC-VII (i.e., 1-9-9-7)

Looked at in this way, we can say something about each of the four decimal groups:

- Each group can contain only three possible symbols—we will call them U (unit size), F (five size), and T (ten times the unit size).
- Legal combinations of the three symbols are as follows:
  - UT (e.g., IX, XC)
  - UF (e.g., IV, XL)
  - {Unit group}—up to four repetitions of the unit (e.g., III, XX)
  - F (e.g., V, L)
  - F{Unit group} (e.g., VII, LXXX)

Now, the next thing we can do is write two functions—the purpose of which is to tell us where a group ends:

```
int UnitGroup(const char szN[],int nStart,char cUnit);
int DecimalGroup(const char szN[],int nStart,char cUnit,char
cFive,char cTen);
```

The arguments for the two functions are as follows:

- szN: A string containing the Roman numeral
- nStart: Our current position in the string (0 is the first character)
- cUnit: The unit symbol (e.g., I,X,C,M)
- cFive: The five symbol for the current position (e.g., V,L,D)
- cTen: The ten symbol for the current position (e.g., X,C,M)

The return values for the UnitGroup() and DecimalGroup() functions are the character positions immediately after the current group. If no match for the type of group each function is looking for can be found, the functions just return nStart. These two functions are presented in Example 9.11.

EXAMPLE 9.11

UnitGroup() and DecimalGroup() functions

```
/* Unit group finds the end of a group of Roman numeral symbols matching cUnit
(in szN[], starting at nStart)returning the position of the end. If more than 4
are present, it returns nStart+4 (because a legal numeral can have no more than
4 of a given digit in a row). If there is no match, it just returns nStart. */
int UnitGroup(const char szN[],int nStart,char cUnit)
{
    int i;
    cUnit=(char)toupper(cUnit);
    for(i=0;i<4 && toupper(szN[nStart+i])==cUnit;i++){}
    return nStart+i;
}

/* Unit group finds the end of a group of Roman numeral symbols representing
a single decimal digit. cUnit is the unit symbol for that digit (e.g., 'I'),
cFive is the five symbol for that digit (e.g., V), and cTen is the ten symbol
(e.g., X). It returns the starting position in the string of the next decimal
place, or nStart if there is no match. */
int DecimalGroup(const char szN[],int nStart,char cUnit,char cFive,char cTen)
{
    int nPos=nStart;
    cUnit=(char)toupper(cUnit);
    cFive=(char)toupper(cFive);
    cTen=(char)toupper(cTen);
    // cFive and cTen may be '\0' for thousands place
    if (cFive !=0 && toupper(szN[nStart])==cFive)
        nPos=UnitGroup(szN,nStart+1,cUnit);
    else if (toupper(szN[nStart])==cUnit) {
        if (cTen!=0 && toupper(szN[nStart+1])==cTen) nPos=nStart+2;
        else if (cFive!=0 && toupper(szN[nStart+1])==cFive) nPos=nStart+2;
        else nPos=UnitGroup(szN,nStart,cUnit);
    }
    return nPos;
}
```

We immediately notice a few things about these functions:

- They are much smaller than IsLegalRoman1().
- Virtually all the comments relate to the arguments, as opposed to how the code works, because once you understand what the functions are supposed to do, their actual implementation is relatively trivial.

TEST YOUR UNDERSTANDING 9.7:

Identify how each line of code in UnitGroup() and DecimalGroup() corresponds to our rules for decimal places (using U, F and T).

Naturally, it is not really fair to compare the size of the two functions to IsLegalRoman1(), because we haven't included IsLegalRoman2(). That function, however, turns out to be pretty trivial, as shown in Example 9.12.

EXAMPLE 9.12

IsLegalRoman2()—elegant approach

```
// tells whether a Roman numeral, in szNum[], is legal
bool IsLegalRoman2(const char szNum[])
{
    unsigned int nStart=0;
    nStart=DecimalGroup(szNum,nStart,'M',0,0);
    nStart=DecimalGroup(szNum,nStart,'C','D','M');
    nStart=DecimalGroup(szNum,nStart,'X','L','C');
    nStart=DecimalGroup(szNum,nStart,'I','V','X');
    if (nStart==0 || nStart!=strlen(szNum)) return false;
    return true;
}
```

The IsLegalRoman2() function is simple in its operation. Because we know that Roman numerals are written higher to lower, left to right, we:

- Process each decimal group, in descending order.
  - If a group isn't present, the DecimalGroup() function returns to the original position, and we go to the next group.
  - If a group is present, nStart gets moved to the start of the next group.
- Once we have processed all the decimal places, we test to see whether we are at the end of the string containing the numeral—by comparing nStart to strlen(szNum).
  - If we are, it was a valid string—and all the groups were processed successfully, and in order.
  - If we are not at the end of the string, we were stopped by an invalid character somewhere, which means we'll be returning **false.**

The procedure is illustrated for the integer MCMVII (1907) in Figure 9.3.

9.5.4: Roman2Int Function

Once we know a string containing a Roman numeral is legal, actually finding the value is practically trivial. Our basic algorithm is as follows:

- Read in a numeral digit.
- If its value is >= to the value of the digit that follows, add the digit to the total.
- If its value is < than the digit that follows, subtract the value.

The function can be prototyped as follows:

```
unsigned int Roman2Int(const char szNum[]);
```

The return value is the value of the Roman numeral in szNum, or 0 if the numeral is illegal. For example:

- Roman2Int("MCMLXXXIII") would return 1983.
- Roman2Int("MIM") would return 0, because it is an illegal number form.

The function is presented in Example 9.13.

| FIGURE 9.3 | IsLegalRoman("MCMVII") Illustration |

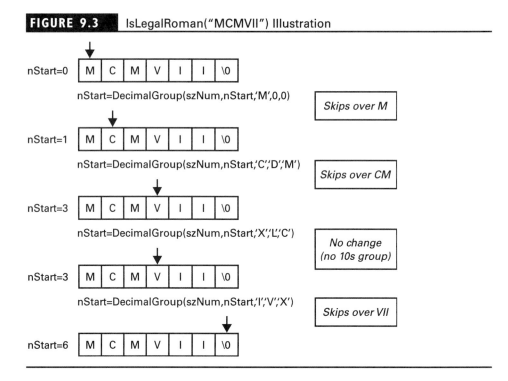

| EXAMPLE 9.13 |

Roman2Int() function

```
// returns the integer value of a Roman numeral in szNum,
// or 0 if the numeral is illegal
unsigned int Roman2Int(const char szNum[])
{
    unsigned int nTotal=0;
    int i;
    if (!IsLegalRoman2(szNum)) return 0;
    for(i=0;szNum[i]!=0;i++) {
        unsigned int nVal=NumeralValue(szNum[i]);
        unsigned int nNext=NumeralValue(szNum[i+1]);
        if (nVal<nNext) nTotal=nTotal-nVal;
        else nTotal=nTotal+nVal;
    }
    return nTotal;
}
```

9.6: REVIEW AND QUESTIONS

9.6.1: REVIEW

Algorithm is a term for a procedure that we use to solve computational problems. Iterative algorithms tend to rely on loops. (Another form of algorithm, recursive, is the subject of Chapter 15.)

The simplest iterative algorithms typically involve sequences of numbers. Such sequences can refer to values that change over time, such as capital in a typical financial calculation, or elements in a mathematical series (e.g., factorial or Fibonacci numbers). When working with such sequences, the programmer often has the choice of holding values in an array or in temporary variables. The choice made will depend upon factors such as whether we will be using the series more than once (in which case an array to hold the values might be preferable), and if memory is limited (in which case variables may be preferred).

Financial series almost always follow a particular pattern:

```
Value[t] = Value[t-1] + CashAdded[t] -
CashSubtracted[t]
```

The trick is to determine the sources of cash (e.g., interest, fees, contributions) and whether each sign is positive or negative. In most calculations, the signs are reversed for the two parties (e.g., what is positive from the borrower's perspective is negative from the lender's perspective).

Many algorithms work on a divide-and-conquer principle, breaking a single large problem into many smaller problems—each of which is much easier to solve. A good example of such a problem is binary search, used to find a value in a sorted array. The principal behind the algorithm is intuitive. Given a sorted search space (e.g., array, phone book), you start by testing the middle:

- If you match, you're done.
- If your test is higher than the value at the middle, you throw away the lower half and concentrate on the upper half.
- If your test is lower than the value at the middle, you throw away the upper half and concentrate on the lower half.
- You then set your new test location (e.g., array coefficient, page number) to the middle of the half that you did not throw away.

You keep repeating this process until either you find what you're looking for or your top and bottom are next to each other—meaning that what you are looking for is not there.

Similar to binary search is the successive approximation algorithm. This approach is usually used to compute continuous functions (e.g., the loan payment associated with a given principal, interest, and loan term). In order to use the function, you need:

- An upper bound and a lower bound of the value you're searching for
- A function that tells you whether your guess is too low or too high

You also need to be sure that the domain you are searching doesn't oscillate (e.g., like a sine wave)—technically, the term is *monotonic*—so that only one answer is possible.

The successive approximation algorithm we presented does the following:

- It takes our value range and chooses a point in the middle.
- It uses the test function to tell us whether our guess is too high or too low.
- It changes the range so that we only search the upper half (if our guess was too low) or lower half (if our guess was too high).
- The process repeats until the upper and lower bound are within a specified amount of each other.

The final topic discussed was the importance of choosing a good representation in designing an algorithm. The problem discussed was interpreting Roman numerals (e.g., writing a kind of ator() library function). The code demonstrated that writing the algorithm without a good representation led to code that was ugly and could easily have contained bugs. Choosing a better representation led to code that was much more compact and that would have (almost) certainly run.

9.6.2: GLOSSARY

algorithm A method of solving a particular problem

binary search A technique for searching a sorted array that works by dividing the array in half until the sought-after value is found or the remaining array is one element in size

brute force method Any method that attempts to solve a problem using pure processing power, and does not take advantage of problem characteristics that could make the solution process more efficient

divide-and-conquer A process in which a problem is broken down into separate parts that are solved independently

Fibonacci sequence A sequence in which every number is the sum of the previous two numbers in the sequence

sequence An array or other collection where the value of each element is dependent on the values of other elements in the array, based upon their position

successive approximation An algorithmic technique that estimates some desired value and, through a series of iterations, grows continually closer to some desired final result

9.6.3: QUESTIONS

1. *Net Present Value:* The net present value of a stream of cash flows is just the sum of each payment in the stream at time t, multiplied by the factor:

$$1/(1+r)^t$$

where r is the discount rate (i.e., the interest rate being used) and t is period. Suppose we have the following function prototype:

```
double NPV(double Pmts[],double
    dRate,int nPeriods);
```

where Pmts[] is an array holding the payments (+ or −) in each period, dRate is the discount rate we are using, and nPeriods is the number of payments in the array. Write the NPV() function.

2. *Factorial:* N factorial, sometimes written N!, is a sequence where each element is computed as follows:

```
N!  ➔  N*(N-1)*(N-2)*...*3*2*1
```

For example, 1! is 1, 2! is 2, 3! is 6, 4! is 24, 5! is 120, and so forth. Write a function that computes the factorial sequence with the following prototype:

```
unsigned int Factorial(unsigned int nVal);
```

where nVal is the number whose factorial value we want to compute and the function returns the computed value. What are the pros and cons of using unsigned integers in this computation?

3. *Logistic Function:* One of the most heavily studied sequences in the field of chaos research is based on the logistic function, which is sometimes used to model animal populations. The function is generally presented along the following lines:

$$P_t = k * P_{t-1} (1-P_{t-1})$$

where P_t is a value between 0 and 1, t is the sequence number, and k is a constant (the most interesting behaviors occur when $2.2 < k < 4$). Write a function prototyped as follows:

```
double Logistic(unsigned int nT,double
    dK,double dP0);
```

The function should return the value of the series at time nT, assuming a constant of dK and an initial value (i.e., the value of the series at period 0) dP0 where $0 < dP0 < 1$.

4. *Reaching Limit of a Sequence.* In finance, a formula stating that the total present value of an infinite series of payments of $1, discounted at rate r (greater than 0 and less than 1), is given as:

```
1/(1-r)
```

Write and test a function that returns the number of periods that you have to receive payment before reaching some specified percentage of that total value (e.g., 90%). The function should be prototyped as follows:

```
unsigned int ValuePeriod(double
    dRate,double dPercent);
```

where dRate is the discount rate used (see Question 1 for information on discounting) and dPercent is the percent of the final value we are looking for. Have your test program prepare a table showing how this value varies based on interest rate and percent of value, such as:

	Target 85%	Target 90%	Target 95%
6% discount			
8% discount			
10% discount			

Check to make sure your values seem to make sense.

5. *More Efficient Fibonacci Function:* The function used to compute the Fibonacci sequence, discussed in Section 9.2.1, would be exceptionally inefficient if we wanted to compute more than one sequence of numbers during our program (because we recomputed it each time). Rewrite the function using the following prototype:

```
unsigned int FibNew(unsigned int
    nPos,unsigned int arVals[]);
```

The function should return the value of the sequence at position nPos (assuming the sequence starts at 0). The arVals[] array will hold the values of the sequence that we have already computed *except* that arVals[0] will hold the maximum sequence value we have computed (which isn't any problem, because we know the value of position 0 is always 1). When the function is called, it should:

- Check nPos to see whether it is less than arVals[0]. If it is, we just return the value in arVals at postion nPos.

- If nPos>arVals[0], we should start at the last element computed and continue computing the sequence until we reach nPos. We should then update arVals[0] to reflect the fact that nPos values have been computed.

You can test your function by comparing its return value to that of the function presented in Section 9.2.1. (Substantial extra credit should be awarded to anyone who can come up with a plausible business situation in which this function would be even remotely useful.)

In-Depth Problems

6. *Mortgage Amortization:* Using the successive approximation algorithm discussed in this chapter, and the analysis of the problem in Section 9.4.1, create your own function to compute a mortgage payment, prototyped as follows:

```
double Payment(double dRate,unsigned
    int nPeriods,double dAmount);
```

with dRate as interest rate (consistent with periods), nPeriods as the number of periods, and dAmount as the amount of the mortgage.

7. *APR Computation:* The APR (effective annual percentage rate) on a loan can be different from the nominal interest rate charged on a loan as a result of fees and other expenses (e.g., taxes) that are paid to obtain the loan. One way it can be computed is to take the total cash flows associated with the loan and then determine the discount rate for which the NPV (see Question 1)

becomes 0. Write and test an APR function that is prototyped as follows:

```
double APR(double dLoan,double
    dFees,double dPmt,unsigned int nTerm);
```

The function should compute the APR associated with a given loan amount (dLoan, assumed to be received at period 0), set of fees (dFees, assumed to be paid out at period 0), and payment amount (dPmt, assumed to be paid from period 1 to period dTerm). After figuring out reasonable values for upper and lower bounds, use successive approximation to find an interest rate that brings the NPV function to 0.

8. *Advanced APR Computation:* Write and test an APR function, such as that presented in Question 7, that is prototyped as follows:

```
double APR(double dLoan,double
    dFees,double dNRate,unsigned int
    nTerm);
```

The return value and arguments are the same as for the earlier function except that the nominal interest rate (i.e., the rate quoted on the loan) is provided, instead of the actual payment. That means you will need to compute the payment (e.g., use Question 6 with dNRate, dTerm, and dLoan as arguments) before beginning the determination of interest rate.

9. *Logarithm (base 10):* The pow(double dVal,double dPower) function in math.h returns the value of dVal raised to dPower. The logarithmN function is defined such that:

```
pow(N, logarithm_N(dVal)) is equal to
    dVal
```

Define a function:

```
double log10(double dVal);
```

that uses successive approximation and the pow() function to compute the logarithm. You should test that dVal > 1–E15, and is less than 1+E15, which will allow you to set your upper bound at +15 and your lower bound to –15.

10. *Extended Roman Numerals:* Assume that an archaeologist just unearthed a scroll, penned by RESI (Roman Empire Standards Institute) that instituted the following new symbols:

```
F =   5,000
T =  10,000
B =  50,000
H = 100,000
```

Using the files in Roman.h and Roman.cpp as a starting point, extend the Roman2Int function to accommodate these symbols.

Pointers and Complex Arrays

EXECUTIVE SUMMARY

Chapter 10 focuses on the subject of pointers—the ability to manipulate addresses—which is the source of many of C++'s greatest strengths and weaknesses. Up to this point in the book, we finessed the subject of pointers, noting only that an address is a natural way of identifying the start of an array, such as a character string. In this chapter, the full potential that pointers provide to the programmer will be explored.

The chapter begins by examining how pointers are declared, how to place useful addresses into pointers, and how to get the data to which a pointer "points." The subject of pointer arithmetic—what happens when you apply arithmetic operators such as addition and subtraction to addresses—is explored. We then return to the subject of arrays, introduced much earlier in the book, and extend the concept to multidimensional arrays and arrays of pointers, spending some time considering what each representation technique is best for. We then examine the strong kinship between a pointer variable and an array name, noting their many similarities and their one key difference. Finally, we test our understanding of pointers and arrays using a *memory grid*, a teaching tool that makes the abstract concepts of addressing and memory organization more concrete.

LEARNING OBJECTIVES

Upon completing this chapter, you should be able to:

- Declare and initialize pointers
- Access the data that a pointer refers to
- Describe the basic arithmetic operations that can be performed on pointers, such as adding integers and subtracting pointers from each other
- Explain the organization of multidimensional arrays and how to access data within them
- Describe the organization of arrays of pointers
- Distinguish between situations appropriate for multidimensional arrays versus arrays of pointers
- List the ways in which pointers are similar to array names and the ways in which they differ
- Identify addresses and values in a simple map of memory for array and pointer expressions

10.1: NATURE OF A POINTER

When we introduced the concept of an array, we explained that an address in memory was the most natural way to refer to an array. Because all the elements in an array are *contiguous* in memory—meaning that they follow one another with no space in between—if you know the address of the first array element and the size of each array element (in bytes), you can easily determine the location of any other element in the array.

TEST YOUR UNDERSTANDING 10.1:

If the start of an array of 1-byte characters buf[80] is located at address 0x1000 in memory, where would buf[10] be located (remember to convert the 10 to hex before specifying the address)? How would that change if buf[80] was an array of double real numbers, starting at the same address? What key fact would you need to know about a double to answer the question?

Addresses can be used for many other things besides telling us where an array starts, however. In this section we examine *pointers*, variables that we declare to hold a memory address, instead of an actual value.

C and C++ are relatively unusual among computer languages in that they allow programmers to manipulate the values of memory directly, using variables defined to hold addresses instead of actual values. Using these variables, the C/C++ programmer can write code of unparalleled efficiency. Compiled with a good compiler, well-written C/C++ code is nearly as efficient as assembly language (and more so, as application size grows).

Pointers also have a downside, however. Because they provide a direct pathway to memory, and because memory contains practically everything that keeps the computer going—including the operating system, program code, and application data—writing data to just one bad address can cause severe problems to practically any program that happens to be running when the error occurs. On the PC, the introduction of operating systems (such as MS Windows NT, 2000, and XP) that are designed to protect applications from each other, made the situation markedly better than it used to be. Still, it is probably a good rule of thumb to save any data that you care about (such as your taxes, or that 23-page term paper on medieval footwear that you need to hand in tomorrow) before you start running untested code that uses addresses. *Don't say I didn't warn you.*

10.1.1: Pointers as Variables

A pointer is declared just like any other variable, except an asterisk is placed in front of the variable name to let the compiler know that the variable will hold an address, instead of a value. For example, in the code:

```
char *cpointer;
double val,*pval;
```

cpointer is declared as a pointer that will hold the address of a character. Similarly, val is declared as a double, while pval is declared as a variable that will hold the address of a double.

From the preceding illustration, it is apparent that whenever we declare an address, we must also declare the type of data that we expect to find at that address. The two main benefits of doing so are, first, that it allows us to perform pointer arithmetic (to be discussed later in this chapter), and second, that it gives the compiler the ability to ensure that we aren't doing anything obviously incorrect. For example, consider the strcpy library function that we discussed in earlier chapters. It is declared as follows:

```
char *strcpy(char *dest,const char *src);
```

Suppose that, in our code, we called the function as follows (using the variables cpointer and pval as already defined):

```
strcpy(cpointer,pval);
```

The compiler would look at the first argument and, because it was expecting a pointer to a character and that is how cpointer is defined, it would move on. Then it would examine the second argument. Although pval is an address, the way it is defined we would expect to find 8-byte double-precision real numbers at the address pval. The strcpy function, however, expects the address of a character string, so it doesn't seem to make sense that we are giving it the address of a double. Thus, the compiler will do its job, and issue a warning. As the programmer gains experience, such warnings come to be deeply appreciated. By telling us the exact line where our code doesn't make sense, the compiler saves us minutes, hours, or days of searching to figure out why we are ending up with such weird characters in the string pointed to by cpointer after we call the function.

Despite the fact the C++ requires us to specify the type of each pointer we use, an address is an address, regardless of what it points to. Thus, in the preceding declarations, the actual variables cpointer and pval are going to be the same size. On a typical PC, Windows 95 or above, those pointers will both be 4 bytes long—even though a char is 1 byte and a double is 8 bytes on the same machine. The bottom line: the length of the address tells you nothing about the size of the house there.

To say a final word on the subject, it is an extremely bad idea to make assumptions in your code that depend on an address being a particular size (e.g., 4 bytes). The size of a pointer is not specified by the C/C++ programming languages—meaning it can change as hardware evolves. If you need to know how large a pointer is, use the sizeof operator, introduced in Chapter 8, Section 8.3.2. Don't just code assuming 4 bytes, because that happens to be what it is today.

TEST YOUR UNDERSTANDING 10.2:

If the size of a pointer is 4 bytes, what does that tell you about the maximum amount of memory that will be available on the machine (given that every byte of memory must have a unique address)? In the very early 1980s, the CP/M machines that preceded the IBM-PC had 2-byte addresses. What does that tell you about the most memory those machines could hold?

10.1.2: Initializing the Value of a Pointer

When you declare a pointer, you are not setting aside any memory for the data it will point to.

Some statements are so important that they warrant constant repetition. So let's say it again, altogether now:

> *When you declare a pointer, you are not setting aside any memory for the data it will point to!*

Let us consider what this statement means by looking at a series of declarations, and figuring out what they are actually doing:

```
short int i,parray[10],*pi;
char *mypointer,c1,carray[80];
unsigned char uc2;
```

If we look at the first line, we are declaring three variable names. The variable i refers to a single short integer, taking up 2 bytes of memory (in Visual Studio .NET). The variable parray, on the other hand, refers to an array of 10 short integers (say 20 bytes of memory). When parray is used by itself, as we have already said, it refers to the address where that 20 bytes of memory start.

What about pi? Well, based on what we already know (especially given the statement that was repeated), we can deduce two things:

- Somewhere in memory we have set aside enough room to hold an address (probably 4 bytes).
- Whatever value is currently contained in those 4 bytes has nothing to do with anything useful. Most likely, it is the address of a random location in memory—an address that our system may not even have installed (e.g., if the address is hex 0xCCCCCCCC, a favorite of the Visual Studio debugger, it probably doesn't exist unless you have more than 3 gig of RAM installed).

From the second of these facts, we can quickly deduce a third fact. It is extremely unlikely that anything good will come of using the pointer pi until we get the address of a short integer we want to access into it.

The four common ways of getting an address into a pointer are as follows:

1. Applying the & operator to a variable name or array element (or, more generally, any lvalue)
2. Calling a function that returns an address or changes a pointer reference argument
3. Assigning the value from another pointer or array name
4. Assigning the value from a pointer arithmetic expression

We devote an entire chapter section to pointer arithmetic expressions, so we will concentrate on only the first three of these methods now. A number of indirect ways of assigning addresses to pointers can also be used (e.g., passing pointer addresses into functions, copying memory). These methods will be introduced later on in the book, as they are needed.

The & Operator   The & operator can be applied to any C++ expression referring to a value in memory, sometimes referred to as an lvalue, a term introduced in passing when we discussed the assignment operator (i.e., any value that it makes sense to put on the left-hand side of an assignment statement). Up to this point in the book, we have seen two types of lvalue expressions: variable names and references to array elements (e.g., parray[3]). To provide a simple example, the & operator could be used as follows:

```
char c1='c',carray[80]="Hello, World";
char *pc1,*pc2;
pc1=&c1;
pc2=&carray[6];
```

In this example, pc1 would contain the address of c1 by the time we reach the end of the code. If we went to that address, we would find a 'c' (the integer 97, according to the ASCII coding scheme) there. Similarly, pc2 would contain the address of element 6 (zero-based, of course!) of the array named carray. If we went to that address, we would find a space (ASCII value of 32).

TEST YOUR UNDERSTANDING 10.3:

If we changed the last line of our example to pc2=&carray[7], what value would we find if we went to the address contained in pc2 (character and integer versions)?

The & operator can also be applied to pointers. For example, the expression &pc1 is perfectly legal. Its interpretation is "the address in memory where the (4-byte) pointer pc1 is located." You should notice that it is very different from the *value* of pc1, which is "the address in memory where the (1-byte) character c1 is located." The relevance of this distinction will become clearer when we turn our attention to complex arrays, later on in the chapter.

Calling a Function Many functions, particularly string functions, return an address as a value. You can, therefore, use such a function call to acquire the address to assign to your pointer. We illustrate this call by considering the strstr standard library function (creating your own version of this function is an exercise at the end of the chapter).

TEST YOUR UNDERSTANDING 10.4:

If the array ar1 begins at address 0x00001000, what would the address in the pointer *found* be after the fragment in Example 10.1 was run?

EXAMPLE 10.1

strstr function

char *strstr(const char *s1,const char *s2);

The strstr function is a standard C library function that searches the string pointed to by its first argument (i.e., s1) for the first occurrence of the second string (i.e., s2). If it finds the substring, it returns the address within s1 where the occurrence begins. If not, it returns the NULL pointer, signifying no value.

Consider the following fragment of code:

```
char ar1[80]="The quick brown fox";
char *found;
found=strstr(ar1,"ow");
```

After the last line is executed, the pointer found will contain an address that points to the string "own fox".

In C++ (but not C), it is also possible to assign a value to a pointer argument that is passed as a reference to a function, for example:

```
void ElementAddress(char *&pEle,const char *ar,int nPos)
{
    pEle=&ar[nPos];
}
```

Calling this function will result in the first argument taking on the address of the element of ar[] at position nPos. Notice that the & in the function header, which declares pEle to be a reference, serves an entirely different purpose from the & in the body, which is the operator that takes the address of element ar[nPos].

Assigning the Value from Another Pointer or Array Name   Because pointers are variables, they can be assigned to each other. Array names refer to the address where the array starts, which means that these names can also be used to get values into pointers. Consider the following fragment of code:

```
char c1='c',carray[80]="Hello, World";
char *pc1,*pc2;
pc1=carray;
pc2=pc1;
```

The variables pc1 and pc2 would both end up referring to the same address—the address where carray starts.

The assignment of addresses between array names and pointers does not work in the opposite direction, however. The code:

```
carray=pc1;          /* definitely *not* legal */
```

will lead to compiler errors. The problem is that carray is not a variable. Instead it has a value assigned to it by the compiler (and then adjusted by the linker and loader) based upon the translation of the program to machine language. To use an analogy, variables are like data on a chalkboard: we can constantly write new values and erase existing ones. Array names, in contrast, are like addresses carved into a stone facade. We can read them easily enough, but we can't change them. We will return to this point when we consider the relationship between arrays and pointers.

Initializing a String Pointer   Because they are so useful in C/C++, NUL terminated strings are given special treatment as far as initialization is concerned. We have already seen this in arrays, where we can write:

```
char howdy[10]="hello";
```

instead of writing:

```
char howdy[10]={'h','e','l','l','o','\0'};
```

which is how we initialize other arrays.

String notation, using double quotes, can also be used to initialize pointers. To understand how this differs from initializing an array, consider the following two statements:

```
char howdy[10]="hello";
char *hi="hello";
```

In the first of these statements, the compiler will set up code that creates a 10-character array, then effectively perform a strncpy of "hello" into the array, initializing the last 4 characters in the array to the NUL terminator. In the second:

■   The variable hi, a (4-byte) pointer is first created.

- The compiler counts the number of characters in "hello" and then, somewhere in memory, creates an array of that size (at least 6 bytes).
- "hello" is then used to initialize the newly created array.
- Finally, it takes the address of the array it just created and places that address in the pointer hi.

This more elaborate process of initializing a pointer has some significant practical repercussions. Specifically, most compilers assume a double-quoted string to be constant, meaning it should not be changed. As a consequence, the following code fragment, which attempts to change "hello" to "jello" creates an access violation:

```
char *hi="hello";
hi[0]='j';
```

In Visual Studio .NET, this particular access violation results in an exception, causing the program to stop running.

The best way to avoid such a violation is either:

- To declare string variables as arrays, if you know you are going to change them
- To use the const qualifier when declaring pointers to strings that should not be changed (e.g., const char *hi="hello";)

Both of these approaches avoid the problem. Which one is better depends entirely on the situation.

TEST YOUR UNDERSTANDING 10.5:

What do you suppose would happen if you wrote the following code and then compiled it?

```
const char *hi="hello";
hi[0]='j';
```

If you really wanted to turn "hello" to "jello", how would you need to declare the string?

10.1.3: Retrieving the Value of a Pointer

Little purpose would come from placing addresses in pointers if we could not then retrieve the values at those addresses. In fact, for the most part, we usually care little about the actual addresses that are stored in a pointer. These addresses can easily change every time we run our program, depending upon where it is loaded in memory. Thus, getting data values from the location specified by a pointer, also called **dereferencing** a pointer, is an important task.

Two operators are typically used to get addresses from pointers, the * operator (sometimes referred to as the *indirection* operator, or the *dereferencing* operator) and the familiar brackets we already learned to use with arrays.

Dereferencing a Pointer with the * Operator   If you place an * operator in front of a pointer (or any expression that returns an address), the resulting expression refers to the value contained at that address. The type of pointer being dereferenced will, of course, determine the type of value returned. For example, in the following code fragment:

```
char c1='c',carray[80]="Hello, World";
char *pc1,*pc2;
pc1=&c1;
pc2=&carray[3];
carray[2]=*pc1;
*pc1=*carray;
```

The line *carray[2]=*pc1* will change the first l in "Hello, World" to a 'c' (which is the value that pc1 points to). The line **pc1=*carray* is even more interesting. The right-hand side (*carray) refers to the character at the address specified by carray—which is the first element of the array, or 'H'. The left-hand side (*pc1), refers to the data that pc1 points to, which turn out to be the variable c1. So, this line has the same effect as writing:

```
c1='H';
```

In other words, executing the line of code **pc1=*carray* actually changes the value in c1. This ability to change variable values by using their addresses turns out to be one of the most important capabilities that pointers provide us with.

TEST YOUR UNDERSTANDING 10.6:

In the code fragment just discussed, what would the following expressions do?

```
carray[8]=*pc2
*pc2=carray[1]
```

Would it matter what order we did them in?

When you initially encounter the asterisk used to perform dereferencing, it may seem like too much of a good thing. After all, that same asterisk is used to declare a variable as a pointer (as well as being used for multiplication). The choice of the asterisk as a dereferencing operator was intentional, however. To understand why, consider the following declaration:

```
int i1,*i2,i3;
```

As we know by now, this declaration specifies that i1 is an integer, i2 is a pointer to an integer, and i3 is an integer. You could read the declaration in another way, however. You could say we are declaring i1 to be an integer, *i2 to be an integer, and i3 to be an integer. Notice the subtle difference here: while i2 is a pointer, *i2 would, in fact, refer to an integer. Thus, it makes some sense to use the same notation for declaring pointers and dereferencing them—particularly when only a limited number of special characters is available for the language to use!

Using Brackets We already know how to use brackets to get elements from an array. Well, good news! We can use that exact same approach to retrieve data from a pointer. In fact, every time we used brackets inside a string function in previous chapters, that is exactly what we were doing. When we pass array names into functions, C++ creates a temporary local pointer to refer to the address of the array inside the function. In fact, C++ almost never passes a copy of an entire array into a function. Why copy all that data when the address will take us to where we want to go?

TEST YOUR UNDERSTANDING 10.7:

Given that we can use array notation instead of the * operator to deref-erence pointers, the code fragment presented earlier could be rewritten:

```
char c1='c',carray[80]="Hello, World";
char *pc1,*pc2;
pc1=&c1;
pc2=&carray[3];
carray[2]= pc1[0];
pc1[0]= carray[0];
```

Explain the changes. How would you rewrite the following lines?

```
carray[8]=*pc2
*pc2=carray[1]?
```

The equivalence of [] and * notation will be further explored when we consider pointer arithmetic.

10.1.4: The NULL Pointer

Sometimes we need to indicate that a pointer points to nothing. Perhaps we want to show that it has not been initialized. Or, perhaps, we want to signal a function call was unsuccessful (such as a call to strstr in Example 10.1 that did not find a matching substring). The problem is that once you define a variable, any variable, it always has *some* value, whether it is a valid value or not. And invalid pointer values are prodigiously dangerous, because they usually point to memory locations where your program has no business going.

To get around this problem, a constant NULL (case sensitive) has been defined. Its value is usually the address 0x00000000, but is only guaranteed to be so in C++, not C. Whenever a pointer has been assigned the value of NULL, it is assumed not to point to anything. One common example of its use is testing function return values.

The fact that NULL is defined does not, in and of itself, guarantee us against improperly initialized pointers. If the programmer calls functions that can return NULL, it is always a good idea to check them. Attempting to write data to NULL will almost always lead to an

---

EXAMPLE 10.2

Checking strstr return values

Consider the following fragment of code:

```
char ar1[80]="The quick brown fox jumped over the lazy dog";
char ar2[80];
char *found;
DisplayFormatted("Enter a string to seach for: ");
InputString(ar2);
found=strstr(ar1,ar2);
if (found==NULL) DisplayFormatted("The value you are looking for was not found!");
else {
    DisplayFormatted("The value you are looking for is found: ");
    DisplayFormatted("%s",found);
}
```

If the user types in "lazy" in response to the gets, it will send the following to the screen:

The value you are looking for is found: lazy dog

If the user types in "horse" instead, it will send the following to the screen:

The value you are looking for was not found!

exception that will halt your application in its tracks. Students just learning programming should take heart, however. On older machines, particularly DOS and earlier versions of MS Windows, the situation was even worse. The address 0000:0000 was actually quite important on those machines, holding key operating system routines. As a result, when you wrote data to an address specified by a pointer that inadvertently contained NULL, you invariably wiped out your keyboard interrupts and temporarily turned your PC into a noisy and poorly styled paperweight that had to be turned off, then rebooted (which took five minutes or so). The silver lining to that cloud was that most of us battered in that fashion eventually learned to check for NULL. That way, we only wreaked havoc on our systems a manageable four or five times a day. (Any less would have meant we just weren't trying hard enough.)

10.1.5: Pointers as Function Arguments

Using pointers as arguments to functions solved a key limitation of C functions. When we first considered functions, we noted that C functions couldn't change the values of their arguments (the exception of references, in C++, being duly noted). The explanation given was that function arguments are copied into local variables before they are used within the function. Thus, the only *direct* way to get information from a function was through its single return value. And only getting a single value back from a function is very limiting.

Passing in a pointer to a function allows us to sidestep the single return value limitation. Instead of passing in the actual variable we want to change, we pass in the address of that variable—in other words, a pointer to that variable. Although the function cannot change the value of the pointer itself (i.e., it can't change the address where the data are located), it can dereference the pointer, allowing it to change the value of the variable we were interested in.

Toupper vs. MakeUpper As an example, consider the following Toupper() and MakeUpper() functions:

```
char Toupper(char in) {
    if (in>='a' && in<='z') in=in-'a'+'A';
    return in;
}
void MakeUpper(char *pin) {
    if (*pin>='a' && *pin<='z') *pin=*pin-'a'+'A';
    return;
}
```

Suppose, these functions were called from a code fragment specified as follows:

```
char c1='a',c2='b',c3;
c3=Toupper(c1);
MakeUpper(&c2);
```

After calling the code, c1 would have the value 'a' (unchanged), c3 would have the value 'A' (from the return value of Toupper), and c2 would have the value 'B' (changed by MakeUpper).

In-Depth: sscanf A good example of a function that takes pointers as arguments because it needs to change their values is the **sscanf** function, which acts as a type of inverse function to sprintf (see Chapter 7, Section 7.3.2). The arguments to the function are:

- A string to be scanned

- A formatting string, similar to that used for sprintf. Common format specifiers include:
  - %d – decimal integer
  - %x – hexadecimal integer
  - %i – integer (sscanf tries to figure our the format by looking for leading characters, such as 0x)
  - %s – NUL terminated string; sscanf assumes a string ends at the first white character, such as a ' ' or tab
  - %[*count*]c – One or more characters, specified by the optional count parameter (e.g., %20c); often used to read strings of known length that contain white characters
  - %f – double precision real numbers
  - Nonformat specifier codes are treated as literal characters. If the string being scanned does not contain characters matching the literals in the correct position, no further arguments are scanned.
- A set of pointer arguments (whose number depends on number of % argument specifiers in the formatting string) whose values are set when the first argument string is scanned

The function returns the number of arguments successfully scanned.

Because sscanf takes the specified inputs and placed them into its arguments, pointers to those arguments (rather than the arguments themselves) must be passed. The following code illustrates the difference:

```
char buf[80];
char str[80]="Hello!"
int i1=21,i2=14,i3=55;
sprintf(buf,"%d %d  %d %s",i1,i2,i3,str);
i1=i2=i3=0;
strcpy(str,"Goodbye!");
sscanf(buf,"%d %d %d %s",&i1,&2,&i3,str);
// restores i1, i2, and i3 to their original values and
// replaces "Hello!" in str
```

To display the values of i1, i2, and i3, the variables themselves are passed as arguments. To restore those values by scanning buf, their addresses need to be passed. Because str is an array, it is already passed in as an address to sprintf(), and is passed the same way to sscanf().

An example showing a simple pair of functions that converts between integer and string formatted dates is shown in Example 10.3. The "integer format" date is in the form YYYYMMDD. For example, 18 July 2004 would be 20040718. The text formatted date is simply the standard U.S. "MM/DD/YYYY" format.

The ScanDate() function reads three integers that must be separated by / characters (because the sscanf() function specifies them in the format string). Argument addresses must be used to set the values. If three arguments are successfully scanned, it then:

- Adjusts the year for two-digit dates
- Updates the days-per-month array (Months[]) for leap years (changing February to 29)
- Checks that the day number is valid for the specified month

---

EXAMPLE 10.3

Reading and writing dates using sscanf() and sprintf()

```
int ScanDate(const char *buf)
{
    int Months[]={31,28,31,30,31,30,31,31,30,31,30,31};
    int nM,nD,nY;
    if (sscanf(buf,"%d/%d/%d",&nM,&nD,&nY)!=3 || nY<0) return 0;
    // creating a Y2K problem
    if (nY<50) nY+=2000;   //
    if (nY<100) nY+=1900;  //
    // adjusting for leap years—occurs
    // 1) every 4 years except for years divisible by 100
    // 2) in years divisible by 400
    if (nY%400==0) Months[1]=29;
    else if (nY%100!=0 && nY%4==0) Months[1]=29;
    // checking valid month and day
    if (nM<1 || nM>12) return 0;
    if (nD<1 || nD>Months[nM-1]) return 0;
    return nY*10000+nM*100+nD;
}

void DateString(char *szTarget,int nDate)
{
    int nY=nDate/10000;
    int nD=nDate%100;
    int nM=(nDate/100)%100;
    sprintf(szTarget,"%i/%i/%i",nM,nD,nY);
}
```

If all tests are successful, it returns an integer date.

The DateString() function takes the integer date and breaks it up into year, month, and day components. The modulus operator can be used effectively here because of the manner in which dates are formatted. It then uses sprintf—which uses variable values, not addresses, to construct the string.

Side Effects   The changing of a value pointed to by an argument of a function is sometimes called a side effect. Code that makes extensive use of side effects is often much more difficult to understand and debug than code that relies purely on return values. The reason is that when you call a function, you don't necessarily expect it to make changes to its arguments. As a result, you may use the same values passed in as arguments later on in your code, without realizing they have been changed. This problem can be particularly vexing when you are using functions you did not write, such as library functions.

One way of addressing the problem of which arguments are modified and which are not is to use the **const** modifier in front of the pointer declaration (e.g., const char *arg1 instead of char *arg1). If the **const** modifier is present, a compiler error will be produced if the function attempts to change the dereferenced value of the pointer. In general, it is good programming practice to use the **const** modifier any time you do not expect to change the value that an argument points to. **const** can also modify a reference argument.

What would be a better way of specifying each of the following definitions for standard C/C++ library functions that we have covered?

- int strlen(char *str)
- char *strcpy(const char *dest,char *src);
- int strcmp(char *s1,char *s2);

10.1.6: The *void* Pointer and Pointer Type Casting

Throughout this section, we emphasized the advantages of specifying a type for every pointer we declare. At times, however, it is convenient to declare a pointer that can point to anything. The most common examples of situations in which such general pointers are useful include the following:

- *Generic memory functions.* C/C++ provides a number of functions for initializing and copying the contents of memory. These memory functions can be used on all data types (including C structures, to be defined later). For that reason, their arguments are generally pointers.

- *Generic collection objects.* Advanced programming techniques, some of which are touched on in the SwapSort lab exercise of this chapter, often require that complex collections of data be created, such as lists of data elements and lookup tables. Using void pointers, it is possible to write generic functions that can be used to create and maintain these collections.

void * When such general purpose addressing is needed, a special pointer type, void *, is available. You can directly assign any type of pointer to a **void pointer** without a compiler warning. For example:

```
int myarray[10];
void *parray;
parray=myarray;
```

It is up to you, the programmer, however to keep track of the type of data assigned to the void pointer. The program cannot determine that information for itself.

If you have a void pointer, you can also assign it to a typed pointer—once again, assuming you know what type of data the void pointer actually points to. Because void pointers have no inherent type, you will normally need to assign them into a typed pointer before you can do anything useful with them. To illustrate, consider the C standard library's memset function, as shown in Example 10.4.

Does Memset code in Example 10.4 code initialize the block from start to end, or end to start? Would this code continue to work properly on a machine where the character size was 2 bytes?

Type Casting Pointers When moving between pointer types, a compiler warning will often be produced. In C, which is much more flexible in this regard than C++, assigning a const void pointer to any other type of pointer (including void) that is not const will generate such a message. In C++, assignments across types (including void pointers to other pointers) will generate warnings or errors.

EXAMPLE 10.4

The memset function

The standard library function memset takes a block of memory and initializes every byte within it to a single value. Although the actual C declaration is slightly different, the function *could* be prototyped as follows:

```
void *memset(void *addr,unsigned char c,int bytes);
```

where *addr* is the starting address of the memory we are initializing, *c* is the character we are initializing it to and *bytes* is the number of bytes we are initializing. It returns *addr* (the same address being passed in), although the return value is rarely used.

The memset function provides a convenient means of initializing large objects, such as arrays. For example, in the code fragment that follows:

```
int bigarray[10000];
memset(bigarray,0,10000*sizeof(int));
```

the call to memset initializes every byte in bigarray to 0.

Our own version of the memset function (Memset) could be defined as follows:

```
void *Memset(void *addr,unsigned char c,int bytes)
{
    unsigned char *pblock=addr;
    // the above line will generate a C++ warning, to be explained later
    while(bytes->0) pblock[bytes]=c;
    return addr;
}
```

By assigning the void pointer *addr* to *pblock,* we are able to access every byte in the block of interest.

TEST YOUR UNDERSTANDING 10.10:

Why would the line of code:

```
unsigned char *pblock=addr;
```

found in the memset function (Example 10.4) compile without warning in C, yet lead to an error in C++?

The reason for such warnings/errors is that the compiler wants to focus your attention on the possibly dangerous thing you are doing—taking an address of one type and putting it into a pointer of another type. Pointer-to-pointer assignments are usually warnings, not errors, and so a number of "avoidance" behaviors are available to you, such as ignoring the warning or turning the compiler warning settings off. The problem with the first, ignoring the warning, is that it desensitizes you (like the boy who cried wolf), so you end up ignoring all warnings—including the ones that would save you hours or days in finding code problems. The second approach, turning the warning settings off, is even worse. It's like telling your doctor not to inform you of any areas of concern found during a routine physical, just because some of those concerns might turn out to be unfounded.

So, how do you get rid of a warning when you know the code is correct? Similar to what we did when errors surfaced during numeric conversions, we can type cast the pointers. Pointer type casting involves placing the correct pointer type (within parentheses) directly in front of the pointer being converted. Type casting to eliminate a warning that we know is "okay" is illustrated in the simple implementation of the standard library function memcpy that follows.

EXAMPLE 10.5

The memcpy function

The standard library function memcpy takes a block of memory and copies it, byte by byte, to another location. Effectively, then, it is the same as strcpy, except you specify how many bytes are to be copies instead of copying until the NUL terminator is reached. Although the actual C/C++ declaration is slightly different, the function *could* be prototyped as follows:

```
void *memcpy(void *dest,const void *src,int bytes);
```

where *dest* is the starting address of the block we are copying to, *src* is the starting address of the block of memory we are copying from, and *bytes* is the number of bytes we are copying. It is critically important, for this particular function, that the *src* and *dest* blocks of memory do not overlap. The function returns *dest* (the same address being passed in), although the return value is rarely used.

The memcpy function provides a convenient means of moving data between large objects, such as arrays. For example, in the code fragment that follows:

```
double bigarray1[10000],bigarray2[10000];
memset(bigarray1,0,10000*sizeof(double));
memcpy(bigarray2,bigarray1,10000*sizeof(double));
```

the call to memset initializes every byte in bigarray1 to 0. The call to memcpy then copies all the bytes in bigarray1 into bigarray2—effectively doing the same thing.

Our own version of the memcpy function (Memcpy) could be defined as follows:

```
void *Memcpy(void *dest,const void *src,int bytes)
{
    unsigned char *p1,*p2;
    p1=dest;
    p2=(unsigned char *)src;
    while(bytes-->0) p1[bytes]=p2[bytes];
    return dest;
}
```

The type cast, in the lines *p2=(unsigned char *)src* is required because src is defined as const, whereas p2 is not.

TEST YOUR UNDERSTANDING 10.11:

In Example 10.5, why doesn't the line of code *p1=dest* require a type cast in C? Would it require a type cast in C++?

A number of memory-related functions, return void pointers. You will always want to type cast the return values of such functions in C++. As a result, it is good programming practice to type cast all conversions across pointer types (even void), whether or not they generate warnings.

Type Casting Pointers in C++ Type casting using parentheses, as already described, works in C++ just as it works in C (except that C++ requires you to do it nearly all the time). The main danger with the "standard approach" to type casting is that the compiler accepts the programmer's type cast as "the gospel," even if the programmer has made a logic error in doing so. For example, after a const pointer has been type cast to non-const pointer, the program can then make changes to the memory whose address was contained in the const pointer—defeating the protection declaring a pointer as const is supposed to give you. In another example, by casting pointers between inherently different types (e.g., float and int), you can convince the compiler to allow you to put memory of one type that's supposed to be used for another type. Unless you know what you are doing, this activity is a formula for trashing memory.

When doing advanced object-oriented programming in C++, a programmer's reliance on type casting increases dramatically. In C, the major motivation for type casting pointers is to get rid of warnings. In C++, however, how a pointer is type cast can significantly change how a function executes. For this reason, a number of more sophisticated type casting operators, such as **static_cast** and **dynamic_cast** are provided for safer type casting. As with all object-oriented features of C++, discussion of these operators is postponed until the end of the text.

10.1: SECTION QUESTIONS

1. What is the main potential drawback of using pointers in your code?
2. One advantage of declaring pointer types is the ability to perform pointer arithmetic. What is the other advantage?
3. Is taking addresses the only use of the & operator in C/C++? If not, how do you suppose C/C++ decides what operator to use when it encounters &?
4. What does the term *dereferencing* a pointer mean?
5. Explain the possible motivations for declaring a **void** pointer.
6. Why is it a good idea to type cast all pointer conversions, even if the C++ compiler does not require you to?

10.2: POINTER ARITHMETIC

Once you accept the fact that bracket notation can be used in place of the * for dereferencing pointers, the whole concept of pointer arithmetic becomes much less mysterious. We begin the topic by examining what happens when integers are added and subtracted from pointers, then we move on to other arithmetic operations. Finally, we show the precise correspondence between **array notation** and * notation.

10.2.1: Adding and Subtracting Integers from Pointers

When we observed, in Section 10.1.3, that we could substitute bracket notation for pointer notation, we concluded that the following expressions are equivalent for any variable p1 declared to be a pointer:

```
*p1 ≡ p1[0]
```

Given this equivalence, it is natural to wonder what, if any, equivalences exist for coefficient values other than 0, such as 1, 2, 3, and so on. As it turns out, a direct equivalence is available that is both straightforward and elegant.

For any pointer p1, and any integer i, the following expressions are precisely equivalent:

```
*(p1 + i) ≡ p1[i]
```

This identity is probably *the single most important thing you need to remember if you want to master pointers.* Moreover, this equivalence turns out to be mandated by the design of typical C/C++ compilers. In these compilers, whenever an expression in bracket notation is encountered, it is translated to **pointer (*) notation** before the expression is actually compiled. In other words, pointer notation can be viewed as the "natural" notation for address dereferencing.

TEST YOUR UNDERSTANDING 10.12:

Given that pointer notation is the natural notation for dereferencing, would you expect the following fragment of code to compile?

```
char x,y,arrc[]="Howdy";
x=arrc[2];
y=2[arrc];
```

Explain why or why not. If it would compile, what would the values of the variables x and y be after running the fragment?

Given that *(p1+i) is the same as p1[i], we can then make some deductions about the expression p1+i. Specifically, we know:

1. Because we get a value by putting an asterisk in front of it, p1+i must be an *address*.

2. Because the value at the address p1+i points to is always p1[i], the address at p1+i must be the same as &p1[i]. In other words, p1+i must point to the ith element (zero-based) of the array.

   These two deductions allow us to make some further deductions:

   ```
   (1) (p1+i)  ≡ &p1[i]   ➜ What we deduced already
   (2) *(p1+i) ≡ p1[i]    ➜ Our initial identity
   (3) &*(p1+i) ≡ &p1[i]  ➜ We apply the & operator to both sides
   ```

   Given (1) through (3), we can come up with two important conclusions:

   - The & and * are *inverse* operators, which means that if you apply one right after the other, they cancel each other out. We can see this effect by comparing (1) and (3).
   - The address produced by adding the integer i to an address is the address of the ith element of the array.

Here, then, is pointer arithmetic in a nutshell:

> **Pointer Arithmetic:** *If you take an address p1, then add an integer i to it, the resulting address will be the value of p1 plus i * sizeof the type of object p1 points to.*

The easiest way to illustrate pointer arithmetic is by looking at a few examples.

Having determined what happens to an address when an integer is added to it, subtraction is no different. We simply take the integer we are subtracting, multiply it by the size of the data being pointed to, and subtract the result from the initial address.

TEST YOUR UNDERSTANDING 10.13:

Suppose that p1 is a pointer to a **char,** and contains the address 0x00001000. Suppose that d1 is a pointer to a **double,** and also happens to contain the address 0x00001000. For any integer k, which of the following two statements is true:

- p1+k*sizeof(d1) refers to the same address as d1+k

EXAMPLE 10.6

Adding integers to addresses

Assume the following declarations have been made somewhere in the program:

```
char *p1,*p2;
double *d1,*d2;
float *f1,*f2;
short int *s1,*s2;
int *i1,*i2;
```

Assume, as well, that at the time we reach the following block of code in the program, p1==0x00001000, d1==0x00002000, f1==0x00003000, s1==0x00004000, and i1==0x00005000.

```
p2=p1+2;
d2=d1+2;
f2=f1+2;
s1=s1+2;
i1=i1+2;
```

After the preceding block of code, and assuming the normal sizes for **char** and **int**, we would find the following tests would all be true:

```
p2==0x00001002
d2==0x00002010
f2==0x00003008
s2==0x00004004
i1==0x00005008
```

The values are arrived at because 2*1 is 2 (p2), 2*8 is 0x10 (d2), 2*4 is 8 (f2 and i1), and 2*2 is 4 (s2).

- p1+k*sizeof(double) refers to the same address as d1+k

  Given the values of p1 and d1 above, and if k==1, what would the values of (a) p1+k*sizeof(d1), (b) p1+k*sizeof(double), and (c) d1+k be for code compiled with Visual Studio .NET?

10.2.2: Other Arithmetic Operations on Pointers

Besides integer addition and subtraction, a few other pointer arithmetic operations are commonly seen. Of greatest interest are the application of increment/decrement operators (++ and --) to pointers and what is accomplished by subtracting two addresses. It is also useful to note some operations that are illegal with addresses.

Increment/Decrement Operations on Pointers   As was discussed in an earlier chapter, the increment operator i++ is a shorthand way of writing the expression:

```
i = i+1;
```

Similarly, the decrement operator i-- is the same as writing:

```
i = i-1;
```

Given what we already know about pointer arithmetic, it then follows that:

1. Incrementing a pointer causes a pointer to hold a new address that is the original address plus the size of the object being pointed to.

2. Decrementing a pointer reduces the original address by the size of whatever is being pointed to.

One important limitation on the use of the increment/decrement operators is that they cannot be applied to array names. The reason for this limitation is that the address referred to by an array name cannot be changed (as already noted), because doing so would be tantamount to telling C/C++ to relocate the array in memory. Since ++ or -- change the argument they are applied to, the compiler will generate an error if they are applied to an array name.

A common use for the increment/decrement operator is iterating through an array without using subscripts, as is shown in the example that follows.

TEST YOUR UNDERSTANDING 10.14:

In Example 10.7, why is the pi++ in the for loop legal, even though pi is declared as const? What changes would we need to make to this function if we wanted to create a version that summed an array of double values?

Subtracting Pointers   When you subtract two pointers, the result is an integer specifying the "distance" between the two pointers. How to interpret that distance can be deduced as follows.

Suppose p1 and p2 are both defined as pointers of the same type. Further suppose that p1=p2+x, where x is an integer. Then:

p1=p2+x   ➜   Given

p1-p2=x   ➜   Subtracting p2 from both sides

It follows, then, that x represents the number of "elements" between the two addresses. Stated another way:

> When two pointers of the same type are subtracted, the result is an integer that represents the difference in the actual addresses (in bytes) divided by the size of the object being pointed to.

EXAMPLE 10.7

Summing the elements in an array of integers

Suppose we wanted to write a function that would determine the sum of an array of integers of a specified size. The function could be prototyped as follows:

```
int TotalInts(const int *pi,int count);
```

Where the return value would be the total, pi refers to the starting address of the array, and count is the number of elements in the array. The following code could be used to implement the function, using the increment operator instead of coefficients:

```
int TotalInts(const int *pi,int count)
{
    int total;
    for(total=0;count-->0;pi++) total=total+*pi;
    return total;
}
```

Normally, such arithmetic will be guaranteed accurate only if the values come from the same array. Doing so guarantees that the remainder, after dividing the number of bytes by the size of the object, will be 0. Otherwise, the remainder is discarded.

TEST YOUR UNDERSTANDING 10.15:

What would the expression &p1[6]-&p1[5] return for any non-void pointer p1?

Illegal Operations   A number of operators are illegal when addresses are involved.

- *Adding two addresses:* There is no reasonable way to interpret what it would mean to add two addresses, so the operation is illegal.
- *Subtracting two pointers of different types:* Subtracting two pointers of different types makes no sense, because we don't know which size to divide the difference in addresses by. In Visual Studio .NET doing so leads to a warning. If the warning is ignored—always a bad idea—the size of the first pointer in the subtraction is used to determine the result.
- *Subtracting a pointer from an integer:* There is no reasonable way to interpret this operation, so it is illegal.

Normally, very little motivation can be found to write code that attempts these illegal operations, because they don't make any sense. Decades of programming experience teach us that using code whose intent is entirely unknown to its author will almost never lead to the solution of a programming problem.

10.2.3: Summary of Pointer Arithmetic

The effects of the different pointer arithmetic operations are summarized in Table 10.1.

TABLE 10.1   Pointer Arithmetic Operations

First Argument	Operator	Second Argument	Effect
Address	+/–	Integer	Takes the integer times the size of the object being pointed to and adds it to (or subtracts it from) the address
Integer	+/–	Address	
Address	–	Address	Takes the difference between the two addresses, in bytes, and divides them by the size of the objects being pointed to; can only be used on pointers of the same type, and would normally be relevant only for pointers in the same array
Integer	–	Address	Illegal
Address	+	Address	Illegal
Address	++/––	(N/A)	Postfix: Returns the value of the address, then adds/subtracts the size of the object being pointed to/from the address; cannot be used on array names (whose address cannot be changed)
(N/A)	++/––	Address	Prefix: Adds/subtracts the size of the object being pointed to/from the address and returns the resulting address; cannot be used on array names (whose address cannot be changed)

10.2: SECTION QUESTIONS

1. If d1 is a pointer to a **double,** and contains the address 0x00001050, what address would the expression d1-4 evaluate to?

2. Pointer arithmetic is also called address arithmetic. Why is "address arithmetic" a more accurate term, given our definition of a pointer?

3. We think of the increment operator (++) as taking its argument and adding 1 to it. Why is what happens slightly more complicated when the argument being incremented is a pointer?

4. If d1 and d2 are both pointers to double, and d1==0x00001f30 and d2=0x00001ebc, what would the expression d1-d2 return? Can you tell whether these values are from the same array?

5. If arr is declared as follows: *int arr[10]* and arr begins at address 0x00001000 in memory, what would happen if the expression arr++ was encountered in the code?

10.3: COMPLEX ARRAYS

Up to this point, we limited our discussions to *one-dimensional arrays*. Such arrays are powerful, and many things can be done with them. C/C++ provides even more powerful representational tools, however, that include multidimensional arrays and, even more importantly, arrays of pointers. In this section, we examine these more complex array types, and consider what they can be used for.

10.3.1: Multidimensional Arrays

A multidimensional array is an array that is declared and accessed with more than one coefficient. In programming languages that do not allow programmers to access addresses, such as FORTRAN, COBOL, and BASIC, the ability to define multidimensional arrays can be a useful capability. Although C and C++ also support the definition of multidimensional arrays, their utility is dramatically reduced by the ability to use arrays of pointers in their place. (The reason arrays of pointers are usually better than multidimensional arrays will become clearer later in this section, and when we discuss dynamic memory in Chapter 12.)

To understand the nature of a multidimensional array, it is helpful to think visually. If we think of a variable as a point in memory, then our standard array can be visualized as a line of these points in a row. Its single coefficient represents a point on the line, and just as we refer to a line as one-dimensional, we refer to an array with one coefficient as one-dimensional. A two-dimensional array has two coefficients, usually referred to as a row and a column, and can be visualized as a table (which is, of course, a two-dimensional object). In order to reach a particular piece of data, we need to supply a row number and a column number (both zero-based in C/C++, naturally). A three-dimensional array has three coefficients, and can be visualized as a three-dimensional cube or rectangle. To get a piece of data in such an array, you need three numbers, representing the X, Y, and Z coordinates. An illustration of these different array types is provided in Figure 10.1. Multidimensional arrays in C/C++ are not, however, limited to three dimensions. The process of adding dimensions can go on indefinitely, with as many dimensions being added as needed (although beyond three is hard to visualize and harder to draw).

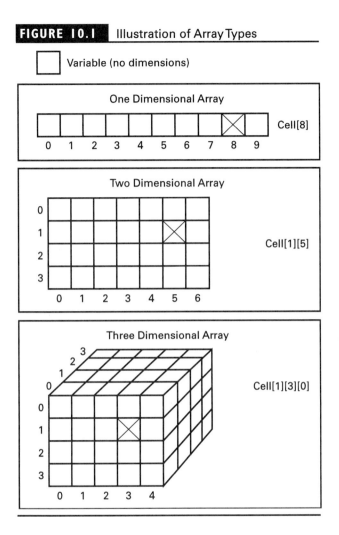

FIGURE 10.1 Illustration of Array Types

A number of characteristics of C/C++ multidimensional arrays need to be understood before they can be used effectively:

- Arrays are declared, and coefficients accessed, using separate brackets for each coefficient (see Figure 10.1). This format differs from many programming languages, where commas are often used to separate coefficients.

- Arrays are stored in row-major order. For example, if you view the first coefficient of a two-dimensional array as the row, and the second as the column, then all the data for a specific row are stored before the data for the next row.

- If a reference is made to a multidimensional array with less than the declared number of coefficients, the reference itself refers to an array.

The first two of these characteristics are relatively straightforward. The third, however, takes a bit more explanation.

Partial Coefficients in Multidimensional Arrays   Suppose we have a two-dimensional array defined as follows:

```
char screen[25][80];
```

Such an array might, for example, hold the contents of an old PC-based text screen (which had 25 rows and 80 columns). If we were to refer to element screen[5][17], we would be talking about the character at the 6th row, 18th column (assuming, like most humans, we start at 1 when we talk about text screen positions). But what if we just referred to screen[5]? Given that we stated that coefficients are stored in row-major order, screen[5] would seem to refer to the entire row. That, in fact, is how C/C++ interprets it. And, because the row is an array of 80 characters, screen[5] is—effectively—an array name.

TEST YOUR UNDERSTANDING 10.16:

Explain why the following code is legal:

```
char screen[25][80];
char *pscreen;
pscreen=screen[5];
```

Would the assignment *pscreen=screen* also be legal? Why or why not?

Initializing Multidimensional Arrays   We have already seen that one-dimensional arrays can be initialized with a comma-separated list of values. For example:

```
int myarray[10]={1,4,6,7,8};
```

would initialize the first five elements of the array myarray to 1, 4, 6, 7, and 8, respectively, with the remaining elements being initialized to 0.

For multidimensional arrays, the same initialization process applies, however nested brace-enclosed collections are used for the different dimensions. For example:

```
int array3[2][3][2]={{{1,2},{3,4},{5,6}},
{{7,8},{9,10},{11,12}}};
```

Note that this order also reflects the order in which the array elements would be stored in memory.

TEST YOUR UNDERSTANDING 10.17:

In the previous example, what would be the value of example, array3[1][2][0]? What would be the value of array3[0][1][1]? Given what you know about C/C++'s disregard of array boundaries, and how multidimensional arrays are stored, what would you expect the value of array3[0][3][1] to be?

10.3.2: Arrays of Pointers

The array of pointers is one of the most powerful representational techniques in the C/C++ language family. Conceptually, it differs little from a normal, one-dimensional array—the difference being that the elements are pointers to data elements, instead of the actual data elements themselves. This distinction is illustrated in Figure 10.2, where the actual array is the column of addresses on the left, while the data being referenced are the random strings on the right.

A particularly important aspect of the diagram in Figure 10.2 is the fact that while the array itself is contiguous and in order, there is no reason that the memory addresses being

FIGURE 10.2 An Array of Character Pointers

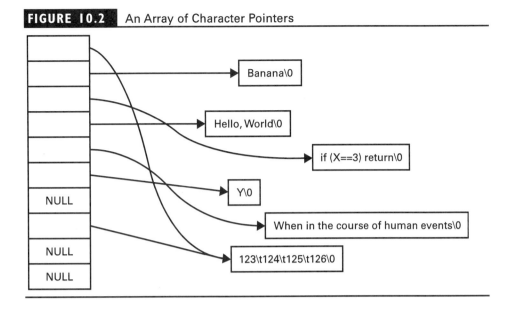

referenced should be contiguous, or even in order. Thus, while Array[1] points to the string "Banana", and Array[2] points to the string "if (X==3) return", there is no basis for assuming anything about where the two strings ("Banana" and "if (X==3) return") are located in memory. They could be anywhere.

Declaring an Array of Pointers Declaring an array of pointers is straightforward. You simply declare an array, then place an asterisk in front of the name. For example:

```
int *array1[10];
char *array2[4]={"Hello","World","It\'s","me"};
```

In the first example, we are declaring an array of 10 pointers to integers. In the second, we are declaring an array of 4 pointers to characters. In addition, in the second case, we are telling the compiler to create constant strings in memory and then assign each of their addresses to one of the pointers. Just as with any other array, had we left the 4 out of the declaration, the compiler would have counted the number of elements and used that count to size the array.

TEST YOUR UNDERSTANDING 10.18:

Suppose the second declaration had been specified as follows:
```
char *array2[10]= {"Hello","World","It\'s","me"};
```
What do you suppose would have happened, given your understanding of how arrays are initialized?

Passing an Array of Pointers as an Argument to a Function As with any C/C++ data object, the ability to pass it as an argument to a function is critical. Because C and C++ do not normally make copies of array arguments, it makes sense that we will use a pointer. But how will that pointer be declared?

To understand the declaration of a pointer to an array of pointers, it is useful to return to how we handled an array. For example:

```
char array1[80];
char *parr1=array1;
```

If the same logic were to hold, it would then appear that:

```
char *array2[80];
char **parr2=array2;
```

This declaration was accomplished simply by placing an extra asterisk in front of both of the original expressions. It also turns out that it is precisely how we create a pointer to an array of pointers (or to a multidimensional array).

TEST YOUR UNDERSTANDING 10.19:

In Example 10.8, what advantages are there to having a function such as FindDay() take the array to be searched as an argument, as opposed to making it a static global array? (*Hint:* Think flexibility and designing code for the international environment.) What modifications to this function would be required to make it suitable for searching any array of strings?

10.3.3 Higher Order Arrays of Pointers

Adding even more flexibility to the C/C++ language is the ability to declare multilevel arrays of pointers—that is, arrays of pointers that point to other arrays of pointers. Although such complexity takes a while to get used to, it does offer an extremely powerful tool for representing data.

Conceptually, arrays of arrays of pointers look something like the illustration in Figure 10.3. The initial array contains pointers that point to other arrays of pointers which,

---

EXAMPLE 10.8

Linear search

Suppose we wanted to write a search routine that looked for a matching string in an array of pointers, say days of the week, and returned the array coefficient of the matching element (or –1 if there was no match). For example, our array might be declared as follows:

```
char *days[]={"Monday","Tuesday","Wednesday","Thursday","Friday",
"Saturday","Sunday"};
```

Our function could be declared as follows:

```
int FindDay(const char *day,const char **dayarray);
```

We could then write the function as follows:

```
int FindDay(const char *day,const char **dayarray)
{
    int i;
    for(i=0;i<7 && strcmp(dayarray[i],day)!=0;i++) {};
    if (i==7) return -1;
    else return i;
}
```

in turn, point to character strings. The declaration of the array in Figure 10.3 would be something like:

```
char **Plants[5];
```

where the 5 represents the number of elements in the first (leftmost) array. The remaining arrays and the strings would then need to be established somewhere else. (Normally such arrays would be created using dynamic memory, discussed in Chapter 12.)

Following the same line of logic used for single dimension arrays of pointers, if we needed to pass it into a function, or declare a pointer to it, we would simply have to add an additional asterisk. For example, the following fragment of code creates a pointer to the Figure 10.3 array.

```
char **Plants[5];
char ***pplant=Plants;
```

There is no mechanical limit to the number of levels of indirection (e.g., pointers to pointers to pointers to pointers, etc.) that can be declared. From a practical standpoint,

FIGURE 10.3 An Array of Arrays of Pointers

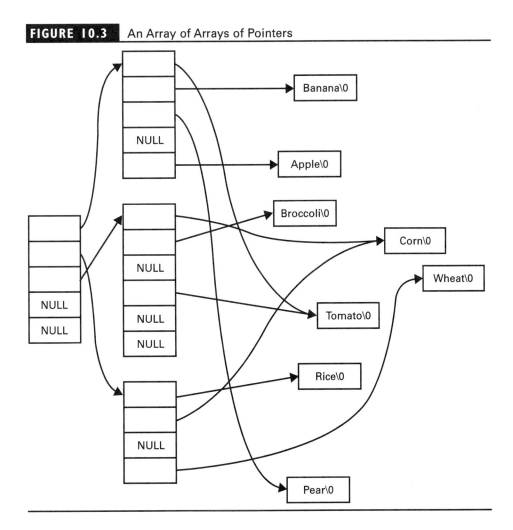

however, more than three asterisks tend to numb the mind of even experienced programmers. When greater depth of indirection is needed, other representational techniques (such as C structures and C++ classes) are usually used. (We see how arrays and other objects can be incorporated into structures in Chapter 11.)

10.3: SECTION QUESTIONS

1. Given your understanding of multidimensional arrays and their initialization, would the following declaration work:

   ```
   char screen[25][80]={"Hello","world","I\'m","back."};
   ```

   If it would work, what would it do?

2. When declaring a multidimensional array, and leaving the compiler to determine the size of the coefficient (e.g., similar to int test[]={1,2,3}; for single dimensional arrays), what coefficient would it make sense to leave empty, the left or the right?

3. Why might arrays of pointers usually be preferable to multidimensional arrays when dealing with "real-world" data?

10.4: IN DEPTH: MEMORY GRID EXERCISES

Becoming comfortable with pointers is not an instantaneous process. Even programmers experienced in other languages normally find that all the brackets, asterisks, ampersands, and parentheses take a bit of getting used to. The exercises that follow are intended to assist the more advanced C/C++ student in attaining a comfort level with pointers and complex arrays.

10.4.1: Introduction to the Memory Grid

A memory grid, as defined in this book, is simply a snapshot of simulated memory with each byte written as a two-digit hexadecimal integer. The easiest way to explain how they work is by using an example.

We begin by supposing there is a hypothetical block of memory with contents specified according to Figure 10.4. In this grid, the left-hand column contains the address in memory of the first byte in the row, with the addresses of subsequent bytes being offset by the column headers.

For example, the address of the first byte in the first row is 0x10002000, and its value is 0x03. The second byte in the first row (0x5B) has the address 0x10002001. The last byte in the first row (0x10) has the address 0x1000200F. And so forth...

We then overlay a set of declarations on the grid. For example:

```
short int arint[6];
char *p1;
char *parr[4];
char c1,c2;
long nv1;
char bytes[10];
```

Finally, we need to assert four things about these declarations:

1. They are located in memory in the order in which they are declared.

FIGURE 10.4   Grid of Hypothetical Memory

	0	1	2	3	4	5	6	7	8	9	A	B	C	D	E	F
0x10002000	03	5B	06	0E	06	00	00	00	E1	00	5C	00	9B	20	00	10
0x10002010	30	20	00	10	70	20	00	10	50	20	00	10	90	20	00	10
0x10002020	00	00	00	00	00	00	00	00	00	00	00	00	00	00	00	00
0x10002030	49	44	00	54	00	00	00	00	00	00	00	4E	05	00	68	69
0x10002040	04	00	00	00	01	00	00	00	00	00	00	00	00	00	00	00
0x10002050	4C	4E	41	4D	45	00	00	00	00	00	00	43	09	00	68	69
0x10002060	14	00	00	00	01	00	00	00	00	00	00	00	00	00	00	00
0x10002070	46	4E	41	4D	45	00	00	00	00	00	00	43	1D	00	68	69
0x10002080	14	00	00	00	01	00	00	00	00	00	00	00	00	00	00	00
0x10002090	41	44	44	52	45	53	53	00	00	00	00	43	31	00	68	69
0x100020A0	28	00	00	00	01	00	00	00	00	00	00	00	00	00	00	00

2.   They are contiguous in memory (i.e., no filler spaces are left between variables—such spaces often being put in by most "real-world" compilers to increase memory access efficiency).

3.   Integers and pointers are organized with low-order bytes in low addresses.

4.   The starting address of the array arint (i.e., &arint[0]) is 0x10002000.

Of these four assertions, only the third needs further clarification before we proceed with the example. Within memory, the bytes that make up a multibyte integer (e.g., short, long, int) or an address could conceivably be organized in two ways. The first, high-order byte in low address, would mean the integer 0x12345678 would appear in memory as:

        0x12 0x34 0x56 0x78

which is the same order in which we wrote it. In this case, the most significant byte in the integer (0x12) is in the lowest memory address. Hence the description: high byte in low memory. Another way to store the integer, however would be to store the least significant byte (i.e., 0x78) in the lowest memory address, which effectively reverses the digits. Using this scheme, the same integer would appear as:

        0x78 0x56 0x34 0x12

This scheme, sensibly, is called low byte in low memory. It also happens to be the way that Intel-based PCs store integers and pointers. Thus, whenever an integer or pointer value is retrieved from our grid, the bytes must be reversed. Such reversal is not necessary for character strings (which are always stored left to right, as they are written). Similarly, we will avoid **double** and **float** variables in these grids, because the many minutes it would take to translate just one IEEE floating point value to its decimal form would seem to offer few benefits.

To ensure that these concepts are clear, let us consider some examples:

Example 1:

Q. What is arint[4]?

A. Because &arint[0] is 0x10002000 (the top of the grid), we would find arint[4] at address 0x10002008 (because short integers are two bytes). Going to that address and taking two bytes (once again, because arint[4] is a short integer), we find the bytes E1 00.

Because integers are stored in reverse order, the final value is 0x00E1. (Conversion to decimal, if desired, is left as an exercise for the reader—finding the right hex byte values usually serves the purposes of the grid exercise.)

Example 2:

Q. What is &c1?

A. The expression &c1 is going to be an address in memory. To find that address, we will need to figure out how much space is taken up by the declarations before it. We can do that as follows:

```
short int arint[6]   → 0x0C bytes (6 * 2)
char *p1             → 0x04 bytes (assuming 4-byte pointers)
char *parr[4];       → 0x10 bytes (again, assuming 4-byte pointers)
```

The declaration of c1 follows parr. Therefore &c1==0x10002000+0x0C+0x04+0x10. The result is 0x10002020.

Example 3:

Q. What is c1?

A. This question is simple, given that we already know where c1 is located. Because c1 is declared as a character, we simply go to that address (0x10002020) and retrieve the character value, which is 0x00.

Example 4:

Q. What is *p1?

A. From Example 2, we can deduce that p1 is located at address 0x1000200C. Taking the 4-byte pointer and reversing the bytes, we find that p1==0x1000209B. Because p1 is a char pointer, the * causes us to go to the address in p1 and return the character, which is 0x43 (or 'C')

Example 5:

Q. What is arint+5?

A. We have asserted that arint begins at 0x10002000. We must, therefore, add 5 to that address. In doing so, however, we must not forget the rules of pointer arithmetic, which state that the integer must be multiplied by the size of the object pointed to. In this case, that size is 2 (short int), so the answer is 0x1000200A.

TEST YOUR UNDERSTANDING 10.20:

What would we need to multiply 3 by to determine the value of the expression parr+3?

10.4.2: Memory Grid Walkthrough

Walkthrough available in grid1.wmv

Assume the memory contents and layout of memory specified in Section 10.4.1.

Expressions: Evaluate the following expressions (integer values can be left in hex):

#	Expression	Value
1	nv1	
2	&nv1+3	
3	parr[2]	
4	*parr[0]	
5	bytes	
6	arint[1]+arint[2]	
7	&c2+3	
8	bytes[arint[4]–241]	
9	*(&nv1+3)	
10	*(parr[3]+arint[2])	

Functions: Assume the behavior of the various library functions discussed in this book. Fill in the following table (*Return* means you should specify the return value, *Action* means you should describe the action). In the event a function call is illegal, specify "illegal" for your answer. *In the event an action would change memory, you may assume memory is restored to its original state by the time the next function is called.*

Function Call	Type of Answer	Answer
strlen(p1)	Return	
strlen(parr[3])	Return	
DisplayFormatted("%s",parr[1])	Action	
strlen(c1)	Return	
strcpy(p1,parr[3])	Action	
strcmp(parr[0]+32,parr[2])	Return	
strlen(parr[2]+2)	Return	
DisplayFormatted("%s",parr[2]+2)	Action	
strcpy(parr,parr+1)	Action	
DisplayFormatted("%s",*parr)	Action	

10.5: IN DEPTH: POINTER ARRAY EXAMPLES

In this section, we present a couple of examples that use pointer arrays. The first, Shuffle, describes an algorithm for randomizing an array of pointers. The second, Tokenize, introduces a versatile function for taking a complex expression, such as a line from a text file, and breaking it into its component pieces, known as tokens.

10.5.1: Shuffle

 Walkthrough available in Shuffle.wmv

Sometimes you need to randomize the order of elements in an array. For example, if you were writing a game program, you might want to sort a deck of cards. This type of task can be accomplished relatively easily, provided you know how to insert an element into an array and you are aware of the C/C++ stdlib function rand(), which generates a random integer.

The two functions used in the Shuffle demonstration are ShuffleArray() and InsertVal(). They are presented in Example 10.9.

The ShuffleArray() function takes two arguments: the array being shuffled (arVals[]) and the number of elements in the array (nCount). It works as follows:

- We have an array, arTemp[], that is available for scratch space. In our demo, it is defined at the file scope.
- We generate a series of nCount random numbers, using the C/C++ stdlib.h function rand(), then set the position of insertion (nPos) as the modulus of the random number divided by the current number of elements in our array. We then take a value from arVals[] and insert it at position (nPos) in arTemp[].
- Once we have added all nCount elements, we copy arTemp[] into arVals[].

The InsertVal() function takes four arguments: the array where the insertion is to take place (arVals[]), the void pointer to be inserted (*pVal), the position of insertion (nPos), and the size of the array (nMax). The function works as follows:

EXAMPLE 10.9

Shuffling an array

```
void *arTemp[MAXSHUFFLE];

void ShuffleArray(void *arVals[],int nCount)
{
    int i,nPos;
    for(i=0;i<nCount;i++) {
        if (i>0) {
            int nRand=rand();
            nPos=nRand%i;
        }
        else nPos=0;
        InsertVal(arTemp,arVals[i],nPos,i);
    }
    for(i=0;i<nCount;i++) arVals[i]=arTemp[i];
}

void InsertVal(void *arVals[],void *pVal,int nPos,int nMax)
{
    if (nPos<nMax) memmove(arVals+nPos+1,arVals+nPos,sizeof(void *)*(nMax-nPos));
    arVals[nPos]=pVal;
}
```

- Unless the insertion is at the end of the array (i.e., nPos==nMax), it makes space for the insertion with a call to memmove(), which works just like memcpy (Example 10.5) except source and destination can overlap. (Also see end of chapter question 8.) The size argument is just the difference between the array size and insertion point (i.e., the number of elements that need to be moved) times the size of each array element, which is just sizeof(void*).
- Having made space, we place the value pointer (pVal) at the insertion position.

Code to test the function is presented in Example 10.10. The function works by initializing an array of fruit names, copying them into a temporary array, shuffling the temporary array, then printing the results. The process is then repeated (to verify randomizing the same array twice leads to a different order). The results of running that code are presented in Figure 10.5.

EXAMPLE 10.10

Calling code for shuffle demonstration

```
void ShuffleDemo()
{
    int i;
    char *arFruit[12] = {"Orange", "Apple", "Pear", "Banana", "Tangerine", "Kumquat",
        "Lemon", "Pineapple", "Grapefruit", "Grape", "Cherry", "mango"};
    char *arShuffled[12];
    memmove(arShuffled,arFruit,12*sizeof(char *));
    ShuffleArray((void **)arShuffled,12);
    DisplayString("Shuffle Demo:");
    NewLine();
    for(i=0;i<12;i++) {
        DisplayString("Original: \"");
        DisplayString(arFruit[i]);
        DisplayString("\"\tSorted: \"");
        DisplayString(arShuffled[i]);
        DisplayString("\"");
        NewLine();
    }
    NewLine();
    memmove(arShuffled,arFruit,12*sizeof(char *));
    ShuffleArray((void **)arShuffled,12);
    DisplayString("Repeating Shuffle Demo:");
    NewLine();
    for(i=0;i<12;i++) {
        DisplayString("Original: \"");
        DisplayString(arFruit[i]);
        DisplayString("\"\tSorted: \"");
        DisplayString(arShuffled[i]);
        DisplayString("\"");
        NewLine();
    }
}
```

FIGURE 10.5 Shuffle Demonstration Output

10.5.2: Tokenize

 Walkthrough available in Tokenize.wmv

One of the great strengths of C/C++ is its ability to work with low-level data, such as raw strings. As a result, we often use the language to process input strings from files or users. One important step that is nearly always required in such applications is tokenizing—the breaking up of strings into component pieces (known as tokens). For example, before we could begin to interpret an expression such as:

    "CAPITAL[T] = (1+INT_RATE)*CAPITAL[T-1] + INCOME[T]"

we would probably want to break it up into its component pieces, for example,

    "CAPITAL","[","T""]","=","(","1","+","INT_RATE",")", etc.

How we decide to break it up is likely to depend on what we plan to use the results for. Anytime we break up a string, however, we will likely need to address certain issues, such as the following:

- Are there special break characters? So we don't have to write spaces between every token, certain characters can be defined to automatically break up tokens (e.g., '+' or ','). Alternatively, we might choose to identify characters that *don't* break up tokens, for example, letters, numbers, and special characters, such as '_'.

- Are there characters that keep tokens together? For example, the " and ' are often used to allow tokens containing white space and break characters to be defined, such as "Hello, World."

- Are there certain break characters that can be combined? For example, in C/C++, the '<' and '=' characters are both break characters. When they appear together, however, it's easier to work with them if they come out as a single token (i.e., as "<=" instead of "<" and "=").

With these points in mind, we will create a fairly powerful tokenizing function that can be customized to break up many different types of expressions. This function will prove useful in many places later in the book.

Operation   The Tokenize() function discussed here operates in the following manner:

- It takes a string in a buffer as one of its arguments.
- It breaks the string up into tokens, using NUL terminators.
- It fills a string array with the start address of each token.

In doing so, it makes a number of assumptions:

- Any nonprinting character (except those within quoting delimiters, such as " or ') is assumed not to be part of a token.

- Any nonwhite character that is not between 'A' and 'Z', 'a' and 'z', or '0' and '9' is assumed to start a new token—unless the character is explicitly defined to be a nonbreaking character (default nonbreaking characters are '.' and '_').

- If a delimiting character is encountered (defaults are " and '), all characters that follow are assumed to be part of the same token until a matching delimiting character is encountered. Because the ending delimiter must match the starting delimiter, it is possible to enclose apostrophes (') within double quotes, or double quotes within apostrophes (see Figure 10.6 for example).

- The leading delimiter in a delimited token (e.g., a token within quotes) is included in the token, while the ending delimiter is NUL'ed out. Thus, the quoted string "Hello" within an expression would come back as the token "Hello (see Figure 10.6). This feature can prove to be a useful device when translating expressions—because it is easy to ignore the leading character of a string if it is not wanted (i.e., just add 1 to the address), but it can be tedious to strip off the trailing delimiter.

The operation of the function is illustrated in Figure 10.6.

Implementation   The Tokenize() demonstration application consists of a number of functions, along with some global variable definitions that serve as default values for the function. The function and global data prototypes are presented in Example 10.11.

The external (global) variables have the following significance:

- *szBreaks:* A string containing all the nonalphanumeric characters (i.e., characters that aren't letters and numbers) that are not break characters. It turns out to be a more economical way to handle breaking characters than specifying them individually.

- *szDelimiters:* A string containing the characters that can be used to delimit a token that contains blanks or break characters. These characters would normally

| **FIGURE 10.6** | Output of Tokenize() Function Test |

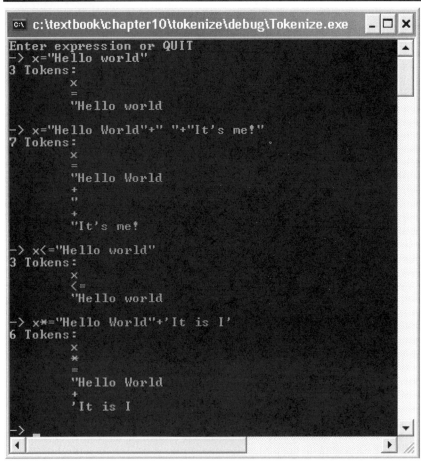

be quotes or apostrophes, but might also include special charters so that one could delimit strings using notation such as %This is a string%. The tokenizer assumes that the same character will start and end each string.

- *arJoins[]:* A lexically (i.e., using ASCII ordering) sorted array containing break strings of break characters that we want to combine, such as "<=" or "&&".
- *nJoinCount:* A constant integer that contains the number of join strings in arJoins.

The values for these global variables are presented in Example 10.12. It is worth noting that nJoinCount is computed by the compiler—using the sizeof operator—so that additional join strings (such as "++" or "+=") could be added without modifying the count. It is critical, however, that any new strings be added in the right order (using ASCII sorting) because binary search is used to find out whether a given operator encountered in the expression being tokenized is present.

Two simple helper functions, JoinLen() and IsBreak(), are defined to make the Tokenize() function itself more compact. JoinLen() incorporates a typical binary search

---

EXAMPLE 10.11

Prototypes and declarations from Tokenize.h

```
extern const char *szNonBreaks;
extern const char *szDelimiters;
extern const char *arJoins[];
extern const int nJoinCount;

int Tokenize(char *src,char *arDest[],
    const char *szNonB,const char *szDel,
    const char **arJn,int nJoinC);

/* in C++, this would be natural place to use default arguments,
such as:

int Tokenize(char *src,char *arDest[],
    const char *szNonB=szNonBreaks,const char *szDel=szDelimiters,
    const char **arJn=arJoins,int nJoinC=nJoinCount);

*/

size_t JoinLen(const char *szTok,const char *arJ[],int nEnd);
bool IsBreak(char cChar,const char *szNonB);
```

EXAMPLE 10.12

Values for Tokenize() default values

```
const char *szNonBreaks="_.";
const char *szDelimiters="\"\'";
// arJoins must be lexically sorted...
const char *arJoins[]= {
    "!=","&&","<=","==",">=","||"
};
const int nJoinCount=sizeof(arJoins)/sizeof(char *);
```

---

function in order to determine the length of a token that starts with a break character. The default length is, naturally, 1. But, as we have already noted, some operators (such as <= and &&) consist of more than one character. JoinLen() takes the following arguments:

- *szTok*: A pointer to the position in the string being tokenized where a break character was encountered
- *arJ[]*: A sorted array of strings containing the combined breaks
- *nEnd*: A count of elements in the combined break array

The function presented in Example 10.13 returns 1 unless the expression contains a sequence of characters that matches one of the strings in the arJ[] array—in which case it returns the length of the matching sequence. The IsBreak() function, also shown in Example 10.13, takes two arguments:

- *cChar:* The current character being examined in the expression

EXAMPLE 10.13

Tokenize helper functions

```
// simple binary search for tokens; naturally, arJ must be sorted
size_t JoinLen(const char *szTok,const char *arJ[],int nEnd)
{
    int nStart=0;
    if (nStart>=nEnd) return 1;
    if (memcmp(szTok,arJ[nStart],strlen(arJ[nStart]))<=0) return 1;
    while(nEnd-nStart>1) {
        int nTest=(nStart+nEnd)/2;
        int nFlag=memcmp(szTok,arJ[nTest],strlen(arJ[nTest]));
        if (nFlag>0) nStart=nTest;
        else if (nFlag<0) nEnd=nTest;
        else nStart=nEnd=nTest;
    }
    if (nStart==nEnd) return strlen(arJ[nEnd]);
    else return 1;
}

bool IsBreak(char cChar,const char *szNonB)
{
    if ((cChar>='A' && cChar<='Z') || (cChar>='a' && cChar<='z') ||
        (cChar>='0' && cChar<='9') || (strchr(szNonB,cChar)!=0))
            return false;
    return true;
}
```

- *szNonB:* A string containing characters specifically defined to be nonbreaking characters

The function returns false if the character is alphanumeric (a letter or a number) or matches one of the specified nonbreaking characters. Otherwise, it returns true.

The Tokenize() function, presented in Example 10.14, illustrates a situation in which the default argument capability that C++ provides (and C doesn't) would be nice to have. The function takes six arguments:

- *src:* The string being tokenized
- *arDest:* An array of string pointers that holds the positions where each token begins in src
- *szNonB:* String containing nonbreaking characters
- *szDel:* String containing delimiting characters
- *arJn[]:* Array containing allowable joined-break strings (e.g., <=, &&)
- *nJoinC:* Count of elements in arJn[] array

The function begins by examining its last four arguments. For any of these arguments where the value is specified to be 0 (or −1, for the last argument, which is an integer), it uses the associated global default value. It means a call to the function:

```
int nCount=Tokenize(buf,arToks,0,0,0,-1);
```

will result in the global defaults being used. Otherwise, the programmer calling the function can customize it to the special needs of the expression being tokenized.

EXAMPLE 10.14

Tokenize() function

```
int Tokenize(char *src,char *arDest[],
            const char *szNonB,const char *szDel,
            const char **arJn,int nJoinC)
{
    size_t nPos=0;
    int nCount=0;
    size_t nLen=strlen(src);
    // setting arguments to global defaults if not specified
    szNonB =((szNonB==0) ? szNonBreaks :   szNonB);
    szDel =((szDel==0) ? szDelimiters : szDel);
    arJn = ((arJn==0) ? arJoins : arJn);
    nJoinC = ((nJoinC==-1) ? nJoinCount : nJoinC);
    while(src[nPos]!=0)
    {
        if (src[nPos]<=' ') {
            src[nPos]=0;
            nPos++;
        }
        else if (strchr(szDel,src[nPos])!=0) {
            // find position of delimiter (e.g., " or ') within szDel string
            char *pDel=strchr(szDel,src[nPos]);
            size_t nOff=pDel-szDel;
            for(nPos++;src[nPos]!=0 && src[nPos]!=szDel[nOff];nPos++){};
            if (src[nPos]==0) return -1; // unbalanced delimiter
            src[nPos]=0; // NUL out matching delimiter
            nPos++;
        }
        else if (IsBreak(src[nPos],szNonB)) {
            size_t nJLen=JoinLen(src+nPos,arJn,nJoinC);
            memmove(src+nPos+nJLen+1,src+nPos+nJLen,nLen-nPos-nJLen+1);
            src[nPos+nJLen]=0;
            nPos=nPos+nJLen+1;
            nLen++;
        }
        else {
            while(src[nPos]>' ' && !IsBreak(src[nPos],szNonB)) nPos++;
            if (src[nPos]>' ') {
                memmove(src+nPos+1,src+nPos,nLen-nPos+1);
                src[nPos]=0;
                nPos=nPos+1;
                nLen++;
            }
        }
    }
    for(nPos=0;nPos<nLen;nPos++) {
        if (src[nPos]!=0) {
            arDest[nCount]=src+nPos;
            nCount++;
            while(src[nPos]!=0 && nPos<nLen) nPos++;
        }
    }
    return nCount;
}
```

Like many C/C++ library functions (e.g., strlen), the function uses size_t whenever a memory range (e.g., a string length) is specified. It also assumes that src and arDest[] are large enough to hold the tokens after the process. A sufficient size can be assured if the size of the src array is at least twice the size of the expression being tokenized, and arDest[] has as many elements as src has characters.

TEST YOUR UNDERSTANDING 10.21:

Explain why the maximum size of the src after a call to Tokenize() can be no more than twice the expression's initial length.

The basic operation of the function is as follows:

- *nPos* is used to keep track of the current position in the expression string, and *nLen* is used to keep track of the length of the expression. This length can change because whenever a break character is encountered, NUL terminators must be inserted into the string to separate the tokens. For example, "X=Y" becomes 'X','0','=','0','Y' (i.e., "X\0=\0Y") to separate the = sign (a break character) from the other tokens.

- We loop until src[nPos]==0, the end of the·string. Within the loop:
  - We first NUL out any white characters we find—conveniently located below the space character in ASCII.
  - We next check for string delimiter characters. If one is found, we increment nPos until we find the matching delimiter (or the end of the string). We then NUL out the matching delimiter and increment nPos. If the end of the string was encountered, we return −1 to signal an invalid expression. We use pointer arithmetic to figure delimiter matches. Because strchr() returns the address in a string where a matching character was found, subtracting the address where we found the match from the start of the string tells us the position (nOff) within the string. For example, if we matched the first delimiter, its address would be the same as the delimiter string, so the offset would be 0.
  - We next check for a break character. If found, we use the JoinLen() function to determine whether it is the beginning of a multicharacter operator (e.g., >=, &&). We then move the remainder of the src string following the break character (or multicharacter string) over one position to the right (using memmove) and insert a NUL terminator, incrementing nLen because we added a character to our src expression.
  - Otherwise, we loop until a white character, break character, or delimiting character is found. If the character that ends the token is not white, we insert a NUL terminator, the way we did after a break character.

- Once our first loop is completed, we enter a second loop that populates the arDest[] array. The loop goes through the expression string looking for non-NUL characters (recall that all white characters were replaced by NUL terminators in the first loop). When it finds it, it:
  - Puts the address at the current position (specified by nCount) in arDest[].

       ▪ Increments nCount to prepare for the next token.

       ▪ Skips over all non-NUL characters, to reach the end of the token.

    ■ Once all token start positions have been placed in arDest[], the function returns nCount.

10.6: IN DEPTH: SWAP SORT PROGRAMMING LAB

As we discovered when studying binary search in Chapter 9, it is much more efficient to search for values in a sorted array than in an unsorted array. Up to this point, however, we have not discussed how the array gets sorted in the first place. In this lab, we introduce the concept of a **swap sort** (aka, exchange sort and bubble sort). Although the swap sort algorithm is notoriously inefficient, it serves our purposes for the time being.

When data are to be sorted, arrays of pointers often turn out to be more useful than arrays of data. For one thing, pointers are all the same size (unlike strings), so swapping them around is easier. For another, structures (introduced in Chapter 11) often take up a lot of memory, and it is a waste of processing time to keep moving them around. Furthermore, in real-world applications, the data being sorted are usually on disk—and it is very inefficient to move such data around. Thus, our swap sort algorithm will focus on the task of sorting an array of pointers to strings.

10.6.1 Swap Sort Overview

Swap sort happens to be one of those simple algorithms that, given enough time, most of us could have come up with on our own. The principle is simple:

1. An unsorted array is passed into the sorting function.

2. The sorting function enters a loop that goes through all the elements of the array, starting at position 1 (we refer to it as the first pass). If the value of any element is less than the one located prior to it in the array, the two elements are swapped.

3. After the pass is complete, the process is completed—the only difference being that on the second pass the algorithm stops at one less than the size of the array. The reason for considering one less element is that the largest element in the area of the array being sorted will always float to the top (like a bubble in water, hence the alternate name "bubble sort")—because it will be continuously be swapped with its neighbor until the end of the pass. Thus, after a pass of N elements, we know that the largest element has bubbled up to element N, so the next pass only needs to go as far as element $N - 1$.

4. The sorting function is complete, and returns, when one of two conditions have been met: (1) a pass occurs without any swaps, or (2) the size of the area being sorted, N, reaches 1.

The swap sort algorithm can be implemented for any type of data, provided a function can be defined that determines whether one data item is greater than another. For the current lab, we will write a swap sort function that sorts an array of pointers to strings. Thus, we can think of the process as looking like Figure 10.7.

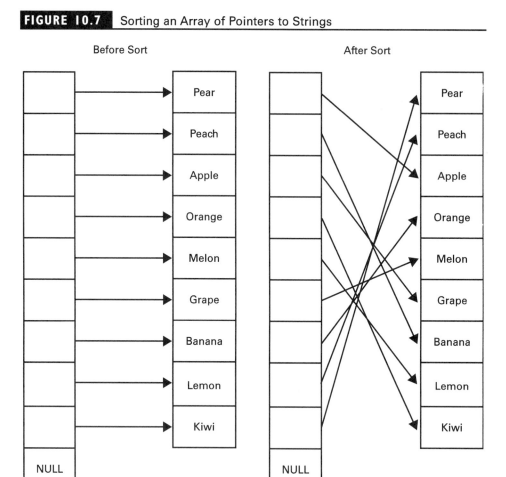

FIGURE 10.7 Sorting an Array of Pointers to Strings

10.6.2: Swap Sort Specifications

The data to be sorted using the swap sort routine will be an array of pointers to string that will have a NULL pointer after the last element. The following can be used as a test data source (corresponding to Figure 10.5):

```
char *fruit[] = {
    "Pear",
    "Peach",
    "Apple",
    "Orange",
    "Melon",
    "Grape",
    "Banana",
    "Lemon",
    "Kiwi",
    NULL
};
```

The functions to be written are as follows:

---

void PrintArray(const char **ar);

Arguments: An array of strings (with a NULL in the final position). The function does not return a value.

Description: Iterates through an array of pointers to strings and prints each string, until a NULL is encountered.

---

void Swap(const char **ar,int i1,int i2);

Arguments: An array of strings (ar), and two positions within that array (i1 and i2) that are to be swapped.

Description: Swaps the contents of two elements in an array of pointers. Only the pointers themselves are swapped, the data pointed to is untouched.

---

void SwapSort(const char **ar);

Arguments: An array of strings (with a NULL in the final position). The function does not return a value.

Description: Performs a *case-insensitive* swap sort on the array that is passed in as an argument.

Highlights:

1. The function should first make a pass through the data to determine how many elements there are (which can be done by looking for the NULL pointer that signifies the end of the data).
2. Within the bubble sort routine, the library function stricmp should be used to determine whether one element is larger than another. The function Swap, defined by the programmer, should be used to swap elements.

The *main()* function should:

1. Have the fruit[] array declared and initialized as a local variable.
2. Call *PrintArray* to demonstrate the initial order.
3. Call *SwapSort* to sort the array.
4. Call *PrintArray* once again, to show the array has been sorted.

10.7: REVIEW AND QUESTIONS

10.7.1: REVIEW

Pointers are variables that hold addresses, instead of values. They are declared just like normal variables, except an * is placed in front of the variable name. For example:

```
int *i1;
```

would declare i1 to be a pointer to an integer—meaning it holds an address that is (presumed to be) the address of an integer. One fact is critical to remember when you declare a pointer:

When you declare a pointer, you are not setting aside any memory for the data it will point to.

This fact is critical to remember, because a common mistake made by programmers is to use a pointer that has not been initialized. Just like a variable, however, a pointer always has a value. In the case of a pointer, however, until it has been initialized you are pointing to a random location in memory. A constant, NULL, is often used to signify that a pointer does not contain an address. In C++, NULL is guaranteed to be 0. In C, it is nearly always so.

Pointers are always initialized according to the type of data they are expected to point to. This consistent usage allows the compiler to check that appropriate pointer types are used (e.g., in function calls) and also permits pointer arithmetic. One type of pointer, **void ***, is permitted to point to anything. This type of pointer is most often used for generic memory functions (e.g., memcpy, memset) and for generic collections.

The four common ways of assigning an address to a pointer are as follows:

1. Applying the & operator to a variable name or array element (or, more generally, any lvalue)

2. Calling a function that returns an address

3. Assigning the value from another pointer or array name

4. Assigning the value from a pointer arithmetic expression

Two common ways can be used to get the value that a pointer refers to, known as *dereferencing*:

1. The * operator, placed in front of the pointer (e.g., *i1 gets the value i1 points to).

2. The [] operator, placed after the pointer (e.g., i1[0] gets the value i1 points to).

These two approaches are completely equivalent. In fact the following relationship is *always* true:

$$*(p1 + i) \equiv p1[i]$$

where p1 is any address (e.g., pointer or array name) and i is any integer. This relationship always holds and is the basis of pointer arithmetic.

Pointer arithmetic is the algebra of adding pointers and integers. Because of the correspondence between [] and * notation, it is constrained to operate as follows:

> Whenever a pointer and an integer are added together, the result is an address that is equal to the original address plus the integer*the size of the object pointed to.

The easiest way to visualize its operation is to think of pointer arithmetic as jumping from element to element in an array. It is also possible to subtract two pointers:

> Whenever two pointers are subtracted, the result is the number of elements (i.e., objects) between the two pointers (equivalent to the difference in addresses divided by the size of the objects pointed to).

Pointer arithmetic only makes sense when applied to objects in the same array.

Another important tool provided by C/C++ is the ability to define complex arrays, which we define as multidimensional arrays or arrays of pointers. Conceptually, a single array can be visualized as a row of values, while a multidimensional array can be visualized as a table, a 3-D

table, or an even more complex table—depending on the number of dimensions.

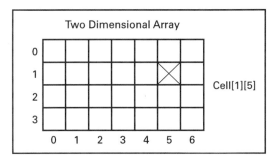

Two Dimensional Array

Cell[1][5]

Each row of a multidimensional array is, itself, treated as an array. For example, in the preceding example, if Cell were a 2-dimensional array of integers:

Cell   Refers to the address of the start of the array (type int **)

Cell[1]   Refers the address of row one, an array of integers (type int*)

Cell[1][5] Refers the value at the cell indicated with an X (type int)

Arrays of pointers tend to be more flexible than multidimensional arrays. Conceptually, they can be visualized as a table of 4-byte address values (under current compilers), which point to data that can be anywhere in memory, as illustrated here:

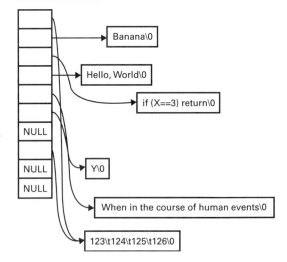

Multidimensional arrays of pointers can also be defined.

A tool that can be helpful in visualizing pointers is the memory grid. You can create a grid by taking a collection of bytes (representing memory), then overlaying a hypothetical set of declarations over the bytes. The tool is particularly useful in becoming practiced in resolving complex memory references.

10.7.2: GLOSSARY

array notation   A method of accessing data associated with a pointer or array name using brackets, equivalent to pointer notation in its effect

const   A declaration modifier that, when used in front of a pointer, prevents that pointer from subsequently being used to change its associated value (i.e., being dereferenced and changed)

dereferencing   Acquiring the value associated with an address

initialize   To set a variable to its initial value, often while the variable is being declared

NULL pointer   A pointer used to signify that it is not pointing anywhere—usually to the 0 position in memory (although this 0 value is guaranteed only for C++)

pointer arithmetic   The rules for applying arithmetic (+ and –) operators on integers and addresses. It is defined in such a way that these arithmetic operations always lead to results consistent with array notation

pointer notation   A method of accessing data or addresses associated with a pointer using the * (dereferencing) operator

sscanf()   A library function that takes a text string and extracts data from it using a formatting string similar to that used by sprintf()

swap sort   A sorting algorithm where one value is sorted for another

void pointer   A pointer (or memory address) not specified to be pointing to any specific type of data

10.7.3: QUESTIONS

1.   *Rewriting common string functions:* In the earlier chapters of this book, we introduced a number of common C library functions that could also be implemented by the user. Rewrite and test the implementations of the following functions using pointer notation, instead of array notation:

- Strlen—Chapter 6, Section 6.5.1
- Strcpy—Chapter 7, Section 7.2.2
- Strcmp—Chapter 7, Section 7.2.3
- Stricmp—Chapter 7, Section 7.2.5

In your implementations, make sure you eliminate all brackets, replacing them with * notation. (*Hint:* In some cases, you may be able to get rid of iterator integers in loops, and just increment the pointers themselves.)

2.   *Memcmp:* The C function memcmp() compares two blocks of memory—using their ASCII codes—and returns a result comparable to strcmp() (see Chapter 7, Section 7.2.3). It is prototyped roughly as follows:

```
int memcmp(const void *addr1,const
    void *addr2,size_t nCount);
```

The arguments addr1, addr2 are the start addresses of the two blocks to be compared, and nCount is the number of bytes to be compared. (The main difference between memcmp and strncmp is that NUL terminators are ignored, and all bytes are always compared.)

Create and test your own version of memcmp(), using the following prototype:

```
int Memcmp(const void *addr1,const
    void *addr2,int nCount);
```

(*Hint:* The technique for handling void pointers in Memset, Example 10.4, and Memcpy, Example 10.5, can be useful in this regard.)

3.   *Strchr:* The C library function strchr works like strstr (see Example 10.1) except that it looks for a character inside a string. It is prototyped as follows:

```
char *strchr(const char *str,char c);
```

For example, a call to the function:

```
strchr("Hello, World",',');
```

would return a pointer to the middle of the first string that would display as ", World". If the character is not present, it returns NULL.

Create and test your own version of the function, Strchr, using the same arguments.

4.   *Strstr:* Implement your own version of strstr (see Example 10.1), prototyped as follows:

```
char *Strstr(const char *s1,const
    char *s2);
```

(*Hint:* If you have not already done so, implement Memcmp() from Question 2 or use the library version. If you use this function effectively, Strstr becomes easy to write.)

5.   *Stristr:* Create and test a case-insensitive version of Strstr() called Stristr(). (*Hint:* Consider implementing a case-insensitive version of Memcmp, called Memicmp, in which case the function becomes a trivial modification of Strstr.)

6.   *Find:* Create and test a function Find() that works like strstr() except that it returns the position within the first string of the second string, or –1 if it is not there. For example:

```
Find("Hello, World","ll");
// returns 2
Find("Hello, World",",");
// returns 5
Find("Hello, World","x");
// returns -1
```

This function is prototyped as follows:

```
int Find(const char *str1,const
char *str2);
```

(*Hint:* Be sure to use strstr within your function and think about how pointer arithmetic could be used to get the integer position within the string from the address.)

7. *CountStrings:* Create and test a function, CountStrings(), that counts the number of independent (i.e., non-overlapping) occurrences of its second argument within its first argument. For example:

```
CountStrings("Yellow is the color"
"of mellow Hello","ll");
// returns 3
CountStrings("xxxxxx","xxx");
// returns 2 (non-overlapping) //
occurrences
CountStrings("Hello World", "x");
// returns 0
```

(*Hint:* Definitely use your own or the library version of strstr() to do this task efficiently.)

8. *Memmove:* Memcpy() as defined in Example 10.5, suffers from the same problem as strcpy when source and destination overlap (see Strmove, in Chapter 7, Section 7.5.1, for details). Create and test your own version of the C library function memmove, called Memmove (modeled after Strmove), which will copy a block of memory properly even when source and destination overlap. The prototype of the function is as follows:

```
void *Memmove(void *pDest,void
*pSrc,int nBytes);
```

where pDest is the address of the destination block, pSrc is the address of the source block, and nBytes is the number of bytes being moved.

9. *Replsub:* Create and test a function Replsub() with the following prototype:

```
char *Replsub(char *buf,const char
*str,const char *sub)
```

The function should find the first occurrence of str in buf and replaces it with sub. For example, if buf contains "Hello World", str contains "o", and sub contains "ooo", then buf will contain "Hellooo World" after the function is called. The function should return the address in buf where the replacement occurred (similar to what strstr returns when looking for a string). (*Hint:* This function can be really nasty to implement unless you use memmove, in which case three or four lines of code is usually enough.)

10. *Replall:* Create and test a function Replall() with the following prototype:

```
void Replall(char *buf,const char
*str,const char *sub)
```

The function should find *every* occurrence of str in buf and replace it with sub. For example, if buf contains "Hello World", str contains "o", and sub contains "ooo", then buf will contain "Hellooo Wooorld" after the function is called. (*Hint:* Implement Replsub first and this function becomes a lot easier.)

11. *Modified Tokenize:* The Tokenize() function in Example 10.14 assumes that every nonletter, nonnumber character is a break character. Create an alternative version of the function where you specify break characters (as the third argument), instead of specifying nonbreak characters. You may continue to assume that white characters are always breaking characters, and that the remaining arguments and return value are the same. (*Hint:* Be sure to modify the right function!)

In-Depth Questions

12. *Date Sort:* Suppose you were given an array of strings containing U.S. format date values, such as "7/4/03" (July 4th, 2003). Modify the SwapSort routine so it would put these values in order. (*Hint:* The trick is going to be revising your comparison function.)

CHAPTER 11

Structures

EXECUTIVE SUMMARY

Chapter 11 examines structures, a construct for organizing related data elements that are similar to the *objects* of OOP. We have already seen how arrays allow us to maintain collections of data elements of the same type. Using structures, we can also maintain collections of data that are of different types.

The chapter begins by presenting the basic concept of a C structure, and briefly explaining its relationship to the more general C++ object. How to declare a structure is then presented, along with the concept of composition. The . and -> operators for accessing individual data elements within a structure are discussed. We then consider how structures can be organized in memory, revisiting the memory grid with structures included in memory along with other data types. Two walkthroughs that use structures are presented. The first, a simple table of employees, demonstrates basic operations, such as getting data into and out of structures. The second example, an in-depth lab that builds on the dBase file lab of Chapter 8, looks at the use of structures in binary files.

LEARNING OBJECTIVES

Upon completing this chapter, you should be able to:

- Explain the nature of a C/C++ structure and its relationship to C++ objects
- Declare a simple structure
- Declare a structure that is composed with other structures
- Access the individual elements within a structure, starting either with a structure object or a structure pointer
- Distinguish between situations requiring the . or -> operator
- Describe the basic manner in which C++ structures are placed in memory
- Implement functions to retrieve and change the data within a structure
- Implement structures to manage collections of other types of data

11.1: WHAT IS A STRUCTURE?

A structure is a construct used for organizing data. Used effectively, structures can help the programmer manage the complexity of applications as they grow ever larger. In this section, we look at the nature of a structure from a conceptual perspective, contrasting it with an object. Subsequent sections detail the declaration and use of structures in C/C++.

11.1.1: Nature of a Structure

Up to this point in the text, we have learned a lot of ways of representing information within our programs. Using the C/C++ fundamental data types, along with arrays and pointers, we can—with a little bit of work and creativity—come up with our own representations for most pieces of data we commonly encounter.

Although we may celebrate how far we have come, we should also feel a certain uneasiness, knowing that something is missing. Consider, for example, the most common method of accessing and storing information on computers: the database table. All of us have worked with tables, such as the example in Table 11.1. But how would we represent such a table in a program?

Given the techniques already covered, our best approach would probably be to create a series of parallel arrays (or arrays of pointers), with one array for each column. For a simple 7-column table, that might be manageable. But what about the 97-column table we use to hold personnel data on an individual employee? Or the 43-column table we use to hold product information? Or the 143-column table that we use to save and categorize sales leads? Quickly, we see the limitations of parallel arrays. In real-world situations they are a pain in the neck to use.

But, you might counter, why not just leave databases to applications such as SQL and Access? After all, why should we bring tables of data into our programs when we have perfectly good tools to manage them? This excellent point does not, however, solve our problem. We need to bring information from our database into our program if we want to use it—even if we limit ourselves to one row at a time. But here's the rub: even bringing the data from one row (record) of our previously mentioned sales lead table would require that we declare and name 143 different data elements. And we can't use an array as a way to avoid assigning names, because the data come in different types (e.g., integers, real numbers, strings, dates, times, Booleans). And think about trying to pass the information about a single sales lead to a function. How would you like to work with a function that had 143 arguments?

Conceptually, then, our problem is clear. Although arrays give us the ability to represent columns of a table nicely, we need some other tool to represent the rows of table. That is the role played by a structure.

> *Definition:* A structure is a construct for representing a collection of data elements all related to a common entity.

The practical effect of this definition is that when we define a structure, we are defining a compound data type. Each of the individual *data elements* (sometimes called *data*

TABLE 11.1		Typical Database Table				
Last Name	**First Name**	**Gross Pay**	**Fica**	**U.S. W/H**	**State W/H**	**Insurance**
Washington	George	3000	180	450	150	175
Adams	Abigail	2500	150	375	125	175
Jefferson	Tom	4000	240	600	200	175
Madison	Dolly	2000	120	200	67	125
Madison	Jimmy	1500	90	150	50	125
etc...						

members or *data fields*) is tied together by a common thread—they are all associated with some common theme—technically referred to as an *entity*. In the case of our database example, the theme or entity is what the row signifies (in the case of Table 11.1, for example, the entity might be the biweekly pay data for a given employee).

Two other terms are useful in referring to structures:

- A **structure definition** is a description of the data and organization used in a particular structure. In our database example, it is the equivalent of a table definition—specifying the name, type, and order of the columns in our table.

- An **object** or **instance** of a given structure is an actual collection of data elements, organized according to our structure definition, that is related to a specific entity. In our database example, our object or instance would be the complete contents of an actual row in the table.

11.1.2: Structures vs. Objects

By using the term *object* to refer to a collection of data organized according to a structure definition, we seem to be implying that structures are somehow related to OOP. In fact, when we use structures within our C/C++ programs, we are engaging in a primitive form of OOP. Indeed, this text intentionally tries to apply structures in its examples in ways that will naturally lead to the development of the OOP philosophy.

So how are structure objects and OOP objects different? We go into this issue in greater detail in Chapter 13, when we introduce C++ objects. The biggest difference is relatively easy to understand, however:

> Structure objects are collections of data; OOP objects are collections of data *and functions*.

What does it mean to have a function associated with an object? To get a basic idea, return to the example in Table 11.1. This table looks like a simplified version of the information used to create a paycheck. A piece of data is missing however: the actual amount of the paycheck. One reason that information might not be stored is simple: It can be calculated with a simple formula:

```
NetPay=GrossPay-FICA-US W/H-StateW/H-Insurance
```

Not only does using the formula save us some storage space, it also eliminates the possibility that someone might get into our data and modify the NetPay amount (i.e., the amount on the paycheck), making it inconsistent with the other values.

Now suppose you are a programmer working on an application that uses a "Pay" structure such as that represented by the columns of Table 11.1.

- If you do not know how to compute net pay, and your Pay object does not have net pay explicitly included as a data element, then you are at an impasse.

- If the Pay structure were a true object, on the other hand, part of the object definition could include a function that would return the value of NetPay. When applied to an object, that function would cause the formula to be computed using the data values contained within that object (e.g., the field values for a specific row). Furthermore, you—as the user of the object—wouldn't need to know the nature of the formula being applied, or even if the result came from a formula or was just the return of existing data.

In other words, when using a true OOP object, the user of that object can often ignore the complexities of what data are being stored within the object and how they are being stored. When we are dealing with structures, however, we do not have that luxury.

11.1: SECTION QUESTIONS

1. Explain how a structure serves a purpose similar to an array.
2. How does a true object (in the sense of OOP) extend the notion of a C structure?
3. Can data be associated with a C/C++ structure definition?

11.2: DECLARING A STRUCTURE

In this section, we learn how to create a structure definition in C/C++. We also learn how one structure definition can include other structure elements, a process called composition. Finally we present a simple structure declaration sample.

11.2.1: The struct Construct: Defining a Structure

Declaring a structure definition involves placing a series of standard data declarations within a struct construct. The basic framework is as follows:

```
struct structure-name {
    standard-data-declarations
};
```

It should be noted that the semicolon at the end of the definition is important—as we find out later.

For example, if we wanted to declare a structure to hold some basic information about individual employees in a firm, it might look like the following:

```
struct employee {
    unsigned int nId;
    char szLastName[30];
    char szFirstName[30];
    unsigned int nYearHired;
    double dSalary;
    bool bActive;
};
```

It is important to note that a construct in this form specifies the *structure definition*—it does not create any actual objects. Such definitions are normally included in header files, and perform the same basic purpose as two other types of constructs we have seen in such files:

- Function prototypes
- **extern** variable declarations

11.2.2: Declaring a Structure Object

Once a structure has been defined, you can use two ways to create actual objects of that structure type. One is associated with the definition itself, the other can be done anywhere.

Combining Definition and Object Creation   One way to declare an object is to place an object name after the right brace, but before the semicolon, in the structure. For example:

```
struct employee {
    unsigned int nId;
    char szLastName[30];
    char szFirstName[30];
    unsigned int nYearHired;
    double dSalary;
    bool bActive;
} empSmith, empJones;
```

This code creates two objects, empSmith and empJones, both organized according to the employee structure. To describe them, we would normally say that empSmith and empJones are both employee objects.

It is fairly unusual to declare objects in conjunction with the structure definition. The problem is that such definitions are normally placed in header files (as already noted) so that different source files in a project can share them. As soon as you share a file that creates an object, however, you get one of those pesky "already defined" linker errors.

In fact, the ability to declare objects before the semicolon in a structure definition mainly turns out to be an annoyance. It is one of the few places in C/C++ where you have to have a semicolon after a closing brace. On those occasions that you forget the semicolon—and it is nearly impossible not to forget it every once in a while—you will be greeted by hundreds of compiler errors. These errors are caused by the fact that until a semicolon is found, the compiler assumes that everything following your structure is an object name—including function prototypes, variable declarations, preprocessor instructions, function definitions, other structure definitions, you name it.

Thus, if you get hundreds of unexpected errors compiling a simple program, always check your structure definitions for ending semicolons before wasting a lot of time on trying to interpret the errors.

Creating Objects After the Declaration   Fortunately, a much more convenient way can be used to create objects. Once the compiler has processed the structure definition (e.g., by loading the .h file), you can define objects at any subsequent time just the way you define other variables, by writing:

struct *structure-name object-name;*

For example, the same two structure objects created earlier could also be created as follows:

```
struct employee empSmith,empJones;
```

In C++, the **struct** keyword can be omitted, although we will continue to use it for consistency.

Once a structure object has been created, you can perform certain operations on it as if it were a normal data type. Specifically:

- You can assign it to another object of the same type (e.g., empSmith=empJones;).
- You can pass it into a function—in this case, a local copy is created just like any other C function argument (unless it is passed by reference in C++).

- You can return it from a function.

On the other hand, certain things can't be done with structure objects that can be done with other primitive data types:

- You can't apply test operators to compare them (e.g., empSmith<empJones is illegal).
- You can't apply arithmetic operators to them—or any other operator except assignment (e.g., empSmith+empJones is illegal).

All of these rules can cease to apply when structure objects are extended to become OOP objects in C++. Indeed, the internal mechanisms for handling structures in C++ can be vastly different from those of C. As long as the programmer sticks with C syntax for structures when defining them in C++, however, these rules remain valid.

Initializing Structure Objects   When a structure object is being created, it can be initialized using a process similar to that already discussed for arrays (Chapter 3, Section 3.1.2). Braces {} are used to surround the list, and the individual items in the list are used to initialize the elements in the order they are declared. Thus:

```
struct employee {
    unsigned int nId;
    char szLastName[30];
    char szFirstName[30];
    unsigned int nYearHired;
    double dSalary;
    bool bActive;
};
struct employee empSmith={101,"Smith","Joan",1999,100000,true};
```

would initialize the nId member to 101, the szLastName member to "Smith", and so on.

In doing initialization, two important rules apply:

- The item on the initialization list must be appropriate for the data type of the member being initialized.
- If not all elements are initialized (e.g., fewer items appear on the list than in the structure), remaining elements of the object are initialized to the zero-equivalent (just as they are for array initializations).

It is important to note that you cannot initialize declarations within the structure definition itself. For example, it is illegal to write:

```
struct bad_struct {
    char szName[80]="Smith"; // illegal
    double dPay=100000; // also illegal
};
```

The reason is that when you are defining a structure, no memory is set aside to initialize. It is only once an object has been created that you have a chunk of memory that you can initialize with values.

11.2.3: Composing Structures

Composition is the ability to embed structures within other structures. To get the basic idea, suppose you were an automobile manufacturer trying to create a data structure to summarize the information about an automobile. You might discover—as you went around to the various departments—that a number of structures were already used in existing programs, such as less simplistic versions of the ones shown in Example 11.1.

Naturally, you would like your "car" structure to contain all the information in these various structures. So how do you set up this master structure?

Composition   C/C++ provides a simple mechanism for embedding one structure within another, called composition. To compose a structure within another structure, you just declare a structure object within your main definition. For example, we could create our car structure as follows:

```
struct car {
    unsigned int nSerialNo;
    struct engine e;
    struct body b;
    struct interior in;
    struct epa_safety safe;
};
```

In defining the car structure in this manner, members for all the data from the other structures are created whenever we create a car object.

EXAMPLE 11.1

Example automobile structures

```
struct engine {
    unsigned int nCylinders;
    double dVolume;
    double dTorque;
    char szManufacturer[40];
};

struct body {
    char szColor[20];
    unsigned int nWheelbase;
    unsigned int nCubicCargo;
};

struct interior {
    bool bLeather;
    bool bDigitalConsole;
    bool bCDPlayer;
    char szColor[20];
};

struct epa_safety {
    double dMPG_city;
    double dMPG_highway;
    bool bSideAirbags;
    unsigned int nSafetyRating;
};
```

In order to compose a structure within another structure, the embedded structure:

- Must have been previously defined.
- Must not be the same as the outer structure, which would be the memory equivalent of standing between two mirrors facing each other.

It is also possible to actually define structures within other structures, both with and without names, to create compositions. Because we will have little need for these capabilities, we will not present them.

Initializing Composed Structures Initializing structures with embedded structures requires us to use initialization lists embedded within our main initialization list. For example:

```
struct car mycar= {10210, //nSerialNo
    {6,4.1},                       // engine initializers
    {"Hunter Green",81,183},       // body initilizers
    {false,false}                  // interior initializers
};          // we stopped before initializing epa_safety
```

As was the case with other initializations, any elements not initialized are set to their zero equivalents.

Alternatives to Composition It is possible to use data from one structure in another without composition. The most obvious way is to declare a pointer with the structure. For example, a revised version of the car structure could be declared as follows:

```
struct car_pointer {
unsigned int nSerialNo;
    struct engine *pe;
    struct body *pb;
    struct interior *pin;
    struct epa_safety *psafe;
};
```

Declared in this way, we could create a car_pointer object as follows:

```
struct engine e1={6,4.1};
struct body b1={"Hunter Green",81,183};
struct interior in1={false,false};
struct epa_safety epa1={0.00};
struct car_pointer mycarptr={10210,&e1,&b1,&in1,&epa1};
```

The main differences between using composition and a pointer to another structure are as follows:

- When structures are composed, the life of the embedded structure is identical to that of the main structure.
- When a pointer to a structure is used, changes made to the referenced structure (e.g., updates to values) are immediately available.

If a particular object cannot exist outside of the main structure—such as a structure specifying something unique to the object being declared, such as a multipart VIN number structure—it makes sense to compose it. If, on the other hand, the object has its own existence, such as a radio that could be replaced with another radio at the customer's request, a pointer to a separate structure may make sense.

11.2: SECTION QUESTIONS

1. Why do we usually declare objects in a different place from where we define structures?

2. Why can't we compose a structure with itself?

3. Why can we assign (i.e., =), but not test (e.g., <, >) or perform arithmetic (e.g., +, –) on structure objects?

4. Should a structure be able to point to another structure of the same type? For example, should the following definition be allowable?

```
struct test {
    int nVal;
    struct test *pTest;
};
```

11.3: ACCESSING DATA IN A STRUCTURE

Now that we have discussed how to create objects and initialize them, we need to consider how to make them useful—and that means being able to get data into them and out of them.

11.3.1: Accessing Data in a Structure Object

Once we have a structure object, it is relatively rare that we would be interested in dealing with the entire object at once. Much more likely, we are going to be interested in accessing or setting individual data elements within our object. For this purpose, the period (.) operator is defined.

Accessing Top-Level Elements   The basic structure for accessing a data element within a scalar object is as follows:

```
object-name . member-name
```

For example, if empSmith is an employee object (as defined in Section 11.2.1), then:

```
empSmith.nId
```

refers to the specific value of the nId member of the empSmith object. Similarly, the expression:

```
empSmith.szLastName
```

refers to the starting address of the szLastName[] array, which is part of the structure. On the other hand:

```
empSmith.szLastName[0]
```

refers to the first character in that array.

The values of object elements that we access are lvalues, just like array elements, which means that they can be used on the right- and left-hand side of assignment statements. For example:

```
int nVal=empSmith.nId;              // places Smith's ID in nVal
empSmith.nId=105;                   // sets Smith's ID to 105
strcpy(empSmith.szLastName,"Smyth."); // sets Smith's last name to
                                    // "Smyth"
```

Accessing Composed Elements   Where structures are composed, we refer to the name of the composed object as a **member,** then use another dot to refer to the element within that embedded object. For example, using the definition of the car structure from Section 11.2.3:

```
struct car mycar= {10210,{6,4.1}, {"Hunter Green",81,183},
  {false,false}};
int nWheel=mycar.b.nWheelbase;
// nWheel is now 81
```

To understand the reasoning behind the expression:

- We first look at the car structure and find that b refers to an embedded body object.
- This object is the third member element in the car structure, so it is initialized by the third element in the initialization list ➜ {"Hunter Green",81,183}.
- Looking up the definition of the body structure (in Example 11.1), we find that the nWheelbase member of that structure is the second element within the body structure, meaning it was initialized by the second element in our initialization list, which is 81.

TEST YOUR UNDERSTANDING 11.1:

Identify the values of the following expressions, given the preceding code fragment:

```
mycar.nSerialNo
strlen(mycar.b.szColor);
strlen(mycar.in.szColor);
mycar.e.dVolume;
```

11.3.2: Accessing Data from a Structure Pointer

The procedure for accessing element data using a structure pointer is similar to that used for accessing data from an object. The only difference is that we use the -> operator, instead of the dot.

Accessing Top-Level Elements   The basic form for accessing elements using a pointer to a structure is as follows:

```
structure-pointer -> member-name
```

For example:

```
struct employee empSmith={101,"Smith","Joan",1999,100000,true};
struct employee *pEmp=&empSmith;
int nYear=pEmp->nYearHired;
// nYear is now 1999
int nLen=strlen(pEmp->szFirstName);
// nLen is now 4
```

Notice, the fact that we use the -> operator with a pointer on the left has no effect on the value we are accessing. In fact, all four of the following expressions are *exactly* equivalent given the preceding code:

```
empSmith.nId ≡ pEmp->nId ≡ (&empSmith)->nId ≡ (*pEmp).nId
```

They all refer to the same precise value in memory. The only thing that determines whether you need a dot or an arrow is whether you have an object (dot) or a pointer (arrow) on the left. Some additional good news is that the compiler message you get when you use the wrong operator is pretty easy to understand.

Accessing Composed Elements   When you have a pointer to a structure, accessing composed elements is exactly the same as when you have an object itself, except your left-hand operator is the arrow (->). If the element you are referencing is a pointer to a structure itself (as it was in our definition of the car_pointer structure in Section 11.2.3) you will need to use the arrow operator to get element values from the object pointed to. These various combinations are presented in Example 11.2.

Although it initially seems complicated, the same rule applies anywhere in an expression:

- If what is to the left of the operator is an actual object—or an expression equivalent to an object, such as (*object-pointer)—the dot operator is used.

- If what is to the left evaluates to the address of an object, the arrow (->) is used.

In both cases, it is the value of the data element that is returned by the expression.

11.3.3: Employee Data Input and Output

Walkthrough available in SimpleEmp.wmv

Our SimpleEmp demonstration uses the same employee structure defined in Section 11.2.2 (see Example 11.3). In addition, it defines three functions:

- *void EmployeeTest()*: Initializes, displays, edits, then redisplays an employee object, to demonstrate the effect of the two functions for displaying and editing.

EXAMPLE 11.2

Accessing elements in embedded objects and pointers

```
struct engine e1={6,4.1};
struct body b1={"Hunter Green",81,183};
struct interior in1={false,false};
struct epa_safety epa1={0.00};
struct car_pointer mycarptr={10210,&e1,&b1,&in1,&epa1};
struct car mycar= {10210,    //nSerialNo
    {6,4.1},                  // engine initializers
    {"Hunter Green",81,183}, // body initilizers
    {false,false},    // interior initializers
};
struct car *pCar=&mycar;
struct car_pointer *pCptr=&mycarptr;
// mycar is object, b is embedded object
int nWheel0=mycar.b.nWheelbase;
// pCar is pointer, b is embedded object
int nWheel1=pCar->b.nWheelbase;
// mycarptr is object, pb is embedded pointer to object
int nWheel2=mycarptr.pb->nWheelbase;
// pCptr is pointer, pb is embedded pointer to object
int nWheel3=pCptr->pb->nWheelbase;
```

EXAMPLE 11.3

Employee structure

```
#define MAXNAME 30

struct employee {
    unsigned int nId;
    char szLastName[MAXNAME];
    char szFirstName[MAXNAME];
    unsigned int nYearHired;
    double dSalary;
    bool bActive;
};
```

- *void DisplayEmp(struct employee emp)*: Displays the values of the employee structure passed as an argument to the console.
- *void InputEmp(struct employee *pEmp)*: Prompts the user to change each element in the employee object pointed to by pEmp. A pointer is passed to allow changes to the actual object.

The three functions used in the application are presented in Example 11.4. The SimpleIO routines are used to provide IO support.

The DisplayEmp() function is a straightforward example of how data values can be extracted from a structure object. Because the emp object is passed by value, the function operates using a temporary copy of the object. Any changes we make to the object inside the function would be lost when the function returns, and the object's memory is reclaimed by the stack.

The InputEmp() is a bit more interesting. Among its key features:

- A pointer is passed to allow us to make changes that impact the empSmith object in the calling function.
- No matter what type of data is required for each element, the user input is taken as a string that goes into a temporary buffer (buf). Two reasons explain this design choice:
  - By checking to find out if the string was empty, we can allow the original (default) value to be retained. This interface is as close to "user-friendly" as we can come in a console application.
  - Our two strings in the employee structure (szLastName and szFirstName) are both a lot shorter than the width of the screen. That causes a potential concern: The user might type in something longer than they could handle. Using a buffer, we can copy the values into szLastName and szFirstName, limiting their size to MAXNAME. This way, no matter how much the user types, we will still be safe.

Figure 11.1 shows the console display of a test session with EmployeeTest().

EXAMPLE 11.4

Functions in the SimpleEmp application

```
void EmployeeTest()
{
    struct employee
    empSmith={101,"Smith","Joan",1999,100000,true};
    DisplayEmp(empSmith);
    NewLine();
    InputEmp(&empSmith);
    NewLine();
    DisplayEmp(empSmith);
}

void DisplayEmp(struct employee emp)
{
    DisplayFormatted("ID: %i\n",emp.nId);
    DisplayFormatted("%s, %s\n",emp.szLastName,emp.szFirstName);
    DisplayFormatted("Salary: $%.2f\n",emp.dSalary);
    DisplayFormatted("Year Hired: %i, Status: %s\n",emp.nYearHired,
        (emp.bActive) ? "Active" : "Former");
}

void InputEmp(struct employee *pEmp)
{
    char buf[MAXLINE];
    DisplayString("\nHit enter to accept existing
    values...\n\n");
    DisplayFormatted("Last Name [%s]: ",pEmp->szLastName);
    InputString(buf);
    if (strlen(buf)>0)strncpy(pEmp->szLastName,buf,MAXNAME);
    DisplayFormatted("First Name [%s]: ",pEmp->szFirstName);
    InputString(buf);
    if (strlen(buf)>0)strncpy(pEmp->szFirstName,buf,MAXNAME);
    DisplayFormatted("Salary [%.2f]: ",pEmp->dSalary);
    InputString(buf);
    if (strlen(buf)>0)pEmp->dSalary=atof(buf);
    DisplayFormatted("Year hired [%i]: ",pEmp->nYearHired);
    InputString(buf);
    if (strlen(buf)>0)pEmp->nYearHired=atoi(buf);
    DisplayFormatted("Still active (Y or N) [%s]: ",
        (pEmp->bActive) ? "Yes" : "No");
    InputString(buf);
    if (strlen(buf)>0)pEmp->bActive=(buf[0]=='y' || buf[0]=='Y');
}
```

FIGURE 11.1 Output of EmployeeTest() function

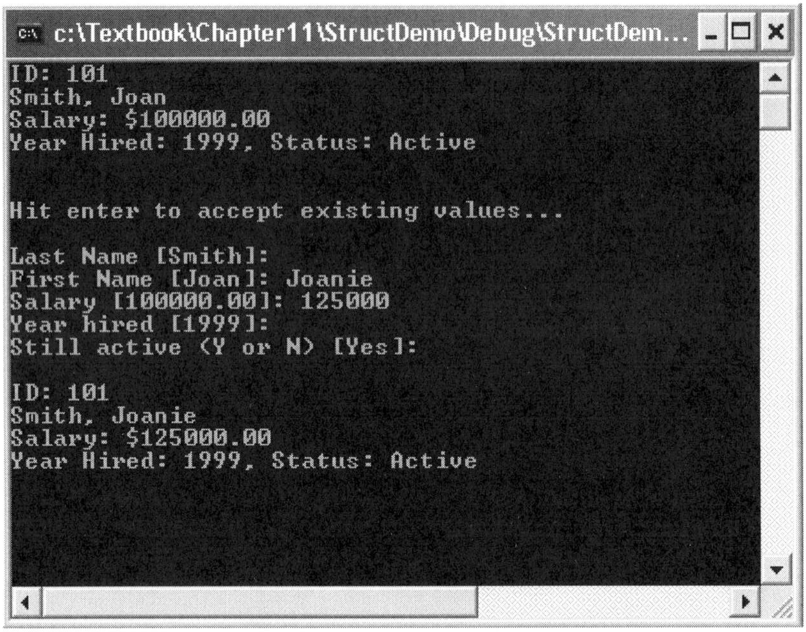

```
c:\Textbook\Chapter11\StructDemo\Debug\StructDem...
ID: 101
Smith, Joan
Salary: $100000.00
Year Hired: 1999, Status: Active


Hit enter to accept existing values...

Last Name [Smith]:
First Name [Joan]: Joanie
Salary [100000.00]: 125000
Year hired [1999]:
Still active (Y or N) [Yes]:

ID: 101
Smith, Joanie
Salary: $125000.00
Year Hired: 1999, Status: Active
```

11.3: SECTION QUESTIONS

1. Why is mixing up the . and -> operators to access data inside a structure usually not too great a problem?

2. If pEmp is a pointer to an employee structure, what are two alternative notations you could use to get the last name string out of it that would use the . (instead of the ->) operator?

3. Why do we pass an object into DisplayEmp() but a pointer into InputEmp() in Example 11.4. If we wanted to pass a pointer into DisplayEmp(), could we do so? If yes, what would be the best way to prototype the function?

4. In Example 11.2, we saw two different ways of accessing wheelbase information:

   ```
   pCar->b.nWheelbase
   mycarptr.pb->nWheebase
   ```

   Explain the difference between the two accesses.

11.4: ARRAYS OF STRUCTURES

Even though an individual structure would allow us to represent a row of a table, such as Table 11.1, we need to represent a collection of structures if we want to manage the whole table. Up to this point, the technique we used for representing such collections is an array.

Fortunately, **arrays of structures** and pointers to structures are treated exactly the same as arrays of fundamental data types. Structures present the additional issue of member access, however, so it is useful to present some examples.

11.4.1: Arrays of Structures

Suppose, instead of a single employee, you wanted to hold the data for 100 employees in your application. This task could be accomplished by declaring an array of employee objects, such as:

```
struct employee arEmp[100];
```

Accessing Array Element Values Once declared in this fashion, individual elements of individual objects can be accessed. For example, the ID of the second element (third employee) would be accessed using:

```
arEmp[2].nId
```

Because element accesses are lvalues, this declaration could appear on either the left- or right-hand side of an assignment operator.

Array names of arrays of structures are also treated the same as any other array name—they refer to the address where the array starts. Therefore, the following two expressions refer to the identical value in memory:

```
arEmp->nId  ≡  arEmp[0].nId
```

Also, like any other array name, you cannot change the address where the array starts.

TEST YOUR UNDERSTANDING 11.2:

Why is the arrow (->) operator used in arEmp->nId while the dot (.) operator is used in arEmp[0].nId?

Initializing Array Element Values All the rules for initializing arrays and structures that we have already applied can be used to initialize arrays of structures. Specifically, the array initialization is accomplished by a list of comma-separated elements within braces {}. Because the **elements** are structures themselves, they are also initialized within nested braces. For example, we could initialize the first four elements of our array of employees as follows:

```
struct employee arEmp[100]={
    {101,"Smith","Joan",1999,100000,true},
    {102,"Brown","Franklin",2001,60000,false},
    {103,"Green","Mary",1988,45000,true},
    {111,"Johnson","Jeremy",2002,75000,true},
};
```

Naturally, if composed objects were present, additional nesting levels would be required within the structure braces.

Structure Array Sample A sample routine, demonstrating a structure array (and the use of the DisplayEmp() function from Example 11.4), is presented in Example 11.5.

The console output produced by running the function is presented in Figure 11.2.

11.4.2: Arrays of Structure Pointers

Our concept of an array of pointers also extends to arrays of structure pointers. For example, we could declare an array of 100 pointers to employee objects as follows:

```
struct employee *arpEmp[100];
```

EXAMPLE 11.5

EmployeeArrayTest()

```
void EmployeeArrayTest()
{
    int i;
    struct employee arEmp[100]={
        {101,"Smith","Joan",1999,100000,true},
        {102,"Brown","Franklin",2001,60000,false},
        {103,"Green","Mary",1988,45000,true},
        {111,"Johnson","Jeremy",2002,75000,true},
    };
    for(i=0;i<4;i++) {
        DisplayEmp(arEmp[i]);
        NewLine();
    }
}
```

FIGURE 11.2   Output from EmployeeArrayTest() function

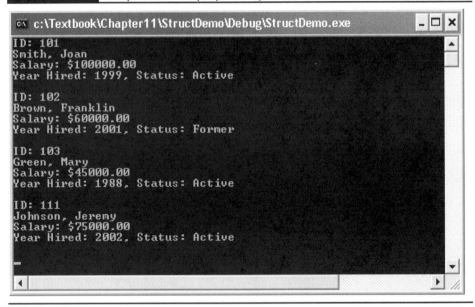

Because the elements of an array declared in this fashion are pointers, not structure objects, to access individual member values, the arrow (->) operator needs to be used. For example, to access the ID for the structures pointed to by the second pointer in the array (array element 1), we would use the following expression:

```
arpEmp[1]->nId
```

Because our array name, already defined, is actually a pointer to a pointer, the following two expressions are equivalent:

```
(*arpEmp)->nId  ≡  arpEmp[0]->nId
```

This equivalence is precisely consistent with the rules we established for dereferencing pointers in Chapter 10.

As we also mentioned in Chapter 10, a big advantage of arrays of pointers over arrays of structures occurs when we want to sort them. Example 11.6 creates a four-element array of pointers and demonstrates how it can be used to order the display of existing structures.

The highlights of how the function works are as follows:

- We declare and initialize an array, arEmp, exactly the same as was done in Example 11.5.
- We create a four-element array of pointers, arPtrEmp. We initialize it using structures in arEmp (pointer arithmetic is used to get their address) in a different order. Specifically, the pointers refer to:
  - arPtrEmp[0] points to arEmp[2]
  - arPtrEmp[1] points to arEmp[3]
  - arPtrEmp[2] points to arEmp[1]
  - arPtrEmp[3] points to arEmp[0]
- We loop through the four elements of the arPtrEmp array and display them. Because these elements are pointers, we need to dereference them (using the * operator) in order to pass them into DisplayEmp(), which expects a value, not a pointer.

The output of the function is presented in Figure 11.3.

TEST YOUR UNDERSTANDING 11.3:

Instead of using pointer arithmetic to initialize the values in the arPtrEmp array, how could we have used the & operator to get the addresses of the elements in arEmp?

EXAMPLE 11.6

EmployeePointerArrayTest() function

```
void EmployeePointerArrayTest()
{
    int i;
    struct employee arEmp[100]={
        {101,"Smith","Joan",1999,100000,true},
        {102,"Brown","Franklin",2001,60000,false},
        {103,"Green","Mary",1988,45000,true},
        {111,"Johnson","Jeremy",2002,75000,true},
    };
    struct employee *arPtrEmp[4]={arEmp+2,arEmp+3,arEmp+1,arEmp};
    DisplayString("Pointer Array Test:\n\n");
    for(i=0;i<4;i++) {
        DisplayEmp(*arPtrEmp[i]);
        NewLine();
    }
}
```

FIGURE 11.3   Output from EmployeePointerArrayTest()

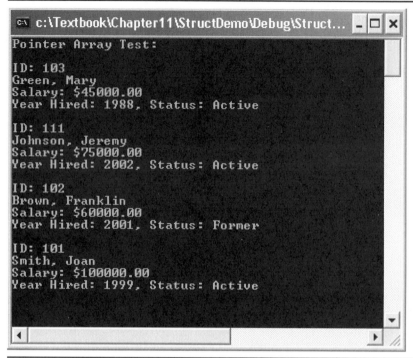

11.4: SECTION QUESTIONS

Suppose we had the following arrays defined:

```
struct employee ar1[10];
struct employee *ar2[10];
// some initialization code…
```

1. Write two different expressions that would take element 2 of ar1 and place its address in element 3 of ar2.

2. Write two different expressions for assigning the object data pointed to by element 1 of ar2 into element 5 of ar1.

3. Write two different expressions that return the second (element 1) character in the last name (szLastName) of element 3 of ar1.

4. Write an expression that could be used to test whether the first name (szFirstName) of the employee of element 8 of ar1 matches the first name of the employee pointed to by element 0 of ar2.

5. Write an expression that tests whether element 7 of ar2 points to ar1 element 6.

6. Write an expression to tell whether the data in element 7 of a2 are the same as that in ar1 element 6.

11.5: IN DEPTH: SERIALIZING STRUCTURES

 Walkthrough available in EmpBinary.wmv

In this section, we introduce techniques for reading and writing structures to a file stream, a process sometimes referred to as serialization. We will continue to use the SimpleIO functions, introduced in Chapter 8, for this purpose.

11.5.1: Approaches to Reading and Writing Structures in C++

The process of writing structure data to files and reading it back is a straightforward extension of the rules for reading and writing primitive data types, such as integers and real numbers. We can take two basic approaches to loading/saving structures:

- *Brute force:* The entire structure is saved and loaded as a single block of data.
- *Element-by-element:* The individual elements of the structure are saved and loaded.

The brute force method, illustrated in Example 11.7, is the simpler of the two methods. It takes advantage of the fact that a structure—like an array—is stored contiguously in memory, and that the sizeof operator can be used to find how many bytes are used to hold the entire structure.

Using the brute force method is generally not recommended for two reasons:

- *Many structures contain pointers.* When these pointers are loaded from disk, they typically contain addresses that are entirely irrelevant to the current state of the program.
- *Disaster can result if brute force is used for true C++ objects.* C++ objects—of which structures will turn out to be the simplest form—frequently contain embedded information (such as virtual function pointers) that will be corrupted if structures are loaded and saved as blocks. Attempting to do so will frequently lead to program crashes.

Having noted that block structure saving and loading is generally not desirable, a programmer should also be aware that it is encountered relatively frequently when simple structures are being used.

The element-by-element approach to saving and loading structure data is generally the best way to deal with serializing structure data. As illustrated in Example 11.8, it involves dealing with each data element individually.

EXAMPLE 11.7

Brute force approach to loading and storing structures

```
void SaveEmployeeBrute(STREAM &out,const struct employee *pEmp)
{
    WriteBlock(out,pEmp,sizeof(struct employee));
}
void LoadEmployeeBrute(STREAM &in,struct employee *pEmp)
{
    ReadBlock(in,pEmp,sizeof(struct employee));
}
```

EXAMPLE 11.8

Element-by-element saving and loading functions

```
void SaveEmployee(STREAM &out,const struct employee *pEmp)
{
    WriteInteger(out,pEmp->nId);
    SaveString(out,pEmp->szLastName);
    SaveString(out,pEmp->szFirstName);
    WriteInteger(out,pEmp->nYearHired);
    WriteReal(out,pEmp->dSalary);
    WriteInteger(out,(int)pEmp->bActive);
}
void LoadEmployee(STREAM &in,struct employee *pEmp)
{
    pEmp->nId=ReadInteger(in);
    LoadString(in,pEmp->szLastName);
    LoadString(in,pEmp->szFirstName);
    pEmp->nYearHired=ReadInteger(in);
    pEmp->dSalary=ReadReal(in);
    pEmp->bActive=(ReadInteger(in)!=0);
}
void SaveString(STREAM &out,const char *sz)
{
    WriteInteger(out,(int)strlen(sz)+1);
    WriteBlock(out,sz,((int)strlen(sz)+1)*sizeof(char));
}
void LoadString(STREAM &in,char *sz)
{
    int nCount;
    nCount=ReadInteger(in);
    ReadBlock(in,sz,nCount*sizeof(char));
}
```

A number of advantages come with the element-by-element approach:

- Elements requiring special care (e.g., pointers) can be skipped, or handled individually, using whatever special logic is required.
- Where data types are embedded (e.g., strings, composed structures), additional functions can be called. In Example 11.8, this feature is illustrated with the calls to the LoadString() and SaveString() functions, used to handle NUL terminated strings, within the LoadEmployee() and SaveEmployee() functions.

11.5.2: Reading and Writing Collections of Structures

The basic procedure for serializing collections of structures is straightforward. Normally, it involves two steps:

- Saving/loading information defining the collection being serialized (most commonly, the number of elements in the collection)
- Serializing the elements themselves

Once again, a programmer can choose between a brute force (Example 11.9) and element-by-element (also called object-by-object) approach (Example 11.10).

EXAMPLE 11.9

Brute force save and load functions for an array of employees

```
bool SaveEmployeesBrute(const char *szName,
  const struct employee *pArr,int nCount)
{
    STREAM out;
    // open for writing, truncate
    if (!Open(out,szName,false,true,true,false)) {
        return false;
    }
    WriteInteger(out,nCount);
    WriteBlock(out,pArr,nCount*sizeof(struct employee));
    Close(out);
    return true;
}

int LoadEmployeesBrute(const char *szName,struct employee *pArr)
{
    STREAM in;
    int nCount;
    // open for reading, don't truncate
    if (!Open(in,szName,true,false,false,false)) {
        return -1;
    }
    nCount=ReadInteger(in);
    ReadBlock(in,pArr,nCount*sizeof(struct employee));
    Close(in);
    return nCount;
}
```

The brute force functions (Example 11.9) may provide some speed advantages, but have little else to recommend them, because the objects themselves are saved as blocks. Moreover, when collections are being saved, the complexity of the brute force and object-by-object functions (Example 11.10) are usually similar (provided a function to save individual objects is available). Thus, the second approach is nearly always preferable.

11.5: SECTION QUESTIONS

1. What is the difference between saving a structure as a block and saving it element-by-element? Under what circumstances might it make sense to save a structure as a block?

2. What is the near-universal approach for saving collections of data (e.g., arrays)?

3. How would you normally go about writing serializing functions for a structure that has another structure composed within it?

4. How would we need to go about changing the functions in this section if we wanted to load and save structures using a text file?

EXAMPLE 11.10

Object-by-object save and load functions for an array of employees

```
bool SaveEmployees(const char *szName,
  const struct employee *pArr,int nCount)
{
    STREAM out;
    int i;
    // open for writing, truncate
    if (!Open(out,szName,false,true,true,false)) {
       return false;
    }
    WriteInteger(out,nCount);
    for(i=0;i<nCount;i++) {
       SaveEmployee(out,pArr+i);
    }
    Close(out);
    return true;
}

int LoadEmployees(const char *szName,struct employee *pArr)
{
    STREAM in;
    int nCount,i;
    // open for reading, don't truncate
    if (!Open(in,szName,true,false,false,false)) {
       return -1;
    }
    nCount=ReadInteger(in);
    for(i=0;i<nCount;i++) {
       LoadEmployee(in,pArr+i);
    }
    Close(in);
    return nCount;
}
```

11.6: IN DEPTH: STRUCTURES IN THE MEMORY GRID

In this section, we extend out memory grid exercises (Chapter 10, Section 10.4) to include structures.

11.6.1: Structures in Memory

What are we doing when we define a structure? Essentially, we are establishing a road map of memory that will be used when we create an actual object. Take, for example, the following structure:

```
struct field {
    char szName[11];
    char cType;
    short nPos;
    short nCode;
    char nLen;
    unsigned char reserved[15];
};
```

How much memory would it take to hold an object of this type? We can determine the minimum amount by adding the size of each element, as shown in Table 11.2.

Let us further assume that the bytes for these different elements happen to be laid out contiguously in memory (which, coincidentally, happens to be true for the field structure, when compiled using Visual Studio .NET). In this case, we could map the various elements to positions in memory grid, if we knew the starting position of the structure, as illustrated in Figure 11.4.

sizeof Operator and Structures As we mentioned in passing, in Chapter 10, Section 10.4, the compiler will often insert spaces when groups of variables are being declared to achieve efficiency. The same is true when it lays out structures. As a result, the minimum size of a structure that we used in Figure 11.4 would not necessarily be the actual size used by the compiler. The compiler might, for example, add an extra byte here or there, to ensure that number members were stored at even addresses, more efficient for access and retrieval purposes. In C++, the situation can become even more complicated, because the information stored in a "true" object (as opposed to a simple structure) may include "invisible" information, such as virtual function pointers. Having made these important qualifications, however, the notion that a structure is just the collection of its individual components, laid out contiguously in memory, is a pretty useful mental model.

Even if our compiler assigned the members in structures to the exact locations we predicted, it would still be pretty cumbersome to add up element sizes to determine the total number of bytes required by a structure. Fortunately, the C/C++ **sizeof operator,** introduced in

TABLE 11.2	Minimum Size of Field Object	
Element	**Size, in Bytes**	**Starting Position**
szName[11]	11	0x00
cType	1	0x0B
nPos	2	0x0C
nCode	2	0x0E
nLen	1	0x10
reserved[15]	15	0x11
Total:	**32**	

FIGURE 11.4 Map of Field Struct in Memory

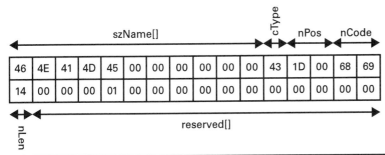

Chapter 8, can be used to determine the exact amount of memory required by structure. Its use for structures and other elements is illustrated in Example 11.11.

11.6.2: Example Memory Grid with Structures

Assume we have the following declarations:

```
short int arint[6];
char *p1;
struct field *parr[4];
struct field fld;
struct field arr[3];
```

EXAMPLE 11.11

Application of the sizeof operator

```
void SizeofDemo()
{
    int n0,n1,n2,n3,n4,n5,n6,n7,n8,n9,n10,n11,n12;
    short i;
    char *pVal="Hello, World";
    char buf[80]="Hello, World";
    struct employee arEmp[100];
    struct employee *arPtrEmp[4];
    n0=sizeof(struct field);
    // n0 is 32
    n1=sizeof(int);
    // n1 is 4
    n2=sizeof i;
    // n2 is 2 (i is a short)
    n3=sizeof(pVal);
    // n3 is 4 (size of a char *)
    n4=sizeof(buf);
    // n4 is 80 (size of the array)
    n5=sizeof(struct employee);
    // n5 is 88, size of a single struct
    n6=sizeof arEmp;
    // n6 is 8800, 100*size of a single struct
    n7=sizeof(arEmp[1]);
    // n7 is 88
    n8=sizeof(arPtrEmp);
    // n8 is 16 (4 elements * 4 byte pointer)
    n9=sizeof(arPtrEmp[0]);
    // n9 is 4 (size of a pointer)
    n10=sizeof(*arPtrEmp[0]);
    // n10 is 88 (structure size)
    n11=sizeof(*pVal);
    // n11 is 1, size of a character
    n12=sizeof strlen(pVal);
    // n12 is 4, size of the size_t return value of strlen
    return;
}
```

Also assume these data elements are contiguous in memory, and arint begins at 0x10002000. Finally, assume the memory grid as shown in Figure 11.5.

Using the same procedures outlined in Chapter 10, Section 10.4, we can then create a table of where our variables begin, presented as Table 11.3:

Examples   Before proceeding to the problems, let us consider some examples (omitting the leading 0x1000 from addresses, for convenience):

Example 1:

Q. What is fld.cType?

A. **4E.** The fld field structure object starts at 2020 (from Table 11.3). cType begins at position 0x0B within the structure (from Table 11.2). Therefore, we want the value of byte 202B, which is 4E ('N').

Example 2:

Q. What is fld.reserved?

A. **0x10002031.** Following the same procedure, we can locate the fld.reserved array as starting at 2031. Because we specified the name of an array, without any coefficients, that starting address is also our answer.

Example 3:

Q. What is strlen(arr[2].szName)?

A. **7.** We know that arr begins at 2040. Because each field structure object is 32 (0x20) bytes, it follows that &arr[1] is 2060, and &arr[2] is 2080. The szName[] array begins at the start of the structure, so we count bytes until we reach the NUL terminator:

```
41 44 44 52 45 53 53 00
```

There are 7 bytes.

Example 4:

Q. What is pArr[2]->nLen?

A. **0x14.** pArr begins at 2010, and is an array of pointers. Therefore, &pArr[1]==2014, &pArr[2] is 2018. The pointer at that location (reversing the bytes) is 0x10002040, or 2040 in our shorthand. So we go to the structure at 2040, then add 0x10 to find nLen. The value at 2050 is 0x14 (20, base 10).

FIGURE 11.5   Grid of Hypothetical Memory

	0	1	2	3	4	5	6	7	8	9	A	B	C	D	E	F
0x10002000	03	5B	06	0E	06	00	00	00	E1	00	5C	00	8B	20	00	10
0x10002010	20	20	00	10	60	20	00	10	40	20	00	10	80	20	00	10
0x10002020	49	44	00	54	00	00	00	00	00	00	00	4E	05	00	68	69
0x10002030	04	00	00	00	01	00	00	00	00	00	00	00	00	00	00	00
0x10002040	4C	4E	41	4D	45	00	00	00	00	00	00	43	09	00	68	69
0x10002050	14	00	00	00	01	00	00	00	00	00	00	00	00	00	00	00
0x10002060	46	4E	41	4D	45	00	00	00	00	00	00	43	1D	00	68	69
0x10002070	14	00	00	00	01	00	00	00	00	00	00	00	00	00	00	00
0x10002080	41	44	44	52	45	53	53	00	00	00	00	43	31	00	68	69
0x10002090	28	00	00	00	01	00	00	00	00	00	00	00	00	00	00	00

TABLE 11.3	Size and Starting Position of Variables

Variable	Size, in Bytes	Starting Position
arint[]	12	0x10002000
p1	4	0x1000200C
pArr[]	16	0x10002010
fld	32	0x10002020
arr	96	0x10002040

Example 5:
Q. What is arr+5?

A. **0x100020E0.** We figured out that arr begins at 2040 (Table 11.3). We need to add 5 to that. In doing, so, however, we must not forget the rules of pointer arithmetic. Specifically, the 5 must be multiplied by the size of the elements in the array (32 bytes each, or 0x20). 5*0x20 is 0xA0, so the result is 20E0. This value is not on our grid, but the question doesn't require us to know what is there—because it evaluates to an address.

11.6.3: Memory Grid Walkthrough

Walkthrough available in grid2.wmv

Assume the memory contents and layout of memory specified in Section 11.5.2. Evaluate the following expressions (integer values can be left in hex):

#	Expression	Value
1	fld.nLen	
2	arr–>cType	
3	&pArr[2]	
4	&(fld–>cType)	
5	arr–1	
6	pArr[0]+2	
7	&(pArr[3]–>szName)	
8	strlen(pArr[1]–>szName)	
9	fld.szName+3	
10	pArr[2]–>reserved[3]	

11.7 IN DEPTH: EMPDATA WALKTHROUGH

Walkthrough available in EmpData.wmv

Using the structures we already defined, we can create a simple employee database with the ability to add, edit, delete, list, load, and save employees.

11.7.1: Overview of EmpData Application

The employee database application manages an array of employee structure objects, allowing you to maintain the list with a collection of routines to add, edit, delete, and list employees. Its interface consists of the same character-driven menu we have already seen, as illustrated in Figure 11.6.

FIGURE 11.6 Interface of EmpData Application

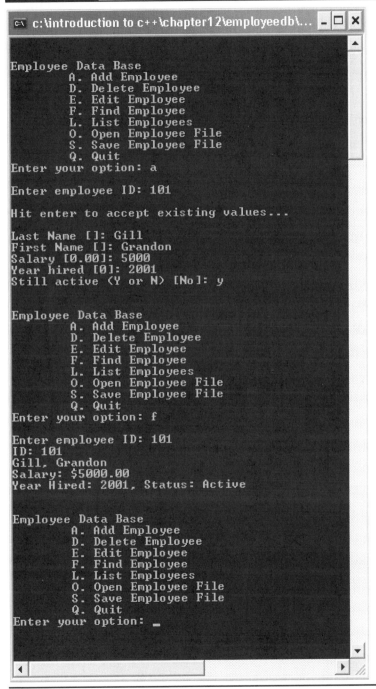

At the heart of the application is an EmpData structure, which holds an array of employee objects, plus a counter that tells us how many elements are in the array. It is shown in Example 11.12.

The application consists of nine functions, described in Table 11.4, as well as other functions previously presented in the chapter.

As noted in the descriptions in Table 11.4, the EmpData application requires that every employee have a unique ID. This requirement forces us to do some checking when data come in and go out. (It also explains why ID was omitted from the InputEmp() function in Example 11.4.)

11.7.2: Walkthrough

We will now examine the main interface, search, display, and editing functions in the EmpData application. We then consider the problem of testing the application.

Main Interface The basic interface for the EmpData application is the same character-driven menu (using a large case construct) that we have seen several times already. It is modeled after the MainMenu function (Chapter 6, Section 6.6.2) and implemented in the function EmpMain(). Because we have seen the same basic implementation many times, the source code is not presented here (but is included in the EmpData.cpp in the Chapter11\EmpData folder on the CD).

Search Most of the functions in the EmpData application need to be able to locate an employee's position in the array of employees using the employee's ID. Locating the position is accomplished by the FindEmployee() function, shown in Example 11.13. The PromptForId() function is also shown (a trivial function requesting an employee ID from the user) because the two routines are generally used in conjunction with each other.

The FindEmployee() function looks for an ID using a linear search of the employee structures. If it cannot find a matching ID, it returns −1, otherwise it returns the position in the array where the match was found. Such linear search is an inefficient approach, especially as the number of employees gets larger.

Display Individual employee object data are displayed using the DisplayEmp() function (already presented in Example 11.4). The ListEmployees() function, presented in

---

EXAMPLE 11.12

EmpData structure

```
#define MAXEMPLOYEES 100

#include "Employee.h"

struct EmpData {
    int nCount;
    struct employee arEmp[MAXEMPLOYEES];
};
```

TABLE 11.4	Function Descriptions for EmpData Application
Name	**Description**
EmpMain	void EmpMain();
	Implements a character-driven menu for selecting the various options and quitting.
PromptForId	unsigned int PromptForId();
	Asks the user for an employee ID and returns the value as an unsigned integer.
FindEmployee	int FindEmployee(const struct EmpData *pData,unsigned int nId);
	Searches for an employee object whose ID matched nId in the pData–>arEmp[] array, returning its position in the array if found, and –1 otherwise.
ListEmployees	void ListEmployees(const struct EmpData *pData);
	Lists all the employees in the pData–>arEmp[] array, using the DisplayEmp function (Example 12.4).
AddEmployee	void AddEmployee(struct EmpData *pData);
	Adds an employee with a unique ID to the pData–>arEmp[] array, incrementing pData–>nCount.
EditEmployee	void EditEmployee(struct EmpData *pData,unsigned int nId);
	Allows the user to edit the employee object with the ID (nID) contained in the pData–>arEmp[] array.
DeleteEmployee	bool DeleteEmployee(struct EmpData *pData,unsigned int nId);
	Allows the user to edit the employee object with the ID (nID) contained in the pData–>arEmp[] array (after asking the user to confirm), decrementing pData–>nCount. It returns **true** if the ID is found, **false** otherwise.
SaveAll	bool SaveAll(const char *szName,const struct EmpData *pData);
	Saves the collection of employees, pointed to by *pData*, to a binary file named *szName*. It returns **true** if successful, **false** otherwise.
LoadAll	bool LoadAll(const char *szName,const struct EmpData *pData);
	Loads a collection of employees from a binary file named *szName*, placing it in the structure pointed to by *pData*. It returns **true** if successful, **false** otherwise.

Example 11.14, simply iterates through the array of employees, calling the DisplayEmp() function on each one.

Editing Data   Our database can be edited in three ways: by adding employees, deleting employees, and by editing the contents of a given employee object. To make the problem a bit more interesting, a constraint was introduced: Each employee must have a unique ID. This requirement complicates the adding and editing routines, in particular:

- *Adding:* Before an employee is added, we must ensure that the employee's ID is not already in place.
- *Editing:* Care must be taken to ensure that the employee's ID is not changed during editing (or, at least, not changed to an ID that is already present).

EXAMPLE 11.13

PromptForId() and FindEmployee() functions

```
/* PromptForID() asks the user for an Employee ID */
unsigned int PromptForId() {
    unsigned int nId;
    DisplayString("Enter employee ID: ");
    nId=(unsigned int)InputInteger();
    return nId;
}


/* FindEmployee() looks for an employee ID (nId). If found, it
  returns the array position in pData->arEmp.
  If not, it returns -1 */
int FindEmployee(const struct EmpData *pData,unsigned int nId)
{
    int i;
    for(i=0;i<pData->nCount && nId!=pData->arEmp[i].nId;i++){}
    if (i==pData->nCount) return -1;
    return i;
}
```

EXAMPLE 11.14

ListEmployees() function

```
/* ListEmployees() displays a list of all employees */
void ListEmployees(const struct EmpData *pData)
{
    int i;
    for(i=0;i<pData->nCount;i++) {
        NewLine();
        DisplayEmp(pData->arEmp[i]);
    }
    if (i==0) DisplayString("No employees entered...\n");
}
```

In the adding routine, AddEmployee(), shown in Example 11.15, prompted for an ID prior to commencing the editing and addition. Once a valid ID is provided, the function:

- Assigns the ID to a temporary employee object, called emp.
- Calls the InputEmp() function to permit the non-ID elements to be edited (explaining why the ability to edit ID was not included in InputEmp() when it was presented in Example 11.4).
- Upon completion of editing, it assigns the temporary object to the next available position in the pData->arEmp array (the pArray->nCount element).
- It then increments pArray->nCount to signify we have a new employee.

The EditEmployee() function, presented in Example 11.16, avoids the problem of changing the ID by a design decision—preventing InputEmp() from having access to the nId member of the structure.

EXAMPLE 11.15

AddEmployee() function

```
/* EditEmployee() allows an employee to be added to
to the table and edited */
void AddEmployee(struct EmpData *pData)
{
    struct employee emp={0};
    bool bvalid=false;
    while(!bvalid) {
        unsigned int nId=PromptForId();
        if (FindEmployee(pData,nId)>=0) {
            char buf[MAXLINE];
            DisplayString("ID that you entered already exists."
                " Try again? (Y or N): ");
            InputString(buf);
            if (toupper(buf[0])=='N') bvalid=true;
        }
        else {
            emp.nId=nId;
            InputEmp(&emp);
            pData->arEmp[pData->nCount]=emp;
            pData->nCount++;
            bvalid=true;
        }
    }
}
```

EXAMPLE 11.16

EditEmployee() function

```
/* EditEmployee() allows the user to edit the data
for the employee whose ID passed (nID) */
void EditEmployee(struct EmpData *pData,unsigned int nId)
{
    int nPos=FindEmployee(pData,nId);
    if (nPos<0) {
        DisplayString("Employee ID does not exist...\n");
    }
    else InputEmp(pData->arEmp+nPos);
}
```

The most interesting aspect of the EditEmployee() function is how access was provided to the specific element in the call:

```
InputEmp(pData->arEmp+nPos)
```

Pointer arithmetic was used here, although it could also have been written:

```
InputEmp(&(pData->arEmp[nPos]))
```

which might be viewed as slightly clearer.

The deletion of employee objects is the most complex of the functions in the application. When a deletion is performed, all the elements above the deleted element in the array need to be moved down. This situation is almost exactly the same as was discussed in the overlapping Strcpy example (Chapter 7, Section 7.2.2), so a nearly identical loop is used in DeleteEmployee (shown in Example 11.17). After the deleted employee is copied over, the pData->nCount variable is decremented.

The DeleteEmployee() function could have been much smaller except that the design decision was made to show the user the contents of the object being deleted (and prompt the user for confirmation), before performing the deletion. This extra query for user confirmation is probably a pretty good idea in routines that perform a permanent deletion using a value that could easily be mistyped, such as ID.

Loading and Saving   The functions for serializing (i.e., loading and saving) the collection of employee objects are presented in Example 11.18.

These functions essentially serve as wrappers around the functions already developed to load and save employee structure objects presented in Examples 11.8 and 11.10. In the case of the LoadAll() function, an effort is made to restore the original count of employees in the event the attempt to load employees fails. You would normally want to design such a feature into an application, because entering incorrect file names is fairly common—particularly in text-based interfaces.

EXAMPLE 11.17

DeleteEmployee() function

```
/* DeleteEmployee() removes an employee from the pData->arEmp
array, prompting the user first to be sure it's okay. It returns
true if the employee's ID (nID) is found, false otherwise */
bool DeleteEmployee(struct EmpData *pData,unsigned int nId)
{
    int nPos=FindEmployee(pData,nId);
    if (nPos<0) {
        DisplayString("Employee ID does not exist...\n");
        return false;
    }
    else {
        char buf[MAXLINE];
        DisplayEmp(pData->arEmp[nPos]);
        NewLine();
        DisplayString("Are you sure? (Y or N): ");
        InputString(buf);
        if (toupper(buf[0])=='Y') {
            int i;
            for(i=nPos;i<pData->nCount-1;i++) {
                pData->arEmp[i]=pData->arEmp[i+1];
            }
            pData->nCount--;
        }
    }
    return true;
}
```

EXAMPLE 11.18

SaveAll() and LoadAll() functions

```
/* SaveAll() saves the collection of employees pointed to by
   pData into a binary file named szName */
bool SaveAll(const char *szName,const struct EmpData *pData)
{
    return SaveEmployees(szName,pData->arEmp,pData->nCount);
}

/* LoadAll() loads a collection of employees, saved in binary format in a file
   named szName, into an EmpData structure pointed to by pData. It returns
   false if the file cannot be open. */
bool LoadAll(const char *szName,struct EmpData *pData)
{
    int nOld=pData->nCount;
    pData->nCount=LoadEmployees(szName,pData->arEmp);
    if (pData->nCount<0) {
        pData->nCount=nOld;
        return false;
    }
    else return true;
}
```

Testing the Application   Using a technique called redirection, we can automate some of our testing. Redirection involves telling the program to take its standard input from a text file or send its standard output to a text file, or both. In .NET, it is accomplished by opening the project properties dialog, choosing "Debugging" properties, and supplying command line arguments. An argument of < file-name causes the text file to be used for input. An argument of > file-name causes output to be sent to a file, instead of the console. To test some sample data, just create a text file such as TestEmp.txt (Example 11.19) and supply:

> < TestEmp.txt

as a command line argument. Instead of prompting you for input, it will use the lines of the file instead. You can then add lines to the file to perform more extensive testing.

TEST YOUR UNDERSTANDING 11.4:

Given the interface of the EmpData application (e.g., Figure 11.6), explain what the TestEmp.txt file accomplishes.

11.8: IN DEPTH: DBF STRUCTURES LAB EXERCISE

 Walkthrough available in DBFStruct.wmv

This exercise involves modifying the .DBF binary file viewer (originally presented in Chapter 8, Section 8.5) so that it uses structures.

11.8.1: Specifications

The specifications for the lab exercise include the data structures, functions, and interface to be implemented to complete the exercise. These specifications assume the reader is already familiar with Chapter 8, Section 8.5. Ideally, the lab described in Chapter 8, Section 8.5.3, will have been implemented.

EXAMPLE 11.19

TestEmp.txt

```
a
101
Gill
Grandon
100000
2001
y
a
102
Gill
Clare
50000
1992
n
a
103
Brown
Jeff
15000
1968
y
1
d
103
y
1
q
```

Data Definitions Two structures will need to be defined as part of the exercise:

- *field*: A structure that holds a single field definition. The field structure presented in Section 11.6.1 can be used for this purpose. The nPos member should be used to hold the starting position of the field within the record buffer.
- *dbf*: A structure to hold the entire database definition, including:
  - Values such as record length, date modified, number of fields, etc.
  - A STREAM object that will be opened to the .DBF file
  - An array of field definitions (*Hint:* Because dBase III files were limited to 128 fields, you can use that as the size of the array.)

Functions The functions to be implemented are listed in Table 11.5.

Interface The interface for the lab exercise is to be identical to that described in Chapter 8, Section 8.5.3.

11.8.2: Procedure

The following procedure is recommended to implement the lab exercise:

| TABLE 11.5 | Functions to Implemented "DBF Structures" Lab Exercise |

void DisplayLoop(const char szFile[])

The driver function for the application, it takes the name of the DBF file (i.e., Films1999.dbf) as its only argument. The function should:

- Declare a local dbf structure object.
- Open the DBF file using the OpenDBF() function.
- Enter a loop that prompts the user for a record number. Within that loop:
  - If the user enters an invalid record number, it should display an error message.
  - If the user enters 0, it should break out of the loop.
  - If the user enters a valid record number, it should:
    1. Move to the appropriate position in the file (computed using the data start position and the record length).
    2. Load the record data into a buffer, which can be done with ReadBlock() and the record length. If you size the buffer at 4001 characters (the maximum dBase record size), you should never have to worry about too many bytes being read.
    3. Call the DisplayRecord() function to cause the actual record data to be displayed.
- Close the database by calling CloseDBF().

void DisplayRecord(const struct dbf &db,const char szRecord[])

Displays all the field data for a given record. Its arguments are the dbf structure (*db*) and character string containing the currently active record (*szRecord*). The function will consist of a single loop, which iterates through the individual field values. Within the loop, the function will:

- Extract the actual data from the szRecord[] array. The GetField() function, presented in Chapter 8, Section 8.4.1, Example 8.8, could be used to extract the data.
- Display the field name, followed by the associated data.

bool OpenDBF(const char szFile[],struct dbf &db)

Opens the file named szFile as a binary read stream using the STREAM object embedded in the db structure. The function should then:

- Load relevant information (e.g., record length, number of records, number of fields, date modified) into the dbf structure.
- Load definitions for all fields into the field object array embedded within the dbf structure.

If successful, the function should return **true,** otherwise it should return **false.**

void CloseDBF(struct dbf &db)

Closes the open file stream embedded in the dbf structure, then sets all data items (e.g., record length, number of records, number of fields) to 0.

■ Create the field and dbf structures, placing their definitions in an include file. The field structure should be defined first in that file, to avoid error messages (because it is to be composed within the dbf structure). You will also need to include SimpleIO.h within the header file, because an embedded STREAM object is present in the dbf structure definition.

- Write the OpenDBF() function. Test it within a simple main() function, using the debugger to make sure the proper information is being loaded.
- Create your DisplayLoop() function, omitting or commenting out the call to DisplayRecord(), using the debugger to make sure that the proper data are loaded when the user specifies a record number.
- Write the DisplayRecord() function, then test the application.

11.9: REVIEW AND QUESTIONS

11.9.1: REVIEW

A structure is a technique for creating a data object that is a collection of different data elements. Conceptually, a structure is like the layout of a database table, with each element being a separate column. A data object, on the other hand, is like a row (record) in that table. The object contains the actual data.

Defining a structure in C/C++, which serves to identify how memory is to be laid out without actually creating any objects, is done using the following syntax:

```
struct structure-name {
    data-declarations...
};
```

where **struct** is a keyword, *structure-name* is the name the programmer chooses to give to the structure (which must be unique within a particular program) and *data-declarations...* are a collection of one or more declarations—identical as to how they would appear within a function, except that they cannot be initialized. The individual declarations that make up a structure are called elements or, sometimes, members.

To create an actual structure object, a syntax just like any other declaration is used (except the struct keyword must be present in C, although not in C++):

```
struct structure-name obj-name ;
```

where *structure-name* is the name given to a previously defined structure, and *obj-name* is the name being given to the object, which can be any legal variable name. It is also possible to declare arrays of objects, pointers to objects, and arrays of pointers to objects, and so forth, just as would be done with any other variable. It is also possible to declare structure objects by listing them after a structure definition, before the final semicolon. This practice is not typical, however, because structure definitions are normally placed in header (.h) files, and actually declaring objects in a header file usually leads to multiple-definition linker errors.

Within a structure definition, it is possible to declare another structure, in which case the process is called composition. The rules for composition are the same as for declaring a structure—the structure being composed within another structure must have been previously defined.

Structures can be initialized using braces, just like arrays. The order and type of the elements in the initializing list must match the order and type of the declarations within the structure. If a composed element of the structure or an array inside the structure is to be initialized, its initialization must be nested in braces.

To access data elements within a structure object, two operators are used, the . (period) and -> (arrow) operators. They are applied as follows:

```
structure-object . element-name OR
structure-object-pointer -> element-name
```

where *structure-object* can be a variable defined as a structure, an array element, or a dereferenced pointer. (It can also refer to composed object members of a structure.) A *structure-object-pointer* refers to the address of a *structure-object*. In both cases, the result is the value of the specific element. Which operator is used (. or ->) is determined entirely by whether the expression to the left of the operator is an object or a pointer (address).

Structure data are usually serialized (i.e., loaded from and saved to a file stream) by creating a function that saves and loads data element-by-element. It is possible to save a structure as a single block of memory, provided:

- No embedded pointers are contained within the structure.
- The structure is not a true C++ object (with member functions).

The best approach to serializing is usually to write separate functions for loading and saving each data element. Objects with composed structures can then call the loading or saving functions that have been written for each embedded element.

Conceptually, a structure definition tells the compiler how to organize bytes in memory, while still being able to treat an entire structure object as a unit for purposes of assignment, passing the structure into functions, and returning a structure. Consider the following definition, for example:

```
struct field {
    char szName[11];
    char cType;
    short nPos;
    short nCode;
    char nLen;
    unsigned char reserved[15];
};
```

This definition would imply memory to be laid out something along the following lines within the object itself:

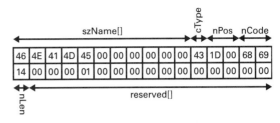

The precise layout will be determined by the compiler—with spaces sometimes being added for efficiency. In C++, the actual object layout can be even more complicated, with room set aside for "invisible" embedded pointers.

11.9.2: GLOSSARY

array of structures   An array of structure objects that is conceptually similar to a table in a database, with each object representing a record

element   A specific item of data in an array (referenced by coefficient) or a specific data item within a structure (referenced by name)

member   An alternative name for an element within a structure, more commonly used in OOP

object   A block of memory, organized according to a particular structure definition, that contains data elements. In C++, objects also normally include a set of functions that can be performed on those data elements

serialization   The process of reading and writing data to a file stream in sequential fashion in order to save or retrieve the complete object

sizeof operator   An operator, evaluated by the compiler, that returns the total memory size required for a particular data type, variable, or object

struct   The keyword used to specify that the {} enclosed block of declarations that follow is to be used to determine how a structure is laid out. If no block follows, the names following the structure name are to be created as objects, object pointers, or arrays

structure (or object) declaration   The process of specifying that an object, based on a particular structure definition, is to be created

structure definition   The process of defining how a structure will be laid out in memory, without creating any actual objects

11.9.3: QUESTIONS

The following questions (1–10) need to be done in sequence and are designed to create an application similar to EmpData (Section 11.6).

1.   *Designing a Structure:* Assume you are down with the flu, and are going to send a friend (or spouse) to the store for you to pick up some things you really need. Naturally, you will need to write up a list. Create an empty project and begin by defining a structure that could be used to hold the information for each item on the list.

This task may be slightly trickier than it looks, because among the types of things that you certainly want to communicate are things such as (a) what type of item is it, (b) where to find the item, (c) does it have to be a specific brand, (d) what is the maximum price you are willing to pay, and so on.

2.   *Creating I/O functions:* Create and test a pair of functions, modeled after DisplayEmployee() and InputEmployee() to allow display and edit of list items.

3.   *Creating a Menu:* Create a function, modeled after EmpMain, that will be the interface of your application.

4.   *Create a Collection Structure:* Create a structure called ShoppingData, modeled after the EmpData structure that will hold a collection of your list items. Create a global object of that type and populate it with some test data by initializing it with 10 or so item elements (using braces, as shown in Section 11.4.1). Create and test a ListItems function that displays all the items on your list.

5.   *Write a FindItem function:* Write and test a function that finds the list item for a particular item type (e.g., "PaperTowel").

6. *Write an AddItem function:* Write and test a function that adds an item to the list. It should not add any item of a type that is already in the list. Note that this task is somewhat different from the employee example, because ItemType will—presumably—be a string, whereas the employee ID was an integer.

7. *Write a RemoveItem function:* Write and test a function that removes an item from the list. You should design your function so it finds the list item based on item type, and has an argument that specifies whether the user should be prompted. For example, it might look like:

```
bool RemoveItem(struct ShoppingData
    *pList,const char *szType,bool nPrompt);
```

where it returns true (1) if successful, false (0) if it is not.

8. *Write an EditItem function:* Write and test a function that edits an item. One thing that you must think about here is to be sure that the item type doesn't change when it is edited or—if it does—that the new item type is not already in the list.

In-Depth Questions

9. *Write SaveItem and LoadItem functions:* Write and test a pair of functions that saves and loads an individual item using a binary file stream.

10. *Write SaveList and LoadList functions:* Write and test a pair of functions that saves and loads the entire list using a binary file stream.

At this point you have a full application comparable to the EmpData application.

The next five questions build on the 1999 film database, introduced in Chapter 8, Sections 8.4 and 8.5. They involve loading data into a structure from different text file formats.

11. Create a structure, Film, that can be used to hold the data for a particular video in the database.

12. Create a function, FilmFixed(), that will load the data for a film from a single line of the fixed text format Film1999.txt file. The function should be prototyped as follows:

```
bool FilmFixed(const char *szLine,
    struct Film *pFilm);
```

It should extract the data from the line of text, and place that data into the structure specified by pFilm.

13. Create a function, FilmTabbed(), that will load the data for a film from a single line of the tab-delimited format Film1999.tab file. (A tab-delimited file uses the tab character to separate data.) The function should be prototyped as follows:

```
bool FilmTabbed(const char *szLine,
    struct Film *pFilm);
```

It should extract the data from the line of text, and place those data into the structure specified by pFilm. You should examine the file in a text editor before you attempt to process it. The Tokenize() function (presented in Chapter 10, Section 10.5.2) should be helpful for implementing your function.

14. Create a function, FilmDelim(), that will load the data for a film from a single line of the comma separated variable file Film1999.csv. (A CSV file uses commas to separate data elements and, typically, uses " " to mark the start and end of fields.) The function should be prototyped as follows:

```
bool FilmDelim(const char *szLine,
    struct Film *pFilm);
```

It should extract the data from the line of text, and place those data into the structure specified by pFilm. You should examine the file in a text editor before you attempt to process it. The Tokenize() function (presented in Chapter 10, Section 10.5.2) should be helpful for implementing your function.

15. Modify the DisplayFilm() function (presented in Chapter 8, Section 8.4.1, Example 8.9) so it takes a Film structure as an argument, instead of a line of text from the file. The new prototype should be:

```
void DisplayFilm(const struct Film
    *pFilm);
```

Modify the ListFilms() function (presented in Chapter 8, Section 8.4.1, Example 8.7) so it looks at the file extension (*Hint:* Look at the last three characters of the file name.) then:

- Calls the appropriate loading function— FilmFixed(), FilmTabbed(), or FilmDelim()—to load the data into a local Film structure object.
- Calls DisplayFilm() to display the data.

CHAPTER 12

Memory Management

EXECUTIVE SUMMARY

Chapter 12 examines how we can acquire additional memory from the operating system, referred to as *dynamic memory,* and how that memory needs to be managed. The use of such memory proves to be critical to effective programming, because relatively few real-world applications can be constructed entirely out of arrays whose size can be determined in advance. Using such dynamic memory, however, also presents certain challenges that need to be understood. A program that leaks memory can, over time, affect every other program running on the same computer.

The chapter begins by reviewing the two forms of memory we have already introduced—local memory and static (or global) memory—then contrasts these with dynamic memory. The functions and operators used to acquire and release such memory are then presented. The design of structures that contain pointers to dynamic memory elements is considered. A dynamically resizing array of pointers is presented as a walkthrough. Finally, a lab exercise that extends the employee application of Chapter 11 is specified.

LEARNING OBJECTIVES

Upon completing this chapter, you should be able to:

- Explain the differences between the three major memory types: static, local, and dynamic
- Identify the strengths and weaknesses of dynamic memory
- Acquire and release memory for various data elements in C++
- Explain the issues associated with structures that incorporate pointers to dynamic memory
- Implement a simple dynamic array of pointers, explaining how it differs from a static or local array of pointers
- Implement a simple database that uses dynamic memory

12.1: DYNAMIC MEMORY

Dynamic memory is memory that we acquire from the operating system while our program is running. The ability to utilize such memory frees us from the limitation of having to predefine the size of all our arrays. Such flexibility proves to be crucial as our programs become more complex.

In this section, we contrast dynamic memory with the other forms of memory we have already seen: local memory and static (global) memory. We then turn to the issues of scope and duration of the different memory types.

REAL-WORLD EXAMPLE

PC programs before dynamic memory

To understand the importance of dynamic memory, it is useful to think about what life was like without it. Not all programming languages provide access to dynamic memory. FOR-TRAN, for example, does not. In the early 1980s, before C and databases were widely supported, FORTRAN was often used to write business applications on PCs. The practical implications of this limitation became obvious to anyone wanting to buy business software, such as an accounting application, off the shelf. The "requirements" section on the box tended to be quite large. Not only would it include normal requirements—such as processor type, operating system, and RAM requirements—it would also include a list of software "limits," such as:

- 50 employees
- 100 G/L account categories
- 10 asset categories
- 100 vendors
- 200 customers
- etc.

The reason for such limits was that the application declared internal arrays to hold the various data elements it used. Each one of these arrays had to be sized in advance. This pre-sizing made program design difficult, because you had to decide on each separate limit while ensuring that total program memory was kept within acceptable limits (e.g., 512K). It also challenged the consumer: finding the right business software could be a frustrating process. A program with the previously mentioned specifications, for example, would not have been suitable for a small five-employee company with ten vendors and *300 customers* because just one of the limits had been exceeded.

12.1.1: Types of Memory

Up to this point in the text, we dealt with two forms of memory:

- **Static memory,** allocated when the program starts running
- **Local memory,** acquired and released as functions are called and returned

To understand the third type of memory, *dynamic memory,* it is useful to develop a mental model of how a simple operating system might organize memory. Such an example is presented in Figure 12.1.

Figure 12.1, which is an extension of the stored program model introduced in Chapter 1, shows memory as being divided into three conceptual areas:

1. *Program Area:* Contains the actual program code (i.e., machine language) for all the programs we have running.
2. **Frame Area:** The second area, the frame area, contains data associated with each process that is running. Within each process block, we have two types of space: the space for the static data that is required by the process *and* the space set aside to hold the stack to be used by each executable program.
3. **The Heap:** The remaining memory that is not being used by the operating system, programs, and running processes.

FIGURE 12.1 Simple Memory Organization Scheme

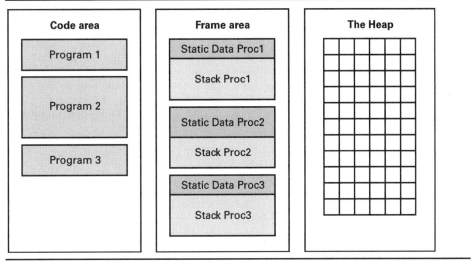

Simple operating systems may use a one-to-one correspondence between processes and programs. In more sophisticated operating systems, however, the correspondence between process data and programs is much more complex. In Windows, for example, multiple processes may access the same program code.

Up to this point, we have only used the first two areas in our programs. The problem with limiting ourselves to code and frame areas is that once a process starts running, the space set aside for these areas does not ordinarily change. Even the stack—which we think of as growing and contracting—is actually static in size. In Visual Studio .NET, for example, a default stack size of 1 meg for each C++ .exe program is used (although there is a build setting that can be used to change the size for a given project). What is changing, as functions are called and as they return, is the percentage of the available stack that our program is using. The practical impact of a fixed stack size is to limit the number of active function calls (and associated local variables) that can be active while our program is running. Occasionally, a program will experience a "stack overflow" purely because it has too many local variables declared. In such a situation, a build setting can be used to adjust the stack size.

If we are going to get more memory while our program is running, its source will have to be "the heap." The heap is managed by the operating system (or by intermediate libraries that interact with the operating system), which means we have to ask the OS to give us the chunk of memory we need. Correspondingly, when we are done with the memory (e.g., the user closes an open document while the program is running), we also need a way to give the memory back.

12.1.2: Scope and Lifetime of Memory

As has already been mentioned in several earlier chapters, the **scope** of a variable name refers to its visibility within a program. C and C++ are perfectly content to allow local variables to "hide" existing variables with the same name—either global variables or other local variables. Hiding variables is demonstrated in Example 12.1.

EXAMPLE 12.1

Demonstration of variable scope

```
// static variable, file scope (i-global)
int i=5;

void ScopeDemo()
{
    DisplayFormatted("Static i == %i\n",i);
    {
        // here's another i—hiding the global i (i-local)
        int i;
        for(i=0;i<5;i++) {
            DisplayFormatted("%i.\t",i);
            {
                // here's another i (i-inner) hiding i-local
                int i;
                for(i=0;i<4;i++)
                {
                    DisplayFormatted("(%i)",i);
                }
                NewLine();
            }
        }
    }
}
```

A Scoping Demonstration   Example 12.1 defines the variable i three times—once as a global variable, once as a variable local to the function ScopeDemo(), and once interior to the outer for loop. The output from the function is shown in Figure 12.2.

The scope and lifetime of each version of i is different:

- *i-global* exists for the duration of the program. Its scope is limited to that portion of the file that comes after its definition, unless *extern int i;* appears in an .h file, in which case the scope is the project (or at least every file including that particular header).
- *i-local* has a lifetime that begins right after the first PrintFormatted statement() and ends right before ScopeDemo() returns. Its scope is the block that defines its duration—excepting the block in which i-inner takes precedence.
- *i-inner* has a lifetime that starts and ends five times within the ScopeDemo() function. With each iteration of the outer loop, it is created anew. Just as the iteration ends, it is destroyed. Its scope is the block in which it is created. During time in which i-inner is in scope, i-local and i-global are both hidden. They continue to exist. You just can't access them by name.

C++ Scope Features   The fact that variables can be hidden by other variables, without warning, is a programming feature that can definitely lead to some unanticipated opportunities to enhance your debugging skills. It can also be inconvenient to discover that you can't get at a variable's value because some local variable happened to use the same

FIGURE 12.2   Output from ScopeDemo

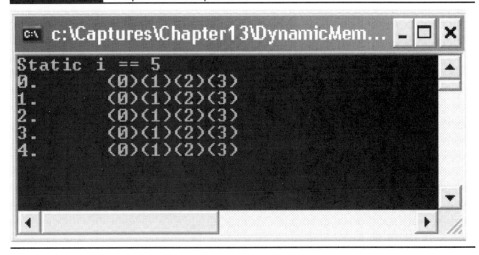

name. C++ adds a couple of capabilities not present in C that makes the situation slightly less cumbersome:

- The scope resolution operator (::) can be used to access static global variables, even when local variables of the same name are in scope. For example, ::i would always refer to the global i, even in our inner loop.

- Namespaces, already mentioned in the context of **cout,** use the scope resolution operator to disambiguate identical names (e.g., std::cout can be used to identify the one globally defined version of cout within the std namespace).

In general, we will avoid the need for these features by avoiding ambiguous names.

Dynamic Memory Scope and Lifetime   Dynamic memory has scope and life-time properties different from local and global variables. In the first place, in C++ we always acquire our dynamic memory in the form of a pointer. As a result, to the extent that scoping issues exist, they apply to the pointer name, not the data themselves. (And because the pointer name is likely to be a local or global variable, the same rules apply.)

The lifetime of dynamic memory is also different. Its lifetime starts when you request it from the operating system. Its lifetime ends when you give it back to the operating system (or, if you forget to do so, when your program ends).

The fact that you have to give back dynamic memory when you are done with it makes C/C++ quite different from many other languages (such as Java and C#). Placing this responsibility on the programmer has two practical consequences:

1. *Efficiency:* It can lead to significant efficiency gains for memory-intensive pro-grams, as compared with other languages that must stop to perform "garbage collection" of unused memory.

2. *Memory Leaks:* A "memory leak" occurs where a program loses track of the memory it allocated, and therefore cannot give it back.

The second of these consequences should be of particular concern to C/C++ program-mers. Even a program with relatively modest memory leaks can degrade the performance of every program running on the same system. If you run a program with memory leaks long enough, even small leaks will eventually add up. The result: the heap gets used up and the OS starts using the hard disk as its emergency source of new RAM (aka virtual memory). Because the hard drive can easily be 10,000 times slower than RAM (on a good day), once virtual memory comes into play, operations that previously took a second can take three hours. And that coffee grinder whine the drive starts to emit when being used as a virtual memory source doesn't do much good for your nerves, either.

12.1: SECTION QUESTIONS

1. What are the biggest advantages of static memory?
2. What are the biggest advantages of local memory?
3. What are the biggest advantages of dynamic memory?

12.2: MANAGING DYNAMIC MEMORY IN C++

The facilities for managing dynamic memory in C++ involve two operators:

- **new**: used to allocate new memory for a data element or array
- **delete**: used to release the memory

12.2.1: Acquiring Memory in C++

The **new operator** provides a powerful, type-safe tool for acquiring memory from the operating system. The three common forms of the operator are as follows:

```
new data-type ;
new data-type [ nCount ] ;
new data-type ( initialization-list ) ;
```

The last of these forms is strictly for OOP usage. As a result, we only consider the first two here. Examples of these two forms are:

```
char *pC,*pArr;
pC=new char;
pArr=new char[80];
```

In functional form, the two versions of the new operator can be prototyped roughly as follows:

```
data-type *operator new(data-type);
data-type *operator new(data-type,unsigned int nCount);
```

The first form is used to acquire a single data element. The second form, using array brackets, is used to allocate an array of nCount elements. Both versions return a pointer to the data type being allocated.

Checking for NULL (or 0, in C++) after **new** is applied is not normally necessary. A failure of **new** generates a memory exception, which has the effect of preventing the code that follows it from being executed.[1] Thus, a test for NULL will have no effect.

---

[1] Unless the programmer explicitly suppresses the behavior, such as through the use of std::nothrow. For example:
```
char *pNew=new (std::nothrow) char[80];
```
In this case, a NULL return would need to be tested.

Although not having to test for NULL may initially sound like good news, it presents a bit of a problem when using C++ purely for the purposes of structured programming. The proper way to handle an exception is inherently object-oriented (because exceptions throw an exception object). Unfortunately, not handling exceptions properly invariably leads to a program crash (often displaying that annoying window asking whether you want to send a message to Microsoft). So, you have to live dangerously when your programs call **new** until you move to the next level, and start using OOP.

12.2.2: Releasing Memory in C++

The **delete operator** returns memory (acquired with **new**) to the operating system. The operator actually comes in two versions:

```
delete object-pointer ;
delete [] array-pointer ;
```

In use, it appears as follows:

```
char *pC,*pArr;
pC=new char;
pArr=new char[80];
delete pC;
delete [] pArr;
```

When you are deleting objects with **delete,** you need to keep track of whether the object was allocated as an array. Using **delete** on an array object, or using **delete** [] on a nonarray object leads to "undefined behavior." And as we know by now, this message is not good.

12.2: SECTION QUESTIONS

1. In what ways does C++ memory allocation seem awkward to use in the context of structured programming?
2. What are the implications of new and delete being operators, instead of functions?
3. How would you allocate an array of 100 char pointers using new?

12.3: MANAGING DYNAMIC MEMORY FOR STRUCTURES

The basic principle of managing dynamic memory for structures is identical to managing any other form of dynamic memory. Many structures incorporate pointers to other dynamic memory objects, however. Some care must be taken in allocating and releasing the memory for such structures, if memory leaks are to be avoided. In this section, we examine both simple structures and structures that manage their own memory.

12.3.1: Acquiring Memory for Structures

Memory for C++ structures is acquired using **new** just as it is for basic data types. For example:

```
struct employee *pEmp=new employee;
struct employee *pArr=new struct employee[10];
```

The first expression allocates and constructs a single employee (pEmp). The second allocates and constructs an array of ten employees (pArr).

Once a structure has been allocated, it should be initialized. When we reach the OOP section of the text, we will see how constructor functions can be defined to perform this type of initialization automatically. For a pure structure, however, we could also define a function—such as that shown in Example 12.2—to perform the initialization.

Structures with Embedded Dynamic Memory   It is quite common to incorporate pointers to other dynamic memory objects within a structure. For example, we might rewrite the previous employee structure as:

```
struct employee_rev {
    unsigned int nId;
    char *pszLastName;
    char *pszFirstName;
    unsigned int nYearHired;
    double dSalary;
    bool bActive;
};
```

We could use the dynamic memory to hold the last and first names. The advantage of this approach is that:

1. We don't waste space for short names.
2. We are not limited to 30 characters for very long names.

Where a structure manages dynamic memory, however, it is critical that the managed memory be released prior to releasing the structure itself. In OOP, this process will

---

EXAMPLE 12.2

Initializing C++ structure element by element

```
#define MAXNAME 30

struct employee {
    unsigned int nId;
    char szLastName[MAXNAME];
    char szFirstName[MAXNAME];
    unsigned int nYearHired;
    double dSalary;
    bool bActive;
};

void DemoEmpInit(struct employee *pEmp)
{
    pEmp->nId=0;
    memset(pEmp->szLastName,0,MAXNAME*sizeof(char));
    memset(pEmp->szFirstName,0,MAXNAME*sizeof(char));
    pEmp->nYearHired=0;
    pEmp->dSalary=0.0;
    pEmp->bActive=false;
}

//   normally, such initialization will be part of an OOP constructor function
```

normally be performed within a destructor function that can be written by the programmer. In structured programming, our best bet would be to write a special function to do the job. Example 12.3 illustrates a C++ function that could be used to release the memory for an employee structure.

Obviously, the problem with just deleting the structure is that doing so would cause us to lose our pointers to the two name strings.

Programming Tip for Working with Dynamic Structures   When working with dynamic structures in C++, you can save yourself a lot of debugging time if you always define two functions for each type of structure you create:

- A function that you always use when you allocate memory for a structure
- A function that you always use when you delete memory for a structure

When working with true objects in C++, the construction and destruction of structure objects will normally be accomplished using OOP constructor and destructor functions.

12.3: SECTION QUESTIONS

1. Why is it a good idea to allocate and free structures in special functions, instead of just calling new and delete when needed?
2. Why will we normally not write independent functions for allocating and freeing structures in C++?
3. What does it mean to say a structure manages dynamic memory? Why is it particularly important to be careful in your memory management if you are using structures that manage dynamic memory?
4. Why is it not a good idea to initialize C++ structures using memset?
5. If you are managing a dynamic array of pointers inside a structure, how is it likely to be declared?

12.4: DYNAMIC ARRAY OF POINTERS WALKTHROUGH

Walkthrough available in DynArray.wmv

In this section, we present a structure that manages a dynamically resizing array of pointers. Understanding the mechanics of such a structure is a good way to start gaining insights into the many collections provided by the C++ STL.

EXAMPLE 12.3

Releasing managed memory in employee_rev structures

```
void DeleteEmpRev(struct employee_rev *pEmp)
{
    delete [] pEmp->pszLastName;
    delete [] pEmp->pszFirstName;
    delete pEmp;
}
```

12.4.1: Dynamically Resizing Array of Pointers

The DynArray project implements a structure that manages a dynamically resizing array of void pointers. Using this structure, we can hold a collection of any type of object, not worrying about the size of the collection.

DynArray Structure   The DynArray structure, presented in Example 12.4, provides the access point to our dynamic array.

The structure is simple, with only three elements:

- *nSize:* Keeps track of the number of elements currently being used in the array
- *nCount:* Keeps track of the number of elements available in the array
- *pData:* pointer to the actual array of pointers we are managing

The conceptual view of the structure is presented in Figure 12.3.

In the example, the dynamic array is currently 16 elements in size (nCount), although only 7 elements are in active use (nSize). These 7 element point to 7 objects (of undetermined type) in memory.

Because nCount is larger that nSize, we can continue to add elements to the array without resizing. When nSize==16, however, our next addition will require us to resize. To avoid endless calls to **new,** we normally do such resizing in blocks. In this example, the block size for resizing is the value of the parameter DYNBLOCKSIZE (see Example 12.4), which was set to 16.

12.4.2: DynArray Function Summary

The nine functions included in the DynArray project are summarized in Table 12.1.

Only the first three of the functions manage dynamic memory.

Example   A demonstration program, illustrating these functions in operation, is presented in Example 12.5.

The console output from running the functions is presented in Figure 12.4.

The DynArray functions that specifically involve memory allocation and deallocation are presented in Example 12.6.

The ReallocArray() function is the only one of the three functions that is not entirely straightforward. C++ does not provide a function for resizing a block of memory directly, so we perform the allocation function manually, as follows:

EXAMPLE 12.4

DynArray structure

```
#define DYNBLOCKSIZE 16

struct DynArray {
    int nSize;
    int nCount;
    void **pData;
};
```

FIGURE 12.3 Conceptual View of Dynamic Array Structure

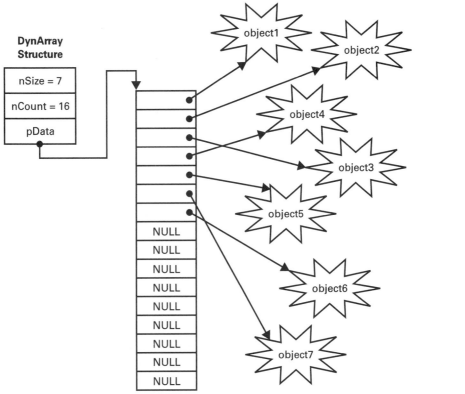

- We compute the target size (taking nNewSize and computing the nearest even multiple of DYNBLOCKSIZE that is greater than or equal to the specified value), assigning the target size value to nRealSize.
- We allocate a new array (pNew), using the **new** operator.
- We determine how many elements we will copy over: the smaller of the new size (nNewSize) and the existing size (pA->nCount).
- We use a loop to copy over the elements from the old pointer array (pA->pData) to the new one (pNew).
- We delete the old pointer array.
- We assign the new pointer array to pA->pData, and update the pA->nCount and pA->nSize values to their new values.

Example 12.7 contains functions that do not directly call memory functions. The GetAt() and SetAt() functions are simple data access functions. Although the programmer could easily use the data arrays in the structure directly, using these functions provides two benefits:

1. Both functions perform bounds checking—eliminating one of the most common problems plaguing C and C++ programmers.

TABLE 12.1	DynArray Functions
Function	**Description**
CreateDynArray()	*struct DynArray *CreateDynArray();* Creates an empty DynArray structure, with nCount and nSize set to 0 and the pData pointer set to NULL.
ReallocArray()	*void ReallocArray(struct DynArray *pA,int nNewSize);* Sets the number of elements in the dynamic array to the specified count, resizing the array if necessary. Actual size is set to an even multiple of DYNBLOCKSIZE.
FreeDynArray()	*void FreeDynArray(struct DynArray *pA);* Frees the DynArray structure, after freeing the dynamic array of pointers.
GetAt()	*void *GetAt(const struct DynArray *pDyn,int i);* Returns the value of the element at position i in the pointer array. An assertion failure is produced if the coefficient is illegal.
SetAt()	*void SetAt(struct DynArray *pDyn,void *pData,int i);* Sets the value of the element at position i in the pointer array to the value pData. An assertion failure is produced if the coefficient is illegal.
Add()	*void Add(struct DynArray *pDyn,void *pData);* Places a new element (pData) at the end of pointer array, resizing if necessary and incrementing nSize.
InsertAt()	*void InsertAt(struct DynArray *pDyn,void *pData,int i);* Places a new element (pData) at position i in the pointer array, moving all elements at position i and above up one position. The array is resized if necessary and nSize is incremented. An assertion failure occurs if the position i is > nCount.
RemoveAt()	*void RemoveAt(struct DynArray *pDyn,int i);* Removes the element at position i in the pointer array, moving all elements at position i and above down one position. nSize is decremented. An assertion failure occurs if the position i is >= nSize.
SetSize()	*void SetSize(struct DynArray *pDyn,int i);* Sets the size of the array by calling ReallocArray().

2. By controlling how the structure is accessed, these functions provide a useful chokepoint for debugging activities. Naturally, this benefit is valid only if the programmer *always* uses the functions to control access.

The Add() and Insert() functions both resize the array (if necessary), before adding/inserting an element in the array. Where they differ is that InsertAt():

- Needs to verify the insertion position is valid.
- Needs to move elements out of the way. (It starts from the highest position in the array and moves down toward the insertion point to avoid corrupting memory, as discussed in Chapter 7, Section 7.2.2.)

Both functions ultimately use SetAt() to place the data in the array.

EXAMPLE 12.5

DynArray function demonstration

```
void DynArrayDemo()
{
    int i;
    struct DynArray *pD=CreateDynArray();
    Add(pD,"Hello");
    Add(pD,"World!");
    Add(pD,"me");
    for(i=0;i<pD->nCount;i++) {
        DisplayFormatted("%s ",(char *)GetAt(pD,i));
    }
    NewLine();
    InsertAt(pD,"It\'s",2);
    for(i=0;i<pD->nSize;i++) {
        DisplayFormatted("%s ",(char *)GetAt(pD,i));
    }
    NewLine();
    RemoveAt(pD,1);
    for(i=0;i<pD->nSize;i++) {
        DisplayFormatted("%s ",(char *)GetAt(pD,i));
    }
    NewLine();
    SetAt(pD,"I",2);
    for(i=0;i<pD->nSize;i++) {
        DisplayFormatted("%s ",(char *)GetAt(pD,i));
    }
    NewLine();
    FreeDynArray(pD);
}
```

FIGURE 12.4   Console Output from Demonstration Program

c:\Captures\Chapter13\DynamicMem...

```
Hello World! me
Hello World! It's me
Hello It's me
Hello It's I
```

EXAMPLE 12.6

Memory-related functions in DynArray

```
struct DynArray *CreateDynArray()
{
    struct DynArray *pAr=new struct DynArray;
    pAr->nSize=0;
    pAr->nCount=0;
    pAr->pData=NULL;
    return pAr;
}

void ReallocArray(struct DynArray *pA,int nNewSize)
{
    int nRealSize=DYNBLOCKSIZE*((nNewSize+DYNBLOCKSIZE-1)/DYNBLOCKSIZE);
    void **pNew=new void *[nRealSize];
    int nCopySize=(nNewSize<pA->nSize) ? nNewSize : pA->nSize;
    if (pA->nCount>0) {
        int i;
        for(i=0;i<nCopySize;i++) pNew[i]=pA->pData[i];
        delete pA->pData;
    }
    pA->pData=pNew;
    pA->nSize=nNewSize;
    pA->nCount=nRealSize;
}

void FreeDynArray(struct DynArray *pA)
{
    delete [] pA->pData;
    delete pA;
}
```

The RemoveAt() function is similar to InsertAt() in that it must:

- Verify its coefficient is legal.
- Move elements as a result of a change in the array.

Because RemoveAt() performs a deletion, however, it iterates from the deletion point to the end of the array.

The SetSize() function simply makes a call to ReallocArray().

12.4.3: DynArray Wrapup

The benefits of using a DynArray object instead of an actual array of pointers are:

- Dynamic resizing
- Bounds checking

Both of these features are extremely helpful in achieving high programming productivity.

EXAMPLE 12.7

DynArray functions not involving memory allocation

```
// returns the pointer value at position i, asserting i is legal
void *GetAt(const struct DynArray *pDyn,int i)
{
    assert(i<pDyn->nSize);
    if (i<0 || i>=pDyn->nSize) return NULL;
    return pDyn->pData[i];
}

// sets the pointer value at position i to pData, asserting i is legal
void SetAt(struct DynArray *pDyn,void *pData,int i)
{
    assert(i>=0 && i<pDyn->nSize);
    if (i<0 || i>=pDyn->nSize) return;
    pDyn->pData[i]=pData;
}

// adds pointer pData to the end of the array
void Add(struct DynArray *pDyn,void *pData)
{
    if (pDyn->nSize==pDyn->nCount) ReallocArray(pDyn,pDyn->nSize+1);
    else pDyn->nSize++;
    if (pDyn->nSize>pDyn->nCount) return; // If reallocation failed...
    SetAt(pDyn,pData,pDyn->nSize-1);
}

// inserts the pointer pData at position i, moving existing element up
// asserts i is legal
void InsertAt(struct DynArray *pDyn,void *pData,int nPos)
{
    int i;
    assert(nPos>=0 && nPos<=pDyn->nSize);
    if (nPos<0 || nPos>pDyn->nSize) return;
    if (pDyn->nSize==pDyn->nCount) ReallocArray(pDyn,pDyn->nSize+1);
    else pDyn->nSize++;
    if (pDyn->nSize>pDyn->nCount) return; // If reallocation failed...
    for(i=pDyn->nSize-1;i>nPos;i--) {
        pDyn->pData[i]=pDyn->pData[i-1];
    }
    SetAt(pDyn,pData,nPos);
}
```

(Continues)

The disadvantages of using a DynArray object over a pure array of pointers are:

- Slightly slower performance
- Inability to use standard array accessors []

In Chapter 14, we will discuss how to overload operators, eliminating the second of these issues. Furthermore, performance is not a major issue for many types of programming. As a consequence, dynamic arrays—based on the principles described in this walkthrough—

EXAMPLE 12.7 (CONTINUED)

```
// Removes the pointer at position i, moving existing element down
// Asserts i is legal
void RemoveAt(struct DynArray *pDyn,int nPos)
{
    int i;
    assert(nPos>=0 && nPos<pDyn->nSize);
    if (nPos<0 || nPos>=pDyn->nSize) return;
    for(i=nPos;i<pDyn->nSize-1;i++) {
        pDyn->pData[i]=pDyn->pData[i+1];
    }
    pDyn->nSize—;
}


// Sets the array to the specified size
void SetSize(struct DynArray *pDyn,int i)
{
    ReallocArray(pDyn,i);
}
```

are commonly provided in C++ class libraries (such as the **vector** template class) and are used by programmers in preference to true arrays for program safety reasons.

12.5: IN DEPTH: DYNAMIC EMPLOYEE DATABASE LAB

The dynamic employee programming lab involves modifying the EmpData application (Chapter 11, Section 11.6) to use a dynamic memory array.

12.5.1: Overview of EmpDyn Application

The dynamic employee database application is based on the EmpData sample (Chapter 11, Section 11.7) that manages an array of employee structure objects, allowing you to maintain the list with a collection of routines to add, edit, delete, list, load, and save employees. In this lab, the objective is to replace the fixed array of employees incorporated into the main structure with a dynamic array.

At the heart of the application is an EmpDyn structure, which holds an array of employee objects, plus a counter that tells us how many elements are in the array. It is shown in Example 12.8.

The structure is similar to the EmpData structure, except:

- arEmp is now a pointer to a dynamic array, instead of a fixed size array
- nCount keeps track of the size of the array (instead of the old fixed constant MAXEMPLOYEES)
- nSize keeps track of the number of employees

The application consists of nine functions, described in Table 12.2. Those that are largely unchanged from the EmpData project (with the exception of changing the structure name from EmpData to EmpDyn) are indicated with an *.

EXAMPLE 12.8

EmpDyn structure

```
#define EMPBLOCK 16

#include "Employee.h"

struct EmpDyn {
    int nCount;
    int nSize;
    struct employee *arEmp;
};
```

12.5.2: Instructions

The lab can be performed using the following procedure:

- Assemble the EmpData files in a new project, and test it to make sure it is working properly.
- Do a "Search and Replace in Files" to replace EmpData with EmpDyn.
- Modify the EmpDyn structure so it reflects the change to a dynamic array (see Example 12.8).
- Write the InitializeEmployees() function (which should be nearly trivial).
- Write the ResizeEmpArray() function.
- Modify the AddEmployee() function to test for available size and incorporate dynamic resizing.
- Modify the LoadAll() function so that it deletes the existing array of employees, then creates a new array based on the number of employees saved in the file.
- Modify the EmpMain() function to initialize and clean up the array.

12.5.3: Import and Export

To create functions that import and export your employee data, you can use three common text formats:

- Fixed width format
- Tab-delimited format
- Comma-separated variable (CSV) format

(Details on these formats can be found in Chapter 11, end-of-chapter questions 11–15.)

Functions   You will be implementing eight functions (as well as making necessary modifications to the EmpMain() function to implement the interface). The basic idea is that two driver functions (ImportEmp and ExportEmp) will use the file extension (.txt, .tab, or .csv) to determine the appropriate format. These driver functions will handle the actual loading

TABLE 12.2	Function Descriptions for EmpDyn Application

Name	Description
EmpMain	*void EmpMain();*
	Implements a character-driven menu for selecting the various options and quitting. Should call InitializeEmp() near the beginning of the routine, and ResizeEmpArray() with a 0 nMax parameter before exiting, to prevent memory leaks.
PromptForId*	*unsigned int PromptForId();*
	Asks the user for an employee ID and returns the value as an unsigned integer.
FindEmployee*	*int FindEmployee(const struct EmpDyn *pData,unsigned int nId);*
	Searches for an employee object whose ID matches nId in the dynamic pData->arEmp array, returning its position in the array if found, and –1 otherwise.
ListEmployees*	*void ListEmployees(const struct EmpDyn *pData);*
	Lists all the employees in the pData->arEmp array, using the DisplayEmp function (Chapter 12, Example 12.4).
AddEmployee	*void AddEmployee(struct EmpDyn *pData);*
	Adds an employee with a unique ID to the pData->arEmp array, incrementing pData->nCount. If the arEmp array is full, calls ResizeEmpArray() with pData->nSize+EMPBLOCK as the new size.
EditEmployee*	*void EditEmployee(struct EmpDyn *pData,unsigned int nId);*
	Allows the user to edit the employee object with the ID (nID) contained in the pData->arEmp[] array.
DeleteEmployee*	*bool DeleteEmployee(struct EmpDyn *pData,unsigned int nId);*
	Allows the user to edit the employee object with the ID (nID) contained in the pData->arEmp[] array (after asking the user to confirm), decrementing pData->nCount. It returns **true** if the ID is found, **false** otherwise.
SaveAll*	*bool SaveAll(const char *szName,const struct EmpData *pData);*
	Saves the collection of employees, pointed to by pData, to a binary file named szName. It returns **true** if successful, **false** otherwise.
LoadAll	*bool LoadAll(const char *szName,const struct EmpData *pData);*
	Loads a collection of employees from a binary file named szName, placing it in the structure pointed to by pData. It returns **true** if successful, **false** otherwise.
InitializeEmployees	*void InitializeEmployees(struct EmpDyn *pData)*
	Initializes the pData->nCount to 0 and the pData->arEmp pointer to NULL.
ResizeEmpArray	*voidResizeEmpArray(struct EmpDyn *pData,int nMax)*
	Resizes the arEmp dynamic array, changing the pData->nSize appropriately. pData->nCount is not affected, unless the new nMax is less than the old count, in which case pData->nCount is reduced to the value of nMax. Calling ResizeEmpArray() with a 0 size should delete the arEmp array, and cause the arEmp pointer to be set to NULL.

or saving of lines from/to the files, while specialized functions ExportXXX and ImportXXX (where XXX refers to the format) will do the actual formatting or extraction.

The functions are specified in Table 12.3.

Instructions   The recommended way to implement these functions is as follows:

- Create a test data set of employees to work with in an application such as MS Access or MS Excel. Both of these packages will allow you to export your data in all three formats (i.e., fixed format text, tab-delimited, and comma-separated variables).

- Write the import functions one at a time. Two functions already written, Get Field() (Chapter 8, Section 8.4.1, Example 8.8, used to extract data from fixed length text format) and Tokenize() (Chapter 10, Section 10.5.2, Examples 10.12. and 10.13, used to extract data from delimited strings) will be especially helpful in this respect.

TABLE 12.3	Import/Export Functions
Name	**Description**
ImportEmp	*bool ImportEmp(const char *szFile,struct EmpDyn *pData);*
	Opens then reads the text file szFile line-by-line, calling one of three extraction functions based upon the file extension. Once each employee is read, it should be added to the *pData* object using the same process used for loading data from a binary file. Returns **false** if the file cannot be opened, **true** otherwise.
ImportTxt	*bool ImportTxt(const char *szLine,struct employee *pEmp);*
	Extracts employee data from the string szLine, which was read from a fixed format text file, and places it in the pEmp structure. Returns **false** if the extraction fails, **true** otherwise.
ImportTab	*bool ImportTab(const char *szLine,struct employee *pEmp);*
	Extracts employee data from the string szLine, which was read from a tab-delimited text file, and places it in the pEmp structure. Returns **false** if the extraction fails, **true** otherwise.
ImportCsv	*bool ImportCsv(const char *szLine,struct employee *pEmp);*
	Extracts employee data from the string szLine, which was read from a comma-separated variable text file, and places it in the pEmp structure. Returns **false** if the extraction fails, **true** otherwise.
ExportEmp	*bool ExportEmp(const char *szFile,const struct EmpDyn *pData);*
	Opens then writes existing employee data to the text file szFile, calling one of three formatting functions based upon the file extension. Returns **false** if the file cannot be opened, **true** otherwise.
ExportTxt	*void ExportTxt(char *szLine,const struct employee *pEmp);*
	Translates employee data from the pEmp object into a fixed field width format and places them in the string szLine (which will then be written to a text file in ExportEmp).
ExportTab	*void ExportTab(char *szLine,const struct employee *pEmp);*
	Translates employee data from the pEmp object into a tab-delimited format and places them in the string szLine (which will then be written to a text file in ExportEmp).
ExportCsv	*void ExportCsv(char *szLine,const struct employee *pEmp);*
	Translates employee data from the pEmp object into a comma-separated variable format and places them in the string szLine (which will then be written to a text file in ExportEmp).

- Write the export functions one at a time. For these functions, use of sprintf() (Chapter 7, Section 7.3.3) can make the process much easier, although the strcat() function can also be used.

- Test your export functions both by reading the files using your import functions and by loading them into Excel/Access.

12.6: REVIEW AND QUESTIONS

12.6.1: REVIEW

Three memory types can be used in a C++ program:

- *Static memory:* Memory set aside when a program begins running and freed when it ends. Examples of this type of allocation include global variables.

- *Local or automatic memory:* Memory allocated on the stack (aka frame) that is available while a function (or block within a function) is being executed, but is removed once the function returns. An example is local variables.

- *Dynamic memory:* Memory provided from "the heap," a memory pool made available to all processes by the operating system, which can be requested by a program and must also be returned.

Dynamic memory is different from the other two forms in several ways. First, it must be explicitly requested when needed, and returned when no longer needed. Failure to return dynamic memory can lead to a memory leak that can slow system performance dramatically. Second, it continues to exist until the program returns it to the O/S—even if the program has lost any way to access it. Third, it is always acquired and returned using a pointer.

In C++, memory is acquired and released using operators. The **new** operator, which acquires memory, can be applied in three ways:

```
new type ;
new type [ count ] ;
new type ( arguments... ) ;
```

The *type* refers to any primitive (e.g., int) or user-defined (e.g., structure) type name. The last version of the new operator is relevant only to OOP, so we consider only the first two, which are distinguished by whether we are allocating memory for an array of data objects or just an individual object.

To return memory in C++, we use the **delete** operator. It comes in two forms:

```
delete pointer ;
delete [] pointer ;
```

The second should always be used for arrays (even arrays of one element), the first for scalars. The version of **new** called to acquire memory determines the appropriate **delete** version. Using the wrong version can lead to an exception.

Dynamic memory is often used within a structure as a substitute for dimensioning an array. When done this way, it is wise to define special functions for creating and deleting the structures, so as to avoid inadvertent memory leaks. (In C++, this task is often done with constructor and destructor functions.)

12.6.2: GLOSSARY

automatic memory   Another name commonly used for local, or frame-based, memory

delete operator   Similar to the free() function in C language, it will return the select object to the operating system, thereby making the memory available for other programs

dynamic memory   Memory acquired from the operating system on demand, and freed when no longer needed

frame area   The area in memory used for local data by each process that is running, organized according to the principles of a stack

heap   The space that the operating system has available for supplying memory to processes

local memory   Memory with a limited scope that is automatically released once execution of the particular function or block is finished

new operator   Used by C++ to acquire space for an object or array of objects

scope   The portion of a program where the variable is available for use, determined by the visibility and the lifetime of the variable

static memory   Memory that exists for the duration of a program, such as globally defined data in C/C++

12.6.3: QUESTIONS

The following ten questions all involve creating dynamic memory strings:

1. *StrRest function.* Create and test a function, prototyped as follows:

```
char *StrRest(const char *src,
    int nPos);
```

that creates a new NUL terminated string, allocated using dynamic memory, from its argument src, that consists of the characters in original string starting at nPos. If nPos is >= to the length of the original string, it should return an empty string (i.e., a 1-byte array containing a NUL terminator).

2. *StrLeft function.* Create and test a function, prototyped as follows:

```
char *StrLeft(const char *src,
    int nCount);
```

that creates a new NUL terminated string, allocated using dynamic memory, from its argument src, that consists of the left nCount characters in original string. If nCount is >= to the length of the original string, it should return a copy of the original string.

3. *StrRight function.* Create and test a function, prototyped as follows:

```
char *StrRight(const char *src,
    int nCount);
```

that creates a new NUL terminated string, allocated using dynamic memory, from its argument src, that consists of the rightmost nCount characters in original string. If nCount is >= to the length of the original string, it should return a copy of the original string.

4. *StrMid function.* Create and test a function, prototyped as follows:

```
char *StrMid(const char *src,
    int nPos,int nCount);
```

that creates a new NUL terminated string, allocated using dynamic memory, from its argument src, that consists of nCount characters from original string starting at position nPos. If nPos >= the length of the original string, it should return an empty string (see StrRest, in Question 1). If nCount + nPos is >= to the length of the original string, it should return a copy of the original string starting at nPos.

5. *StrConcat function.* Create a function, prototyped as follows:

```
char *StrConcat(const char *src1,
    const char *src2);
```

that creates a new NUL terminated string, allocated using dynamic memory, by concatenating its two arguments, src1 and src2.

In this section, we create a structure that manages a dynamically allocated NUL terminated string.

6. *The String struct.* Create a structure that manages a string, defined as follows:

```
struct String {
    char *pStr;
};
```

Create and test three different functions for initializing the structure as follows:

```
struct String *CreateEmpty();
// allocates memory for an empty,
// initialized String
struct String *Create(const char *str);
// creates a String structure with a
// copy of str
struct String *Copy(const struct String *s);
// creates a new String that's a
// copy of s
```

7. *Remove.* Create and test a function that cleans up the memory managed by a String structure, then deletes/frees the structure itself, prototyped as follows:

```
void Remove(struct String *str);
```

8. *Assign.* Create and test a function that assigns one String object to another, prototyped as follows:

```
const String *Assign(struct String
    *dest,const struct String *src);
```

Consistent with similar functions (e.g., strcpy), the function should assign its second argument to its first argument, then return a pointer to its second argument. One thing you should be sure to check for: Make sure it doesn't crash in the event the programmer attempts to assign a String object to itself.

9. *String manipulators:* Implement and test the following functions, based on the definitions provided in Questions 1–4:

```
struct String *Rest(const struct
    String *src,int nPos);
struct String *Left(const struct
    String *src,int nCount);
struct String *Right(const struct
    String *src,int nCount);
struct String *Mid(const struct
    String *src,int nPos,int nCount);
```

In each case, the function should use the src argument for the string to be manipulated, but should create a new String object, initialized with a NUL terminated string created consistent with the operation. (Hint: The functions you developed in Questions 1–4 can be used for this purpose.)

10. *String concatenation.* Implement and test a function Concat that adds its second argument to the end of its first argument (similar to what was done in Question 5). The function should be prototyped as follows:

```
void Concat(struct String *dest,
    const struct String *added);
```

Note that unlike the previous functions, this function changes its dest argument by adding the NUL terminated string from *added* to whatever was initially in *dest*. It does not return a new String object. Feel free to use the StrConcat function developed in Question 5 within your solution.

PART 3

OBJECT-ORIENTED PROGRAMMING

Encapsulation

EXECUTIVE SUMMARY

Chapter 13 examines how we can extend the concept of a structure to create encapsulated objects, also called abstract data types (ADTs). Organizing programs around encapsulated objects, rather than functions, is the primary difference between object-oriented programming and structured programming (which was the focus of Chapters 1 through 12). The ability to define these objects also represents the most significant extension made to C in the design of C++.

The chapter begins with an overview of object-oriented programming, defining three characteristics of OOP design: encapsulation, inheritance, and polymorphism. We then present the mechanisms for creating member functions and data, explaining member visibility (public, protected, and private). Object construction and destruction are then discussed. Two commonly used member qualifiers, static and const, are then examined. The unified modeling language (UML) representation of a class, generated using FlowC, is then presented, and some principles of encapsulated design are introduced. Finally, a series of examples and lab exercises using an encapsulated version of the employee structure introduced in Chapter 11 is presented.

LEARNING OBJECTIVES

Upon completing this chapter, you should be able to:

- Explain the basic concepts of encapsulation, inheritance, and polymorphism
- Apply simple member functions
- Define inline and regular member functions
- Explain public, protected, and private visibility
- Write constructor and destructor functions for C++ classes
- Understand what is meant by a const member, and explain appropriate uses
- Understand what is meant by a static member, and explain appropriate uses
- Draw a UML class diagram for a basic C++ class
- List some elementary principles of object-oriented design
- Create simple applications using encapsulated objects

13.1: INTRODUCTION TO OBJECTS AND OBJECT-ORIENTED PROGRAMMING

In this section, we introduce the basic OOP concepts of encapsulation, inheritance, and polymorphism—focusing on how to apply existing objects, rather than on how to define new ones. This presentation will be organized into three topics:

- Encapsulation
- Inheritance
- Polymorphism

These topics reflect the three main characteristics that distinguish OOP from structured programming. Before discussing them, however, it is useful to understand how OOP evolved.

13.1.1: Evolution of OOP

As we become more and more ambitious in the applications we design and build, the obstacle we ultimately face is always the same: complexity. Complexity limits the size of the applications we can build before we find them impossible to debug. It also limits our ability to share and maintain code. As a consequence, the evolution of programming technique has always reflected changing approaches to overcoming the complexity barrier. Roughly speaking, these techniques have evolved through three stages:

1. *Construct-oriented approaches:* These approaches attempt to reduce complexity by avoiding the use of constructs that make code confusing—such as the jump (goto statement) and multiple exit points (returns, breaks). Code developed using this approach often exhibits an almost linear flow, moving from construct block to construct block, and is relatively easy to read. The construct-oriented approach, often seen in programs written in older languages such as FORTRAN and COBOL, is typified by large functions that closely model the modular structure of an application.

2. *Function-oriented approaches*: Retaining the structured programming practices of the construct-oriented approach, the function-oriented approach also attempts to break modules into collections of small, self-contained, functions— often using data structures to pass complex arguments. This approach, which has been the central approach adopted by this textbook in Chapters 1 through 12, offers two major advantages over a pure construct-oriented approach: (1) self-contained functions are easier to understand and document; and (2) use of self-contained functions tends to promote reuse through the development of libraries. Programmers who are experienced in using languages such as C and Pascal nearly always adopt a function-oriented style.

3. *Object-oriented approaches*: The object-oriented approach employs all the practices of function-oriented programming, but changes the locus of organization

from modules and functions to "objects." These objects incorporate a mixture of data and functions. Properly designed, they can be quite self-contained (helping to manage complexity), offer the same benefits of reusability provided by libraries, and provide additional benefits in the form of extendibility, using a process called inheritance.

It is best to view these three approaches as evolutionary, not alternatives. The function-oriented approach cannot be used effectively unless a construct-oriented approach is in place. Similarly, OOP employs the function-oriented approach—often to extremes—with the main distinction being its use of the "object" as an organizing entity.

The choice of programming approach tends to be dictated by three factors:

- Complexity of the problem being solved
- Tools (e.g., languages) to be used
- Experience of the developers or development team

For simple problems, any of the three approaches can be used. Thus, tools and experience tend to determine which approach will be used. As problems become more complex, however, the construct-oriented approach (e.g., writing the program in one, well-commented, 5,000 line main() function) tends to give way to function-oriented approaches and, ultimately, object-oriented approaches.

We now turn to the some of the characteristics that C++ provides to support the object-oriented approach.

13.1.2: Encapsulation

Encapsulation is a design style whereby data and program elements are combined to form a single, self-contained object. C++ supports encapsulation by starting with a basic C structure (referred to as a class) and adding various capabilities, the most important of which are the following:

1. The ability to associate functions, as well as data elements, with **class** (structure) definitions. Collectively, data and function elements are referred to as *class members*. Frequently, we will refer to **data members** and *function members* when we need to distinguish between the two categories of members.

2. The ability to define functions that are automatically invoked when an object is created or destroyed. These functions are referred to as **constructor functions** and **destructor functions.**

3. The ability to specify accessibility of member data and member functions. Normally, accessibility is used to distinguish between the **interface** of an object—the set of features available to a developer who wants to embed that object within an application—and its **implementation,** which is the internal construction of the object that is normally of interest mainly to the programmer who developed the object.

We will now consider the first of these capabilities, class membership, from the object user's perspective.

The C++ concept of class members is a straightforward extension of the simple structure that we presented in Chapter 11 (indeed, the **struct** keyword in C++ can be used to create a C++ class). The data members of a class are exactly the same as the data elements of a structure. For example, the following declaration:

```
struct emp_pay0 {
    int nEmpId;
    double dGrossPay;
    double dBenefitContributions;
    double dFica;
    double dTax;
    double dNetPay;
};
```

would be a perfectly legal class in C++. The members of that class would be nEmpId, dGrossPay, dBenefitContributions, dFica, and so on—all of which would be data members.

Where C++ extends the simple structure is in its ability to make functions, as well as data, part of a class (or structure) definition. For example, in C++, we might see the structure definition revised as follows:

```
struct emp_pay1 {
    int nEmpId;
    double dGrossPay;
    double dBenefitContributions;
    double dFica;
    double dTax;
    double NetPay();
    void ComputeFica(double dRate);
};
```

In emp_pay1, then, the dNetPay data member in emp_pay0 has been replaced by what looks like (and is) a function prototype, NetPay(). A second function prototype, ComputePay(double dRate), is also embedded in the structure definition. They are not, however, the same type of function definitions and declarations that we have seen up to this point. They are, instead, **member functions**—meaning that they are meaningful only when applied to a specific object.

The emp_pay1 class would be a legal object declaration in C++, as we shall see shortly. Declared in this way, the process for applying member functions is almost exactly the same as that used for accessing structure data, which we already learned. For example:

```
int main(char argc,char *argv[])
{
    emp_pay1 e1,*pe1;
    e1.dGrossPay=1000;
    e1.dBenefitContribution=50;
    e1.ComputeFica(0.076);
    e1.dTax=0.15*e1.dGrossPay;
    pe1=&e1;
    cout << "The employee's net pay is " << pe1->NetPay() << endl;
    return 0;
}
```

The first thing you should notice in main() is the declaration line. Up to this point in the text, we would have written it as:

```
struct emp_pay1 e1,*pe1; // also legal
```

Although we could have included the **struct** keyword, it is not necessary in C++ when we are creating objects (but it would be required in a C program). Adding member functions to our structure makes the structure itself incompatible with C syntax anyway, so we will use the more compact C++ notation for the rest of the text.

The next thing that you should notice is the similarity between member function access and structure data access, evident from the use of e1. For example, when we wanted to call the member function ComputeFica() using the object e1, the same dot notation employed to get at structure data was used:

```
e1.ComputeFica(0.076);
```

Similarly, when we wanted to call the NetPay() function, and we wanted to use an object pointer (pe1), we used the following syntax:

```
pe1->NetPay()
```

The arrow (->) operator was used here because the left-hand side was a pointer, just as was done in Chapter 11.

Naturally, when we start defining our own C++ classes, we need answers to a number of questions, the most obvious being: Where would ComputerFica() and NetPay()actually be defined (since all we have is a prototype within the structure itself)? These types of questions will be addressed later in the chapter. Just knowing how to access member functions that have already been defined, however, is very powerful. It is, for example, sufficient to allow us to use the C++ file I/O system directly (the subject of Chapter 17), instead of Simple IO.

13.1.3: Inheritance

Inheritance is the ability to define a class using members of another class as a starting point. To understand the types of benefits this capability provides, let us refine our example of an employee object. Suppose, we have an employee class defined as follows:

```
struct employee {
    int nEmpId;
    int nSSN;
    char szLName[30];
    char szFName[30];
    char cMI;
    double dGrossPay;
    double dBenefitContributions;
    double dFica;
    double dTax;
    double NetPay();
};
```

Here, we just added some useful information—such as Name and SSN—to our earlier class. Now suppose, as well, that in addition to "standard" employees, we also have another special type of employee, executives, who receive a bonus in stock options in addition to their gross pay. One way we could accommodate this category would be to create an independent structure for executive pay. For example, we could define an executive class as follows:

```
struct executive1 {
    int nEmpId;
    int nSSN;
```

```
            char szLName[30];
            char szFName[30];
            char cMI;
            double dGrossPay;
            double dBenefitContributions;
            double dFica;
            double dTax;
            double dOptionShares;
            double dEstValuePerOption;
            double NetPay();
            double OptionValue() ;
      };
```

This class is, as should be evident, quite similar to our earlier employee class. The only change is that we added members to take care of the bonus information (shown in bold).

Alternatively, we could use composition to define our executive object. For example:

```
      struct executive2 {
            struct employee emp;
            double dOptionShares;
            double dEstValuePerOption;
            double OptionValue() ;
      };
```

Although creating a brand new executive class using the executive1 approach would work, two significant disadvantages come from defining the new class in this manner.

- If you ever wanted to keep a collection of all your employees, you would need to maintain separate collections (e.g., lists or arrays) for your standard employees and your executives. Similarly, if you developed a function that took an employee as an argument, you would need to create a separate version of the function to handle executives. The problem here is that even though we know an executive is a type of employee, by creating a separate class we hide that fact from our computer.

- If you ever made a change to your employee class (e.g., adding a health insurance ID number), you would need to make the same change to the executive class if you wanted to maintain consistency between them.

Similarly, the composition (executive2) suffers from the first of these disadvantages, and also a second disadvantage—the awkward syntax required to get at employee data within an executive2 object, for example:

```
      executive2 e2;
      char szLast=e2.emp.szLName;
```

Inheritance provides an elegant solution that is an improvement over both the executive1 and executive2 approaches. Using inheritance, we would define our executive class by specifying that an executive inherits from employee, which is done as follows:

```
      struct executive :  public employee
      {
            double dOptionShares;
            double dEstValuePerOption;
            double OptionValue();
      };
```

The **: public employee** in the definition states that whenever we create an executive object, we automatically include all the members that are associated with an employee. As a result, the only members that we need to include with the definition are those that we are adding, or those that we are changing. (In our example, they are the same members that we bolded when we defined executive from scratch.)

TEST YOUR UNDERSTANDING 13.1:

With executive as defined in this section, would the following code produce a compiler error?

```
executive e1;
e1.nSSN=0;
```

Why or why not?

The relationship we establish using inheritance is sometimes called an "is a" or "is-a" relationship, so named because an executive "is a(n)" employee. Such a relationship solves the problems of defining executive independent of employee because:

- A collection containing pointers or references to employees can also include executives, because executives are a kind of employee.
- Functions that take employee pointers or references as arguments can also take executives, for the same reason.
- If we were to enhance our employee class, when we recompile our executive class it would automatically be enhanced as well—because the inheritance in the definition causes the revised version of the employee class to be used.

Naturally, our example would not limit us to inheriting executives. We could define other classes, such as salesperson, that inherit from employee but have additional information, such as sales and commission rate. C++ even allows for multiple inheritance—inheriting members from more than one class—that might be used to create classes such as sales_executive (inheriting both from executive and salesperson).

Naturally, many subtleties are associated with inheritance and are discussed in greater detail in Chapter 16.

13.1.4: Polymorphism

Polymorphism is the ability to define member functions that are called in a way that is context sensitive. In a Microsoft Foundation Classes (MFC) Windows program, for example, dozens of functions named OnMouseMove() may define how various windows—all of which inherit from a common class called CWnd—behave when the mouse moves over them. Polymorphism allows the specific version of the function being called to vary according to what type of window the mouse is passing over (which could be a button, menu, dialog box, etc.).

To understand how polymorphism might be used, suppose that we wanted to create a member function for our employee objects (including inherited classes, such as executive) that returned total compensation. We could do this task within the employee class relatively easily, for example:

```
double TotalCompensation(); // would be defined to return
the value of dGrossPay
```

For executive objects, on the other hand, the function might be slightly more complex, because we need to include option value in addition to pay, for example:

```
double TotalCompensation(); // would need to return
// dGrossPay+OptionValue();
```

Suppose, as well, that we have an array of pointers to employee objects (including pointers to executives and any other types of employees we might have defined) called arEmps containing nCount elements, and want to determine the total compensation for the whole company. A function to perform this computation might look as follows:

```
double TotalCompanyCompensation(struct employee **arEmps,
    int nCount)
{
    double dTotal=0.0;
    int i;
    for(i=0;i<nCount;i++)
        dTotal=dTotal+arEmps[i]-->TotalCompensation();
    return dTotal;
}
```

Without polymorphism, this function would call the simple version of the TotalCompensation() function for every employee (regardless of whether it was an executive type of employee). Where polymorphism is present, on the other hand, each object would call its own version of the function (e.g., employee objects would call the simple version, executive objects would call the version that includes stock option value).

Polymorphism is present only when inheritance is used to define objects. For this reason, we will consider it, in greater depth, in Chapter 16.

13.1: SECTION QUESTIONS

1. Why is the transition from construct-oriented programming to object-oriented programming that took place between the early 1960s and mid-1990s best considered "evolutionary" rather than "revolutionary"?

2. What are some advantages that an encapsulated object provides over the use of separate functions and structures in terms of managing program complexity?

3. What are some advantages of inheritance in managing program complexity?

4. Under what circumstances are polymorphism likely to be particularly useful?

13.2: DEFINING MEMBER FUNCTIONS

In this section, we introduce the key capability required to implement encapsulation: the ability to define member functions. We begin by identifying the key similarities between member functions and the global functions that were the focus of Chapters 1 through 12. We then look at some important differences between member functions and global functions: establishing member access, using the **this** pointer, and overloading member functions. Our main focus in this section will be on describing the mechanics of implementing member functions. Toward the end of the chapter (Section 13.5) we will step back and introduce some general principles of object design.

13.2.1: Defining Member Functions

Defining member functions has both similarities and differences to the global C++ function definitions we have already seen. Initially, we will concentrate on the many similarities. For example—like the global C++ functions we have already seen—member functions:

- Have the standard *return-value name(arguments)* format we have already seen (with two important exceptions)
- Can have default arguments
- Can be overloaded
- Can be defined as either regular or inline functions

The last of these similarities warrants the most discussion, because we have not previously talked much about inline functions. Whenever we define a C++ function, we have the choice of making it a regular or inline function, using the **inline** keyword. The difference determines how the function is stored and called, and its practical implications to the programmer relate mainly to efficiency.

When a regular function is compiled (as we have discussed in earlier chapters, starting with Chapter 1), the code for that function is placed in a single location. When a function call is encountered in your code, the compiler then generates the machine language instructions to call that function (pushing arguments on the stack and jumping to the function). The main advantage is that only one copy of each function needs to be stored. The main disadvantage is the overhead associated with making the call.

If an **inline** keyword is used when defining a function, this disadvantage no longer applies. Instead, a copy of the entire function is made each time a call is encountered in the program. The resulting code can be slightly more efficient, but may also be quite a bit larger (if many calls are made to the particular inline function). The way inline functions are implemented also has an important practical implication: Because the definition of the function needs to be available to every source file that calls it, inline functions are normally defined in an .h (header) file, rather than in a .cpp file.

Defining Inline Member Functions   Because this book focuses on clarity, rather than efficiency, there was no need to introduce inline functions up to this point. In defining member functions, however, inline functions are often used. In fact, any function whose definition appears in the class/structure definition itself is—by default—going to be implemented as an inline function. For example, in the following emp_pay2 structure, the NetPay() member function definition has been implemented as an inline member:

```
struct emp_pay2 {
    int nEmpId;
    double dGrossPay;
    double dBenefitContributions;
    double dFica;
    double dTax;
    double NetPay() {return dGrossPay-dBenefitContributions-
        dFica-dTax;}
    void ComputeFica(double dRate);
};
```

This structure differs from the previously defined emp_pay1 (Section 13.1.2) in that the line prototyping the NetPay() function:

```
double NetPay();
```

has been replaced by a full definition. For example:

```
double NetPay() {return dGrossPay-dBenefitContributions-dFica-dTax;}
```

By looking at the function, it is obvious that the variables used in the example have the same names as some of the emp_pay2 structure member variables. What may be less obvious is where they get their values from. To understand better, recall that NetPay(), as a member function, will always operate on some emp_pay2 object—it cannot be called by itself. In other words, within a global function such as main, a call such as:

```
emp_pay2 e2;
// some initialization
double dVal=e2.NetPay();
```

would be legal, whereas:

```
emp_pay2 e2a;
// some initialization
double dVal=NetPay();
```

would *not* be legal (just as writing dGrossPay by itself would not be legal, whereas e2a.dGrossPay would be fine).

The implications then are that when we call a member function, the variables used inside the function can take their values from the object it is being applied to. Thus, the call:

```
double dVal=e2.NetPay();
```

would have the same effect as writing:

```
double dVal=e2.dGrossPay-e2.dBenefitContributions-e2.dFica-e2.dTax;
```

given they way we defined NetPay().

Just as we can reference member data with a member function, we can also reference other member functions. To see this capability, consider the emp_pay3 structure defined as follows:

```
struct emp_pay3 {
    int nEmpId;
    double dGrossPay;
    double dBenefitContributions;
    double dFica;
    double dTax;
    double dAutoPayments;
    double NetPay() {return dGrossPay-dBenefitContributions-
    dFica-dTax;}
    double PayCheckAmount(){return NetPay()-dAutoPayments;}
    void ComputeFica(double dRate);
};
```

In this structure, the NetPay() function is called from within the PayCheckAmount() function (from which automatic payments, such as insurance or mortgage deductions, have been subtracted). Applying the function in an example:

```
emp_pay3 e3;
// some initialization
double dCheck=e3.PayCheckAmount();
// accomplishes the same thing as...
dCheck=e3.NetPay()-e3.dAutoPayments;
// accomplishes the same thing as...
dCheck= e3.dGrossPay-e3.dBenefitContributions-e3.dFica-e3.dTax -
    e3.dAutoPayments;
```

Defining Regular Member Functions A regular member function is defined in a .cpp file, the same as the global functions we have already seen. The main difference in how the definitions appear is in the use of the scope resolution operator to identify what class a function is associated with. For example, the ComputeFica() member might be defined as follows in a .cpp file:

```
void emp_pay3::ComputeFica(double dRate) {
    dFica=dGrossPay*dRate;
}
```

In this case, the *emp_pay3::* tells the compiler that we are defining a member function of the emp_pay3 structure. Having done so, it knows that the dFica and dGrossPay referenced within the function are member variables (and does not give us undefined variable errors).

Choosing Between Inline and Regular Member Functions It usually does not make a great deal of difference to the compiler whether a member function is defined to be inline or regular. In fact, if an inline function is too large, some compilers will implement the function as a regular function (regardless of how the programmer coded it).

Three potential advantages come with making all functions "regular" in nature:

- Greater consistency is achieved—you never have to wonder which file your implementation is in.
- Your code is more pure if you don't mix function declarations and definitions.
- When selling your code to others as a compiled library and header file, the less code you include in the header, the harder it is for the purchaser to reverse engineer your program.

If performance suffers, you can also redefine the function by using the inline keyword and placing it in the header file outside the class definition. For example, if we redefined ComputeFica() as follows:

```
inline void emp_pay3::ComputeFica(double dRate) {
    dFica=dGrossPay*dRate;
}
```

and placed it under our emp_pay3 structure definition in the header file, we could accomplish the same thing as including the function definition within the structure definition.

Some arguments can also be made for making short member functions inline:

- Potential performance benefits may be gained.
- Many C++ member functions are short (e.g., one line), and it often saves time to include them in the class definition—as well as making it easier to see what they are doing.
- Other languages, such as Java, incorporate all member function definitions within the overall class definition. Writing C++ classes in this way will often make it easier to convert your code to these other languages.

The bottom line is that the choice between inline and regular function definitions has little practical impact on the programmer. The choice is mainly one of style, as suggested in Style Sidebar 14.1.

STYLE SIDEBAR 14.1	Inline vs. Regular Function Definitions

Camp	Position	Justification
Super scruffy	Whatever feels best at the time.	Since the compiler makes the ultimate decision, why should I worry?
Scruffy	It's okay to define functions in the header as long as they aren't too long.	Some gains in efficiency may come from using header functions. Also, it is easier to modify functions in the header because the declaration and body are in the same place. When header functions get too large, however, it can make the header hard to read.
Middle ground	It's reasonable to define certain categories of functions as header functions (such as simple data access members) but the default should always be to define functions in the .cpp file.	Consistent practice never hurts, but which practice is chosen can—to some extent—be determined by convenience.
Neat	Your class declaration should not include any function definitions. If performance requires inline functions, they should be added below the class definition.	The consistency clarity of your code should be a separate issue from its efficiency.
Neat freak	Inline functions should always be avoided.	Purity rules. If your program runs so slowly that it needs inline functions to make performance adequate then you should be complaining to your supervisor that the problem is impossible.

13.2.2: Access Specifiers

Walkthrough available in MAccess.avi

When defining a class or structure, the C++ programmer implicitly or explicitly specifies the accessibility of each member function and data element. By controlling accessibility, class designers can distinguish between the interface of a class and its implementation. Using an automobile as an example:

- The "interface" consists of those elements of the car that the driver (e.g., user) interacts with, such as the steering wheel, pedals, controls, and instrumentation panel.
- The implementation includes elements such as the drive train and electrical system—those elements of the car that the typical driver doesn't need to know about and probably shouldn't play with.

Member Access   Three keywords specify member access:

- **public:** Specifies that the member data or member function can be accessed any time an object is available.
- **private:** Specifies that the member data or member function can *only* be accessed within other member functions of the class.
- **protected:** Specifies that the member data or member function can *only* be accessed within other member functions of the class (or classes that inherit from the class).

In this text, we nearly always limit ourselves to public and protected access, which are by far the most common forms.

The easiest way to illustrate how access works is to compare a **struct** with the same definition implemented as a **class.** In order to achieve backward compatibility, the default access to members of a **struct** is **public,** which means the structure and P0Test() function shown in Example 13.1 will run perfectly.

Replacing the **struct** keyword with the more commonly used **class** keyword—which defaults to **private** access—leads to many problems. The errors are listed in Example 13.2.

These errors identify the following problems, all of which are a result of the fact that P0test() is not a member of the Person00 class, and therefore can only access members declared to be **public:**

```
1) Person00 p0={"Grandon","Gill",0,48,250};
```

You are not allowed to initialize data for which access is private.

```
2) p0.FullName(buf);
```

You are not allowed to call a member function that is declared to be private.

```
3) DisplayFormatted("First: %s, Last: %s, Full: %s\n",
     p0.szFName,p0.szLName,buf);
```

You are not allowed to access data members that are declared to be private.

We can eliminate these problems by inserting a single **public:** access specifier, as shown in Example 13.3. This specifier also has the effect of rendering our class declaration *identical* to the structure definition in Example 13.1.

> In C++, the only difference between a **class** object and a **struct** object is the default access.

For this reason, in this text we use **class** when declaring C++ objects with member functions, and reserve the use of **struct** for objects that only include data (such as the structures of Chapter 11).

Given that private/protected data access can lead to lots of errors—all of which go away when public access (or a **struct**) is used—it is reasonable to ask "Why not just make everything public?" To understand why making everything public is a bad idea, you must go back to why OOP evolved in the first place: to handle problems too complex for other techniques. A key challenge of managing complexity is in knowing where to direct your attention. If you are a programmer, using a class library designed by some other programmer, one of your first questions will always be: Which of the hundreds (or thousands) of available members should I be accessing in my program?

The public/protected declaration provides a useful starting point. Any member (function or data) declared to be public is intended for use by programmers who are using the class. Protected and private members, on the other hand, should not be accessed directly.

EXAMPLE 13.1

struct access demonstration

```
struct Person00 {
    char szFName[40];
    char szLName[40];
    char cMI;
    int nAge;
    int nWeight;
    void FullName(char *szBuf) {
        char szMI[2]={cMI};
        strcpy(szBuf,szFName);
        strcat(szBuf," ");
        if (szMI[0]>' ') {
            strcat(szBuf,szMI);
            strcat(szBuf," ");
        }
        strcat(szBuf,szLName);
    }
};

int P0test()
{
    Person00 p0={"Grandon","Gill",0,48,250};
    char buf[80];
    p0.FullName(buf);
    DisplayFormatted("First: %s, Last: %s, Full: %s\n",
        p0.szFName,p0.szLName,buf);
    return 0;
}
```

EXAMPLE 13.2

Errors compiling Person00 defined as a class

Compiling...
PersonMain.cpp
C2552: 'p0' : non-aggregates cannot be initialized with initializer list
    'Person00' : Types with private or protected data members are not aggregate
C2248: 'Person00::FullName' : cannot access private member declared in
class 'Person00'
    see declaration of 'Person00::FullName'
    see declaration of 'Person00'
C2248: 'Person00::szFName' : cannot access private member declared in class
'Person00'
    see declaration of 'Person00::szFName'
    see declaration of 'Person00'
C2248: 'Person00::szLName' : cannot access private member declared in class
'Person00'
    see declaration of 'Person00::szLName'
    see declaration of 'Person00'

EXAMPLE 13.3

Person00 class with public access

```
class Person00 {
public: // changes access of all declarations that follow
    char szFName[40];
    char szLName[40];
    char cMI;
    int nAge;
    int nWeight;
    void FullName(char *szBuf) {
        char szMI[2]={cMI};
        strcpy(szBuf,szFName);
        strcat(szBuf," ");
        if (szMI[0]>' ') {
            strcat(szBuf,szMI);
            strcat(szBuf," ");
        }
        strcat(szBuf,szLName);
    }
};
```

By so declaring them, the class designer effectively stuck a "No user-serviceable parts inside" sticker on the member. Although the specification (like the sticker) will do nothing to prevent a determined programmer from accessing the data or function, the wise programmer will take heed.

Based on this discussion, it seems like a bad idea to make our entire Person00 class public. So how do we get at the data we need (e.g., to print the name)? One approach is to define public member functions specifically designed to allow us to access whatever data we need. Not surprisingly, functions of this type are often referred to as **accessor functions.**

In our example, we had three problems:

- We could not initialize our structure.
- We could not call the FullName() member, because it was private.
- We could not get at the last name and first name data members in order to print them.

In Example 13.4, we rewrite the class Person00 class as Person01 with some strategic functions defined.

To solve these problems, we take the following steps:

- Implement a function Initialize() that allows us to set the values in our structure. The function includes default arguments, so that you only need to know first name and last name to call it.
- Set access to FullName() as **public,** because we see no reason it needs to be private.
- Create a series of accessor functions that allow us to get the values of the different data elements—the First(), Last(), MI(), Age() and Weight() functions.
- In our new test function, P1test(), we only call the public functions.

EXAMPLE 13.4

Person class with accessor functions defined

```
class Person01 {
protected: // changes access of all declarations that follow
    char szFName[40];
    char szLName[40];
    char cMI;
    int nAge;
    int nWeight;
public:
    void FullName(char *szBuf) {
        char szMI[2]={cMI};
        strcpy(szBuf,szFName);
        strcat(szBuf," ");
        if (szMI[0]>' ') {
            strcat(szBuf,szMI);
            strcat(szBuf," ");
        }
        strcat(szBuf,szLName);
    }
    void Initialize(const char *szF,const char *szL,
                        char cM=0,int nA=-1,int nW=-1) {
            strncpy(szFName,szF,40);
            strncpy(szLName,szL,40);
            cMI=cM;
            nAge=nA;
            nWeight=nW;
        }
        const char *First(){return szFName;}
        const char *Last(){return szLName;}
        char MI(){return cMI;}
        int Age(){return nAge;}
        int Weight(){return nWeight;}
};

int P1test()
{
    Person01 p1;
    p1.Initialize("Grandon","Gill",0,48,250);
    char buf[80];
    p1.FullName(buf);
    DisplayFormatted("First: %s, Last: %s, Full: %s\n",
        p1.First(),p1.Last(),buf);
    return 0;
}
```

If you look at the Person01 class, the most "dangerous" aspect of the class is probably the name arrays (szFName[] and szLName[]) , which could be overflowed by a programmer who didn't know they were limited to 40 characters. To protect our class, we do two things:

- In the Initialize() function, we use strncpy() to limit the characters copied to the available space (40 characters each).
- In the First() and Last() functions, we return the addresses of the arrays as constant character pointers (const char *) making it harder for the class user/programmer to write data to them.

Naturally, the cost of improving class safety is the time it takes to write the various accessor functions. Fortunately, such functions are so easy to write that the time it takes to write them is negligible. In Section 13.5 we will further discuss the benefits of limiting member access.

In-Depth: friend Specifier From time to time, we find ourselves in situations where we want to maintain certain data/function member protection as a general rule, but really need access to those members within a particular function or class. Such access can be provided using the **friend** keyword.

As an example, suppose we want to maintain the fully private nature of our Person00 class, but still want to call a function that accessed private members. Declaring that function to be a friend, within the class declaration, would allow us to accomplish this objective. This call is illustrated in Example 13.5.

Because all members within the Person00r1 function are protected, the P0r1test function would generate a series of errors except for its declaration as a **friend.** (Even declared as a friend, the compiler would not allow the initialization list used in the original P0Test, presented in Example 13.1.)

The friend specifier can also be used to specify access for a class or an individual function within a class. Example 13.6 shows a simple class (TestR2) defined with a single member (the P0r2Test() function). By making the class, (or just the function itself), a friend, access to protected members can be obtained as illustrated in Example 13.6.

As a general rule, the friend specifier is not usually necessary (it is most commonly encountered in operator overloading, the topic of Chapter 14). Most often, the need for a friend specification can be avoided by defining additional accessor functions.

13.2.3: The *this* Pointer

Because member functions operate on objects, and objects exist in memory, it stands to reason that the object to which a member function is being applied has an address. In C++, a variable named **this** containing that address is automatically defined whenever a regular member function is called.

For the most part, the **this** pointer serves relatively little useful purpose. Example 13.7 illustrates the point by showing how the inline Initialize() member function, originally defined in Example 13.4 could be rewritten as InitializeThis(), which uses the **this** pointer to access each member element.

Similar to the **friend** specifier, the **this** pointer tends to have certain limited uses. We will see the most common of the pointer in Chapter 14, Section 14.2, when we discuss assignment operator overloading.

EXAMPLE 13.5

Use of friend specifier to provide access to private members

```
class Person00r1 {
protected:
    char szFName[40];
    char szLName[40];
    char cMI;
    int nAge;
    int nWeight;
    void FullName(char *szBuf) {
        char szMI[2]={cMI};
        strcpy(szBuf,szFName);
        strcat(szBuf," ");
        if (szMI[0]>' ') {
            strcat(szBuf,szMI);
            strcat(szBuf," ");
        }
        strcat(szBuf,szLName);
    }
    friend int P0r1test();
};

int P0r1test()
{
    Person00r1 p0;
    strncpy(p0.szFName,"Grandon",40);
    strncpy(p0.szLName,"Gill",40);
    p0.cMI=0;
    p0.nAge=48;
    p0.nWeight=250;
    char buf[80];
    p0.FullName(buf);
    DisplayFormatted("First: %s, Last: %s, Full: %s\n",
        p0.szFName,p0.szLName,buf);
    return 0;
}
```

13.2.4: Member Function Overloading

Member functions have all the capabilities of normal C++ functions. In particular member functions can be:

- *Overloaded:* Different versions of a member function with the same name can be defined.

- *Assigned Default Argument Values:* Default values for arguments, from right to left, can be specified (e.g., cM, nA, and nW in Initialize(), as shown in Example 13.7).

As was noted in Chapter 4, Sections 4.3.2 and 4.3.3, the compiler must be able to distinguish which version of a function to call using its arguments.

EXAMPLE 13.6

Granting friend access to a class or class member

```
class TestR2
{
public:
    int P0r2test();

};

class Person00r2 {
protected:
    char szFName[40];
    char szLName[40];
    char cMI;
    int nAge;
    int nWeight;
    void FullName(char *szBuf) {
        char szMI[2]={cMI};
        strcpy(szBuf,szFName);
        strcat(szBuf," ");
        if (szMI[0]>' ') {
            strcat(szBuf,szMI);
            strcat(szBuf," ");
        }
        strcat(szBuf,szLName);
    }
    // either option alone will work
    friend class TestR2;
    friend int TestR2::P0r2test();
};

// Declaration of class member function given friend access to
// Person00r2 class
int TestR2::P0r2test()
{
    Person00r2 p0;
    strncpy(p0.szFName,"Grandon",40);
    strncpy(p0.szLName,"Gill",40);
    p0.cMI=0;
    p0.nAge=48;
    p0.nWeight=250;
    char buf[80];
    p0.FullName(buf);
    DisplayFormatted("First: %s, Last: %s, Full: %s\n",
        p0.szFName,p0.szLName,buf);
    return 0;
}
```

EXAMPLE 13.7

Using the *this* pointer

```
void Initialize(const char *szF,const char *szL,
        char cM=0,int nA=-1,int nW=-1) {
    strncpy(szFName,szF,40);
    strncpy(szLName,szL,40);
    cMI=cM;
    nAge=nA;
    nWeight=nW;
}

void InitializeThis(const char *szF,const char *szL,
        char cM=0,int nA=-1,int nW=-1) {
    strncpy(this->szFName,szF,40);
    strncpy(this->szLName,szL,40);
    this->cMI=cM;
    this->nAge=nA;
    this->nWeight=nW;
}
```

13.2: SECTION QUESTIONS

1. Why is the *class-name::* scope resolution operator required when defining functions in the .cpp file but not within the class?

2. Why must class members be accessed using the . and -> operators outside of member functions, yet those operators are not required to access members within member functions?

3. Would it make sense to declare a large function that is called in many places from within your program as an inline function?

4. Under what circumstances would it matter whether access for a particular member data element were declared to be private versus protected?

5. What are some good reasons for not making all class members (data and functions) public?

6. Explain why the need for a friend specification can often be avoided by defining additional accessor functions.

7. Explain why this->nAge, (*this).nAge, and nAge are all precisely equivalent when used within a Person01 member function.

8. Why is any global function called with a structure or structure pointer as an argument a good candidate for a member function if you are moving to OOP?

13.3: CONSTRUCTOR AND DESTRUCTOR FUNCTIONS

In addition to defining regular member functions, C++ allows us to define functions that are automatically invoked whenever an object is created (*constructor functions*) or destroyed (*destructor functions*). These functions can be powerful tools, allowing the programmer to automate many allocation and cleanup functions that would otherwise require careful thought in a program.

13.3.1: Constructor Functions

Whenever we create an object from a C++ class, a constructor function is called to initialize the contents of that object. Such constructors can either be created implicitly (by the compiler) or explicitly (by the programmer, which is done by giving a member function the same name as the class itself).

Implicitly Created Constructors   If our class has no constructor functions explicitly defined by the programmer, two types of public constructors are created automatically:

- A **default constructor,** which simply creates the object and does no initialization
- A **copy constructor,** which makes a byte-for-byte copy of the object being created

Assume, for example, we've defined the following very simple class:

```
class MyClass
{
    int nData;
};
void MySimpleFunc(MyClass obj);
```

Because the programmer has not defined any constructor functions, situations in which the default constructor would be invoked include:

```
MyClass obj1;
MyClass *pObj1=new MyClass;
```

The copy constructor, on the other hand, gets called whenever we need to copy an existing object in order to create a new object. Continuing the previous example, because no constructors have been defined, the automatically created copy constructor would be invoked in each of the following situations:

```
MyClass obj2=obj1; // the contents of obj2 are initialized
// by copying obj1
MyClass pObj2=new MyClass(obj2); // initializes the new
// object to obj2 contents
MySimpleFunc(obj1); // a copy of obj1 is made when passed
// into the function
```

In our discussions of structures in Chapter 11, we took advantage of the fact that these two constructors are automatically created for us when we create pure structures. The real power of C++ constructors, however, derives from our ability to define our own.

TEST YOUR UNDERSTANDING 13.2:

Would a copy constructor have been invoked if our function MySimpleFunc() had been prototyped in the following ways?

```
void MySimpleFunc(MyClass *pObj);
void MySimpleFunc(Myclass &obj);
```

Why or why not?

Explicitly Defined Constructors   If a programmer decides the implicit constructors do not accomplish what is needed (and it is rare that they do!), it is possible to define one or more constructors explicitly by prototyping one or more functions having *the same* *name as the class, and no specified return value.* In fact, constructor (and destructor) functions are the only C++ functions that do not have any return specification (i.e., not even void, to indicate that no value is returned).

To illustrate the explicit definition of constructors, it is useful to consider an example:

```
class emp_pay4 {
public:
    emp_pay4(){ nEmpId=0; }
    emp_pay4(int nID,double dPay=0.0) {
        nEmpId=nID;
        dGrossPay=dPay;
    }
protected:
    int nEmpId;
    double dGrossPay;
    double dBenefitContributions;
    double dFica;
    double dTax;
    double NetPay() {
        return dGrossPay-dBenefitContributions-dFica-dTax;
    }
    void ComputeFica(double dRate);
};
```

In the emp_pay4 structure as defined here, we find two constructor functions (using the C++ function overload capability, which applies to constructors as well as other C++ functions) :

```
emp_pay4(){ nEmpId=0; }
```

and

```
emp_pay4(int nID,double dPay=0.0) {
    nEmpId=nID;
    dGrossPay=dPay;
}
```

The first is invoked whenever an object is created with no argument. For example:

```
emp_pay4 e1;
emp_pay4 *pEmp=new emp_pay4;
emp_pay4 *parEmp=new emp_pay4[5];
```

The first line would cause e1 to be created with the first constructor, which would then initialize the nEmpID member of the object e1 to 0. The second line would cause a dynamic object (once again, with the nEmpID member set to 0) to be allocated. The last line would cause an array of emp_pay4 objects to be created, with the first constructor being called five times (for each of the five objects).

To invoke a constructor defined with arguments, parentheses are used—similar to a function call. For example, in the following declarations:

```
emp_pay4 e2(101,68000.00), e3(102);
emp_pay4 *pNew=new emp_pay4(103,75000);
emp_pay4 arEmp[5]={emp_pay4(104,97000),emp_pay4(105)};
```

both e2 and e3 would be created using the second constructor. In the case of e2, the nEmpId member would be initialized to 101, while the dGrossPay value would be initialized to 68000.00. In the case of e3, the nEmpId of the new object would be 102, while the default argument value of 0.00 would be used to initialize dGrossPay. In the second line, the dynamically allocated object assigned to pNew would have nEmpId initialized to 103 and dGrossPay initialized to 75000.

It is also possible to call the constructors with arguments when initializing arrays with an aggregate list, as shown in the line:

```
emp_pay4 arEmp[5]={emp_pay4(104,97000),emp_pay4(105)};
```

In this case, the second constructor is called on the first two elements of the five-element array. The first constructor (with no arguments) is then called for the remaining three elements.

When the new operator is used to create an array, only a constructor with no arguments can be used. If one is not available, the operation will fail.

As soon as a programmer defines any explicit constructors, the implicit default constructor is no longer defined, although a copy constructor is still created. This feature can be important because certain operations (such as allocating an array of objects with new, as just noted) require a default constructor. For this reason, a programmer will normally want to define a default constructor (i.e., a constructor with no arguments) whenever *any* constructor is defined.

TEST YOUR UNDERSTANDING 13.3:

Explain what the following operation would do, given our definition of emp_pay4:

```
emp_pay4 ep=e2;
```

13.3.2: Destructor Functions

Unlike constructor functions, only one destructor function can be declared for a given class. It is automatically invoked whenever an object is released. For example:

- When a local variable goes out of scope, such as occurs when a function returns.
- When a program ends—at which time destructor functions are called for all static variables.
- When the **delete** operator is applied to objects that were created dynamically using the **new** operator (see Chapter 12, Section 12.3).

Although you virtually never "call" a destructor function, you need to be aware of the types of activities that are performed during object release. In C++ file stream objects, for example, the destructor function is often defined so that it automatically closes the file associated with the object. In many destructors, memory managed by the class will be released as part of the destruction process. This function will be illustrated in Section 13.3.3.

The implicit destructor function does nothing. To define a destructor function, you use the class name preceded by a tilde. For example:

```
class emp_pay5 {
public:
    emp_pay5(){ nEmpId=0; }
    emp_pay5(int nID,double dPay=0.0) {
        nEmpId=nID;
        dGrossPay=dPay;
    }
    ~emp_pay5(){}
```

```
protected:
    int nEmpId;
    double dGrossPay;
    double dBenefitContributions;
    double dFica;
    double dTax;
    double NetPay() {
        return dGrossPay-dBenefitContributions-dFica-dTax;
    }
    void ComputeFica(double dRate);
};
```

In the emp_pay5 class, the destructor (which doesn't actually do anything) is defined in the line:

```
~emp_pay5(){}
```

Empty destructors are relatively common (in which case they don't need to be over-ridden, because the implicit version works just fine). If a class manages memory—typically found in classes that contain pointers as members—the destructor will generally contain delete statements to return that managed memory to the heap.

13.3.3: Person Class with Dynamic Names

Walkthrough available in PersonDynamic.avi

To illustrate the use of constructors and destructors, we define a new version of the Person class, Person02. The implementation of Person02 differs from that of Person01 in several ways:

- Instead of storing first and last names in embedded arrays, the class uses pointers to dynamic memory. One advantage of doing so is eliminating the 40-character name limit in Person01.
- Explicit constructors and a destructor have been defined to manage the memory for the names.

The Person02 class is presented in Example 13.8.

The changes made to the Person02 class include the following:

- Member variables were renamed so that each begins with m_ (e.g., nAge became m_nAge). Although this change has no effect on program performance, it is consistent with Microsoft's convention for naming member variables. The benefit of doing so is that it becomes easier to keep track of what are member variables (versus local variables and global variables) within member functions.
- The m_pszFName and m_pszLName members are redefined as pointers.
- Two constructor functions have been defined: a default constructor and a constructor that allows variables to be explicitly initialized.
- A destructor function has been defined that deletes the contents of the m_pszFName and m_pszLName arrays. This function eliminates the possibility of memory leaks that would occur if a Person02 object were deleted without taking care of the name strings in memory.
- The Initialize() function was substantially modified.

EXAMPLE 13.8

Person class managing dynamic names

```cpp
class Person02 {
public:
    Person02(){
        m_pszFName=0;
        m_pszLName=0;
    }
    Person02(const char *szF,const char *szL,
            char cM=0,int nA=-1,int nW=-1){
        m_pszFName=0;
        m_pszLName=0;
        Initialize(szF,szL,cM,nA,nW);
    }
    ~Person02() {
        delete [] m_pszFName;
        delete [] m_pszLName;
    }
protected: // changes access of all declarations that follow
    char *m_pszFName;
    char *m_pszLName;
    char m_cMI;
    int m_nAge;
    int m_nWeight;
public:
    void FullName(char *szBuf) {
        char szMI[2]={m_cMI};
        strcpy(szBuf,m_pszFName);
        strcat(szBuf," ");
        if (szMI[0]>' ') {
            strcat(szBuf,szMI);
            strcat(szBuf," ");
        }
        strcat(szBuf,m_pszLName);
    }
    void Initialize(const char *szF,const char *szL,
            char cM=0,int nA=-1,int nW=-1) {
        delete [] m_pszFName;
        m_pszFName=new char[strlen(szF)+1];
        strcpy(m_pszFName,szF);
        delete [] m_pszLName;
        m_pszLName=new char[strlen(szL)+1];
        strcpy(m_pszLName,szL);
        m_cMI=cM;
        m_nAge=nA;
        m_nWeight=nW;
    }
    const char *First(){return m_pszFName;}
    const char *Last(){return m_pszLName;}
    char MI(){return m_cMI;}
    int Age(){return m_nAge;}
    int Weight(){return m_nWeight;}
};
```

The heart of the changes made to the Person02 class are in the Initialize() functions. Now that the class uses dynamic memory to hold the name strings, each time a string is changed, the old string is deleted and a copy of the new name is made and assigned to the appropriate pointer. For example:

```
delete [] m_pszFName;
m_pszFName=new char[strlen(szF)+1];
strcpy(m_pszFName,szF);
```

was used to create a new string m_pszFName string from the function argument szF. Even though this code would have problems if we ran out of memory (because we don't handle memory exceptions, as noted in Chapter 12), if the memory is available, we know the m_pszFName string will be long enough to handle the szF argument, so we use strcpy() to make the copy, as opposed to:

```
strncpy(szFName,szF,40);
```

previously used in the Person01 version.

TEST YOUR UNDERSTANDING 13.4:

Why is it critical that m_pszLName and m_pszFName be initialized to 0 before Initialize() is called in the second version of the Person02 constructor?

Despite the implementation differences between Person01 and Person02, the two classes are nearly identical as far as the interface is concerned. In other words, the public members available to a programmer using a Person02 object are essentially the same as those for a Person01 object. The practical implication is that anywhere a Person01 object was used, we should be able to change it to a Person02 object without affecting the program. Thus, given that the test code for the Person01 class (from Example 13.4) was as follows:

```
int P1test()
{
    Person01 p1;
    p1.Initialize("Grandon","Gill",0,48,250);
    char buf[80];
    p1.FullName(buf);
    DisplayFormatted("First: %s, Last: %s, Full: %s\n",
        p1.First(),p1.Last(),buf);
    return 0;
}
```

we should be able to replace the first line with:

```
Person02 p1;
```

without producing any errors (compiler or runtime). This supposition, in fact, proves to be the case.

TEST YOUR UNDERSTANDING 13.5:

One interface enhancement is made in transforming the Person01 to the Person02 class, and one interface capability has been lost. What are they? (*Hint:* Examine all the public members and find one that can be called in Person02, but not Person01. Think about the implicitly defined members and figure out which is no longer accessible.)

13.3: SECTION QUESTIONS

1. When MyClass was defined in Section 13.3.1, the two implicit constructors that were created could have been defined as follows:

```
MyClass(){}
MyClass(const MyClass &ref) { (*this)=ref;}
```

Explain why these two constructors do the same thing as the explicit constructors.

2. Assume the following class has been defined:

```
class Simple {
    public:
        Simple(int nVal){m_nVal=nVal;}
    protected:
        int m_nVal;
}
```

Explain which of the following lines will work and which will fail:

a. Simple s1;

b. Simple s2(5);

c. Simple *p3=new Simple(10);

d. Simple *p4[5]=new Simple[5];

e. Simple s5[]={Simple(15),Simple(20),Simple(30)};

f. Simple s6=s2;

3. Assume the following class is defined:

```
class AClass {
    AClass(){m_cVal=0;}
    char m_cVal;
}
```

What would be the problem with the following declaration?

```
int main(int argc,char argv[])
{
AClass a;
return 0;
}
```

How could this problem be solved?

4. What two problems could result if we wrote the following Person02 member function?

```
void Person02::First(const char *szF) {
    m_pszFName=szF;
}
```

Rewrite the First() function in Question 4 to eliminate the problem.

13.4: CONST AND STATIC QUALIFIERS

Three qualifiers are only relevant to member functions: **const, static,** and **virtual**. The last of these, **virtual**, is relevant only when inheritance is present, and is discussed in Chapter 16. We now turn our attention to the first two.

13.4.1: const Member Functions

When declaring a member function, it is possible to append a **const** keyword to the declaration. For example, consider the following class:

```
class SimpleName {
public:
    SimpleName(const char *sz){Name(sz); }
    void Name(const char *sz){strncpy(m_szName,sz,40);}
    const char *Name() const {return m_szName;}
protected:
    char m_szName[40];
};
```

The second version of the Name() function is declared as follows:

```
const char *Name() const {return m_szName;}
```

In this function, we note two **const** keywords. The first, beginning the declaration, we have already seen many times: it indicates that the return value is a constant character string. The second **const,** therefore, is the one of interest here.

A member function followed by a const qualifier signifies that calling the member function will not change any data in the object to which the function is being applied.

The compiler takes a const declaration seriously. Any member function that is so declared:

- Cannot change the values of any member data.
- Cannot call any member functions that are not likewise declared to be const.

Furthermore, if an object, object reference, or object pointer is declared to be const, only const member functions can be applied to it. For example, the following code would produce an error:

```
SimpleName nm("grandon");
const SimpleName *pN=&nm;
cout << pN->Name() << endl; // OK, displays "grandon" to
// the screen
pN->Name("Grandon"); // error is generated
```

The problem here is that pN is declared to be const, and therefore attempting to call the Name(const char *) function, as is done on the last line, is illegal. Calling the Name() version, as is done on the third line, is fine however. If the version of Name() with no arguments is defined as const, you can apply it to a const pointer.

If a member function is declared to be const in the header file, its definition in the .cpp must have the same qualifier. For example, if we choose not to define Name() inline, its definition would appear as follows:

```
const char *SimpleName::Name() const
{
    return m_szName;
}
```

If you leave off the const in the definition header, a compiler error will result. The error is because it is possible to define two member functions that differ only in const specification.

The **const qualifier** is a powerful tool in ensuring the integrity of your code. It puts the compiler to work for you—making sure that you only change your objects when you think you are changing your objects. Used haphazardly, however, it can create intricate networks of error messages that can take hours (even days) to resolve. To illustrate how such problems can arise, let us refer back to our Person02 class (Example 13.8) and suppose we wanted to write a function to compare two person objects to see whether they have the same name. Such a function (modeled after a strcmp() in return value) might be defined as follows:

```
int PersonCmp(const Person02 &p1,const Person02 &p2)
{
    int nCmp=stricmp(p1.Last(),p2.Last());
    if (nCmp!=0) return nCmp;
    return stricmp(p1.First(),p2.First());
}
```

The function is simple: it first compares the last names and returns the difference unless they are equal, in which case it returns a comparison of the first names. Because PersonCmp() is not a member function or friend, we use the public member functions to get at the first and last names.

When we compile PersonCmp(), we get the errors listed in Example 13.9.

These errors are pretty typical of const errors. The underlying problem is that the Person02::First() and Person02::Last() member functions are not defined to be const. As a result, we cannot apply them to const objects, such as the two arguments of the function, p1 and p2.

The way the errors are expressed by the compiler makes slightly more sense than:

```
C2662: Jeepers, creepers! There's a lead pipe in the con-
servatory…
```

but only slightly. As we know from Section 13.2.3, a **this** pointer is created every time a member function is invoked. If a Person02 member has no specifier, the pointer is of type:

```
Person02 *this;
```

If, on the other hand, the member function is const qualified, the pointer is declared as follows:

```
const Person02 *this;
```

Because p1 and p2 are declared as const references in the function header, only the second type of this pointer can be created from them. That declaration leads to an error whenever we try to create a **this** pointer that is not const.

Returning to our problem, we ask a more practical question: How do we solve it? The two possible approaches are the sleazy, shortsighted approach and the thoughtful

---

EXAMPLE 13.9

Errors compiling PersonCmp()

C2662: 'Person02::Last' : cannot convert 'this' pointer from 'const Person02' to 'Person02 &'
    Conversion loses qualifiers
C2662: 'Person02::First' : cannot convert 'this' pointer from 'const Person02' to 'Person02 &'
    Conversion loses qualifiers

approach. As luck would have it, the first of these is the simplest. We redefine our function as follows:

```
int PersonCmpSleazy(Person02 &p1, Person02 &p2)
{
    int nCmp=stricmp(p1.Last(),p2.Last());
    if (nCmp!=0) return nCmp;
    return stricmp(p1.First(),p2.First());
}
```

By removing the two const qualifiers on the function arguments, we no longer limit ourselves to calling const member functions, and the errors go away. The problem with this approach is that we make changes to our function that we know should not be necessary—because a comparison function should not be changing its arguments.

A much better approach would be to look at the function and see whether the errors make sense given what the function is supposed to do. As it turns out, they don't make sense, which means our problem is really with the Person02 class itself. To correct this problem, we need to make sure that any function members that actually are const are declared that way, which leads to the Person03 class, shown in Example 13.10.

The changes in Person03 are relatively subtle. Six member functions could be const qualified:

```
void FullName(char *szBuf) const;
const char *First() const;
const char *Last() const;
char MI() const;
int Age() const;
int Weight() const;
```

Once we make these changes, Person03 objects can be passed into the PersonCmp() function and no error messages appear.

TEST YOUR UNDERSTANDING 13.6:

Explain why four of the Person03 member functions could not be const qualified.

13.4.2: The static Qualifier

As introduced in Chapter 12, the term **static** is normally used to refer to data that are initialized and then remain available until a program ends. Global variables, for example, are static.

The **static** keyword is commonly encountered in a C++ program in three places:

- In local variable declarations within a function
- In member data declarations within a structure or class
- Within class member function declarations

Before looking at how **static** applies to member functions, it is useful to examine its data-related implications.

static Variables in Functions   When a variable is declared static within a function, it is created and initialized the first time the function is called, and maintains its value even after the function returns. In other words, even though the variable goes out of scope when the function ends (i.e., we cannot access it by name), it still continues to exist in memory. To illustrate how it differs from local variables, consider the function defined in Example 13.11.

EXAMPLE 13.10

Person03 class with const qualifiers

```
class Person03 {
public:
    Person03(){
        m_pszFName=0;
        m_pszLName=0;
    }
    Person03(const char *szF,const char *szL,
                                char cM=0,int nA=-1,int nW=-1){
        m_pszFName=0;
        m_pszLName=0;
        Initialize(szF,szL,cM,nA,nW);
    }
    ~Person03() {
        delete m_pszFName;
        delete m_pszLName;
    }
protected: // changes access of all declarations that follow
    char *m_pszFName;
    char *m_pszLName;
    char m_cMI;
    int m_nAge;
    int m_nWeight;
public:
    void FullName(char *szBuf) const {
        char szMI[2]={m_cMI};
        strcpy(szBuf,m_pszFName);
        strcat(szBuf," ");
        if (szMI[0]>' ') {
            strcat(szBuf,szMI);
            strcat(szBuf," ");
        }
        strcat(szBuf,m_pszLName);
    }
    void Initialize(const char *szF,const char *szL,
                        char cM=0,int nA=-1,int nW=-1) {
        delete m_pszFName;
        m_pszFName=new char[strlen(szF)+1];
        strcpy(m_pszFName,szF);
        delete m_pszLName;
        m_pszLName=new char[strlen(szL)+1];
        strcpy(m_pszLName,szL);
        m_cMI=cM;
        m_nAge=nA;
        m_nWeight=nW;
    }
    const char *First()const {return m_pszFName;}
    const char *Last()const {return m_pszLName;}
    char MI()const {return m_cMI;}
    int Age()const {return m_nAge;}
    int Weight()const {return m_nWeight;}
};
```

EXAMPLE 13.11

SimpleCounter() function

```
void SimpleCounter()
{
    int nLocal=1;
    static int nStatic=1;
    cout << "Call count: " << nLocal << " (Local), "
            << nStatic << " (Static)" << endl;
    nLocal++;
    nStatic++;
}
```

The first time the SimpleCounter() function is called, nLocal is created and initialized to 1, as is nStatic. Thereafter, each time the function is called (while the program continues running), the process is repeated for nLocal, but nStatic retains its previous value. As a consequence, when the function is called 10 times from a loop, the output shown in Figure 13.1 results.

static Variables in Structures and Classes   Data members in classes or pure structures declared to be static are somewhat similar in spirit to their function counterparts. They are constructed the first time any object of the class is created, and then remain until the program ends.

What makes static members unique (and occasionally useful) among data members is the fact that all objects share a single copy of the data member. This way, static data members can keep track of global call information, such as the number of active objects in the class. This capability is illustrated by the ObjCounter class, in Example 13.12, where the m_nCount variable is declared as a public, static member. The output from running the test function, TestCount(), is presented in Figure 13.2.

As demonstrated by the output, when ObjCounter objects are constructed, the constructor function increments the m_nCount static member. Similarly, when objects are deleted, the counter is decremented. This rule applies to both individual objects and to

FIGURE 13.1   Output of SimpleCounter() Called from a Loop 10 Times

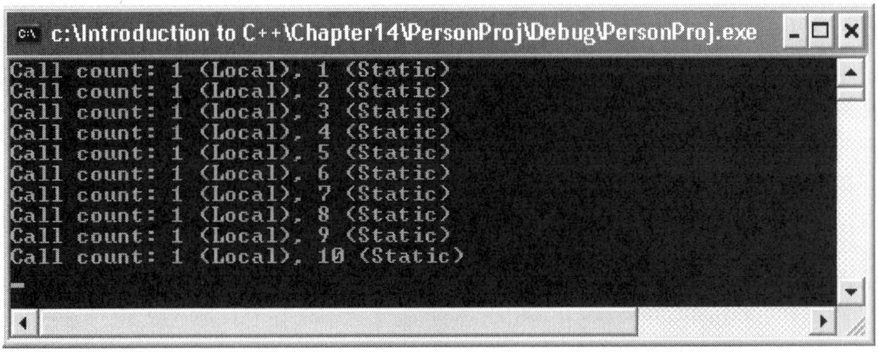

```
c:\Introduction to C++\Chapter14\PersonProj\Debug\PersonProj.exe
Call count: 1 (Local), 1 (Static)
Call count: 1 (Local), 2 (Static)
Call count: 1 (Local), 3 (Static)
Call count: 1 (Local), 4 (Static)
Call count: 1 (Local), 5 (Static)
Call count: 1 (Local), 6 (Static)
Call count: 1 (Local), 7 (Static)
Call count: 1 (Local), 8 (Static)
Call count: 1 (Local), 9 (Static)
Call count: 1 (Local), 10 (Static)
```

EXAMPLE 13.12

ObjCounter header and source files

```cpp
// ObjCounter.h header file
#pragma once

class ObjCounter
{
public:
    ObjCounter(void);
    ~ObjCounter(void);
    static int m_nCount;
};

void TestCount();
```

```cpp
// ObjCounter.cpp source file
#include "objcounter.h"
#include <iostream>
using namespace std;

// static members must be initialized outside the class definition
int ObjCounter::m_nCount=0;

ObjCounter::ObjCounter(void)
{
    m_nCount++;
}

ObjCounter::~ObjCounter(void)
{
    m_nCount--;
}

void TestCount()
{
    cout << ObjCounter::m_nCount << " is initial object count" << endl;
    ObjCounter obj1;
    cout << ObjCounter::m_nCount << " after obj1 created" << endl;
    ObjCounter *pArr=new ObjCounter[10];
    cout << ObjCounter::m_nCount << " after pArr initialized" << endl;
    delete [] pArr;
    cout << ObjCounter::m_nCount << " after pArr deleted" << endl;
}
```

arrays—where the constructor is called as many times as there are elements in the array (e.g., ten times in the example).

One important consideration regarding static variables is the need to initialize them outside the class in which they are declared. In this respect, they are like global variables—the structure declaration allows their name and type to be shared but memory must be

FIGURE 13.2 Results of Running TestCount() Function

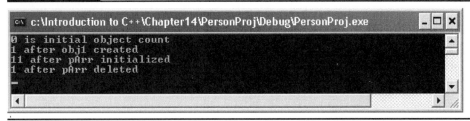

allocated for them in one, and only one, place as was done in Example 13.12 in the ObjCounter.cpp file, with the line:

```
int ObjCounter::m_nCount=0;
```

If you do not have an int initialization statement in one (and only one) of your source files, an "unresolved external" linker error will result.

TEST YOUR UNDERSTANDING 13.7:

Given the manner in which static variables are declared, what are the implications for member access?

static Member Functions A member function qualified as **static** is shared by all the objects in the class, just like a static data member. A number of practical implications follow:

- Because a static member function is not associated with any particular object, you cannot access non-static member data or member functions from within it without supplying an object.

- The **const** qualifier cannot be applied to a static member function, because it cannot—by its nature—make changes to an associated object.

- The **this** pointer cannot be accessed within a static member because it has no associated object.

- You don't need to have an object in order to call a static member function.

In all of these respects, a static member function is just like an ordinary function—not like a member function at all. However, the following three reasons explain why it might make sense to define a static member function instead of a regular global function:

- Placing a static function within a class is like giving it the class as a namespace, and could prevent name collisions with other functions having the same name.

- Use of static functions can allow you to create applications in which all functions and data (except the main() function) are associated with objects. Indeed, in languages such as Java, declaring static member functions is the *only* way to implement general functions.

- Unlike regular functions, private and protected members can be accessed within static functions. This capability can be useful when objects are passed into the function as arguments or are created within the function.

In Example 13.13, a static member function, Count(), has been added to the ObjCounter class. In addition, in order to call the function within TestCount(), the scope resolution operator needs to be applied.

EXAMPLE 13.13

ObjCounter class with static member function

```cpp
// ObjCounter.h header file, modified with Count() member
#pragma once

class ObjCounter
{
public:
    ObjCounter(void);
    ~ObjCounter(void);
    static int m_nCount;
    static int Count(){return m_nCount;}
};

void TestCount();
```

```cpp
// ObjCounter.cpp source file
#include "objcounter.h"
#include <iostream>
using namespace std;

// static members must be initialized outside the class definition
int ObjCounter::m_nCount=0;

ObjCounter::ObjCounter(void)
{
    m_nCount++;
}
ObjCounter::~ObjCounter(void)
{
    m_nCount--;
}
void TestCount()
{
    cout << ObjCounter::Count() << " is initial object count" << endl;
    ObjCounter obj1;
    cout << ObjCounter::Count() << " after obj1 created" << endl;
    ObjCounter *pArr=new ObjCounter[10];
    cout << ObjCounter::Count() << " after pArr initialized" << endl;
    delete [] pArr;
    cout << ObjCounter::Count() << " after pArr deleted" << endl;
}
```

13.4: SECTION QUESTIONS

1. Why wouldn't it make sense to declare a regular (nonmember) function as const?
2. Why could failing to properly declare a single member function as const have a ripple effect on other member functions?
3. Can you ever assign values to a member variable within a const member function?
4. How are static member variables like global variables?
5. Explain why the const qualifier makes no sense for a static member function
6. If only public static member variables can be declared, does the same apply to static member functions?

13.5: INTRODUCTION TO OBJECT-ORIENTED DESIGN AND UML

In Chapters 1–12, the flowchart was used as a tool for visualizing the design of functions and programs. As we start to program with objects as our principal organizing construct, however, the traditional ANSI flowchart becomes increasingly less relevant. In this section, we introduce the concept of the unified modeling language (UML), summarize a few principles of object-oriented design and programming practice that have emerged in the chapter, and show how FlowC can be used to design C++ classes.

13.5.1: What Is UML?

The **unified modeling language,** or **UML,** is an evolving standard for designing complex systems and object-oriented applications. Unlike flowcharting—which offers the opportunity for direct translation from diagram to code—UML designs usually operate at a higher level of abstraction. They serve to organize and clarify complex programming and systems problems without proving a mechanical means of implementing the solution.

Although the UML standard continues to evolve, under the direction of the Object Management Group (OMG, at http://www.omg.org), certain vendors—such as Rational Software, acquired by IBM in 2003—have taken a leading role in its development and in incorporating it into products. Although many diagrams exist, the OMG uses three categories:

- *Structural diagrams,* illustrating various aspects of the overall structure of an application or system
- *Behavior diagrams,* illustrating interactions between objects and transitions between object states
- *Model management diagrams,* illustrating subsystems and models within the overall system or application

The most commonly used diagrams in OOP design are the first two, structural diagrams that illustrate how classes are defined and interrelate, and behavior diagrams that illustrate how classes respond to events and messages from other classes.

In this text, we limit ourselves to considering some of the simple structural diagrams, the basic class diagram, and the generalization/specialization (inheritance) diagram. The first, the basic class diagram, is a rectangular box divided into three parts: (1) the class name, (2) the data members of the class, and (3) the function members of the class. An

FIGURE 13.3 Basic Class Diagram for Person03 Class

Class: Person03
Data members:
char *m_pszFName
char *m_pszLName
char m_cMI
int m_nAge
int m_nWeight
Function members:
+   Person03()
+   Person03(char *szF,char *szL,char cM=0,char nH=–1,char nW=–1)
+   void FullName(char *szBuf) const
+   void Initialize(const char *szF,const char *szL,char cM=0,char nA=–1,char nW=–1)
+   const char * First() const
+   const char * Last()
+   char MI() const
+   int Age() const
+   int Weight() const

example of such a diagram, created with FlowC, is presented in Figure 13.3. The second type of diagram relates to inheritance, and will be introduced in Chapter 16.

In addition to listing the names of the data and function members, the FlowC version of the diagram provides additional information, such as function arguments. In addition, the characters on the left indicate member access, where # is protected and + is public (– is also commonly used to indicate private access). Where a member function or data is static, the $ symbol is also present.[1]

13.5.2: Some Object-Oriented Design Principles for C++

During the course of this chapter, a number of comments have been made regarding reasonable design and programming practices for creating object-oriented C++ programs. Some of the most significant of these are as follows:

- *Think encapsulated:* The best C++ classes are designed as self-contained units. Such design encourages both abstract thinking and enhances reusability. One mechanical step you can take to help this process along is to *write every class with its own .h file and .cpp file.* Even though this practice can lead to dozens (or hundreds) of files in even modest applications, it is much easier to move classes between applications when they are in separate files.

- *Differentiate between interface and implementation:* Use the public/protected access specifiers that C++ provides to make it clear what is internal to the class

---

[1] The basic representation used to design this diagram was found at http://www.rational.com/uml/resources /quick/plainposter.jsp (accessed July 7, 2002).

and what is available to programmers using the class. Also, do not assume you are only doing a favor for *other* programmers by designing your classes in this way. It can prove useful when you are using your own classes, as well.

- *Design your classes as if the implementation could change at any minute:* In an "ideal" class, you can protect all your data, making only member functions part of the interface. It is easy to write accessor functions, and it is amazing how often they turn out to be useful, as was illustrated by the move from Person02 to Person03, where we changed almost everything about how the class was constructed without changing the interface.

- *Use naming conventions to reduce cognitive strain:* Simple things, such as beginning member variable names with m_ and data type abbreviations (as we have suggested here) can dramatically reduce the amount of thinking you need to do when you are programming. Remember, the reason OOP was developed was to help manage increasing program complexity. By choosing consistent names, you can avoid unnecessary complexity. Three weeks after you write the class you will have forgotten nearly everything about the class you wrote and will be grateful for any help you can give yourself.

- *Design your classes so the compiler can help you find errors:* Capabilities that C++ offers, such as the const qualifier, can require some thought and their use may even slow down the initial writing of code. As code gets more and more complex, however, the initial writing effort takes less and less of your time (as a percentage of total time). Locating bugs becomes the biggest challenge. Using tools such as const qualification can surface errors in your design—and attach a line number to them!

We extend these principles further when we introduce the other main object-oriented programming capabilities (inheritance and polymorphism) in Chapter 16.

13.5.3: Creating in Classes in FlowC

 Walkthrough available in FlowCObject.avi

Classes can be added to FlowC just as functions and structures can be added. Because classes are designed to be self-contained, however, they are only rendered in UML form in the project window (as shown in Figure 13.3). To edit a class, you must open a class window (from the main menu, the right click menu, or by double clicking the UML summary). The class view, shown in Figure 13.4, contains a declaration box that will display all member variables and a collection of function flowcharts for the function members. Once in a class view, you add and move between functions just as if it were a project view.

FlowC can generate the C++ code for any class constructed within it, as shown in Figure 13.5. Consistent with common C++ practice, FlowC creates two files for each class: a header file containing the definition and a .cpp containing the implementation of any functions not declared to be inline. Classes included in a project can be exported to a folder containing a Visual Studio .NET project and then brought into the project.

Although FlowC is not intended to be a full-fledged design tool, it can be useful for creating a skeletal project with class declarations and function **stubs** (functions that take the proper arguments and return a dummy value but have not been implemented). It will also be used, from time to time, in the rest of the text for purposes of illustration.

FIGURE 13.4 Class View in FlowC

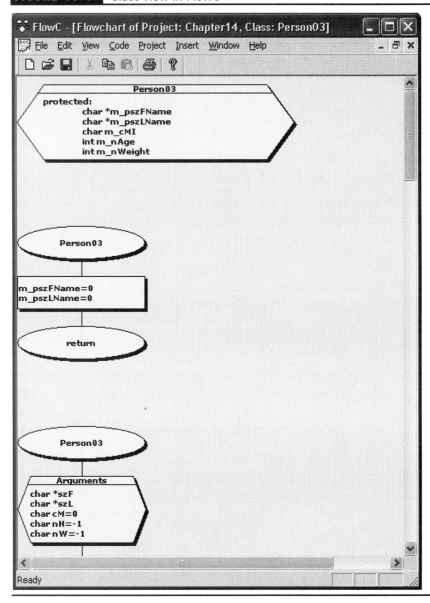

FIGURE 13.5   FlowC Code Generation

```
FlowC - [C code for Project: Chapter14]
File  Edit  View  Code  Project  Insert  Window  Help

class Person03
{
protected:
    char *m_pszFName
    char *m_pszLName
    char m_cMI
    int m_nAge
    int m_nWeight
public:
    Person03();
    Person03(char *szF,char *szL,char cM=0,char nH=-1,char nW=-1);
    void FullName(char *szBuf) const;
    void Initialize(const char *szF,const char *szL,char cM=0,char nA=-1,char nW=-1)
    const char * First() const;
    const char * Last();
    char MI() const;
    int Age() const;
    int Weight() const;
    ~Person03();
};
// Target:Person03.cpp
/* Person03.cpp: Person03 Class Implementation */
// Included C/C++ libraries
#include <stdlib.h>
#include <iostream>
#include <fstream>
using namespace std;
#include "Person03.h"
 Person03::Person03()
{
    m_pszFName=0;
    m_pszLName=0;
    return;
}
 Person03::Person03(char *szF,char *szL,char cM=0,char nH=-1,char nW=-1)
{
    // No action taken
    return;
}
void Person03::FullName(char *szBuf) const
{
    char szMI[2]={cMI};
    strcpy(szBuf,m_pszFName);
    strcat(szBuf," ");
    if(szMI[0]>' ') {
        strcat(szBuf,szMI);
```

Ready

13.5: SECTION QUESTIONS

1. What does it mean when we say that UML operates at a higher level of abstraction than flowcharting?

2. What key pieces of information are conveyed by a basic UML class diagram?

3. What recommended design and programming practices particularly help to reduce the cognitive strain on the programmer when designing and using C++ classes?

4. What recommended design and programming practices particularly help to reduce debugging time for C++ classes?

5. What does it mean to use FlowC to "create a skeletal project with class declarations and function stubs"?

13.6: ENCAPSULATION EXERCISES

Walkthrough available in EmpClass.avi

In this section, we consider how to transform code that worked with structures into encapsulated objects. Specifically, we walk through the transformation of structure-based code for an employee database—originally developed in Chapter 11, Section 11.6.2—into two classes. A lab is then presented for transforming the implementation of that database into one that utilizes dynamic memory (paralleling the lab presented in Chapter 12, Section 12.5).

13.6.1: A Simple Employee Class

In Chapter 11, Example 11.3, we introduced a simple structure to hold employee data. That structure, presented here in Example 13.14, is a pure structure. To work with the structure, we developed a series of functions, the prototypes of which are also presented in Example 13.14. Our first objective is to transform this collection of data and functions into an encapsulated class.

A number of aspects of the transformation of the employee structure (Example 13.14) to a class (Example 13.15) are quite straightforward, and are applicable to almost any conversion from structured to object-oriented programs:

- Member data should be made protected by default, and it makes sense to rename it for consistency (e.g., using the m_ prefix convention often found in Microsoft code).

- Simple (one line) accessor functions can be written for setting and accessing member data.

- Any function that takes a structure as an argument can easily be rewritten as a member function. The procedure involves:
  - Removing the structure reference or pointer from the argument.
  - If the reference or pointer argument was const, adding the const qualifier to the member declaration.

- Any function related to the class that does not take a structure as an argument can be made static.

EXAMPLE 13.14

Employee structure from Chapter 12

```
#define MAXNAME 30

struct employee {
    unsigned int nId;
    char szLastName[MAXNAME];
    char szFirstName[MAXNAME];
    unsigned int nYearHired;
    double dSalary;
    bool bActive;
};

void DisplayEmp(struct employee emp);
void InputEmp(struct employee *pEmp);
void SaveEmployee(STREAM &out,const struct employee *pEmp);
void LoadEmployee(STREAM &in,struct employee *pEmp);
void SaveString(STREAM &out,const char *sz);
void LoadString(STREAM &in,char *sz);
```

In addition to these functions, it also makes sense to define one or more constructor functions for initializing data. As we will discuss further in Chapter 14, it is also frequently convenient to have a function that copies an object. It is not unreasonable to call such a function Copy(), and pass it a constant reference to the object we are making a copy of.

The results of making these changes are presented in Example 13.15.

The revised class consists of the following:

- Two constructors, a default and one that allows all data elements to be initialized.
- A Copy() function used to copy the contents of another object.
- Rewritten Save(), Load(), Display(), and Input() functions. In each case, we dropped "Employee" or "Emp" from the name (because, being a member it's obvious what type of data we are operating on), and we removed the structure reference from the argument. For two of the functions, Save() and Display(), we added const qualifiers since they are not going to change the object they are applied to (unlike Edit() and Load(), which will change the object by their very nature).
- SaveString() and LoadString() are brought into the class as static members, because they aren't applied directly to an object. It is debatable whether they should be made part of the class at all—they could be used to load and save strings from any source—but we do so here for the purposes of demonstration.
- A pair of accessor functions is defined for each member data element. The first (const qualified) is used to return the value from the object. The second is used to set the value.

Most of our member functions are quite straightforward. Two of our new functions, the constructor and the Copy() function, are presented in Example 13.16. These functions set member data values in two different ways—the constructor using the variables themselves and the Copy() function using the accessor functions that were defined. Of these two

EXAMPLE 13.15

Employee class after modifications

```
// employee class
#define MAXNAME 30

class employee
{
public:
    employee(){m_nId=0;}
    employee(int nId,const char *szL,const char *szF,
        unsigned int nY=2003,double dSalary=0.0,bool bActive=true);
    void Copy(const employee &emp);
    // modified functions
    void Save(STREAM &out) const;
    void Load(STREAM &in);
    void Display() const;
    void Input();
    static void SaveString(STREAM &out,const char *sz);
    static void LoadString(STREAM &in,char *sz);

    // accessor functions
    unsigned int Id() const {return m_nId;}
    void Id(int n){m_nId=n;}
    const char *LastName() const {return m_szLastName;}
    void LastName(const char *sz){strncpy(m_szLastName,sz,MAXNAME);}
    const char *FirstName() const {return m_szFirstName;}
    void FirstName(const char *sz){strncpy(m_szFirstName,sz,MAXNAME);}
    unsigned int YearHired() const {return m_nYearHired;}
    void YearHired(int n){m_nYearHired=n;}
    double Salary() const {return m_dSalary;}
    void Salary(double d){m_dSalary=d;}
    bool Active() const {return m_bActive;}
    void Active(bool b){m_bActive=b;}

protected:
    unsigned int m_nId;
    char m_szLastName[MAXNAME];
    char m_szFirstName[MAXNAME];
    unsigned int m_nYearHired;
    double m_dSalary;
    bool m_bActive;
};
```

approaches, the accessor function approach is generally preferred. In this illustration, for example, using the accessor for FirstName() and LastName() allows you to avoid worrying about overrunning the m_szLastName and m_szFirstName arrays. The accessor automatically ensures that too many characters are not copied.

The types of changes made to the earlier functions are all similar in nature. For this reason, we examine the "before" and "after" for just two of them: the InputEmp () function (which became the Input() member function) and the SaveEmployee() function

---

EXAMPLE 13.16

Constructor and Copy() functions

```
employee::employee(int nId,const char *szL,const char *szF,
          unsigned int nY,double dSalary,bool bActive)
{
    m_nId=nId;
    strncpy(m_szLastName,szL,MAXNAME);
    strncpy(m_szFirstName,szF,MAXNAME);
    m_nYearHired=nY;
    m_dSalary=dSalary;
    m_bActive=bActive;
}

void employee::Copy(const employee &emp)
{
    Id(emp.m_nId);
    LastName(emp.m_szLastName);
    FirstName(emp.m_szFirstName);
    YearHired(emp.m_nYearHired);
    Salary(emp.m_dSalary);
    Active(emp.m_bActive);
}
```

(which became the Save() member function). The Input() group is shown in Example 13.17; the Save() group in Example 13.18.

The two Input() functions are nearly identical except for a single change: wherever pEmp-> was present in the original function, it has been removed. Our member names now represent the values from the object we are operating on. The same applies for the Save() family. Of note here is the const qualifier applied to the definition of the Save() member. Saving an object should not normally require modifying it. The qualification makes the compiler check to be sure that we aren't using any improper functions inside of Save(), or setting member variable values.

A slightly more significant change had to be made to the EmployeeTest() function used to test employee input and display. The old and new versions of these functions are presented in Example 13.19.

The changes to the object version include the following:

■ Because we cannot initialize protected members with an aggregate list, our multi-argument version of the constructor is invoked in its place. Specifically:

```
struct employee empSmith={101,"Smith","Joan",1999,100000,true};
```

becomes:

```
employee empSmith(101,"Smith","Joan",1999,100000,true);
```

■ Rather than passing our object in as an argument to various functions, we apply the member to it. For example:

```
InputEmp(&empSmith);
```

becomes:

```
empSmith.Input();
```

EXAMPLE 13.17

InputEmp() and Input() member functions

```
void InputEmp(struct employee *pEmp)
{
    char buf[MAXLINE];
    DisplayString("\nHit enter to accept existing values...\n\n");
    DisplayFormatted("Last Name [%s]: ",pEmp->szLastName);
    InputString(buf);
    if (strlen(buf)>0)strncpy(pEmp->szLastName,buf,MAXNAME);
    DisplayFormatted("First Name [%s]: ",pEmp->szFirstName);
    InputString(buf);
    if (strlen(buf)>0)strncpy(pEmp->szFirstName,buf,MAXNAME);
    DisplayFormatted("Salary [%.2f]: ",pEmp->dSalary);
    InputString(buf);
    if (strlen(buf)>0)pEmp->dSalary=atof(buf);
    DisplayFormatted("Year hired [%i]: ",pEmp->nYearHired);
    InputString(buf);
    if (strlen(buf)>0)pEmp->nYearHired=atoi(buf);
    DisplayFormatted("Still active (Y or N) [%s]: ",
        (pEmp->bActive) ? "Yes" : "No");
    InputString(buf);
    if (strlen(buf)>0)pEmp->bActive=(buf[0]=='y' || buf[0]=='Y');
}

void employee::Input()
{
    char buf[MAXLINE];
    DisplayString("\nHit enter to accept existing values...\n\n");
    DisplayFormatted("Last Name [%s]: ",m_szLastName);
    InputString(buf);
    if (strlen(buf)>0)strncpy(m_szLastName,buf,MAXNAME);
    DisplayFormatted("First Name [%s]: ",m_szFirstName);
    InputString(buf);
    if (strlen(buf)>0)strncpy(m_szFirstName,buf,MAXNAME);
    DisplayFormatted("Salary [%.2f]: ",m_dSalary);
    InputString(buf);
    if (strlen(buf)>0)m_dSalary=atof(buf);
    DisplayFormatted("Year hired [%i]: ",m_nYearHired);
    InputString(buf);
    if (strlen(buf)>0)m_nYearHired=atoi(buf);
    DisplayFormatted("Still active (Y or N) [%s]: ",
        (m_bActive) ? "Yes" : "No");
    InputString(buf);
    if (strlen(buf)>0)m_bActive=(buf[0]=='y' || buf[0]=='Y');
}
```

EXAMPLE 13.18

SaveEmployee() and Save() member functions

```
void SaveEmployee(STREAM &out,const struct employee *pEmp)
{
    WriteInteger(out,pEmp->nId);
    SaveString(out,pEmp->szLastName);
    SaveString(out,pEmp->szFirstName);
    WriteInteger(out,pEmp->nYearHired);
    WriteReal(out,pEmp->dSalary);
    WriteInteger(out,(int)pEmp->bActive);
}

void employee::Save(STREAM &out) const
{
    WriteInteger(out,m_nId);
    SaveString(out,m_szLastName);
    SaveString(out,m_szFirstName);
    WriteInteger(out,m_nYearHired);
    WriteReal(out,m_dSalary);
    WriteInteger(out,(int)m_bActive);
}
```

EXAMPLE 13.19

Structure and Object versions of EmployeeTest()

```
// structure version
void EmployeeTest()
{
    struct employee empSmith={101,"Smith","Joan",1999,100000,true};
    DisplayEmp(empSmith);
    NewLine();
    InputEmp(&empSmith);
    NewLine();
    DisplayEmp(empSmith);
}

// object version
void EmployeeTest()
{
    employee empSmith(101,"Smith","Joan",1999,100000,true);
    empSmith.Display();
    NewLine();
    empSmith.Input();
    NewLine();
    empSmith.Display();
}
```

Naturally, not all transformations of structured programs to classes will be as mechanical as the preceding, which was facilitated by the fact that the task of working with employees is naturally suited to object representation.

13.6.2: In Depth: An Employee Collection Class

The EmpData application (presented in Chapter 11, Section 11.6) involves creating a simple database for loading and saving employee objects. The original structure being modified was prodigiously simple (shown in Example 13.20, along with function prototypes).

The revised class, shown in Example 13.21, is fairly straightforward but has a number of new member functions whose purpose is not immediately obvious.

The most important of these new member functions are the GetAt() and GetValue() members. The two functions have an identical purpose: accessing a pointer to a particular employee object in the m_arEmp[] array. What differentiates them is that one—GetValue()—returns a const employee object and is const qualified, while the other returns a regular pointer and is not const qualified. The implication is as follows:

- If you need to access an employee in a const qualified member function, use the GetValue() version.
- If you need to access an employee, then change the value of that employee, use the GetAt() version.

This distinction is evident by comparing the Save() and Load() members, as shown in Example 13.22.

Because saving the employees does not require modifying them, GetValue() is used to iterate through the count of employees, so each can be saved to the stream. In Load(), however, GetAt() is used to acquire the pointer into which data from the stream will be loaded.

Most of the remaining member functions are the result of straightforward transformations of the original functions—similar to those shown in Section 13.6.1. Two functions,

---

EXAMPLE 13.20

Original EmpData structure

```
#define MAXEMPLOYEES 100

#include "Employee.h"

struct EmpData {
    int nCount;
    struct employee arEmp[MAXEMPLOYEES];
};

unsigned int PromptForId();
void ListEmployees(const struct EmpData *pData);
void AddEmployee(struct EmpData *pData);
void EditEmployee(struct EmpData *pData,unsigned int nId);
bool DeleteEmployee(struct EmpData *pData,unsigned int nId);
int FindEmployee(const struct EmpData *pData,unsigned int nId);
bool SaveAll(const char *szName,const struct EmpData *pData);
bool LoadAll(const char *szName,struct EmpData *pData);
```

EXAMPLE 13.21

EmpData class

```
class EmpData
{
public:
    EmpData(){m_nCount=0;}
    employee *GetAt(int i) {
        if (i<0 || i>=m_nCount) return 0;
        return m_arEmp+i;
    }
    const employee *GetValue(int i) const {
        if (i<0 || i>=m_nCount) return 0;
        return m_arEmp+i;
    }
    int Count() const {return m_nCount;}
    static unsigned int PromptForId();
    void ListEmployees() const;
    void AddEmployee();
    void EditEmployee(unsigned int nId);
    bool DeleteEmployee(unsigned int nId);
    int FindEmployee(unsigned int nId) const;
    bool Save(const char *szName) const;
    bool Load(const char *szName);
protected:
    int m_nCount;
    employee m_arEmp[MAXEMPLOYEES];
};
```

---

however, require us to do more major changes. The problem is that when we defined constructors for the employee object, we altered our implicit ability to assign one employee to another—a subject addressed in greater detail in the next chapter. As a result, functions that previously assigned one structure to another (e.g., DeleteEmployee(), AddEmployee(), etc.) no longer compile. To get around this issue, we replace the assignment operator with a call to the employee::Copy() function. The before and after versions of the AddEmployee() functions are presented in Example 13.23.

13.6.3: In Depth: Dynamic Employee Lab Exercise

In Chapter 12, Section 12.5, a lab exercise was presented that involved replacing the Chapter 11 version of the employee database, which used predefined arrays to hold all data, with one that used dynamic memory. In this lab exercise, the objective is simple:

- Reimplement the employee and EmpData classes so that they use dynamic arrays.
- *Make no changes to the public interface of either class.*

The new classes will be defined as shown in Examples 13.24 and 13.25. In both cases, the only public function change was the addition of a destructor function.

In implementing the classes, pay particular attention to the following:

- The changes made between Person01 (Example 13.4) and Person02 (Example 13.8) in this chapter
- The discussion of dynamic arrays in Chapter 12, Section 12.4

EXAMPLE 13.22

Save() and Load()

```
bool EmpData::Save(const char *szName) const
{
    STREAM out;
    int i;
    // open for writing, truncate
    if (!Open(out,szName,false,true,true,false)) {
        return false;
    }
    WriteInteger(out,m_nCount);
    for(i=0;i<Count();i++) {
        GetValue(i)->Save(out);
    }
    Close(out);
    return true;
}

bool EmpData::Load(const char *szName)
{
    STREAM in;
    int i;
    // open for reading, don't truncate
    if (!Open(in,szName,true,false,false,false)) {
        return false;
    }
    m_nCount=ReadInteger(in);
    for(i=0;i<Count();i++) {
        GetAt(i)->Load(in);
    }
    Close(in);
    return true;
}
```

EXAMPLE 13.23

Before and after versions of AddEmployee functions

```
/* AddEmployee() allows an employee to be added to
to the table and edited */
void AddEmployee(struct EmpData *pData)
{
    struct employee emp={0};
    bool bvalid=false;
    while(!bvalid) {
        unsigned int nId=PromptForId();
        if (FindEmployee(pData,nId)>=0) {
            char buf[MAXLINE];
            DisplayString("ID that you entered already exists. Try again?"
            "(Y or N): ");
            InputString(buf);
            if (toupper(buf[0])=='N') bvalid=true;
        }
        else {
            emp.nId=nId;
            InputEmp(&emp);
            pData->arEmp[pData->nCount]=emp;
            pData->nCount++;
            bvalid=true;
        }
    }
}
/* After: object version */
void EmpData::AddEmployee()
{
    employee emp;
    bool bvalid=false;
    while(!bvalid) {
        unsigned int nId=PromptForId();
        if (FindEmployee(nId)>=0) {
            char buf[MAXLINE];
            DisplayString("ID that you entered already exists. Try again?"
            "(Y or N): ");
            InputString(buf);
            if (toupper(buf[0])=='N') bvalid=true;
        }
        else {
            emp.Id(nId);
            emp.Input();
            m_arEmp[m_nCount].Copy(emp);
            m_nCount++;
            bvalid=true;
        }
    }
}
```

EXAMPLE 13.24

Revised employee class

```
class employee
{
public:
    employee();
    employee(int nId,const char *szL,const char *szF,
        unsigned int nY=2003,double dSalary=0.0,bool bActive=true);
    ~employee();
    void Copy(const employee &emp);
    // modified functions
    void Save(STREAM &out) const;
    void Load(STREAM &in);
    void Display() const;
    void Input();
    static void SaveString(STREAM &out,const char *sz);
    static void LoadString(STREAM &in,char *sz);

    // accessor functions
    unsigned int Id() const {return m_nId;}
    void Id(int n){m_nId=n;}
    const char *LastName() const {return m_szLastName;}
    void LastName(const char *sz){strncpy(m_szLastName,sz,MAXNAME);}
    const char *FirstName() const {return m_szFirstName;}
    void FirstName(const char *sz){strncpy(m_szFirstName,sz,MAXNAME);}
    unsigned int YearHired() const {return m_nYearHired;}
    void YearHired(int n){m_nYearHired=n;}
    double Salary() const {return m_dSalary;}
    void Salary(double d){m_dSalary=d;}
    bool Active() const {return m_bActive;}
    void Active(bool b){m_bActive=b;}
protected:
    unsigned int m_nId;
    char *m_szLastName;
    char *m_szFirstName;
    unsigned int m_nYearHired;
    double m_dSalary;
    bool m_bActive;
};
```

EXAMPLE 13.25

Revised EmpData class

```
class EmpData
{
public:
    EmpData();
    ~EmpData();
    employee *GetAt(int i);
    const employee *GetValue(int i) const;
    int Count() const {return m_nCount;}
    static unsigned int PromptForId();
    void ListEmployees() const;
    void AddEmployee();
    void EditEmployee(unsigned int nId);
    bool DeleteEmployee(unsigned int nId);
    int FindEmployee(unsigned int nId) const;
    bool Save(const char *szName) const;
    bool Load(const char *szName);
protected:
    int m_nSize;
    int m_nCount;
    employee *m_arEmp;
};
```

13.7: REVIEW AND QUESTIONS

13.7.1: REVIEW

The C++ programming language is based upon an OOP approach to programming. An OOP approach typically exhibits three characteristics:

- *Encapsulation:* The combination of data and functions into self-contained objects, operating independently, or nearly independently, of each other.

- *Inheritance:* The ability to define objects using the characteristics and structure of other objects as a starting point.

- *Polymorphism:* The presence of functions or messages where the same function/message applied to different objects can produce distinctly different behaviors (depending on the type of object to which the function/member is applied).

In a C++ class or struct, every data member or function member is defined to be either accessible to programmers using the class (*public*) or inaccessible to programmers using the class (*private, protected*). In addition, other classes or functions can be declared to be *friend* functions/classes, meaning that they are granted access to nonpublic members when they use objects of the class.

By controlling accessibility to members, class designers can distinguish between the interface of a class and its implementation. One common design choice often made by object-oriented programmers during class design is to hide the internal data structure of objects by making all data members private/protected, and including only member functions in the interface. Thus, programmers who use an existing class, such as the C++ standard library classes, will nearly always be applying member functions to class objects, rather than directly accessing the internal data of those objects. Designing classes in this way tends to promote long-term stability, allowing internal data structures to change with system changes (e.g., hardware, operating system) while the original interface to the object is supported.

Member functions also have certain characteristics not associated with regular C++ functions. Member functions qualified as **const** do not change any data in the object to which they are applied. Member functions qualified as **static** are not applied to any particular object, making them roughly equivalent to regular C++ functions declared in a namespace.

Every C++ class has one or more constructor functions, used to initialize objects when they are created, and a single destructor function. If no constructor function is explicitly defined, two public constructors—one taking no arguments and one doing a byte-by-byte copy of an object of the same type—are implicitly defined. As soon as the programmer defines any constructor, the implicit default constructor ceases to be available. Constructor functions can be identified by virtue of the fact that they have the same name as the class itself, and no return values. These constructors can be used both in standard declarations and in dynamic memory allocation by supplying arguments in parentheses. Only a default constructor—a constructor that takes no arguments—can be used to allocate dynamic arrays of objects.

The destructor function for a class takes no arguments and is normally defined to perform cleanup operations, such as releasing dynamic memory allocated by the class itself and closing any open files. An implicit destructor that does nothing is defined if none is specified by the programmer. Destructor functions are not called explicitly, but instead get called as a side effect of operations such as deletion and variables going out of scope.

In designing object-oriented applications or systems, the unified modeling language (UML) is sometimes used. This language consists of a variety of diagrams that can be used to describe application structure, activities, and system organization. A common UML diagram is the basic class diagram, which identifies the data and function members of a class, along with their access specification (i.e., public, private, protected). FlowC can be used to create rudimentary basic class diagrams.

In the course of explaining the basic approach to encapsulation provided by C++, a number of recommendations for designing object-oriented applications were illustrated:

- *Think encapsulated:* The best C++ classes are designed as self-contained units.

- *Differentiate between interface and implementation:* Use the public/protected access specifiers to make it clear what is internal to the class and what is available to programmers using the class.

- *Design your classes as if the implementation could change at any minute:* In an "ideal" class, you can protect all your data, making only member functions part of the interface.

- *Use naming conventions to reduce cognitive strain:* Simple things, such as beginning member variable names with m_ and data type abbreviations can dramatically reduce the amount of thinking you need to do when you are programming.

- *Design your classes so the compiler can help you find errors:* Capabilities that C++ offers, such as the const qualifier, can require some thought and their use may even slow down the initial writing of code, but they provide a long-term payback as complexity grows.

13.7.2: GLOSSARY

accessor functions Member functions specifically designed to provide access to data members within the class

class A definition of the organization of an object, similar to a structure definition in C/C++, but typically including functions as well as data elements

const qualifier A keyword placed at the end of a member function's header declaration specifying that calling the function will not change object data

construct-oriented programming An approach to programming dominated by the use of branching and looping constructs. Programs organized in this fashion tend to rely heavily on the main() function

constructor function A function used to initialize an object when it is declared. In C++, such functions can be identified by virtue of the fact that they have the same name as the class, and no return value

copy constructor A constructor function that initializes the object being constructed by copying the data in another object

data member A member of a structure or class that defines data to be stored in all objects based upon that class

default constructor A constructor function used to create an object if no arguments are specified in the object's declaration

destructor function A function that is called whenever an object is released (e.g., goes out of scope, is deleted); normally performs cleanup operations such as releasing memory from managed data members and closing any associated file streams; in C++, such functions can be identified by the same name as the class, preceded by a tilde (~), and no return value

encapsulation The ability to combine data and code into a self-contained object

friend A function or class that is granted access to non-public members of another class as part of the declaration of the other class

function-oriented programming An approach to programming in which the primary means of organizing the program is based around the creation of self-contained functions; structured programming in C/C++ tends to be organized along these lines

implementation The internal construction of an object; of greatest interest to the object's designer

inheritance The ability to define new objects using existing objects as a starting point

interface The collection of data and function members associated with an object that is available to any programmer

using that object (much the way a user interface represents the set of tools provided for a user's interaction with an application); typically, an object's interface is the only part of a well-constructed object that is relevant to anyone not involved with the object's internal design

member function A function that is defined as part of a class and operates upon objects declared to be of that class, applied using the same . and -> operators that are used to access elements of structures

object-oriented programming An approach to programming in which the primary tool for organizing programs is the self-contained object, which allows data and functions to be encapsulated into a single unit

polymorphism The ability to define objects that respond to the same message (e.g., a command sent by another object) differently according to the nature of the receiving object

private class member A member of an object that cannot be altered by any other class or object, considered to be part of the object's implementation

protected class member A private member of an object that cannot be altered by any other class or object unless that class inherits it from the original class

public class member A member of an object that can be accessed by other objects, considered to be part of the object's interface

static qualifier A keyword placed before a member's declaration specifying that the data or function is shared by all objects in the class, and is not applicable to a single object (the way normal member functions and data are)

stub A function placed in a project as a placeholder, while the project is being programmed; normally stubs take the proper arguments used for the final function, but return a dummy value

unified modeling language (UML) A language consisting of a variety of diagrams that can be used to describe application structure, activities, and system organization

13.7.3: QUESTIONS

Questions 1–6 involve the creation of an encapsulated class to hold time values. The basic UML class diagram for the completed class is presented below.

Basic UML Diagram for Time Class

Class: Time
Data members:
double m_dTime
bool m_b24Hour
Function members:
+   Time()
+   Time(double dTime)
+   Time(int nHour,int nMinute,int nSecond,boolbPM=false)
+   int Hour() const
+   int Minute() const
+   int Second() const
+   bool AmPm() const
+   void AmPm(bool b12)
+   bool Pm() const
+   void GetTime(char szTime[]) const
+   bool SetTime (const char szTime[])
+   void SetToNow()
+$ static void CurrentTime(Time &timVal)

1. *Data and constructors.* Create a basic class containing two protected data members:

■   m_dTime should be a double whose decimal portion represents the percentage of the day complete (e.g., 0.3333 is 8 AM, 0.75 is 6 PM).

■   m_b24Hour is a Boolean value signifying whether hour values returned are on a 12-hour (AM/PM) or 24-hour clock.

Create three constructors, (1) a default constructor that initializes the time to 12 AM (i.e., 0.00), (2) a constructor that takes a double and assigns it to the m_dTime value, and (3) a constructor that computes the time fraction for an hour, minute, second combination that is passed in. If bPM is true, the hour should be interpreted as PM on the AM/PM setting, and m_b24Hour should be set to false. Otherwise, set m_b24Hour to true.

2. *AM/PM accessor functions.* Add a pair of accessor functions named AmPm for setting the value of m_b24Hour (which should be false if AmPm() is true).

3. *Some more accessor functions.* Add const qualified member functions that return the following values:

■   The hour associated with the m_dTime time value. *Note:* This value should never be greater than 12 if m_b24Hour is true. Otherwise, it should never be greater than 23. Also, note that when m_b24Hour is true, the hour value can be affected even in the AM time period (i.e., 12:30 AM).

■   The minute associated with the current time (0 to 59).

■   The second associated with the current time (0 to 59).

■   Pm() is set to true if the hour is returned using the AM/PM system and it is a PM value.

4. *Getting a time string.* Write a function GetTime() that takes the current time and places it, in text form, in a buffer that is passed in. You should format the string according to whether a 24-hour clock is used. (*Hint:* This function is definitely an occasion where sprintf is quite convenient.)

5. *In-depth: Setting a time string.* Write a function SetTime() that takes a sting containing the time (e.g., "3:00:45 PM"), determines its fractional value, then uses that to set the value of m_dTime. (*Hint:* This task is not as hard as it sounds if you use the Tokenize() function introduced in Chapter 10, Section 10.5.2.) The function should return false if it cannot interpret the time string passed in.

6. *In-depth: Getting system time.* Write a static member function, CurrentTime(), that retrieves the system time, then translates it into a Time object (passed in as an object reference). Also use that function within a member function SetToNow() that sets the time value of the object to which it is applied to the current time. To access the system time, the basic approach is as follows:

■   Include <time.h> in your source file.

■   To get the time, write the following code:

```
time_t theTime=time(NULL);
struct tm *pTm, tmData;
pTm=localtime(&theTime);
// Copying data from static
//structure
tmData=(*pTm);
```

■   Use the Visual Studio .NET system to find out more about the tm structure(its elements are presented in Example 13.26). This structure contains the information you will need to determine your time value.

EXAMPLE 13.26

tm Structure Definition

```
struct tm {
int tm_sec; /* seconds after the minute - [0,59] */
int tm_min; /* minutes after the hour - [0,59] */
int tm_hour; /* hours since midnight - [0,23] */
int tm_mday; /* day of the month - [1,31] */
int tm_year; /* years since 1900 */
int tm_wday; /* days since Sunday - [0,6] */
int tm_yday; /* days since January 1 - [0,365] */
int tm_isdst; /* daylight savings time flag */
 };
```

Note: After reading about the functions available in time.h, you may decide to change how you implement your GetTime() and SetTime() functions.

Questions 7–10 involve creating an encapsulated Date class. The basic UML class diagram for this class follows.

Basic UML Class Diagram for Date Class

Class: Date
Data members:
unsigned long m_nDate
Function members:
+   Date()
+   Date(int nY,int nM,int nD)
+   int Month() const
+   void Month(int nM)
+   int Day() const
+   void Day(int nD)
+   int Year() const
+   void Year(int nY)
+   int JulianDate() const
+   void GetDate(char szTarget[],int nFormat) const
+   bool SetDate(const char * szDate)
+   int DaysBetween(Date &dateVal) const
+   void SetToToday()
+$ static bool LegalDate(int nY,int nM,int nD)

7. *Data, constructors, and accessors.* Create a basic Date class containing a protected member m_nDate, and unsigned integer specifying the date in the form YYYYMMDD (e.g., 23 July 2004 would be 20040723). As shown in Figure 13.7, create two constructors and accessor pairs for Month(), Day(), and Year().

8. *LegalDate function.* Create a static LegalDate() member that returns true unless a specific year, month, day combination is not legal. Naturally, the challenge with this function is identifying leap years, because it changes what is legal for February. Use the following rule:

- If a year is divisible by 400, it is a leap year.
- Otherwise, if it is divisible by 100 it is *not* a leap year.
- Otherwise, if it is divisible by 4 it is a leap year.
- Otherwise, it is not a leap year.

You may want to call this function in your constructor and other accessor functions to ensure that invalid dates are not set.

9. *JulianDate() and DaysBetween() members.* Write a member function that computes the Julian date (i.e., numeric value of the day, where 1 Jan is 1, 2 Jan is 2, 1 Feb is 32, etc.) for a particular day. Once this function is complete, create a DaysBetween() function that returns the number of days between the object date and the functions argument, returning the value as an integer.

10. *In-depth: GetDate(), SetDate(), and SetToToday() functions.* Write functions modeled after the GetTime(), SetTime(), and SetToNow() functions in the Time class (Questions 4–6). For your GetDate() function, define at least two different string formats for the date, which can be passed in using the second argument (nFormat). Your SetDate() function should be able to successfully interpret both formats.

Questions 11 and 12 involve designing your own classes around loosely specified guidelines. They assume completion of Questions 1–10 (although the design portion can be done without actually implementing the Time and Date classes).

11. *Create a DateTime class.* Design and implement a class that composes a Date and Time object. It should not contain any public data members. (*Hint:* Much of the work on this class will involve writing simple accessor functions.)

12. *Create a TimeSpan class.* This class should hold a double value, expressed in days and fractional days, that is computed when either Date, Time, or DateTime objects are subtracted from each other.

Operator Overloading

EXECUTIVE SUMMARY

Chapter 14 examines the rather unique capability that C++ provides for defining operators. Used appropriately, operator overloading can improve code clarity and speed the process of coding. Used excessively, it can render the programmer's code nearly incomprehensible. Although most operator overloading can be done at the discretion of the programmer, one type of overload—overloading the assignment operator—is virtually mandated in many programming situations. For this reason, we cannot ignore operator overloading.

The chapter begins by showing the mechanics of operator overloading, both within a class and outside it. We then explore assignment operator overloads—the most critical overload—in some detail. In doing so, we also discuss the copy constructor, which is virtually always defined in conjunction with the assignment operator. We then proceed through a series of progressively more complex examples, beginning with an overload of the insertion and extraction operators, followed by an overload of the bracket operator used to create a void pointer array class. Finally, we develop a fully functional encapsulated NUL terminated string class, called the GString class, which overloads almost a dozen different operators (including a type cast). These final exercises are particularly intended to provide the reader with insights into the nature of the **standard template library (STL)** classes, which we explore in greater depth in Chapter 15.

LEARNING OBJECTIVES

Upon completing this chapter, you should be able to:

- Explain the relationship of the functional notation for operators—adopted in Chapter 4—to operator overloading
- Create overloads for binary operators
- Create overloads for unary operators, including the type cast
- Discuss the specific challenges faced when overloading the assignment operator
- Explain the relationship between the assignment operator and the copy constructor and how they can be implemented together
- Explain how a bracket overload can make an object look like an array
- Overload the operators necessary to make a NUL terminated string class look like a string object in other programming languages

14.1: OVERLOADING AN OPERATOR

 Walkthrough available in Overload.wmv

In this section, we consider why operator overloading can be a useful programming technique, then consider the mechanics involved with such overloading. The functional form we adopted for describing operators in Chapter 4 will facilitate our discussion of the latter topic.

14.1.1: Why Overload Operators?

To set up the operator overload problem, let's define a simple class called MyInt that has a single data member—an integer. This class is presented in Example 14.1, along with a main() function that attempts to add two MyInt objects together.

Not surprisingly, when we tried to compile this program, the compiler had some harsh words for us:

```
C2784: 'std::reverse_iterator<_RanIt> std::operator
       +(_Diff,const std::reverse_iterator<_RanIt> &)' : could
       not deduce template argument for 'const
       std::reverse_iterator<_RanIt> &' from 'MyInt'
C2784:'std::_Ptrit<_Ty,_Diff,_Pointer,_Reference,_Pointer2,_Reference2>
       std::operator +(_Diff,const
       std::_Ptrit<_Ty,_Diff,_Pointer,_Reference,_Pointer2,_Reference2>
       &)' : could not deduce template argument for 'const
       std::_Ptrit<_Ty,_Diff,_Pointer,_Reference,_Pointer2,_Reference2>
       &' from 'MyInt'
C2676: binary '+' : 'MyInt' does not define this operator or a
       conversion to a type acceptable to the predefined operator
```

(At least, they would probably be harsh if we could make any sense of them at all.)

EXAMPLE 14.1

MyInt class and attempt to apply it in main()

```
class MyInt
{
public:
    MyInt(void){m_nInt=0;}
    MyInt(int nVal){m_nInt=nVal;}
    ~MyInt(void){};

    int Value() const {return m_nInt;}

protected:
    int m_nInt;
};

int main(int argc,char *argv[])
{
    MyInt m1(7),m2(5),m3;
    m3=m1+m2;
    return 0;
}
```

In effect, what the compiler is telling us is that even though we may "understand" what should happen when you add two MyInt structures together, the compiler certainly doesn't. Fixing this type of problem is what operator overloading is all about.

If a one-word justification for the necessity of overloading operators in C++ were required, the word would be *strings*. Up to this point, we have been forced to use a number of distinctly programmer-hostile functions every time we wanted to work with text data, including:

- *strcpy* or *strdup*, every time we really wanted to say String1=String2
- strcmp, every time we wanted to test if String1>String2 or String1==String2 or String1<=String3 and so forth
- strcat, every time we really wanted to write String1+String2

Most languages supply built-in support for **string objects** (as opposed to NUL terminated strings)—meaning these operators can be applied to strings as part of the language. In C++, however, we need operator overloading to achieve the same effect.

The benefits of operator overloading are not entirely limited to implementing strings, however. Our ability to overload the assignment operator, for example, can be used to fine-tune how we manage memory and how our classes can be used. These benefits, however, are mainly relevant to advanced programming.

The "big picture" is that if a language supplies a nice set of built-in operators for handling strings, it probably doesn't need to support operator overloads.

14.1.2: Regular Operator Overloads

Regular operator overloads—overloads that are not defined within a class—use the same functional form we introduced in Chapter 4. For instance, in the MyInt class of Example 14.1, it is reasonable that when we add two MyInt objects together, we would like to return a third object with the m_nInt members of the two original objects added together. Written as a function, it would look like the following:

```
MyInt operator+(const MyInt &v1,const MyInt &v2) {
    MyInt v3;
    v3.m_nInt=v1.m_nInt+v2.m_nInt;
    return v3;
}
```

What we are saying here is the following:

- When we add two MyInt objects together, a third MyInt object will be returned.
- The addition does not change the arguments on either side (which is why it makes sense to make them const references—although just making copies also would have worked).
- The returned MyInt object will have an m_nInt member equal to the sum of the m_nInt members of the two arguments.

Now, at this point it is reasonable to be a bit skeptical. After all, should we be using the + operator (inside the function) when the whole purpose is to overload the + operator? The answer is a resounding yes. The + operator used inside the function adds two elements that hold integer values—and, of course, adding integers is a capability that is built into C++. The + operator we just overloaded, on the other hand, allows us to add two MyInt objects—something that C++ would be clueless about otherwise.

It gets even better, however. Working with MyInt objects might be a bit of a pain, so perhaps we should be able to add integers to them directly. Doing so, it turns out, is easy. Just overload the + operator a few more times and mix int values and MyInt values, as shown in Example 14.2.

<u>**TEST YOUR UNDERSTANDING 14.1:**</u>

Why do the three operator overloads need to be defined as friend functions?

EXAMPLE 14.2

MyInt with overloaded + operators and main() function

```
class MyInt
{
public:
    MyInt(void){m_nInt=0;}
    MyInt(int nVal){m_nInt=nVal;}
    ~MyInt(void){};

    int Value() const {return m_nInt;}
    friend MyInt operator+(const MyInt &v1,const MyInt &v2) {
        MyInt v3;
        v3.m_nInt=v1.m_nInt+v2.m_nInt;
        return v3;
    }
    friend MyInt operator+(const MyInt &v1,int n2) {
        MyInt v3;
        v3.m_nInt=v1.m_nInt+n2;
        return v3;
    }
    friend MyInt operator+(int n1,const MyInt &v2) {
        MyInt v3;
        v3.m_nInt=n1+v2.m_nInt;
        return v3;
    }

protected:
    int m_nInt;
};

int main(int argc,char *argv[])
{
    MyInt m1(7),m2(5),m3,m4,m5;
    m3=m1+m2;
    m4=m3+9;
    m5=2+m4;
    return 0;
}
```

The fact that three overloads, and not four, need to be defined when mixing MyInt and primitive data elements is worth considering. Looking at the three overloads, we see:

```
MyInt operator+(const MyInt &v1,const MyInt &v2);
MyInt operator+(const MyInt &v1,int n2);
MyInt operator+(int n1,const MyInt &v2);
```

Looking at these overloads, we see the missing combination is:

```
MyInt operator+(int n1,int n2);
```

The problems that allowing such an overload would cause should be immediately evident. If allowed, everywhere in your program where two integers were added, a MyInt object would immediately be produced. The situation would get ugly fast.

In fact, C++ prevents you from doing a number of overloads, including the following:

- Overloads that would change the behavior of any of the built-in operators when applied to primitives
- Overloads involving operators that aren't predefined in C++ (i.e., you can't invent your own operators)
- Overloads that would really screw up the language, such as the . operator for selecting members and the scope resolution operator (::)

In addition, you cannot alter operator precedence. This restriction can make some overloads inconvenient—requiring strange use of parentheses to apply the overloaded operator.

For the most part, the operators most commonly overloaded as regular functions are:

- **Insertion** (<<) and **extraction** (>>) in the context of sending objects to and from streams
- Test operators (particularly == and !=) used to compare objects from the same or related classes

Examples of both types of overload for the MyInt class are presented in Example 14.3. The insertion/extraction overloads allow a MyInt object to be saved to a SimpleIO stream using the << operator, or read from the stream using a >> operator. Because we use the same operators for normal I/O in C++, overloading these operators makes perfect sense. Similarly, the ability to compare two objects for equality applies to most objects.

Other operators (such as arithmetic operators) can, of course, be overloaded. The main issue here is one of whether the overload reduces, or adds to, confusion. What would it mean, for example, to overload the multiplication operator for two employee objects? Thus, operator overloading should be limited to situations with a reasonably natural interpretation of what the overload is supposed to be doing.

14.1.3: Class Member Operator Overloads

In addition to using regular or friend functions to overload operators, it is also possible to overload operators as member functions. In fact, some operators (such as the assignment operator) need to be overloaded in this way.

When defining member overloads, one less argument is normally required in the function header, because the object being operated on is implicitly available. For example,

---

EXAMPLE 14.3

MyInt stream and test overloads

```
STREAM &operator<<(STREAM &out,const MyInt &val)
{
    WriteInteger(out,val.m_nInt);
    return out;
}

STREAM &operator>>(STREAM &in,MyInt &val)
{
    val.m_nInt=ReadInteger(in);
    return in;
}

bool operator==(const MyInt &v1,const MyInt &v2) {
    return (v1.m_nInt==v2.m_nInt);
}
bool operator==(const MyInt &v1,int n2) {
    return (v1.m_nInt==n2);
}
bool operator==(int n1,const MyInt &v2) {
    return (n1==v2.m_nInt);
}
```

---

if we wanted to make our subtraction (−) operator overload a class member, it could be defined as follows:

```
MyInt operator-(const MyInt &v1) {
    MyInt v3;
    v3.m_nInt=m_nInt-v1.m_nInt;
    return v3;
}
```

In this case, in the following code fragment:

```
MyInt a1(5),a2(2),a3;
a3=a1-a2;
```

the subtraction would effectively be equivalent to the call:

```
a3=a1.operator-(a2);
```

In fact, the expression a1.operator-(a2) will compile and run properly (amazingly enough). Using the functional form instead of the operator form in actual code would, however, be considered an odd programming practice.

One disadvantage of making binary operators a class member is that it limits your ability to mix data types on either side. For example, even though we defined three overloads for our + operator, our − operator is limited to two overloads:

```
MyInt MyInt::operator-(const MyInt &v1);
MyInt MyInt::operator-(int n1);
```

The effect of this would be that we can't subtract a MyInt object from an integer. For this reason, we normally define binary member functions outside of the class.

Increment/Decrement Operators   As first mentioned in Chapter 4, the increment and decrement operators are a bit tricky because they can appear on either side of the object they are applied to. For example:

```
x1++
++x1
```

To address this problem, the postfix version of the overload function is given an extra argument (of type int) for the sole purposes of distinguishing it from the prefix version, as illustrated in the overload definitions shown in Example 14.4.

The other difference between prefix and postfix overloads is that the prefix overload can return a reference to the original object (because the return value is made available after the increment takes place), which requires the use of the **this** pointer. It also allows a prefix increment to be used on the left-hand side of an assignment, as shown in the last line of the following code fragment:

```
MyInt i1(10),i2(10),i3,i4,i5(25);
i3=i1++;
i4=++i2;
++i5=i1;
```

The fact that the code is legal, however, does not mean that it is particularly useful, because the assignment will wipe out the value just incremented, as well as rendering the code completely opaque.

TEST YOUR UNDERSTANDING 14.2:

What are the values for the m_nInt members of i1, i2, i3, i4, and i5 going to be after the preceding code fragment executes?

Type Cast Operator   Another operator normally overloaded as a member is the type cast operator. The syntax for the overload is a bit odd, as what follows the operator keyword also serves as the return type. For example, we could overload the (int) type cast for MyInt (within the class declaration) as follows:

```
operator int () const {
    return m_nInt;
}
```

EXAMPLE 14.4

Prefix and postfix increment operator overloads

```
MyInt &MyInt::operator++() {
    m_nInt++;
    return *this;
}

MyInt MyInt::operator++(int) {
    MyInt r;
    r.m_nInt=m_nInt;
    m_nInt++;
    return r;
}
```

With this type cast in place, we could use a MyInt object virtually anywhere that an int would normally be used. For example:

```
MyInt t1(50);
int nVal=t1;
```

would compile and, when run, would result in nVal being set to 50.

TEST YOUR UNDERSTANDING 14.3:

Explain how nVal becomes 50 in the preceding code fragment.

14.1: SECTION QUESTIONS

1. Explain the two ways you could rewrite the + overload of two MyInt objects so it did not have to be a friend.
2. Why must you understand classes before operator overloading becomes useful?
3. What operator overloads should be applicable if it makes sense to sort a class (e.g., to perform binary search)?
4. Why wasn't the operator==overload, presented in Section 14.1.2, declared as const?
5. Explain why the **this** pointer may be needed in some operator overloads.
6. Why is it generally better to pass const references as arguments for operator overloads than actual objects?

14.2: ASSIGNMENT OPERATORS AND COPY CONSTRUCTORS

 Walkthrough available in CopyAndAssign.wmv

In many situations in a C++ program, a copy of an object is made. Examples include the following:

- When an assignment operation takes place
- When an object is created by initializing it to another object
- When an object is passed into a function
- When a function returns an object
- When an object is composed within another object being copied or assigned

Because copying is so common, the compiler automatically creates a copy constructor and an assignment operator for a class in most circumstances. The problem is, the versions it creates are often so flawed that they are counterproductive. As a result, the programmer must often write copy constructors and assignment overloads.

14.2.1: A Copying Problem

To illustrate the problem caused by improperly defined copying, we design a simple class to manage a NUL terminated string that will become the basis of the lab exercise in Section 14.4. This class is presented in Example 14.5.

The class manages a character pointer buffer, m_pBuf, that points to a NUL terminated string. It consists of the following:

- Two constructor functions: a default constructor and one that initializes the string

---

EXAMPLE 14.5

The GString00 class

```
class GString00
{
public:
    GString00(void) {
        m_pBuf=0;
    }
    GString00(const char *szVal) {
        m_pBuf=0;
        Set(szVal);
    }
    ~GString00(void) {
        delete [] m_pBuf;
    }
    void Display() const {
        if (m_pBuf) DisplayString(m_pBuf);
        else DisplayString("(Null)");
    }
    void Set(const char *szVal) {
        delete [] m_pBuf;
        m_pBuf=new char[strlen(szVal)+1];
        strcpy(m_pBuf,szVal);
    }
protected:
    char *m_pBuf;
};
```

- A destructor function that releases the buffer when the object is destroyed
- A Display() member that uses SimpleIO to display the string value
- A Set() member that deletes the existing buffer, then allocates memory for a new one

At face value, the class seems perfectly reasonable. But run the code in Example 14.6 and the output in Figure 14.1 appears, followed immediately by an assertion failure. What is the problem?

The behavior of the program initially seems to defy the laws of logic. Stepping through it in the debugger, you would find that the TestSet() function seems to work perfectly (as is evident from the output in Figure 14.1) and yet when we return from the function, the str variable has been corrupted. This result is particularly surprising when we called TestSet() and str was passed in by value—so nothing we did inside the function should have affected it.

Welcome to the world of bad copies! What actually happened is as follows:

- When the function was called, str was passed in by value—and we did not define a copy constructor—so the implicit copy constructor was used to make a copy for use within the function. The implicit copy was, byte-for-byte, the same as str, meaning that we then had two copies of the GString00 object that pointed to the same buffer.

EXAMPLE 14.6

Main and TestSet() function

```
int main(int argc,char *argv[])
{
    GString00 str("Hello World");
    TestSet(str,"It\'s a new world!");
    str.Display();
}

void TestSet(GString00 str,const char *pStr)
{
    DisplayString("Old value: ");
    str.Display();
    NewLine();
    str.Set(pStr);
    DisplayString("New value: ");
    str.Display();
    NewLine();

}
```

FIGURE 14.1   Output From Example 14.6

- Within the function everything worked fine except for one thing: when we called SetAt() we deleted the old buffer (which, unfortunately was the buffer that the str in main() still pointed to).
- When we called str.Display() in main, it pointed to the corrupted buffer—leading to the peculiar display and the assertion failure.

At this point, we could easily blame our call to Set() within the TestSet() function. To see whether this call format was really the problem, we comment it out and rerun the code with the functions shown in Example 14.7.

The result? Exactly the same output (excepting the "It's a new world!" part) followed by the same crash! This sequence seems really odd, because we didn't call any function that could have modified str. Or, at least, that's what we think.

The explanation is as follows:

- As noted previously, the local copy of str in TestFunction() pointed to the same buffer as the version of str in main.

EXAMPLE 14.7

Revised test code

```
int main(int argc,char *argv[])
{
    GString00 str("Hello World");
    TestSet(str,"It\'s a new world!");
    str.Display();
}

void TestSet(GString00 str,const char *pStr)
{
    DisplayString("Old value: ");
    str.Display();
    NewLine();
//  str.Set(pStr);
//  DisplayString("New value: ");
//  str.Display();
//  NewLine();

}
```

- When we returned from TestSet(), the destructor was called on the local object—as always happens when local variables go out of scope. The result: our hapless buffer was deleted by the destructor function, instead of by Set().
- When we returned to main(), str again pointed to memory that had been released.

So, how do we solve this problem? We need to write our own **copy constructor**—one that makes a duplicate copy of the buffer instead of duplicating the address in m_pBuf. For reasons we will see shortly, it is convenient to do this task with two functions (although it could easily be done in one). These functions are shown in Example 14.8.

As soon as the compiler sees a constructor function with a single reference to a const object of the type being constructed, its implicit copy constructor is discarded. What *our* copy constructor does is to set m_pBuf to 0 (to ensure we don't try to delete an uninitialized pointer), then it calls Set(), which makes a copy of the buffer. When we pass an object with this copy constructor into SetTest(), the copy within SetTest() has its own buffer—a

---

EXAMPLE 14.8

Copy constructor and Copy() member

```
GString00(const GString00 &str) {
    m_pBuf=0;
    Copy(str);
}
void Copy(const GString00 &str) {
    Set(str.m_pBuf);
}
```

---

copy of the original buffer—to play with, so nothing that happens within the function will affect the str object in main().

So, when do you need to define your own copy constructor? The general rule for implicit copy constructors is as follows:

- If composed objects have their own copy constructors, these constructors are used.
- If they do not, a byte-by-byte copy is made.

Some circumstances under which implicit copy constructors are not generated are difficult to keep track of (e.g., if any composed member has a private or protected copy constructor).

For practical purposes, almost any time your class members call **new** and **delete** to manage embedded data, if you want a copy made, you need to write your own copy constructor. And, chances are, you will need one:

- If you intend to pass objects into functions or return them from functions (pointers and references don't require copy constructors, however)
- If you intend to place them in collections, such as the vector template, discussed in Chapter 15
- If you intend to initialize them with other objects
- If you intend to assign them to other objects using an assignment operator overload

We now turn to the last of these situations.

14.2.2: Overloading the Assignment Operator

Because assignment and copying are similar, it stands to reason that once a copy constructor has been defined, the **assignment operator** definition will be similar. In fact, if you put the major copying work into some function (that we have chosen to call Copy() here), you can just call that function from both places. In fact, it is tempting to define the GString00 assignment operator as follows:

```
const GString00 &GString00::operator=(const GString00 &rhs){
    Copy(rhs);
    return *this;
}
```

This particular function will work nearly all of the time. But one problem can make it fail. Consider, for example, the code in Example 14.9, which produces the output in Figure 14.2.

Tracing the two bad output lines, we find the problem is in a2 and pb. As it happens, these variables refer to the same object. With the line of code:

```
*pb=a2;
```

we were, in effect, writing a2=a2 (which would have led to the same problem). The source of the difficulty is as follows:

- When an object is assigned to itself, the Set() function is called with a pointer to the same buffer that is to be modified.
- That buffer is immediately deleted, which corrupts it.
- When memory is allocated, we are just making a copy of corrupted memory of indeterminate length—which is not good.

EXAMPLE 14.9

main() and TestAssign functions

```
int main(int argc,char *argv[])
{
    GString00 str("Hello World");
    TestSet(str,"It\'s a new world!");
    str.Display();
    TestAssign();
}

void TestAssign()
{
    GString00 a1("Hello!"),a2("World"),a3,a4,a5;
    GString00 *pa=&a1,*pb=&a2;
    a3=a1;
    a4=a2;
    a5=*pa;
    *pb=a2;
    NewLine();
    DisplayString("Assignment Results:");
    NewLine();
    a1.Display();
    NewLine();
    a2.Display();
    NewLine();
    a3.Display();
    NewLine();
    a4.Display();
    NewLine();
    pa->Display();
    pb->Display();
}
```

FIGURE 14.2   Assignment Failure Output When Running Code in Example 14.9

Two ways of handling this problem are a thoughtful way and a simple mechanical way that works for virtually every assignment overload. The "thoughtful" way involves changing the Set() function so the copy is made before the deletion occurs. Unfortunately, it does not generalize well to other assignment situations.

The simple mechanical way involves testing to see whether a self-assignment is being made and, if it is, simply returning. This test could be implemented as follows:

```
const GString00 &GString00::operator=(const GString00 &rhs){
    if (this==&rhs) return *this;
    Copy(rhs);
    return *this;
}
```

The & operator, applied to a reference, gives the address of the referenced object, which means we are not self-assigning *unless* the address of the reference matches the **this** pointer. Furthermore, if a Copy() function has been written, this particular overload can be used for almost any class. And, of course, with the modification our test code now runs flawlessly.

14.2.3: General Framework for Assignment and Copy Constructors

Combining what we found in Sections 14.2.1 and 14.2.2, we can propose a general skeleton that can be used for virtually all assignment/copy constructor overloads:

- Write a function Copy() that does the appropriate element-by-element copying. Its prototype should be as follows:

    ```
    void Copy(const ClassName &ref);
    ```

- Use the following framework for the copy constructor:

    ```
    ClassName::ClassName(const ClassName &ref)
    {
        // initialize any pointers that might be deleted to 0
        Copy(ref);
    }
    ```

- Use the following framework for the assignment operator overload:

    ```
    ClassName &ClassName::operator=(const ClassName &ref)
    {
        if (this==&ref) return *this;
        Copy(ref);
        return *this;
    }
    ```

Finally, if you *don't* want a copy constructor defined (e.g., because you see no need for your complex object ever to be copied), place an empty copy constructor as a private or protected member. Doing so prevents an implicit copy constructor from being used (and the compiler will give you an error if you accidentally try to copy your object).

14.2: SECTION QUESTIONS

1. Would the problems initially encountered with TestSet() have occurred if we had passed str in as a reference?

2. If constructor problems are encountered, can they be solved by eliminating the delete operations in the destructor function?

3. What is the principal pitfall of implementing assignment overloads?

4. What is the main benefit of having an assignment overload return a reference to the object being assigned?

5. What makes understanding assignment overloads particularly important?

6. Why does it make sense to always overload both the assignment operator and copy constructor if you are going to overload either one?

14.3: OPERATOR OVERLOADING DEMONSTRATIONS

In this section we will walk through two operator overloading examples. Both involve building on previously developed classes. The first is a simple insertion/extraction overload for employee objects—complicated by the lack of a copy constructor. The second involves the creation of a fully functional encapsulated void pointer array class—demonstrating an overload of the [] (bracket) operator.

14.3.1: Adding Operators to Employee Objects

Walkthrough available in EmployeeOps.wmv

In Chapter 13, Sections 13.6.1 and 13.6.2, we walked through the encapsulation of *employee* objects and an *EmpData* class to manage a collection of employees. In doing so, we glossed over some rather awkward code.

Assignment and Copy Constructor Overload For example, in the EmpData::AddEmployee() member (originally presented in Example 13.23, presented here in Example 14.10), when we appended the new employee to the array, the code was the following:

```
emp.Id(nId);
emp.Input();
m_arEmp[m_nCount].Copy(emp);
m_nCount++;
bvalid=true;
```

In the line:

```
m_arEmp[m_nCount].Copy(emp);
```

what we really wanted to write was:

```
m_arEmp[m_nCount]=emp;
```

To write the clearer version, however, we need an assignment operator overload.

As it turns out, inserting an assignment operator is prodigiously easy to do, because we had the foresight to write a Copy() function already. All we need to do is follow the pattern presented in Section 14.2.3, as shown in Example 14.11.

Because the employee class, as implemented in Chapter 13, Section 13.6.1, stored names in arrays declared within the class, it has no member pointers that need to be set to 0 in the copy constructor. (Overloading assignment and copy constructors for the EmpData class are left as part of an end-of-chapter exercise.)

EXAMPLE 14.10

EmpData::AddEmployee function

```
void EmpData::AddEmployee()
{
    employee emp;
    bool bvalid=false;
    while(!bvalid) {
        unsigned int nId=PromptForId();
        if (FindEmployee(nId)>=0) {
            char buf[MAXLINE];
            DisplayString("ID that you entered already exists. Try again? (Y or N): ");
            InputString(buf);
            if (toupper(buf[0])=='N') bvalid=true;
        }
        else {
            emp.Id(nId);
            emp.Input();
            m_arEmp[m_nCount].Copy(emp);
            m_nCount++;
            bvalid=true;
        }
    }
}
```

EXAMPLE 14.11

Employee copy constructor and assignment overload

```
employee(const employee &emp) {
    Copy(emp);
}
const employee &operator=(const employee &emp) {
    if (&emp==this) return *this;
    Copy(emp);
    return *this;
}
```

Insertion/Extraction Overloads   By making a practice of overloading the >> and << operators for binary loading and saving of any objects we intend to serialize, we can eliminate the mental strain of remembering "What did we call that function?"

Insertion/extraction overloads have to be done outside our class, because common practice dictates the stream object will always be on the left when these operators are applied (which means that a class member overload would need to be done in the stream object's class, whatever that is).

TEST YOUR UNDERSTANDING 14.4:

Explain why a member overload, as opposed to a regular function overload, would have to be in the stream class.

As a first attempt, we simply try a naïve overload along the following lines:

```
STREAM operator>>(STREAM in,employee &emp) {
    emp.Load(in);
    return in;
}
STREAM operator<<(STREAM out,employee &emp) {
    emp.Load(out);
    return out;
}
```

When we try these overloads, however, we get the following error message from the compiler:

```
error C2558: class 'std::basic_fstream<_Elem,_Traits>' : no
copy constructor available or copy constructor is declared
'explicit'
    with
    [
        _Elem=char,
        _Traits=std::char_traits<char>
    ]
```

The specifics of the message become (slightly) clearer after we talk about C++ I/O in Chapter 17. For now, however, what should catch our eyes are the words "copy constructor." What the message says, in effect, is that we cannot copy a STREAM object that is passed into a function or returned from a function.

How do we address this problem? If we look back to Example 14.3, we discover we already have the answer. Because references don't involve making copies, we can pass in and return references. The modified overloads are:

```
STREAM &operator>>(STREAM &in,employee &emp) {
    emp.Load(in);
    return in;
}
STREAM &operator<<(STREAM &out,employee &emp) {
    emp.Load(out);
    return out;
}
```

What is particularly remarkable about this process is that we can do it having no idea how STREAM objects are implemented.

14.3.2: The PtrArray class

Walkthrough available in PtrArray.wmv

In Chapter 12, Section 12.4, we implemented a structure that managed a dynamic array of void pointers. As an "array," however, it had a big disadvantage—you couldn't access elements using the [] operators.

In this walkthrough, we create a PtrArray class that encapsulates our DynArray structure and overloads the [] and assignment operators. The resulting class has an interface nearly identical to that of the CPtrArray that is provided as part of the **Microsoft Foundation Classes (MFC)**. It also provides a useful starting point for understanding the vector<> template, introduced in Chapter 15.

Declaration   The declaration of the class is presented in Example 14.12.

Interface   The class interface is reminiscent of the DynArray application—intentionally so. The main changes include the following:

- A default and copy constructor are added, along with a destructor.
- A Copy() function and assignment overload are provided.
- Two overloads of the bracket operator are provided—for use in const and non-const operations.
- A RemoveAll() function is added, to clean out the array.
- The ReallocArray() function is protected—meaning we don't want programmers to call it directly (which is fine, because the public SetSize() accomplishes the same purpose).

In addition, two functions were removed: CreateDynArray() and FreeDynArray(). They are no longer needed as a result of the available constructors and destructors.

The test functions—using the old DynArray structure from Chapter 12, Example 12.5—and one for the PtrArray class are contrasted in Example 14.13. These two functions produce identical output.

Of particular interest in comparing DynArrayDemo() and PtrArrayDemo() is how much cleaner the latter is. Two aspects of the code, in particular, are much more convenient:

- We don't need to explicitly allocate and free PtrArray objects—the constructor and destructor do that for us.

EXAMPLE 14.12

PtrArray class declaration

```
class PtrArray
{
public:
    PtrArray();
    PtrArray(const PtrArray &ar);
    ~PtrArray();
    const PtrArray &operator=(const PtrArray &ar);
    void Copy(const PtrArray &ar);
    void *&operator[](int);
    void *&operator[](int) const;
    void *GetAt(int i) const;
    void SetAt(int i,void *pData);
    void Add(void *pData);
    void InsertAt(int i,void *pData);
    void SetSize(int i);
    int GetSize() const;
    void RemoveAt(int i);
    void RemoveAll();
protected:
    int m_nCount;
    int m_nSize;
    void **m_pData;
    void ReallocArray(int nNewSize);
};
```

EXAMPLE 14.13

DynArray and PtrArray test functions

```
void DynArrayDemo()
{
    int i;
    struct DynArray *pD=CreateDynArray();
    Add(pD,"Hello");
    Add(pD,"World!");
    Add(pD,"me");
    for(i=0;i<pD->nSize;i++) {
        DisplayFormatted("%s ",(char *)GetAt(pD,i));
    }
    NewLine();
    InsertAt(pD,"It\'s",2);
    for(i=0;i<pD->nSize;i++) {
        PrintFormatted("%s ",(char *)GetAt(pD,i));
    }
    NewLine();
    RemoveAt(pD,1);
    for(i=0;i<pD->nSize;i++) {
        DisplayFormatted("%s ",(char *)GetAt(pD,i));
    }
    NewLine();
    SetAt(pD,"I",2);
    for(i=0;i<pD->nSize;i++) {
        DisplayFormatted("%s ",(char *)GetAt(pD,i));
    }
    NewLine();
    FreeDynArray(pD);
}

void PtrArrayDemo()
{
    int i;
    class PtrArray ar;
    ar.Add("Hello");
    ar.Add("World!");
    ar.Add("me");
    for(i=0;i<ar.GetSize();i++) {
        DisplayFormatted("%s ",(char *)ar[i]);
    }
    NewLine();
    ar.InsertAt(2,"It\s");
    for(i=0;i<ar.GetSize();i++) {
        DisplayFormatted("%s ",(char *)ar[i]);
    }
    NewLine();
    ar.RemoveAt(1);
    for(i=0;i<ar.GetSize();i++) {
        DisplayFormatted("%s ",(char *)ar[i]);
    }
    NewLine();
    ar.SetAt(2,"I");
    for(i=0;i<ar.GetSize();i++) {
        DisplayFormatted("%s ",(char *)ar[i]);
    }
    NewLine();
}
```

■ We can access elements of PtrArray objects using brackets. For example:

```
DisplayFormatted("%s ",(char *)GetAt(pD,i));
```

becomes

```
DisplayFormatted("%s ",(char *)ar[i]);
```

Implementation   Much of the implementation of the PtrArray class was built by applying the type of mechanical changes mentioned in Chapter 13, Section 13.6.1, to the DynArray structure. These changes included the following:

■ Renaming member data with the m_ prefix

■ Removing DynArray structure objects passed in as arguments

■ Making any function that previously took a const DynArray reference or pointer as an argument a const qualified member

■ Replacing direct accesses of data with calls to member functions, wherever practical

The member functions for which most or all changes were made in this manner are presented in Example 14.14.

Newly introduced member functions are presented in Example 14.15. Of these functions, the only two that are not self explanatory are the [] operator overloads. Here, the question of greatest interest is not how they work (which should be evident from inspection). Rather, it is why are two needed?

The reasoning for defining two [] overloads is as follows. When the C++ compiler encounters a [] operator (or any member function for that matter), it can tell whether it is being applied to a const object. If so, it calls the const version. If not, it calls the non-const version. The fact that both do the same thing is irrelevant to the compiler.

With both operators defined, however, we can then use bracket operators within our GetAt() (const) and SetAt() (non-const) members, as shown in Example 14.16. Doing so ensures that every public access we make to the array of void pointers will go through the bracket overload. Ensuring that all access and setting operators ultimately go through a single function can prove to be a useful debugging tool as programs get more complex.

TEST YOUR UNDERSTANDING 14.5:

Why do we use the syntax (*this)[i] in the GetAt() and SetAt() functions?

The final significant change made to the class was the addition of a RemoveAll() member and a change to the ReallocArray() function, shown in Example 14.17.

In the DynArray structure, RemoveAll() would have been a dangerous function—calling it on an uninitialized DynArray structure would probably generate an exception—because the pData element would not be 0. Our PtrArray class ensures the m_pData pointer is set to zero upon construction (and RemoveAll() was part of the MFC CPtrArray interface the PtrArray class was modeled on), so it made sense to add it to our class. Given that the RemoveAll() function was available, it also made sense to call it if ReallocArray() is passed as a new size.

TEST YOUR UNDERSTANDING 14.6:

Explain why, from the class user's perspective, calling SetSize(0) is equivalent to calling RemoveAll().

EXAMPLE 14.14

Member functions that were mechanically adapted from DynArray

```
// returns number of active pointers in the array
int PtrArray::GetSize() const {
    return m_nSize;
}
// adds pointer pData to the end of the array
void PtrArray::Add(void *pData)
{
    if (m_nCount==m_nSize) ReallocArray(m_nSize+1);
    else m_nSize++;
    if (m_nSize>m_nCount) return; // If reallocation failed...
    SetAt(m_nSize-1,pData);
}
// inserts the pointer pData at position i, moving existing element up
// asserts i is legal
void PtrArray::InsertAt(int nPos,void *pData)
{
    int i;
    assert(nPos>=0 && nPos<=m_nSize);
    if (nPos<0 || nPos>m_nSize) return;
    if (m_nSize==m_nCount) ReallocArray(m_nSize+1);
    else m_nSize++;
    if (m_nSize>m_nCount) return; // if reallocation failed...
    for(i=m_nSize-1;i>nPos;i—) {
        SetAt(i,GetAt(i-1));
    }
    SetAt(nPos,pData);
}
// removes the pointer at position i, moving existing element down
// Asserts i is legal
void PtrArray::RemoveAt(int nPos)
{
    int i;
    assert(nPos>=0 && nPos<m_nSize);
    if (nPos<0 || nPos>=m_nSize) return;
    for(i=nPos;i<m_nSize-1;i++) {
        SetAt(i,GetAt(i+1));
    }
    m_nSize—;
}
// Sets the array to the specied size
void PtrArray::SetSize(int i)
{
    ReallocArray(i);
}
```

EXAMPLE 14.15

New member functions in the PtrArray class

```
PtrArray::PtrArray(){
    m_pData=0;
    m_nCount=0;
    m_nSize=0;
}
PtrArray::PtrArray(const PtrArray &ar) {
    m_pData=0;
    Copy(ar);
}
PtrArray::~PtrArray() {
    RemoveAll();
}
const PtrArray &PtrArray::operator=(const PtrArray &ar) {
    if (&ar==this) return *this;
    Copy(ar);
    return *this;
}
void PtrArray::Copy(const PtrArray &ar) {
    RemoveAll();
    SetSize(ar.GetSize());
    for(int i=0;i<ar.GetSize();i++) {
        SetAt(i,ar[i]);
    }
}
void *&PtrArray::operator[](int i) {
    assert(i>=0 && i<m_nSize);
    return m_pData[i];
}
void *&PtrArray::operator[](int i) const {
    assert(i>=0 && i<m_nSize);
    return m_pData[i];
}
```

EXAMPLE 14.16

GetAt() and SetAt() members of PtrArray

```
// returns the pointer value at position i
void *PtrArray::GetAt(int i) const
{
    return (*this)[i];
}
// sets the pointer value at position i to pData
void PtrArray::SetAt(int i,void *pData)
{
    (*this)[i]=pData;
}
```

EXAMPLE 14.17

Revised ReallocArray() function

```
void PtrArray::ReallocArray(int nNewSize)
{
    if (nNewSize==0) {
        RemoveAll();
    }
    else {
        int nRealSize=DYNBLOCKSIZE*((nNewSize+DYNBLOCKSIZE-1)/DYNBLOCKSIZE);
        void **pNew=new void *[nRealSize];
        int nCopySize=(nNewSize<m_nCount) ? nNewSize : m_nCount;
        if (m_nSize>0) {
            for(int i=0;i<nCopySize;i++) {
                pNew[i]=m_pData[i];
            }
            delete m_pData;
        }
        m_pData=pNew;
        m_nCount=nRealSize;
        m_nSize=nNewSize;
    }
}

void PtrArray::RemoveAll() {
    delete [] m_pData;
    m_pData=0;
    m_nCount=0;
    m_nSize=0;
}
```

14.4: LAB EXERCISE: THE GSTRING CLASS

Walkthrough available in GString.wmv

Near the outset of the chapter, the assertion was made that if it weren't for strings, we probably wouldn't have operator overloads. In this section, the reader can develop a complete class that encapsulates a NUL terminated string and provides a lot of bells and whistles. Indeed, in some ways its features compare favorably to those of the STL **string** class that will be introduced in the next chapter.

14.4.1: Overview

Before the STL was widely adopted as the C++ standard, Visual C++ developers using strings in their applications frequently used **CString** objects, defined as part of the MFC. The GString class presented here is an attempt to develop a string implementation that closely mimics the CString class and offers two advantages:

- The MFC CString class is quite well designed and provides an excellent vehicle for practicing operator overloads.

- After completing the GString class, the reader will be completely conversant in the CString interface, should he or she ever decide to engage in MFC programming.

The nice features of GString objects include the following:

- Automatic assignment from NUL terminated strings
- Automatic type casting to constant NUL terminated strings
- Support for comparison operators (e.g., >, ==, !=) with other GStrings and NUL terminated strings
- Ability to concatenate with other GStrings and NUL terminated strings using the + operator
- Access of individual characters using the [] operator
- >> and << support for text output
- >> and << support for serializing to a binary stream
- Various substring generation members, such as Left(), Right() and Mid()

The class declaration is shown in Example 14.18.

14.4.2: Interface and Implementation Issues

In this section, we consider the interface of the GString class, then address some implementation issues.

Interface   The GString interface is relatively straightforward. The GStringDemo function, presented in Example 14.19, demonstrates all but the I/O features.

The output of running GStringDemo() is presented in Figure 14.3.

Implementation Issues   Most of the functions required to implement the GString class are just a line or two long. A few, however, warrant some additional explanation, particularly the protected members, which—by their very nature—are defined largely at the discretion of the programmer.

```
friend OUTPUT &operator<<(OUTPUT &out,const GString &str1);
friend INPUT &operator>>(INPUT &in,GString &str1);
friend STREAM &operator<<(STREAM &out,const GString &str1);
friend STREAM &operator>>(STREAM &in,GString &str1);
```

The SimpleIO **OUTPUT** and **INPUT** streams are objects of the same type as **cout** and **cin**, as will be discussed in Chapter 17. These overloads, therefore, provide us with text I/O. The **STREAM** overloads should, therefore, load and save the data in binary form. (*Hint:* The LoadString() and SaveString() functions introduced in Chapter 11 accomplish the type of loading and saving required.)

```
void Copy(const char *bufnew);
```

deletes the existing GString buffer, then creates a copy of *bufnew* to assign to *m_szBuf*. It can be called from many other member functions (including the Copy(const GString &) function), but is not necessary for the class user, because assignment can be used in its place.

```
void SubstituteBuf(char *bufnew);
```

works like the protected copy but simply assigns *bufnew* to *m_szBuf*, without copying it. You would never want to make a function like this one accessible to a programmer just

EXAMPLE 14.18

GString declaration

```
class GString
{
public:
    GString(){m_szBuf=0;}
    GString(const char *p);
    GString(const GString& sz);
    ~GString();
    const GString &operator=(const GString &stringSource);
    const GString &operator=(const char *pszSource);
    void Copy(const GString &sz);

    operator const char * () const {return m_szBuf;}

    friend bool operator==(const GString& s1,const GString& s2);
    friend bool operator==(const GString& s1,const char *s2);
    friend bool operator==(const char *s1,const GString& s2);
    friend bool operator!=(const GString& s1,const GString& s2);
    friend bool operator!=(const GString& s1,const char *s2);
    friend bool operator!=(const char *s1,const GString& s2);
    friend bool operator<(const GString& s1,const GString& s2);
    friend bool operator<(const GString& s1,const char *s2);
    friend bool operator<(const char *s1,const GString& s2);
    friend bool operator>(const GString& s1,const GString& s2);
    friend bool operator>(const GString& s1,const char *s2);
    friend bool operator>(const char *s1,const GString& s2);
    friend bool operator<=(const GString& s1,const GString& s2);
    friend bool operator<=(const GString& s1,const char *s2);
    friend bool operator<=(const char *s1,const GString& s2);
    friend bool operator>=(const GString& s1,const GString& s2);
    friend bool operator>=(const GString& s1,const char *s2);
    friend bool operator>=(const char *s1,const GString& s2);

    friend OUTPUT &operator<<(OUTPUT &out,const GString &str1);
    friend INPUT &operator>>(INPUT &in,GString &str1);
    friend STREAM &operator<<(STREAM &out,const GString &str1);
    friend STREAM &operator>>(STREAM &in,GString &str1);

    int GetLength() const;
    char operator[](int i) const;
    char GetAt(unsigned int i) const;

    void Empty();
    bool IsEmpty() const;

    friend GString operator+(const GString& str1,const GString& str2);
    friend GString operator+(const GString& str1,const char *s2);
    friend GString operator+(const char *s1,const GString& str2);

    int Find(const char *str1) const;
```

(Continues)

EXAMPLE 14.18 (CONTINUED)

```
    GString Mid(int i) const;
    GString Mid(int i,int j) const;
    GString Left(int i) const;
    GString Right(int i) const;

protected:
    char *m_szBuf;
    void Copy(const char *bufnew);
    void SubstituteBuf(char *bufnew);
    void Concat(const char *s1,const char *s2);
};
```

using the class, but it can be quite convenient when writing some of the substring and concatenation functions.

*void Concat(const char *s1,const char *s2);*

sets the GString object's buffer to a newly concatenated string, consisting of s1 followed by s2. It would not serve a useful purpose for a class user, but it can be used in all the + operator overloads.

14.4.3: Procedure

A reasonable procedure for programming the GString class would be the following:

- *Start with the final version of GString00 (from Section 14.2.2).* This code will handle copying and assignment. You might also want to implement the protected Copy(), which can then be called from your public copy and many other functions.

- *Implement the type cast operator.* Use the operator from Section 14.1.3 as a guide—yours will be every bit as trivial.

- *Implement the comparison operators.* Done properly, all of these operators will be nearly identical and in a single line of code. Don't hesitate to use library functions. By this time, you probably have enough code to begin testing.

- *Implement the stream operators for text and binary I/O.* If it is helpful, you may assume that no string will be more than 32,000 characters long. Use the SimpleIO functions unless you are already familiar with Chapter 17.

- *Implement GetLength().* Another one-line call to a library function.

- *Implement the [] operator.* This operator should return a character from the GString object at the specified position. Make it return 0x00 if an invalid position is specified. The GetAt() function does the same thing.

- *Implement Empty() and IsEmpty().* Empty() releases a string, setting m_szBuf to 0. IsEmpty() tells whether a string is empty, returning true if it is, false otherwise.

- *Implement Find().* This function returns the position where it finds a substring matching its argument in the object it is applied to. It returns −1 if no matching substring is found.

EXAMPLE 14.19

GStringDemo function

```
void GStringDemo()
{
    char buf[80]={0};
    GString s1,s2,s3,s4,s5,s6,s7,s8;
    s1="This is ";
    s2="a test";
    s3=s1+s2;
    cout << s3 << endl;
    s4="AARDVARK";
    s5="ZEBRA";
    s6="aardvark";
    s7="zebra";
    s8=s7;
    if (s4<s5) cout << s4 << " is less than " << s5 << endl;
    else cout << s4 << " is greater than or equal to " << s5 << endl;
    if (s6<s5) cout << s6 << " is less than " << s5 << endl;
    else cout << s6 << " is greater than or equal to " << s5 << endl;
    if (s7==s8) cout << s7 << " equals " << s8 << endl;
    else cout << s7 << " does not equal " << s8 << endl;
    if (s7!=s5) cout << s7 << " does not equal " << s5 << endl;
    else cout << s7 << " equals " << s5 << endl;
    if (s4<"ABC") cout << s4 << " is less than " << "ABC" << endl;
    else cout << s4 << " is greater than or equal to " << "ABC" << endl;
    // basic_string members
    cout << endl << "Individual characters in " << s6+": ";
    for(int i=0;i<s6.GetLength();i++) {
        cout << s6[i] << " ";
    }
    cout << endl << "Left 2 characters in " << s6+": " << s6.Left(2);;
    cout << endl << "Remaining characters in " << s6+
        " (starting at position 4): " << s6.Mid(4);
    cout << endl << "Three characters in " << s6+
        " (starting at position 4): " << s6.Mid(4,3);
    cout << endl << "Last 5 characters in " << s6+": " << s6.Right(5);
    // setting up not found constant
    cout << endl << "Length of " << s6 << " is " << s6.GetLength();
    int nPos=s6.Find("var");
    if (nPos!=-1) cout << endl << "Found \'var\' in " << s6;
    else cout << endl << "Did not find \'var\' in " << s6;
    nPos=s5.Find("var");
    if ((int)nPos!=-1) cout << endl << "Found \'var\' in " << s5;
    else cout << endl << "Did not find \'var\' in " << s5;
    strcpy(buf,s6);
    cout << endl << "Copy of string in buffer is: " << buf << endl;
    return;
}
```

| FIGURE 14.3 | Output after Running GStringDemo Function |

```
c:\Captures\Chapter15\GStringApp\Debug\GStringApp.exe
This is a test
AARDVARK is less than ZEBRA
aardvark is greater than or equal to ZEBRA
zebra equals zebra
zebra does not equal ZEBRA
AARDVARK is less than ABC

Individual characters in aardvark: a a r d v a r k
Left 2 characters in aardvark: aa
Remaining characters in aardvark (starting at position 4): vark
Three characters in aardvark (starting at position 4): var
Last 5 characters in aardvark: dvark
Length of aardvark is 8
Found 'var' in aardvark
Did not find 'var' in ZEBRA
Copy of string in buffer is: aardvark
```

- *Look at the Chapter 12 end-of-chapter exercises, Questions 1–10.* These questions discuss implementing structure versions of the remaining functions you will be writing.

- *Implement the + operator.* In order to implement + efficiently, you may want to define a protected Concat() function, such as that described in 14.4.2, which can be called from all three overloads.

- *Implement the substring members.* If you write the Mid() member first, it can be used inside the Left() and Right() members.

14.5: REVIEW AND QUESTIONS

14.5.1: REVIEW

C++ allows you to specify how its operators will work when applied to the classes that you create. This powerful capability makes it possible to implement classes that behave like flexible strings and arrays.

Operator overloads are specified using the operator functional form introduced in Chapter 4. Thus, an overload of the + operator would tend to look this way:

```
ClassType operator+(const ClassType
    &a1,const ClassType &a2);
```

The function body would then be called whenever an expression was encountered where two ClassType objects were separated by a plus sign. In general, it is better to use references than actual objects in defining operator overloads,

because they involve less copying overhead when called and don't need an available copy constructor.

Operators can either be overloaded as regular functions (often specified as friend functions in the class to which they apply) or as member functions. When an operator is overloaded as a member, one less argument is specified, because the object to which the operator is applied is implicitly available to class members. For binary operators, it means the LHS of the operator needs to be an object of that class. This requirement can be a limitation for binary operators that relate different types of values (e.g., const char * and string objects), so such operators tend to be defined as regular or friend functions.

Some of the limitations on operator overloading include the following:

- Overloads that would change the behavior of any built-in operators when applied to primitives
- Overloads involving operators that aren't predefined in C++ (i.e., you can't invent your own operators)
- Overloads that would really screw up the language, such as the . operator for selecting members and the scope resolution operator (::)
- Overloads cannot alter operator precedence

Certain overloads require special syntax. Two important examples are:

- The postfix ++ and −− operators, which have an extra int argument that is not used in order to distinguish them from the prefix versions
- The **type cast overload,** where the operator name and return value are combined, as in:

```
operator const char*()
```

The most critical (and common) operator overload is that of the assignment operator. Although the compiler normally creates an implicit version of the assignment operator, this version is typically "wrong" for classes that manage their own pointers and can cause quite subtle bugs. Part of the problem is that assignment and copying operations may not always be self-evident to the programmer—often occurring invisibly as functions are called and returned, and during the use of template classes.

Because the assignment operator and copy constructor are nearly identical, they are virtually always implemented together (and should be). A general framework for their implementation is as follows:

- Write a function Copy() that does the appropriate element-by-element copying. Its prototype should be as follows:

```
void Copy(const ClassName &ref);
```

- Use the following framework for the copy constructor:

```
ClassName::ClassName(const ClassName
  &ref)
{
  // initialize any pointers that
  // might be deleted to 0
  Copy(ref);
}
```

- Use the following framework for the assignment operator overload:

```
ClassName
&ClassName::operator=(const
ClassName &ref)
{
  if (this==&ref) return *this;
  Copy(ref);
  return *this;
}
```

14.5.2: GLOSSARY

assignment operator   The operator used to assign a value to its LHS argument, it is nearly always overloaded in conjunction with a copy constructor

copy constructor   A constructor function that initializes the object being constructed by copying the data in another object

CString   An encapsulated string implementation provided with the MFC.

extraction operator   Another name for the >> or input operator

INPUT   The name used by SimpleIO to refer to an input text stream

insertion operator   Another name for the << or output operator

Microsoft Foundation Classes (MFC)   A library of C++ classes provided by Microsoft as part of Visual Studio

.NET that is particularly well suited for developing MS Windows applications

OUTPUT   The name used by SimpleIO to refer to an output text stream

string object   An object instantiating the STL string class, more generally, can refer to any encapsulated string object, such as MFC CString objects

standard template library (STL)   The most commonly used standard C++ library, offering various collection objects, strings and file stream encapsulations

STREAM   The name used by SimpleIO to refer to a file stream, input or output, typically used for serializing data in binary form

type cast overload   An operator that is called when an object is type cast explicitly or implicitly (e.g., by being passed as an argument to a function)

14.5.3: QUESTIONS

Questions 1–2 involve enhancing the MyInt (Section 14.2.1) class.

1. *MyInt += operator.* Overload the += operator within the MyInt class.

2. *MyInt bool type cast.* Write a type cast that casts a MyInt object to bool using the normal C++ rules for true and false.

Questions 3–7 involve enhancing the PtrArray (Section 14.3.2) and GString (Section 14.4) classes.

3. *Array of integers.* Create a new class by modifying PtrArray class that holds an array of integers.

4. *Array of strings.* Create a new IntArray class by modifying PtrArray class that holds an array of GString objects.

5. *Case-insensitive strings.* Create a new IString class by modifying GString class to make it case-insensitive. Make sure all members are case-insensitive.

6. *GString minus operator.* Overload the − operator for the GString class. It should take its RHS and remove it, if found, from the LHS string, returning a new string with the RHS removed. Implementations for mixed GString and const char * arguments should be supplied.

7. *GString += and −= operators.* Overload the += and −= operators (consistent with the + operators already defined and − operators specified in Question 6) for the GString class.

Questions 8–10 involve enhancing the employee and EmpData classes as originally presented in Chapter 13, Sections 13.6.1 and 13.3.2. It assumes the modifications in Section 14.3.1 have been made.

8. *Overloading EmpData operators.* Add a copy constructor, assignment operator, and insertion/extraction (<< and >>) operator overloads to the EmpData class, making its interface consistent with the employee class. (Hint: You will also want to define a Copy() member, naturally.)

9. *Replacing the EmpData embedded array.* Replace the embedded array of employees in the EmpData class with a PtrArray member (as defined in Section 14.3.2). Implement the change so that the EmpData interface does not change.

10. *Replace employee embedded name string arrays with GString objects.* Change the employee class implementation so that the last name and first names are stored as GString arrays. The only interface changes you should make are to have the LastName() and FirstName() functions return GString objects, i.e.:

```
GString LastName() const;
GString FirstName() const;
```

Note: As long as the employee interface is maintained, you should not have to change EmpData.

Questions 11–14 involve overloading operators related to the Date, Time, DateTime, and TimeSpan classes developed in Questions 1–12 of Chapter 13.

11. *Overload subtraction for the time class.* Add a friend operator overload to the Time class (Chapter 13, Questions 1–6) that returns a real number when one time class is subtracted from another. The result should correspond to a fraction of a day, and may be positive or negative.

12. *Overload addition and subtraction for the Date class.* Add a series of friend overloads to the Date class (Chapter 13, Questions 7–10) that perform the following operations:

Arg1	Op	Arg2	Result
Date	−	Date	**int**, indicating days between the two dates
Date	−	int	Date, the LHS date with the number of days subtracted
Date	+	int	Date, the LHS date with the number of days added
int	+	Date	Date, the RHS date with the number of days added

13. *Overload addition and subtraction for the DateTime class.* Add a series of friend overloads to both the DateTime class (Chapter 13, Question 11) and TimeSpan (Chapter 13, Question 12) class that perform the following operations:

Arg1	Op	Arg2	Result
DateTime	−	DateTime	TimeSpan, indicating distance between the two dates
DateTime	−	TimeSpan	DateTime, the LHS date with the TimeSpan subtracted
DateTime	+	TimeSpan	DateTime, the LHS date with the TimeSpan added
TimeSpan	+	DateTime	DateTime, the RHS date with the TimeSpan added

14. *Overload += and −= for the DateTime class.* Add a series of member overloads to both the DateTime class (Chapter 13, Question 11) and TimeSpan (Chapter 13, Question 12) class that perform the += and −= operations. The results should be consistent with the table in Question 13.

Templates, Strings, and Vectors

EXECUTIVE SUMMARY

Chapter 15 examines the concept of a C++ template and presents two common templated classes from the C++ standard template library (STL): the string and the vector. Although this textbook has, thus far, focused on the mechanics of C++ programming, the practical realities of programming dictate that library classes be used extensively in our programs. Indeed, homegrown classes that do general purpose tasks—such as maintaining collections of other objects—should generally be avoided.

The chapter begins with an overview of the STL, then explains, in general terms, the nature of a template. A brief In-Depth section illustrates how a simple template can be constructed, and how the process works. The next major section introduces the STL **string** object, a useful templated class that allows us to move away from the mechanics of working with NUL terminated CStrings. The string member functions are also contrasted with those of the GString object, developed in Chapter 14, Section 14.4. A general survey of collections is then presented, followed by a discussion of the vector template collection. Two general classes are developed in walkthroughs: a Person class that holds data related to an individual, and a vector-based sorted collection of employees. The chapter concludes with a lab exercise that implements a Company class, an exercise that continues in Chapter 16.

LEARNING OBJECTIVES

Upon completing this chapter, you should be able to:

- Explain the origins and purpose of the STL
- Create objects based on a C++ template class
- Describe the basic approach to creating a C++ template
- Identify the key elements of the STL **string** interface and use them
- Explain what is meant by *collection shapes*
- Describe the properties of an iterator
- Create vector-based objects
- Compose vector-based collections inside other classes

15.1: INTRODUCTION TO THE STL

Chapter 15 is intended to serve two purposes. The first is to provide a broad overview of the C++ STL. The second is to provide a practical introduction to the **string** and **vector<>** template classes. In this section, we focus on the first objective. We begin with a quick overview of how the **STL (standard template library)** evolved and what its evolution means for programmers. We then provide an overview of what is meant by a template. Finally, we provide a more in-depth look at how templates can be created.

15.1.1: Evolution of Standard C++ Libraries

Although Bjarne Stoustrup developed the initial version of C++ programming language in the early 1980s, many of the most important aspects of the language did not become commercially available until the mid-1990s, culminating in the adoption of the ISO standard in 1998.

The most important of the changes that transformed the language in the mid-1990s was the incorporation of support for templates and namespaces into C++ compilers. In the Visual Studio family, for example, template support began with version 4.0, introduced in the 1995–1996 time frame. With template capability built into the compiler, it became possible to include the standard template library—originally developed at Hewlett-Packard and then placed in the public domain—with the compiler. The new compiler capabilities also made it possible for Microsoft to develop its own alternative proprietary template-based libraries (e.g., the Active Template Library, or ATL) that could be used as an alternative to the MFC for developing MS Windows applications and components.

What makes templates in general, and the STL in particular, so important is the way they enhance our ability to create type-safe collections of data and perform I/O. In Chapter 17, we will focus on the use of the STL to perform C++ I/O. In this chapter, we consider how templates can be used to enhance our collections.

Because the STL has, with some modifications, been incorporated into the C++ ISO standard, the original C++ standard library—designed, for the most part, in the early 1980s—is no longer widely used. Programmers need to be aware, however, that one remaining vestige of the old libraries can be found in the include files of some compilers. Specifically, a preprocessor statement such as:

```
#include <iostream>
including namespace std;
```

ensures the modern (STL) version of the I/O libraries is used. On the other hand, writing:

```
#include <iostream.h>  // note the .h (and no need to
// include a namespace).
```

may result in the old libraries being used. Because no benefit derives from using the old libraries when writing new code, it makes sense to be careful not to inadvertently place the .h extension in C++ include statements intended to use the STL library.

15.1.2: What Is a Template?

A **template** is, in effect, a factory for creating source code. The two forms of templates are function templates and class templates. Function templates are factories that generate new function definitions on demand. Class templates generate new classes. In this chapter, we focus on the latter, because class templates are the basis of the STL capabilities we are most interested in.

So what do we mean by a factory? When you create a normal C++ class, you are creating source code that will be compiled. When you create a C++ class template, on the other hand, you are creating instructions that will cause the compiler to generate appropriate source code when it is needed.

The best way to understand why class factories might be useful is to draw upon an example from Chapter 14. In Section 14.3.2, we developed a PtrArray class that provided an easy-to-use object for holding collections of pointers. The collection designed for void pointers could, in effect, hold pointers to any type of object. The problem is that once you make the pointers void, you lose the type checking capability of C++. What would be nice, then, would be to generate different versions of the PtrArray class to hold different types of pointers (e.g., EmployeePtrArray to hold employee objects, PersonPtrArray to hold person objects, and so forth).

In fact, we can even go a step further. In the Chapter 14 end-of-chapter exercises, Question 3 required you to modify the PtrArray class to hold an array of integers and Question 4 required you to modify the class to hold an array of GString objects. If you did these exercises, you perhaps noticed a surprising thing: if you just went through and changed every void * in the class definition to an int (or GString), you were almost completely done. What templates do is allow us to define classes in such a way that we can create these alternative versions automatically.

You can tell a template class by the presence of < and > in the definition. What goes between the < and > is a comma separated list of elements that are normally either class names or constants. The **vector<>** template, for example, is discussed in Section 15.4 and is used to create an array object much like the PtrArray. When you declare a variable:

```
vector<int> ar1;
```

the resulting object ar1 becomes, in effect, an array of integers. The declaration:

```
vector<GString> ar2;
```

on the other hand, creates a vector array object (holding a collection of GString objects) called ar2. Finally, the declaration:

```
vector<void*> ar3;
```

creates a vector array object holding void pointers called ar3. In three lines of code, then, we used templates to generate three different classes.

The **string** object is also templated, but this fact is hidden from us because the STL used a synonym for the template declaration instead of the declaration itself (something easily done in C++ using a typedef). If you traced through the compiler include files, you would discover that every time you write **string**, it is equivalent to writing:

```
basic_string<char>
```

which means our **string** object holds one-byte characters. A **wstring** type is also supported by the STL, designed to hold two-byte characters, such as Unicode. You might think of it as being specialized as:

```
basic_string<short>
```

Such typedef synonyms are used extensively in defining I/O names, allowing them to maintain a reasonably high level of compatibility with pretemplate code based on the original C++ standard library.

15.1.3: In Depth: Defining a Simple Template

 Walkthrough available in GArray.wmv

To better understand what templates are, it is useful to take a quick look at how a class template can be created. Many of the subtleties to "professional-grade" template definition (e.g., defining embedded iterator classes) are far beyond the scope of this textbook. Nonetheless, it can be relatively simple to create a powerful template if you have a well-designed class to start from.

We begin with the PtrArray class (Chapter 14, Section 14.3.2), which is a fairly ideal candidate for a template class for two reasons:

- Collections, such as arrays, are the type of object most commonly templated.
- We already know, from the Chapter 14, Questions 3 and 4, that it is easy to modify the PtrArray class to hold other types of data.

Template Parameters   The first decision associated with designing a template is the choice of parameters for the template. Naturally, one thing we want to control is the type of data being stored in the array, so it will have to be a parameter (and, for the vector template class, it is the only parameter). Often, it is useful to specify a second parameter that identifies how data will be passed into certain functions, such as Add(), SetAt(), and InsertAt(). As we know, when we pass objects into a function, a copy is made (unless it is passed in as a pointer or a reference). Making such copies, however, can add to the overhead associated with using the class when large objects are stored. For this reason, it is often nice to be able to specify that certain functions take references as values. We return to this discussion shortly, when we look at the actual code.

Based on the fact that we seem to need two parameters, we specify our template class as GArray<T,A>, where T is the data type being stored, and A is how it is passed into functions as an argument. (Not coincidentally, it will make the resulting template quite similar to the CArray<T,A> template provided with the MFC.)

Our GArray<T,A> template will allow us to create a wide range of type-safe arrays. For example:

```
GArray<int,int> ar1;
```

would declare an array of integers named a1.

```
GArray<void*,void*> ar2;
```

would create an array of void pointers, effectively identical to the PtrArray class.

```
GArray<employee,employee&> ar3;
```

would create an array of employee objects. In this template, where employee values were passed into key functions, they would be passed in as references. Finally:

```
GArray<GString,const char*> ar4;
```

would create an array of GString objects. When we passed GString objects into function, such as Add(), however, the argument would be a const char *, allowing us write code such as:

```
ar4.Add("Hello, World!");
```

This mixing of T and A data types is made possible by virtue of the fact that our GString class has built in type cast and constructor functions that provide for const char * arguments. On the other hand, if we made the following declaration:

```
GArray<GString,int> ar5;
ar5.Add("Hello");
```

we would get the following error (on the Add() line) when we compiled:

```
C2664: 'GArray<class GString,int>::Add' : cannot convert
parameter 1 from 'char [6]' to 'int'

This conversion requires a reinterpret_cast, a C-style cast,
or function-style cast
```

This error message tells us that that the compiler cannot figure out how to turn the string into an integer argument, as required by the A (second) template parameter. On the other hand, if we called it:

```
ar5.Add(17);
```

we would get something along the lines of the following lengthy error message:

```
C2679: binary '=' : no operator found which takes a right-
hand operand of type 'int' (or there is no acceptable con-
version)
        c:\Program Files\Microsoft Visual Studio
        .NET\Vc7\include\xlocale(582) : while compiling class-
        template member function 'void
        GArray<T,A>::SetAt(int,int)'
        with
        [
            T=GString,
            A=int
        ]
        c:\Program Files\Microsoft Visual Studio
        .NET\Vc7\include\xmemory(111) : while compiling class-
        template member function 'GArray<T,A>::GArray(void)'
        with
        [
            T=GString,
            A=int
        ]
        c:\Introduction to C++\Chapter16\GArray\GArray.cpp(67) :
        see reference to class template instantiation
        'GArray<T,A>' being compiled
        with
        [
            T=GString,
            A=int
        ]
```

What this message tells us is that it cannot figure out how to convert between GString and int within the SetAt() function (which was called within the Add() function). It demonstrates an important fact about templates: the parameters you supply *must* make sense.

<u>**TEST YOUR UNDERSTANDING 15.1:**</u>

In Chapter 14, Section 14.3.1, we tried to overload the input (extraction) operator for employee objects as follows:

```
STREAM operator>>(STREAM in,employee &emp);
```

Explain the following compiler error message that resulted:

```
error C2558: class 'std::basic_fstream<_Elem,_Traits>' : no copy
constructor available or copy constructor is declared 'explicit'
    with
    [
        _Elem=char,
        _Traits=std::char_traits<char>
    ]
```

Template Construction   If you have a working class as a model for your template, constructing the template version can be relatively straightforward. Three basic steps are necessary:

- You place a template declaration in front of your class declaration and every member function in the .cpp file. This declaration is of the form template<*parameter-type-list*>. For example, in our illustration:

  ```
  template<class T,class A>
  ```

  specifies that both the parameters T and A are going to be type names (they don't have to be actual class names).

- Everywhere that you have an old class name inside the class definition itself, replace it with the *template-name*. Outside of the definition (including member function definitions in the .cpp file), replace it with the full template specifier *template-name<parameter-list>*. In our example, it would be GArray<A,T>.

- Go through your class and member function definitions and replace data types with the appropriate parameter name. In our example, you could do a global search-and-replace of "void *" with T (because it will be holding T type objects instead of the original void * objects), then make selective replacements of function arguments with A.

- Move all member functions in the .cpp file into the .h file, under the class definition. This command is required because the compiler needs to access the full function definitions every time a template member is called.

At this point, you can start testing your template by declaring some objects. Normally, this activity will surface some modifications of things you didn't think about. (The GArray<> template didn't require any, but it is pretty unusual not to require any modifications.) The declaration and a few member functions are presented in Example 15.1.

These definitions are identical to those in the PtrArray class, except for the changes we discussed. We also see the A parameter was used in the three functions used to add data to the array (the Add(), SetAt(), and GetAt() functions), while the T parameter was used everywhere else that void * originally occurred.

Examining the template, we can conclude an additional important fact. Any object for which we wanted to use this template would need the following:

- An assignment overload, because the SetAt() function uses assignment to set array elements

- A copy constructor, because GetAt() member returns a copy of the object

EXAMPLE 15.1

GArray<> declaration and selected numbers

```
template<class T,class A>
class GArray
{
public:
    GArray();
    GArray(const GArray &ar);
    ~GArray();
    const GArray &operator=(const GArray &ar);
    void Copy(const GArray &ar);
    T &operator[](int);
    T &operator[](int) const;
    T GetAt(int i) const;
    void SetAt(int i,A pData);
    void Add(A pData);
    void InsertAt(int i,A pData);
    void SetSize(int i);
    int GetSize() const;
    void RemoveAt(int i);
    void RemoveAll();
protected:
    int m_nCount;
    int m_nSize;
    T *m_pData;
    void ReallocArray(int nNewSize);
};

template<class T,class A>
GArray<T,A>::~GArray() {
    RemoveAll();
}
template<class T,class A>
T GArray<T,A>::GetAt(int i) const
{
    return (*this)[i];
}
template<class T,class A>
void GArray<T,A>::SetAt(int i,A pData)
{
    (*this)[i]=pData;
}

template<class T,class A>
const GArray<T,A> &GArray<T,A>::operator=(const GArray &ar) {
    if (&ar==this) return *this;
    Copy(ar);
    return *this;
}
```

If the classes being used in the template do not meet the requirements of the template, compiler error messages (such as the ones earlier in the section) will be generated when template members are called. The compiler will not generate error messages for template functions that are not used; it error-checks only the source code it generates from the template, not the template itself.

To demonstrate the GArray<> template, we use three different versions of the same test code used to demonstrate the PtrArray class. These versions are identical except that each uses a different data type:

```
GArray<void*,void*>
GArray<char*,char*>
GArray<GString,const char *>
```

The first function is presented in Example 15.2. The output of running all three functions is shown in Figure 15.1.

EXAMPLE 15.2

First GArray<> demonstration function

```
void GArrayDemo1()
{
    int i;
    GArray<void*,void*> ar;
    ar.Add("Hello");
    ar.Add("World!");
    ar.Add("me");
    for(i=0;i<ar.GetSize();i++) {
        DisplayFormatted("%s ",(const char *)ar[i]);
    }
    NewLine();
    ar.InsertAt(2,"It\'s");
    for(i=0;i<ar.GetSize();i++) {
        DisplayFormatted("%s ",(const char *)ar[i]);
    }
    NewLine();
    ar.RemoveAt(1);
    for(i=0;i<ar.GetSize();i++) {
        DisplayFormatted("%s ",(const char *)ar[i]);
    }
    NewLine();
    ar.SetAt(2,"I");
    for(i=0;i<ar.GetSize();i++) {
        DisplayFormatted("%s ",(const char *)ar[i]);
    }
    NewLine();
}
```

FIGURE 15.1   Output from Three Versions of GArrayDemo() Function

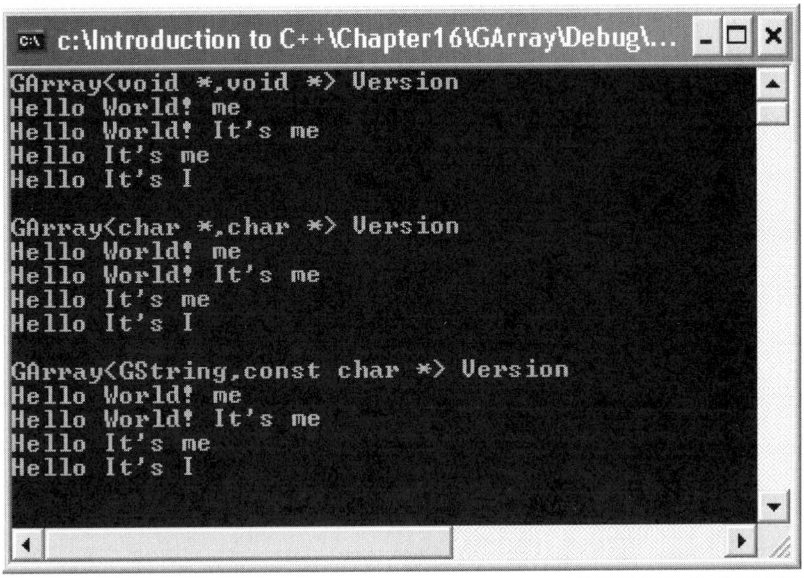

```
c:\Introduction to C++\Chapter16\GArray\Debug\...

GArray<void *,void *> Version
Hello World! me
Hello World! It's me
Hello It's me
Hello It's I

GArray<char *,char *> Version
Hello World! me
Hello World! It's me
Hello It's me
Hello It's I

GArray<GString,const char *> Version
Hello World! me
Hello World! It's me
Hello It's me
Hello It's I
```

15.1: SECTION QUESTIONS

1. What is the relationship of the STL to the original C++ standard library?
2. Why is it sometimes difficult to tell whether an object has been created from a template class?
3. Why are templates sometimes described as factories?
4. Do you need to know how to create templates in order to use them?
5. Why does it sometimes make sense to separate type and argument specifications in a template definition?
6. Do you think you would have any problem specifying the following template?

    GArray<STREAM, STREAM&>

15.2: THE string STL CLASS

Walkthrough available in STLString.wmv

The **string** object, derived from the basic_string<> template class, is probably the most commonly used class in C++ programs. Using **string** objects, the NUL terminated strings that originated in C can be largely replaced. Moreover, a member is available for converting string objects to NUL terminated strings, should that be useful for backward compatibility.

15.2.1: string Overview

Among the characteristics that differentiate **string** objects from NUL terminated strings are the following:

- Support for assignment from other **string** objects and NUL terminated strings

- Support for comparison operators (e.g., >, ==, !=) with other **string** objects and NUL terminated strings
- Ability to concatenate with other **string** objects and NUL terminated strings using the + operator
- Access of individual characters using the [] operator
- >> and << support for text output

Overall, the most important difference between **string** objects and NUL terminated strings is that **string** objects can be treated just like the other primitive data types (e.g., integers and real numbers). This capability not only simplifies C++ programming, it also makes it much more like programming in other languages, such as Basic or Java.

Whenever you use **string** objects in your program, you must include the C++ STL string library file with the statement:

```
#include <string>
using namespace std;
```

Omitting the .h is particularly critical in this case, because "string.h" refers to the C-string library (with prototypes of strcpy, strlen, strcat, etc.) and not the **string** object.

15.2.2: string Interface

The STL **string** interface is like the GString interface presented as a lab exercise in Chapter 14 (Section 14.4). A demonstration routine illustrating the use of string objects is presented in Example 15.3. The output from running the routine is presented in Figure 15.2.

Some differences from the GString interface (aside from naming conventions) include:

- No automatic type cast goes from **string** objects to const char *. The c_str() member function needs to be called instead.
- The **string** object copy() function copies characters into a buffer instead of setting the string to its argument.
- The **string** object empty() function tests whether a string is empty instead of emptying it.
- The **string** object has a generous collection of searching functions, including find(), find_ first_not_of(), find_ first_of(), find_last_not_of(), and find_ last_of().

15.2.3: string Operators and Members

As we begin to use more and more library classes, it becomes increasingly important that the reader start to use the excellent online language documentation provided by Visual Studio .NET (and on the MSDN Web site) for understanding class members, as opposed to relying too heavily on a textbook for reference purposes. Unlike any textbook, the language documentation supplied by .NET tends to be complete and up-to-date—at least as far as the Microsoft version of the compiler is concerned.

Unfortunately, the nature of some of the STL class objects makes it easy to miss parts of the relevant description. Such oversight is particularly likely for string and standard I/O objects where many of the templated classes have synonyms, or where inheritance is present (a specific problem for the standard I/O classes).

In the case of the **string** object, to find all the relevant members and operators supported by the class, you need to look in two places: under **string** and under **basic_string** (which is the template class used to derive strings).

EXAMPLE 15.3

Demonstration of string features

```
void StringDemo()
{
    char buf[80]={0};
    string s1,s2,s3,s4,s5,s6,s7,s8;
    // initializing from NUL terminated string
    s1="This is ";
    s2="a test";
    // demonstrating concatenation
    s3=s1+s2;
    cout << s3 << endl;
    cout << s3 + " of concatenation" << endl << endl;
    // comparison demonstration
    s4="AARDVARK";
    s5="ZEBRA";
    s6="aardvark";
    s7="zebra";
    s8=s7;
    if (s4<s5) cout << s4 << " is less than " << s5 << endl;
    else cout << s4 << " is greater than or equal to " << s5 << endl;
    if (s6<s5) cout << s6 << " is less than " << s5 << endl;
    else cout << s6 << " is greater than or equal to " << s5 << endl;
    if (s7==s8) cout << s7 << " equals " << s8 << endl;
    else cout << s7 << " does not equal " << s8 << endl;
    if (s7!=s5) cout << s7 << " does not equal " << s5 << endl;
    else cout << s7 << " equals " << s5 << endl;
    if (s4<"ABC") cout << s4 << " is less than " << "ABC" << endl;
    else cout << s4 << " is greater than or equal to " << "ABC" << endl;
    cout << endl << "Individual characters in " << s6+": ";
    // using length() member
    for(unsigned int i=0;i<s6.length();i++) {
        // accessing individual characters
        cout << s6[i] << " ";
    }
    // using copy() member to get a substring
    s6.copy(buf,2);
    cout << endl << endl << "Left 2 characters in " << s6+": " << buf << endl;
    cout <<  "Three characters in " << s6+" starting at offset 2: "
        << s6.substr(2,3) << endl << endl;
    // testing find() member function
    unsigned int nPos=s6.find("var");
    if ((int)nPos!=-1) cout << endl << "Found \'var\' in " << s6;
    else cout << endl << "Did not find \'var\' in " << s6;
    nPos=s5.find("var");
    if ((int)nPos!=-1) cout << endl << "Found \'var\' in " << s5;
    else cout << endl << "Did not find \'var\' in " << s5 << endl;
    // converting string object to NUL-terminated string
    strcpy(buf,s6.c_str());
    cout << endl << "Copy of string in buffer is: " << buf << endl;
    return;
}
```

| **FIGURE 15.2** | Output from StringDemo() Function of Example 15.3 |

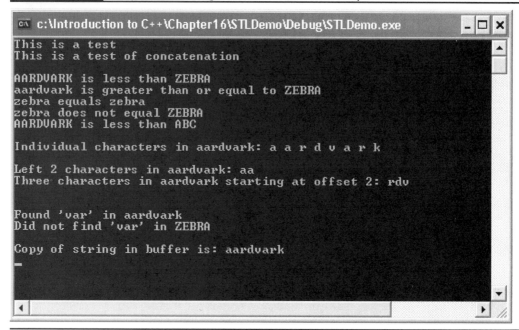

```
c:\Introduction to C++\Chapter16\STLDemo\Debug\STLDemo.exe
This is a test
This is a test of concatenation

AARDVARK is less than ZEBRA
aardvark is greater than or equal to ZEBRA
zebra equals zebra
zebra does not equal ZEBRA
AARDVARK is less than ABC

Individual characters in aardvark: a a r d v a r k

Left 2 characters in aardvark: aa
Three characters in aardvark starting at offset 2: rdv


Found 'var' in aardvark
Did not find 'var' in ZEBRA

Copy of string in buffer is: aardvark
```

Using this documentation, we can identify the operators overloaded for string objects, which are summarized in Table 15.1.

Of the more than thirty string member functions, many of which are quite limited in their usage, some of the more commonly used are summarized in Table 15.2.

15.2: SECTION QUESTIONS

1. Why does it make sense to create the string object from a template?
2. What do you need to do in order to pass string objects into NUL terminated string functions such as strcmp()?
3. Can string objects be saved directly to binary files?
4. Why do string objects appear in two places in the Visual Studio .NET reference documentation?
5. Why is it better to use string objects than your own homegrown string class (e.g., GString)?
6. What is the problem with using #include <string.h> instead of #include<string> when you want to use string objects?

15.3: INTRODUCTION TO COLLECTIONS

When you think of objects in the context of object-oriented programming, it is natural to think of self-contained objects such as employees or your typical row (record) in a database table. Although these types of objects are certainly important, as your programs grow

TABLE 15.1	String Operators, Compiled from the Visual Studio .NET Documentation	

Operator	Arguments	Purpose

==
!=
>
<
>=
<=
	LHS & RHS:
	   string
	   const char *
	   (at least one string must be present)
		Performs a character comparison, using ASCII character sequence

=	LHS:
	   string
	RHS:
	   string
	   const char *
		Assigns a value to the string on the LHS

+	LHS & RHS:
	   string
	   const char *
	   (at least one string must be present)
		Returns a new string that is the result of concatenating the LHS and RHS arguments

+=	LHS:
	   string
	RHS:
	   string
	   const char *
		Equivalent to LHS=LHS+RHS

<<	LHS:
	   ostream (OUTPUT)
	RHS:
	   string
		Sends a string to a text output stream, such as cout

>>	LHS:
	   istream (INPUT)
	RHS:
	   string
		Extracts a string from a text input stream, such as cin

[]	integer argument	Returns the character at the specified position in the string, but will not generate an exception

more and more complex, less and less of your time will be spent on the objects themselves. What will really challenge you is managing collections of objects.

Take, for example, a program such as FlowC. The "flash" of the program is the graphics, the shadowing, the fonts. As a practical matter, however, building in these capabilities took about 3 percent of the development time—if that. The challenge of programming involves doing things such as developing a data structure for managing the various elements that go into a function, for managing the functions attached to a class, and for managing the classes attached to a project. Every time the user touches an element, the

TABLE 15.2	Selected String Member Functions, Compiled from Visual Studio .NET Documentation	
Operator	**Arguments**	**Purpose**
append push_back	1. string | const char *	Concatenates argument to the end of the string (like += operator)
c_str	None	Returns a const char * to a buffer whose contents are the same as those of the string; similar to a const char * type cast
clear erase	None (clear) 1. offset=0 (erase) 2. count=0 (erase)	Empties the contents of a string Allows an optional specified range of the string to be emptied
copy	1. char * 2. count 3. offset=0	Copies characters (arg2) from a string to a character buffer (arg1), starting at a specified position (arg3)
find find_first_not_of find_first_of find_last_not_of find_last_of rfind	1. char | const char * | string 2. offset=0	Performs various searches for a substring within the string, starting at position offset; returns character offset where found or value < 0 (when type cast to signed integer) (rfind starts searching at the end of the string and moves forward)
insert	1. offset 2. string | const char *	Inserts a string at the specified offset position within the string object (*Note*: other overloads also exist)
length size	None	Returns length of the string
replace	1. offset 2. count 3. string | const char *	Replaces count characters, starting a position offset with a string (arg3)
substr	1. offset 2. count	Returns a string that is a substring of the object, starting at offset with up to count characters
swap	1. string	Swaps contents with its argument

collection class managing it needs to ensure that nothing was done that negatively affected its integrity—such as changing a function name to one that was already in use. Then there is the matter of layout—each construct needs to manage a collection of its own drawing objects, plus the collection of drawing objects for embedded constructs. To add to the overall challenge, each graphic view needs to maintain a collection of layout elements telling it where each box, diamond, oval, line, and text element should be placed.

In this section, we precede our discussion of the vector template class (Section 15.4) with a more general discussion of how we maintain collections.

15.3.1: Collection Shapes

Excluding the structure—which can be viewed as a collection of data elements of different types—we have only used one collection type so far in this text: the array. Now the array is certainly a powerful collection, especially if we encapsulate it and template it to make it type safe (e.g., the GArray or vector templates). But an array is only one form of collection among many more. Indeed, aside from I/O, collections are the most important part of the STL. In this section, we turn to the question of what makes a particular collection appropriate.

A **collection** is defined by its *shape*. By shape, we refer to a set of characteristics that describe the set of capabilities available for accessing and modifying the collection and the elements within. Two performance issues are particularly important contributors to shape: (1) the time it takes to apply a given capability, such as finding a particular element, and (2) how that time changes as the collection grows. In Chapter 9, Section 9.3.2, for example, we found that sorting an array could change search time from linear (proportional to N) to logarithmic (proportional to $\log N$). This characteristic distinguishes the array shape from the sorted array shape. Looking at all the shape characteristics of a given collection helps us decide whether it is appropriate for a given task.

Many collections support some form of linear access (i.e., accessing one element at a time, in an order determined by the collection), also known as sequential access. Other characteristics that help define a **collection's shape** include the following:

- *Random access, by position:* An array allows you to move directly to any element in the collection (if you know the position of the element)—like moving the reader on a CD. Other collections (e.g., the linked list) do not; to get to an element in the middle you have to trace through all the intervening elements.

- *Random access, by value (keyed access):* How long it will take to find a given element based upon some key value of that element is usually expressed as a fraction of collection size. Lookups can be further broken down into time to find exact matches (e.g., looking up the name associated with a social security number, so nearby SSNs are irrelevant) and approximate matches (e.g., looking up how to spell a word in a dictionary), which can be very different.

- *Insertion time:* How long it takes to insert an element into the collection is also sometimes broken into insertion at front, insertion at back, and insertion in the middle.

- *Deletion time:* How long it takes to remove an element from the collection. Similar to insertion, front, back, and middle deletions may be distinguished.

The most common shapes are array-based, linked list, tree, and lookup table.

Array-Based Collections: vector, deque, and Sorted Array The array-based collections are comparable to the GArray we already discussed. These collections provide efficient access of elements by position. When we need to insert/delete elements anywhere but the end, however, we need to move all the elements following the insertion/deletion. This process requires a loop that will be proportional to array size in time. For example, if the array has N elements, an insertion in the middle will require $N/2$ elements to be moved—which is proportional to N. As a consequence, arrays can become inefficient when data sets grow very large unless we are always adding elements to the end.

Access by content in arrays tends to be linear (i.e., proportional to the number of elements in the array). If the array has been sorted, however, access can become logarithmic, as was discussed in Chapter 9, Section 9.3.2.

Linked List: list The linked list collection shape typically ties its elements together with pointers, as illustrated in Figure 15.3.

| **FIGURE 15.3** | Singly and Doubly Linked Lists |

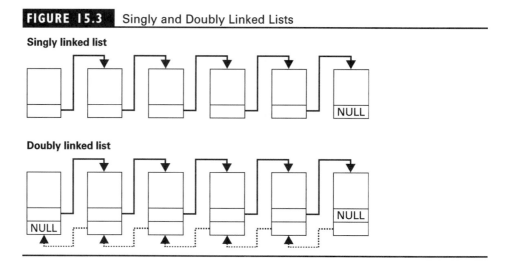

The shape makes insertion/deletion of elements anywhere in the list relatively fast, because we don't have to move the existing elements, just splice the pointers to add the new element to the chain or remove an existing element.

Conceptually, a list is like a tape cassette, as opposed to an array—which is like a CD. What this analogy means is that it offers no random access: to access a list element by position you need to start at the beginning (or end, if the list is **doubly linked**) and jump from link to link until you reach the desired content—making keyed access linear (which is as bad as it gets). As a result, lists are typically used for sequential processing or as an underlying shape for implementing queues or stacks.

Trees   The tree shape uses element pointers, the way a list does. Unlike a list, however, each tree element—often referred to as a **node**—has at least two pointers that allow the tree to branch out, as shown in Figure 15.4 for a binary tree (i.e., a tree where each node has two branches).

An important subcategory of trees is sorted trees. In Figure 15.4, for example, the elements are arranged such that for every node, the left-hand pointer points only to nodes with values less than or equal to the node's value, while the right-hand pointer points only to nodes of greater value. Arranged in this way, access by content becomes roughly logarithmic. It is also possible to make access by position (i.e., **random access**) logarithmic.

The STL map template behaves like a sorted tree. It is a useful shape in situations where keyed elements are frequently added and removed—insertions/deletions can occur in logarithmic time (i.e., the time it takes to find them), as opposed to the linear time required for array insertion/deletions. For this reason, trees are often used as the underlying shape for holding information such as database index tables.

Lookup Table: hash_map (MS Extension to STL)   The primary characteristic of the lookup table shape is that it allows for keyed access to elements that is virtually independent of collection size. On the downside, however, such speed only applies to exact matches. Whereas a sorted array or **tree** stores elements with similar keys nearby (e.g., their key may begin with the same few letters), in a typical lookup table implementation,

FIGURE 15.4 A Sorted Binary Tree

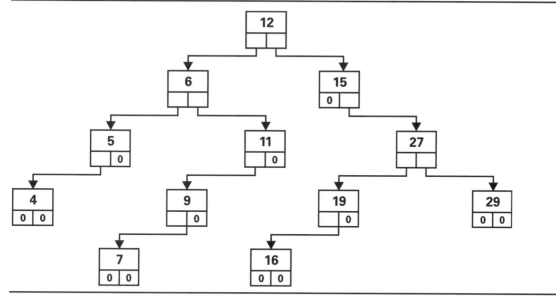

similar elements tend to be randomly scattered throughout the table, as illustrated by the keys array in Figure 15.5. This characteristic makes the shape a good choice where exact matches are required (e.g., accessing information by customer number or SSN), and a bad choice in situations where adjacent elements are of interest (e.g., a dictionary used to look up word spellings).

A typical lookup table uses a technique called **hashing.** One way to implement a hashing algorithm, illustrated in Figure 15.5, is to have two parallel arrays—one containing pointers to key values and the other containing pointers to the actual data associated with the key. A function takes the key as an argument and then generates a "hash code" to determine the position of the key and data pointers in the parallel arrays. The nature of the hash code function tends to lead to the apparent randomness in key distribution—which accounts for the shape's inability to access data keyed with similar but not identical keys.

Summary In Table 15.3, we present some common collection types, the associated STL objects, and their characteristics. Of these collections, the STL **vector, list,** and **map** are the most commonly used.

15.3.2: Iterators

Regardless of a collection's shape properties, it is usually desirable to have the ability to go through the set of elements in linear fashion. To do so, STL collection classes holding sequences of objects automatically define an **iterator** object type whenever a template class is created. The purpose of the iterator object is to allow you to move through the collection sequentially using a common interface that applies to all collections. Iterator variables can be declared as follows:

```
template-name<parameters>::iterator   variable-name;
```

| **FIGURE 15.5** | Typical Parallel Array Lookup Table Organization |

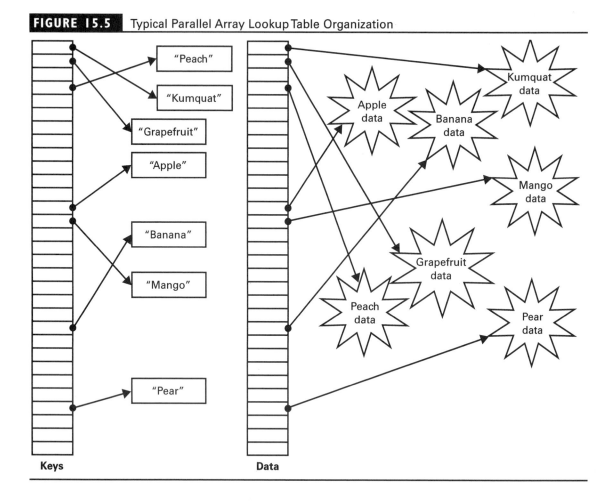

The interface of the iterator should be familiar to C++ programmers—it is used exactly like a pointer. In other words, if nPos is declared as an iterator:

- *nPos accesses the collection element at that position.
- nPos[offset] accesses collection elements for shapes supporting random access.
- *(nPos+offset) also accesses collection elements for shapes supporting random access.
- nPos++ moves the iterator to the next element in the collection.
- nPos−− moves to the previous element in the collection.

In addition, two class member functions are defined for use with iterators:

- begin() returns the iterator value at the start of the collection.
- end() returns a special iterator value signifying that we incremented the last element of the collection.

TABLE 15.3	Common Collection Types and Their Shape Characteristics	
STL Object	**Collection Description**	**Shape Characteristics**
deque **vector**	Dynamic array-type objects that provide random access and can grow efficiently when elements are added to the end; deque also supports fast adds at the beginning	Random access: yes Keyed access: no Insert/Delete at beginning: linear (vector) Insert/Delete at beginning: fast (deque) Insert/Delete in middle: linear Insert/Delete at end: fast
User-implemented *sorted array*	Sorted array, using vector or deque objects	Random access: yes Exact keyed access: logarithmic Approximate keyed access: logarithmic Insert/Delete: linear+
list	A collection of objects linked together in a conceptual chain that permits efficient element insertion and deletion	Random access: no Keyed access: linear Insert/Delete: fast
queue	A collection, normally used for processing elements in sequence, that only allows elements at both ends to be accessed; implemented as an adapter that is attached to some other underlying shape	Random access: no Keyed access: no Insert/Delete at beginning: fast Insert/Delete in middle: no Insert/Delete at end: fast
stack	A collection, normally used for processing elements, allowing only elements at the end to be accessed, in LIFO (last-in, first-out) order; implemented as an adapter that is attached to some other underlying shape	Random access: no Keyed access: no Insert/Delete at beginning: no Insert/Delete in middle: no Insert/Delete at end: fast
User-implemented *sorted tree* *map*	A collection of objects linked together to permit efficient searching, addition, and deletion	Random access: no Exact keyed access: logarithmic Approximate keyed access: logarithmic Insert/Delete: logarithmic
hash_map	A lookup table, normally implemented with a technique called hashing, that allows keyed elements to be accessed rapidly, and independently of the table size	Random access: yes Exact keyed access: size-independent Approximate keyed access: no Insert/Delete: fast

As an example, consider **string** objects. Because they are collections of characters, individual characters can be accessed using iterators in addition to the [] notation or the at() member. In fact, the following two code fragments accomplish precisely the same result:

```
// character access using length and [] overload
for(unsigned int i=0;i<s6.length();i++) {
    // accessing individual characters
    cout << s6[i] << " ";
}
```

and

```
// character access using iterator
string::iterator iter;
for(iter=s6.begin();iter!=s6.end();iter++) {
    // accessing individual characters
    cout << *iter << " ";
}
```

The principal advantage of using iterators to access class elements is their consistency across shapes. Therefore, if you know how to iterate through a vector using an iterator, you can do the same thing in a list or map. In addition, the STL provides various flavors of iterators (e.g., reverse iterators, random access iterators) whose availability varies by shape.

15.3: SECTION QUESTIONS

1. Is a collection's shape best viewed as an interface or implementation property?
2. As elements are added to the end of a dynamic array (e.g., a GArray object), we periodically need to resize it. Would the same be true of a list shape?
3. Why does it make sense to implement stacks and queues on top of other collections?
4. Why does the STL fail to provide a standard tree collection?
5. What are the principal advantages of creating an iterator data type with each template class?
6. Describe any obvious drawback of the iterator interface.
7. Does the fact that iterators act like pointers indicate that they are pointers?

15.4: THE vector<> STL CLASS

 Walkthrough available in Vector.wmv

The vector<> template class can be used to encapsulate an array of virtually any type of object for which an assignment operator is available. Its flexibility allows it to substitute for most arrays normally used in programs—greatly increasing code integrity in the process.

15.4.1: vector Overview

Among the characteristics that differentiate **vector**<> objects from standard arrays are the following:

- Dynamic resizing as elements are added (using the insert() and push_back() members)
- Ability to remove elements (using the remove() and pop_back() members)
- Bounds checking performed as elements are accessed using the [] operator
- size() operator returns the number of elements in the **vector**
- Access can be performed using an iterator

Whenever you use **vector** objects in your program, you must include the C++ STL vector library file with the statement:

```
#include <vector>
using namespace std;
```

15.4.2: vector<> Interface

The **vector<>** interface is similar to that of the *PtrArray* and *GArray<>* classes that were presented in Chapter 14, Section 14.3.2, and in Section 15.1.3. Some differences include:

- The vector<> template defines an iterator in addition to supporting the [] overload and allows us to go through the elements of an array many different ways. For example:

```
vector<string> arText;
// initialization omitted
for(i=0;i<arText.size();i++) {
    cout << arText[i] << " ";
}
```

and

```
// iterator using "pointer arithmetic" style
for(i=0;i<arText.size();i++) {
    cout << *(arText.begin()+i) << " ";
}
```

and

```
vector<string>::iterator iter;
// using same approach as string example
for(iter=arText.begin();iter!=arText.end();iter++) {
    cout << *iter << " ";
}
```

- vector<> template insertion requires an iterator to identify the insertion point.

A demonstration of the **vector<>** interface, creating and then performing operations of an int vector, followed by a string vector, is shown in Example 15.4. The output from running the demonstration function is presented in Figure 15.6.

15.4.3: vector<> Member Functions

The **vector<>** member functions are similar to those of the **string** and other collection classes. Some of the more important members are summarized in Table 15.4.

15.4: SECTION QUESTIONS

1. Why would we want to use vector<> objects in place of true C++ arrays wherever we can? What cost might come from doing so?
2. What does it mean when we say a vector<> collection is type safe?
3. If iter is the name of an iterator, what does iter[3] refer to? Are any restrictions put on the use of brackets with iterators?
4. Explain the arText.begin()+3 in the expression:
   arText.insert(arText.begin()+3,"Is");
5. Where do the member names pop_back() and push_back() likely derive from?
6. What is the difference between a vector's capacity and its size?

EXAMPLE 15.4

Demonstration of vector<> template class

```
void VectorDemo()
{
    vector<int> arSquares;
    // ading values to end of vector
    for(unsigned int i=1;i<=10;i++) {
        arSquares.push_back(i*i);
    }
    cout << endl <<  "Test of integer array!" << endl;
    for(i=0;i<arSquares.size();i++) {
        cout << i+1 << '\t' << arSquares[i] << endl;
    }
    vector<string> arText;
    // inserting values at the start of the vector
    string s0("Me"),s1("It\'s"),s2("World"),s3("Hello");
    arText.insert(arText.begin(),s0);
    arText.insert(arText.begin(),s1);
    arText.insert(arText.begin(),s2);
    arText.insert(arText.begin(),s3);
    cout << endl << "First string vector test:" << endl;
    for(i=0;i<arText.size();i++) {
        cout << arText[i] << " ";
    }
    cout << endl;
    // inserting values at position 3
    arText.insert(arText.begin()+3,"Is");
    // replacing a value
    arText[2]="It";
    // removing an element
    arText.erase(arText.begin()+1);
    cout << endl << "Second string vector test:" << endl;
    // iterator using "pointer arithmetic" style
    for(i=0;i<arText.size();i++) {
        cout << *(arText.begin()+i) << " ";
    }
    vector<string>::iterator iter;
    cout << endl << endl << "Third string vector test:" << endl;
    // using same approach as string example
    for(iter=arText.begin();iter!=arText.end();iter++) {
        cout << *iter << " ";
    }
    cout << endl;
    return;
}
```

FIGURE 15.6   Output of VectorDemo() Function

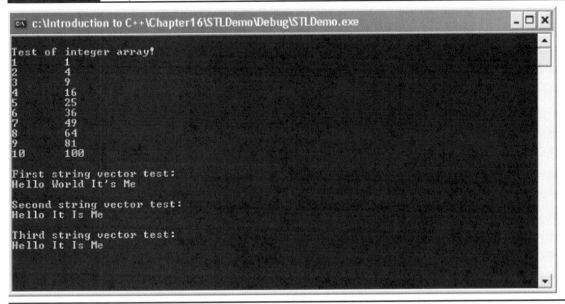

```
c:\Introduction to C++\Chapter16\STLDemo\Debug\STLDemo.exe

Test of integer array!
1       1
2       4
3       9
4       16
5       25
6       36
7       49
8       64
9       81
10      100

First string vector test:
Hello World It's Me

Second string vector test:
Hello It Is Me

Third string vector test:
Hello It Is Me
```

TABLE 15.4   Selected vector<> Member Functions, Compiled from Visual Studio .NET Documentation

Operator	Arguments	Purpose
assign	1. vector	Replaces the contents of the vector with its argument
begin	None	Returns an iterator that can be used for random access (i.e., supports [] operators) to the first element of the vector
capacity	1. None	Number of available elements before the vector must resize
clear erase	None (clear) 1. iterator (erase) 2. iterator=end() (erase)	Empties the contents of a vector Allows an optional specified range of the vector to be emptied
end	None	Returns an iterator representing the position beyond the data in the array
insert	1. iterator 2. element-object	Inserts an element at the specified position within the vector (*Note*: other overloads also exist)
pop_back	None	Removes last element in the vector
push_back	1. element-object	Adds element to the end of the vector
reserve	1. element-count	Sets the minimum size of the vector before resizing must occur
size	None	Returns number of elements in the vector

15.5: TEMPLATE OBJECT EXERCISES

In this section, we develop two relatively simple classes, a Person class and a collection class that maintains a sorted array of pointers to Person objects. These two classes will later be used extensively in the Video Store lab exercise presented at the end of Chapter 16. Before beginning with these classes, however, we will overload the >> and << operators for loading and saving string objects.

15.5.1: Loading and Saving String Objects

In order to complete the exercises in this chapter and the next, it is convenient to overload the output/insertion (<<) and input/extraction (>>) operators for loading and saving strings to a file. To make them easy to access, we make them inline functions in a file called utils.h, the contents of which are presented in Example 15.5.

In the output (insertion) overload we do the following:

- Save the length of the string (+ 1 character to include the NUL terminator) after truncating it to no more than MAXSTRINGLEN-1 characters.
- Copy the (truncated, if necessary) characters into a text buffer using the **string** copy() member.
- Save the buffer to the strm.

EXAMPLE 15.5

string object overloads in utils.h

```
// utils.h: contains useful utility functions
#include <string>
#include "SimpleIO.h"

#define MAXSTRINGLEN 32001

inline STREAM &operator<<(STREAM &strm,const string &str) {
    int nLen=(int)str.length();
    nLen=(nLen>MAXSTRINGLEN-1) ? MAXSTRINGLEN-1 : nLen;
    WriteInteger(nLen+1);
    char buf[MAXSTRINGLEN]={0};
    str.copy(buf,nLen);
    WriteBlock(strm,buf,nLen+1);
    return strm;
}

inline STREAM &operator>>(STREAM &strm,string &str) {
    int nVal=ReadInteger(strm);
    char buf[MAXSTRINGLEN]={0};
    nVal=(nVal>MAXSTRINGLEN-1) ? MAXSTRINGLEN-1 : nVal;
    ReadBlock(strm,buf,nVal);
    str=buf;
    return strm;
}
```

The input (extraction) proceeds in similar fashion:

- We read the integer length.
- We truncate (if necessary) to protect our buffer.
- We read the string into our buffer.
- We assign our buffer to the string.

TEST YOUR UNDERSTANDING 15.2:

Why should it never be necessary to truncate the strings we are reading in?

15.5.2: A Person Class

Walkthrough available in Person.wmv

The Person object we are creating here is a simple object—having only first name and last name data members. In Chapter 16, however, we will be taking this class and using it as a basis for an inheritance network. For this reason, we include quite a number of member functions, in addition to normal accessor functions and overloads, such as the following:

- Input() and Display(): Intended for console-oriented I/O
- Get() and Print(): Intended for I/O from a fixed text file
- Load() and Save(): Intended for I/O from a binary file
- Key(): Returns a combination of last name and first name intended to be a unique identifier for collections
- FixedString(): Generates a fixed length string containing last name and first name of a type consistent with what the Get() function reads from a file
- Overloads of << and >> for binary file load and save
- Overloads of << and >> for fixed text file load and save

The header file for the class is presented in Example 15.6.

By now, virtually everything in the header should be familiar. A few comments:

- The Key() function uses concatenation to develop a lookup key for our Person. This function will be used in Section 15.5.3.
- The IsValid() function is used to detect a valid load—in this case a "valid" person cannot have an empty last name. We don't use this function until Chapter 16.
- The >> and << operator overloads don't need to be friend functions, because we are just wrapping them around public member functions.

The Person functions themselves are also, for the most part, quite simple. The binary file functions could not be simpler, as shown in Example 15.7.

Because we overloaded the << and >> operators for binary load/save of **string** objects in Section 15.5.1, our Load() and Save() members take advantage of this fact. And, as already noted, we just wrap our Person << and >> operators around those functions.

The Input() and Display() functions, presented in Example 15.8, are equally trivial. Input() uses the SimpleIO functions to read in the data. To make it useful as an editing function, it displays the existing values for the data members (if any) by contatenating [

EXAMPLE 15.6

Person class declaration (Person.h)

```
class Person
{
public:
    Person(void);
    virtual ~Person(void);
    Person(const Person &pers) {
        Copy(pers);
    }
    const Person &operator=(const Person &pers) {
        if (&pers==this) return *this;
        Copy(pers);
        return *this;
    }
    void Copy(const Person &pers) {
        m_szLastName=pers.m_szLastName;
        m_szFirstName=pers.m_szFirstName;
    }

    string LastName() const {return m_szLastName;}
    void LastName(const char *szName){m_szLastName=szName;}
    string FirstName() const {return m_szFirstName;}
    void FirstName(const char *szName){m_szFirstName=szName;}

    string Key() const {return m_szLastName+","+m_szFirstName;}
    bool IsValid() const {return !m_szLastName.empty();}

    void Input();
    void Display() const;
    void Get(INPUT &in);
    void Print(OUTPUT &out) const;
    string FixedString() const;
    void Load(STREAM &strm);
    void Save(STREAM &strm) const;

protected:
    string m_szLastName;
    string m_szFirstName;
};

INPUT &operator>>(INPUT &in,Person &pers);
OUTPUT &operator<<(OUTPUT &out,const Person &pers);
STREAM &operator>>(STREAM &strm,Person &pers);
STREAM &operator<<(STREAM &strm,const Person &pers);
```

EXAMPLE 15.7

Person binary loading and saving members

```
void Person::Load(STREAM &strm)
{
    strm >> m_szLastName;
    strm >> m_szFirstName;
}


void Person::Save(STREAM &strm) const
{
    strm << m_szLastName;
    strm << m_szFirstName;
}

STREAM &operator>>(STREAM &strm,Person &pers)
{
    pers.Load(strm);
    return strm;
}
STREAM &operator<<(STREAM &strm,const Person &pers)
{
    pers.Save(strm);
    return strm;
}
```

EXAMPLE 15.8

Person input and display members

```
void Person::Input() {
    char buf[1024];
    DisplayString("Last Name: ");
    if (!m_szLastName.empty())
        DisplayString(("["+m_szLastName+"] ").c_str());
    InputString(buf);
    if (buf[0]!=0) m_szLastName=buf;
    DisplayString("First Name: ");
    if (!m_szFirstName.empty())
        DisplayString(("["+m_szFirstName+"] ").c_str());
    InputString(buf);
    if (buf[0]!=0) m_szFirstName=buf;
}

void Person::Display() const
{
    cout << "Last Name:\t" << LastName() << endl;
    cout << "First Name:\t" << FirstName() << endl;
}
```

and] around the existing value to create a new string. Then it uses the c_str() member and converts it for passing into the SimpleIO DisplayString() function. For example:

```
if (!m_szLastName.empty())
    DisplayString(("["+m_szLastName+"] ").c_str());
```

If the user hits return (causing an empty string to be placed in buf), the function does not modify the exiting value.

In Display() we don't even bother with SimpleIO. Because **string** objects have the << and >> text stream operators already overloaded as part of the STL, we just send them to cout.

The fixed format members, Get(), Print(), and FixedString() require slightly more explanation. The idea behind them is to create paired functions for writing and reading fixed text. The write function, Print(), calls FixedString(), which in turn does the following:

- Creates a buffer filled with 40 space characters.
- Assigns the buffer to a string, str.
- Uses the replace() member to replace however many spaces are required with the last name, starting at position 0. The call LastName().substr(0,20) prevents more than 20 characters for the last name.
- Uses the replace() member to replace however many spaces are required with the first name, starting at position 20.
- Returns the resulting string.

The reading function, Get(), does the following:

- Reads a line from the stream.
- Assigns that line to a string (szBuf).
- Uses the substr() member to extract the last name and first name strings from the buffer.
- Calls the Trim() function (defined in utils.h and shown in Example 15.9), which removes any trailing white characters in the two strings.

These write and read functions are presented in Example 15.10.

15.5.3: A Sorted Person Array

Walkthrough available in PersonArray.wmv

The PersonArray class is designed to maintain an array of keyed Person objects—allowing no duplicate objects in the array.

EXAMPLE 15.9

Trim() function in Utils.h

```
inline void Trim(string &str) {
    int nLen=(int)str.length()-1;
    while(nLen>=0 && str[nLen]<=' ') nLen--;
    str.erase(nLen+1);
}
```

EXAMPLE 15.10

Person members for fixed format I/O

```
string Person::FixedString() const
{
    char buf[1024]={0};
    int i;
    for(i=0;i<40;i++) buf[i]=' ';
    string str=buf;
    str.replace(0,LastName().substr(0,20).length(),LastName().substr(0,20));
    str.replace(20,FirstName().substr(0,20).length(),FirstName().substr(0,20));
    return str;
}

void Person::Get(INPUT &in) {
    char buf[1024];
    GetLine(in,buf,1024);
    string szBuf=buf;
    m_szLastName=szBuf.substr(0,20);
    Trim(m_szLastName);
    m_szFirstName=szBuf.substr(20,20);
    Trim(m_szFirstName);
}

void Person::Print(OUTPUT &out) const
{
    PrintLine(out,FixedString().c_str());
}

INPUT &operator>>(INPUT &in,Person &pers) {
    pers.Get(in);
    return in;
}

OUTPUT &operator<<(OUTPUT &out,const Person &pers)
{
    pers.Print(out);
    return out;
}
```

Interface   The PersonArray interface includes a variety of features:

- An Add() member used to add a Person pointer to the array. Other insertion members are not included in the interface because, in a sorted array, a given element should only be in one position.
- Several different overloads of the Find() member, causing a binary search of the array to be conducted and a Person pointer returned if a match is found.
- Two types of overloads of the [] operator:
  - [int] returns the element pointer at the specified position in the array.

■ [string] returns the element pointer with the key matching the string (or 0 if no match is found).
- A Remove() member that removes a specified key, deleting the associated Person object.
- A RemoveAll() member that removes all Person elements and deletes them.
- Load() and Save() members for binary serialization, as well as overloads of the >> and << operators.

Some test code that uses the class is presented in Example 15.11. The output from a run where five names were entered is presented in Figure 15.7.

Implementation   The implementation of the PersonArray class is similar to what we have seen before except for its use of insertion sort to keep its elements in order. We first make the actual collection that holds the data—a vector<Person*> object—a protected member, and then limit modifications to additions and removals. All functions that return a Person * return that pointer as a const value—meaning it should not be changed. (To change a person object, you'd need to remove it, modify it, and then add it back.)

The class declaration, in PersonArray.h, is presented in Example 15.12. One aspect of the interface design was that many versions of the same member are provided—the only difference being variation in how the argument is presented (e.g., const char * vs. string&). The main purpose of the various versions is to make access for the programmer more convenient.

The most critical function of the class is the protected FindPos() function both, shown in Example 15.13. The function implements binary search, as discussed in Chapter 9, Section 9.3.2. The significance of its return value is as follows:
- If it finds the key, it returns the position of the key.
- If it doesn't find the key, it returns the position where the key would be located.

Many other member functions then use the result of the search. The public functions for locating keyed values, both Find() functions and text overloads of the [] operator, are presented in Example 15.14. All return 0 if the key is not found, and all do little more than provide convenient packaging around FindPos(). In this way, the function ensures that any error found in our binary search routine needs to be fixed in only one place.

The routines for addition and deletion just provide a wrapper around the vector<Person*> object's own interface. They are presented in Example 15.15.

In the case of the two overloads of the Add() member, two different purposes are being accomplished:
- The Add(Person *) takes a Person pointer to the actual object that is being added to the collection, which should have been created with the **new** operator.
- The Add(const Person&) overload, in contrast, actually creates a new object by making a copy of the argument that was passed. This feature would be useful where a Person has been edited, for example.

Both return −1 if the addition fails.

The Add(Person *) member performs what is called an insertion sort. Instead of adding elements at the end of the array, it finds the position where they would be if they were present (the value returned by then FindPos() member), then inserts them there. It is actually a reasonably efficient sort (roughly $N * \text{Log } N$), and is much better than swap sorting (Chapter 10, Section 10.6), which is about N^2.

EXAMPLE 15.11

Test function using PersonArray class

```
void TestPersonArray()
{
    PersonArray ar;
    DisplayString("To stop entering people, make a person\'s last name \'99\'");
    NewLine();
    Person pers;
    while(pers.LastName()!="99")
    {
        pers.Input();
        if (pers.LastName()=="99") continue;
        int nPos=ar.Add(pers);
        if (nPos<0) {
            DisplayString("Duplicate person encountered!");
            NewLine();
        }
        else {
            DisplayFormatted("Person added at position %i",nPos);
            NewLine();
        }
    }
    int i;
    NewLine();
    DisplayString("Printing array contents:");
    NewLine();
    for(i=0;i<ar.Size();i++) {
        cout << i << ". " << ar[i]->Key() << endl;
    }
    // test [] lookup and remove
    DisplayString("Enter LastName,FirstName values to test lookup and removal"
      " (99 to end)");
    NewLine();
    string LName;
    while(LName!="99")
    {
        char buf[256];
        InputString(buf);
        LName=buf;
        if (LName=="99") continue;
        const Person *p=ar[LName];
        if (p==0) {
            DisplayString("Not found!");
            NewLine();
        }
        else {
            p->Display();
            NewLine();
            ar.Remove(p->Key().c_str());
        }
    }
    NewLine();
    DisplayString("Printing array contents:");
    NewLine();
    for(i=0;i<ar.Size();i++) {
        cout << i << ". " << ar[i]->Key() << endl;
    }
}
```

FIGURE 15.7 Output from a TestPersonArray() Function

In the case of the Remove() members, the RemoveAt(int) does the actual removal and deletion of the Person being removed. The various Remove() overloads just package the call to RemoveAt() in different ways.

RemoveAll() does a complete removal: deleting all elements then calling clear on the vector<Person*> object itself. This function is called in the destructor and before loading data from a binary file. As we emphasize throughout the text, whenever the same task needs to be performed in more than one place, it makes sense to define a function.

The Load() and Save() members, along with their >> and << overloads, are presented in Example 15.16. In each case, they take advantage of the fact that we have already implemented serialization on our Person object. So, consistent with our general philosophy for collections, we just save/load the collection size, then loop through the elements calling save/load on each. The >> and << overloads, in turn, are identical to those implemented in the Person class.

EXAMPLE 15.12

Person Array class declaration (PersonArray.h)

```
class PersonArray
{
public:
    PersonArray(void);
    ~PersonArray(void);

    const Person *operator[](int) const;
    const Person *operator[](const char *) const;
    const Person *operator[](const string &szKey) const;
    const Person *Find(const char *szKey,int &nPos) const;
    const Person *Find(const char *szKey) const;
    const Person *Find(const string &szKey) const;

    int Add(Person *);
    int Add(const Person &pers);
    void Remove(const char *szKey);
    void RemoveAt(int nVal);
    void Remove(Person *p);
    int Size() const;
    void RemoveAll();

    void Load(STREAM &strm);
    void Save(STREAM &strm) const;

protected:
    vector<Person*> m_arp;
    int FindPos(const string &szKey) const;
    int FindPos(const char *szKey) const;
};

STREAM &operator>>(STREAM &strm,PersonArray &ar);
STREAM &operator<<(STREAM &strm,const PersonArray &ar);
```

EXAMPLE 15.13

FindPos() member functions of PersonArray class

```
// implements binary search
int PersonArray::FindPos(const char *szKey) const {
    int nLower=0,nUpper=(int)m_arp.size();
    if (m_arp.size()==0 || m_arp[0]->Key()>=szKey) return 0;
    while(nUpper-nLower>1) {
        int nTest=(nUpper+nLower)/2;
        if (m_arp[nTest]->Key()<szKey) nLower=nTest;
        else if (m_arp[nTest]->Key()>szKey) nUpper=nTest;
        else return nTest;
    }
    return nUpper;
}
```

EXAMPLE 15.14

Find() member functions of the PersonArray class

```
const Person *PersonArray::Find(const string &szKey) const{
    return Find(szKey.c_str());
}

const Person *PersonArray::Find(const char *szKey,int &nPos) const
{
    nPos=FindPos(szKey);
    if (nPos==Size() || m_arp[nPos]->Key()!=szKey) return 0;
    return m_arp[nPos];
}

const Person *PersonArray::Find(const char *szKey) const {
    int nPos;
    return Find(szKey,nPos);
}

const Person *PersonArray::operator[](const char *szKey) const {
    return Find(szKey);
}

const Person *PersonArray::operator[](const string &szKey) const {
    return Find(szKey.c_str());
}
```

One capability not added to the PersonArray class (although presented as an end-of-chapter exercise) is the copy construct/assignment operator. This decision was intentional, for two reasons. First, collections such as this one could, potentially, get quite large, so we should be reluctant to see them copied when a reference would suffice. Second, there's no obvious reason why we should need to make a copy of this particular collection.

As a result of this decision, both the constructor and destructor functions for the class are simple, as shown in Example 15.17, along with the two remaining overloads/functions, both of which are trivial in nature.

We turn next to a lab that incorporates the PersonArray into a Company class.

15.6: LAB EXERCISE: COMPANY CLASS

Walkthrough available in Company.wmv

In this section, we implement a simple class that we call the Company class. Its primary purpose is to manage a collection of employees who, for the time being, will be implemented as Person objects. This class is relatively straightforward to build, and will be an important building block of the inheritance lab exercise at the end of Chapter 16.

15.6.1: Class Overview

The Company class is, for the most part, a class that manages a collection of employees. Furthermore, for the time being, we will just treat our newly created Person object as an employee, although we will be extending what constitutes an employee in Chapter 16.

EXAMPLE 15.15

PersonArray addition and removal member functions

```cpp
int PersonArray::Add(Person *pers) {
    int nPos;
    if (Find(pers->Key().c_str(),nPos)) return -1;
    vector<Person*>::iterator iter=m_arp.begin();
    m_arp.insert(iter+nPos,pers);
    return nPos;
}

int PersonArray::Add(const Person &pers) {
    Person *p=new Person(pers);
    int nRet=Add(p);
    if (nRet<0) delete p;
    return nRet;
}


void PersonArray::Remove(const char *szKey) {
    int nPos;
    if (!Find(szKey,nPos)) return;
    RemoveAt(nPos);
}

void PersonArray::Remove(Person *p) {
    assert(p!=0);
    Remove(p->Key().c_str());
}

void PersonArray::RemoveAt(int nPos)
{
    assert(nPos>=0 && nPos<(int)m_arp.size());
    if (nPos<0 || nPos>Size()) return;
    delete m_arp[nPos];
    vector<Person*>::iterator iter=m_arp.begin();
    m_arp.erase(iter+nPos);
}

void PersonArray::RemoveAll()
{
    for(int i=0;i<(int)m_arp.size();i++) {
        delete m_arp[i];
    }
    m_arp.clear();
}
```

EXAMPLE 15.16

Load and save members of PersonArray

```
void PersonArray::Load(STREAM &strm)
{
    RemoveAll();
    int nVal=ReadInteger(strm);
    for(int i=0;i<nVal;i++) {
        Person *pers=new Person;
        strm >> *pers;
        m_arp.push_back(pers);
    }
}

void PersonArray::Save(STREAM &strm) const
{
    WriteInteger(strm,Size());
    for(int i=0;i<Size();i++) {
        strm << *(m_arp[i]);
    }
}

STREAM &operator>>(STREAM &strm,PersonArray &ar)
{
    ar.Load(strm);
    return strm;
}
STREAM &operator<<(STREAM &strm,const PersonArray &ar)
{
    ar.Save(strm);
    return strm;
}
```

EXAMPLE 15.17

Constructor, destructor, and remaining functions

```
PersonArray::PersonArray(void)
{
}

PersonArray::~PersonArray(void)
{
    RemoveAll();
}

const Person *PersonArray::operator[](int i) const {
    assert(i>=0 && i<(int)m_arp.size());
    if (i<0 || i>Size()) return 0;
    return m_arp[i];
}

int PersonArray::Size() const {
    return (int)m_arp.size();
}
```

The basic functionality we want to extend to the class is the following:

- The ability to add and remove employees
- The ability to find an employee using a lookup key
- The ability to edit employees
- The ability to load and save company data to a binary file stream
- The ability to import and export employees from a fixed length text file format

Most of these functionalities already exist within the PersonArray class. The major job in the lab is, therefore, to implement the Company interface through which PersonArray capabilities are implemented.

15.6.2: Class Specifications

The key functions to be implemented for the Company class are described in Table 15.5.

Most of the "useful" class members perform tasks comparable to that of the PersonArray class. A few additional members include the following:

```
virtual void Menu() const;
```

The Menu() option should display the options (10–12, 101–107) and descriptions to the screen. For example:

```
1   - Change Name
10  - Display all data
11  - Load
12  - Save
101 - Add an Employee
102 - Remove an Employee
103 - Edit an Employee
etc.
```

This particular implementation will help us when we start inheriting the Company class in Chapter 16.

```
virtual bool Option(int nOption);
```

Takes the integer value of an option typed in by the user and calls the appropriate top-level function (e.g., implemented with a case statement). The function should return **true** unless the option selected is not one of the valid option numbers (i.e., 101–108), in which case it should return **false**. For example:

```
switch(nOption)
{
    case 101:
    {
        AddEmployee();
        break;
    }
    case 102:
    {
        RemoveEmployee();
        break;
    }
    // More options
    default:
    {
```

TABLE 15.5	Top-Level Menu Options for Company Class

Menu Option No.	**Top-Level Company Functions**
1	**void ChangeName() const** Used to change the name of the Company object. Prompts user for new name.
10	**void DisplayAll() const** Displays the company name and all the Employee objects.
11	**void LoadFromFile()** Prompts the user for a file name, opens the file for reading, then loads the Company data from the file.
12	**void SaveToFile() const** Prompts the user for a file name, opens the file for writing, then saves the Company data to the file.
101	**void AddEmployee()** Prompts the user for an Employee ID and, if the ID is valid (i.e., not already present), allows the user to edit and add the Employee to the PersonArray collection.
102	**void RemoveEmployee()** Calls FindEmployee(true) to access the Employee object, displaying the data. Prompts the user for a confirmation and, if the user confirms, removes the Employee object from the PersonArray collection.
103	**void EditEmployee()** Calls FindEmployee(false) to access the Employee object, then allows the user to edit the Employee.
104	**Person *FindEmployee(bool bDisplay=true) const** Prompts the user for an Employee ID and, if the ID is valid returns a pointer to the employee. If bDisplay is true, displays the Employee object's data.
105	**void ListEmployees() const** Displays the data for all employees in the PersonArray, one employee per line.
106	**void ImportEmployees()** Prompts the user for a file name (presumably a text file), then loads the fixed format employee records into the PersonArray.
107	**void Export Employees() const** Prompts the user for a file name (presumably a text file), then saves the employee records from the PersonArray in a fixed text format.
N/A	**void Interface()** Enters a loop that displays a menu (i.e., calling the Menu() function), prompts the user for an option number, then selects one of the preceding options (i.e., calling the Option() function).

```
                return false;
        }
    }
    return true;

    void ImportEmployees(INPUT &in);
    void ExportEmployees(OUTPUT &out) const;
```

Uses the argument to save or load employees using a text stream in fixed text format. Obviously, it should be the same format already supported by the Person object. These functions can be used with sample data provided in the lab folder.

```
const Person *GetEmployee(int i);
int EmployeeCount() const;
```

Allows random access of employees, in place of defining an iterator. Although we could overload the [] operator for this purpose as well, thinking of a company as an array of employees doesn't really clarify the problem. In Chapter 16, we will make enhancements to the class (through inheritance) that would cause the notation to become positively confusing.

The declaration that should be used for the Company class is presented in Example 15.18. Only simple accessor functions have been omitted, which should be defined according to the conventions you have already seen many times. No copy constructor or assignment overload is required, for the same reasons presented in the design of the PersonArray class.

15.6.3: Instructions

The Company class has enough members so that you need to be a bit methodical about testing. You should begin writing a simple Menu() function that lists the specified options, and an Option() function that implements the selection of the option. You can then write an Interface() function that should contain a nonterminating loop that works roughly as follows:

- Calls Menu() to display the options if some local display variable (e.g., bDisplay) is true
- Sets the display variable to **false**
- Displays the prompt, which is not part of the Menu() (the reason involves facilitating inheritance in Chapter 16, as we shall see)
- Prompts the user for the option, read in as a NUL terminated string
- Checks for an empty line—if so, it sets the display variable to **true** (causing the menu to refresh the next iteration of the loop)
- Checks for the 'Q' option and returns **true** if found
- If not 'Q', sends the integer value to the Option() function
- If Option() returns **false**, informs the user that the option was illegal and sets the display variable to **true**

The screen display for a Company object when the Interface() member is called should be roughly the same as Figure 15.8.

Once your Interface() function is implemented, you are free to choose the order of implementation. A reasonable order would be:

- Adding an employee
- Employee() and EmployeeCount(), useful in many of the other functions
- Listing employees
- Loading and saving employees (saving you lots of subsequent typing)
- Deleting employees
- Editing employees (Recall that when you edit an employee, you could be changing its name. As a result, a common procedure is to delete then add the employee after the edit has been performed.)

EXAMPLE 15.18

Company class declaration

```cpp
class Company
{
public:
    Company(void);
    virtual ~Company(void);

    virtual void RemoveAll();

    // top-level functions
    void ChangeName();
    void DisplayAll() const;
    void LoadFromFile();
    void SaveToFile() const;
    void AddEmployee();
    void RemoveEmployee();
    void EditEmployee();
    Person *FindEmployee(bool bDisplay=true) const;
    void ListEmployees() const;
    void ImportEmployees();
    void ExportEmployees() const;
    void Interface() const;

    // useful functions in class
    bool AddEmployee(const Person &pers);
    void RemoveEmployee(const char *szKey);
    void RemoveEmployee(const string &szKey);
    Person *FindEmployee(const char *szKey) const;
    Person *FindEmployee(const string &szKey) const;

    void Load(STREAM &strm);
    void Save(STREAM &strm) const;

    Person *GetEmployee(int i) const;
    int EmployeeCount() const;

    // called from Interface()
    void Menu() const;
    bool Option(int nOption);

    void ImportEmployees(INPUT &in);
    void ExportEmployees(OUTPUT &out) const;

protected:
    PersonArray m_arPerson;
    string m_szCompanyName;
};

STREAM &operator>>(STREAM &strm,Company &ar);
STREAM &operator<<(STREAM &strm,const Company &ar);
```

FIGURE 15.8   Example Company::Interface() Display

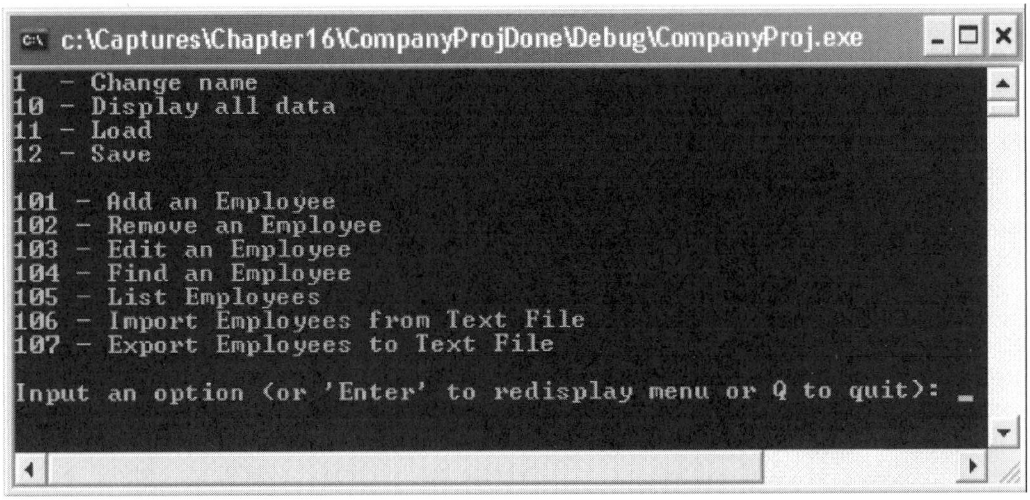

- Exporting employees (Check the file with a text editor once you have created it.)
- Importing employees

During this process, do not change how the Company class is declared. We will be modifying it in the next chapter.

15.7: REVIEW AND QUESTIONS

15.7.1: REVIEW

The standard template library (STL)—which began to be widely supported by compilers in the mid-1990s and became part of the ISO standard in 1998—has largely replaced the original C++ class libraries developed in the early 1980s. When STL classes are included, the .h in the #include statement is typically omitted. This omission is important to be aware of, because adding the .h can lead to the wrong header being accessed. For example:

```
#include <string>
```

accesses the STL **string** implementation, whereas:

```
#include <string.h>
```

accesses the headers that support the standard C NUL terminated string functions.

As the name suggests, the STL is based around the C++ template feature. A template is language capability that allows code for classes and functions to be generated automatically, based on supplied parameters. Template parameters are provided as a comma-separated list between < and > symbols, and may be either data types or constants. They serve to specify the way the templated code is generated. For example, the declaration:

```
vector<int> ar1;
```

serves to declare a dynamic array of integers, generating appropriate source code. On the other hand:

```
vector<string> ar2;
```

declares an array of string objects, and would then generate a different set of source code. As part of compilation and linking, duplicated code generated by template usage is removed—one of the major challenges of implementing development tools that support templates.

During the compilation process, template inconsistencies are detected only as template class objects are declared and used—and the types of errors generated can vary based on the parameters supplied. For example, a template may only work with classes that support assignment overload.

The STL **string** is a templated basic_string<> object designed to work with 1-byte characters. It supports all the standard string operators, including comparison (>, <, <=, >=, != and ==), assignment (=, +=), concatenation (+), character element access([]), and insertion/extraction using a text stream (<< and >>). It also provides member functions for searching and generating substrings. With **string** objects available, it is possible to avoid the awkward syntax required for working with strings that has been around since the introduction of C in the late 1960s and early 1970s.

Collections are a critical part of OOP. To describe a collection, we refer to its "shape," which is a set of properties that relate to its performance across a variety of collection access and modification activities. The STL supports a variety of collection shapes, each of which has its own performance properties:

- *Array* shapes, such as **vector<>**, provide random access but relatively slow insertion/deletion except at the end.

- *Linked List* shapes, such as **list<>**, are efficient only for sequential access but provide for highly efficient insertion/deletion anywhere in the collection.

- *Lookup Table* shapes, such as **hash_map<>**, provide efficient content-based lookup for keyed data (exact matches only) in a collection.

- *Stack and Queue* shapes, such as the **stack<>** and **queue<>**, limit collection access to LIFO (last-in, first-out) and FIFO (first-in, first-out), respectively, and are normally implemented using another collection shape, such as a **list<>** or **vector<>**.

In addition, some common collection shapes tend to be user-implemented, such as the ***sorted array*** and ***tree.***

STL collections holding sequences of objects support a template-specific iterator data type. Once an iterator has been declared, it supports sequential access to collection elements using an interface closely reminiscent of standard pointer arithmetic. For example:

- *nPos accesses the collection element at that position.

- nPos[offset] accesses collection elements for shapes supporting random access.

- *(nPos+offset) also accesses collection elements for shapes supporting random access.

- nPos++ moves the iterator to the next element in the collection.

- nPos—moves to the previous element in the collection.

In addition, two class member functions are defined for use with iterators:

- begin() returns the iterator value at the start of the collection.

- end() returns a special iterator value signifying that we incremented the last element of the collection

The two primary advantages of using iterators are: (1) the programmer can use the same approach to gain access to elements in different shapes, and (2) using iterators can reduce the number of code changes required if the programmer changes an object's underlying collection shape.

The vector<> template implements a type-safe dynamic array object for data types supporting assignment and copying. Its interface includes a [] overload to get at individual elements, along with a variety of insertion and deletion members. A number of advantages of using vector<> objects over true C++ arrays include the following:

- Dynamic resizing as elements are added (using the insert() and push_back() members).

- Ability to remove elements (using the remove() and pop_back() members).

- Bounds checking performed as elements are accessed using the [] operator.

- size() operator returns the number of elements in the **vector.**

- Access can be performed using an iterator.

To create an iterator for use with a vector<> collection, the declaration:

```
vector<type>::iterator iter-var-name ;
```

is made, with *type* matching the type used to create the template object you intend to apply the iterator to. Thereafter, the begin()member of the template object can be used to initialize the iterator. This same procedure applies to other shapes, including **string** objects (where the iterator accesses characters within the string).

The only drawback of using vector<> and string<> objects in place of true arrays and NUL terminated strings is one of performance. On today's computers, however, the performance costs tend to be slight when contrasted with the benefits of code clarity and safety gained from using STL objects.

15.7.2: GLOSSARY

Active Template Library (ATL) A collection of template-based classes, developed by Microsoft, primarily aimed at developing components and applications in a Windows-based environment

bounds checking Ensuring that array positions outside the valid coefficients of the array are not accessed

collection A set of objects that is managed by some other object, the collection object

collection shape The set of performance properties for collection access and modification that determines a collection's most appropriate uses

doubly linked list A linked list shape that supports processing from front-to-back or back-to-front

dynamic resizing The ability of a collection to change its size, as necessary, to accommodate the addition and removal of elements

first-in, first-out (FIFO) Collection access in which elements are processed in the order in which they were added (see **queue<>**)

hashing An algorithm supporting keyed access to data using a coding function to position elements for fast access

iterator An object that can be used to traverse the elements of a collection using a pointer-style interface; each STL collection template defines an iterator data type as part of its implementation, and a common interface is used for all iterators

last-in, first-out (LIFO) Collection access in which elements are added most recently are processed before previously added elements (see **stack<>**)

list<> An STL template class that supports a linked list

linked list A collection shape that supports sequential processing and rapid insertion and deletion of internal elements; conceptually, it can be viewed as a chain of elements linked together by pointers

lookup table A common term used to describe a mapping of keys to objects, normally implemented using a hashing algorithm

map<> An STL template class that supports keyed lookup using an underlying tree shape

node A term commonly used to refer to an element contained in a tree shape

queue<> An STL template class that implements waiting line (FIFO) access to collection members, built on top of some other underlying shape

random access The ability to access elements in a collection without traversing other elements, often implemented with the [] operator

serialization A term frequently used to refer to loading and saving objects in binary form

shape See *collection shape*

singly linked list A linked list shape that supports processing from front-to-back only

stack<> An STL template class that implements stack (LIFO) access to collection members, built on top of some other underlying shape

Standard Template Library (STL) A library of template-based objects that began to replace the original C++ standard libraries in the mid-1990s and became part of the ISO standard in 1998

string An STL template class that implements an encapsulated string object

template A parameterized way to declare a class or function in C++ that causes source code to be generated when a template object/function is created with specified parameters; templates are sometimes likened to code factories

tree A collection shape that supports rapid insertion and deletion of internal elements and access by content and position that is more efficient than that afforded by a linked list; conceptually, it can be viewed as an "organization chart" of elements linked together by pointers, with each parent node potentially pointed to two or more child nodes; trees may be sorted or unsorted

vector<> An STL template class that implements a dynamic array; it takes a single parameter, the data type of the array elements

15.7.3: QUESTIONS

1. *PersonArray collection shape.* Although the PersonArray class was implemented as a sorted vector<>, another shape would have been even more appropriate. Using the general shape descriptions, identify a shape that would have allowed even faster access. Under what foreseeable circumstances would that alternative shape be less attractive?

2. *Tree performance.* Justify why access by content in a sorted tree is logarithmic. (*Hint:* Contrast what would happen when searching a sorted tree with what happens in binary search of an array.)

3. *Copying PersonArray.* Implement a copy constructor and assignment operator for the PersonArray class implemented in Section 15.5.3. (*Hint:* Don't forget that the class expects to have its own copies of the Person objects it manages.)

4. *String trimming.* Implement an LTrim() function, modeled after Trim() in Example 15.9, that trims leading blanks from a string and returns the result.

5. *Case change.* Implement MakeUpper() and MakeLower() functions that are prototyped as follows:

```
void MakeUpper(string &str);
void MakeLower(string &str);
```

The functions should make their argument strings entirely upper/lowercase.

Questions 6–10 involve enhancing the employee and EmpData classes as originally presented in Chapter 13, Sections 13.6.1 and 13.6.2. These modifications parallel the modifications made in Chapter 14, Questions 8–10.

6. *Replace employee embedded name string arrays with string objects.* Change the employee class implementation so that the last name and first names are stored as STL string objects. The only interface changes you should make are to have the LastName() and FirstName() functions return string objects. For example:

```
string LastName() const;
string FirstName() const;
```

Note: As long as the employee interface is maintained, you should not have to change EmpData.

7. *Using a vector<employee> template array.* Replace the embedded array of employees in the EmpData class with a *vector<employee>* member. Implement the change so that the EmpData interface does not change.

8. *Overloading EmpData operators.* After making the modification in Question 7, add a copy constructor, assignment operator, and insertion/extraction (<< and >>) operator overloads to the EmpData class, making its interface consistent with the employee class. (*Hint:* You will also want to define a Copy() member, naturally.)

9. *Using a vector<employee*> template array.* Replace the embedded array of employees in the EmpData class with a *vector<employee*>* member. Implement the change so that the EmpData interface does not change. How does implementing the internal collection using pointers differ from using objects?

10. *Overloading EmpData operators (when employee objects are managed as pointers).* After making the modification in Question 9, add a copy constructor, assignment operator, and insertion/extraction (<< and >>) operator overloads to the EmpData class, making its interface consistent with the employee class. (*Hint:* The effect will be similar to Question 3.)

In-Depth Questions

Questions 11–15 are intended to build upon the DBF Structures lab exercise (Chapter 11, Section 11.7). The objective is to create three classes providing the same functionality as the structures and functions defined in that exercise. They assume the reader is familiar with the exercise in Section 11.7, as well as the dBase lab in Section 7.5.

11. *Creating a Field class.* Create a Field class that encapsulates the field structure of Section 11.7. The field name should be stored as an STL string, with that and all other data elements being protected. In addition to a full set of accessor functions, a Load() member function should be defined as follows:

```
void Field::Load(STREAM &strm);
```

This function should load a field definition from a .DBF file (you may assume the file pointer has been properly positioned). Overload the >> operator as well, to accomplish the same purpose. Because this exercise focuses on creating a reader only, no corresponding Save() member is required. Copy constructors and assignment also need to be implemented. You should also define a bool IsValid() member that checks to see that the field name is not empty, and its length > 0, returning false if they are not.

12. *Creating a FieldSet class.* Create a FieldSet class that manages a vector<Field> collection of fields. In addition to a full set of accessor functions, a Load() member function should be defined as follows:

```
void FieldSet::Load(STREAM &strm,
    int nCount);
```

This function should load nCount field definitions from a .DBF file. (You may assume the file pointer has been properly positioned at the beginning of the field definition section of the .DBF file.) You should also overload the [] operator as follows:

```
Field operator[] (int) const;
Field operator[] (const char *) const;
Field operator[] (const string &) const;
```

The first should return a field based on its position in the table. The two text-based versions should return a field matching the name between the brackets. For all the operators, if the argument is invalid (i.e., invalid position, matching field name not found), the function should return a field object with an empty name.

13. *Creating a Header class.* Create a Header class that holds the information from the 32-byte header block in .dbf file. In addition to a full set of accessor functions, a Load() member function should be defined as follows:

```
void Header::Load(STREAM &strm);
```

This function should reposition the strm pointer to the beginning of the file (if necessary), then load the header information into the appropriate Header members.

14. *Creating a DbfTable class.* Create a DbfTable class that contains an embedded Header and FieldSet. In addition to a full set of accessor functions, a Load() member function should be defined as follows:

```
void DbfHeader::Load(STREAM &strm);
```

This function should load the Header object and then, using the calculated field count, load the FieldSet object. You should also overload the [] operator as follows:

```
string operator[] (int) const;
string operator[] (const char *) const;
string operator[] (const string &) const;
```

The first should return a string that contains the entire record whose number (1 based) is passed in as an argument (i.e., 1 is the number of the first record). It should also set an internal string member (which can be used to implement subsequent field value accesses) to the same string. The two text-based versions take a field name as an argument and return the field value, extracted from the currently loaded record string. For all the operators, if the argument is invalid (i.e., invalid record number, matching field name not found), the function should return an empty string.

In addition to the composed objects, the DbfTable should included (at a minimum):

- A STREAM member that holds the .DBF file stream
- A bool member that keeps track of whether a DBF table is open
- A string member to hold the contents of the current record (as previously noted)
- An integer member keeping track of the currently loaded record in the table

In addition to the operator overloads, the DbfTable should include (at a minimum):

- bool Open(const char *): Opens the DBF file and loads the Header and RecordSet information, returning true if the operation was successful and the data valid.
- void Close(): Closes the current table if it is open (should also be called in the destructor function).
- void Record(int i): Loads the specified record from the file and sets the internal record string. If the record number is invalid, the current record string should be emptied.
- string Field(const char *szFieldName): Returns text value of the field in the currently active record (specified by field name), returning an empty string if it is invalid.
- string Field(int nFieldNumber): Returns text value of the field in the currently active record (specified by number), returning an empty string if it is invalid.
- void DisplayFields(): Displays all field name—field value pairs for the currently loaded record, one pair per line.
- void List(vector<string> &ar): For all records, lists the values of the fields whose names are in ar, one line per record (i.e., tabular form).

You should also write a series of accessor functions to get information from the embedded objects (e.g., a RecordCount() member that accesses RecordCount() from the Header object). Finally, you should write a main() function to test your members as you develop them.

15. *Add an interface to the DbfTable() class.* Add a RunMenu() member to your class to implement a menu that provides the following options to the user:

```
O. Open a DBF table
C. Close the current DBF table
G. Go to a record number
D. Display the record contents
F. Display a field value
L. List records for specified
   fields
Q. Quit
```

Only options O and Q should be displayed if the current table is closed. Only options C through Q should be displayed if a table is open.

Implement each menu option in a select construct, gathering the required data from users and calling the appropriate member functions.

Inheritance and Polymorphism

EXECUTIVE SUMMARY

Chapter 16 introduces the use of inheritance in C++, the final fundamental capability of the language to be introduced in this text. Inheritance provides important representational and computational capabilities not otherwise offered by structured languages. It is particularly well suited to promoting code reuse and providing a means for representing certain types of abstract relationships between different types of data.

The chapter begins with a brief overview of inheritance in general terms, contrasting it with composition. We then explore how inheritance relationships can be specified in a C++ program, and how initialization is accomplished when inherited objects are constructed. The **static_cast** and **dynamic_cast** C++ operators are also explained. We then turn to the subject of polymorphism and how polymorphic member functions differ from other member functions. The final language capability introduced is multiple inheritance, which is presented with a series of cautions because its use can lead to unexpected problems. The chapter concludes with an extended lab exercise, building upon the Person/Company classes introduced in Chapter 15.

LEARNING OBJECTIVES

Upon completing this chapter, you should be able to:

- Explain the benefits of inheritance
- Explain how inheritance differs from composition
- Create a simple UML generalization/specialization diagram using FlowC
- Create inherited classes in C++
- Control construction in inherited classes
- Differentiate between polymorphic and regular member functions
- Call base class member functions within other member functions
- Explain the use of the virtual keyword in polymorphism and multiple inheritance
- Explain the pros and cons of multiple inheritance
- Use inheritance to create a network of classes as part of an application

16.1: INTRODUCTION TO INHERITANCE

Inheritance provides a powerful tool for defining abstract data types (ADTs). Instead of starting with a "blank slate" when we create a class, we can use one or more previously defined classes as a starting point. This capability provides two important benefits:

1. It promotes reuse of existing objects.
2. It implements a new form of relationship between objects that can be useful in visualizing certain types of programming situations.

In this section, we explore inheritance from a general perspective.

16.1.1: What Is Inheritance?

Inheritance is the ability to define a class using a previously defined class as a starting point. In creating an inherited definition, we are usually trying to accomplish two types of objectives:

- *Adding* capabilities that are not present in the original class
- *Overriding* behaviors in the original class that are not appropriate in the inherited class

To illustrate these capabilities, let us suppose we want to define a series of classes to encapsulate different animals. We might begin by defining a series of member functions to access key data elements relevant to all animals, such as:

- Body temperature (e.g., warm-blooded or cold-blooded)
- Does it lay eggs? (true or false)
- Does it give live birth? (true or false)

In addition, we would probably need some members relevant to specific animals or groups of animals, which might include aspects such as:

- Running speed
- Swimming speed
- Hair color

We might also find it useful to view our classes in a taxonomy, organizing our classes into groups and subgroups with common characteristics. This form of organization is, in fact, what biologists do when they define a genus, species, subspecies, and so on, and assign different organisms to them. It is also the same principle used in a C++ inheritance hierarchy. An example is presented in Figure 16.1.

In this hierarchy, we start with a class called Animal having three function members, BodyTemp() (e.g., "warm-blooded" or "cold-blooded"), LiveBirth() (e.g., true or false) and LaysEggs() (e.g., true or false). Although these members are attributes of the class (meaning that all Animal objects have values for them), no meaningful default values exist because hundreds of thousands of animals fall into both categories of each value.

When we specialize to the Mammal and Fish classes, on the other hand, we may override the values for a certain attribute. For example, if we have a Mammal object, we can generally say:

- LiveBirth() returns true

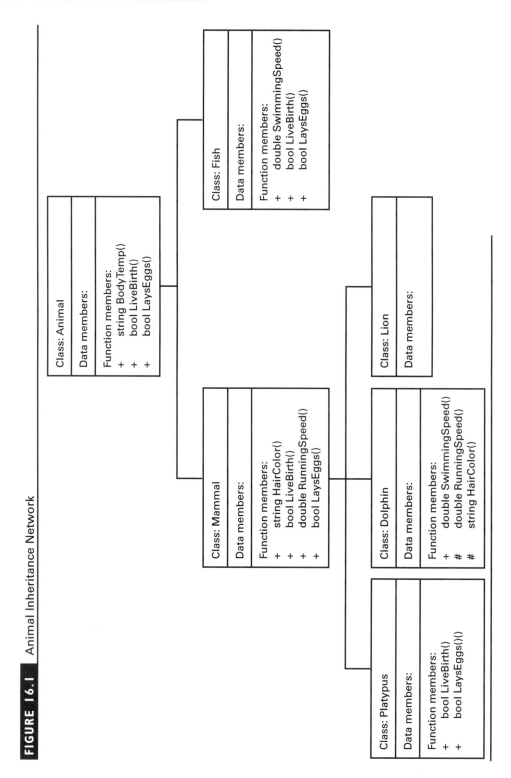

FIGURE 16.1 Animal Inheritance Network

- LaysEggs() returns false
- BodyTemp() is "Warm-Blooded"

It might also make sense to add another member, HairColor(), because mammals generally have hair and, perhaps, RunningSpeed(), reflecting the fact that the vast majority of mammals live on land. These members are both examples of adding capabilities not present in the base class.

Similarly, for the Fish objects, we would probably default to:

- LiveBirth() returns false
- LaysEggs() returns true
- BodyTemp() is "Cold-Blooded"

It might also make sense to add another member, SwimmingSpeed(), reflecting the fact that the vast majority of fish live in water.

Now, if we were to move down a level to actual species—done in this example for three select mammals—we can start to see the need for override. In the case of a Lion object, we are done—lions fit the default for the mammal class very well. All we need to do is initialize relevant members with data reflecting things such as running speed and the color of the lion's fur. When we specialize to a Platypus object, on the other hand, we need to override the default returns for LiveBirth() and LaysEggs(), because the duck-billed platypus is one of a handful of mammals that actually lays eggs.

Similarly, in the case of the Dolphin, the RunningSpeed() member is no longer applicable and HairColor() doesn't really seem that applicable either (although they might have a strand of hair here or there). Removing an inherited member is usually not allowed in inheritance mechanisms so we might do the next best thing: make it protected to remove it from the class interface. It would also make sense to add a SwimmingSpeed() attribute to the Dolphin object.

16.1.2: Benefits of Inheritance

Three principal benefits come with using inheritance in writing programs: conceptual, reuse, and organizational. We briefly consider all three.

Conceptual Taxonomies, such as the Animal taxonomy of Figure 16.1, were used for centuries before OOP was invented as a means of organizing and clarifying relationships between entities. The ability to model such relationships in our code can provide the same type of clarification benefits to both class designers and class users.

An example of such a hierarchy can be found in Figure 16.2, which shows the graphic objects provided by the Microsoft Foundation Classes (MFC). The principal drawing object is a window, encapsulated using the CWnd class. A programmer almost never uses a pure CWnd object, however. Instead, selections from the dozens of specialized window classes—all of which inherit from CWnd—are actually used in the programs we write. Because we know these specialized windows inherit from CWnd, however, we don't have to learn a new interface for each object. Members for common activities, such as repositioning a window, are established at the CWnd class level. It means that the process for sizing and positioning a combo box will be essentially the same as that for sizing and repositioning our main view window, or the frame window

FIGURE 16.2 MFC Window-Object Hierarchy (from MS Visual Studio .NET Documentation)

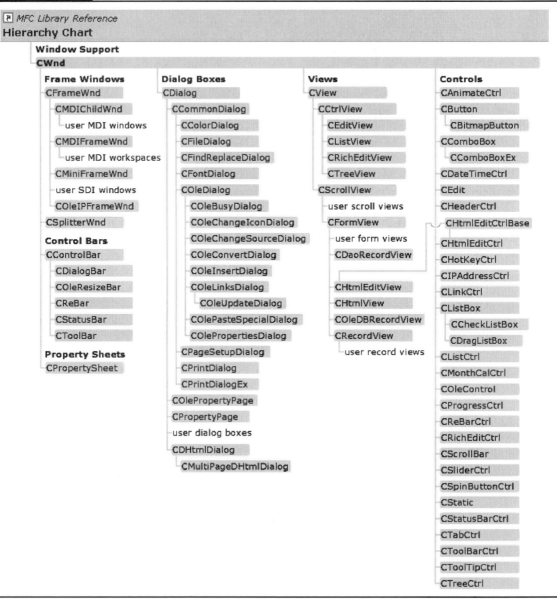

that encloses it. Use of a hierarchy also tends to simplify documentation, because only the additions and overrides made in each class need to be explained.

Reuse The other related benefit of inheritance is the way it promotes reuse of code. Throughout this text, we emphasize using existing code wherever possible. Unfortunately, the way such reuse has typically been accomplished—copying the code from one place, dropping it in another place, then editing the copy—does not scale well. As we reuse more and more code, from more and more different sources, we find some inherent weaknesses of copies. For example:

- In working on our copy, we often discover some ways to improve the original code, and make the changes while we are working. Unfortunately, these changes are *only* made in the copy, because we don't have time to go back and change the original.
- While we are working on our copy, someone else improves the original—perhaps removing a defect or adding an enhancement. We don't get word of the improvement, so our edited copy continues to be based on substandard code.

Although inheritance doesn't entirely solve these kinds of problems, it is a good start. Using inheritance, we don't copy the original code, we inherit from it. The changes we make are, therefore, in the form of the additions or overrides, so whenever we need a capability built into the object we're inheriting from—known as the base class—we call the original code, not some copy.

Some important implications of this process include the following:

- When we discover a defect in the base class, we fix the original base class code, not some copy we made of that code.
- When the base class is enhanced, as soon as we recompile our programs those enhancements become available to any code using the base class.

Naturally, using inheritance to promote reuse comes with an important caveat: The interface of all classes in our hierarchy must be preserved. As soon as some programmer comes along and "enhances" a class by pulling out some outdated member function, our code may stop working because we happened to be using that function. It is fine to add members to a class—but removing them is a no-no. The need to preserve the interface also helps to explain why public member functions are so much preferable to public member data in a class. If your data elements are public, you cannot change how they are implemented (e.g., moving from 1-byte to 2-byte characters) without changing the interface. When data access is implemented using member functions, on the other hand, we can build necessary conversions into our rewritten member functions to support the old interface, while adding new member functions (or new overloads) to support the additional functionality provided by the new data type. In fact, you will often see member functions with an Ext appended to their name in the MFC. In most cases, these functions are the result of extensions to the MFC classes that were renamed to avoid conflicts with the original interface.

Organizational   A particularly strong case for inheritance exists where an application can benefit from maintaining a collection of related objects of different types in a single collection (and, in turn, can allow us to exploit polymorphism, discussed in Section 16.3).

Suppose, for example, we are building a program to keep track of the residents of a zoo. Somewhere in the application, we are likely to have a collection (e.g., a vector) containing all the animals. If all inherit from a common source (e.g., Animal) this collection is easily done with:

```
vector<Animal*> arAll;
```

The reason it is possible is that any time inheritance is used, **base class** pointers can also point to inherited objects. Thus, the following assignments would all be legal and would not generate any errors or warnings:

```
Lion myLion;
Lion *pLion=&myLion;
Mammal *pMammal=&myLion;
Animal *pAnimal=&myLion;
```

It means that if you have a collection of objects, all of which inherit from some base class, you can use base class pointers to hold all the elements in the collection.

The ability to use a base class pointer (or reference) to keep track of many objects is so useful that we sometimes create abstract classes at the top levels of the hierarchy to act as position holders and to help define and organize lower levels. What makes a class abstract is that we never intend to create objects from it—only from its **child classes.**

Examples of classes that would likely be abstract classes in the Figure 16.1 hierarchy are Animal, Mammal, and Fish. Whereas Lion, Dolphin, and Platypus refer to actual types of animals—images that spring into your mind when you hear the names—the term *mammal* typically generates no such mental image. Rather, it serves to organize our collection of animals, along with other classes such as Insect, Amphibian, and Primate.

16.1.3: Inheritance vs. Composition

Inheritance is not the only way to take advantage the capabilities of one class within another. We have already seen many examples of another technique, first introduced in Chapter 11, Section 11.2.3, called composition. In composition, we embed one object within another—thereby making it possible to use the embedded object's data and members within the outer object.

Although inheritance and composition offer many of the same benefits, we also note some important differences:

- When inheriting from another class, the default is for the interface of the base class to become almost entirely available within the class being created. In other words, all public members and data in the base class become public members and data in the new class.

- When composing a class, it is more typical to make the embedded object a private data member, then implement whatever interface members are appropriate.

The choice between inheritance and composition is not always clear-cut (unless the need to maintain a polymorphic collection exists). The first question to ask is normally the following: Does an is-a relationship exist? The answer can be determined by making the statement:

```
A(n) X object is a(n) Y object
```

where X is the new object and Y is the base object. For example, in Figure 16.1, we could make the statement:

```
A Lion is a Mammal
```

and the statement makes sense. It would argue for inheritance, rather than composition.

An is-a relationship is not the only criterion for choosing between inheritance and composition. Another practical issue is the degree to which we actually want to inherit the entire interface of the base class. For example, in the PersonArray walkthrough presented in Chapter 15 (Example 15.12) we composed a vector<Person*> object within our PersonArray class to implement a sorted array. Now, it makes perfect sense to say:

```
A PersonArray is a vector<Person*>
```

which suggests inheritance could have (or, possibly, should have) been used. The problem here is we specifically did not want a number of the vector<> members to be accessible, such as insert(), because their improper use by the programmer could lead to the array getting out of order. Thus, if we chose to inherit from vector<Person*>, we would need to make a lot of members private or use the "private" inheritance capability of C++ (to be discussed), both of which tend to negate many of the benefits of inheritance.

Another potential barrier to using inheritance is where many is-a relationships exist. For example, we might have one species taxonomy (such as Figure 16.1) and another taxonomy based on preferred environment (e.g., sea creature, land creature, air creature) and yet another based on preferred food source (e.g., fish eater, meat eater, plant eater). Now each of the following statements makes sense:

```
A Dolphin is a Mammal
A Dolphin is a Sea Creature
A Dolphin is a Fish Eater
```

To implement them in an inheritance network, however, you need multiple inheritance—meaning the ability of a class to inherit characteristics from more than one base class. Even though such multiple inheritance is supported by C++ (unlike Java and C#, which do not support multiple inheritance), its use is fraught with perils once you start trying to do it (as will be discussed in Section 16.4). For this reason, where many such relationships need to be preserved, composition is often a better alternative.

16.1.4: Inheritance in FlowC

FlowC also allows elementary inheritance relationships to be diagrammed, in a form similar to the UML generalization/specialization diagram (e.g., Figure 16.1). The steps required to create a diagram are relatively simple:

- To establish an inheritance relationship, you simply specify one or more base classes in the same dialog where member variables are added.
- To display the diagram, select a particular class, right click it, and chose inheritance net.

How the net will be displayed depends, to some extent, on what class is clicked. Figure 16.1, for example, was the inheritance net for Animal. If you selected Lion, on the other hand, the net in Figure 16.3 would be produced. The reason for the difference is that FlowC displays the direct parents and all children for the class selected. Thus, because Lion has only parents, the appearance is linear, whereas Animal provides the entire taxonomy.

16.1: SECTION QUESTIONS

1. Why might a zoologist argue that Dolphin is really an abstract class?
2. In the statement:

    The choice between inheritance and composition is not always clear-cut (unless the need to maintain a polymorphic collection exists).

    Why does the polymorphic collection make the choice more clear-cut?
3. If you need to override a lot of members to make an inherited class work, what might that tell you about your hierarchy?
4. Explain the concerns you might have in creating a sorted array (e.g., the PersonArray) by inheriting from a vector<>.

5. Does making a member protected remove it from the class?

6. How would multiple inheritance impact the display of a class such as Lion (Figure 16.3) in FlowC?

16.2: INHERITANCE IN C++

Walkthrough available in Employee1.wmv

In this section we examine how single inheritance relationships can be established in C++. We begin by presenting a simple inheritance scenario, and then consider some variations, including:

- Public versus private inheritance
- Issues in overriding member functions and data
- Controlling initialization in inheritance

In the two subsequent sections, we address the additional issues of implementing polymorphism (Section 16.3) and multiple inheritance (Section 16.4).

16.2.1: Establishing an Inheritance Relationship

FIGURE 16.3   Lion Inheritance Net

Class: Animal
Data members:
Function members: +   string BodyTemp() +   bool LiveBirth() +   bool LaysEggs()

Class: Mammal
Data members:
Function members: +   string HairColor() +   bool LiveBirth() +   double RunningSpeed() +   bool LaysEggs()

Class: Lion
Data members:

To demonstrate how easy it is to establish an inheritance relationship, we return to the Person class introduced in Chapter 15, Section 15.5.2, and the PersonArray class, introduced in Chapter 15, section 15.5.3. As you may recall:

- The Person class implemented a simple object, with a last name and a first name.

- The PersonArray implemented a sorted array of person objects.

As a lab exercise, we then embedded the PersonArray in a Company class, intended to represent the employees in our company.

Unfortunately, our Person class is a pretty lame excuse for an employee object. (Actually, it's a pretty lame excuse for a Person object as well, but we'll let that slide for now.) At a minimum, we would want our employees to have an employee ID and a title (or position name). At this point, we have two choices:

- We could create a brand new Employee class from scratch (perhaps starting with a renamed copy of the Person.cpp and Person.h files), which would mean we also need to create a brand new EmployeeArray class collection.

- We could create an Employee class by inheriting from the Person class. It would mean that an Employee object was—by definition—also a Person object, so we could still use our PersonArray for storing the collection.

Naturally, the second approach seems like less work and, therefore, is likely to be the more attractive.

Implementing inheritance is simple in C++. When declaring the class, we simply add a : (colon) after the class name, followed by a comma-separated list of classes we intend to inherit from with access specifiers (usually public or private). In the case of our Employee class, we are only inheriting from one class and we will want public access to all members (other access types are considered in Section 16.2.3). The Employee class definition is presented in Example 16.1.

Looking at the definition—our first attempt—we see that we are defining an Employee to be a Person with the following data members added:

- An ID string (m_szID)
- A Title/Position string (m_szPosition)

After making this change, we can then go into our PersonArray test function (originally presented in Chapter 15, Example 15.11) and change the local pers object from a Person to an Employee, as shown in Example 16.2. After adding:

```
#include "Employee.h"
```

to the top of the .cpp file, the program will then compile and run.

If you run the program, however, you will quickly see that running and doing what we want are two different things. Because our change to the Person class to create an Employee only involved adding members, our member functions such as Input() still operate as if we were dealing with a Person object. In other words, while we may be able to hold ID and position information in our new Employee class, we don't have any way of getting that information into the class if we use inherited Person members. Thus, we need to discuss overriding members.

16.2.2: Overriding Member Functions

Whenever you inherit from a class, you will typically find that some member functions work just fine, while others need to be modified. In the case of creating our new Employee class,

---

EXAMPLE 16.1

Employee class, first version

```
#include "person.h"

class Employee :
    public Person
{
public:
    Employee(void);
    virtual ~Employee(void);

    string ID() const {return m_szID;}
    void ID(const char *sz){m_szID=sz;}
    string Position() const {return m_szPosition;}
    void Position(const char *sz){m_szPosition=sz;}

protected:
    string m_szID;
    string m_szPosition;
};
```

EXAMPLE 16.2

Change of Person to Employee in demonstration function

```
void TestPersonArray()
{
    PersonArray ar;
    DisplayString("To stop entering people, make a person\'s"
    "last name \'99\'");
    NewLine();
    Employee pers; // changed from Person to Employee
    while(pers.LastName()!="99")
    {
        pers.Input();
        if (pers.LastName()=="99") continue;
        int nPos=ar.Add(pers);
        if (nPos<0) {
            DisplayString("Duplicate person encountered!");
            NewLine();
        }
        else {
            DisplayFormatted("Person added at position %i",nPos);
            NewLine();
        }
    }
    // etc...
```

---

the only Person members that work just fine (for the time being) in the new class are the simple accessor functions: LastName(), FirstName(), Key(), and IsValid(). All our remaining functions—Input(), Display(), Get(), Print(), Load(), Save(), even our constructors—need to be overridden if they are going to be appropriate for handling Employee objects.

To override a member function, all you need to do is declare one or more member functions with the same name as the function you are overriding. You should also be aware that as soon as you override one function with a given name, any overloaded versions in the base class cease to be part of the public interface. As a consequence, one way to "hide" inherited members that aren't relevant (e.g., RunningSpeed() for a Dolphin) is to make a single version of the function, with no arguments, private.

Simple Overrides Given all the changes that need to be made, it is reasonable to question the benefits of inheritance at this point. But overriding a member function is different from rewriting from scratch. Take, for example, our Person::Display() function. That function was originally written as:

```
void Person::Display() const
{
    cout << "Last Name:\t" << LastName() << endl;
    cout << "First Name:\t" << FirstName() << endl;
}
```

What we want to do is not so much throw away that function as to add additional items in our Employee::Display() version of the function. Fortunately, C++ allows us to call the base class version of the function within an override by using the scope resolution operator. As a result, our new Employee::Display() member can be written as:

```
void Employee::Display() const
{
    cout << "ID:\t" << ID() << endl;
    Person::Display();
    cout << "Position:\t" << Position() << endl;
}
```

What we have done here is to sandwich the Person::Display() function call between the ID display and the position display. In fact, we can use the same approach in many of our I/O functions, as shown in Example 16.3. The approach fails, however, for one function: Get(), which is used to read a line from a fixed format text file. The problem here is that the Person::Input() function reads a line from a text file but does not give us access to the line that was read. As a result, if we call the base class from a fixed format file containing one employee per line, we lose access to the ID and position data. We will return to this problem shortly.

TEST YOUR UNDERSTANDING 16.1:

In all our Employee I/O functions, we chose to sandwich the Person data between our ID and position members. Is it necessary that all I/O functions handle the data in the same order?

The same basic approach of calling the base class can also frequently be applied to constructor functions and assignment overloads—which are not inherited (more about inheriting constructors will be presented in Section 16.2.4). In the case of our Employee object, we clearly needed to do something about these issues, because in our Person base class version, only the names are copied. The modified versions are presented in Example 16.4—with the only real change being made to the Copy() function, which calls the Person::Copy() base class. We need, however, to duplicate the assignment and copy constructor code, however, because—as we noted at the start of the paragraph—these functions are not inherited.

Benefits of Base Class Calls   The benefits of using base class member functions extend beyond saving us a bit of coding. They can dramatically enhance our ability to modify code. As an example, suppose we decided to add a phone number to our original Person class. This change would, of course, entail modifications to nearly all of our original Person member functions, to accommodate assignment, loading, saving, displaying, and input of the new piece of data. If, however, our Employee class always calls the base class in its functions, we can often enhance the Person class *without making any changes to the Employee class*. This will be demonstrated by adding a phone number member.

This situation brings us back to the Get() member of the Employee class. In the Person class, Get() was defined as shown in Example 16.5. We could not call this function in Employee (because we would lose access to the file line), so our first attempt at rewriting the function (also shown in Example 16.5) looks like a more complicated version of the original.

TEST YOUR UNDERSTANDING 16.2:

Why will the Employee version of the Get() function in Example 16.4 cease to work properly when we introduce a phone number into the Person class?

EXAMPLE 16.3

Employee I/O functions calling the base class

```
void Employee::Input() {
    char buf[1024];
    DisplayString("ID: ");
    InputString(buf);
    m_szID=buf;
    Person::Input();
    DisplayString("Position: ");
    InputString(buf);
    m_szPosition=buf;
}
void Employee::Display() const
{
    cout << "ID:\t" << ID() << endl;
    Person::Display();
    cout << "Position:\t" << Position() << endl;
}
void Employee::Load(STREAM &strm)
{
    strm >> m_szID;
    Person::Load(strm);
    strm >> m_szPosition;
}
void Employee::Save(STREAM &strm) const
{
    strm << m_szID;
    Person::Save(strm);
    strm << m_szPosition;
}
string Employee::FixedString() const
{
    char buf[1024]={0};
    int i;
    for(i=0;i<30;i++) buf[i]= ' ';
    string str=buf;
    str.replace(0,ID().substr(0,10).length(),ID().substr(0,10));
    str.replace(10,Position().substr(0,20).length(),Position().substr(0,20));
    string pers=Person::FixedString();
    str.insert(10,pers);
    return str;
}

void Employee::Print(OUTPUT &out) const
{
    PrintLine(out,FixedString().c_str());
}
```

EXAMPLE 16.4

Employee overloaded constructor and assignment functions

```
Employee(const Employee &pers) {
    Copy(pers);
}
const Employee &operator=(const Employee &pers) {
    if (&pers==this) return *this;
    Copy(pers);
    return *this;
}
void Copy(const Employee &pers) {
    Person::Copy(pers);
    m_szID=pers.m_szID;
    m_szPosition=pers.m_szPosition;
}
```

EXAMPLE 16.5

Person and Employee Get() member functions, version 1

```
void Person::Get(INPUT &in) {
    char buf[1024];
    GetLine(in,buf,1024);
    string szBuf=buf;
    m_szLastName=szBuf.substr(0,20);
    Trim(m_szLastName);
    m_szFirstName=szBuf.substr(20,20);
    Trim(m_szFirstName);
}

void Employee::Get(INPUT &in) {
    char buf[1024];
    GetLine(in,buf,1024);
    string szBuf=buf;
    m_szID=szBuf.substr(0,10);
    Trim(m_szID);
    m_szLastName=szBuf.substr(10,20);
    Trim(m_szLastName);
    m_szFirstName=szBuf.substr(30,20);
    Trim(m_szFirstName);
    m_szPosition=szBuf.substr(50,20);
    Trim(m_szPosition);
}
```

The problems that can be caused by this type of design are sufficiently severe that it is probably worth redesigning the base class to ensure greater consistency. One way to redesign is to look at the Person::Print() function, which broke the writing process into two steps: preparing a string (the FixedString() function) and writing the data to the file (the Print() function). This two-stage process allowed us to call the Person::FixedString() within our Employee::FixedString() function, as previously shown in Example 16.2.

We can modify the Get() member of the Person class using the same process, using another overload of the FixedString() function, as shown in Example 16.6 (with the m_szPhone member already added).

With the base class revised in this fashion, we can then make effective use of the base class FixedString() member within our Employee class, as illustrated in Example 16.7. This function:

- Extracts the ID from positions 0–9
- Creates a substring of the Person information, then calls Person::FixedString() to extract that information
- Extracts the Position/Title information from the portion of the string following the Person segment

TEST YOUR UNDERSTANDING 16.3:

Explain the role of nPersonStr in the Employee::FixedString() function. How well will this function accommodate changes to the Person base class?

Overriding Design Principles In considering this example, a number of good programming practices related to overriding are illustrated:

- In a child class, always call the base class member function whenever it is feasible to do so. This approach shortens code and enhances reliability.

EXAMPLE 16.6

Revised Person Get(), FixedString(), and FixedLength() members

```
void Person::Get(INPUT &in) {
    char buf[1024];
    GetLine(in,buf,1024);
    string szBuf=buf;
    FixedString(szBuf);
}

void Person::FixedString(string &str)
{
    m_szLastName=str.substr(0,20);
    Trim(m_szLastName);
    m_szFirstName=str.substr(20,20);
    Trim(m_szFirstName);
    m_szPhone=str.substr(40,15);
    Trim(m_szPhone);
}
```

EXAMPLE 16.7

Revised Get() and FixedString() members of the Employee class

```
void Employee::Get(INPUT &in) {
    char buf[1024];
    GetLine(in,buf,1024);
    string szBuf=buf;
    FixedString(szBuf);
}

void Employee::FixedString(string &str) {
    int nPersonStr=(int)Person::FixedString().length();
    m_szID=str.substr(0,10);
    Trim(m_szID);
    Person::FixedString(str.substr(10,nPersonStr));
    m_szPosition=str.substr(10+nPersonStr,20);
    Trim(m_szPosition);
}
```

- Design every class with overriding by child classes in mind. It is surprising how often a class that you thought was only a child becomes a parent. (e.g., the Dolphin class mentioned in the end-of-section exercises for Section 16.1).

- When you discover yourself overloading a function where you cannot call the base class—but would like to—consider redesigning the base class if you have access to it. No matter how experienced you are, you almost never get all the members constructed exactly right the first time.

16.2.3: In Depth: Public vs. Private Inheritance

Walkthrough available in Protected.wmv

When the **public** keyword is used in specifying an inheritance derivation, as shown in Example 16.1, the access specifiers of the resulting class are as follows:

- **public** base-class members remain public.
- **protected** base-class members remain protected.
- **private** base-class members become inaccessible.

This behavior is normally what we want—and it is also why **protected** access is more common than **private** access.

It is also possible to specify protected or private derivation, for example:

```
class MyClass : protected BaseClass {...etc...};
```

or

```
class MyClass : private BaseClass {...etc...};
```

When the **protected** derivation specifier is used:

- **public** base-class members become protected.

- **protected** base-class members remain protected.
- **private** base-class members become inaccessible.

When the **private** derivation specifier is used:

- **public** base-class members become private.
- **protected** base-class members remain private.
- **private** base-class members become inaccessible.

As a practical matter, then, any time you use a derivation other than public, you hide the entire interface of the derived class. The only exception occurs when no constructor is declared, in which case the implicit constructor will be public.

Although it is not immediately obvious why one would want to hide the entire interface of a child class, we have actually seen an example where this approach could have been used. In the PersonArray class (Chapter 15, Example 15.12), we managed a vector<Person*> object within the class. As noted in Section 16.1.3, however, it makes sense to say:

```
A PersonArray is a vector<Person*>
```

The problem with public inheritance was, however, that too many vector<Person*> members could mess up our order. By using private or protected inheritance, however, we could hide those members from the class user, then expose only those that were safe. As illustrated in Example 16.8, only those vector members we allowed are exposed. As is also evident from the example, many of these implementations consist of little more than calls to the base class (vector<Person*>) members.

Because private and protected derivation do not offer many coding or reusability benefits over composition—and are generally less well understood by programmers—we use composition throughout this text in situations where it might be possible to use private or protected inheritance.

16.2.4: In Depth: Initialization During Inheritance

Up to this point, when we needed to initialize member variables, we did so in the body of our constructor functions. For example, we could define a constructor to initialize the members of our Person object as follows:

```
Person(const char *szL,const char *szF,const char *szP) {
    m_szLastName=szL;
    m_szFirstName=szF;
    m_szPhone=szP;
}
```

Unfortunately, this approach has two limitations that present problems from time to time:

- It provides us with no way to invoke base class constructors other than the default constructor, which is called as part of the construction process for the child class.
- It will not allow us to initialize any data member declared const.

To get around these limitations, the new ISO standard for C++ allows us to specify initializations that take place during construction as part of an **initialization list** that precedes the body of the constructor. The basic format is as follows:

```
ClassName(arguments) : initializer-list { constructor-body }
```

EXAMPLE 16.8

PersonArray class using protected inheritance

```
class PersonArray : protected vector<Person*>
{
public:
    PersonArray(void);
    ~PersonArray(void);

    const Person *operator[](int) const;
    const Person *operator[](const char *) const;
    const Person *operator[](const string &szKey) const;
    int push_back(Person *);
    int push_back(const Person &pers);
    void erase(int nVal);
    void erase(const char *szKey);
    void erase(Person *p);
    int size() const;
    void clear();

    const Person *Find(const char *szKey,int &nPos) const;
    const Person *Find(const char *szKey) const;
    const Person *Find(const string &szKey) const;
    void Load(STREAM &strm);
    void Save(STREAM &strm) const;

protected:
    int FindPos(const string &szKey) const;
    int FindPos(const char *szKey) const;
};

// Examples of implemented functions
const Person *PersonArray::operator[](int i) const {
    return vector<Person*>::operator[](i);
}

    int PersonArray::size() const {
    return (int)vector<Person*>::size();
}
void PersonArray::erase(int nPos)
{
    assert(nPos>=0 && nPos<(int)size());
    if (nPos<0 || nPos>size()) return;
    delete (*this)[nPos];
    iterator iter=begin();
    vector<Person*>::erase(iter+nPos);
}
void PersonArray::clear()
{
    for(int i=0;i<(int)size();i++) {
    delete (*this)[i];
    }
    vector<Person*>::clear();
}
```

(Continues)

EXAMPLE 16.8 (CONTINUED)

```
int PersonArray::push_back(Person *pers) {
    int nPos;
    if (Find(pers->Key().c_str(),nPos)) return -1;
    vector<Person*>::iterator iter=begin();
    insert(iter+nPos,pers);
    return nPos;
}
```

Two types of items can be contained in this list:

1. Base class constructors
2. Member variable names

Argument lists that are valid for a constructor appropriate to the data being initialized can follow each initializer list item. For example, suppose we wanted to write a constructor for our Employee object that could be used to initialize all the values. Two approaches to writing the constructor—without and with an initializer list—are shown in Example 16.9. The initializer version calls the three-argument Person constructor we just defined, and then initializes the two remaining member variables.

TEST YOUR UNDERSTANDING 16.4:

Rewrite the preceding three-argument Person constructor using an initialization list.

EXAMPLE 16.9

Employee constructor without and with initializer list

```
// using body of the constructor
Employee(const char *szI,const char *szL,
    const char *szF,const char *szP,const char *szT)
{
    m_szID=szI;
    m_szLastName=szL;
    m_szFirstName=szF;
    m_szPhone=szP;
    m_szPosition=szP;
}

// using initializer list
Employee(const char *szI,const char *szL,
    const char *szF,const char *szP,const char *szT) :
        Person(szL,szF,szP),
        m_szID(szI),
        m_szPosition(szT)
{
    // no initializations in body are required
}
```

The primary advantage of using initializer lists—which are becoming increasingly common in commercial C++ code—is that they allow the base class to be called even for constructor functions. As noted previously, they also *must* be used if a class contains const member variables.

16.2.5: In Depth: Type Casting Inherited Objects in C++

The technique we used thus far for type casting is the (type-specifier) format that originated in the C programming language. Although this technique remains widely used, C++ offers two templated operators that are much safer to use for type casting:

- static_cast<*type-specifier*>
- dynamic_cast<*type-specifier*>

The **static_cast**<> operator is used to do a type cast on any type of expression, but performs no runtime checking. As a consequence, it is similar in effect to the old C-style use of parentheses, and should only be used where the casting is sure to work. For example:

```
Person *p1;
Employee *e1=new Employee;
p1=static_cast<Person*>(e1);
```

In this illustration, we can be confident that the type cast is valid because we know an Employee object is, by inheritance, also a Person object. It is sometimes called an upcast.

The **dynamic_cast**<> operator, in contrast, is only used on pointers and references. It does, however, perform a runtime check to ensure that the pointer or reference being checked can be cast to the type-specifier template argument. If the type cast is consistent, it is performed. If not, and the type-specifier is a pointer, a NULL value (0) is returned. If the type-specifier is a reference, an exception is generated.

Suppose, for example, we have a Customer class that inherits from Person just as the Employee does (as part of the lab exercise in Section 16.6). Then consider the following code fragment:

```
Person *p1,*p2;
Employee *e1=new Employee,*e2,*e3;
Customer *c1=new Customer;
p1=static_cast<Person*>(e1);
p2=static_cast<Person*>(c1);
e2=dynamic_cast<Employee*>(p1); // e2 will now have the same
// address as e1
e3= dynamic_cast<Employee*>(p2); // e3 will now have the
// address 0
```

In the case of the dynamic cast of p1, the address in p1 points to an Employee object so that address is returned. In the case of the dynamic cast of p2, however, the runtime check done by the program determines that p2 does not point to an Employee object, so a 0 (NULL value) is returned. Moving from a parent to a child is sometimes called a **downcast.**

16.2: SECTION QUESTIONS

1. If emp is an Employee object created from the definition in Section 16.1, would emp.LastName() be a valid expression?

2. Given that the Person and Employee copy constructors are identical, why do we need to override the copy constructor for an Employee?

3. Why does making a single overridden member function private have the effect of making all member functions of that name inaccessible?

4. Following the rules we have already been given, what would happen if you declared a member variable in the child class with the same name as one in the base class?

5. What OOP design principle from Chapter 13 do the principles for overriding in Section 16.2.2 particularly relate to?

6. Why would protected/private inheritance tend to be particularly relevant to specialized collections?

7. Aside from obvious use in initializing const members, why are constructor initialization lists desirable from a design perspective?

8. Implement a simple static member of the Employee class, prototyped as follows:

```
bool Employee::IsEmployee(void *p);
```

that uses dynamic casting to return true or false depending upon whether the argument p is pointer to an employee object.

16.3: POLYMORPHISM IN C++

 Walkthrough available in Animals.wmv

Polymorphism is the ability to define functions that will be called according to the object to which they are being applied at run time. The primary benefit we get from this capability is being able to maintain collections of objects using pointers or references to some base class without losing all their inherited capabilities. In this section, we examine a simple polymorphism example, and then consider the subject of abstract classes, ending with some general rules regarding when to specify polymorphism.

16.3.1: Implementing Polymorphism in C++

The easiest way to understand polymorphism is to look at a simple example, which uses part of the Animal hierarchy introduced in Section 16.1. Suppose we define Mammal, Lion, and Platypus objects as shown in Example 16.10.

Consider, then, the simple test code presented in Example 16.11. What we would (ideally) like to see are the lines:

```
A Platypus Doesn't give live birth
A Lion Gives live birth
A Platypus Doesn't give live birth
A Lion Gives live birth
```

Our reasoning that the second pair should echo the first is that the second pair simply uses dereferenced pointers to the objects used in the first pair. Aren't dereferenced pointers always the same as the objects they point to?

The answer is no, as illustrated by the actual output from the function in Figure 16.4. This outcome, in a nutshell, is what happens when we don't have polymorphism.

EXAMPLE 16.10

Mammal, Lion, and Platypus classes

```
class Mammal : public Animal
{
public:
    Mammal(void){}
    virtual ~Mammal(void){}

    string Name() const {return string("(Generic mammal)");}

    bool LiveBirth() const {return true;};
    bool LaysEggs() const {return false;}
};

class Lion : public Mammal
{
public:
    Lion(void){}
    virtual ~Lion(void){}
    string Name() const {return string("Lion");}
};

class Platypus : public Mammal
{
public:
    Platypus(void){}
    virtual ~Platypus(void){}

    bool LiveBirth() const {return false;};
    bool LaysEggs() const {return true;}
    string Name() const {return string("Duck-billed Platypus");}
};
```

The problem is as follows. When we assigned the addresses of the platypus (p) and lion (l) objects to pM1 and pM2 pointers, the operation was perfectly legal for these reasons:

```
A Platypus is a Mammal
A Lion is a Mammal
```

However, when the compiler sees pM1->Name() or pM2->Name() all it knows is that the object pointed to is a Mammal object, so it calls the Mammal() version of the Name() function in both cases. The same is also true for the LiveBirth() member.

Even though this operation makes sense to the compiler, it is definitely not what we want. Instead, we want the program at run time to determine what type of Mammal object pM1 and pM2 point to and—based on that information—call either the Platypus or Lion versions of the Name() and LiveBirth() members.

EXAMPLE 16.11

Animal demonstration test code

```
void TestAnimal()
{
    Platypus p;
    Lion l;
    Mammal *pM1,*pM2;
    cout << "A " << p.Name() <<
        (p.LiveBirth() ? " Gives live birth" : " Doesn't give live birth")
        << endl;
    cout << "A " << l.Name() <<
        (l.LiveBirth() ? " Gives live birth" : " Doesn't give live birth")
        << endl;
    pM1=&p;
    cout << "A " << pM1->Name() <<
        (pM1->LiveBirth() ? " Gives live birth" : " Doesn't give live birth")
        << endl;
    pM2=&l;
    cout << "A " << pM2->Name() <<
        (pM2->LiveBirth() ? " Gives live birth" : " Doesn't give live birth")
        << endl;
}
```

FIGURE 16.4   Output from TestAnimal()

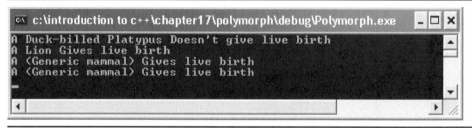

Implementing Polymorphism   To implement polymorphic behavior in a function, all we need to do is use the **virtual** keyword when we declare the Name() and LiveBirth() functions in the Animal class. What **virtual** does is the following:

- It creates a pointer—sometimes referred to as a **thunk**—that gets embedded in each object of that class (or any child classes) that points to the specific function to be called. The collection of object thunks is frequently held in an array called a **vftable** (i.e., virtual function table).

- When the compiler encounters a call to a **virtual function,** instead of coding the call directly, it writes code that calls whatever function is pointed to by the thunk embedded in the object.

The practical result is that when we change the definition of Mammal to that of Example 16.12, the output of Figure 16.5 results.

EXAMPLE 16.12

Revised Mammal definition

```cpp
class Mammal : public Animal
{
public:
    Mammal(void){}
    virtual ~Mammal(void){}

    virtual string Name() const {return string("(Generic mammal)");}

    virtual bool LiveBirth() const {return true;};
    virtual bool LaysEggs() const {return false;}
};
```

FIGURE 16.5 Output of TestAnimal() with Revised Mammal Class Definition

Common Polymorphism Errors   Although the appropriate use of the **virtual** keyword implements polymorphic behavior nicely, we still need to be aware of a few issues. First, any functions inherited from a virtual function need to match the function prototype exactly. Subtle differences, such as differing return types or a missing/extra const qualifier totally negate the process. For example, if the Platypus member:

```cpp
bool LiveBirth() const {return false;}
```

were changed to:

```cpp
int LiveBirth() const {return false;}
```

the result would be a fairly common error message from the compiler:

```
error C2555: 'Platypus::LiveBirth': overriding virtual func-
tion return type differs and is not covariant from
'Mammal::LiveBirth'

    see declaration of 'Mammal::LiveBirth'
```

If, on the other hand, we committed the sin of omitting the **const** qualifier in our Platypus LiveBirth() function, making it:

```cpp
bool LiveBirth() {return false;}
```

we would get the output in Figure 16.6.

The problem here is that the compiler thinks the new LiveBirth() (missing the const) is a different overload from our original virtual function in Mammal. As a result, it calls the Mammal version because no override is in place in the Platypus class.

FIGURE 16.6	Erroneous Output Resulting from Missing const Qualifier

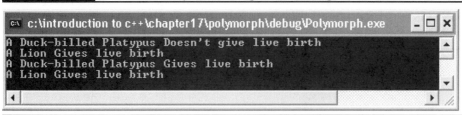

Disabling Polymorphism   A second polymorphism issue involves situations where we want to call the base class member, instead of calling the virtual member. Suppose, for example, we had a collection of Mammal objects and wanted to identify any unusual members. For this identification, we might want to compare each object's LiveBirth() and LaysEggs() members with the default values for Mammals.

To disable polymorphic behavior, the scope resolution operator can be used to specify the version of the polymorphic function to be called. As a demonstration, consider the revised version of TestAnimal() presented in Example 16.13.

The two if constructs at the end compare the polymorphic LaysEggs() and LiveBirth() return values with their return values as specified in the Mammal class. The output that results is shown in Figure 16.7.

The virtual Destructor Function   Whenever you are going to be handling polymorphic collections of objects, one function you will definitely want to make virtual is the destructor function. The reason is that the destructor is called whenever the **delete** operator is applied. If the destructor is not polymorphic, the destructor for the pointer type used to hold the collection (e.g., Mammal) will be used, as opposed to the destructor for the object type (e.g., Platypus). This situation can be particularly problematic where a child class manages memory data not managed by the base class.

16.3.2: Abstract Classes

Although our Mammal hierarchy doesn't exactly qualify us to be zoologists, it does provide a rather powerful demonstration of polymorphism in C++. However, we need to be aware of a few conceptual problems with the hierarchy:

- The "(Generic Mammal)" name specified in the Mammal class is a really lousy default value for classes that inherit from Mammal. If the programmer doesn't know the name of a mammal, he or she shouldn't be creating a class for it!
- Nothing in our code prevents us from creating a Mammal object. The question is, do we really want to mix classification objects with actual animal objects?

These issues were previously mentioned in Section 16.1, at which time it was suggested we might somehow distinguish between an "abstract" class and a normal class.

C++ gives us an easy mechanism for creating an abstract class—just specify one or more virtual member functions to be a pure virtual function, which is done by writing = 0 after the function declaration in the header file.

EXAMPLE 16.13

Revised TestAnimal() function

```
void TestAnimal()
{
    Platypus p;
    Lion l;
    Mammal *pM1,*pM2;
    pM1=&p;
    cout << "A " << pM1->Name() <<
        (pM1->LiveBirth() ? " Gives live birth" : " Doesn't give live birth")
        << endl;
    pM2=&l;
    cout << "A " << pM2->Name() <<
        (pM2->LiveBirth() ? " Gives live birth" : " Doesn't give live birth")
        << endl;

    if (pM1->LaysEggs()==pM1->Mammal::LaysEggs() &&
        pM1->LiveBirth()==pM1->Mammal::LiveBirth()) {
            cout << "A " << pM1->Name() << " is a typical mammal!" << endl;
    }
    else {
            cout << "A " << pM1->Name() << " is an unusual mammal!" << endl;
    }
    if (pM2->LaysEggs()==pM2->Mammal::LaysEggs() &&
        pM2->LiveBirth()==pM2->Mammal::LiveBirth()) {
            cout << "A " << pM2->Name() << " is a typical mammal!" << endl;
    }
    else {
            cout << "A " << pM2->Name() << " is an unusual mammal!" << endl;
    }
}
```

FIGURE 16.7   Output from Revised TestAnimal()

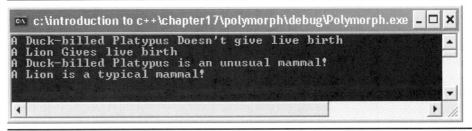

The creation of pure virtual functions is illustrated in Example 16.14, which includes an Animal class from which Mammal inherits. The features that should be noted include the following:

- Animal is an abstract class, with the member functions Name(), LiveBirth(), and LaysEggs() all declared as pure virtual functions.

EXAMPLE 16.14

Animal class hierarchy with abstract Animal and Mammal classes

```cpp
class Animal
{
public:
    Animal(void);
    virtual ~Animal(void);

    virtual string Name() const = 0;

    virtual bool LiveBirth() const = 0;
    virtual bool LaysEggs() const = 0;
};

class Mammal : public Animal
{
public:
    Mammal(void){}
    virtual ~Mammal(void){}

    virtual bool LiveBirth() const {return true;};
    virtual bool LaysEggs() const {return false;}
};

class Lion : public Mammal
{
public:
    Lion(void){}
    virtual ~Lion(void){}
    string Name() const {return string("Lion");}
};

class Platypus : public Mammal
{
public:
    Platypus(void){}
    virtual ~Platypus(void){}

    bool LiveBirth() const {return false;};
    bool LaysEggs() const {return true;}
    string Name()const {return string("Duck-billed Platypus");}
};
```

- Mammal no longer has a Name() function. It can be omitted because the pure virtual function in the Animal base class is—in effect—a promise that any class that can be turned into an object will have a Name() function implemented. Because Mammal doesn't have a name, it follows that we should get an error if we try to create a mammal. If we try, in fact, we get the following compiler error:

```
error C2259: 'Mammal' : cannot instantiate abstract class
     due to following members:
     'std::string Animal::Name(void) const' : pure virtual
     function was not defined
     see declaration of 'Animal::Name'
```

Thus, defining pure virtual functions has solved both of our conceptual problems.

TEST YOUR UNDERSTANDING 16.5:

Why didn't we pull LiveBirth() and LaysEggs() from the Mammal definition the way we removed Name()?

So far, we showed why it is conceptually beneficial to be able to declare Animal and Mammal as abstract classes. What we have yet to explain is why declaring pure virtual functions is a good way to accomplish this task.

Essentially, declaring a pure virtual function does two things:

- As we saw with the Mammal construction error, it sets up a contract to implement the function for all objects we intend to create, giving an error if we try to create a class missing one or more pure member definitions.

- It allows us to call that member function on any pointer or reference object that is of the base class type or a child of that type. For example, because we know the Name() function is going to be available for any object we create, the compiler lets us call it on Animal or Mammal pointers—even though we know those classes don't have an actual definition for Name() in place.

It is this second capability that makes polymorphism so powerful when collections of objects are being maintained. If, for example, we had a vector<Animal*> collection, we could call the Name() function on each member to get a list of names. We could also create an IsUnusual() function for each member that could identify if it is typical of its parent class.

16.3.3: Polymorphism Design Issues

As we have seen, using the virtual specifier C++ makes it possible to specify which members are polymorphic and which are not. An obvious question to ask, therefore, is why not make every member virtual? Doing so would, in fact, mimic the behavior of many other OOP languages (such as Java).

Essentially, two reasons explain why making every C++ member virtual would be considered a sloppy programming practice:

1. *Overhead:* It takes slightly more time to call a virtual function than it does a nonpolymorphic function. Although the difference is usually fairly trivial, why be wasteful?

2. *Conceptual:* When you declare a function virtual you are stating, in effect, "I believe I'll eventually declare some child class that will override this function." If

this is, in fact, your intention, then fine. If, on the other hand, you don't think you will ever be overriding a particular function, you can make that assertion in your code by *not* making it virtual. Then, when you come back to your class a year later, you can use the member declarations to help clarify (in your own mind) what you were thinking when you designed the class.

The bottom line is that a function should generally be virtual if:

- It is likely to be overridden at some future time.
- It is a function you are likely to want to use in a collection of objects based upon some abstract class.
- It is a destructor function, unless you know the object will never be used as part of a collection and doesn't manage any memory internally.

Any member function that doesn't meet any of these three criteria can—and probably should—be left as a nonvirtual function for reasons of efficiency and clarity.

16.3: SECTION QUESTIONS

1. Why are polymorphic functions particularly useful in collections?
2. Why does the presence of virtual functions render the memory-mapped view of a structure inaccurate?
3. Why are compiler error messages about undefined pure virtual functions a good thing?
4. In an intermediate abstract class, when does it make sense to write a definition for a pure virtual function that has been inherited, rather than leaving it to be defined in child classes?
5. If you were to define a Fish class, what might it look like?
6. Of the reasons not to make every member function polymorphic, which is more convincing: the performance or the conceptual?
7. Why is the destructor function usually polymorphic?

16.4: IN DEPTH: MULTIPLE INHERITANCE IN C++

Walkthrough available in Multi.wmv

Multiple inheritance is the ability to define classes that inherit characteristics from more than one base class. Although it can be a powerful tool, its use also leads to a number of subtle problems that have led to its being omitted from many other languages, such as Java and C#. In this section, we look at how to define multiple inheritance, some of the problems associated with it, and techniques for minimizing those problems.

16.4.1: What Is Multiple Inheritance?

To illustrate the type of scenario in which multiple inheritance might be useful, let us return to our animal hierarchy and consider the case of the mule. A mule is an animal that results from breeding a horse and a jackass. Mules are also born sterile, meaning they neither give live birth nor lay eggs. As a consequence of their origin, it might make sense to define a Mule object as inheriting from both Horse and Jackass classes, as illustrated in Figure 16.8, overriding the LiveBirth() member.

Although this approach seems straightforward enough at first, it actually introduces a number of subtleties. For example:

- Both the Horse and the Jackass objects have a Name(). Which one of these should Mule() inherit as a default? (The same would apply to any member where Horse and Jackass members return different values, such as the RunningSpeed() member.)

- If Horse and Jackass have data members with the same name, which of the data members should take precedence in the Mule object, or should both be included?

FIGURE 16.8 Multiple Inheritance of a Mule

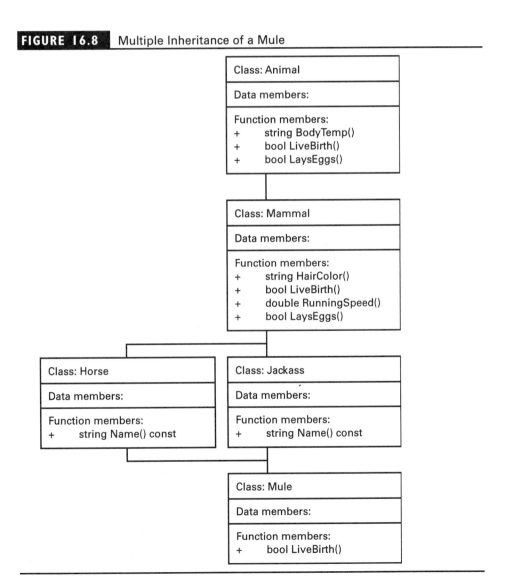

Now we could argue that part of the problem here is that we haven't used a good example. After all, because a Mule is a crossbreed, it is reasonable to complain that neither of the two statements:

```
Mule is a Horse
Mule is a Jackass
```

is strictly true. However these types of problems can surface every time we employ multiple inheritance, which is one of the primary complaints leveled against the technique. Thus, where multiple inheritance is used, you need to be alert to the possible occurrence of these issues.

16.4.2: Implementing Multiple Inheritance

Implementing **multiple inheritance** in C++ is quite straightforward: you simply add comma-separated:

```
derivation-specifier class-name
```

items after the first inheritance specification, where *derivation-specifier* can either be **public**, **private,** or **protected**. For example, the following declaration would create a Mule class using multiple inheritance from Horse and Jackass:

```
class Mule :
    public Horse , public Jackass
{
public:
    Mule(void){}
    virtual ~Mule(void){};

    bool LiveBirth() const {return false;}
};
```

Ambiguities in Multiple Inheritance Unfortunately, the preceding multiple inheritance leads immediately to problems. For example, assuming that both Horse and Jackass have Name() members, the code fragment:

```
Mule m;
cout << "The default name for a Mule is " << m.Name() << endl;
```

will produce an error message:

```
error C2385: ambiguous access of 'Name' in 'Mule'
    could be the 'Name' in base 'Horse::Name'
    or the 'Name' in base 'Jackass::Name'
```

This problem could—and should—be solved by overriding the Name() member in Mule. As we already noted, Name() is not the type of member for which natural defaults apply.

Another way we could eliminate the problem is using the scope resolution operator. For example, the code fragment:

```
Mule m;
cout << "One default name for a Mule is " <<
m.Horse::Name() << endl;
cout << "One default name for a Mule is " <<
m.Jackass::Name() << endl;
```

will compile without errors, and will lead to the names "Horse" and "Jackass" being returned, respectively, by the two Name() calls.

The situation can become even more complex when we inherit data. Suppose, for example, we define Horse, Jackass, and Mule as shown in Example 16.15. Once again, we run into ambiguity problems if we call RunningSpeed(), because both Horse and Jackass versions exist. The way we implemented running speed introduces another problem, however. If we examine our Mule class in the debugger, we discover that we now have two data elements called m_nRunningSpeed, as shown in Figure 16.9—one created from Horse and one created from Jackass—that also have different values. (The figure also shows that we have two parallel sets of vftable arrays holding the thunks for our virtual functions.)

EXAMPLE 16.15

Horse, Jackass, and Mule definitions with data member

```
class Horse :
    public Mammal
{
public:
    Horse(void){m_nRunningSpeed=40;}
    virtual ~Horse(void){};

    virtual RunningSpeed() const {return m_nRunningSpeed;}

    string Name() const {return string("Horse");}
protected:
    int m_nRunningSpeed;

};

class Jackass :
    public Mammal
{
public:
    Jackass(void){m_nRunningSpeed=25;}
    virtual ~Jackass(void){};

    virtual RunningSpeed() const {return m_nRunningSpeed;}

    string Name() const {return string("Jackass");}
protected:
    int m_nRunningSpeed;

};

class Mule :
    public Horse , public Jackass
{
public:
    Mule(void){}
    virtual ~Mule(void){};

    bool LiveBirth() const {return false;}
};
```

FIGURE 16.9 A Mule Object (m) Shown in the Debugger

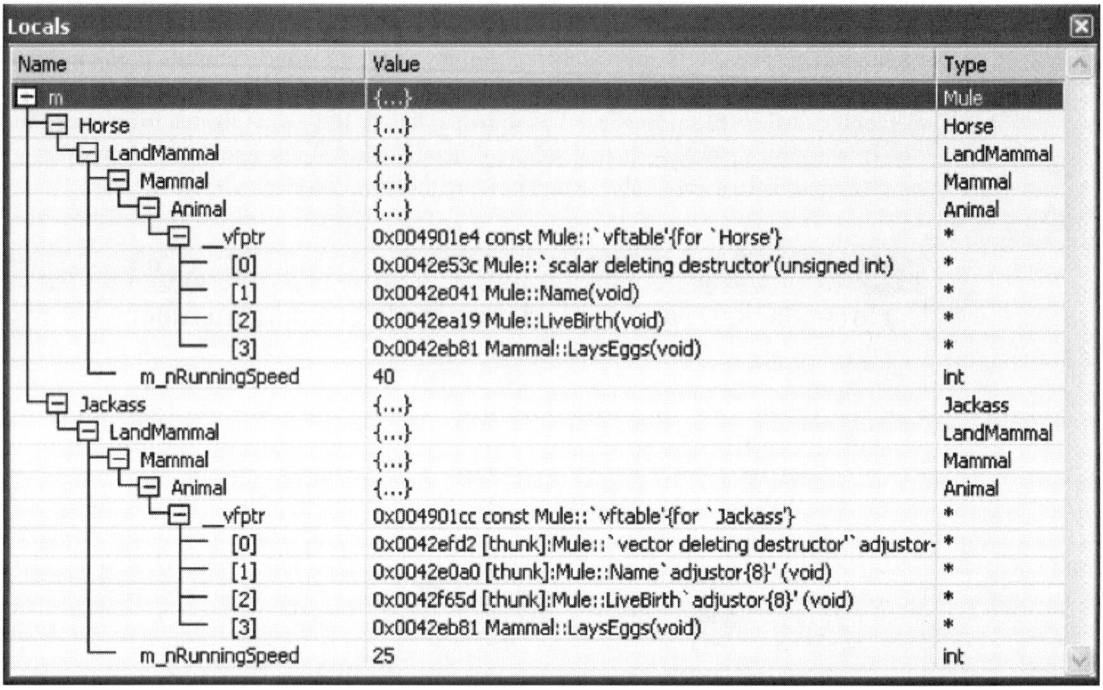

Name	Value	Type
⊟ m	{...}	Mule
⊟ Horse	{...}	Horse
⊟ LandMammal	{...}	LandMammal
⊟ Mammal	{...}	Mammal
⊟ Animal	{...}	Animal
⊟ __vfptr	0x004901e4 const Mule::`vftable'{for `Horse'}	*
[0]	0x0042e53c Mule::`scalar deleting destructor'(unsigned int)	*
[1]	0x0042e041 Mule::Name(void)	*
[2]	0x0042ea19 Mule::LiveBirth(void)	*
[3]	0x0042eb81 Mammal::LaysEggs(void)	*
m_nRunningSpeed	40	int
⊟ Jackass	{...}	Jackass
⊟ LandMammal	{...}	LandMammal
⊟ Mammal	{...}	Mammal
⊟ Animal	{...}	Animal
⊟ __vfptr	0x004901cc const Mule::`vftable'{for `Jackass'}	*
[0]	0x0042efd2 [thunk]:Mule::`vector deleting destructor'` adjustor-	*
[1]	0x0042e0a0 [thunk]:Mule::Name` adjustor{8}' (void)	*
[2]	0x0042f65d [thunk]:Mule::LiveBirth` adjustor{8}' (void)	*
[3]	0x0042eb81 Mammal::LaysEggs(void)	*
m_nRunningSpeed	25	int

The problem here is that unless you specify otherwise, C++ will create complete copies of all objects inherited using multiple inheritance. The practical consequence is that when you inherit casually from classes in the same hierarchy, you can get a lot of duplicate data and other members.

virtual Inheritance C++ does provide us with a mechanism for avoiding the duplication of members and data when multiple inheritance occurs using classes from the same hierarchy. Typically, the solution involves a mixture of design and the **virtual** keyword. When this keyword precedes the derivation specifier (public, private or protected) during inheritance, it causes any of its data/function members that would be duplicated during multiple inheritance to be consolidated. In our hierarchy, for example, it really doesn't make sense to establish independent RunningSpeed() functions in our Horse and Jackass classes. We could, instead, create an intermediate class—LandMammal—that introduces RunningSpeed(), then use the virtual keyword when Horse and Jackass inherit from it, as shown in Example 16.16.

If we were to run the following code fragment:

```
Mule m;
cout << "The default speed for a Mule is " <<
m.RunningSpeed() << endl;
```

the value 25 would now be displayed for running speed. The value is established because when a Mule object is created, the default constructor for a Horse object is called (setting m_nRunningSpeed to 40), after which the default constructor for a Jackass object is called

EXAMPLE 16.16

Mule Classes with virtual inheritance

```cpp
class LandMammal :
    public Mammal
{
public:
    LandMammal(void){}
    virtual ~LandMammal(void){};

    virtual RunningSpeed() const {return m_nRunningSpeed;}

protected:
    int m_nRunningSpeed;
};

class Horse :
    virtual public LandMammal
{
public:
    Horse(void){m_nRunningSpeed=40;}
    virtual ~Horse(void){};

    string Name() const {return string("Horse");}
};

class Jackass :
    virtual public LandMammal
{
public:
    Jackass(void){m_nRunningSpeed=25;}
    virtual ~Jackass(void){};

    string Name() const {return string("Jackass");}
};

class Mule :
    public Horse , public Jackass
{
public:
    Mule(void){}
    virtual ~Mule(void){};

    string Name() const {return string("Mule");}
    bool LiveBirth() const {return false;}
};
```

(overwriting the old value by setting m_nRunningSpeed to 25). As a consequence, the 25 remains when initialization is complete.

If we examine the new Mule (m) object in the debugger, as shown in Figure 16.10, we see that the duplicate copies of m_nRunningSpeed are no longer present (and the two vftable arrays, used to store thunks, are at the same address—meaning there's only one array).

16.4.3: The Interface Style of Multiple Inheritance

Although virtual inheritance solves some of the problems of multiple inheritance, it is not a cure-all. For example, our LandMammal class works fine until you encounter a Hippopotamus—an animal that spends most of its time in water but goes foraging for food at night. All of a sudden, we have to start joining LandMammal and WaterMammal abstract classes. Then we find ourselves wondering, "Is swimming speed for a mammal such a different concept from swimming speed for a fish?" The next thing you know, we're trying to multiple-inherit fish and mammals to get the relevant characteristics.

Problems such as these led to other C++-derived languages—most notably Java and C#—to eliminate multiple inheritance in favor of interfaces. When a class implements an interface, it is essentially creating a contract (with the compiler) to provide bodies to specified functions. In this way, an interface is much like a pure virtual function. Furthermore, once a class implements an interface, that fact can be used in the context of polymorphic collections—which is one of the main benefits of using inheritance as well.

Because C++ supports multiple inheritance, it does not need formal interfaces. Nonetheless, as a matter of programming style, you can choose to limit your use of multiple inheritance to interface-like classes. Such an interface-like class would have a number of characteristics:

- It would not be part of the hierarchy from which you are doing your most significant inheritance (e.g., the animal hierarchy in our example).

FIGURE 16.10 Mule Object Display after Virtual Inheritance Is Implemented

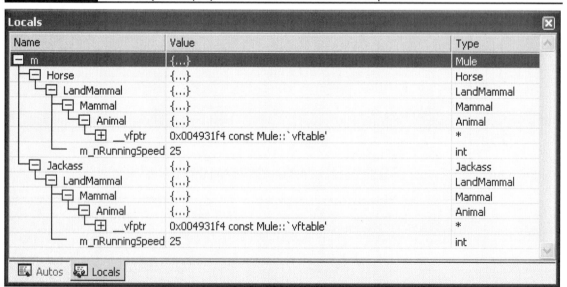

■ The "interface class" would consist entirely of pure virtual function members—no implemented functions and no data members.

Writing your code in this way, you gain two benefits:

1. You eliminate the ambiguities associated with multiple inheritance.
2. You make your code much easier to rewrite in other languages (e.g., Java, C#) should that ever be necessary.

As an example, in our animal hierarchy we might create some habitat-related interface classes, such as LandDweller and SeaDweller. These classes would then be defined along the lines of the classes in Example 16.17.

The member functions in these classes are all pure virtual functions, which eliminates any ambiguity regarding which version of a function needs to be called. It will always have to be implemented in the class inheriting the interface.

Although the interface approach does not lend itself to default values, it does allow for collections to be created based on interface inheritance. As a result, in addition to collections based on our original hierarchy (e.g., collections of mammals, fish, amphibians, etc.), we could also have collections of land-dwellers, sea-dwellers, veldt-dwellers, carnivores, herbivores, and collections based on whatever other interfaces we cared to define.

In the case of our Hippopotamus mammal, we might define the class as inheriting from Mammal, while—at the same time—inheriting from the "interface" classes LandDweller and RiverDweller, from which it would gain members such as RunningSpeed() and SwimmingSpeed(). Although not a perfect approach, this use of interface classes both reduces some of the complexities of multiple inheritance and increases the potential portability of our code to other languages.

EXAMPLE 16.17

Example "interface" classes

```cpp
class LandDweller
{
public:
    LandDweller(void);
    ~LandDweller(void);
    virtual int RunningSpeed() const =0;
    virtual string PreferredTerrain() const =0;
    virtual string FootType() const =0;
};

class SeaDweller
{
public:
    SeaDweller(void);
    ~SeaDweller(void);
    virtual int SwimmingSpeed() const =0;
    virtual string PreferredWaterTemp() const =0;
    virtual string PropulsionMachanism() const =0;
};
```

16.4: SECTION QUESTIONS

1. Explain why the Mule example presented in the text is not, from a conceptual standpoint, a perfect case of multiple inheritance.
2. What is the particular challenge presented by multiple inheritance from classes within the same hierarchy?
3. Why do members that serve as natural default values present a more difficult multiple inheritance challenge than variables that tend to be class-specific?
4. What data issue does the virtual keyword tend to eliminate in a multiple inheritance environment?
5. What multiple inheritance issue does the virtual keyword fail to address?
6. If we had written the Mule class definition in Example 16.16 as follows:
    ```
    class Mule : public Jackass, public Horse {...definition...}
    ```
    would its format have had any effect on the resulting Mule class?
7. Could you develop a hierarchy of interface classes?

16.5: KEYED ARRAY DEMONSTRATION

Walkthrough available in KeyArray.wmv

In this demonstration, we show how we can use inheritance to make classes more general. Our specific focus will be on taking the PersonArray, developed in Chapter 15 (Example 15.12) and making it suitable for storing sorted collections of nearly anything. We present this process in three steps. First, we create a CKey abstract class that can be inherited by any class that needs to be sorted. Next, we rework the PersonArray, renaming it KeyArray, to make it suitable for organizing a collection of any object that inherits from the Key class. Finally, we create a KeyTable (that inherits from the KeyArray), which can be used to keep an ordered collection of any objects—whether or not they inherit from Key.

16.5.1: The CKey Abstract Class

The CKey abstract class is simple, as shown in Example 16.18. It consists of two pure virtual functions, Key(), which return a string that will be used as the key, and NewCopy(),

---

EXAMPLE 16.18

The CKey class

```
class CKey
{
public:

    CKey(void){}
    virtual ~CKey(void){}
    virtual string Key() const = 0;
    virtual CKey *NewCopy() const = 0;
};
```

which returns a copy of the object it is applied to. (The purpose of the second of these functions will be addressed in Section 16.5.2.)

Why define such a trivial class? The reason is simple. When we created the PersonArray class (Example 15.12), we were maintaining a sorted vector<> of object pointers to Person elements. But was anything really special about Person objects used in that array? In fact, all that mattered was that a Key() member be available. As a result, any class that inherits from CKey—either single or multiple inheritance—could be handled by the PersonArray. As a prelude to our next step—transforming the PersonArray to a KeyArray—we change our Person class so that it inherits from CKey, which requires only adding the : public CKey to the class declaration, and adding the NewCopy() member. For example:

```
#include "Key.h"
class Person : public CKey
{
    Person *NewCopy() const {return new Person(*this);}
    // rest of the class remains unchanged
};
```

The reason this change is so simple is that we already have a Key() function implemented in the Person class, which is the only requirement added by inheriting from the abstract Key class.

In the case of our Employee class (Example 16.1), the class will work without *any* changes, because it already has an is-a relationship with CKey through the Person base class. However, for an Employee object, the employee ID probably provides a better key than the last name, first name combination we have been using. So, it makes sense to override the Key() member in the employee class. We also would want to override the NewCopy() member. The resulting changes are as follows:

```
class Employee :   public Person
{
public:
    Employee *NewCopy() const {return new Employee(*this);}
    string Key() const {return ID();}
    // remainder of class unchanged
};
```

The effect of the Key() override is that when we add Person objects to our KeyArray class—to be created next—they will be stored in alphabetical order by name. Employee objects, on the other hand, will be stored in ID order.

16.5.2: The KeyArray Class

The KeyArray class starts as a modification of our PersonArray class (created in Chapter 15, Example 15.12) to work with CKey objects instead of Person objects. A reasonable first pass would be to take the PersonArray code and do two search-and-replace steps:

- Replace PersonArray with KeyArray.
- Replace Person with CKey.

When we make these replacements, we get a pretty clean compile, with errors on only a few lines. One error we can fix relatively quickly. The other, unfortunately, requires some serious design rethinking.

The first error we encounter is in the memory allocation line (first line) of the Add() member:

```
int KeyArray::Add(const CKey &pers) {
    CKey *p=new CKey(pers);
    int nRet=Add(p);
    if (nRet<0) delete p;
    return nRet;
}
```

The message reads:

```
error C2259: 'CKey' : cannot instantiate abstract class
    due to following members:
    'std::string CKey::Key(void) const' : pure virtual func-
    tion was not defined
```

When we think about it, this error message makes sense—we designed CKey to be an abstract class. As a consequence, it stands to reason that we cannot apply the **new** operator to it directly.

Fortunately, we already built in the solution for this problem. If we copy an object as part of the Add() routine, and we implement a NewCopy() member as part of our CKey interface, we can just replace the first line in the Add() function with:

```
CKey *p=pers.NewCopy();
```

The polymorphic NewCopy() function will then call the proper constructor for the type of object being passed in.

We get essentially the same message on another line, this time on the memory allocation within the loop in the Load() function:

```
void KeyArray::Load(STREAM &strm)
{
    RemoveAll();
    int nVal=ReadInteger(strm);
    for(int i=0;i<nVal;i++) {
        CKey *pers=new CKey;
        strm >> *pers;
        m_arp.push_back(pers);
    }
}
```

This error, unfortunately, has no easy solution (except to reimplement the entire class as a template class, presented as an in-depth question at the end of the chapter). The problem is as follows:

- When we were adding an element to our KeyArray, we had a model we could use for creating our object—which could be a Person, an Employee, or (as we will find later) a Customer, Film, or Rental object. We didn't have to know what type because the NewCopy() function creates the appropriate type of object using polymorphism.

- When we load objects, however, we will not know what type of object is being loaded until we look at the data, because nothing in our KeyArray class prevents us from mixing object types. (This problem did not come up in our PersonArray class because we knew we would be loading and saving Person objects.)

Various approaches can be used to solve this problem. One might be to "grow your own" solution. For example, you could:

- Assign a unique code to identify each type of object inheriting from CKey.
- When saving the object, save its code first (e.g., the way we saved the number of elements in a collection), then save the object data.
- When loading the object, read the code first and then, in some static function consisting of a giant case construct, use the code to determine the appropriate class to create, after which the class data could be loaded.

Another approach would be to inherit from a predefined class that, essentially, does the preceding steps for you. An example of such a class is the CObject MFC class, used as a base class for nearly all MFC objects. Unfortunately, no standard C++ class is available for this purpose.

Yet another approach—and the approach we shall take—is to "punt" and simply remove serialization from our KeyArray class. This approach creates a more compact class, whose declaration is shown in Example 16.19. The implementation of the functions is not shown, because they are exactly the same as those in Chapter 15, Section 15.5.3, after doing the name substitutions and changing the line in the Add() member.

EXAMPLE 16.19

KeyArray class declaration

```
class KeyArray
{
public:
    KeyArray(void);
    ~KeyArray(void);

    const CKey *operator[](int) const;
    const CKey *operator[](const char *) const;
    const CKey *operator[](const string &szKey) const;
    const CKey *Find(const char *szKey,int &nPos) const;
    const CKey *Find(const char *szKey) const;
    const CKey *Find(const string &szKey) const;

    int Add(CKey *);
    int Add(const CKey &pers);
    void Remove(const char *szKey);
    void RemoveAt(int nVal);
    void Remove(CKey *p);
    int Size() const;
    void RemoveAll();

protected:
    vector<CKey*> m_arp;
    int FindPos(const string &szKey) const;
    int FindPos(const char *szKey) const;
};
```

Removing serialization from KeyArray may seem to be a pretty drastic step, but it is not as bad as it seems. When designing OOP applications, adding capabilities incrementally (through inheritance) often proves to be a powerful technique. We now turn to the creation of such a class, the EmployeeArray.

16.5.3: The EmployeeArray Class

The EmployeeArray class inherits from KeyArray and adds serialization of objects—which we know will be Employee objects—along with a Display() member that shows its contents and various << and >> overloads. The class declaration is shown in Example 16.20.

Besides adding I/O to the EmployeeArray class, one other major change was made: an override of the two Add() members to take Employee objects as arguments, instead of the more general CKey objects. Because the Add() member is the only way to get objects into the collection, it ensures we will only have Employee objects in the vector<CKey*> collection m_arp. This function is critical, because our serialization operations will crash and burn if non-Employee objects are present. The overrides themselves are simple, however. They just call the base class versions.

TEST YOUR UNDERSTANDING 16.6:

Why didn't we override all the remaining CKey-related member functions the way we overloaded Add()?

The members that we added to support I/O are nearly identical to those we developed for the original PersonArray class. These members are presented in Example 16.21.

The critical changes necessary to the original PersonArray versions are as follows:

■   We create a new Employee object (instead of a Person object) when we are loading.

EXAMPLE 16.20

EmployeeArray declaration

```
class EmployeeArray :
    public KeyArray
{
public:
    EmployeeArray(void);
    virtual ~EmployeeArray(void);

    int Add(Employee *pEmp){return KeyArray::Add(pEmp);}
    int Add(const Employee &emp){return KeyArray::Add(emp);}

    void Load(STREAM &strm);
    void Save(STREAM &strm) const;
    void Display() const;

};

OUTPUT &operator<<(OUTPUT &out,const EmployeeArray &emp);
STREAM &operator>>(STREAM &strm,EmployeeArray &emp);
STREAM &operator<<(STREAM &strm,const EmployeeArray &emp);
```

EXAMPLE 16.21

EmployeeArray I/O members

```
void EmployeeArray::Load(STREAM &strm)
{
    RemoveAll();
    int nVal=ReadInteger(strm);
    for(int i=0;i<nVal;i++) {
        Employee *pers=new Employee;
        strm >> *pers;
        m_arp.push_back(pers);
    }
}
void EmployeeArray::Save(STREAM &strm) const
{
    WriteInteger(strm,Size());
    for(int i=0;i<Size();i++) {
        strm << *((Employee *)(m_arp[i]));
    }
}
void EmployeeArray::Display() const
{
    for(int i=0;i<Size();i++) {
        cout << *((Employee *)(m_arp[i])) << endl;
    }
}
STREAM &operator>>(STREAM &strm,EmployeeArray &ar)
{
    ar.Load(strm);
    return strm;
}
STREAM &operator<<(STREAM &strm,const EmployeeArray &ar)
{
    ar.Save(strm);
    return strm;
}
```

■ We type cast the CKey pointers to Employee pointers in the Save() and Display()
members, because we know that only Employee objects are being stored.

We now have a specialized array for storing Employee data. (Prior to performing the
lab in Section 16.6, you should replace the PersonArray in your Company object with the
EmployeeArray.)

TEST YOUR UNDERSTANDING 16.7:

Could any of the C++ type cast operators be beneficial, rather than
using the old C syntax in the expression ((Employee *)(m_arp[i]))?

16.5.4: The KeyTable Class

Our KeyArray class has two areas of inflexibility that place significant limitations on its use:

1. Only objects inheriting from CKey can be placed in it.

2. Only one key can be specified per object (e.g., once we choose ID as a key for the employee class, we can no longer do an alphabetical sort by name).

To address these limitations, we now create a KeyTable class that can be used to generate a sorted array of any objects.

KeyValPair Class   At the heart of our KeyTable is a small helper class, the KeyValPair class, which we use to associate keys with pointers to anything. The implementation of this class is straightforward and is presented in Example 16.22.

KeyTable Declaration   Because the KeyValPair class inherits from CKey, it can be used directly in a KeyArray collection. For our purposes, however, we choose to hide the KeyValPair implementation by creating a new KeyTable class that inherits from KeyArray. It changes the members so that keys and associated data pointers are added and retrieved directly, and KeyValPair objects are used for internal purposes only. The class declaration for this purpose is shown in Example 16.23.

EXAMPLE 16.22

KeyValPair helper class

```
class KeyValPair :    public CKey
{
public:
    KeyValPair(void){m_pVal=0;}
    KeyValPair(const char *szKey,void *pVal){
        m_szKey=szKey;
        m_pVal=pVal;
    }
    KeyValPair(const string &szKey,void *pVal){
        m_szKey=szKey;
        m_pVal=pVal;
    }
    KeyValPair(const KeyValPair &pair){Copy(pair);}
    virtual ~KeyValPair(void){}
    const KeyValPair &operator=(const KeyValPair &pair) {
        if (&pair==this) return *this;
        Copy(pair);
        return *this;
    }
    void Copy(const KeyValPair &pair) {
        m_szKey=pair.m_szKey;
        m_pVal=pair.m_pVal;
    }
    void *Value() const {return m_pVal;}
    // required members
    KeyValPair *NewCopy() const {return new KeyValPair(*this);}
    string Key() const {return m_szKey;}
protected:
    string m_szKey;
    void *m_pVal;
};
```

EXAMPLE 16.23

KeyTable class declaration

```
class KeyTable :
    public KeyArray
{
public:
    KeyTable(void);
    virtual ~KeyTable(void);

    void *operator[](int) const;
    void *operator[](const char *) const;
    void *operator[](const string &szKey) const;
    void *Find(const char *szKey,int &nPos) const;
    void *Find(const char *szKey) const;
    void *Find(const string &szKey) const;

    void *Value(int i) const;
    string Key(int i) const;

    int Add(const string &szKey,void *val);
    int Add(const char *szKey,void *val);

};
```

Interface   The highlights of the changes to the interface are as follows:

- Our Find() members and [] overloads now return the data pointer associated with a given key string or position.
- Our Add() function takes a key and the data we want to associate with it as arguments.
- The Value() and Key() member functions are added to allow us to access the key string and pointer value of each element.

Suppose, for example, we wanted to get an alphabetical list of our employees. Unfortunately, the Employee class uses ID as a key, so just displaying the contents of an EmployeeArray won't help us. On the other hand, we can create a KeyTable and add the Employee objects to that table using the Person::Key() version of the member—which will return the last name, first name string. This task is illustrated in the following code fragment:

```
int i;
EmployeeArray ar;
// add some data to the previous array (omitted)
KeyTable tab;
for(i=0;i<ar.Size();i++) {
    Employee *pEmp=(Employee *)ar[i];
    tab.Add(pEmp->Person::Key(),pEmp);
}
for(i=0;i<tab.Size();i++) {
    Employee *pEmp=(Employee *)tab[i];
    pEmp->Display();
}
```

The nice thing about KeyTable is that you are not limited to individual existing member functions; you can make up your own keys. For example, if you wanted a sort by department, and by name within each department, if your Employee has a Department() member that returns the department name, you could put the elements in the table as follows:

```
for(i=0;i<ar.Size();i++) {
    Employee *pEmp=(Employee *)ar[i];
    tab.Add(pEmp->Department()+pEmp->Person::Key(),pEmp);
}
```

One problem that could occur using the KeyTable is duplication. Even though we know we will never have two employees with the same ID, it is possible they could have the same first and last names. To deal with this type of issue, you can simply append a value to the string that you know is unique, for example:

```
for(i=0;i<ar.Size();i++) {
    Employee *pEmp=(Employee *)ar[i];
    tab.Add(pEmp->Person::Key()+pEmp->Key(),pEmp);
}
```

You could even create a unique sequence number, for example:

```
for(i=0;i<ar.Size();i++) {
    Employee *pEmp=(Employee *)ar[i];
    char buf[80]={0};
    sprintf(buf,"%i",i);
    tab.Add(pEmp->Person::Key()+buf,pEmp);
}
```

Implementation Because of the similarity between a KeyArray and a KeyTable, the overrides required are relatively modest. The most substantial change is to the Add() members, which construct local KeyValPair objects prior to calling the base class version of Add(), as shown in Example 16.24.

The two new members, Key() and Value(), make a call to the base class [] to access the associated KeyValPair object stored in the array, then return the Key() or Value() member from the object. The main thing of interest in these functions, shown in Example 16.25, is how they call the base class version of the operator using its functional form.

The remaining overloads, provided purely for user convenience, all ultimately end up calling the Value() function if the key is found. (The void * is what is of interest, not the

---

EXAMPLE 16.24

KeyTabl::Add() member functions

```
int KeyTable::Add(const string &szKey,void *val)
{
    KeyValPair pair(szKey,val);
    return KeyArray::Add(pair);
}
int KeyTable::Add(const char *szKey,void *val)
{
    KeyValPair pair(szKey,val);
    return KeyArray::Add(pair);
}
```

EXAMPLE 16.25

Key() and Value() member functions

```
void *KeyTable::Value(int i) const {
    KeyValPair *pVal=(KeyValPair *)KeyArray::operator [](i);
    return pVal->Value();
}
string KeyTable::Key(int i) const {
    KeyValPair *pVal=(KeyValPair *)KeyArray::operator [](i);
    return pVal->Key();
}
```

KeyValPair pointer, which is used for internal purposes only.) These keys are presented in
Example 16.26.

16.6: VIDEO STORE LAB EXERCISE

Walkthrough available in VideoStore.wmv

The Video Store application is designed to demonstrate the construction of an application
that makes extensive use of inheritance and collections of objects. It builds upon the
Company class, developed in a Chapter 15 lab exercise (Section 15.6).

EXAMPLE 16.26

Find() and [] overload members of KeyTable

```
void *KeyTable::operator[](int i) const {
    return Value(i);
}
void *KeyTable::operator[](const char *szKey) const {
    return Find(szKey);
}
void *KeyTable::operator[](const string &szKey) const {
    return Find(szKey);
}
void *KeyTable::Find(const char *szKey,int &nPos) const {
    if (!KeyArray::Find(szKey,nPos)) return 0;
    return Value(nPos);
}
void *KeyTable::Find(const char *szKey) const {
    int nPos;
    if (!Find(szKey,nPos)) return 0;
    return Value(nPos);
}
void *KeyTable::Find(const string &szKey) const {
    int nPos;
    if (!Find(szKey.c_str(),nPos)) return 0;
    return Value(nPos);
}
```

16.6.1: Overview

At the heart of the Video Store application are three major classes that manage collections of objects. The Company class, already discussed, manages a collection of Employee objects. The Store class inherits from Company and manages an additional collection of Customer objects. Finally, the VideoStore class manages two additional collections—Film objects and Rental objects—allowing the user to check out and return films. The basic structure of the application (data members only) is shown in Figure 16.11.

Each one of the three collection classes has its own interface, implemented though an Interface() function that calls a Menu() function to display a list of options available, then calls an Option() function to call the relevant member function. Because of the inheritance relationships present, the number of options supported by the menus grows from parent to child, as shown in Figures 16.12, 16.13, and 16.14.

16.6.2: Specifications

The complete Video Store application requires three major classes (Company, Store, and VideoStore), four unit classes (Employee, Customer, Film, and Rental), and four unit collection classes (EmployeeArray, CustomerArray, FilmArray, and RentalArray). We begin by discussing the unit classes, which are the simplest.

Unit Classes Four fundamental object types are managed within the complete Video Store application: Employee, Customer, Film, and Rental. The Employee class has been developed within the text of this chapter. We, therefore, focus on the remaining classes, which closely parallel Employee.

Like the Employee class, each of the remaining unit classes supports a common set of interface members that are listed in Table 16.1.

All the unit classes ultimately inherit from CKey, making it possible to store them in a KeyArray structure. The inheritance network is presented in Figure 16.15, with only the data members being shown (except for the CKey class).

The unit classes were intentionally designed to be simple and relatively self-explanatory. Some comments, however, are required for each of the classes that need to be implemented:

- **Customer:** Little more than a simplified Employee, its key is the m_szID member, which is called the customer ID.

- **Film:** Each film has a unique film ID code (you may assume no more than ten characters for fixed width processing), a title, and the year released. Only the latter requires any particular thought, since the previous classes only had string data. The utils.h file included with the project contains an Int2String() function that can be useful (particularly for preparing fixed string output).

- **Rental:** The Rental object requires a bit more handling. To begin with, it doesn't have its own built-in key. Instead, you may assume that the combination of date, film ID, and customer ID are—together—unique. Also, the m_nDate (checkout date) and m_nReturned (returned date) are integers

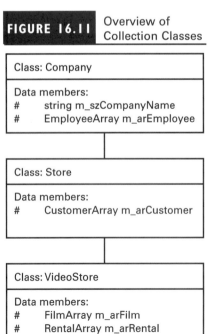

FIGURE 16.11 Overview of Collection Classes

Class: Company

Data members:
string m_szCompanyName
EmployeeArray m_arEmployee

Class: Store

Data members:
CustomerArray m_arCustomer

Class: VideoStore

Data members:
FilmArray m_arFilm
RentalArray m_arRental

FIGURE 16.12 Interface() Menu for Company Object

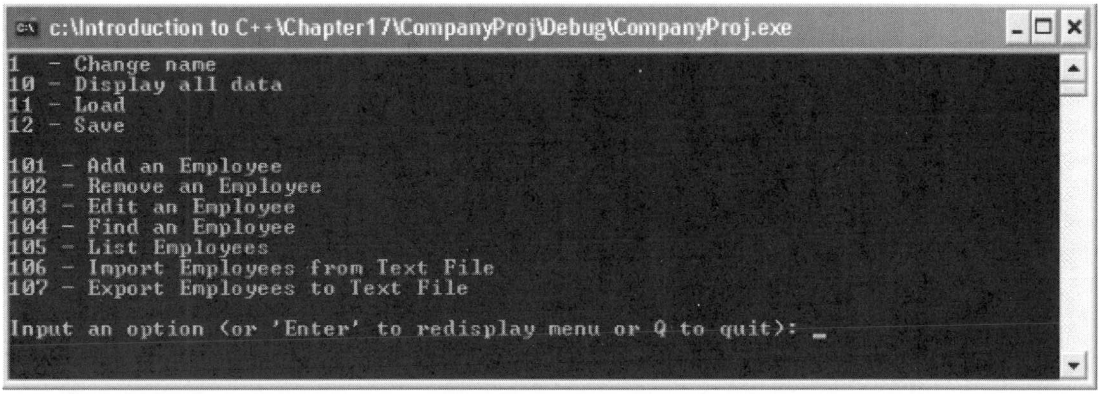

```
c:\Introduction to C++\Chapter17\CompanyProj\Debug\CompanyProj.exe
1   - Change name
10  - Display all data
11  - Load
12  - Save

101 - Add an Employee
102 - Remove an Employee
103 - Edit an Employee
104 - Find an Employee
105 - List Employees
106 - Import Employees from Text File
107 - Export Employees to Text File

Input an option (or 'Enter' to redisplay menu or Q to quit): _
```

FIGURE 16.13 Interface for Store Object

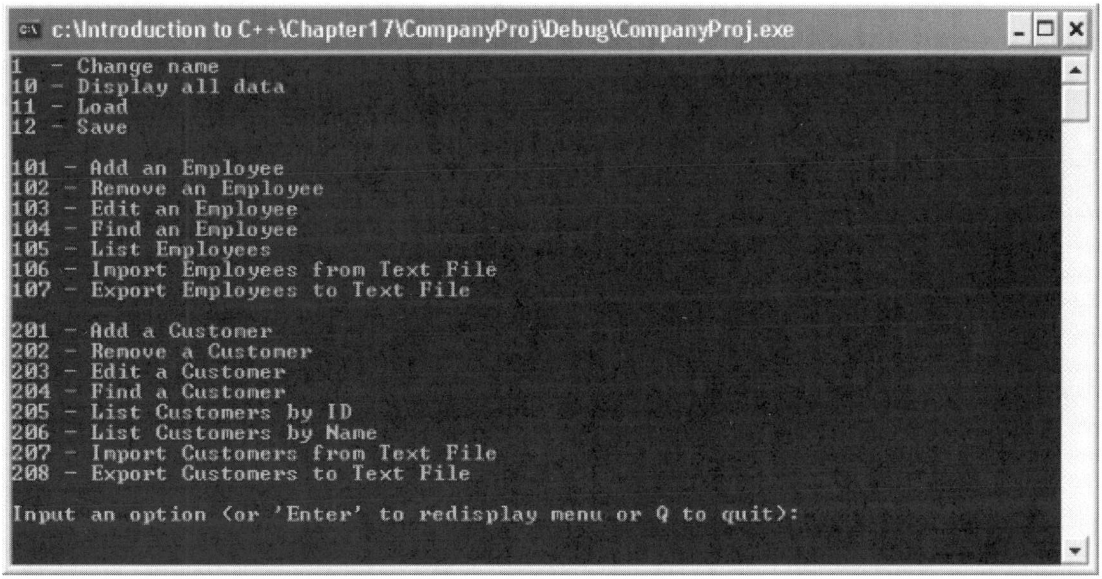

```
c:\Introduction to C++\Chapter17\CompanyProj\Debug\CompanyProj.exe
1   - Change name
10  - Display all data
11  - Load
12  - Save

101 - Add an Employee
102 - Remove an Employee
103 - Edit an Employee
104 - Find an Employee
105 - List Employees
106 - Import Employees from Text File
107 - Export Employees to Text File

201 - Add a Customer
202 - Remove a Customer
203 - Edit a Customer
204 - Find a Customer
205 - List Customers by ID
206 - List Customers by Name
207 - Import Customers from Text File
208 - Export Customers to Text File

Input an option (or 'Enter' to redisplay menu or Q to quit):
```

stored in the format YYYYMMDD (e.g, July 18, 2004, would be 20040718). For convenience, simple (and not very accurate) Date2String() and InputDate() functions are provided in utils.h. The reader is encouraged, however, to implement date classes such as those in the end-of-chapter exercises in Chapters 13 and 14, should time permit.

For each class, you should implement not only the functions listed in Table 16.1, but also appropriate accessor functions for getting and setting data member values.

Unit Collection Classes For each of our unit classes, we create a dedicated collection class—essentially identical in structure and interface to EmployeeArray (Section

FIGURE 16.14 Interface for VideoStore Object

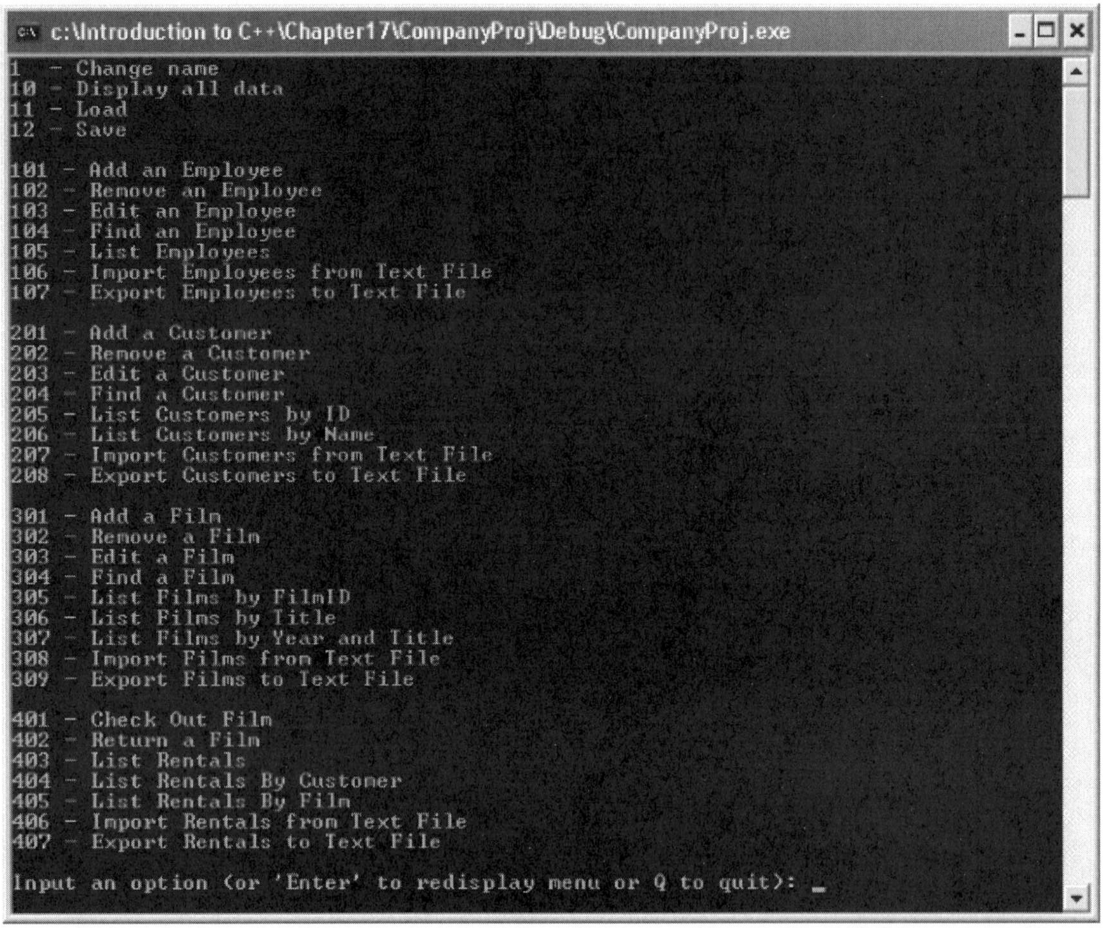

```
c:\Introduction to C++\Chapter17\CompanyProj\Debug\CompanyProj.exe

1   - Change name
10  - Display all data
11  - Load
12  - Save

101 - Add an Employee
102 - Remove an Employee
103 - Edit an Employee
104 - Find an Employee
105 - List Employees
106 - Import Employees from Text File
107 - Export Employees to Text File

201 - Add a Customer
202 - Remove a Customer
203 - Edit a Customer
204 - Find a Customer
205 - List Customers by ID
206 - List Customers by Name
207 - Import Customers from Text File
208 - Export Customers to Text File

301 - Add a Film
302 - Remove a Film
303 - Edit a Film
304 - Find a Film
305 - List Films by FilmID
306 - List Films by Title
307 - List Films by Year and Title
308 - Import Films from Text File
309 - Export Films to Text File

401 - Check Out Film
402 - Return a Film
403 - List Rentals
404 - List Rentals By Customer
405 - List Rentals By Film
406 - Import Rentals from Text File
407 - Export Rentals to Text File

Input an option (or 'Enter' to redisplay menu or Q to quit): _
```

16.5.3). These classes can be created with some creative search-and-replace of the EmployeeArray class. (The alternative is to create a KeyArray template class, as proposed in Question 11 at the end of the chapter.)

Main Classes As noted in the overview, the main classes are Company, Store, and VideoStore. Most of the members of these classes relate to the collections they manage. The Company class, originally developed in Chapter 15, Section 15.6, requires only minimal modifications from its original form. Its top-level interface (essentially repeated from Chapter 15, Table 15.5) is presented in Table 16.2. Only two changes are required from the earlier version: changing the return type of FindEmployee() to an Employee* (instead of a Person*) and changing the underlying collection from a PersonArray to an EmployeeArray.

One additional change that should be made to the Company class is to make certain functions virtual, because we plan to inherit them. These functions include the following:

| **TABLE 16.1** | Members Supported by Unit Classes |

string Key() const

Returns a unique key for maintaining the object in a KeyArray-based collection. The nature of the key depends on the object type

void Input()

Prompts the user for input for each member of the class

void Display() const

Displays the data values for the object

string FixedString() const

Returns a fixed field width representation of the object's data, suitable for export to a text file

void FixedString(const string &str)

Retrieves data from a string containing a fixed width representation of the object, consistent with what was produced by FixedString()

void Load(STREAM &strm)

Loads a unit object stored in a binary file

void Save(STREAM &strm) const

Saves a unit object to a binary file

```
virtual void RemoveAll();
virtual void DisplayAll() const;
virtual void Load(STREAM &strm);
virtual void Save(STREAM &strm) const;
virtual void Menu() const;
virtual bool Option(int nOption);
```

By inheriting these functions in each class, we do not have to change the top-level functions SaveToFile(), LoadFromFile(), and Interface().

The Store class is much like the Company class—particularly because Employee objects are so similar to Customer objects. Its top-level menu options are presented in Table 16.3.

In implementing the Store class, a variety of helpful functions can also be implemented, just as they were for the Company class. In addition to overloading the virtual functions from the Company class, a full set of functions that do not require user I/O should be implemented. For example, in addition to:

```
void AddCustomer();
```

which prompts the user for customer information, we should have:

```
bool AddCustomer(const Customer &pers);
```

which performs the actual addition to the array. The main benefit of having two different functions—one that involves the user and one that doesn't—is that it would allow us to use our Store class in contexts where customers were not coming from the user (e.g., imported from a database), or were not coming from standard input (e.g., a Windows program, where customer data were gathered in a dialog box). Furthermore, having variations

FIGURE 16.15 Inheritance Relationships Among the Unit Classes

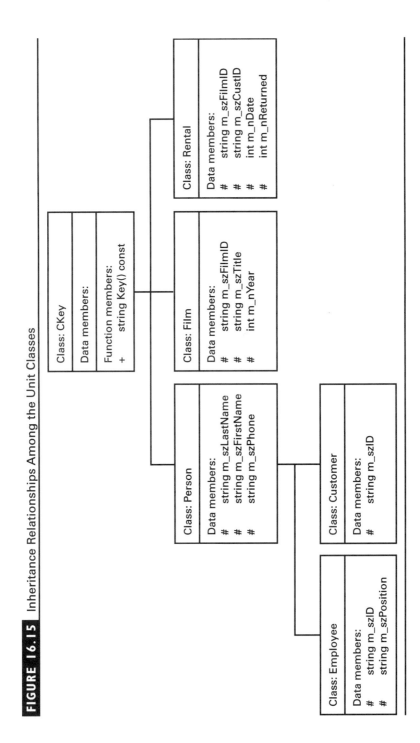

| TABLE 16.2 | Top-Level Menu Options for Company Class |

Menu Option No.	Top-Level Company Functions
1	**void ChangeName() const** Changes the name of the Company object. Prompts user for new name.
10	**virtual void DisplayAll() const** Displays the company name and all the Employee objects.
11	**void LoadFromFile()** Prompts the user for a file name, opens the file for reading, then loads the Company data from the file.
12	**void SaveToFile() const** Prompts the user for a file name, opens the file for writing, then saves the Company data to the file.
101	**void AddEmployee()** Prompts the user for an Employee ID and, if the ID is valid (i.e., not already present), allows the user to edit and add the Employee to the EmployeeArray collection.
102	**void RemoveEmployee()** Calls FindEmployee(true) to access the Employee object, displaying the data. Prompts the user for a confirmation and, if the user confirms, removes the Employee object from the EmployeeArray collection.
103	**void EditEmployee()** Calls FindEmployee(false) to access the Employee object, then allows the user to edit the Employee.
104	**Employee *FindEmployee(bool bDisplay=true) const** Prompts the user for an Employee ID and, if the ID is valid, returns a pointer to the employee. If bDisplay is true, displays the Employee object's data.
105	**void ListEmployees() const** Displays the data for all employees in the EmployeeArray, one employee per line.
106	**void ImportEmployees()** Prompts the user for a file name (presumably a text file), then loads the fixed format employee records into the EmployeeArray.
107	**void Export Employees() const** Prompts the user for a file name (presumably a text file), then saves the employee records from the EmployeeArray in a fixed text format.
N/A	**void Interface()** Enters a loop that displays a menu (i.e., calling the Menu() function), prompts the user for an option number, then selects one of the preceding options (i.e., calling the Option() function).

on the functions isn't much extra work, because we can call the nonuser version from the user version once the user has entered the appropriate data.

The declaration used to create the sample version is presented in Example 16.27.

The VideoStore class manages two collections—Film and Rental objects—and therefore has more top-level functions, as shown in Table 16.4.

The declaration of the VideoStore class used in the sample program is presented in Example 16.28.

TABLE 16.3	Top-Level Menu Options for Store Class

Menu Option No.	Top-Level Store Functions
201	**void AddCustomer()**
	Prompts the user for a Customer ID and, if the ID is valid (i.e., not already present), allows the user to edit and add the Customer to the CustomerArray collection.
202	**void RemoveCustomer()**
	Calls FindCustomer(true) to access the Customer object, displaying the data. Prompts the user for a confirmation and, if the user confirms, removes the Customer object from the CustomerArray collection.
203	**void EditCustomer()**
	Calls FindCustomer(false) to access the Customer object, then allows the user to edit the Customer.
204	**Customer *FindCustomer(bool bDisplay=true) const**
	Prompts the user for a Customer ID and, if the ID is valid returns a pointer to the customer. If bDisplay is true, displays the Customer object's data.
205	**void ListCustomers() const**
	Displays the data for all customers in the CustomerArray, one customer per line.
206	**void ListCustomersByName() const**
	Displays the data for all customers in the CustomerArray in alphabetical order, one customer per line. A good way to implement this is using a KeyTable object, as discussed in Section 17.5.4.
207	**void ImportCustomers()**
	Prompts the user for a file name (presumably a text file), then loads the fixed format customer records into the CustomerArray.
208	**void Export Customers() const**
	Prompts the user for a file name (presumably a text file), then saves the customer records from the CustomerArray in a fixed text format.

16.6.3: Instructions

Although the number of functions to be implemented in the lab exercise is large, few of the individual functions are particularly complex. Indeed, the longest functions are those that do mechanical activities, such as prompting the user for object information, displaying a menu, and routing menu selections.

A good general approach to the exercise is the following:

- Begin by modifying and testing the Company class. Don't move on until you are confident you have the Company working well, and as intended.
- Write the Customer class, using Employee as a starting point. In fact, this class is so simple that a few search-and-replace operations, followed by some deletions (because a Customer doesn't have a position member), will get the job done.
- Develop a CustomerArray class, using the EmployeeArray as a model. Again, the similarity is so strong you can consider living dangerously and postponing testing.

EXAMPLE 16.27

Declaration of Store class

```
class Store :
    public Company
{
public:
    Store(void);
    virtual ~Store(void);

    virtual void RemoveAll();

    // top-level functions
    // all company functions plus
    virtual void DisplayAll() const;
    void AddCustomer();
    void RemoveCustomer();
    void EditCustomer();
    Customer *FindCustomer(bool bDisplay=true) const;
    void ListCustomers() const;
    void ListCustomersByName() const;
    void ImportCustomers();
    void ExportCustomers() const;

    // helpful functions
    bool AddCustomer(const Customer &pers);
    void RemoveCustomer(const char *szKey);
    void RemoveCustomer(const string &szKey);
    Customer *FindCustomer(const char *szKey) const;
    Customer *FindCustomer(const string &szKey) const;

    virtual void Load(STREAM &strm);
    virtual void Save(STREAM &strm) const;

    Customer *GetCustomer(int i) const;
    int CustomerCount() const;

    virtual void Menu() const;
    virtual bool Option(int nOption);

    void ImportCustomers(INPUT &in);
    void ExportCustomers(OUTPUT &out) const;
protected:
    CustomerArray m_arCustomer;
};
```

TABLE 16.4	Top-Level Menu Options for VideoStore Class

Menu Option No.	Top-Level VideoStore Functions
301	**void AddFilm()** Prompts the user for a Film ID and, if the ID is valid (i.e., not already present), allows the user to edit and add the Film to the FilmArray collection.
302	**void RemoveFilm()** Calls FindFilm(true) to access the Film object, displaying the data. Prompts the user for a confirmation and, if the user confirms, removes the Film object from the FilmArray collection.
303	**void EditFilm()** Calls FindFilm(false) to access the Film object, then allows the user to edit the Film.
304	**Film *FindFilm(bool bDisplay=true) const** Prompts the user for a Film ID and, if the ID is valid, returns a pointer to the film. If bDisplay is true, displays the Film object's data.
305	**void ListFilms() const** Displays the data for all films in the FilmArray, one film per line.
306	**void ListFilmsByTitle() const** Displays the data for all films in the FilmArray in alphabetical order by title, one film per line. A good way to implement this is using a KeyTable object, as discussed in Section 17.5.4.
307	**void ListFilmsByYearAndTitle() const** Displays the data for all films in the FilmArray in alphabetical order by title, one film per line. (A good way to implement this function is using a KeyTable object, as discussed in Section 17.5.4.)
308	**void ImportFilms()** Prompts the user for a file name (presumably a text file), then loads the fixed format film records into the FilmArray.
309	**void Export Films() const** Prompts the user for a file name (presumably a text file), then saves the film records from the FilmArray in a fixed text format.

(Continues)

- Develop the Store class. As it turns out, Store and Company manage such similar data types (i.e., Customers and Employees), which means the classes will be very similar.
  - A good starting point is to build the interface first, implementing the Menu() and Option() members. In both cases, you should be able to call the base class and then add the additional capabilities for the Store.
  - The key virtual functions, DisplayAll(), Load(), and Save() (all of which begin by calling the base class), can then be implemented. Be sure to use the serialization capabilities of your unit collection class (CustomerArray) for the last two of these functions.
  - All the Customer management functions can then be implemented, saving ListCustomersByName() until last, at which time you should review the example in Section 16.5.4.

TABLE 16.4	Top-Level Menu Options for VideoStore Class (Continued)

Menu Option No.	Top-Level VideoStore Functions
401	**void CheckOutFilm()**
	Prompts the user for a Film ID and a Customer ID, and if both are found, prompts the user for a checkout date. If the checkout date is valid (you can use the InputDate() function in utils.h as a starting point), a Rental object is created and added to the RentalArray.
402	**void ReturnFilm()**
	Prompts the user for a FilmID, then checks for a Rental object with a matching film ID and a Return date of 0 (i.e., has not been returned), and if it finds such a Rental object, prompts the user for the return date and updates the m_nReturned member to that date.
403	**void ListRentals() const**
	Lists all Rental objects in the RentalArray, one per line. The default order should be checkout date + film ID + customer ID (assuming the Rental Key() member is properly implemented).
404	**void ListRentalsByCustomer() const**
	Provides a listing of film ID and title, grouped by customer ID. The KeyTable will be a definite help in implementing this function, which is reminiscent of grouping in a database report.
405	**void ListRentalsByFilm() const**
	Provides a listing of customer ID and name, grouped by film ID.
406	**void ImportRentals()**
	Prompts the user for a file name (presumably a text file), then loads the fixed format rental records into the RentalArray.
407	**void ExportRentals() const**
	Prompts the user for a file name (presumably a text file), then saves the rental records from the RentalArray in a fixed text format.

- You should now do extensive testing of the Store class to make sure it is working.
- Implement the Film class. The only trick associated with this class is the fact that it has a numeric member (Year). A function in Utils.h, however, converts an integer to a string object, which simplifies the process.
- Implement the Rental class. The trick here is the two date members. Two functions in Utils.h allow you to convert back and forth between user input and the internal date format (YYYYMMDD). You will also need to convert that format to a string object (e.g., "20040718") as part of the key function. The advantage of the integer format is that it sorts in a sensible way.
- Implement the VideoStore class. A good way to postpone the more conceptually difficult portion of this task is to do a first pass implementation that just deals with Film objects (options 301–309) and test it first. Once it is working, you can implement the Rental object management and reports (options 401–407).

Upon completion and testing of the VideoStore class, the lab is complete.

EXAMPLE 16.28

VideoStore class declaration

```
class VideoStore :
    public Store
{
public:
    VideoStore(void);
    virtual ~VideoStore(void);
    virtual void RemoveAll();
    // top-level functions
    // all Store functions plus
    virtual void DisplayAll() const;
    void AddFilm();
    void RemoveFilm();
    void EditFilm();
    Film *FindFilm(bool bDisplay=true) const;
    void ListFilms() const;
    void ListFilmsByTitle() const;
    void ListFilmsByYearAndTitle() const;
    void ImportFilms();
    void ExportFilms() const;
    void CheckOutFilm();
    void ReturnFilm();
    void ListRentals() const;
    void ListRentalsByCustomer() const;
    void ListRentalsByFilm() const;
    void ImportRentals();
    void ExportRentals() const;
    // helpful functions
    bool AddFilm(const Film &pers);
    void RemoveFilm(const char *szKey);
    void RemoveFilm(const string &szKey);
    Film *FindFilm(const char *szKey) const;
    Film *FindFilm(const string &szKey) const;
    virtual void Load(STREAM &strm);
    virtual void Save(STREAM &strm) const;
    Film *GetFilm(int i) const;
    int FilmCount() const;
    Rental *GetRental(int i) const;
    int RentalCount() const;
    virtual void Menu() const;
    virtual bool Option(int nOption);
    void ImportFilms(INPUT &in);
    void ExportFilms(OUTPUT &out) const;
    void ImportRentals(INPUT &in);
    void ExportRentals(OUTPUT &out) const;
protected:
    FilmArray m_arFilm;
    RentalArray m_arRental;
};
```

16.7: REVIEW AND QUESTIONS

16.7.1: REVIEW

Inheritance is a powerful programming capability that promotes abstract thinking, reuse of code, and the ability to handle diverse collections of related objects using polymorphism. The inheritance relationship is also sometimes referred to as the "is-a" relationship, because when ClassB can benefit from inheriting properties from ClassA, it usually makes sense to say:

A ClassB object is a ClassA object.

In this type of inheritance relationship, ClassA is often referred to as the base class or parent class, while ClassB can be called the child class.

In C++, inheritance is implemented by declaring a class, then following the class name with a colon, some inheritance specifiers, and name of the base class. For example:

```
class Child : public Parent {
    // ClassB member are declared,
    // just as they would be in a
    // normal class
};
```

When Child is declared in this way, all of the members of Parent (except private members) can be used within Child objects. Other inheritance derivation specifiers (e.g., protected, private) can also be used. These specifiers hide various Parent members within the Child class, and are considerably less common.

When a Child inherits from a Parent, two types of changes are typically made in the Child class:

- *Additions:* New data and function members can be added to the Child class.
- *Overrides:* The behavior of Parent member functions are changed in the Child class.

Whenever a given function name is overridden in the Child, all Parent overloads of that function become invisible—although they can be called using the scope resolution operator (e.g., Parent::OverrideMemberName() will call the function defined in the Parent class).

A special case of inheritance involves constructor functions. Normally, when a Child object is created, the default (no argument) version of the Parent constructor is called in the process of constructing the Child. To allow greater flexibility, an initialization list may be specified as part of a constructor function. Within that list may be Parent constructor overloads and data member names. For example, the Employee constructor:

```
Employee(const char *szI,
const char *szL,const char *szF,
const char *szP,const char *szT) :
    Person(szL,szF,szP),
    m_szID(szI),
    m_szPosition(szT)
        {
        // no initializations in body
        // are required
        }
```

calls a three-argument version of its base class (Person) constructor, and then specifies constructors for two of its string data members (m_szID and m_szPosition).

When inheritance is present, it can also be useful to replace standard C-style type casting (using parenthesis) with C++ template operators:

- **static_cast**<*target-type*>: Performs a type cast with no runtime checking.
- **dynamic_cast**<*target-type*>: Determines whether the type cast is valid, returning 0 (pointers) or generating an exception (references) if it is not.

A particularly important type of behavior available in inheritance situations is polymorphism. Most commonly used where collections of object pointers or references are present, polymorphic member functions are called according to the nature of the object to which they are applied. For example, if LiveBirth() is a polymorphic function:

```
Mammal *p1=new Lion;
Mammal *p2=new Platypus;
p1->LiveBirth(); // returns true
p2->LiveBirth(); // returns false
p2->Mammal::LiveBirth(); // returns true
```

In this case, even though Mammal returns **true** for LiveBirth(), the platypus pointer returns **false** because the function is overridden (because a platypus lays eggs).

To declare a function polymorphic, the **virtual** keyword is placed in front of its prototype in the class declaration. In our platypus example, if LiveBirth() were *not* declared **virtual**, the following calls would return different values:

```
Platypus plat;
Mammal *p1=&plat;
plat.LiveBirth(); // returns false,
// the Platypus version
p1->LiveBirth(); // returns true,
// the Mammal version
```

A particularly powerful way to organize polymorphic objects is inheritance hierarchies. Often, classes that are never intended to be stand-alone objects are used to structure a framework (e.g., a taxonomy used to create animal objects, where levels such as genus and species are used to classify and organize the hierarchy). Classes never intended to be objects are called abstract classes. In C++, declaring one or more pure virtual functions makes a class abstract. Such functions are implemented by placing = 0; after the function prototype in the class declaration, for example:

```
class CKey {
    virtual string Key() const = 0;
    // etc.
};
```

Until a child of an abstract class provides a body for *all* pure virtual functions, the child class remains an abstract class as well.

In deciding whether to make a function polymorphic, the general rule is that a function should be virtual if:

- It is likely to be overridden at some future time.
- It is a function you are likely to want to use in a collection of objects based upon some abstract class.
- It is a destructor function, unless you know the object will never be used as part of a collection and doesn't manage any memory internally.

Any member function that doesn't meet any of these three criteria can—and probably should—be left as a nonvirtual function for reasons of efficiency and clarity.

Unlike many popular languages (e.g., Java and C#), C++ provides for multiple inheritance, allowing more than one base class to be specified. Multiple inheritance is accomplished by adding comma-separated inheritance specifications in the class declaration, for example:

```
class Mule :
    public Horse , public Jackass
{
    // etc…
};
```

where Mule inherits from Horse and Jackass. Multiple inheritance tends to lead to a number of problems, including the following:

- Ambiguity when members with the same name are present in two or more base classes
- Duplication of data, when data members with the same name are inherited
- Conceptual issues (regarding whether two concurrent is-a relationships actually exist)

The **virtual** keyword, added to the inheritance specification, can eliminate some duplication when two or more base classes come out of the same hierarchy. Another approach is to create interface classes—consisting solely of pure virtual functions—that can guarantee the presence of the member functions desirable for polymorphism, but force the programmer to define the functions in the inherited class (to eliminate ambiguity). Using interface classes as a design principle is also likely to make transporting code to other languages more straightforward.

16.7.2: GLOSSARY

abstract class   A class used to organize an inheritance network, but cannot be the basis of an actual object because it has one or more pure virtual functions

base class   A class whose properties are being inherited in an inheritance relationship (same as parent class)

child class   A class that inherits properties from one or more parent classes

downcast   A type cast from a parent to a child

dynamic_cast<>   A C++ templated operator used as a substitute for the C type cast syntax, a dynamic_cast<> operation does runtime checking to ensure the cast is valid, returning a 0 (pointer) or an exception (reference) if it is not, often used for downcasts

hierarchy   A collection of classes' parent-child relationships

initialization List   A comma-separated list of constructor functions and member names that can be used to initialize objects during construction and is specified as part of a constructor function

interface Class   An abstract class used in multiple inheritance situations that consists solely of pure virtual functions

multiple inheritance   The ability of an object to inherit directly from more than one base class

override   The process of redefining a base class member function in a child class, once a given function name has been overridden, all other overloads that may exist in the base class are hidden

parent class   A class whose properties are being inherited in an inheritance relationship (same as base class)

polymorphism The ability to choose what member function to call at runtime when an object pointer or reference is present, polymorphism allows collections of objects in the same hierarchy to perform different tasks when the same member function is used on each object

private inheritance A form of inheritance in which all public and protected members of the base class become private in the child class

protected inheritance A form of inheritance in which all public and protected members of the base class become/remain protected in the child class

public inheritance A form of inheritance in which all public members of the base class remain public in the child class; private members of the base class are always inaccessible in the child class

pure virtual function A function declared without a body that must be defined in a child class

static_cast<> A C++ templated operator used as a substitute for the C type cast syntax, a static_cast<> operation does no runtime checking (see dynamic_cast<>). Often used for upcasts

thunk A term used for a virtual function pointer embedded in a polymorphic object

upcast A type cast from a child to a parent

vftable[] A term sometimes used to describe the table of function pointers created for virtual functions

virtual function A member function declared to be polymorphic in nature, pointers to these functions are normally implemented as hidden members of objects

virtual inheritance A form of multiple inheritance that combines duplicated member data and functions when two classes in the same hierarchy are both used as base classes

16.7.3: QUESTIONS

1. *Motorized vehicle taxonomy.* Create a hierarchy of motorized vehicles, with attributes such as number of wheels, passenger seating, etc.

2. *Employee and contractor hierarchy.* Create a hierarchy of employee and independent contractor classes, focusing on how pay is calculated (e.g., W2 vs. 1099, exempt vs. nonexempt, hours*wage, salary, commission*sales, etc.). Identify some categories that could benefit from multiple inheritance (e.g., sales manager).

3. *Revised unit object hierarchy.* In the Section 16.6 lab exercise, suppose we decided to add another abstract class to our hierarchy, KeyObject, as shown in the diagram below. What pure virtual member functions would it make sense to place in KeyObject? Would this modification offer any benefits?

4. *Revised unit-array object hierarchy.* In the Section 16.6 lab exercise, suppose we decided to add another abstract class to our hierarchy, KeyCollection, as shown in the diagram below. What member functions would it make sense to place in KeyCollection? Would this modification offer any benefits? (*Hint:* Think about how you needed to modify the EmployeeArray code for each different collection. Properly implemented, the KeyCollection class could be constructed with only one pure virtual function needing to be overridden in each child class.)

KeyCollection Hierarchy

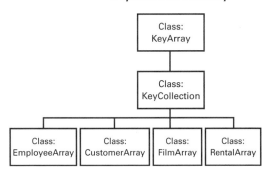

5. *Base class for Company.* Why might you want to inherit the Company class from an abstract base class, instead of starting it from scratch? What member functions would be placed in the class? Can you think of circumstances where it might make sense to define such a base class?

KeyObject Hierarchy

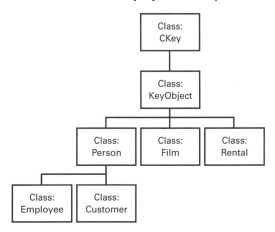

6. *Customer rental records.* Suppose we wanted to keep track of all the films each customer had rented as part of the Customer class. How would we need to modify the Customer class, and would inheritance be a good method for this modification? How would you need to modify the Video Store application to permit this information to be collected?

7. *Enhanced Employee array.* In the EmployeeArray class presented in Section 16.5.3, overload the [] operators so they return Employee * objects.

8. *Sorted array allowing duplicate values.* Create a SortedArray class that inherits from KeyArray and will allow duplicate key values.

9. *Case-insensitive string.* Create an iString class that inherits from string but does comparisons in case-insensitive fashion. One benefit of inheriting here is so that you can do the necessary operator overloads.

10. *Uppercase string class.* Create a uString class that inherits from iString (Question 9) but only allows uppercase characters. You will have to override a number of the iString members here so that each time the string is initialized, all the characters are transformed to uppercase.

In-Depth Questions

11. *KeyArray template.* Recreate the KeyArray as a template with a single data type parameter. What additional capabilities not present in KeyArray can be included in a template version?

12. *KeyTable template.* Recreate the KeyTable as a template class with a single data type parameter (representing the type of data being stored).

13. *Multiple film copies.* How would you need to modify the Video Store application if our store had multiple copies of some of its films? Consider whether inheritance would be the best technique for handling this modification.

14. *Multiple cassette rental transactions.* How would you need to modify the Video Store application to allow for a customer to rent multiple videos in the same transaction? Consider what classes you would want to add and what, if any, use you could make of inheritance.

15. *Video sales.* How would you need to modify the Video Store application to allow for sales of videos, in addition to rentals? Consider what classes you would want to add and what, if any, use you could make of inheritance.

CHAPTER 17

File Stream I/O in C++

EXECUTIVE SUMMARY

Chapter 17 examines how we can use files to load and save data in our applications using C++. The chapter is organized around the same topics as Chapter 8 (Introduction to File Stream I/O), but presents the topics using C++ objects instead of the SimpleIO functions we have relied on. Furthermore, because the basic concepts of streams, text files, and binary files are independent of language, the general discussions of these topics presented in Chapter 8 are not repeated.

The chapter begins with an overview of file I/O in C++ that stresses the practical realities of using I/O objects, without providing a more detailed explanation of their subtleties. The primary purpose of this section is to make C++ I/O objects accessible to readers who wish to use them—in preference to SimpleIO objects. For this reason, it does not assume knowledge beyond pure data structures (Chapter 11). We then consider C++ I/O in greater depth, beginning by introducing the C++ STL object hierarchy. Text-based I/O using the ostream/istream and ofstream/ifstream objects is presented, along with formatting using both C++ manipulators and member functions. Techniques for binary file I/O using the C++ file objects are explored. A walkthrough of the complete SimpleIO implementation is followed by a lab exercise involving the implementation of an encapsulated GFile class (based upon the interface of the MFC CFile class) and a GStdioFile class (based on the MFC CStdioFile class).

LEARNING OBJECTIVES

Upon completing this chapter, you should be able to:

- Apply simple member functions to C++ file objects
- Open and close a file stream in C++
- Read and write text-formatted data using C++ file objects
- Read and write binary data using C++ file objects
- Use member functions to navigate within C++ binary file streams
- Write C++ applications that incorporate binary files
- Encapsulate file I/O operations into a single class

17.1: A QUICK INTRODUCTION TO C++ I/O

Chapter 17 is designed to serve two purposes. The first is to provide the reader with enough information about C++ I/O to perform the exercises and projects throughout the textbook. The second is to provide a deeper understanding of how C++ I/O is performed, with particular emphasis on text formatting capabilities.

We now turn to the first objective. The section presents a "quick and dirty" summary of the practical information required to use C++ for text and binary I/O, without any attempt to explain the underlying mechanics and subtleties. Enough detail is provided, however, so that file I/O in Chapters 9 through 16 can be accomplished using just what is presented here. This section assumes a basic knowledge of structures, but not the full knowledge of objects developed in Chapters 13–16.

17.1.1: Opening a C++ File Stream

C++ file I/O is accomplished using various I/O objects. These objects are declared exactly the way we declared SimpleIO variables in Chapter 8.

Text Streams　　Two types of objects are used most commonly for text I/O in C++ I/O:

```
ifstream    Input file streams
ofstream    Output file streams
```

If we want to use these objects in our code, we need to place:

```
#include <fstream>
using namespace std;
```

at the top of our .cpp file.

The process of declaring a file object closely corresponds to the way that we create a structure object—except that we do not use the **struct** keyword. Once a file object is created, we can then open it, applying the same . operator we learned about for working with structures to the open() *member function*. For example:

```
ofstream myout;
myout.open("SampleFile.txt");
```

After this code fragment, the myout object would be an open file stream to which we could send output.

Failure of file member functions can be tested using another member function: fail(). For example:

```
ifstream myin;
myin.open("SampleInput.txt");
if (myin.fail()) {
    cerr << "The file did not open…" << endl;
    // take appropriate action
}
```

To close a C++ stream, the close member can be used. For example:

```
myin.close();
```

In many cases, however, C++ streams don't have to be closed explicitly. The reason is that when a C++ object goes out of scope, the associated file is automatically closed. For example, consider the following block of code:

```
{
    ofstream myout;
    myout.open("SampleFile.txt");
    myout << "Hello, World!" << endl;
}
```

In this example, which writes "Hello World\n" to a text file named SampleFile.txt, myout does not need to be closed explicitly, because—upon leaving the block—myout goes out of scope and, therefore, closes automatically. As a consequence, the close() member is normally used either when we want to reopen another stream using an existing object, or when we are concerned that another process might want to access the open file, so we need to close it as quickly as possible.

C++ predefines a number of text stream objects that are automatically available:

cout	An ostream object used for standard output
cin	An istream object used for standard input
cerr	An ostream object (that defaults to standard output) used for error messages

These objects (*istream* and *ostream*) actually reside one level above the *ofstream* and *ifstream* in the C++ I/O hierarchy. This proximity proves to be unimportant to programmers, because anything they can do with their own *ofstream* and *ifstream* objects can also be done with *ostream* and *istream* objects (except opening and closing the stream).

In SimpleIO.h, the two type names used for text I/O are INPUT and OUTPUT. They are defined as follows:

```
typedef ostream OUTPUT;
typedef istream INPUT;
```

Defined in this way, the SimpleIO functions that take text input and output streams (e.g., the PrintString() and GetString() functions), can be passed as either standard objects (cin, cout,cerr) or ifstream/ofstream file stream objects opened by the user. This capability makes the functions slightly more flexible than their standard I/O equivalents (the DisplayString() and InputString() functions).

Binary Streams   Three types of objects are most commonly used for binary I/O C++, our first two streams plus a third:

ifstream	Input file streams
ofstream	Output file streams
fstream	Input/Output file streams

The process of opening an *fstream* object is slightly more complicated because we need to be specific about the mode used to open it. It is done by specifying a second argument to the open() member function. C++ uses defined constants to specify opening mode, which are bitwise or'd together. Common combinations of these constants (which must be written in their full form, i.e., ios_base::*constant_name*) are presented in Table 17.1, along with their C equivalents.

An example of opening an existing binary file for I/O operations would, therefore, be:

```
fstream myio;
myio.open("IOExample.bin", ios_base::in | ios_base::out |
    ios_base::binary);
if (myio.fail()) {
    // error handling
}
```

The second open() argument can also be specified for ifstream and ofstream objects (it defaults to ios_base::in and ios_base::out, respectively, if not specified). When specifying a second argument for these objects, the programmer must make sure that the argument is consistent with the stream type (i.e., don't open an ifstream object with an ios_base::out argument, or the operation will fail).

TABLE 17.1	Opening Modes for C++
C++ Equivalent	**Meaning**
ios_base::in	Existing file is to be opened for input
ios_base::in | ios_base::out	Existing file is to be opened for input and output
ios_base::out | ios_base::trunc *or* ios_base::out	File is to be opened for writing and erased if it exists
ios_base::out | ios_base::in | ios_base::trunc	File is to be opened for reading and writing and erased if it exists
ios_base::out | ios_base::app	File is opened for appending in write mode
ios_base::out | ios_base::in | ios_base::app	File is opened for appending in read and write mode
ios_base::binary	File is opened in binary mode, with no end of line translations

17.1.2: C++ Text I/O

Text I/O using the predefined objects **cin, cout,** and **cerr** can be performed using the >> (extraction or input) operator and << (insertion or output) operators for all the primitive C++ types. The usage is identical when using file streams for text I/O.

As we argued in Chapter 8, it is usually better to get a line of text from the user, rather than bringing in data variable by variable, because C++ does not start processing the input typed by the user until the enter key is pressed. A member function of ifstream, called getline(), is generally used in preference to taking input directly from the user with the >> operator. For example:

```
buf[MAXSIZE];
cin.getline(buf,MAXSIZE);
// buf can now be processed to extract the
// necessary information
```

17.1.3: C++ Binary I/O

C++ binary I/O is normally performed on fstream objects. In SimpleIO, this operation corresponds to the STREAM data type.

Reading and Writing Data   C++ provides read() and write() members similar to the SimpleIO ReadBlock() and WriteBlock() functions. These functions take the following arguments:

```
.read(char *buf,int nCount);
.write(const char *buf,int nCount);
```

The only major difference between the C++ versions of the functions and their SimpleIO ReadBlock() and WriteBlock() counterparts is that the C++ functions require a character buffer instead of a void *.

The difference in arguments is significant because it means that a type cast will have to be used any time a .read() or .write() function is called on noncharacter data. For example, to save and load an integer in binary format, the following code could be used:

```
int nTest1=25,nTest2;
ofstream out;
ifstream in;
out.open("TestOut.bin",ios_base::out | ios_base::trunc |
    ios_base::binary);
if (!out.fail()) out.write((char *)&nTest1,sizeof(int));
out.close(); // closing out because we want to reopen it
// for input
in.open("TestOut.bin",ios_base::in | ios_base::binary);
if (!in.fail()) in.read((char *)&nTest2,sizeof(int));
// nTest2 should now contain the integer 25
```

File Positioning Functions C++ provides fstream positioning members equivalent to the SimpleIO SeekReadPosition() and SeekWritePosition() functions:

```
.seekg(unsigned int nPosition);  // moves to specific
// position in input stream
.seekp(unsigned int nPosition);  // moves to specific
// position in output stream
```

A failure of a seek operation can be tested with the fail() member function.

Three member functions are also commonly used to identify our current position in a file stream, all of which are applicable to both text and binary files:

- *unsigned int tellg()*: Returns the current offset from the origin of the file for an input stream.
- *unsigned int tellp()*: Returns the current offset from the origin of the file for an output stream.
- *bool eof()*: Returns true value if we have reached the end of a file stream, and have tried to read past it.

To remember which version of each function is used on each type of stream, think of g for "getting" (i.e., input) and p for "putting" or "printing" (i.e., output).

17.1: SECTION QUESTIONS

1. What typical method is used to check whether an I/O operation has been successful?

2. How is opening a C++ file stream object different from opening a file stream using SimpleIO?

3. If cin, cout, and cerr are object types different from ifstream and ofstream, can we still use the same operators and functions to access our files as we do for the standard objects?

4. How does the buffer (i.e., memory area) used for binary I/O in C++ differ from that used in SimpleIO? What are the practical implications of this difference for the programmer?

5. Why might .getline() be preferable to a series of input/extraction (>>) operators when acquiring complex data from a user?

6. When repositioning a file pointer in a binary file, what do you need to remember in C++ about how the file was opened?

7. Why doesn't C++ have separate functions for standard I/O and file I/O, the way SimpleIO does?

17.2: C++ I/O OBJECTS

In this section, we introduce C++ I/O in a more systematic manner, assuming that the reader is familiar with Chapters 13–16. Although the capabilities of the C++ I/O system extend well beyond what is covered in this text, what we present here will be sufficient to get information to and from the console, and to and from files (both text and binary). We first identify the key objects in the C++ I/O system, then focus on the mechanics of standard and file I/O.

17.2.1: C++ I/O Object Hierarchy

We already noted, back in Chapter 2, that C++ performs its I/O using specialized objects, such as **cout.** Actually, the I/O classes that C++ provides correspond to an inheritance hierarchy, shown in Figure 17.1.

The classes in this hierarchy can be described as follows:

- **ios:** A class containing the common members of all I/O objects. Its main purpose is to act as the top of the input-output system hierarchy, because an object created from the ios class would not have much useful functionality.

- **istream:** A general input object, such as the standard input object **cin.** In addition to the functionality it inherits from ios, it has a number of input-specific members for retrieving character data from a stream, such as get(), getline(), and read(). This class corresponds to the INPUT data type in SimpleIO.

- **ostream:** A general output object, such as the standard output object **cout.** In addition to the functionality it inherits from ios, it has a number of output-specific members, such as put() and write(). This class corresponds to the OUTPUT data type in SimpleIO.

FIGURE 17.1 C++ I/O Object Hierarchy

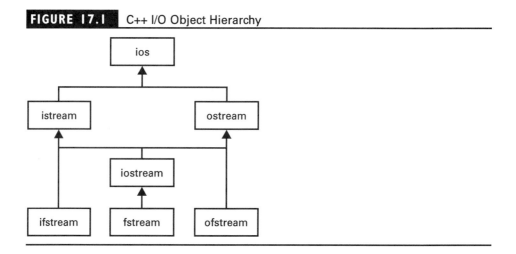

- **iostream:** A general input-output object, inheriting the characteristics of both istream and ostream. Similar to ios, its main purpose is to help organize the inheritance hierarchy.
- **ifstream:** An input file stream, inheriting characteristics from istream and adding the ability to attach and detach the stream from an associated file using open() and close() members.
- **ofstream:** An output file stream, inheriting characteristics from ostream and adding the ability to attach and detach the stream from an associated file using open() and close() members.
- **fstream:** An input-output file stream, inheriting characteristics from iostream and adding the ability to attach and detach the stream from an associated file using open() and close() members. This class corresponds to the STREAM data type in Simple IO.

In addition to the three file stream classes (ifstream, ofstream, and fstream), corresponding classes also perform I/O using a memory buffer (i.e., **istrstream, ostrstream, and strstream**). These classes are not discussed in this text, because the sprintf() function for formatting strings (Chapter 7, Section 7.3.3) can be used to format an output memory buffer, and we have presented a number of functions (e.g., Tokenize(), in Chapter 10, Section 10.5.2) for translating input strings.

Although the preceding hierarchy is a good enough model for the purposes of this chapter, you should be aware that it is something of a simplification (a fact that will become painfully obvious as you start to read the Visual Studio .NET documentation). The problem is that two distinct sets of I/O classes have been defined for C++. The original set of classes was quite faithful to Figure 17.1 in structure. The second set of classes, implemented in the standard template library (STL), uses class templates to create more flexible objects. Such increased flexibility was deemed imperative with the upcoming change in character size (to 2-byte characters) that appears to be inevitable. Using these templates, it was more convenient to define our "class" names (e.g., ostream, istream, fstream) using typedefs (see Chapter 3, Section 3.4.2). As a result, the actual classes being inherited are template classes with names such as basic_ios<char>, basic_fstream<char>, and basic_ostream<char>.

It is worth repeating here that one remaining vestige of the old libraries can be found in the include files of some compilers. Specifically, a preprocessor statement such as:

```
#include <iostream>
including namespace std;
```

ensures the modern (STL) version of the I/O libraries is used. On the other hand, writing:

```
#include <iostream.h>  // note the .h (and no need to
// include a namespace)
```

may result in the old libraries being used. Because no benefit comes from using the old libraries when writing new code, it makes sense to be careful not to inadvertently place the .h extension in C++ include statements using the standard libraries.

17.2.2: Working with I/O Objects

We normally work with I/O objects in one of three ways:

- *Using overloaded operators.* The most frequently used are the >> and << operators.

■ *Using member functions.* Because of the inheritance relationship between the I/O classes specified in Figure 17.1, any object inherits the members of all its parents. For example, any function available for an ios object is available for all I/O objects, while any ostream member is available to ofstream objects, any istream member is available for ifstream objects, and so forth.

■ *Using manipulators.* A number of specialized functions are available that can be applied in the context of >> and << operations. Although the underlying mechanism by which they are applied is beyond the scope of this text, their use is relatively straightforward—they are just inserted into the << or >> operation as if they were data elements. For example, the **hex** manipulator causes any integer output that follows to be displayed in hexadecimal (base 16), while the **dec** manipulator causes integers to be displayed in decimal (base 10). In addition to placing manipulators in stream I/O operations, they can also be applied as stand-alone functions.

The use of overloaded operators and **manipulators** in the PrintHex() function is illustrated in Example 17.1. In this example, the hex manipulator changes the cout object display format to hexadecimal—causing nVal to be printed in hex—and then changes the format back to decimal. An alternative version of the same function, PrintHexModified0(), shows the same manipulators applied to the stream as functions.

Working with Formatting Flags   For many of the I/O operations that we typically perform, several alternative approaches are available. For example, the formatting changes in Example 17.1 could have also been accomplished using member functions, as shown in the functions PrintHexModified1() and PrintHexModified2() in Example 17.2, both of which accomplish the same task.

To understand how the two modified versions of the function work, you need to understand that the base used to print integers is one of many formatting details stored in bit form (in an unsigned integer type named **fmtflags**) for every I/O object. These bits are commonly referred to as the I/O formatting **flags**. (Details on using bits to store information and the bitwise operators can be found in Chapter 4, Section 4.7.4.) To help us in working with these flags, a series of constants have been defined within the **ios_base** class

---

EXAMPLE 17.1

PrintHex() function

```
// prints an integer in hexadecimal format using manipulators in I/O
void PrintHex(int nVal)
{
    cout << hex << nVal << dec;
}

// prints an integer in hexadecimal format using manipulator functions
void PrintHexModified0(int nVal)
{
    hex(cout);
    cout << nVal;
    dec(cout);
}
```

EXAMPLE 17.2

PrintHexModified() function versions using member functions

```
// prints an integer in hexadecimal format using member functions
void PrintHexModified1(int nVal)
{
    cout.unsetf( ios_base::dec );
    cout.setf( ios_base::hex );
    cout << nVal;
    cout.unsetf( ios_base::hex );
    cout.setf( ios_base::dec );
}

// prints an integer in hexadecimal format using flags member
void PrintHexModified2(int nVal)
{
    cout.flags( (cout.flags() & ~ios_base::dec) | ios_base::hex );
    cout << nVal;
    cout.flags( (cout.flags() & ~ios_base::hex) | ios_base::dec );
}
```

(the underlying class for the ios object) that identify the actual bit values for each flag. To access these constants, we specify the class name (ios_base) followed by the C++ scope resolution operator (::), to form an expression such as **ios_base::hex**. This operator is necessary so that C++ can tell the hex formatting constant (used in Example 17.2) from the hex manipulator (used in Example 17.1).

To change the base to hexadecimal, we need to:

- Turn off the flag (bit) that signifies we should display integers in decimal form.
- Turn on the flag bit that signifies we should be printing in hexadecimal.

Upon completing our display, we need to reverse the process to restore decimal formatting.

As illustrated in Example 17.2, this process can be accomplished in two ways. The first, and most direct way, is to use the two ios member functions unsetf() and setf(), which are used to change the values of one or more flags. In PrintHexModified1(), the line:

```
    cout.unsetf( ios_base::dec );
```

causes the decimal flag bit to be turned off (if it is on). The line that follows:

```
    cout.setf( ios_base::hex );
```

then sets the hexadecimal formatting flag. Naturally, we reverse the process after we display our integer.

The second function, PrintHexModified2, works with the entire flag integer. The ios object has two versions of its flags() member function,[1] consistent with our normal approach to defining accessor functions:

- *fmtflags flags() const:* Returns the current flags value (as an unsigned integer).
- *fmtflags flags(fmtflags newflags):* Sets the format flags integer value to its argument, returning the previous flag values.

---

[1] Recall that the typedef fmtflags is, essentially, an unsigned integer used to hold a collection of bits.

To change decimal formatting to hexadecimal, we turn off the decimal bit and turn on the hex bit as follows:

```
cout.flags( (cout.flags() & ~ios_base::dec) | ios_base::hex );
```

To understand this line, it is useful to break down the operation into a series of steps:

- *~ios_base::dec* is going to create an integer with every bit turned on *except* the decimal bit. (For example, ios_base::dec is going to be an integer that equates to a binary number with a single bit set, such as 00000000000000000000001000000000. When we apply the bitwise negation operator, all 0s become 1s and all 1s become 0, producing an integer such as 11111111111111111111110111111111.)

- *cout.flags() & ~ios_base::dec* is going to force the decimal bit off, leaving every other flag bit unchanged as a result of the & operator, because anything &'d with a 1 will be unchanged, and any bit &'d with a 0 will be set to 0.

- (cout.flags() & ~ios_base::dec) | ios_base::hex is going to set the specific hex flag bit, because anything |'d with a 0 will be unchanged, while anything |'d with a 1 becomes 1.

17.2.3: Standard I/O Objects

Three commonly used I/O objects are included in the <iostream> library:

- **cin:** The standard input object, of type *istream*, which defaults to taking input from the keyboard.

- **cout:** The standard output object, of type *ostream*, which defaults to sending information to the screen.

- **cerr:** The standard error object, of type *ostream*, which defaults to sending information to the screen.

17.2.4: Opening and Closing C++ File Stream

The most common I/O objects in a C++ program are ifstream (input file stream), ofstream (output file stream), and fstream (input/output file stream) objects. These streams can be opened in two ways:

- When the stream object is constructed, by using the file name as an argument to the constructor function
- Using the open() member function

Using the Constructor Function to Open Stream Objects As we know, a constructor function is automatically called whenever a C++ object is created. The constructor functions for the file stream objects are of the form:

```
ifstream(const char *szName,
    unsigned int nMode=ios_base::in);
ofstream(const char *szName,
    unsigned int nMode=ios_base::out);
fstream(const char *szName,unsigned int nMode);
```

The two arguments to the constructor are:

- *szName:* A NUL terminated string containing the file name (with path, if necessary).

■ *nMode:* A bitfield containing information on the manner in which the file is to be opened.

For example, the following code could be used to open files test1.txt, test2.txt, and test3.bin as the objects t1, t2, and t3, respectively:

```
ifstream t1("test1.txt");
ofstream t2("test2.txt",ios_base::out | ios_base::trunc);
fstream t3("test3.txt",ios_base::out | ios_base::in |
    ios_base::binary);
```

The allowable bitfield values for the constructor functions are specified in Table 17.2. These values are |'d (bitwise or'd) together to specify the opening mode. Normally, ifstream and ofstream files can be opened without a second argument, because the ios_base::in and ios_base::out are default arguments.

The opening modes in C++ accomplish the same purpose as four Boolean variables supplied to the Open() function in SimpleIO, namely:

```
bool Open(STREAM &file,const char *szName,bool bRead,bool bWrite,
    bool bTrunc,bool bText);
```

The principal differences are that in the C++ open() member, we | the constants together and open() does not return a Boolean result—instead, we have to test for failure.

Using the open() and close() Members The open() member of ifstream, ofstream, and fstream can be used to open an existing stream argument. These functions take the same arguments as the constructor. Thus, the code:

```
fstream t4;
t4.open("test4.txt",ios_base::out | ios_base::in);
```

is equivalent to:

```
fstream t4("test4.txt",ios_base::out | ios_base::in);
```

In addition, a close() member exists to close the stream associated with a given file object. It allows the same object to be used for more than one file. For example, in the code fragment:

```
fstream t5("test5.bin",ios_base::out | ios_base::in |
ios_base::binary);
t5.close();
t5.open("test5.txt",ios_base::out | ios_base::in);
```

t5 is first associated with the binary file test5.bin, then—after the first file is closed—is associated with the text file test5.txt.

TABLE 17.2   Opening Mode Constants

Constant	Meaning
ios_base::in	File is to be opened for input
ios_base::out	File is to be opened for output
ios_base::trunc	File is to be truncated (erased) upon opening
ios_base::ate	Move to the end of the stream upon opening
ios_base::app	All insertions take place at the end of the stream
ios_base::binary	File is opened in binary mode, with no end of line translations (See Chapter 8, Section 8.3.1 for general discussion of text vs. binary files.)

Because the destructor function associated with C++ file objects automatically closes the file when the object goes out of scope or is deleted, the close() member is typically only required when a file needs to be used somewhere else or when we need to reuse the object (as just illustrated) for another file.

17.2: SECTION QUESTIONS

1. Why is it that anything we can do (e.g., apply an operator, invoke a member function) to **cout** can also be done to any ofstream object we declare?

2. What does the fact that I/O flags can be applied to both ostream and istream objects tell us about where those flags are defined?

3. Why does C++ have all these complex names (e.g., ios_base, basic_fstream) floating around?

4. Why don't we need to specify mode constants when opening ifstream and ofstream objects? Could we specify such constants if we wanted to?

5. Why can we often get away without explicitly closing file stream objects that we have opened?

6. When does it makes sense to explicitly call the close() member of a file stream object?

7. How does the way we invoke manipulators differ from the way we invoke member functions?

17.3: TEXT I/O IN C++

Text I/O is the default I/O form in C++ and may be performed on file objects and higher-level objects (e.g., istream and ostream). Output is normally performed using the << operator (sometimes referred to as the output operator or insertion operator). Input is often performed using the >> operator (sometimes referred to as the input operator or extraction operator).

17.3.1: >> and << Operators

The << (output or insertion) operator is overloaded for all the elementary types (e.g., char, int, double, float) and can also be used to output NUL terminated strings and certain types of C++ standard objects (such as the **string** object). Its functional format is:

```
ostream &operator<<(ostream &out,supported-type val);
```

where *supported-type* is any of the primitive C++ data types (along with other types that the programmer may decide to overload).

The >> (input or extraction) operator is also overloaded. It takes data—a text token whose start and end are determined by the presence of white characters, such as space or tab—from its input stream, translates it into the appropriate data type, then sets the argument value. Its functional format is:

```
istream &operator>>(istream &out,supported-type &val);
```

where *supported-type* is any of the primitive C++ data types (along with **string** objects of any other types that the programmer may decide to overload).

Despite its simplicity, the >> (input) operator suffers from two defects:

- It assumes that any string coming in ends as soon as white space is encountered.
- It doesn't start processing the user's input until the Enter key is pressed.

These defects make it reasonable for a programmer to question its use in a real-world program that takes input from the user. It is fine, however, for reading data of known format from a file stream.

17.3.2: The getline() Member

Rather than using the extraction operators, a better approach is to take user input a line at a time using the getline() member function. Because it is a member function for istream classes and inherited classes (e.g., iostream, ifstream, and fstream), it is applied using the . or -> operator. Its functional form is, effectively, as follows:

```
istream &getline(char *buf,int nMax);
```

where buf is the location into which the line of text is to be placed (with a NUL terminator at the end), and nMax is the maximum number of characters to be read. The function return value, a reference to an istream object, is not normally used. It could, however, be applied to create code such as:

```
cin.getline(buf,MAXLINE).getline(buf,MAXLINE).getline(buf,MAXLINE);
```

where each function is successively applied to the return value of its predecessor. Naturally, such code is best avoided for the sake of clarity.

Some examples of getline(), taken from SimpleIO.cpp, are presented in the InputInteger() and InputReal() functions in Example 17.3. In each of the examples, a line

---

EXAMPLE 17.3

Use of getline() member in some SimpleIO.cpp functions

```
// reads an integer from the keyboard, returning the value
int InputInteger()
{
    char buf[MAXLINE];
    cin.getline(buf,MAXLINE);
    return atoi(buf);
}

// reads a real number from the keyboard, returning the value
double InputReal ()
{
    char buf[MAXLINE];
    cin.getline(buf,MAXLINE);
    return atof(buf);
}

// reads a string from the keyboard, placing the value in its argument
void InputString(char str[])
{
    cin.getline(str,MAXLINE);
}
```

of text is retrieved from **cin.** In the case of integer and real number input, the appropriate conversion function is then applied.

17.3.3: I/O Formatting in C++

Many of the benefits of using the >> and << operators in C++ in place of printf and other traditional C I/O functions seem less compelling when complex formatting is required. The problem is not a lack of formatting capability in the standard C++ library—the C++ library is extensive. Rather, the main challenge is that many of the C++ capabilities need to be accessed through a combination of member functions and manipulators that can be quite cumbersome. Nonetheless, with a little patience they can be mastered.

The first step in understanding C++ formatting is recognizing that each I/O stream has, associated with it, a collection of properties. These properties determine how output will be displayed, and input will be interpreted. We already identified one of these properties, the radix (aka, base) that is used to display integers. These properties are controlled using member functions and manipulators. Key member functions for ios objects (and, therefore, inherited by all I/O objects) are presented in Table 17.3. A listing of flag constants and manipulator functions is presented in Table 17.4. Additional information on all these functions is available in the Visual Studio .NET help system (from which the tables have been adapted).

The manipulators presented in Table 17.4 come in two forms. The first form, as we already described, has no arguments, and the manipulator is actually placed into the stream as if it were a keyword. For example:

```
cout << hex << 255;
```

would cause FF to be displayed (255 in hexadecimal). All subsequent integers would then be displayed in hexadecimal until a **dec** manipulator was encountered, or the appropriate flag was set.

The second form of manipulator takes a single argument—usually an integer. For example:

```
cout << setw(20) << 123;
```

It would cause the integer 123 to be displayed with 17 leading spaces (assuming we did not have the left-justify flag set). The prototypes of these manipulators, found in the help system, are odd because each returns its own, specialized data type. You should not be overly concerned, however. It is just a convenient way of tricking the << and >> operators, which are overloaded, to call the function, and then apply the appropriate action to the stream. The mechanics are important only if you need to create your own manipulators.

In addition to the manipulators associated with ios objects (i.e., all input/output objects) listed in Table 17.4, some specific manipulators are also used for input and output streams. The ostream (output) manipulators are:

- **endl:** Generates a newline ('\n') and flushes the file buffer of all output. It is the preferred means of generating new lines in C++, although \n can also generally be used without serious problems.
- **ends:** Creates a white space (' ') to separate character output into separate strings.
- **flush:** Flushes the file buffer of all output.

The istream (input) manipulator is:

- **ws:** Skips over white space before character input is received.

TABLE 17.3	ios Formatting Member Functions (Adapted from Visual Studio .NET Online Help System)	

Member	Arguments	Purpose
fill	None	Returns the character that is used for padding when the text is not as wide as the stream (the default is space, ' ', which is ASCII value 32).
fill	A character (e.g., char)	Specifies the character that will be used for padding when the text is not as wide as the stream.
flags	None	Returns the current flag settings.
flags	A **fmtflags** object (e.g., unsigned int)	Sets the stream flags to the specified bits in its argument. Specific flag constants are listed in Table 18.4.
getloc	None	Returns the active locale object. These objects are complex data structures that encapsulate a wide variety of information useful for displaying data such as dates, times, and currencies in a particular location. A global locale object, with values determined by operating system settings, can be accessed if a program needs to change the settings (e.g., using the imbue() member).
imbue	A **locale** object	Changes the locale (see getloc).
precision	None	Returns the current precision setting of the stream.
precision	A **streamsize** object (e.g., int)	Specifies the number of digits to display in a floating-point number. Equivalent to the .Precision portion of a printf formatting specifier (e.g., "%7.2f").
setf	A **fmtflags** object (e.g., unsigned int)	Turns on the specified flags identified by the 1 bits in the argument.
unsetf	A **fmtflags** object (e.g., unsigned int)	Turns off the specified flags identified by the 1 bits in the argument.
width	None	Sets the default field output width to 0, returning whatever width was previously set.
width	A **streamsize** object (e.g., int)	Sets the minimum field output length for the next item displayed in the output stream, returning the previous width. The purpose of this width value is to specify the minimum number of characters that are printed for each data element. It is similar to the number to the left of the decimal point in printf specifiers (e.g., the 20 values in "%20s", "%20i", and "%20.6lf").

Unlike the flag manipulators, these manipulators perform their activities a single time, and do not produce enduring changes to the input or output stream.

17.3.4: I/O Status in C++

In addition to member functions and formatting flags, the ios class at the top of the C++ I/O hierarchy also provides a series of flags for identifying the status of I/O operations. Some of the key member functions for accessing these states are summarized in Table 17.5, adapted from the Visual Studio .NET help system.

The most commonly used of these members are:

TABLE 17.4	Formatting Flags and Manipulators with Stream Defaults Presented in Bold (Adapted from Visual Studio .NET Online Help System)	
Flag Constant	**Manipulators**	**Purpose**
ios_base::boolalpha	boolalpha **noboolalpha**	Displays and reads Boolean values as "true" and "false" rather than as 0 and 1.
ios_base::dec	**dec**	Displays and reads integer values in decimal (base 10) format.
ios_base::fixed	**fixed**	Displays real numbers using a decimal point, rather than using scientific notation.
ios_base::hex	hex	Displays and reads integer values in hexadecimal (base 16) format.
ios_base::internal	internal	Displays numbers with padding needed to reach the desired width internal to the number—normally before or after the sign (e.g., could change display from " −31" to "− 31").
ios_base::left	left	Left justifies data, with any padding characters placed at the end of the display (e.g., " 31" becomes "31 "). Performs same function as '−' formatting flag in printf (e.g., "%−5i").
ios_base::oct	oct	Displays and reads integer values in octal (base 8) format.
ios_base::right	**right**	Right justifies output, placing any required padding in front of characters if a minimum field width is required (i.e., the same as the default behavior in printf, where "%10s" would produce the output " Hello").
ios_base::scientific	scientific	Uses scientific notation (e.g., 1.2E5) to display real numbers. Real numbers can be read in either form.
ios_base::showbase	showbase **noshowbase**	Uses a prefix to identify the base of an integer value. Decimal values are displayed without a prefix, hexadecimal with the 0x prefix (e.g., 0x1A would be equivalent to 26 in base 10) and octal values are displayed with a leading 0 (e.g., 015 would be equivalent to 13 in base 10).
ios_base::showpoint	showpoint **noshowpoint**	Displays a decimal point for real numbers even when the fractional portion is 0 (e.g., 100 is displayed as 100).

(Continues)

- **eof()**: Returns true if the end of a stream has been reached. This function is frequently used for processing files (such as simple text files) where reading is accomplished line-by-line until the end of the file is reached.
- **fail()**: Returns true if an input or output operation fails for some reason. Such failure can also lead to exceptions being generated.
- **is_open()**: Returns true if a stream is open, false otherwise.

17.3.5: C++ Text I/O Demonstration

Walkthrough available in CppText.wmv

The large number of member functions, manipulators, and flags associated with standard C++ I/O give us great flexibility in how we perform text I/O. In Example 17.4, the MemberDemo() function presents a series of output formatting operations using some sample data. The output from the function is presented in Figure 17.2.

TABLE 17.4	Formatting Flags and Manipulators with Stream Defaults Presented in Bold (Adapted from Visual Studio .NET Online Help System) (Continued)		

Flag Constant	Manipulators	Purpose
ios_base::showpos	showpos **noshowpos**	Forces a plus sign when positive numeric fields are displayed (thereby ensuring consistency with negative numbers), equivalent to the + flag in printf.
ios_base::skipws	skipws **noskipws**	Skips over white characters (e.g., <= ' ') during input operations for character and string data (numeric data always skips leading spaces).
ios_base::unitbuf	unitbuf **nounitbuf**	Forces output buffer to be flushed after every data element is sent.
ios_base::uppercase	uppercase **nouppercase**	Uses uppercase letters to display text for numeric purposes (e.g., scientific notation, hexadecimal numbers). Equivalent to certain uppercase and lowercase type specifiers in printf (e.g., 'x' vs. 'X' and 'e' vs. 'E').
Common Single Argument Manipulators (Require #include <iomanip>)		
—	setbase()	Sets the default base for integer input and output. Allowable argument values are: ios_base::hex, ios_base::dec, and ios_base::oct.
—	setfill()	Sets the fill character used when right-justified fields are displayed. Allowable argument is a character (default is ' ').
—	setprecision()	Sets the precision used in displaying real numbers (similar to the precision specifier in printf, except it only applies to real numbers). Takes an integer argument.
—	setw()	Sets the width specifier used to display the next field (similar to width specifier in printf). Takes an integer argument.

Width Test The first section of the text demonstrates the width() member function, which specifies the minimum width to be used in displaying the next data element being output. The initial code displays some text with different width settings.

```
// width example
out << "Width test:" << endl;
out.width();        // sets width to zero
out << "Width is " << out.width() << endl;
out.width(10);
out << "Width is " << 10 << endl;
out.width(10);
out << "Width is ";
out.width(10);
out << out.width() << endl;
out << setw(20) << "Width is " << 20 << endl;
// using mainpulator to accomplish same thing
out.width(20);
out << "Width is ";
out.width(20);
out << out.width() << endl;
```

TABLE 17.5		Status and Error Member Functions Available for C++ Stream Objects

Member Function	Arguments	Purpose
bad	None	Indicates a loss of integrity in the file stream (equivalent to the boolean value of the expression **rdstate() & ios::badbit**)
clear	None	Clears all error flags, setting the **ios::goodbit** flag
clear	One or more status and error flags, bitwise or'd together	Clears all status and error flags, then sets the specified flag arguments
eof	None	Indicates that the end of a stream has been reached (equivalent to the boolean value of the expression **rdstate() & ios::eofbit**)
fail	None	Indicates a failure to read or write a specified value to a stream (equivalent to the boolean value of the expression **rdstate() & ios::failbit**)
good	None	Indicates a stream is ready for further reading and writing (equivalent to the boolean value of the expression **rdstate() & ios::goodbit**). **ios::goodbit** is set when **ios::badbit**, **ios::eofbit** and **ios::failbit** are all off
is_open	None	Indicates if a stream is open
rdstate	None	Reads the state of bits for flags
setstate	One or more status and error flags, bitwise or'd together	Sets additional flags

As is evident from the corresponding display in Figure 17.2, the default justification is right (i.e., leading spaces are inserted). The width setting only applies to the next item being output, however. Thus, the code:

```
out.width(10);
out << "Width is " << 10 << endl;
```

produces the string: " **Width is 10**". On the other hand, the code:

```
out.width(10);
out << "Width is ";
out.width(10);
out << out.width() << endl;
```

produces the string: " **Width is   10**" because both the "Width is" and 10 are padded with leading blanks to bring them to a width of 10.

To pad with trailing blanks, the ios_base::left flag needs to be set, which is accomplished by turning off the ios_base::right flag—using a bitwise and (&)—and turning on the ios_base::left using a bitwise or (|). The code used to accomplish this task is as follows:

```
// setting up left justify
ios_base::fmtflags nFlags=out.flags();
nFlags=(nFlags & ~ios_base::right) | ios_base::left;
out.flags(nFlags);
```

EXAMPLE 17.4

MemberDemo() function (in CppText.cpp)

```
void MemberDemo(ostream &out)
{
    // width example
    out << "Width test:" << endl;
    out.width();        // sets width to zero
    out << "Width is " << out.width() << endl;
    out.width(10);
    out << "Width is " << 10 << endl;
    out.width(10);
    out << "Width is ";
    out.width(10);
    out << out.width() << endl;
    out << setw(20) << "Width is " << 20 << endl;
    // using mainpulator to accomplish same thing
    out.width(20);
    out << "Width is ";
    out.width(20);
    out << out.width() << endl;
    // setting up left justify
    ios_base::fmtflags nFlags=out.flags();
    nFlags=(nFlags & ~ios_base::right) | ios_base::left;
    out.flags(nFlags);
    out << "Repeating with left justify on:" << endl;
    out.width(20);
    out << "Width is ";
    out.width(20);
    out << 20 << '!' << endl;
    // true/false display test
    out << endl << endl << "True/False display test" << endl;
    (nFlags & ios_base::boolalpha) ?
        out << "Boolean is set to true/false" << endl :
        out << "Boolean is set to 1/0" << endl;
    out << "TRUE is displayed as " << true << " and FALSE as " << false <<
        endl;
    out.setf(ios_base::boolalpha);
    nFlags=out.flags();
    (nFlags & ios_base::boolalpha) ?
        out << "Boolean is set to true/false" << endl :
        out << "Boolean is set to 1/0" << endl;
    out << "TRUE is displayed as " << true << " and FALSE as " << false <<
        endl;
    // Radix (base) test
    out << endl << endl << "Radix (base) test" << endl;
    int nVal=135;
    out << "nVal is " << nVal << " in base 10" << endl;
    out.unsetf(ios_base::dec);
    out.setf(ios_base::hex);
    out << "nVal is " << nVal << " in base 16" << endl;
    out.unsetf(ios_base::hex);
```

(Continues)

EXAMPLE 17.4 (CONTINUED)

```
    out.setf(ios_base::oct);
    out << "nVal is " << nVal << " in base 8" << endl;
    out.unsetf(ios_base::oct);
    out.setf(ios_base::dec);
    nFlags=out.flags();
    nFlags=(nFlags | ios_base::showbase);
    out.flags(nFlags);
    out << "Repeating base demonstration with prefix display set" << endl;
    out << "nVal is " << nVal << " in base 10" << endl;
    out.unsetf(ios_base::dec);
    out.setf(ios_base::hex);
    out << "nVal is " << nVal << " in base 16" << endl;
    out.unsetf(ios_base::hex);
    out.setf(ios_base::oct);
    out << "nVal is " << nVal << " in base 8" << endl;
    out.unsetf(ios_base::oct);
    out.setf(ios_base::dec);
    return;
}
```

FIGURE 17.2 Output from MemberDemo() Function

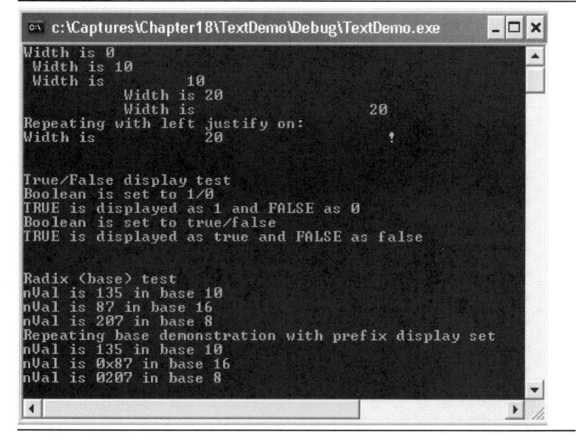

The first line after the comment retrieves the current flag bits. The next line performs the flag change (see Section 17.2.2 for an explanation). The last line sets the output flags to our new settings.

Output Display Type Tests   A number of formatting flags produce significant changes to the way Boolean values and numbers are displayed. The ios_base::boolalpha flag, for example, causes 0 and 1 boolean values to be displayed as 'true' and 'false' as is demonstrated by the following block of code:

```
// true/false display test
out << endl << endl << "True/False display test" << endl;
(nFlags & ios_base::boolalpha) ? /* Test flag on */
   out << "Boolean is set to true/false" << endl :
   out << "Boolean is set to 1/0" << endl;
out << "TRUE is displayed as " << true << " and FALSE as "
      << false << endl;
out.setf(ios_base::boolalpha); /* Setting the boolalpha bit */
nFlags=out.flags();
(nFlags & ios_base::boolalpha) ?
   out << "Boolean is set to true/false" << endl :
   out << "Boolean is set to 1/0" << endl;
out << "TRUE is displayed as " << true << " and FALSE as "
      << false << endl;
```

The conditional operator labeled /* Test flag on */ first checks to see if boolalpha bit is on using the & operator. We then send the values true and false to the display, leading to the display:

TRUE is displayed as 1 and FALSE as 0

The bit was not set, so true and false appear as 0 and 1, because the bit is off. The setf() operator is then used to set the boolalpha bit on (as an alternative, we could have used the flags() member function, as we did to establish left justification). We then repeat our test and see that the display has changed to:

TRUE is displayed as true and FALSE as false

Our output stream would continue to display Boolean values in this fashion until we turn the bit off.

Another example where a flag can radically change how data is displayed involves the radix (i.e., base) to display integers. The following block of code displays the same integer (135) in three different bases by changing dec, hex, and oct flags:

```
int nVal=135;
out << "nVal is " << nVal << " in base 10" << endl;
out.unsetf(ios_base::dec);
out.setf(ios_base::hex);
out << "nVal is " << nVal << " in base 16" << endl;
out.unsetf(ios_base::hex);
out.setf(ios_base::oct);
out << "nVal is " << nVal << " in base 8" << endl;
```

In each case we use unsetf() to remove the existing flag, then setf() to flag our base. The resulting output is:

```
nVal is 135 in base 10
nVal is 87 in base 16
nVal is 207 in base 8
```

We need to use unsetf() (unlike our boolalpha example) because we have more than one base display flag and we need to accommodate more than two possible values.

Another example of a formatting flag is ios_base::show_base, which places a leading 0x in front of hexadecimal integers and a leading 0 in front of octal numbers. In the code, the earlier display is repeated after the flag is set, leading to:

```
nVal is 135 in base 10
nVal is 0x87 in base 16
nVal is 0207 in base 8
```

Using Manipulators to Format Output   Manipulator functions often provide an alternative to member functions for formatting that is less cumbersome. In Example 17.5, the function ManipulatorDemo() accomplishes the same display type formatting done with member functions in Example 17.4.

As already noted, manipulators can be applied in two ways. First, they can be incorporated directly into an input or output operation, such as:

```
out << hex << "nVal is " << nVal << " in base 16" << endl;
```

EXAMPLE 17.5

ManipulatorDemo() function

```
void ManipulatorDemo(ostream &out)
{
    // true/false display test
    out << endl << endl << "Manipulator version of True/False display test" << endl;
    out << "Boolean is set to 1/0" << endl;
    out << noboolalpha << "TRUE is displayed as " << true
        << " and FALSE as " << false << endl;
    out << "Boolean is set to true/false" << endl;
    out << boolalpha << "TRUE is displayed as " << true
        << " and FALSE as " << false << endl;
    // radix (base) test
    out << endl << endl << "Manipulator version of Radix (base) test" << endl;
    int nVal=135;
    out << noshowbase << dec;
    out << "nVal is " << nVal << " in base 10" << endl;
    out << hex << "nVal is " << nVal << " in base 16" << endl;
    out << oct << "nVal is " << nVal << " in base 8" << endl;
    out << "Repeating base demonstration with prefix display set" << endl;
    // using function form of manipulator
    showbase(out);
    dec(out);
    out << "nVal is " << nVal << " in base 10" << endl;
    hex(out);
    out << "nVal is " << nVal << " in base 16" << endl;
    oct(out);
    out << "nVal is " << nVal << " in base 8";
    dec(out);
    // using functional form of endl
    endl(out);
    return;
}
```

Alternatively, they can be applied as functions. For example:

```
hex(out);
out << "nVal is " << nVal << " in base 16" << endl;
```

In fact, the same function is being applied in both cases. Where placed in the stream, however, C++ uses its built-in ability to overload operators as a means of causing the function to execute.

The same member functions and manipulators that can be applied to output streams are also relevant to input streams. In Example 17.6, the same radix changes are made to both input and output.

A sample output from running this function is presented in Figure 17.3.

In the example, the user enters the same number, 64, twice. The second time, however, the hex manipulator was applied to the input stream prior to input in the line:

```
in >> hex >> nVal2;
```

As a result, the 64 was interpreted as 0x64, which is 100 (6 * 16 + 4) in base 10. Both inputs are then displayed in both bases.

EXAMPLE 17.6

IODemo() function

```
void IODemo(ostream &out,istream &in)
{
    int nVal1,nVal2;
    out << endl << endl <<   "Enter an integer: ";
    in >> nVal1;
    out << "Enter the same integer again: ";
    in >> hex >> nVal2;
    out << "The integers you entered were " << nVal1 << " and " << nVal2 << endl;
    out << hex << "The integers you entered were " << nVal1 << " and " <<
     nVal2 << endl;
    dec(in);
    dec(out);
    return;
}
```

FIGURE 17.3   Demonstration of IODemo() Function Input and Output

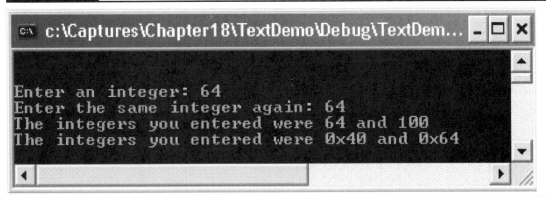

Text File I/O The C++ I/O object hierarchy—consisting mainly of functions that inherit from the root ios object—allows us to treat console text I/O in much the same way that we treat text file I/O. For example, the main function in Example 17.7 shows the MemberDemo() function (of Example 17.4) being called first with cout, then with an ofstream opened as the file "Sample.txt." The contents of the resulting output file, Sample.txt, are presented in Figure 17.4.

In opening the stream, the ofstream constructor was used. The ios_base::trunc argument specified that the file was to be erased upon opening.

EXAMPLE 17.7

main() function for TextDemo project

```
int main()
{
    MemberDemo(cout);
    ManipulatorDemo(cout);
    IODemo(cout,cin);
    ofstream myfile("Sample.txt",ios_base::out | ios_base::trunc);
    MemberDemo(myfile);
    return 0;
}
```

FIGURE 17.4   Contents of Sample.txt After Running the Function

```
Width test:
Width is 0
 Width is 10
 Width is           10
          Width is 20
          Width is                   20
Repeating with left justify on:
Width is             20                    !
True/False display test
Boolean is set to 1/0
TRUE is displayed as 1 and FALSE as 0
Boolean is set to true/false
TRUE is displayed as true and FALSE as false
Radix (base) test
nVal is 135 in base 10
nVal is 87 in base 16
nVal is 207 in base 8
Repeating base demonstration with prefix display set
nVal is 135 in base 10
nVal is 0x87 in base 16
nVal is 0207 in base 8
```

17.3: SECTION QUESTIONS

1. Why do many of the C++ I/O member functions come in pairs (e.g., fill, flags, width, clear)?

2. Why is it better to use manipulators such as **endl** and **ends** to terminate lines and strings than using '\n/ and ' ' characters, which do the same thing?

3. What does the fact that some I/O manipulators (such as **endl** and **ws**) only apply to input or output streams tell you about where they are defined?

4. Given that many formatting options can be accomplished using member functions, manipulators, or through setting flags directly, which is preferred?

5. Why do some formatting commands (e.g., hex) stick, while others only apply to the next item output (the width() member)?

17.4: C++ BINARY I/O

Walkthrough available in CppBinary.wmv

For a discussion of text versus binary files, see Chapter 8, Section 8.3.1.

17.4.1: Reading and Writing Binary Files in C++

C++ provides a read() member function of the istream class and a write() member function of the ostream class that can be used to read and write bytes to a stream. The prototypes of these functions are effectively as follows:

```
istream& read(char *szBuf,int nCount);
ostream& write(const char *szBuf,int nCount);
```

Although quite similar in purpose, they differ from the SimpleIO ReadBlock() and WriteBlock() functions in two important ways:

■ The return value of these functions is not used to signify success or failure of the operation. C++ file I/O is typically uses exception handling, reducing its need to use return values as error flags. Instead, the active stream is returned so that operations can be chained together (as was illustrated for the getline() istream member in Section 17.3.2).

■ The buffer to be read or written to is specified with a character pointer, as opposed to a void pointer. (Actually, the type of pointer used depends on the template definition, but it will always be char throughout this text.)

The second difference creates some practical issues that need to be addressed in code. For example, the following code could be used to write an integer to a stream in SimpleIO:

```
int nTest=144;
STREAM mystream;
// open truncated for binary writing
if (Open("Sample.bin",false,true,true,false))
    WriteBlock(mystream,&nTest,sizeof(int));
```

The corresponding code in C++, however, would generate an error:

```
int nTest=144;
ofstream mystream("Sample.bin",ios_base::out |
  ios_base::trunc | ios_base::binary);
if (mystream.is_open()) mystream.write(&nTest,sizeof(int));
// generates error
```

The problem with the write() operation is that it expects a constant character pointer (const char *), and has been given an integer address (int *) instead. This problem can be remedied in two ways. The first involves using a type cast to tell the compiler everything is okay. For example:

```
mystream.write((const char *)&nTest,sizeof(int));
// no error
```

The other approach would be to copy the data bytes into a character buffer, then write the character buffer to the file. For example:

```
char temp[sizeof(int)];  // creates a 4-byte buffer
memcpy(temp,&nTest,sizeof(int));
mystream.write(temp,sizeof(int));
```

Naturally, when we read in data we run into the same problem. Thus, a typical read might look like:

```
int nTest;
ifstream mystream("Sample.bin",ios_base::in |
ios_base::binary);
if (mystream.is_open()) mystream.write((char *)&nTest,
    sizeof(int));
// char * not const for read
```

Alternatively, we could write the following:

```
char temp[sizeof(int)];  // creates a 4-byte buffer
int nTest;
ifstream mystream("Sample.bin",ios_base::in |
  ios_base::binary);
mystream.read(temp,sizeof(int));
memcpy(&nTest,temp,sizeof(int));
```

It should be noted that either alternative for reading and writing data might lead to some compatibility problems, either across platforms or over time. The problem, as first noted in Chapter 3, is that C++ does not specify sizes for the primitive integer types (e.g., int, char, short, and long). Moreover, the STL classes can also be affected by changes in size. Thus different operating systems and compilers can produce binary files that are inconsistent with each other.

TEST YOUR UNDERSTANDING 17.1:

How would we rewrite the preceding code if the nVal we wanted to read and write were actually a double instead of an int?

One approach to dealing with this type of compatibility problem is to develop special types (e.g., using typedefs) that are of a known size for all systems. Microsoft, for example, defines a number of types in the MFC—such as BOOL, BYTE, WORD, and DWORD—that are guaranteed to remain constant across operating systems and platforms. Such problems do not exist in other popular languages, such as Java, because the language defines the representation of all the elementary types.

Naturally, we can generalize the same rules for reading and writing primitive data types to more complex data types. As an illustration, Example 17.8 contains code for reading and writing data for fifteen pure data employee structures (i.e., no member functions) as a single block.

EXAMPLE 17.8

Function for reading and writing an array of structures

```cpp
#define MAXNAME 30

struct employee {
    unsigned int nId;
    char szLastName[MAXNAME];
    char szFirstName[MAXNAME];
    char cMiddleInit;
    unsigned int nYearHired;
    double dSalary;
    bool bActive;
};

void BinaryCppDemo()
{
    int nCount=10;
    struct employee emparr[15] = {
        {105,"Smith","Anne",'B',1995,125000.00,true},
        {109,"Brown","John",'\0',2000,17000.00,true},
        {102,"Green","Samuel",'C',1991,48000.00,false},
        {115,"Gill","T. Grandon",'\0',2001,54000.00,true},
        {107,"Chancellor","Mary",'K',1997,98000.00,false},
        {104,"Johnson, Jr.","Jerry",'X',1995,32000.00,true},
        {101,"Johnson","Jerry",'X',1988,64000.00,true},
        {108,"Valquist","Elizabeth",'\0',1997,43000.00,true},
        {103,"Gill","Thomas",'R',1995,62000.00,true},
        {106,"Gill","Jonathan",'G',1996,62000.00,true},
    };
    struct employee empin[15];
    fstream bindata;
    bindata.open("TestEmp.bin",ios_base::out | ios_base::trunc |
    ios_base::binary);
    if (bindata.is_open()) {
        bindata.write((const char *)emparr,sizeof(struct employee)*nCount);
    }
    bindata.close();
    bindata.open("TestEmp.bin",ios_base::in | ios_base::binary);
    if (bindata.is_open()) {
        bindata.read((char *)empin,sizeof(struct employee)*nCount);
    }
    return;
}
```

A few comments on this code can be made, particularly in relation to how the same would be accomplished using SimpleIO:

- Because the open() member does not return a Boolean value (unlike the SimpleIO Open() function), we need to explicitly test whether our open was successful, using the is_open() member function.

- Because it is convenient to use a single stream for both reading and writing in this example, we use an fstream object, as opposed to an ofstream for writing and an ifstream for reading. To change how the stream is opened, we use the close() member. Usually, it is safer programming practice to create single direction stream objects (i.e., ifstream and ofstream)—which prevent you from inadvertently mixing up read and write commands—than to use fstream objects unless random access files are being used.

As we already discussed in previous examples, it is generally not a good idea to perform large block I/O in this fashion. It could be disastrous where polymorphic objects are involved. Much more in line with OOP philosophy is to write member functions for loading and saving each class and, within those member functions, save members item-by-item.

17.4.2: Moving Around in a C++ Binary File

The concept of file position is discussed in Chapter 8, Section 8.3.3.

Setting File Position   The function that allows us to change our position in an input file stream is the seekg() member function. The corresponding function for changing position in an output stream is seekp(). The two member functions have two overloads each, and are (effectively) prototyped as follows:

```
istream &seekg(unsigned int nPosition);
// moves to specific position
istream &seekg(int nOffset,unsigned int nOrigin);
// moves relative to origin
ostream &seekp(unsigned int nPosition);
// moves to specific position
ostream &seekp(int nOffset,unsigned int nOrigin);
// moves relative to origin
```

The single argument member functions specify the position in the file using an absolute address, where 0 is the beginning of the file. The two argument versions of each function specify a position in the file relative to a particular point of origin. The three origin constants are:

- **ios_base::cur:** Position is relative to the current position in the file (+ or -).

- **ios_base::beg:** Position is relative to the beginning of the file (effectively acting the same as the single argument version).

- **ios_base::end:** Position is relative to the end of the file (+ or -). + would normally be used only for output streams, because it adds bytes to the end of the stream as part of the positioning operation.

In the event a seek operation fails, the failbit flag is set. This situation can be tested for using the fail() member function.

Determining File Position   Three functions are available to identify our current position in a file, all of which are applicable to both text and binary files:

- *unsigned int tellg():* Returns the current offset from the origin of the file for an input stream.
- *unsigned int tellp():* Returns the current offset from the origin of the file for an output stream.
- *bool eof():* Returns true value if we have reached the end of a file stream, and have tried to read past it.

17.4: SECTION QUESTIONS

1. Why is an fstream object more likely to be useful for binary files than for text files?
2. Would there ever be a reason to open a file containing text as a binary file?
3. What is the difference between saving a structure as a block and saving it element by element? Under what circumstances might it make sense to save a structure as a block?
4. What is the near-universal approach for saving collections of data (e.g., arrays)?
5. Why might changes in integral type sizes (e.g., changing long int from 4 to 8 bytes) be of greater concern for applications using binary files than for those utilizing text files?

17.5: SIMPLEIO WALKTHROUGH

Walkthrough available in SimpleIO.wmv

The SimpleIO library of functions was designed with two purposes in mind:

- To allow functions to be used for I/O purposes, in place of objects, in portions of the text prior to the instruction of C++ classes.
- To create a fairly generic collection of functions reflective of the types of I/O capabilities available in nearly every programming language.

In this section we present a brief walkthrough showing how the SimpleIO collection of functions—that we have been using since Chapter 2—was implemented using C++ stream I/O objects.

17.5.1: Data Types

Typedef statements were used to define three data types within SimpleIO.h:

```
typedef fstream STREAM;
typedef ostream OUTPUT;
typedef istream INPUT;
```

17.5.2: Implementation

The SimpleIO implementation is straightforward (with the sole exception of the Formatting family of functions). We examine this implementation according to groups of functions.

Stream Opening and Closing   The implementation of the Open() and Close() functions is presented in Example 17.9.

The main challenge of the Open() function is translating the four Boolean arguments into the appropriate bitwise or'd constant. This translation is done with a series of conditional operators. The function then returns false either if the fail bit is set, or if is_open() returns false. Both checks were done in case an open file stream was passed in.

The Close() function simply calls the close() member of the file stream.

Console I/O Functions   The console (standard) I/O family of SimpleIO functions is presented in Example 17.10.

The Input versions of the functions all read in a line, using cin.getline(), then translate the input. In the case of the InputCharacter() function, leading white space is removed from the line.

Most of the Display versions just redirect the argument to cout using the insertion operator. The one exception is DisplayFormatted(), which was modeled after the C printf family of functions. The challenge with this function is that it takes a variable number of arguments. The details of unraveling the unknown number of arguments from the stack are beyond the scope of this text but, in essence, what happens is the following:

- The va_start() macro—part of the <stdarg.h> package of C—takes the list of arguments from the stack and packages them into ap.

- ap is passed as an argument into the vsprintf() function, which works exactly like sprintf except data arguments are passed in va_list form.

EXAMPLE 17.9
SimpleIO Open() and Close() family

```
bool Open(STREAM &file,const char *szName,
    bool bRead,bool bWrite,bool bTrunc,bool bText)
{
    ios_base::open_mode nMode=0;
    nMode= ((bRead ? ios_base::in : 0) |
        (bWrite ? ios_base::out : 0) |
        (bTrunc ? ios_base::trunc : 0) |
        (bText ? 0 : ios_base::binary));
    file.open(szName,nMode);
    if (file.fail()) return false;
    return file.is_open();
}
void Close(STREAM &file)
{
    file.close();
}
```

EXAMPLE 17.10

SimpleIO console I/O functions

```cpp
void InputString(char str[])
{
    cin.getline(str,MAXLINE);
}
int InputInteger()
{
    char buf[MAXLINE];
    cin.getline(buf,MAXLINE);
    return atoi(buf);
}
double InputReal()
{
    char buf[MAXLINE];
    cin.getline(buf,MAXLINE);
    return atof(buf);
}
char InputCharacter()
{
    char buf[MAXLINE];
    cin.getline(buf,MAXLINE);
    int i;
    for(i=0;buf[i]>'\0' && buf[i]<=' ' && i<MAXLINE;i++) {};
    if (buf[i]<= ' ') return (char)0;
    else return buf[i];
}
void DisplayString(const char str[])
{
    cout << str;
}
void DisplayCharacter(char cVal)
{
    cout << cVal;
}
void DisplayInteger(int nVal)
{
    cout << nVal;
}
void DisplayReal(double dVal)
{
    cout << dVal;
}
void DisplayFormatted(const char *fmt,...)
{
    char buf[MAXLINE];
    va_list ap;
    va_start(ap,fmt);
    vsprintf(buf,fmt,ap);
    cout << buf;
    va_end(ap);
}
void NewLine()
{
    cout << endl;
}
```

- When vsprintf returns, buf contains the same formatted text it would hold if we had called sprintf, so we send that text to **cout.**
- The va_end() macro is called to return the stack to its appropriate position.

Text Stream I/O Functions The text stream I/O functions are quite similar to console I/O functions, but some subtle differences can be found, particularly in the input side. These differences are as follows:

- Because we may be reading data elements from a text file, it is overly restrictive to assume each data element is going to be on its own line. As a result, we just extract the data from the stream. The design idea behind this practice is that it is much more reasonable to expect (or require) that a text file will meet your *exact* specifications than it is to expect the same thing from a user.
- White space, particularly before strings and at the end of a text file line, can interfere with our ability to read the values we are looking for. To deal with this issue, we use the ws manipulator on the stream, which "eats" white space when reading in a character.

We also use the fail() member of istream to determine whether a getline() has not been successful in the GetLine() function. It is particularly useful when reading a text file line-by-line, as a failure of GetLine() means we reached the end of the file. The Get function family from SimpleIO is presented in Example 17.11.

The Print (output) family of functions is even more straightforward. They are identical to their console counterparts except that they direct their output to their argument (ostream &out) instead of to the predefined object cout. For example:

```
void PrintString(OUTPUT &out,const char *szOut)
{
    out << szOut;
}
```

Binary I/O Functions The SimpleIO binary I/O functions simply package fstream::read() and fstream::write() member calls (indirectly through calling the ReadBlock() function). The reading versions of these functions are presented in Example 17.12.

The fact that more data types (e.g., short, float) are supported by the binary SimpleIO functions is a reflection of the nature of binary storage. For example, when reading and writing numeric text, it usually makes little or no difference if the internal representation is float or double—so we just define one function that handles the most capable type (double). It makes a huge difference in a binary file, however, whether data are stored as a 4-byte real (float) or an 8-byte real (double). So we need functions that handle both (and we need to make sure our write matches our read version).

The writing versions of the SimpleIO binary file functions are presented in Example 17.13.

The final binary file functions supported by SimpleIO are the file positioning functions. They are presented in Example 17.14, and simply repackage fstream calls.

17.6: LAB EXERCISE: GFILE AND GSTDIOFILE

Walkthrough available in GFile.wmv

In this exercise, you can implement your own encapsulated file classes, GFile, and GStdioFile, modeled after the MFC CFile and CStdioFile classes.

EXAMPLE 17.11

Get functions in SimpleIO

```
void GetString(INPUT &in,char *szIn)
{
    in >> ws >> szIn >> ws;
}
void GetBlock(INPUT &in,void *pIn,int nVal)
{
    in.read((char *)pIn,nVal);
}
int GetInteger(INPUT &in)
{
    int nVal;
    in >> nVal;
    return nVal;
}
char GetCharacter(INPUT &in)
{
    char cVal;
    in >> ws >> cVal;
    return cVal;
}
double GetReal(INPUT &in)
{
    double dVal;
    in >> dVal;
    return dVal;
}
bool GetLine(INPUT &in,char *szIn,int nMax)
{
    in.getline(szIn,nMax);
    if (in.fail()) return false;
    return true;
}
```

17.6.1: Overview

When the Microsoft Foundation Classes (MFC) were introduced in the early 1990s, the current STL was not supported, nor was it part of the C++ standard. As a consequence, available standard libraries were considerably less capable than today's. Furthermore, MFC was specifically designed to increase the productivity of Windows programming, which meant the large portion of the C++ I/O libraries that dealt with standard (console) I/O weren't relevant, because Windows applications normally don't use the console for I/O purposes. As a result of these two factors, the MFC introduced some encapsulated file classes: CFile and CStdioFile.

In terms of actual capabilities, the CFile (oriented toward binary I/O) and CStdioFile (oriented toward line-driven text I/O) are relatively comparable to the STL classes discussed in this chapter. As a result, it is a useful exercise to reimplement the MFC interface using STL objects (along the same lines as the GString and GPtrArray exercises of Chapter 12).

EXAMPLE 17.12

Read family of SimpleIO binary file functions

```
bool ReadBlock(STREAM &file,void *buf,int nBytes)
{
    file.read((char *)buf,nBytes);
    return !file.fail();
}
int ReadInteger(STREAM &file)
{
    int nVal;
    if (!ReadBlock(file,&nVal,sizeof(int))) nVal=0;
    return nVal;
}
double ReadReal(STREAM &file)
{
    double dVal;
    if (!ReadBlock(file,&dVal,sizeof(double))) dVal=0.0;
    return dVal;
}
float ReadFloat(STREAM &file)
{
    float fVal;
    if (!ReadBlock(file,&fVal,sizeof(float))) fVal=0.0;
    return fVal;
}
char ReadCharacter(STREAM &file)
{
    char cVal;
    if (!ReadBlock(file,&cVal,sizeof(char))) cVal=0;
    return cVal;
}
short ReadShort(STREAM &file)
{
    short nVal;
    if (!ReadBlock(file,&nVal,sizeof(short))) nVal=0;
    return nVal;
}
```

In developing the MFC CFile class, Microsoft also developed some integer data types that, unlike the C++ types, were guaranteed to stay unchanged through MFC versions and were roughly equivalent to the following:

```
typedef unsigned char BYTE;
typedef unsigned short WORD;
typedef unsigned int UINT;
typedef unsigned int DWORD;
typedef unsigned char BOOL;
```

The CFile >> and << operators were overloaded for these special Microsoft types, along with **double, float, andCString.** The >> and << operators were not overloaded, however, for data types that could change in size as C++ evolved, such as **int** and **char.** For

---

EXAMPLE 17.13

Write family of SimpleIO binary file functions

```
bool WriteBlock(STREAM &file,const void *buf,int nBytes)
{
    file.write((char *)buf,nBytes);
    return !file.fail();
}
bool WriteInteger(STREAM &file,int nVal)
{
    return WriteBlock(file,&nVal,sizeof(int));
}
bool WriteReal(STREAM &file,double dVal)
{
    return WriteBlock(file,&dVal,sizeof(double));
}
bool WriteFloat(STREAM &file,float fVal)
{
    return WriteBlock(file,&fVal,sizeof(float));
}
bool WriteCharacter(STREAM &file,char cVal)
{
    return WriteBlock(file,&cVal,sizeof(char));
}
bool WriteShort(STREAM &file,short nVal)
{
    return WriteBlock(file,&nVal,sizeof(short));
}
```

EXAMPLE 17.14

Positioning functions in SimpleIO

```
bool SetWritePosition(STREAM &file,int nPos)
{
    file.seekp(nPos);
    return !file.fail();
}
bool SetReadPosition(STREAM &file,int nPos)
{
    file.seekg(nPos);
    return !file.fail();
}
```

---

our purposes, in defining a class intended to mimic the MFC CFile class, we can use these definitions and overload for STL **string** objects (instead of MFC CString objects).

17.6.2: Specifications

GFile   Implement a GFile class supporting the interface members listed in Table 17.6. Do your initial implementation by composing an fstream member in your class. As an end-of-chapter exercise, you can reimplement your class by inheriting from fstream.

TABLE 17.6	List of GFile Members (Adapted from CFile Function Documentation in Microsoft Visual Studio .NET)

GFile Members to Be Implemented

GFile(const char *szName,unsigned int nFlags)

Constructs a GFile object from a path or file handle.

Comments: See Open().

---

void Close()

Closes a file.

---

bool Open(const char *szName,unsigned int nFlags)

Safely opens a file. Files are opened as binary files, unless otherwise specified.

Comments: Although the MFC has its own set of open flags (e.g., CFile::modeRead, CFile::typeBinary), you can use the STL flags to specify opening mode. The function should return true if successful, false otherwise. You should probably also inspect the flags coming in (see Chapter 4 for bitwise operations), because some of your members (e.g., Seek functions) need to know whether a file is open for reading or writing or both.

---

long Read(void *pBuf,long nCount)

Reads (unbuffered) data from a file at the current file position. Returns the number of bytes read.

Comments: You should prevent read operations from a write-only file, and return 0.

---

long Write(const void *pBuf,long nCount)

Writes (unbuffered) data in a file to the current file position. Returns the number of bytes written.

Comments: You should prevent write operations to a read-only file, and return 0.

---

long Seek(long nPos,unsigned int nFrom)

Positions the current file pointer. Returns the offset from the beginning of the file.

Comments: Although the MFC has its own set of open flags (e.g., CFile::begin, CFile:current), you can use the STL flags to specify relative positioning.

---

void SeekToBegin()

Positions the current file pointer at the beginning of the file.

---

void SeekToEnd()

Positions the current file pointer at the end of the file.

---

string GetFileName() const

Retrieves the filename of the selected file.

Comments: The MFC returns a CString object, but string will work just fine for this exercise. You should probably store the name as a member when the file is opened.

---

long GetPosition() const

Retrieves the current file pointer.

In addition to the members listed in Table 17.6, your class should support overloads for the >> and << operators for the following data types (see definitions in overview, Section 17.6.1):

```
BYTE
WORD
UINT
DWORD
BOOL
double
float
string
```

These overloads should use binary format.

GStdioFile   The MFC CStdioFile class inherits from CFile and supports line reading and writing, in addition to the CFile members.

The GStdioFile class you develop should do the same. Inheriting from GFile should implement the following members:

- char *ReadString(char *buf,int nMaxCount)
- bool ReadString(string &str)
- void WriteString(const char *str)

ReadString(char *,int) returns a pointer to its buffer argument if successful, 0 otherwise. ReadString(string &str) returns true if successful, false otherwise.

The GStdioFile class should also default to text mode when a file is opened, unless specified otherwise.

17.7: REVIEW AND QUESTIONS

17.7.1: REVIEW

Conceptually, the C++ I/O system can be viewed as an inheritance network of different object types, as illustrated in the following figure (originally Figure 17.1):

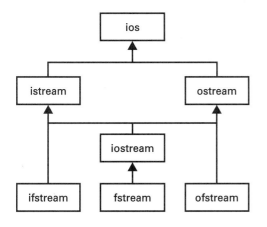

Within this hierarchy, certain types of objects are most commonly used:

- *istream* & *ostream:* Used for standard I/O objects **cin** (istream) and **cout, cerr** (both ostream). Requires <iostream> be included.
- *ifstream:* An input file stream, declared by the programmer and then used to open a file for input. Requires <fstream> be included.
- *ofstream:* An output file stream, declared by the programmer then used to open a file for output. Requires <fstream> be included.
- *fstream:* A general file stream, declared by the programmer then used to open a file for input, output, or input/output. Requires <fstream> be included.

Because ifstream, ofstream, and fstream all inherit properties from istream and ostream, any operator that can be performed using **cout, cin,** and **cerr** can also be performed using the appropriate type of stream object opened by the user.

Text input and output from/to streams is normally accomplished using the >> (input, extraction) and << (output, insertion) operators. When direct input from the user is required, however, the getline() member, applied to any input stream object, is often safer.

Three basic types of functions are used to control I/O formatting:

- Member functions, applied directly to an object, such as cout.width(10)
- Pure manipulator functions, which can either be called with an operator as an argument (e.g., hex(cout) causes cout to display subsequent integers in hexadecimal) or placed in an insertion or extraction operation (e.g., cout << hex; accomplishes the same thing)
- Single argument manipulator functions, which are placed in the stream but also have an argument (e.g., cout << setw(10); which does the same as calling the cout.width(10) member function)

Much I/O formatting is controlled by flags (i.e., bits) that are set on or off for each stream. Some member functions and manipulators allow these flags to be manipulated, providing high levels of I/O control. Tables 17.3 and 17.4 summarized the most important of these functions and manipulators.

Binary files differ from text files in that the data placed in them is usually a direct copy of data in memory (instead of being translated to text form). As a result, they tend to be much more efficient to work with than text files. Implicit in any binary file is a pointer, identifying the position from which the next read or write will start. In C++, binary I/O is accomplished with member functions. Functions commonly used with binary files include:

```
istream-obj.read(char *buf,
    int nCount);
ostream-obj.write(const char
    *buf,int nCount);
```

```
istream-obj.seekg(unsigned int
    nPosition);
ostream-obj.seekp(unsigned int
    nPosition);
istream-obj.tellg()
ostream-obj.tellp()
```

The read() and write() member functions write data directly between a memory buffer and a file stream. Because the buffer is assumed to be an array of bytes (of type **char** in the current version of .NET), it will often need to be type cast. For example:

```
int nVal;
in.read((char *)&nVal,sizeof(int));
```

The two seek member functions, seekg() and seekp(), are used to reposition the file pointer in an input and output file stream, respectively. More complicated versions of the functions, using relative positioning, are also available. The tellg() and tellp() members are used to identify the current position in an input and output stream, respectively. You can remember which version is which by thinking 'g' for "get" (input) and 'p' for "put" or "print" (output).

Using binary files effectively involves some general principles, which include the following:

- When saving an object based on a structure, it is usually safer to save the elements individually than to save the whole structure as a block. The latter can be done without excessive risk, however, if an object is a pure structure and contains no pointers.
- When saving a collection of data, save the number of elements in the collection first, then save the elements themselves. This approach makes reading much easier.
- Avoid making assumptions about object sizes (e.g., sizeof(int)), because size may change in future compiler/OS versions, which could result in file incompatibilities when an application is recompiled.

17.7.2: GLOSSARY

cerr A global ostream object, defined in <iostream>, that defaults to standard output and is typically used for error messages

cin A global istream object, defined in <iostream>, that defaults to standard input

cout A global ostream object, defined in <iostream>, that defaults to standard output

flags A collection of bits associated with all C++ I/O objects that serve primarily to determine subsequent stream formatting

formatted I/O Input and output associated with text streams where the appearance (i.e., format) of the text information must be specified by the programmer

fstream class A class that inherits from the general input/output stream and allows that user to attach a specific file to the stream, most commonly used for binary file I/O

ifstream class A class that inherits from the general input stream and allows that user to attach a specific file to the stream

ios class The base class for all C++ standard I/O objects. Most standard I/O data and member functions are defined in this class

iostream class A class that encapsulates a general input/output stream

istream class A class that encapsulates a general input stream

manipulator A function designed to change the characteristics of an I/O stream, normally used in formatted I/O

ofstream class A class that inherits from the general output stream and allows that user to attach a specific file to the stream

ostream class A class that encapsulates a general output stream

17.7.3: QUESTIONS

Text I/O Questions from Chapter 8

1. *Line counter.* Write and test a function that counts all the lines in a text file. The function should be prototyped as follows:

```
int LineCount(const char
    *szFileName);
```

where szFileName is the name of the file, and the function returns the number of lines.

2. *Word counter.* Write and test a function that counts all the words in a text file. The function should be prototyped as follows:

```
int WordCount(const char
    *szFileName);
```

where szFileName is the name of the file, and the function returns the number of words in the file. For the purpose of this function, any cluster of nonwhite characters separated by one or more white characters from any other cluster is considered a word. For example:

```
"Hello World 123 it's me!"
```

would be considered to have five words. (*Hint:* Write a second function that counts the words in a line and the entire process becomes much easier.)

Binary I/O Questions from Chapter 16

3. *Employee class.* Reimplement the Employee class I/O functions (Example 16.3) using C++ file I/O objects.

4. *EmployeeArray class.* Reimplement the EmployeeArray class I/O functions (Example 16.21) using C++ file I/O separate objects.

5. *Revised GFile class.* Reimplement the GFile class (Section 17.6) so that it inherits from fstream instead of using composition. Consider using protected inheritance, because you are creating your own interface from scratch.

Exercises 6 through 10 involve creating a simple definition or help file system.

6. *Creating a keyword file.* Create a text file formatted along the lines of the illustration at the bottom of the following page. The file should be organized into blocks of text preceded, on a line above, by a keyword enclosed in * characters (or some other character you choose).

7. *KeywordIndex class.* Create a class called KeywordIndex that we will be extending in Questions 8–10. Your initial version of the class should have a member function LoadIndex() that takes a const char * as an argument (the file name of the index file, such as keywords.txt). It should:

- Open the file, which will have to be in binary mode, because we will need position information.

- Read the file line-by-line, identifying each keyword (by virtue of the fact that the line starts and ends with an *). For each keyword, it should:

  - Display the keyword.

  - Display the position of the line immediately following the keyword in the file.

  - Display the number of lines before the next keyword or the end of the file.

- Write a main() function to verify that LoadIndex() works.

8. *KeywordData class.* Create a class called KeywordData that inherits from the CKey class developed in Chapter 16 (Example 16.18). The class should have the data members defined for the following information:

- Key value: A string that will also be the return value of the Key() virtual function

- Key position: The position in the file of the line immediately after the key

- Key lines: The number of lines before the next key

9. *Adding KeyArray to KeywordIndex class.* Add a KeyArray member (see Chapter 16, Section 16.5.2) to the KeywordIndex class. Modify the LoadIndex() function so that instead of printing out the data specified in Question

7, it uses that data to initialize a KeywordData object that is then added to the KeyArray. The function should display an error if any duplicate keywords are encountered.

10. *LookupKeyword() member.* Add a LookupKeyword() member to the KeywordIndex class. The function should take a const char * as an argument. When called, it should:

- Look up the keyword in the KeyArray. If not found, it should display an error message.

- Display the associated text, which should be accomplished by making a direct seek to the position stored in the KeywordData object, then reading the lines from the file and displaying them. (Don't be surprised if extra linefeeds need to be suppressed when you display the lines from the file—it's a side effect of reading text lines in a file open in binary mode.)

Test the class by modifying the main() function you wrote in Question 7.

In-Depth: DBF File Exercise (Binary Files)

11. *DBF Files:* Reimplement the DBF Structures Lab Exercise in Chapter 11, Section 11.7, using C++ file I/O objects.

12. *DBF Classes.* Reimplement the DBF classes, described in Chapter 15, Questions 11–15, using C++ file I/O objects.

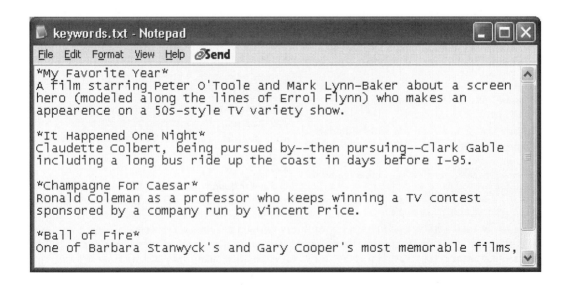

INDEX